VESTED INTERESTS

CROSS-DRESSING & CULTURAL ANXIETY

Vested Interests

CROSS-DRESSING & CULTURAL ANXIETY

Marjorie Garber

ROUTLEDGE
NEW YORK & LONDON

Published in 1992 by

Routledge
An imprint of Routledge, Chapman and Hall, Inc.
29 West 35 Street
New York, NY 10001

Published in Great Britain by

Routledge
11 New Fetter Lane
London EC4P 4EE

Library of Congress Cataloging in Publication Data

Garber, Marjorie
    Vested interests : cross-dressing and cultural anxiety / Marjorie
Garber.
        p.   cm.
    Includes index.
    ISBN 0-415-90072-7
    1. Transvestism. 2. Tranvestites.   I. Title.
HQ77.G37   1991
306.77—dc20   91-20171

British Library Cataloguing in Publication Data

Garber, Marjorie
    Vested interests : cross-dressing and cultural
anxiety.
    I. Title
    306.77

ISBN 0-415-90072-7

FOR BARBARA

CONTENTS

CONTENTS

II. TRANSVESTITE EFFECTS

PICTURE CREDITS

Additional credits appear beside illustrations.

Black-and-white illustrations following page 162:

Make-Up for Beginners, copyright Joost Veerkamp 1987; woodcut from title page of *Hic Mulier: Or The Man-Woman: Being a Medicine to cure the Coltish Disease of the Staggers in the Masculine-Feminines of our Times* (London: J.T., 1620); *Venetian woman with moveable skirt,* 55.503.30, engraving, Italian, ca. 1590, 5 1/2″ × 7 1/2″, the Metropolitan Museum of Art, the Elisha Whittelsey Collection, the Elisha Whittelsey Fund, 1955; *Some Like It Hot,* courtesy of the Museum of Modern Art, New York; *Tootsie, Bringing Up Baby, Yentl,* and *Bedazzled* courtesy of the Museum of Modern Art, New York; George H. Earle, IV, as the Dove Queen in *Come Across,* 1937, photo by Joe Steinmetz, *Town and Country* May 1937; advertisement from the magazine *TV Personals;* Divine in *Female Trouble,* courtesy of the Museum of Modern Art, New York; WAC applying make-up to GI, courtesy of the National Archives, Washington, D.C., photo #111-SC-204637; Olivier being fitted for a drag role, copyright Terry O'Neill; Renée Vivien as page, from the Natalie Barney Collection, Bibliothèque littéraire Jacques Doucet, Paris; Julie Andrews in *Victor/Victoria,* courtesy of the Museum of Modern Art, New York; Romaine Brooks, *Peter (A Young English Girl),* 1970.70, oil on canvas, 1923–1924, 36 1/4″ × 24 1/2″ (91.9 × 62.3 cm), the National Museum of American Art, Smithsonian Institution, gift of the artist; Greta Garbo in *Queen Christina,* courtesy of the Museum of Modern Art, New York; Man Ray, *Marcel Duchamp as Rrose Sélavy,* 57–49–1, photograph, ca. 1920–1921, 8 1/2″ × 6 13/16″, the Philadelphia Museum of Art, the Samuel S. White III and Vera White Collection.

Color illustrations following page 226:

Madonna, *Express Yourself,* photograph by Alberto Tolot, property of Warner Bros. Records; Romaine Brooks, *Una, Lady Troubridge,* 1966.49.6, oil on canvas, 1924, 50 1/8″

× 30 1/8″ (127.3 × 76.4 cm), the National Museum of American Art, Smithsonian Institution, gift of the artist; Elvis in gold lamé, courtesy of Jane and Michael Stern; Frida Kahlo, *Self-Portrait with Cropped Hair*, oil on canvas, 1940, 15 3/4″ × 11″, the Museum of Modern Art, New York, gift of Edgar Kaufmann, Jr.

Black-and-white illustrations following page 290:

Oscar Wilde as Salome, courtesy of Roger-Viollet, Paris; Aubrey Beardsley drawing from: Oscar Wilde, *Salome, a Tragedy in One Act*, trans. Alfred Douglas, illus. Aubrey Beardsley (London: John Lane, The Bodley Head, 1907); engravings of Anne Bonny and Mary Read from: [Daniel Defoe], pseud. Captain Charles Johnson, *Historie der engelsche zee-roovers, beginnende met de geschiedenisse van capiteyn Avery, en zyne makkers* [*The History of the Pirates*], trans. Robert Hennebo (Amsterdam: Hermanus Uytwerf, 1725); Ernest Torrence as Captain Hook, courtesy of the Museum of Modern Art, New York; Betty Bronson and Mary Martin as Peter Pan, courtesy of the Museum of Modern Art, New York; all images of James Barry courtesy of the Royal Army Medical Corps, Aldershot, Hants., Great Britain; Betty Grable in *Mother Wore Tights* and Helmut Berger in *The Damned* courtesy of the Museum of Modern Art, New York; Marlene Dietrich, portrait for *Morocco* (1930); Valentino and Ayres in *The Sheik*, courtesy of the Museum of Modern Art, New York; Elvis Presley in *Harum Scarum*, courtesy of Jane and Michael Stern; Isabelle Eberhardt dressed as an Arab from René-Louis Doyon, *Au Pays des Sables* (Paris: Fernand Sorlot, 1944); Debra Winger in *The Sheltering Sky* copyright 1990, 1991 by Mimmo Cattarinich, all rights reserved, courtesy of Ram Studio Snc, Rome; T. E. Lawrence in Arab clothing, courtesy of the Imperial War Museum, London, photograph #Q 59314; photograph of Elvis and Liberace reproduced by permission of the Liberace Foundation for the Creative and Performing Arts; illustration of Red Riding Hood by Felix Lorioux, from *Les Contes de Perrault* (Paris, 1927).

Jacket: Paul Wunderlich, *Hermaphroditenhemd*, 1973. Reproduced by permission of the artist.

Back Cover: *Androgyny*, courtesy of FPG International Archives, catalogue #H00486.

ACKNOWLEDGMENTS

The writing of this book has been immensely facilitated by the generosity of friends, colleagues, institutions, and interested strangers, who kindly and regularly provided instances of cross-dressing in literature and culture from their reading and personal experience, many though not all of which have found their way into these pages.

Over-the-transom contributions came from unexpected places: the Chair of the Harvard Department of Anthropology described to me his own transvestic adventures among the baboons, whose preference for female human company led him on at least one occasion to cross-dress in the hopes of fooling them into amiability. (They were not deceived.) After an article appeared in the *New York Times Magazine* that made brief mention of my work on cross-dressing, I received several helpful letters, including a manuscript and photographs from a man who had entered a monastery in New York as a way of channeling his impulses to dress in women's clothes. He later left the monastery and began for a time to dress openly as a woman.

My mail was regularly enriched by clippings, cut out of magazines and newspapers, about Phil Donahue in a skirt, or the gang of transvestite underwear thieves in South Florida, or the Billy Tipton affair, or the Waltham-based International Foundation for Gender Education, or the twenty-six year old man in Colorado Springs who enrolled in a high school as a girl and made the all-girl cheerleading squad. To all of those who made my mailbox a constant source of surprise and delight, my very warm thanks.

Two people in particular deserve gratitude and recognition in the making of this book. One is Barbara Johnson, to whom the book is dedicated, who read and commented on every draft, taking time away from her own work to do it; the other is Jennifer Carrell, my research assistant, student, and friend, whose indefatigable labors, acute insights and lively interest in the odd twists and turns of an ever-expanding topic made the writing easy and pleasant. Without Jenny and Barbara this book could not have been written.

Many other friends and collaborators should be mentioned by name: Stephen Orgel, whose friendship and learning were both invaluable in the crafting of the Renaissance portions of the book, and whose own work on English transvestite theater in the

Renaissance was an inspiration; Michael Cooper and Nancy Bauer, who took me to transvestite night clubs and indoctrinated me into the delights of Divine; Nancy Vickers, to whom I am indebted not only for whatever I have come to know about Madonna and George Michael, but also for sharing with me the extraordinary excitement of the move from Renaissance Studies to popular culture; the evening we went to Madonna's *Blond Ambition* concert in Los Angeles, identifiable middle-aged academics in the midst of teenage frenzy, will live for a long time in my memory.

At an early stage Jane Gallop responded with warmth and strong encouragement to the theoretical basis of the project; Terry Castle and Diane Middlebrook both showed welcome interest, and offered much-needed support, at the time the book was being written; Peter Stallybrass and Ann Rosalind Jones gave enthusiastic assent to some of the book's theoretical claims at an important moment in the writing, and have been wonderful friends throughout; Eve Sedgwick, Michael Moon, and Jonathan Goldberg reminded me, in a way both timely and welcome, that transvestism and gay identity were in many ways the same topic; Rebecca Folkman introduced me to the story of Michel Vieuchange; Judith Zeitlin kindly showed me her own work on Chinese transvestite theater and fiction; Deborah Carlin, Susan Gillman, and Amy Kaplan all generously shared materials about slave narratives, gender and culture in American literature; a timely conversation with Henry Finder about *The Silence of the Lambs* led me to realize that Harris's book made the perfect end-piece to a discussion of transvestism, transsexuality, and contemporary fiction and film. Sally and Richard Price enriched my knowledge of anthropology, as did Bill Beeman. David Kastan, Barbara Packer, Cynthia Chase, Rachel Jacoff, Joe Boone, Deborah Nord, Katherine Rowe, Kate Schwarz, Carolyn Dever, Doug Bruster and David Hirsch also gave generously of their time, thought, and clippings, on topics as diverse as sumptuary laws, Amazons, detective fiction, Flora Tristan, the Kinks and John Lyly.

Naomi Schor and Elizabeth Weed were enormously helpful in their editorial comments on "Spare Parts," which appeared in a special issue of *differences*; Julia Epstein and Kris Straub were similarly careful, caring editors of the shortened version of "The Chic of Araby" that is being published in their anthology, *Body Guards*, and I am likewise grateful to Jean Marsden for her comments on "Rosalind the Yeshiva Boy," to appear in her collection, *The Appropriation of Shakespeare*. "Fetish Envy," first presented at the Modern Language Association and then published in *October*, benefited from the good editorial advice of Joan Copjec. The editors of *Nationalisms and Sexualities*, Andrew Parker, Mary Russo, Doris Sommer, and Patricia Yaeger, offered generous responses to "The Occidental Tourist" when it was given as a conference talk, and later when the essay was revised for publication; at the conference itself Gayatri Spivak's comments were especially illuminating and helpful. The chapter on Liberace, Valentino and Elvis, now called "The Transvestite Continuum," was presented as a paper at the Stanford conference on "Gender at the Crossroads" and again at the University of Wisconsin-Milwaukee conference on "The Emotions," both in the spring of 1990; I am grateful to the audiences at both events for

ACKNOWLEDGMENTS

their comments, as I am to the U. C. Berkeley Music Department seminar on gender that also heard and responded to this talk.

Jeanne Newlin and Joseph Keller of the Harvard Theater Collection and Richard Wendorf of the Houghton Library provided expertise, assistance and enthusiasm in the process of selecting and reproducing illustrations. Jennifer Carrell expertly managed the complex process of obtaining permissions for the reproduction of the many pictorial images included here.

I am grateful to the Stanford Humanities Center and to the American Council of Learned Societies for Fellowship support in 1989–90. The year I spent at the Stanford Humanities Center was notable not only for the appeal of its intellectual (and meteorological) climate, but also for the several important and continuing friendships that had occasion to develop in that time and place. Some of those friends have already been mentioned in the list above; to these I want to add Bliss Carnochan, Director of the Stanford Center, whose thoughtfulness and generous spirit were a model of hospitality and friendship.

The Hyder E. Rollins Fund provided generous financial support that has enabled the publication of some of the pictorial images in this book. I am grateful to the Harvard English Department that administers this fund, to Philip Fisher, the Department Chair, and also to the many colleagues in that department who have shown interest in, and support of, my work.

Bill Germano's commitment to and encouragement of this project from first to last has been remarkable. I want to take this occasion to thank him both as an editor and as a friend. Diane Gibbons performed the herculean task of copy-editing with care and grace. Michael Esposito, Charles Hames, Karen Sullivan, and Seth Denbo vigilantly oversaw the book's production. Cheryl Nixon, Carey Monserrate, Liz Scala, Scott Stevens and Susan Thornberg helped out with research at the project's end, as Shuma Chakravarty did at the beginning. Carol Kountz gave generously of her time and talent to the thankless job of proofreading. Rebecca Monroe Novak, Herrick Wales and Karen Friedland, my assistants at the Center for Literary and Cultural Studies, have been a constant source of support.

Rhoda Garber spotted the Paul Wunderlich image that appears on the cover of this book in a shop in St. Paul de Vence; to her I am grateful, as always, for an infinity of things. My debt to Barbara Johnson, whose work and life touch mine at every turn, is inexpressible. Like all our debts, as she knows, this one will take a long time to pay back.

INTRODUCTION:
CLOTHES MAKE THE MAN

Although the logic of anatomy might suggest otherwise, skirts are the traditional garb of women and pants the traditional garb of men—harem bloomers and kilts, the exceptions that prove the rule.

Boston Globe Magazine, August 28, 1988

When you meet a human being, the first distinction you make is "male or female?" and you are accustomed to make the distinction with unhesitating certainty.

Freud, "Femininity"[1]

Dressed as I am in jeans and a sweater, I have no idea to which sex the policemen will suppose me to belong, and must prepare my responses for either decision. I feel their silent appraisal down the corridor as I approach them, and as they search my sling bag I listen hard for a "Sir" or a "Ma'am" to decide my course of conduct.

Jan Morris, *Conundrum: An Extraordinary Narrative of Transsexualism*[2]

Many readers of the *New York Times* were startled recently to learn that one of their most cherished assumptions about clothing and gender was, apparently, without ground. Baby clothes, which since at least the 1940's have been routinely divided along gender and color lines, pink for girls, blue for boys, were, said the *Times,* once just the other way about. In the early years of the twentieth century, before World War I, boys wore pink ("a stronger, more decided color," according to the promotional literature of the time) while girls wore blue (understood to be "delicate" and "dainty"). Only after World War II, the *Times* reported, did the present alignment of the two genders with pink and blue come into being.[3]

Few articles in the *Times* occasioned as much casual astonishment, at least among people of my acquaintance. It was generally known that infants and small children had for hundreds of years been dressed alike, in frocks, so that family portraits from previous centuries made it difficult to tell the young boys from the girls. "Breeching," as a rite of passage, was a sartorial definition of maleness and incipient adulthood, as, in later periods, was the all-important move from short pants to long. Gender differentiation grew increasingly desirable to parents as time went on.[4] By the closing years of the twentieth century the sight of little boys in frilly dresses has become unusual and somewhat risible; a childhood photograph of macho author Ernest Hemingway, aged almost two, in a white dress and large hat festooned with flowers, was itself the focus of much amused critical commentary when reproduced in a best-selling biography—especially when it was disclosed that Hemingway's mother had labeled the photograph of her son "summer girl."[5]

Despite this general awareness of the mutability of infant style, the pink-blue reversal came as something of a shock. In a society in which even disposable diapers had now been gender-color-coded (pink for girls, blue for boys, with anatomically correct extra absorbency in the front or middle) the idea that pink was for boys was peculiarly destabilizing. Notice that it is the connotations of the colors, and not the perception of the genders, that has changed. But what was so particularly fascinating about this detail from the recent history of taste? I think, perhaps, the fact that it reversed a binarism— that it disconcerted not only feelings of tradition, continuity, and naturalness (rather than arbitrariness) of association, but also a way of reading.

The same kind of slightly comic consternation, still on the level of the gender-codes of the child, was produced by the recent discovery of a cross-dressed "Ken" doll ("Barbie" 's long-term boyfriend) in a sealed box sold by the Mattel corporation. Nattily attired in a pink tutu with lace flounces, a handbag slung over his shoulder, Ken stares cheerfully out from the plastic window of a box labeled "My first Ken—He's a handsome prince!" Above his head appears the legend, "So easy to dress!" Offered a regular Ken in exchange, the consumer, who collects Barbies and Kens, declined because she thought the cross-dressed version would be more valuable. Articles on what *Fortune* magazine called "the kinky Ken" made headlines in newspapers and magazines across the country.[6]

Nor, needless to say, are the gender ambiguities of color-coded dress limited to children. In the 1990s, now that television has made the red necktie *de rigueur* for male politicians and custom decrees it as a standard accessory for male professionals—lawyers, professors, and television anchormen—it is somewhat startling to learn that red ties not all that long ago declared their wearers to be homosexuals. The Chicago Vice Commission of 1909 reported that male homosexuals recognized each other by wearing red neckties, a fact that had already been noted in the streets of New York and Philadelphia by the sexologist Havelock Ellis.[7]

When I was in grade school in the 1950s it was *green*, not red, which was for some reason considered to be the "homosexual" color; to wear green inadvertently on a Thursday was to be the butt of jokes all the more tiresome for not being fully understood. These days it is lavender, or purple, that is the color that proclaims gay self-identification—lavender, and also pink, in the pink triangles used by the Nazis to label and stigmatize homosexual men, now defiantly "inverted" by gay activists on T-shirts and buttons as a sign of gay pride. In the period of less than a century the self-identification of gays and lesbians through what Ellis called "the badge of all their tribe"[8] has moved from a covert and localized practice aimed at mutual recognition to a global phenomenon with encompassing political implications. Pink, that "strong, decided" color for boys, now identifies—when they choose it to—gay men and lesbians. What goes around, comes around.

THE CULTURAL POLITICS OF TRANSVESTISM

This book is an attempt to explore the nature and significance both of the "fact" of cross-dressing and of the historically recurrent fascination with it. In the chapters that follow I will explore such varied topics as the relationship between cross-dressing and theatricality; the ways in which clothing constructs (and deconstructs) gender and gender differences; transvestism, power relations, and career paths; cultural misperceptions of gendered costume; transvestism and racism; and the role of cross-dressing in popular culture, high (and low) fashion, and the arts—as well as in the construction of culture itself.

My work on this project has brought me into contact with transvestism in many historical and cultural configurations, from David Bowie, Boy George, and Laurie Anderson to medieval cross-dressed female saints, from the Chevalier d'Eon de Beaumont, whose name provided Havelock Ellis with his preferred term for transvestism, "eonism," to the Tiffany Club of Waltham, Massachusetts, a group of some 350 transvestites, mostly male, middle class, and ninety percent married. "Our largest group is computer engineers," reports a Tiffany spokesperson, "and our second largest is truck drivers. Our biggest contingent is from MIT."[9]

I have also spent a considerable amount of time examining medical discourses about cross-dressing and taking note of their implicit and sometimes explicit gender biases. Medical discourses about transvestism, even those advanced by the establishment within gender identity clinics, are often diametrically at odds with the political discourses of the transvestite-transsexual community. For while doctors find it necessary to distinguish among transvestic syndromes, and especially between transvestites and transsexuals, in order to determine an appropriate course of treatment, transvestites and transsexuals often resist such diagnostic taxonomies for political reasons.

A doctor wants to know whether to perform surgery on the patient, altering the body to conform to an inner sense of gender identity—the most extreme treatment offered for transsexuals—or whether, by contrast, the patient is a transvestite or transvestophile whose pleasure comes from wearing the clothes of the other sex rather than in physically becoming a member of that sex. If, for example, the patient is a male transvestite, whose erotic pleasure comes from the "reassurance" of being a phallic woman, of having a penis *and* dressing in women's clothes, his most reassuring symptom, according to clinicians, is the erection itself; surgery would be a catastrophic, and not a therapeutic, procedure for such patients, since it would remove, not the cause of distress, but the source of pleasure.

For the transvestite-transsexual community, however—a significant population with an active international organization and dozens of local branches from Poughkeepsie to New South Wales—clinical distinctions are divisive rather than helpful. United around issues like the right to shop—access to dresses and nightgowns in large sizes and helpful, courteous sales personnel—this group politically elides such clinical distinctions in favor of effective organization as a neglected minority group. Needless to say, members of the TV-TS community do not think of themselves as "patients," nor do they particularly like the word "transvestite," which seems to imply a compulsive disorder; they prefer "cross-dresser," which suggests a choice of lifestyle.

Although some prominent medical experts from Freud to the present have denied the existence of erotic transvestism in women, many transvestites and transsexuals affirm the reality of pleasure, sexual as well as cultural, in female-to-male as well as male-to-female cross-dressing. What I discuss later on under the rubric of "fetish envy," the desire to be included within Freud's psychoanalytic description of fetishism, assumes a compelling force for people whose cultural identity and visibility is so regularly and authoritatively denied. "We have men who collect lingerie, like full slips; we have women who collect jock straps," says Yvonne Cook, a spokesperson for the International Foundation for Gender Education, a man who considers himself to be a lesbian and who dates a woman who cross-dresses as a man. By the foundation's calculation, six percent of this nation's population are cross-dressers, and (only) one percent transsexuals.[10]

Politics is a relational exercise, however, and if the TV-TS community finds itself at variance with much of the medical community on the question of rights and recognition for cross-gender issues, it has also been critiqued by gay activists who regard some TV-TS groups as homophobic, and voice serious reservations about statistics that suggest that most transvestites are heterosexual. Crucial concerns have been raised by gay theorists about assimilation, stigmatization and the implied desire to erase or scapegoat groups at risk—especially in the age of AIDS.

The story of transvestism in western culture is in fact, as much of this book will attest, bound up with the story of homosexuality and gay identity, from "drag" and "voguing" to fashion and stage design, from the boy actors of the English Renaissance stage to Gertrude Stein and Divine. No analysis of "cross-dressing" that wants to interrogate the phenomenon seriously from a cultural, political, or even aesthetic vantage point can fail to take into account the foundational role of gay identity and gay style. Yet as important as gay culture is to transvestism—and transvestism to gay culture—there are other major areas in which transvestism has also been a defining, and disconcerting, element, an element largely undertheorized, even in the current climate of interest in androgyny, unisex style, historical cross-dressers, and *Tootsie*. Just as to ignore the role played by homosexuality would be to risk a radical misunderstanding of the social and cultural implications of cross-dressing, so to restrict cross-dressing to the context of an emerging gay and lesbian identity is to risk ignoring, or setting aside, elements and incidents that seem to belong to quite different lexicons of self-definition and political and cultural display.

I will return again and again to the relationship between transvestism and gay identity throughout this study. The cultural fascination of cross-dressing, however—as the trivial instance of the cross-dressed Ken doll suggests—is not always *consciously* related to homosexuality, although homosexuality, itself taboo in many contexts, might be viewed as the repressed that always returns.

Why have cultural observers today been so preoccupied with cross-dressing? Why is it virtually impossible to pick up a newspaper or turn on the television or go to the movies without encountering, in some guise, the question of sartorial gender bending? On American television, talk shows have had a field day with the topic. In the last two years, Phil Donahue has broadcast at least sixteen programs on cross-dressing and transsexualism and Geraldo Rivera more than seven, and the question has also been discussed at length by Sally Jessy Raphael and Oprah Winfrey.

In the movies, as well, the 1980's not only produced several new cross-dressing classics (*Tootsie*, *Victor/ Victoria*, *Yentl*, *Torch Song Trilogy*) but also seemed to insert an episode of cross-dressing even in the most unlikely of cinematic contexts: in the sex-and-baseball summer hit *Bull Durham* (where the rookie pitcher wears a garter belt under his uniform), in *White Mischief* (where colonial decadence is figured as a transvestite party), or in *Fatal Attraction* (where little Ellen cross-dresses to play the part of John—"speak-for-yourself"—Alden), to pick three random examples.

Academic studies have likewise shown a marked fascination with cross-dressing. Printed circulars announcing conferences on the topic ("Weekend Conference on Liminality, in History, in Fiction, and on the Stage: Crossdressing, crosscasting, transvestism, boy actors, castrati, hermaphrodites. . . .") have arrived in my mail almost weekly. With the rise of new interdisciplinary studies under the general rubric of "cultural criticism," literary scholars, historians, anthropologists, and others have found in such topics an ideal site for the study of cultural discourses about gender and sexuality.

What are we to make of this evidence of what Freud might have called an "overestimation" of cross-dressing, in high culture and low, as a phenomenon of our time?

TOOT-TOOT-TOOTSIE GOODBYE

Of all the cross-dressing films of the eighties it was Sydney Pollack's *Tootsie* (1982), starring Dustin Hoffman, that most captured the popular imagination—as well as the imagination of literary critics. Indeed, "Tootsie" has become shorthand in some circles for a man who puts himself on parade as a feminist, while retaining, unself-critically, a male-centered view of women.[11] I would like here to take a closer look at *Tootsie* in order to focus on some of the issues that have surfaced around cross-dressing in recent literary criticism.

As many commentators have suggested, the overt "message" of *Tootsie* is that women are better than men. Dorothy Michaels, Hoffman's female character, is much more sensitive, perceptive, sisterly, and professionally successful than Michael Dorsey, the out-of-work actor who in desperation assumes the role of Dorothy. But the subtext, as argued by Elaine Showalter and others, is that men are better than women. A man dressed as a woman can beat out "real women" for a part. As Showalter points out, the success of the film comes primarily "from the masculine power disguised and veiled by the feminine costume. Physical gestures of masculinity provide *Tootsie*'s comic motif of female impersonation. Dorothy Michaels drops her voice to call a taxi, lifts heavy suitcases, and shoves a burly competitor out of the way. Dorothy's 'feminist' speeches too are less a response to the oppression of women than an instinctive situational male reaction to being treated like a woman. The implication is that women must be taught by men how to win their rights."[12] "*Tootsie* does," says Showalter, "have a message for women, although not the one the filmmakers intended. It says that feminist ideas are much less threatening when they come from a man" (139). For this reason, she maintains, "I should make it clear . . . that, to my mind, *Tootsie* is not a feminist film" (136).

In making this argument, Showalter is her usual witty and clear-sighted self. She is one of feminist criticism's most articulate and deeply-read spokespersons, and I mean no disrespect to her when I say that she is here, to coin a phrase, seeing less than the whole picture. For *Tootsie* is indeed not a feminist film. Nor is it a film about a woman, or a man pretending to be woman. It is a film about a transvestite. Its cross-dressed central figure, Michael Dorsey/Dorothy Michaels/Dustin Hoffman, is working within the established Hollywood codes of female impersonation, but for feminists to see *Tootsie* as a film about men's views of women (and of feminism) is to erase or repress any awareness of that which the metadramatic nature of the film constantly stresses: the fact that "Dorothy's" power inheres in her blurred gender, in the fact of her cross-dressing, and not—despite the stereotypical romantic ending—in *either* of her gendered identities. In *Tootsie* transvestism is an enabling fantasy, not merely a joke or a parody, whether the laugh is thought to be on men or on women.

Perhaps because of the time when it appeared, which coincided with an interesting upsurge in feminist criticism among men as well as women, *Tootsie* became a convenient nexus for readings of, and critiques of, mainstream feminism in film. Teresa de Lauretis sees it as one of a recent crop of films whose " 'positive' images of women" (the inner quotation marks are hers) suggest "the social legitimation of a certain feminist discourse, and the consequent viability of its commercial and ideological exploitation."[13] The last page of Vito Russo's book *The Celluloid Closet: Homosexuality in the Movies* laments the fact that "Hollywood is where a timid rehash of *Some Like It Hot* called *Tootsie* can successfully pretend to have something to say about sex roles."[14] Film critic Pauline Kael proposes a possible reading that accords with Showalter's ("It would be easy to say that the movie was itself being condescending to women—that it was suggesting that it took a man to be tough and forthright enough to speak up for women's rights") but finally concludes that Hoffman's triple portrayal of Dorsey, Dorothy, and the TV character Emily Kimberly was carried out in good faith.[15]

Some feminist critics have seen Hoffman's star turn as an example of the preempting of women's roles by men in a Hollywood where there are few enough good parts for actresses. This is very similar to Showalter's argument about male literary critics who wanted to get in on the action and "read like a woman," now that feminism had become respectable and indeed theoretically exciting. In fact, Rebecca Bell-Metereau, like Showalter, notes that in the film Michael Dorsey directly suggests an allegorical reading of the actor as woman: putting on makeup, trying to make himself attractive, sitting by the phone waiting for that all-important call.

What is striking to me about all of these readings of the film is that they erase or look through the cross-dresser, wishing instead to redistribute his/her power: Dustin/ Michael/ Dorothy/ Emily is a man; or an "image of a woman"; or an image of an actor, so that the final deception is lack of deception. All actors are like women in that they depend upon their subordinate positions in Hollywood as women do in society. True enough. But if Hoffman is presented, subtextually, as an actor in *Tootsie*, he is also presented, full frontally, as a cross-dresser. One who dresses for success.

To see the older men who are attracted to Dorothy as fools is to deny the audience's attraction to her; she *is* more attractive, even seductive, in some ways, than any other character in the film. Les the farmer's interest in Dorothy is *not* finally turned into a cruel joke on both of them but rather allows them to indulge in a brief spate of homosocial bonding (with Dorothy as much as Julie the woman-in-the-middle), while the men who stop Dorothy on the street or the dance floor to compliment her on her looks off-camera illustrate something about the power of representation, not about the ludicrousness of gender-misreading. Showalter's resistance to blurred gender, which is one of her consider-able strengths as an ideological critic of and for feminism, manifests itself in a resistance to Dorothy's charms. But we might indeed remember *Some Like It Hot* (1959), where Osgood (Joe E. Lewis) is undeterred by Jerry/Daphne's revelation that he is a man. Osgood's rejoinder, "Nobody's perfect," has become a cliché in the criticism of transvestite theater,[16] but this does not mean that Osgood looks forward to life with Jerry. On the contrary, he blissfully contemplates life with Daphne, whose metamorphic name suggests her nature. To think that Daphne will cease to exist because Jerry has described her situation is to wish away cross-dressing and transvestism as if they had no power in the present. Daphne, like Dorothy, is infinitely more appealing than the male entertainer (Jerry; Michael Dorsey) whose place she has taken. And while it is palpably true—and self-evident to anyone who looks at both films consecutively—that Hoffman patterned many of his mannerisms on Jack Lemmon's, so that his portrayal is not so much that of a man playing a woman as of a man playing a man playing a woman, this should not in itself be a cue for feminist outrage, nor yet for specifically gay protest.

Michael Dorsey, like Joe and Jerry in *Hot*, protests that his cross-dressing is compelled by economic necessity: "I only did it for the work," he says plaintively to both Julie and her father. This is a phenomenon of rationalization which I will discuss later as "the progress narrative." But with Michael as with Jerry, the evidence of the film says otherwise. *Tootsie*, which begins with the camera panning an assorted collection of stage makeup, becomes quickly obsessed with the paraphernalia of male-to-female cross-dressing—as does Michael Dorsey. We see Michael shaving his legs, tweezing his eyebrows, applying mascara and nail polish, fussing with his wig. When Julie asks him why he wears such heavy makeup, he explains that he has "a little moustache problem—too many male hormones." Invited over to Julie's unexpectedly for dinner, he stands in front of his closet in an agony of indecision, dressed in a girdle and pantyhose, flipping through his wardrobe: you can't, he tells his roommate with exasperation, wear white to a casual dinner. After a successful shopping spree he displays his booty: "See this lingerie—you know what it cost?—and the makeup? . . . I have to get up at 4:30, do a close shave . . .". His only regret is that he had to surrender a "beautiful handbag" on sale, because he was "too frightened to fight for it. Now I haven't got a handbag."

Dorsey's usually equable roommate, the playwright Jeff Slater, reads the complexity of Michael's interest in cross-dressing better than the critics: "It is just for the money, isn't it? It's not just so you can wear these little outfits?" At the end of the film we hear a chastened Michael say to Julie that he's still Dorothy: "I just have to learn to do without the dress." But in the final sequence Michael/Dorothy and Julie are still discussing clothes:

> *Julie:* (relenting) Will you lend me that little yellow outfit?
> *Michael:* Which one?
> *Julie:* The Halston.
> *Michael:* (teasing) The Halston? Oh, no, you'd ruin it.

This may be boy-and-girl-talk of the eighties, but it is also more than a little reminiscent of the many recent articles and books on the wives of transvestites.[17] Julie's stages of reaction, from denial to hostility to an interest in Michael/Dorothy's clothes, are paralleled, though obviously with more anguish and anxiety, by the experience of some TV wives. For Julie, of course, this bantering conversation is only a flirtatious game—but games have their own significance, and there is no sense as *Tootsie* closes that Michael's heightened interest in women's clothes is only a ploy.

Just as in Shakespeare's *Twelfth Night* Orsino and Olivia both fall in love not with Viola but with the artifact "Cesario" (Viola—played originally by a boy—dressed in male clothing in imitation of her twin brother), so it is Dorothy Michaels who attracts both characters within the film and audiences who watch it. The Tootsie "role" is that of transvestite. The film rings the (costume) changes on its cross-dressing theme even in the credits, where Franke Piazza is listed as being responsible for "men's costumes," and Jennifer Nichols for "women's costumes." Who, we may ask, does *Dorothy's* clothes? Meanwhile, throughout the film, the refrain of the title song, "Roll, tootsie, roll. Sweet tootsie roll," seems to refer to the insulting, all-purpose diminutive for women employed by the male chauvinist soap-opera director,[18] and specifically addressed, twice, to Dorothy. But any fan of blues or jazz would recognize "tootsie roll" as a term for the phallus. So that "Tootsie" (Dorothy) is again coded as a transvestite, in Freud's description, a "phallic 'woman.' "[19]

The either-or spirit of a certain critical response to *Tootsie* (good for women; bad for women) has been accompanied by a certain tendency toward dismissiveness: the film, say detractors, is slick, mainstream, unthreatening, not really a critique of gender roles, opportunistic and exploitative, a cop-out. It is also, to my mind, a very good film, even richer in detail on reviewing than it is the first few times around. If it is not a critique of gender roles, that may be because it is a critique of gender itself as a category. And if it is slick, unthreatening, mainstream, etc., that may be because *Tootsie*, like Michael/ Dorothy, successfully *passes*, and, in passing, has both its secret pleasure and its cultural effect.

CLOTHES ENCOUNTERS OF THE THIRD KIND

It is curious to note how many literary and cultural critics have recently studied the phenomenon of cross-dressing in literature from the Renaissance to high modernism. The appeal of cross-dressing is clearly related to its status as a sign of the constructedness of gender categories. But the tendency on the part of many critics has been to look *through* rather than *at* the cross-dresser, to turn away from a close encounter with the transvestite, and to want instead to subsume that figure within one of the two traditional genders. To elide and erase—or to *appropriate* the transvestite for particular political and critical aims.

Thus both Sandra Gilbert and Susan Gubar, in separately written articles on male and female transvestism in modernist literature and culture (later combined in a chapter of their jointly authored book), describe the transvestite as in effect a figure for woman: Gubar finds that "cross dressing [is] . . . a dream of prophecy and power" for women like Gertrude Stein and Djuna Barnes, as well as for Woolf's *Orlando*, while Gilbert argues that male modernists like Joyce, Lawrence, and Eliot view transvestism as unsettling and degrading. Gilbert is intrigued by the idea of a "third sex" as it manifests itself in Barnes's *Nightwood*, in the writings of Ursula Le Guin, and in the works of Edward Carpenter, a homosexual gender theorist who wrote in 1908 a book called *Intermediate Sex: A Study of*

Some Transitional Types of Men and Women. But the "third sex" turns out, for Gilbert, to be largely a way of securing power for (and coping with the anxieties of) modernist *women*.[20]

Gilbert's candidates for the third sex are not just any old human subjects but middle-class Western women, what she calls "post-modernist women": the readers, in fact, of post-modernist criticism. But if the third sex is made up exclusively of women, it will go the way of the formerly much-disputed term "Ms.," which denies the criterion of marital status as a socially determinant label, but which is utilized, largely, by the already converted, the educated, middle-class, liberal woman. In order to be maximally effective, "the third sex" must be open to men.

Which is not the same as saying that critics should appropriate the "third sex" *for* men. This is to some extent what Stephen Greenblatt does in his reading of cross-dressing on the Renaissance stage. Greenblatt's essay called "Fiction and Friction" argues that "characters like Rosalind and Viola pass through the state of being men in order to become women. Shakespearean women are in this sense the representation of Shakespearean men." And since the actors in these plays *are* all men, Greenblatt discovers here a "final," "authentic" transvestism, confirming the playfulness of the idea of two sexes and the essential, or essentialized, "fact" of there being only one.[21] As Walter Cohen has pointed out, in Greenblatt's reading of these plays "women" have disappeared.[22] Rosalind and Viola were always already men: boys will be boys. Indeed, the word "boy," conventionally used to describe the players who took the parts of women on the public stage in the English Renaissance, becomes a code word for the "third sex"—here a third sex made up of males, homoerotically attractive to male spectators, rather than a third sex made up of modernist women in trousers.

The "third sex" can be thus assimilated to either the male or the female pole of the hypothetical gender binarism: in either case, it disappears. To argue as Gilbert and Gubar do that "literary women generally persist in seeking . . . a third sex beyond gender" (*Sexchanges*, 365) while "literary men" "express a nausea associated with the blurring of gender boundaries" is once again to divide into two camps, by biological gender rather than by sexual orientation or any other cultural determinant, that complex realm that is articulated and deconstructed by transvestism in literature and culture.

This tendency to erase the third term, to appropriate the cross-dresser "as" one of the two sexes, is emblematic of a fairly consistent critical desire to look away from the transvestite as transvestite, not to see cross-dressing except as male or female manqué, whether motivated by social, cultural, or aesthetic designs. And this tendency might be called an *underestimation* of the object.

For me, therefore, one of the most important aspects of cross-dressing is the way in which it offers a challenge to easy notions of binarity, putting into question the categories of "female" and "male," whether they are considered essential or constructed, biological or cultural. The current popularity of cross-dressing as a theme in art and criticism represents, I think, an undertheorized recognition of the necessary critique of binary thinking, whether particularized as male and female, black and white, yes and no, Republican and Democrat, self and other, or in any other way.

This critique often takes shape, as we have already seen, as the creation of what looks like a third term. Certainly numerous literary texts speculate openly about the "third sex." In his 1835 novel, *Mademoiselle de Maupin*, for example, Théophile Gautier has his sexually ambivalent Théodore write in her (or his) diary: "If ever the fancy takes me to go and find my skirts again in the drawer where I left them, which I very much doubt, unless I fall in love with some young beau, I shall find it hard to lose this habit, and instead of a woman disguised as a man, I shall look like a man disguised as a woman. In truth, neither sex is really mine; . . . I belong to a third sex, a sex apart, which has as yet no name."[23]

Many names have been given to this "third sex" or "third term." Carroll Smith-Rosenberg talks about the development of the concept of the "invert" in the nineteenth century. Renaissance dramatic critics, like Greenblatt and Stephen Orgel, are interested in the construction of the category of the "boy." We could argue that Joan of Arc articulates a "third" category called "maid," or that Maxine Hong Kingston establishes a "third" as "warrior."[24]

The "third" is that which questions binary thinking and introduces crisis—a crisis which is symptomatized by *both* the overestimation *and* the underestimation of cross-dressing. But what is crucial here—and I can hardly underscore this strongly enough—is that the "third term" is *not* a *term*. Much less is it a *sex*, certainly not an instantiated "blurred" sex as signified by a term like "androgyne" or "hermaphrodite," although these words have culturally specific significance at certain historical moments. The "third" is a mode of articulation, a way of describing a space of possibility. Three puts in question the idea of one: of identity, self-sufficiency, self-knowledge.

Let me offer three examples of what I mean by "third" here. They are: the Third World, the third actor, and the Lacanian Symbolic. The Third World is only a "third" in that it does not belong to one or another of two constructed regions, the developed West and what used to be described as the Communist bloc. What the so-called Third World nations have in common is their post-colonial status, their relative poverty, their largely tropical locations, their largely non-Caucasian population, and the fact that they were once subjected to Western rule. Very little else makes the Third World an aggregation; the new nations that came into being as a result of decolonization have in other respects little similarity to one another. "Third World" is a political term, which simultaneously reifies and dismisses a complex collection of entities.

As for the third actor, it will be recalled that this was Sophocles' remarkable contribution to the development of Greek classical drama. A third speaker was added to the protagonist and antagonist, enabling a freer, more dynamic dramaturgy. Yet the "third actor" did not play a single part, but rather several different roles within a given play. Only three speakers conversed on the stage *at a time*, but the number of characters, the number of parts, was not confined to three. A messenger from Corinth disrupts the placid domestic life of Oedipus and Jocasta. A herdsman is compelled to tell them unwelcome news. The third deconstructs the binary of self and other that was itself a comfortable, because commutable and thus controllable, fiction of complementarity. But—or and—it is not itself *a* third *one*; it is rather something that challenges the possibility of harmonious and stable binary symmetry.

The "third" dimension in Lacanian psychoanalysis, the *Symbolic*, is, likewise, not a realm apart, but the transference onto the level of the signifying chain of those binary structures that, in the Imaginary dimension, relate everything back to a fictional "one." Jacques Lacan identifies three dimensions, or orders, in the structure of the human psyche: the Real (that with which, by virtue of the fact that we are *speaking* animals, we have no unmediated relation), the Imaginary, and the Symbolic. The Imaginary is a dimension in which the human subject's relation to himself, and to other people, is structured like, and by, his relation to his mirror image: a dyadic, symmetrical complementarity (whether between child and mirror or between child and mother) based on the fiction of a stable identity, a wholeness, which the mirror instates by equating the self with an *image*. The Symbolic order, what I have been calling the "third," is the register of language, hierarchy, law, and power—the world "out there" to which the human subject must come to relate not only through one-to-one or face-to-face dyads (though these remain inescapable) but through immersion in the codes and constraints of culture. With respect to the mother-child dyad, this "third" is represented by the father and by the prohibition of incest. "The Symbolic order (or language itself)," writes Fredric Jameson, "restructures the Imaginary by introducing a third term into the hitherto infinite regression of the duality of the latter's mirror images."[25]

All three of these examples—the Third World, the third actor, and the Symbolic—involve moving from a structure of complementarity or symmetry to a contextualization, in which what once stood as an exclusive dual relation becomes an element in a larger chain. Thus the United States and the Soviet Union once saw one another, in effect, as rivals dividing up the world, each invested in the fantasy that only the other was in the way. The so-called "Third World," which was always "there," but was invisible to Cold War myopia except as a potential sphere of influence against the encroachment of the "other" superpower, paradoxically contributed to the lessening of Cold War tensions by becoming more politically and economically visible—by (to use a once popular term) "emerging." The Cold War focus on one "other" was thus rendered both impractical and impossible. Likewise the binary, often rivalrous structure of protagonist/antagonist, hero/villain, or even husband/wife in early drama could be disrupted by the manifestation of a "third": the child, the world—in *Oedipus* the locus of history, of "forgotten" knowledge, of the unconscious. The interruption of political events, or of events from the past—an oracle, an unknown herdsman with "news"—the interruption, that is, of things that "exist" in a theatrically conceived space and time but were not present onstage as agents before, reconfigures the relationships between the original pair, and puts in question identities previously conceived as stable, unchallengeable, grounded, and "known."

This interruption, this disruptive act of putting in question, is—as I will be contending throughout this book—precisely the place, and the role, of the transvestite. For all three of these illustrative examples (drawn from the context of world politics—and, since the "Third World" is a largely "non-white" world, from race relations—from theater, and from psychoanalysis and the structure of language) are, as we will see, not just analogies, but also *inextricable* from the functioning of transvestism as such. In fact, the very example Lacan uses to demonstrate his notion of the Symbolic, of the signifying chain, is an example which is directly pertinent to transvestite/transsexual experience as well as to the cultural construction of gender difference.

"URINARY SEGREGATION"

Lacan illustrates the translation of (Imaginary) identities into signifiers in his discussion of "urinary segregation," the triage of bodies performed by the two identical doors labeled "men" and "women" (or, in one New Haven restaurant, "pointers" and "setters") in public accommodations. "The image of twin doors," says Lacan, "symboliz[es], through the solitary confinement offered Western Man for the satisfaction of his natural needs away from home, the imperative that he seems to share with the great majority of primitive communities, by which his public life is subjected to the laws of urinary segregation."[26] Lacan's masculinist vocabulary ("Western *Man*," "the imperative that *he* seems to share") and his colonialist cultural bias ("*Western* Man," "*primitive* communities") frame his tacit assumption that though these signs may be arbitrary, they are not meaningless. He is not concerned with anatomical specifications for gender-tracking. The signs on the doors do not contain pictures of sex organs; they satisfy a desire for cultural binarism rather than for biological certainty. (Indeed, at a recent literary conference in Lausanne, Switzerland, I was amused to find that the two doors were marked with cartoons depicting male and female faces that were so difficult to decipher—and so suggestive in their appearance—that they had to be explained to the conferees in a special announcement from the podium.)

The charming little anecdote Lacan tells to accompany his argument, of two children, a boy and a girl, seated facing each other in a train as it arrives in the station, maintains this oppositional and binary structure: " 'Look,' says the brother, 'we're at Ladies!'; 'Idiot!,' replies his sister [who is facing the other side of the station], 'Can't you see we're at Gentlemen?' " (Lacan, 152). That the two sexes in this story each read the sign of the other is not without interest here. What they see is difference, whether they are conscious of that difference or not.

It is worth pointing out that, as public accommodations more and more often serve a multilingual clientele, the words "men" and "women" or "ladies" and "gentlemen" have been replaced by signs showing a figure dressed in male clothes—trousers—and a figure dressed in female clothes—a skirt or dress. Yet no one (except perhaps transvestites and transsexuals) interprets these signs literally or mimetically. A woman in pants would not ordinarily go through the door marked with a figure in pants, nor would a priest in a soutane or a Hare Krishna advocate in robes head for the door with the skirt.

For transvestites and transsexuals, the "men's room" problem is really a challenge to the way such cultural binarism is read. Cross-dressers who want to pass prefer to read the stick figures literally: those in pants, in there; those in skirts, in here. The public restroom appears repeatedly in transvestite accounts of passing in part because it so directly posits the binarism of gender (choose either one door or the other) in apparently inflexible terms, and also (what is really part of the same point) because it marks a place of taboo. Only little boys (who, as we have seen, have historically in some Western cultures been dressed as girls, until they were "breeched" or put in young men's clothes as a sign of independent maturity) are permitted to "breach" this gender division, in order to accompany their mothers into the women's room. With the advent of more active parenting by fathers it is conceivable that little girls may occasionally find their way into the men's room, but the presence of the urinal (and of the consequent exposure of male genitals) makes this less likely. Thus Dustin Hoffman, in *Tootsie*, reports to his agent that in his cross-dressed persona as "Dorothy Michaels," "I went to the ladies' room—I almost pissed in the sink. I'm in trouble."

In fact, the urinal has appeared in a number of fairly recent films as a marker of the ultimate "difference"—or studied indifference. Early in the film *Cabaret* (1972), Michael York, as an innocent Englishman abroad in Berlin in the early thirties, visits the men's room (clearly marked "*Herren*") of the Kit-Kat Club, and finds himself standing next to a blond chorine at the urinal. We have seen her before in a long shot pulling on her wig. In her full makeup, wig, and low-cut stage costume "she" impassively stares ahead, while York makes a business of seeming matter-of-fact, visibly concealing his very evident double-take. The joke is repeated when the cross-dressed chorine, Elke, is introduced by Liza Minnelli to a fat-cat at one of the nightclub tables. Minnelli has extricated herself from his attentions by whispering that she has "just a little touch of syphilis"; now she and York chortle over the substitution: "Wait till he sees what *Elke's* got." *Cabaret*, a film which uses cross-dressing throughout as both a historically accurate and a theatrically effective sign of German prewar decadence and the ambivalence of Nazi power, situates this initiatory scene of instruction quite deliberately in the men's room. York plays a character who ekes out a living by giving English lessons, but his German learning experience, in which all his up-tight verities and cultural assumptions are finally called into question, starts behind the door marked "*Herren*."

In the case of female impersonators, who want to maintain both the audience's conscious knowledge of their identities as men and the overpowering impression of their femaleness and femininity, the men's room "test" can go the other way, as in a recent film called *The Female Impersonator Pageant* (1985) documenting the crowning of the first annual Female Impersonator of the Year. In the film's opening moments Lyle Waggoner, the male actor who was scheduled to be the announcer for the competition, was heard loudly proclaiming that all beauty contests were alike when the door of the men's room opened to let out a stream of stunning "women," the cross-dressed contestants.

The restroom as site of gender identification accords with a child's earliest training in the use of public accommodations, whether in schools, in airports, or in train or bus stations, and therefore with some of his or her earliest public declarations of gender difference. Lacan's astringently categorical phrase, "urinary segregation," is a reminder at least for citizens of the United States that not too long ago there were separate bathrooms for "white" and "colored" in the southern parts of this country. In other words, this is all about *binaries*. The old binarism, the old division "between the sexes," the ultimate grade school taboo (boys' room/girls' room) becomes a gender test.

For one recent male-to-female transsexual, the test in fact became one of de facto segregation. Barred from the women's room by law school classmates who had known "her" as a man, she was also unwelcome in the men's room in her new female persona and body. The intervention of the law school dean, who permitted her to use *his* bathroom, was a temporary and unsatisfactory solution, since it led to the crossing of yet another taboo boundary, that between faculty and students. Gender and class intersected, with mutually non-beneficial results.[27] It seems particularly ironic, though not for that reason unlikely, that this scenario should play itself out in a law school. I do not know what ultimate solution, if any, was found.

One of the most expressive of the several published memoirs on the transsexual experience is Jan (formerly James) Morris's autobiographical book, *Conundrum*, first published in 1974. Morris now believes that the transsexual era may be ending, that cultural change and other things may have obviated some persons' need to seek a surgical solution to their gender dysphoria.[28] But in her pre-operative condition, when she had been taking hormones and experiencing bodily changes without undergoing the final surgical operation that would construct her anatomically—if not biologically—as a woman, Morris had a number of what might be called "clothes calls." During a trip to South Africa, for example, Morris was told at lunchtime that he had to wear a collar and tie in the dining room, and at dinner that she could not enter wearing trousers. In Mexico a group of housemaids, unable to tell Morris's gender from the "sparse traveler's wardrobe" in the closet, came to the door to ask "Whether you are a lady or a gentleman." "I whipped up my shirt to show my bosom," Morris recounts, "and they gave me a bunch of flowers when I left."[29]

Transsexualism, in fact, is one distinctly twentieth-century manifestation of cross-dressing and the anxieties of binarity, an identifiable site, inscribed on the body, of the question of the constructedness of gender. Transsexual surgery has been performed since 1922, and since the Christine Jorgensen case made headlines in 1953, disrupting the complacency of the "Leave It to Beaver" generation, a remarkable number of novels, memoirs and films have focused on the transsexual as emblem of fear and desire—the fear and desire of the borderline and of technology: *Myra Breckinridge*, the novel and the film; Robert Altman's *Come Back to the Five and Dime, Jimmy Dean, Jimmy Dean*; Brian De Palma's *Dressed to Kill*; *The World According to Garp* (again, both a novel and a film); Angela Carter's *The Passion of New Eve*; the cult film *The Rocky Horror Picture Show*—the list goes on and on. In a chapter called "Spare Parts: The Surgical Construction of Gender" I will discuss transsexual surgery and the gender inequalities of its practice in some detail. Let it suffice to say here that transsexual surgery upped the ante on the two big problems obsessively addressed in medical and cultural discourses: *artifactuality* and *uncertainty*. What did they get, what did they lose, and how could we know what they really were *now*? Not knowing, not being able to know, became, as with the dilemma of the transsexual and the law school restrooms, a source of anxiety—and, in consequence, a battleground for competing vested interests.

The chapters that follow are divided into two long sections, *Transvestite Logics* and *Transvestite Effects*. The reader should not regard them as completely separate or separable, but rather as complementary mirror images of one another. Broadly speaking, *Transvestite Logics* explores the way that transvestism creates culture, and *Transvestite Effects*, the way that culture creates transvestites. Since, as I will argue, one of the most consistent and effective functions of the transvestite in culture is to indicate the place of what I call "category crisis," disrupting and calling attention to cultural, social, or aesthetic dissonances, there has been no attempt here to produce a seamless historical narrative of the "development" of the transvestite figure—indeed, as will quickly become clear, I regard the appropriation of the transvestite as a figure for development, progress, or a "stage of life" as to a large extent a refusal to confront the extraordinary power of transvestism to disrupt, expose, and challenge, putting in question the very notion of the "original" and of stable identity. The rest of this book will be devoted to the exploration of the logics, and the effects, of cross-dressing as an index, precisely, of many different kinds of "category crisis"—for the notion of the "category crisis," I will contend, is not the exception but rather the ground of culture itself.

By "category crisis" I mean a failure of definitional distinction, a borderline that becomes permeable, that permits of border crossings from one (apparently distinct) category to another: black/white, Jew/Christian, noble/bourgeois, master/servant, master/slave. The binarism male/female, one apparent ground of distinction (in contemporary eyes, at least) between "this" and "that," "him" and "me," is itself put in question or under erasure in transvestism, and a transvestite figure, or a transvestite mode, will always function as a sign of overdetermination—a mechanism of displacement from one blurred boundary to another. An analogy here might be the so-called "tagged" gene that shows up in a genetic chain, indicating the presence of some otherwise hidden condition.[30] It is not the gene itself, but its presence, that marks the trouble spot, indicating the likelihood of a crisis somewhere, elsewhere.

In a similar way, I will argue, the apparently spontaneous or unexpected or supplementary presence of a transvestite figure in a text (whether fiction or history, verbal or visual, imagistic or "real") that does not seem, thematically, to be primarily concerned with gender difference or blurred gender indicates a *category crisis elsewhere*, an irresolvable conflict or epistemological crux that destabilizes comfortable binarity, and displaces the resulting discomfort onto a figure that already inhabits, indeed incarnates, the margin. Thus a play like David Henry Hwang's *M. Butterfly*, which tells the story of a male French diplomat and his affair with a male-to-female transvestite singer from the Chinese opera who turns out to be a spy, focuses attention on East-West, Orient-Occident, and gay-straight tensions and redefinitions; that Hwang should choose from current history precisely this story, and that readers and reviewers of his play should regard transvestism as its vehicle rather than its tenor, as, once again, something to be looked *through* on the way to a story about men or women, Asian or European—all of this seems to me symptomatic of category crisis. And we should bear in mind that Hwang's play is based upon a "real" event; that the fantasies unleashed here are cultural forces, not merely "literary" ones.

Likewise, it is, for example, not really surprising to find that there are a remarkable number of transvestite figures in African-American literature—nor is it surprising to find that these figures have been often ignored or marginalized in the crucial and often brilliant discussions of the last years centering on race conflict, miscegenation, and the mulatto/ mulatta.

Category crises can and do mark displacements from the axis of *class* as well as from *race* onto the axis of gender. As we will see shortly, the sumptuary laws that regulated dress for each social class in medieval and Renaissance Europe quickly came as well to regulate and reify dress codes for men and women. Once again, transvestism was the specter that rose up—both in the theater and in the streets—to mark and overdetermine this crisis of social and economic change. In texts as various as *Peter Pan, As You Like It,* and *Yentl*, in figures as enigmatic and compelling as d'Eon and Elvis Presley, George Sand and Boy George, the category crisis and its resultant "transvestite effect" focus cultural anxiety, and challenge vested interests.

What this book insists upon, however, is not—or not only—that cultural forces in general create literary effects, nor even—although I believe this to be the case—that the opposite is also true, but rather that *transvestism is a space of possibility structuring and confounding culture*: the disruptive element that intervenes, not just a category crisis of male and female, but the crisis of category itself.

I

TRANSVESTITE LOGICS

1

DRESS CODES, OR
THE THEATRICALITY OF DIFFERENCE

The distinction between men and women is an important matter to
the state, and so dress and ornament differ according to regulations.
Nowadays women are using weapons as ornaments; in fact, this is prodigious in the extreme. Following this, the Empress Jia affair ensued.
Gan Bao, *Soushen ji* (*Seeking the Spirits*), a record of anomalies and
portents in fourth century China[1]

DRESS CODES AND SUMPTUARY LAWS

All over Europe in the medieval and early modern periods sumptuary laws were
promulgated by cities, towns, and nation states, attempting, with apparently indifferent
success, to regulate who wore what, and on what occasion. The term "sumptuary" is
related to "consumption"; the laws were designed in part to regulate commerce and to
support local industries, as well as to prevent—or at least to hold to a minimum—what
today would be known as "conspicuous consumption," the flaunting of wealth by those
whose class or other social designation made such display seem transgressive.

The idea of a "sumptuary law" designed to regulate dress may seem at first an alien
concept to modern sensibilities, but only if we think of it in national or civic rather than
more local terms. I was brought up with both written and unwritten "dress codes" that
seemed as rigid as any Elizabethan edict. In my middle-class, suburban community girls
were not permitted to wear pants to school, except for "snow pants" in excessively
inclement weather. Boys, if I am remembering correctly, were not allowed to wear shoes
without socks. (That girls *could* wear shoes without socks, and boys *could* wear pants,
makes clear the fact that regulation, rather than another vestimentary or anatomical logic,
was the main object here.)

At college and at some private boarding schools, young women were expected to wear
skirts or dresses to dinner, and young men, shirts and ties, or ties and jackets. (During
the time when this system was breaking down, when I was at Swarthmore College in the
early sixties, several daredevil men in my class appeared at dinner with ties and jackets,

but no shirts; people tell me that at other institutions undergoing similar changes male students came to dinner wearing *only* jackets and ties.)

These "dress codes," remnants of which are still in force in certain restaurants and private clubs, had as their apparent motivation the imposition of discipline, with the implication that you were how you dressed (and would be less likely to hurl buttered rolls across the room if you were wearing a jacket and tie), and also a sense of hierarchy: the school board, or the Deans, or the House Committee, ordained a certain set of behaviors, which happened in this case to be vestimentary. Your submission to those rules signified your acceptance of your position within the hierarchy—which was, to borrow a baseball term, low and inside. Those who preferred to be high and outside declined the hegemonic structure (and membership in the club), and often manifested overt sartorial signs of this self-designated exclusion—by, for example, wearing black, or growing their hair long.

At times of national strife or social change, as, for instance, with the onset of protests against the Vietnam War, aspects of dress often become emblematic of political positions. It would have been surprising to find leftists in those years wearing bow ties, or members of the Young Americans for Freedom sporting black clothes, long hair, or shaggy beards. Yet, as anyone who has gone through these rites of passage can attest, the political/ sartorial and the social/sartorial (or even, perhaps especially, the pubescent/sartorial) have no clear sequence of causality across the board. A young man might begin growing a beard in college because it was forbidden by his high school (or by his parents) and find that his facial hair had become, without his fully being aware of the fact, a politically powerful sign. Sometimes the politics followed the fashion, and sometimes the fashion followed the politics.

Nor are such practices now clearly out of date. In fact dress codes for social regulatory purposes are making something of a comeback, especially in schools and communities where discipline and self-respect are constantly being renegotiated—and where income levels are low. Frank Mickens, the principal of Brooklyn's Boys and Girls High School, made headlines when he banned gold jewelry, removable gold caps for teeth, expensive shearling and leather coats, and personal tape players for his students, who come from neighborhoods that are largely poor and black. A few months later Mickens instituted a shirt-and-tie rule for boys at the school. In accordance with hierarchy, this rule was to be applied first to senior boys, and on Fridays only; a few months later, once the community had become accustomed to this style for its eldest male cohort, all boys would be expected to wear shirts and ties, and not only on Fridays, but every school day. "When the juniors see the seniors doing it, they'll want to be down [i.e., in fashion]," commented one senior man. "Then when the sophomores see the juniors, they'll want to be down with them."[2]

Mickens, a veteran of the letter-of-the-law school of adolescent rule evaders, specified light-colored shirts, and sought donations of suitable shirts and ties from local clothiers so that even the poorest students could comply with the rules. He also initiated talks with girls at the school about a dress code for them, while noting that the male population was in more immediate need of guidance and support. Although the imposition of a mandatory dress code was technically prohibited by school board policy, the idea of the code was enthusiastically supported by both parents and students. One mother told her son that "kids carry themselves a little differently with a shirt and tie on. They walk with a little more respect for themselves," and students suggested that the shirt-and-tie rule would add discipline, and "help people see themselves entering the working world."[3] On Dress for Success Day, the first day the suggested code went into effect, almost all the senior boys wore neckties to school.

As these examples indicate, modern dress codes differ somewhat from sumptuary laws in that their general objective seems to be to class *up*, to enhance upward mobility by requiring a higher standard of dress, whereas the sumptuary laws enacted in Western Europe from the late medieval through the early modern period were designed to keep *down* social climbers, to keep the rising social groups in their sartorial place.[4] In any case, however, when gender enters into such codes, as, inevitably, it does, it is usually as a subset of class, status, rank or wealth—that is to say, as a further concomitant of either the subordination or the commodification of women. If women are conceived of as "status symbols" (or, more recently, as "trophy wives") in their dress, adding to the perceived social luster of their husbands or fathers, sumptuous dress for women becomes a desideratum. If, on the other hand, it is deemed important to put women in their place, rules like "no women in pants" or "ladies must wear hats" or "any woman entering a church must have her shoulders covered" come into force.

Another way in which sumptuary laws may appear to differ from modern dress codes is in their overtly economic and nationalistic or patriotic purposes. Although one of the aims (or, at least, the results) of sumptuary legislation was the subordination of social classes to one another and the sartorial encoding of visible markers for rank and degree, another, related aim was to promote national industries and products and to discourage, at certain times when trade balances were unfavorable, the widespread importation of foreign goods. But even a brief glance at the social history of dress in the twentieth century suggests that political and economic motives are always at work, no matter how much "fashion" may seem to have a will of its own.

According to the *New York Times*, for example, an extremely rigorous dress code remains in force for schoolchildren in contemporary Japan, one of the most highly regulated and regimented of modern societies, through both junior and senior high school. The rules prescribe every aspect of clothing and appearance, from shoes to hair, including the exact width of the pants cuff for boys—with allowances for overweight students—the number of buttons and tucks in pants and skirts and the number of eyelets in shoes. Girls are forbidden to wear ribbons or bright gloves, or to have permanent waves. Boys' hair must be cut short enough not to touch their collars, their ears, or their eyebrows. When a young boy wore pants about one inch narrower than regulation width on a school trip, the article reported, his teacher called his mother, who traveled 370 miles with a new pair of pants and wept in apology before the teacher. Only recently have student protests been vigorous enough for this practice to gain publicity in the West.[5]

In the West as well fashion, if not regulation, has followed economic contingencies in this century. The shorter skirts for women that came in during World War II saved cloth while they afforded women a new look (and perhaps a greater mobility). The invention of nylon in the 1930's, and the replacement of "silk stockings" with "nylons," corresponds to a war industry advance in chemistry. A synthetic fabric designed for parachutes turned out to have the flexibility and strength requisite for women's hosiery, and the silk stockings celebrated by Cole Porter as a metonym of class privilege were democratized, after a fashion, into the nylons bestowed upon civilians by GIs abroad during the war. Both kinds of stockings, however, remained favorite kinds of "payment" to women, by men: what was democratized by this invention was class, not gender. But stockings themselves had, in fact, crossed the gender line a long time before. Silk stockings appear first in England in the wardrobe of Henry VIII, and only much later become primarily associated with women's dress.[6]

As our discussion of sumptuary legislation will make clear, the regulation of gender and rank through dress codes can be a slippery business at a time of widespread social change. Consider what happens when women are admitted to that most regulation-conscious of contexts, the all-male military academy.

The first class of women to enter the U.S. Military Academy at West Point in 1976 quickly became subject to institutional gender paranoia—and to their own. At the Plebe Hop, a required social event held in September, the Academy brought in a rock and roll band, only to register its consternation at the sight of "mirror-image couples dancing in short hair and dress gray trousers."[7] The rule book was swiftly amended; women were still permitted to attend future hops in trousers, but if they wanted to dance they were required to wear uniform skirts.

The Full Dress uniforms supplied for these first female cadets were, significantly, different from those given to the men. The trousers had no back pockets, and the women's coats, unlike the traditional male tailcoats, were cut off at the waist. Both sartorial alterations were intended—or at least so the new cadets speculated—to deemphasize the curve of a woman's buttocks, but the changes in fact called attention to gender differences they were designed to conceal. Three years later the Academy changed its mind—or, at least, its regulations—and issued the women coats with tails.

One female plebe had her face scrubbed till it burned by a superior officer convinced that she was wearing "blush" (though he didn't know the term). Yet a few months later, during Plebe-Parent Weekend, the women cadets were summoned to a mandatory two-and-a-half hour lecture sponsored by the Revlon company, in which professional makeup artists taught them how to apply cosmetics. Apparently the administration had been disconcerted, once again, by the sight of women in trousers and short haircuts—cut weekly by Academy regulation—who didn't look like women. That this special instruction took place during a parental visit suggests that the Academy brass were looking at the new cadets with different, and defensive, eyes.

Nor was this double vision limited to those who set and enforced the dress regulations. A member of the pioneer entering class reported that on her first trip off-post since becoming a cadet she ran in the rain to a local fast food shop. By the time she arrived, her uniform and short hair were drenched; the young woman behind the counter took one look at her and asked, politely, "Can I help you, sir?" Shaken, the cadet rushed out of the shop and locked herself in the bathroom, staring in the mirror. "Did I look like a man? What was West Point doing to me?" Her distress was the greater because the experience marked her as a double outsider. Inside the Academy's grounds she was regarded by hardliners as a misfit because she was a woman; outside, dressed in her military uniform, she was read as a man.

The defining and distorting presence of the "mirror" in these incidents is suggestive. Same and different; self and "other." Just as the Academy looked at its female cadets through the eyes of the parents and the heterosexual social order, just as the woman in her new military uniform looked in the mirror and saw self-difference, saw the question of gender in the eyes of the clerk, so dress codes function in the social world and the world of social hierarchy as structures that simultaneously regulate and critique normative categories like rank (or its civilian counterpart, class) and gender. But the implications of such sartorial codes, as these examples have already suggested, cannot be limited to the social or the economic spheres. With cultural legislation comes cultural legibility, or illegibility—and with them comes, inevitably, the collective and individual paranoia on which much social and psychic life depends. It is not surprising, in view of this, to find that anxiety about cross-dressing is manifested by authoritarian structures (the Academy, the army, the absolute monarch, the local school board) as a sign and symptom of the dissolution of boundaries, and of the arbitrariness of social law and custom.

"NONE SHALL WEAR . . ."

The medieval and Renaissance sumptuary laws, as we have already noted, appear to have been patriotic, economic, and conservatively class-oriented; they sought to restrict the wearing of certain furs, fabrics, and styles to members of particular social and economic classes, ranks, or "states." While protecting, at times, such native industries as the wool trade or the linen trade, and purporting, at least, to guard the public morality against excess and indulgence, these statutes (which also governed food and drink and the playing of sports or games, but were in the main directed at apparel) at the same time attempted to mark out as visible and above all *legible* distinctions of wealth and rank within a society undergoing changes that threatened to blur or even obliterate such distinctions.

The ideal scenario—from the point of view of the regulators—was one in which a person's social station, social role, gender and other indicators of identity in the world could be *read*, without ambiguity or uncertainty. The threat to this legibility was "confusion": "when as men of inferiour degree and calling, cannot be by their attire discerned from men of higher estate."[8] (This was also the intent of what might be called the Nazi dress code, which required male homosexuals to wear pink triangles and Jews to wear armbands marked with yellow stars of David. Indeed the social identification of Jews in Europe by yellow—or sometimes red—scarves or bands goes back as far as medieval times. When in response to Nazi edict the King of Denmark donned a yellow star and urged his compatriots to do likewise, he staged a version of the same "confusion" so alarming to early modern monarchs—this time for moral and political, rather than economic and social, motives.)

From the reign of Edward III until the time of James I, sumptuary legislation in England sought to ensure social legibility and enforce social hierarchy. Queen Elizabeth's reign was the apogee of this move to regulate dress. More royal orders having to do with dress were issued—or at least, have been preserved—from her time than at any other point in English history.[9] It may be useful, therefore, to consider one such proclamation in brief detail, so as to have some idea of the general rhetorical form and force of such laws.

Elizabeth's sumptuary proclamation of August 13, 1597 blamed "the inordinate excess in apparel," which had been decried in "sondry former proclamations"[10] for a falling off in hospitality (since so much was expended on dress), for an increase in crime (since the poorer classes were thought to have been infected by pride, and to have turned to robbery and theft to embellish their wardrobes) and, once again, for the "*confusion* of degree, where the meanest are as richly dressed as their betters" (Jerdan, 247). The proclamation of 1597 had separate categories for men's and women's apparel: each took the form of a long list of proscribed items of dress with an indication of who alone was permitted to wear them. For instance, "none shall wear" (this was the general rubric) "cloth of gold, sylver tissued, silke of purple color" "except" (another rubric) "earls and above that rank and Knights of the Garter in their purple mantles"; or, for women, "none shall wear any" (again, the general rubric) "cloth of silver in kirtles only" "except" "knights' wives and all above that rank." The proclamation ran through the ranks from earls and countesses to gentlemen's wives and men with incomes of 500 marks, specifying appropriate—and inappropriate—materials for headdresses, netherstocks, jerkins, hose, and doublets. The formulation "none shall wear . . . except" carries with it the force of royal edict (compare the Decalogue's "thou shalt not . . .") and the bestowal of favored exceptions. Dress, in other words, was a privilege of rank.

Discussion of sumptuary laws by scholars of Renaissance literature in the 1970's and early 1980's tended to emphasize the implications of such laws for *gender*, especially as reflected in the debates about cross-dressing and the English stage. It is worth remembering, however, that sumptuary legislation was overwhelmingly concerned with wealth or rank, and with gender largely as it was a subset of those categories. (The concept of "class" here, although anachronistic with respect to the social formations of Renaissance England, nonetheless provides a helpful modern analogue). The reversal of emphasis, stressing gender over social status—a reversal that has now itself largely been reversed by more recent scholarship—reflected the temper of the times: the emergence of feminism (and more recently, of gay and lesbian theory) as important forces in the literary academy, and the relative *in*visibility of class within the American ideology of democratic self-realization.

In Elizabethan England "confusion," of both gender and status, became, perhaps inevitably, itself fashionable. An extraordinary passage from the "Homily Against Excess of Apparel" that Elizabeth commanded to be preached in the churches sketches the satiric picture of a representative "Englishman" as one whose national dress *cannot* be characterized.

> Yea, many men are become so effeminate, that they care not what they spend in disguising themselves, ever desiring new toys, and inventing new fashions. Therefore a certain man, that would picture every countryman in his accustomed apparel, when he painted other nations, he pictured the Englishman all naked, and gave him cloth under his arm, and bade him make it himself as he thought best, for he changed his fashion so often, that he knew not how to make it. Thus with our fantastical devices we make ourselves laughing-stocks to other nations; while one spendeth his patrimony upon pounces and cuts, another bestoweth more on a dancing shirt, than might suffice to buy him honest and comely apparel for his whole body. Some hang their revenues about their necks, ruffling in their ruffs, and many a one jeopardizes his best joint, to maintain himself in sumptuous raiment. And every man, nothing considering his estate and condition, seeketh to excel others in costly attire.[11]

Here fashion is the enemy of patriotism as well as of social order and legibility; instead of investing his patrimony on appropriate and seemly necessities—"honest and comely apparel," "his best joint"—this caricature of an Englishman has become his own tailor, and can only be pictured, like an Emperor without clothes, in the process of perpetually reinventing his expensive and fashionable costume. The crescendo of alliteration here ("revenues . . . ruffling in their ruffs"; "jeopardizes his best joint") mimics foppish affectation.

In this passage, we should note, the charge of "effeminacy" against men is not one of transvestism, much less of homosexuality (the word "effeminate" meant something much closer to "self-indulgent, voluptuous," and hence "womanish" or enslaved to women, in the period), but rather one of profligacy. Clothing—and the changeability of fashion—is an index of destabilization, displeasing to the monarch as to the sermonizer, since it renders the Englishman *il*legible, incapable of inscription. The Englishman satirized here is in effect a kind of commodity fetishist, whose obsession with commodity and style ignores the old values: "his estate and condition." Later in the sermon women are equally taken to task: for their self-absorption, for rich apparel, face painting, hair dying, and questionable morals, since though they claim to be making themselves attractive for their husbands they go abroad for admiration, seeking to entice others. What is offensive, then, about excess of apparel for either gender is that it has a deleterious effect upon patriotic pride and upon both the national and the domestic economy.

But notice, particularly, that it is "excess" that is stigmatized and deplored. Excess, that which overflows a boundary, is the space of the transvestite. Dancing shirts, ruffles, face painting—all of the Homily's iconographic indicators of excess could be dislocated from the context of sumptuary laws and rearticulated as signs of another kind of vestimentary transgression, one that violated expected boundaries of gender identification or gender decorum. For one kind of crossing, inevitably, crosses over into another: the categories of "class" and "rank," "estate and condition," which seem to contain and to regulate gender ("earls and above"; "knights' wives"), are, in turn, interrogated by it. As we will see throughout this study, class, gender, sexuality, and even race and ethnicity— the determinate categories of analysis for modern and postmodern cultural critique—are themselves brought to crisis in dress codes and sumptuary regulation. What I will be contending, and seeking to demonstrate, is that the transvestite is the figure of and for that crisis, the uncanny supplement that marks the place of desire.

The biblical injunction from Deuteronomy, "The woman shall not wear that which pertaineth unto a man, neither shall a man put on a woman's garment; for all that do so are abomination unto the Lord thy God" (Deut. 22:5), functioned in effect as another kind of sumptuary law, divinely ordained. Thus, although Queen Elizabeth herself was said to have cross-dressed upon occasion (the legendary story of her appearance at Tilbury in 1588, dressed like an "androgynous martial maiden" to inspire her troops against the Spanish Armada, is only one of the many associations of the Virgin Queen with the Amazons, and other warrior queens), her example was, as so frequently, the exception that would prove the rule.[12] If the Queen could declare in ringing tones that "I know I have the body of a weak and feeble woman, but I have the heart and stomach of a king, and of a king of England too,"[13] the rules were clearly different for commoners. Vives in his *Instruction of a Christian Woman* (1529) cautioned that "A woman shall use no mannes raymente, elles lette hir thinke she hath the mans stomacke," and quoted Deuteronomy to clinch the point.[14] A queen might have a king's stomach, but the ordinary citizen did not possess the privilege of two bodies, and lacking a "man's stomach" (that is, a man's inward emotions, passions, aspirations and desires, as well as a man's organs) she had no business wearing his clothes. This did not prevent female-to-male transvestism from enjoying a London vogue in the last decade of the sixteenth century (as it would again some ten years later), but the practice was at strong variance with the letter of the law, and with the social and "moral" expectations of self-appointed cultural arbiters. This doubtless added appeal to the transgression.

The Deuteronomic injunction against transvestism, the God-ordained dress code, was constantly invoked by Puritans railing against the theater, where cross-dressing was the common practice for boy actors. Thus, for example, in a passage that has been frequently cited by scholars of Renaissance transvestite theater, we find Philip Stubbes complaining in his *Anatomy of Abuses* (1583) that "Our Apparell was given us as a signe distinctive to discern betwixt sex and sex, & therfore one to weare the Apparel of another sex is to participate with the same, and to adulterate the veritie of his own kinde."[15] Confusion, again, was both the threat and the fear. Stubbes deplores, in particular, the wearing of men's styles by women: "Women also there have dublets and jerkins, as men have . . ., buttoned up to the breast, and made with winges, weltes, and pinions on the shoulder poyntes, as mannes apparel is for all the worlde" (*Anatomy*, 68).

Another Puritan and an Oxford Greek scholar, Dr. John Rainolds, was one of many who warned specifically against the contrary case: of men—or rather, boys—wearing the clothes of women. "Beware of beautifull boyes transformed into women by putting on their raiment, their feature, lookes, and facions." Sodomy, homosexuality, sadistic flagellation and male marriage were all, he thought, likely consequences of such behavior—consequences attested by biblical and classical example.[16] For Rainolds, women's clothes act as transferential objects, kindling a metonymic spark of desire: "because a womens garment being put on a man doeth vehemently touch and moue him with the remembrance and imagination of a woman; and the imagination of a thing desirable doth stir up the desire" (Rainolds, 96–97).

We might note that this is a classic description of a fetishistic scenario, in which the woman who is remembered and imagined is the phallic mother. Thus Freud writes about the fetish that it replaces the imagined maternal phallus: "Something else has taken its place, has been appointed its substitute, as it were, and now inherits the interest which was formerly directed to its predecessor . . . What other men have to woo and make exertions for can be had by the fetishist with no trouble at all."[17] But this mechanism of substitution, which is the trigger of transvestic fetishism, is also the very essence of theater: role playing, improvisation, costume, and disguise. In other words, Rainolds, like his fellow antitheatricalists, despite or perhaps because of the hysterical nature of their objections, had intuited something fundamental about the way dramatic representation works—and about the power of the transvestite.

Not only in the theater but also in the streets, the fantasy and fear of transvestism had its visible counterpart. Visible, but not always legible: the "confusion" of degrees and genders was increasingly confounded. During the period 1580 to 1620, as we have already noted, some women as well as men cross-dressed publicly in London, whether for fashion, for comfort, for pleasure, as a stratagem that facilitated theft or other crime, or as a cultural sign of their social position, high or low. The Elizabethan author and playwright Thomas Middleton describes in his *Micro-Cynicon* (1599) an encounter with a male transvestite whom the narrator takes to be a beautiful woman, only to be disabused of this notion when he attempts to have sex with "her." In this case the masquerade was apparently deployed for mercenary reasons, the object of the "painted puppet" in "nymph's attire"—at least according to the narrator—being to elicit money from him. (This example of Elizabethan transvestism—which, according to Middleton, was a common phenomenon in London streets—differs markedly from the "molly-house" culture of the early eighteenth century, in which, as Alan Bray points out, men dressed in women's clothes and makeup not to deceive but to be recognized as homosexuals by other men, in a private, club-like setting. The transvestite of Middleton's narrative is not, or not self-evidently, a homosexual, but rather a trickster seeking to rob his unwary partner.)[18]

Both upwardly mobile citizens' wives and lower-class women, many accused of prostitution or loose living because of their freedom of dress, are cited in the pamphlets—and in the courts. A woman found guilty of dressing in man's attire was sentenced in 1575 to stand on the pillory for two hours dressed in men's clothes, and then sent to Bridewell; another, in 1601, was described in prison records as having a bastard child and going in men's apparel, again as if the two transgressions were related.[19] Yet it seems clear that prostitution and cross-dressing were *alternative* social strategies for social and economic survival.

At the trial of the Puritan William Prynne, Prynne's disapproving view of contemporary *hair dressing*, male and female, was read aloud to the assemblage. Men, he had pointed out with scorn and alarm, now wore curls, while women cut their hair:

> Yett notwithstandinge as our Englishe ruffians are metamorphosed in their deformed, frizlled lockes and hayre, so our Englishe gentle-women, as yf they all intended to turn men outright, and weare the breeches, or to be Popish nunnes, are nowe growne soe farr past shame, past modesty, grace, and nature, as to clipp their hayre like men, with lockes and foretoppes.[20]

Now, this is a very curious accusation. The English gentlewomen are imagined as wishing to turn *either* into *men* or into *nuns*—perhaps because of their clipped hairstyles. Men or nuns—what do these two groups have in common, that they should be envisaged as the hypothetical nightmare transformations of fashionable gentlewomen? Instead of male/female there arises, for the moment, the specter of Protestant/Catholic category crisis. In this case a category crisis *elsewhere*, the virulent anti-Catholicism of the Puritans, is imported and used as a displacement of and for the antifeminism or misogyny of this attack on cross-gender style. It is perhaps no accident that this substitution and replacement should occur at a time when both the sex-and-gender roles of English monarchs, and their religious faith, were under intense scrutiny and pressure. For both of these categories were as much at issue in the time of James I as of his predecessor. And what was largely unconscious, still on the level of the symptom, in the Elizabethan period, became overt and acted out with the coming of James I to the throne.

Despite the continued extravagant and, indeed, increasingly fantastic nature of court dress, sumptuary legislation in James's reign was not only suspended but repealed. The repeal was the result of a struggle between the King and Parliament over prerogative, not a repudiation of the idea of social regulation through dress. Indeed, efforts were made repeatedly throughout the reign to reinstitute some version of the sumptuary laws, but for the same reasons these renewed efforts failed. "None shall wear" was no longer the official dress code of the land.

Yet, even in the absence of sumptuary legislation, feelings ran high in Jacobean England against certain kinds of excess in apparel. "Unisex" styles, and styles that migrated across the spectrum from one gender to another, enjoyed a new vogue. Women and men alike now wore netherstocks (like modern stockings) and high, corked shoes or slippers, called pantoffles, which were hard to keep on the feet and uncomfortable. This fashion may have begun with men, since the Venetian ambassador, writing in 1618, commented that noble English ladies at a masque "all wear men's shoes or at least very low slippers."[21] (Women, however, continued to wear these corked shoes for most of the seventeenth century, despite their discomfort; called choppines or chioppines, the shoes grew to a height of four or five inches from the ground, and must have restricted ease of movement, especially when, by the middle of the century, it became fashionable to wear corked shoes almost twice as long as one's feet.) Members of both sexes wore earrings and carried looking-glasses well into the seventeenth century.[22]

James, notoriously bisexual and extravagant, himself the son of the beheaded Mary Queen of Scots and the adoptive heir of Queen Elizabeth, who sanctioned Mary's execution, was phobic about powerful women—and about women in men's clothes. In 1620 he instructed the Anglican clergy "to inveigh vehemently in their sermons against women wearing broad-brimmed hats, painted doublets, short hair, and even some of them poniards, and, if pulpit admonitions fail, another course will be taken."[23] In the same year, 1620, two pamphlets, *Hic Mulier: Or, the Man-Woman*, and, in rebuttal, *Haec-Vir: Or, the Womanish-Man*, debated the social, moral, and cultural valences of cross-dressing. The author of *Hic Mulier* saw the fashion for men's clothes as a sign not of homosexuality but of a general sexual availability: the cross-dressed woman's "loose, lascivious civille embracement of a French doublet, being all unbutton'd to entice" signified desirability—and desire.[24] In *Haec-Vir* the "mannish woman" gets to speak her piece, and offers a strong assertion of women's rights—an assertion which is complicated rather than clarified by the fact that she offers this opinion when cross-dressed as a man.[25] Is to be free and verbal, then, necessarily to be dressed like a man?

The controversy about cross-dressed acting—did stage plays in which boys wore women's clothing violate Deuteronomy?—was thus part of a continuing Puritan polemic about the immorality of the stage, but it also tapped into larger cultural anxieties, of which the *Hic Mulier* pamphlets were a sign. *Did* clothes, in fact, make the man—or woman?

Was "self-fashioning"—the "forming of a self"—that achievement so consistently claimed as one of the chief distinguishing features of the Renaissance,[26] in fact at the mercy of *fashion*? Of *clothing*?

Let us return for a moment to the figure, from the "Homily Against Excess of Apparel," of the naked Englishman with a bolt of cloth under his arm, instructed to "make [his costume] himself as he thought best, for he changed his fashion so often, that [an artist] knew not how to make it." Renaissance antitheatricalists, in their debates about gender, cross-dressing, and the stage, articulated deep-seated anxieties about the possibility that identity was not fixed, that there was no underlying "self" at all, and that therefore identities had to be zealously and jealously safeguarded.[27]

But what seems clear in all of these speculations—about men in women's clothing and women dressed as men, and even in the label of effeminacy and foppishness—is that the specter of transvestism, the uncanny intervention of the transvestite, came to mark and indeed to overdetermine this space of anxiety about fixed and changing identities, commutable or absent "selves." Transvestism was located at the juncture of "class" and "gender," and increasingly through its agency gender and class were revealed to be commutable, if not equivalent. To transgress against one set of boundaries was to call into question the inviolability of both, and of the set of social codes—already demonstrably under attack—by which such categories were policed and maintained. The transvestite in this scenario is both terrifying and seductive precisely because s/he incarnates and emblematizes the disruptive element that intervenes, signaling not just another category crisis, but—much more disquietingly—a crisis of "category" itself.

TRANSVESTITE SHAKESPEARE (I)

> [A Harvard professor] had asked if future articles would appear in the magazine asserting "that the earth is flat" and that "Queen Victoria was in fact a Peruvian transvestite."
> —Charlton Ogburn, *The Mysterious William Shakespeare: The Myth and the Reality*. Reporting on a letter to the editor of *Harvard Magazine* objecting to Ogburn's controversial article, in which he claimed that the Earl of Oxford was the author of "Shakespeare's" plays[28]

The death of Sir Laurence Olivier on July 11, 1989, was mourned and commemorated as if it were the death of Shakespeare himself—only this time, much more satisfyingly, *with* a body. At a memorial service in Westminster Abbey, where, famously, Shakespeare is *not* buried, although a portrait bust represents him, "the casket," according to the *Boston Globe*, "was surmounted with a floral crown . . . studded with flowers and herbs mentioned in Shakespeare's works: from lavender and savory to rue and daisies."[29]

The parade of dignitaries who moved up the aisle to the fanfare from Sir William

Walton's music to Olivier's film of *Hamlet* included Douglas Fairbanks, Jr., carrying the Order of Merit on a gold-fringed, blue velvet pillow, Michael Caine, carrying Olivier's Oscar (awarded not for any single role, but for "lifetime achievement"), and a host of other actors and actresses (Maggie Smith, Paul Scofield, Derek Jacobi, Peter O'Toole, etc., etc.) bearing such relics as the crown used in the film of *Richard III*, the script of the film *Hamlet*, the laurel wreath in the stage production of *Coriolanus*, and the crown used in the television production of *King Lear*, as well as silver models of the Royal National Theater and the Chichester Festival Theater. That impossible event in literary history, a state funeral for the poet-playwright who defines Western culture, doing him appropriate homage—an event long-thwarted by the galling absence of certainty about his identity and whereabouts—had now at last taken place. Through a mechanism of displacement, the memorial service for Olivier became a memorial service for Shakespeare.

Now, what I want to suggest here is that under these cultural circumstances it is no accident that the Olivier eulogized (even before his death in commemorative essays) is a transvestite Olivier.

At first it might seem surprising that in both print and television obituaries for Olivier— himself arguably the most rampantly heterosexual Shakespearean actor of his generation— he is repeatedly pictured in drag, and described as "girlish." A photo of Olivier as Katherina in a school production of *The Taming of the Shrew* appeared on the NBC Evening News to mark the actor's passing. *Time* magazine commented that "From a list of his acting credits at school (Maria in *Twelfth Night*, Kate in *The Taming of the Shrew*), one imagines that his teachers had already spotted what director Elia Kazan would later cite as Olivier's 'girlish' quality. Throughout his career . . . Olivier would bat his eyes at the audience, soliciting its surrender. But belying those feminine eyes were the cruel, pliant lips, and on them the smile of a tiger too fastidious to lick his chops in anticipation of a tasty meal."[30]

"I may be rather feminine but I'm not effeminate," Olivier once declared,[31] and critic Michael Billington remarks that "he can be masculine and feminine but never neuter" (Billington, 71). He has been compared to Garbo and Dietrich in his sexual ambiguity— a quality, it is claimed, of great actors, though what this asserts is not explained. Nor is Olivier as woman merely an artifact of the tranvestite theater of his same-sex public school. The recent "definitive"[32] biography by Anthony Holden ("author of *Prince Charles*," says the dustjacket) devotes a page of photographs to the great actor in drag, including a full-length photo of a serious-faced middle-aged Olivier in a girdle, high heels, stockings, and padded bra.[33]

Olivier's Malvolio at Stratford in 1955 is said to have been marked by a "dainty, fairy-footed progress across the stage and [a] skittish, faintly epicene lightness," like that of Jack Benny (Billington, 72). (Jewish and working class, this Malvolio, with his crinkly hair and his uncertainty about pronunciation, invoked stereotypes about Jewish effeminacy that are part of the stage heritage of category crisis in ethnic and gender crossover, an essential element in what I will be calling the "transvestite effect.") Kenneth Tynan described Olivier's Richard III, admiringly, as "a bustling spinster" in his dealings with Clarence (Billington, 73), and one critic aptly recalled Neil Simon's lampoon of a flamboyantly gay Richard III in *The Goodbye Girl* as the obverse of Olivier's "sinister amalgam of male power-hunger and female seductiveness" (Billington, 73). The mechanism of displacement in category crisis deployed in and by transvestism is never more acutely emblematized than in Olivier's *Othello*; as Billington notes, "[e]ven at his butchest Olivier slips in hints of a dandified vanity: one remembers that astonishing first entrance in *Othello* with a red rose held gently between thumb and forefinger and with the hips rotating slightly in a manner half way between Dorothy Dandridge and Gary Sobers" (Billington, 75).

This odd emphasis on the feminine and girlish Olivier comes despite—or, perhaps, because of—the fact that Olivier is frequently described as an exceptionally "athletic" Shakespearean actor, and his three marriages are extensively chronicled, as is his career as a movie heartthrob modeled after John Barrymore. As Billington in the same proto-posthumous appreciation recalls, "Olivier's fops leave you in no doubt as to their ultimate masculinity . . . It is a modern fallacy that fops are homosexual. Olivier's two Restoration performances reminded us that in the seventeenth-century finery of apparel and frivolity of manner were compatible with balls" (Billington, 75).

It is not, then, that Olivier is revealed in these representations as effeminate or gay (and, indeed, no similar cult has grown up around his overtly gay contemporary John Gielgud), but rather that he becomes the portrait of triumphant transvestism—no closet queen, but the Queen Elizabeth of his age, and thus a figure for (who else?) Shakespeare himself. If it is the case—and I believe it is—that the transvestite makes culture possible, that there can be no culture without the transvestite because the transvestite marks the entrance into the Symbolic—the eulogizing of Olivier as on the one hand a matinee idol who began his career as a girl (or a "boy actress") and on the other hand as Shakespeare makes compelling, if at first counter-intuitive, cultural sense.

Anyone who has seen a range of Shakespeare productions, from amateur school and college theater to professional repertory companies, will be familiar with the phenomenon of "authentic," "period," or "Elizabethan" dress: ruffs, tights, doublets, and cloaks all around, with trains for the ladies and cap-and-bells and motley for the Fool. This hodge-podge will readily demonstrate the pitfalls of a notion of the "original," which must be constructed backward from portraits and the residual contents of a theater company's wardrobe. Alternatively, to attain "timelessness" rather than museum-style "historical specificity," Shakespeare productions have often been done in "rehearsal clothes" (jeans and black turtlenecks, leotards, sweat suits, and the like), perhaps with an acknowledgment of the fact that in Shakespeare's day plays were generally staged in modern dress.

Elizabethan companies often had the use of the cast-off clothing of great public figures:

in theory, at least, a "King" could wear the costume of a King, or—more likely—a "nobleman" could wear a nobleman's doublet or cloak. The traveler Thomas Platter of Basel reported that "the comedians are most expensively and elegantly apparelled, since it is customary in England, when distinguished gentlemen or knights die, for nearly the finest of their clothes to be made over and given to their servants, and as it is not proper for them to wear such clothes but only to imitate them, they give them to the comedians to purchase for a small sum."[34]

Actors were in effect *allowed* to violate the sumptuary laws that governed dress and social station—on the supposedly "safe" space of the stage. Thus Stephen Gosson, an early antitheatrical pamphleteer, complained that actors dressed in the cast-off clothes of aristocrats mocked their betters. "Overlashing [i.e., extravagance] in apparel is so common a fault," he reported, "that the very hirelings of some of our players . . . jet under gentlemen's noses in suits of silk."[35] The stage was a privileged site of transgression, in which *two* kinds of transvestism were permitted to players: changes of costume that violated edicts against wearing the clothing of the wrong rank as well as the wrong gender. As fools and players were licensed, given official sanction to do that which, unsanctioned, was liable to prosecution, so also licenses to wear clothing forbidden by the various statutes were issued by Queen Elizabeth, as by her predecessors.[36]

Such catalogues of wardrobe details as Autolycus's list of peddler's wares in *The Winter's Tale* ("Golden quoifs and stomachers/ For my lads to give their dears: /Pins and poking-sticks of steel . . ." [4.4.226–27]) or Berowne's self-indicting metaphors of linguistic excess in *Love's Labour's Lost* ("taffeta phrases, silken terms precise, /Three piled hyperboles" now forsworn for "russet yeas and honest kersey noes" [5.2.406–13]) assume a contextual particularity and power when viewed in the context of Renaissance sumptuary laws. Stomachers, "poking sticks" (for the support of ruffs), quoifs for ladies' elaborate court headdresses, three-piled or best-quality velvet, and homespun, domestically produced fabrics like russet and kersey, all had their place in the social and economic hierarchy of dress. But since many of these costume distinctions are unfamiliar and therefore illegible or undecipherable to twentieth-century readers and audiences (they tend, as we have already noted, to coalesce into some ahistorical construct of "Elizabethan dress"), the plays' obsessive emphasis on clothing as a marker of difference is obscured, as the reader's (or director's, or designer's) eye glides absentmindedly past lists of incomprehensible garments in search of moral or emotional (or even sexual or political) context.

Moreover, the *kinds* of difference particularized by the sumptuary laws are themselves governed by a mechanism of displacement, or slippage, that seems to come into play whenever things threaten to get out of hand. It is no accident that sex and degree are the twin categories of classification here, nor that they are rendered both rhetorically and functionally interchangeable. As Natalie Zemon Davis points out in "Women on Top," "varied images of sexual topsy-turvy—from the transvestite male escaping responsibility and harm to the transvestite fool and the unruly woman unmasking the truth" were powerful in early modern Europe "so long as sexual symbolism had a close connection with questions of order and subordination" and "so long as both traditional hierarchical structures *and* disputed changes in the distribution of power in family and political life" served as stimuli for inversion play.[37] Thus Shakespeare's Viola, disguised as a boy, replies to the countess Olivia's question about her parentage, "My state is well;/ I am a gentleman" (*TN* 1.5.278–79), neatly conflating two lies in one.

Twelfth Night is a play as much concerned with status as with gender, and its masquerade centers on not one but two cross-dressers: Viola in her male attire, and Malvolio, imagining himself in his "branch'd velvet gown" (2.5.47–48)—ornamented with an embroidered pattern of leafy branches, an elaborate fashion explicitly forbidden to all persons below the rank of knight in sumptuary statutes from the Yorkist period through the time of Elizabeth[38]—before his final, humiliating appearance in cross-gartered yellow stockings. Malvolio, in other words, is as much a cross-dresser as Viola, but what he crosses is a boundary of rank rather than of gender. His desire is clearly for upward mobility, another kind of coming out of the closet: "There is example for't; the Lady of the Strachy married the yeoman of the wardrobe" (2.5.39–40). Of the two no man's lands, rank seems for *Twelfth Night* (or, *What You Will*) the more socially culpable.

The dual anxieties over gender and status are themselves crossed here. Viola claims for herself the role of "poor monster" (2.2.34), giving substance to Philip Stubbes's complaint that cross-dressed women are "Monsters of both kindes, half women, half men" (*Anatomy*, 73), but it is Malvolio who bears the brunt of the public exposure and social ostracism that result from a violation of the dress code. Again, it seems no accident that his downfall, so elaborately orchestrated by Maria, involves a change of dress, and one that itself substitutes the outdated, fantastical cross-gartering for the upwardly mobile fantasy of the count in his branched velvet gown. Whether we see this exposure of Malvolio as itself displacing a more dangerous monstrosity of gender-crossing (Viola, after all, is allowed to go off in search of her "women's weeds" [5.1.273] or what Orsino even more pertinently calls her "other habits" [387]), or whether the attempted violation of class boundaries, less titillating to a twentieth-century audience, is in Elizabethan context even more daring than the bait-and-switch of gender, the two categories, status and gender, are both clearly marked in the play by costume change of a highly visible and risible kind.

Just as sumptuary laws primarily regulated status rather than gender infractions, so a play like *Twelfth Night* marks the seriousness of Malvolio's transgression as contrasted with Viola's. But—and this is my main point here—this overlay of class or status anxieties onto gender anxieties is exemplary rather than merely "factual" or "historical." What it points toward is the centrality of the transvestite as an index of category destabilization altogether. We are speaking of an underlying psychosocial, and not merely a local or historical, effect. What might be called the "*transvestite effect.*"

One of the cultural functions of the transvestite is precisely to mark this kind of displacement, substitution, or slippage: from class to gender, gender to class; or, equally plausibly, from gender to race or religion. The transvestite is both a signifier and that which signifies the undecidability of signification. It points toward itself—or, rather, toward the place where it is not. The transvestite as object of desire—as, indeed, the embodied construction of mimetic desire—is the manifestation of Freud's concept of the overestimation of the object, as set forth in his essay on narcissism. For the transvestite is there and gone at once. Nobody gets "Cesario" (or "Ganymede"), but "Cesario" (or "Ganymede") is necessary to falling in love. The transvestite on the Renaissance stage, in fact, is not merely a signifier, but also a function.

It is perhaps worth stressing that when we turn to English sumptuary laws, or to Puritan polemicists, to articulate the argument that apparel "is a signe distinctive to discern between sex and sex"—when we stress the category of gender over status—we are prioritizing anxieties that may have been Stubbes's, but are also preoccupations of our own time and culture. *Twelfth Night,* and, indeed, all of Shakespeare's transvestite plays, may occupy the space of transition here between one set of anxieties and the other; this is yet another way of saying that, for us, Shakespeare is the first modern author.

TRANSVESTITE SHAKESPEARE (II)

Cleopatra, said British actress Helen Mirren in *Exposure* magazine, "is the best-written female role ever. She's full of fire and spark and has balls."[39] I presume that Mirren does not merely mean here that historically the role was originally played by a boy, nor yet that the play explicitly acknowledges that fact in the text (*Antony and Cleopatra* 5.2.219–20). "Balls," in Mirren's spirited phrase, does not denote anatomical gender at all; a woman with balls is, and is not, the "phallic woman" of psychoanalytic theory; a woman with balls, or, more exactly, a "female role" with balls, demonstrates in no uncertain terms the power of the transvestite to unsettle assumptions, structures, and hierarchies.[40]

The recent casting of two accomplished actresses in the major Shakespearean roles of King Lear (Marianne Hoppe in Robert Wilson's production of *Lear*[41]) and Falstaff (Pat Carroll in Michael Kahn's *Merry Wives of Windsor* at the Folger Library in Washington[42]) may mark something of a shift in the recognition of the flexible power inherent in the structures of Shakespeare's transvestite theater.

Women have played other Shakespearean male roles to great critical acclaim from the Restoration to the twentieth century. Sarah Siddons was an early Hamlet, and Sarah Bernhardt a famous one. In the nineteenth century alone some fifty professional actresses played the part. Reviews commended the excellence of their portrayals, without any reference to gender cross-casting. No one apparently thought it strange or inappropriate that Bernhardt should play Hamlet, or, for that matter, that Charlotte Cushman or Alice Marriott should play Iago. The modern sense of this cross-dressed portrayal as a stunt or a trick, a dog walking on its hind legs, seems to be a matter of cultural relativism, not of clear-cut historical anomaly, and the recent appearance of Diane Venora in the part of Hamlet suggests that even today such representations are possible, and do not automatically render the whole enterprise suspicious, or, in the common, slightly dismissive parlance, "experimental."

But the roles of Iago and Hamlet are, it might be argued, more stereotypically "feminine" than Lear or Falstaff. What of Iago's jealous possessiveness, so obsessively trained on Othello that it manifests itself as hatred, as well as desire? Or recall the voice-over of Olivier's *Hamlet*: "This is the tragedy of a man who could not make up his mind." To which gender was this dilemma—in 1948, when the film was made—traditionally ascribed?

Sarah Bernhardt remarked that "I cannot see Hamlet as a man. The things he says, his impulses, his actions entirely indicate to me that he was a woman." Max Beerbohm, then drama critic of the *Saturday Review,* retorted by describing her 1899 London production as "Hamlet: Princess of Denmark."[43] The Victorian scholar Edward P. Vining, in an essay entitled *The Mystery of Hamlet*, had revealed that Hamlet had an essentially feminine nature—that is, one that shrank at revenge, feigned madness, and used playacting as a political device—"stratagems that a woman might attempt, and that are far more in keeping with a feminine than with a masculine nature."[44] "The question may be asked," wrote Vining, "whether Shakespeare, having been compelled by the course and exigencies of the drama to gradually modify his original hero into a man with more and more of the feminine element, may not at last have had the thought dawn upon him that this womanly man might be in very deed a woman"?[45] A 1920 German silent film, starring Asta Nielsen, followed Vining's lead and presented Hamlet *as* a woman.[46]

Nonetheless, the casting of women to play such major male roles as Lear and Falstaff might be thought to represent something of an advance, at least in the recognition of women as figures who can personate worldly experience: old men, and men of the world. Marianne Hoppe, an eighty-year old German actress, announced that for Wilson's production "I will not try to play a man, but I will forget I'm a woman. It's difficult being suspended between male and female" (Holmberg, H7). Does this mean that Hoppe wishes to transcend the concept of gender, or to deconstruct it? Pat Carroll described the turning point of her impersonation of Falstaff as the moment when she learned how to swagger. ("I knew the minute I swaggered it was right," she says. "I said, 'Yes, I've seen men do that.' ") As for the Falstaff of the history plays, Carroll notes—apparently without irony—that he is "totally male" and that she "wouldn't dare" try to play him except as an "older man" for whom all the sex was "in his head".[47] Impotence—or fantasy—then, can also be a "feminizing" principle for imagining a dramatic character. Making a woman into a man apparently remains more difficult—in the theater as elsewhere—than discovering the "woman" already within him.

It is arguable—indeed, it has been variously argued by critics over the years—that virtually all of Shakespeare's great characters, from Richard III to Cleopatra, are "suspended between male and female." Cross-casting by modern directors like Wilson, or Mabou Mines' Lee Breuer, who recently staged a cross-cast *King Lear*—like the "original" cross-casting of boys as women on the Elizabethan and Jacobean stage—only brings to the surface the fact that all theatrical gender assignments are, in a way, ungrounded and contingent. Moreover, recent literary and psychoanalytic criticism has tended more and more to see Falstaff—both the Falstaff of the history plays and the Falstaff of *Merry Wives*—as embodying a "feminine principle" or as exhibiting pre-Oedipal symptoms like orality, appetite, and unbounded desire.[48] (And since Falstaff himself cross-dresses in *Merry Wives*, Carroll would also be performing an act of double-crossing or of psychological externalization, showing the "female" side already intrinsic to the Falstaff character even when dressed in male attire.)

So that it is not, after all, that women are seen as more capable of representing a universal "man," but rather that the female or feminine aspects of Lear ("O how this mother swells up toward my heart!/ *Hysterica passio*, down" [2.4.56–57]) and Falstaff are becoming more available, more visible, both to critics and to actors and directors. But the renewed interest in cross-casting, by directors who may or may not have taken cognizance of developments in academic criticism, suggests an intuition about contingent gender roles that is intrinsic, I think, to the enduring success of these Shakespearean characters. The actress and voice coach Kristin Linklater, for example, has assembled a multicultural "Company of Women" which she intends to tour with an all-female *Henry V*, offering a reply in kind both to the patriotic Olivier production of World War II and the post-Falklands, post-Vietnam Kenneth Branagh film.

What seems clear, however—and what I want here to emphasize—is that this capacity for realization onstage lies within the text; that it is not imposed from outside, as a foreign, unwelcome, or overingenious overlay. "Man" and "woman" are *already* constructs within drama; within what is often recognized as "great" drama, or "great" theater, the imaginative possibilities of a critique of gender in and through representation are already encoded as a system of signification.

Transvestite theater is a common, and not an aberrant, phenomenon in many cultures. Indeed, it might be contended that transvestite theater is the *norm,* not the aberration—that what we today regard as "natural" in theatrical representations (men playing men's parts, women playing women) is itself a peculiar troping off, and from, the transvestite norm. When actresses first appeared upon the Restoration stage in England it was said that the actor Edward Kynaston was more effective at playing female roles than any woman could be: "Mr. Kynaston," wrote John Downes, "being then very young, made a compleat Female Stage Beauty, performing his Parts so well . . . that it has since been disputable among the Judicious, whether any Woman that succeeded him so sensibly touch'd the Audience as he."[49]

Consider such canonical moments of greatness in the history of drama as the ancient

Greek theater; the public theater of the English Renaissance; Kabuki and Noh theaters in Japan; the Chinese opera. This is a short list which could easily be made longer. But it is enough to give the sense that transvestism and theater are interrelated, not merely "historically" or "culturally," but psychoanalytically, through the unconscious and through language. Transvestite theater *is* the Symbolic on the stage. In other words, the phenomenon of cross-dressing within theatrical representation, whether in the Dame and Principal Boy of the English pantomime, or in the popularity of films like *Victor/Victoria*, *Tootsie*, and *Some Like It Hot* (all films about acting and making a living through transvestite disguise on the stage), or indeed in the mode—increasingly chic today—of female impersonation *as* theater, may be not only a commentary on the anxiety of gender roles in modern culture, but also—and perhaps primarily—a back-formation: a return to the problem of representation that underlies theater itself.

Transvestite theater recognizes that *all* of the figures onstage are impersonators. The notion that there has to be a naturalness to the sign is exactly what great theater puts in question. In other words, there is no ground of Shakespeare that is not already cross-dressed.

2

CROSS-DRESS FOR SUCCESS

Dukakis didn't get to the podium listening to a pack of pompous, supposedly wired know-it-alls. He got there by hard work and old tricks and, unless he's caught wearing one of Judy Garland's old dresses, he's going to be the next president of the United States.

Mike Barnicle, *Boston Globe*, July 24, 1988[1]

Longtime jazz clarinetist Artie Shaw gripes about today's musicians. "Now Madonna goes out there in a jock strap and that's called music," groaned Shaw, celebrating his 80th birthday last week. "It isn't music."

San Francisco Chronicle, May 24, 1990[2]

TV GUIDE

In his 1977 best-seller, *The Woman's Dress for Success Book,* John T. Molloy cautions professional women against trying to imitate men. A full-page sketch illustrates the "Imitation Man Look," complete with man's fedora, shirt, tie, and pinstriped or chalk-striped suit; these items of clothing are labeled in the sketch, with arrows pointing from the words to the offending hat, tie, and suit, while the words *"Never wear,"* so reminiscent of Queen Elizabeth's sumptuary proclamations, appear in bold type above them.

Molloy takes issue with the "women in industry," who have advised businesswomen on how to dress:

Their experience generally came down to "I don't know what else to do, so I'll imitate men around me." And they wore things like pinstriped suits with vests.

My research indicates that a three-piece pinstriped suit not only does not add to a woman's authority, it destroys it. It makes her look like an "imitation man," and that look always fails.

The "imitation man look" does not refer to looking tough or masculine. The effect is more like that of a small boy who dresses up in his father's clothing. He looks cute, not authoritative. . . . The same thing applies to women. When a woman wears certain clothes with male colors or patterns, her femaleness is accentuated. She frequently looks more diminutive. And this reduces her authority. My testing showed that some men find the "imitation man" look sexy. Other men are completely turned off by it. In either case a woman's authority is diminished.

This is a prime example of why research is necessary. Obviously those fashion designers who turn out "imitation man" clothes and call them career apparel are advancing only their own careers.[3]

Unlike John T. Molloy. It is interesting that in arguing for a costume that would add to a woman's authority, Molloy feels constrained to put down the authority of "women in industry," replacing their professional expertise with his own ("This is a prime example of why research is necessary"). Instead of fashion designers who advance their own careers, we have a testimonial to Molloy's own "scientific method" of what he calls "wardrobe engineering" (Molloy, 21).

Molloy's point of view, however, is not naively unreflective, despite the breeziness of his style. The subject position he speaks from is that of the male employer or colleague, and in a section called, "Sexism? No!" he points out that at the time of the book's writing, 1977, men dominate the power structure. "If women control a substantial hunk of the power structure in ten or fifteen years, I will write a book advising men how to dress in a female-dominated environment" (Molloy, 32). In other words, this self-described "classic 'how to' book" is grounded in the dynamics of economic power and influence. Vests and pants on women are "ultrasexy," according to both Molloy's personal taste and his research ("I was starting to think that I might be a little weird," he confesses, but "I'm happy to report that our research shows I'm normal" [Molloy, 71]). They are therefore not businesslike, although vests, in particular, are "very effective" garments "when you are interested in being appealing," especially when they are tight and in a different color from that of the suit. Many businesswomen who have sat in on his lectures, Molloy tells us, "now don their contrasting vests at the end of the business day" (Molloy, 77).

Molloy's book is unselfconsciously aimed at upwardly mobile lower middle- to middle-class women in business, and does not hesitate to prescribe a "uniform" for all business and professional women, that of the "skirted suit and blouse" (Molloy, 35). "Men with Old Money," "Men with New Money," army officers, blue-collar workers, professors, and dentists all come in for their share of slightly acerbic analysis ("Male professors like the dowdy look"; "Young dentists seem to be under the influence of novocaine. Almost nothing turns them on" [Molloy, 161, 162]).

1977 seems a long time ago in some ways, less long in others. The uniform of the skirted suit and blouse has come and gone, and I am not sure whether or not male professors still like the dowdy look, but they certainly see less of it than they used to. While women do not yet control a substantial hunk of the power structure, their control has significantly increased since 1977, and the relationship of women to power dressing and the "imitation man look" has undergone some changes. In an article in the New York Times Magazine entitled "His, Now Hers," Judith Waters, "a psychologist who has studied the role clothes play in business and private life," is quoted as saying that "The woman confident enough to wear a man's shirt is announcing, in effect, 'I'm so feminine, that I can wear men's clothing and you will not for a minute mistake me for a man.' "[4]

Indeed, the power shoe may now be on the other foot. Another recent *Times* fashion article observes that "competitive power dressing" now seems to pit men against women. "Men find it necessary to dress up to the level of women, who are now vying for the same raises, promotions and perquisites, but with vastly more fashionable wardrobes." "When a woman shows up in a great-looking Armani suit, for instance, she looks assertive and assured," says the men's fashion director of Saks Fifth Avenue, a woman. "The man sitting next to her feels he has to keep up. So he tends to get the new suit so he will look better."[5] And in a book called *Twenty Nine Reasons Not to Go To Law School* a recent woman law school graduate, now an editor, describes a "dress for success seminar" at Boalt Hall Law School at the University of California, in which the student placement director advised women interviewing with large law firms to "strive for the look of 'asexual femininity.' " When she saw her classmates earnestly taking notes, the author recalls, "I knew I didn't belong there."[6]

Even in the title of this law school seminar, however, Molloy's influence continues to be felt. It is probably not an exaggeration to regard his books, with their insidiously catchy titles, as the premier examples of dress codes and sumptuary regulations for the American middle and lower middle classes. Here instead of a monarch or a parliament the regulating body is the marketplace, but legibility, lack of "confusion," and social acquiescence to type are what remain at stake. And as with earlier sumptuary legislation, the category of class begins, almost imperceptibly, to cross over into adjacent categories like sexuality and gender.

Thus *Dress for Success*, Molloy's first book, aimed at men, had warned against haircuts that made young men—in this case, young lawyers—look "effeminate," at least to senior partners in the law firm. "The most successful face," Molloy notes, with regret at the fact ("I hate to tell you this")

is masculine and elongated, neither too heavy nor too thin, without prominent features. In short, the perfect WASP face. Slight faces are judged as being effeminate and round faces as being ineffectual. That's the bad news. The good news is that hair can help . . . .[7]

As this example suggests, Molloy's cultural taxonomies are straightforwardly and unapologetically about class, race, sexuality, and ethnicity. Thus he sizes up the "bizarre" dress codes of California by detailing the sad story of a successful carpet salesman whose wardrobe consisted of "a velvet jacket, slacks, and a shirt open a fair way down." When this man moved to New York, the clash of cultures proved disastrous: "By his third day on the job his boss had already received two calls objecting that the previous salesman had been replaced by a 'homosexual' " (Molloy, 1975, 132). Call this ethnocentrism, call it homophobia, and you will be right; Molloy, who does not endorse social prejudice, nonetheless calls it, above all, bad for business.

In the 1977 volume he argued—again, with the self-help profit motive clearly and disarmingly in full view—that a separate book on women's clothing (i.e., the present one) was necessary, despite the fact that ill-advised fashion writers had used material from his first book, *Dress for Success*, as the basis for their advice to women. Black raincoats, he insists, are not déclassé (and a badge of lower middle-class status) for women, although they are for men. "What all this means is that you can't use research on men's clothing as a basis for determining the effect of women's clothes" (Molloy, 32). Ergo, the second book.

One particular group of women, however, did look with profit at Molloy's original handbook for men. The authors of *Information for the Female-to-Male Crossdresser and Transsexual* cite Molloy specifically and by name when they address the problem of "How to Look 30 When You Are 30." "The biggest problem when going female-to-male is that a 30-year-old female, when crossdressed as a man, can end up looking like a 14-year-old boy. What can the female-to-male crossdresser do to look older?" This problem, as we've seen, was considered by Molloy in his discussion of the "imitation man look," in which the woman in male clothes is described as diminutive, like a small boy in his father's clothing, "cute, not authoritative." But the "imitation man look," with modifications, here has an interested clientele. It makes sense, therefore, that the authors of this pamphlet go to Molloy's first book, and not his second, for advice:

> Says John T. Molloy in *Dress for Success*: "One of the major problems with small men who are very young is that people still are tempted to address them as, 'Hey, kid!' To overcome this, they should only wear super-adult garments." Molloy, who did extensive research on the impressions made by clothing, offers these suggestions to the small young man who wishes to project an authoritative figure in the business world: "The best shirt for the small man is the solid white; the best shoes are traditional wingtips; the best coats are heavy and luxurious, such as camel hair. They should only wear rich-looking attire, and they should be neat to the point of being precise." He suggests wearing only ties that are very expensive—"ties that obviously would not be available to a boy." Stay away from sporty ties (such as paisley) and wear only serious ties (Ivy League, polka dot).[8]

Moreover, it is not only Molloy who is cited as an authority. In the section on "Body Language" readers are advised that "*Gentleman's Quarterly* suggests showing more cuff beneath the suit jacket to make the hands appear larger" (*Information*, 24). A menswear conversion chart lists women's sizes and the equivalent sizes for men's pants, shirts, sweaters and jackets, with a mail-order address for small sized men's shoes.

Like Molloy's in tone and in the apparent class of its intended audience (lower middle to middle), *Information for the Female-to-Male Crossdresser and Transsexual* is a how-to book that knows its time (1985) and fills a need. This invaluable and immensely readable little guide begins by pointing out what seems, in hindsight, obvious: that a lot more published material is available about the male-to-female than the female-to-male cross-dresser. Indeed, as we have already noted, psychologists and psychiatrists still deny the existence of female-to-male transvestites, alleging that any woman who consistently cross-dresses as a man is actually a transsexual—that is, a woman who wishes that she were a man. Dr. Robert Stoller, the most frequently cited authority on this question (whose views are quoted in the pamphlet), observes that

> there are an extremely rare number of females who dress all the time as men, live as men, work as men—in fact, pass unrecognized in society as men. Are they not transvestites? No—and again one must be careful that one is not merely quibbling with words. These women are transsexuals, quite comparable to male transsexuals. They wish to be males, that is to have a body in every way male, and to live in all ways as a man does. They cannot stomach sexual relations with men; they are aroused only by women. Men's clothes have no erotic value whatsoever; these people have no clothing fetish.[9]

For Stoller, then, women who wear men's clothes really want to *be* men—and in this society, who can blame them? They are not even psychotic—their desires are perfectly "natural." According to most doctors, male transvestites derive sexual excitement—and erections—from wearing women's underclothing, but women are regarded as having not *sexual* but *cultural* desires—desires that the culture and its doctors understand. For Stoller the penis is the *"sine qua non,"* or, as he repeatedly describes it, the *insignia* of maleness, and the index, in erection, of sexual excitement. Since women do not have penises, and do not (sic) have erections, they are not demonstrably erotically excited by male clothing, and therefore are not transvestites. Women who cross-dress must thus fall into two other categories: the occasional, recreational cross-dresser who does not wish or try to pass, and the transsexual.

I will come back to this rather circular taxonomic reasoning later in my argument. I mention it here only because Stoller's rhetorical putting-under-erasure of female transvestism is cited in *Information for the Female-to-Male Crossdresser and Transsexual* together with a similar quotation from Dr. Harry Benjamin, who is described as "The Father of Transsexuals" (*Information*, 11). Both quotations are followed by a heartfelt rhetorical question which sets forth the rationale and the need for the present volume: "Is it any wonder that the female crossdresser hesitates to come forward? It would be quite a stigma to be known as the world's first and only woman who gets off on jockey shorts!"[10] Examples from Nancy Friday's *My Secret Garden* and from two other accounts of fetishistic female transvestism assure the female cross-dresser that "yes, there are others like her . . . There are women who become aroused by wearing men's underwear, by slipping on a man's starched white shirt or wingtip shoes" (*Information*, 10). The tone of this reassurance, and its semi-anecdotal quality, is again reminiscent of Molloy, whose books may have served as a model; the genre of *Information for the . . . Crossdresser* is that of the self-help or how-to-manual. It is not addressed to physicians or to literary theorists, but rather to women who wish to dress successfully as men on a regular basis. Its intended audience, whether "the woman trying to pass as a man," or "the pre-operative female-to-male transsexual who has yet to begin hormone therapy" (*Information*, 22), can find here some concrete and indispensable tips. In other words, although the content of the pamphlet, and its implications, are profoundly political, its tone and style are not. It is a social document, deliberately upbeat in spirit, dedicated to problem solving and morale building at the most local and private level.

The chapter called "How to Look 30 When You Are 30," which nicely carnivalizes the usual fashion-magazine advice to women on how to look younger, proposes a number of specific solutions, grouped under the headings of "Clothing," "Face, Hair," "Body Language," "Clothing and Shoe Sizes" (with a conversion chart), "Breast Binding," "The Crotch," and "The Men's Room."

For the face, the pamphlet suggests shaving the peach fuzz on women's faces (men don't have any), and advises that acne may actually be a help: "That pimply, pitted look is very masculine. And too much sun causes the skin to age faster, forms wrinkles, creates a leathery look . . . exactly what you want" (*Information*, 23). Pumping iron is proposed as a way of making the knuckles and veins on the backs of the hands stand out more. The section on breast binding is matter-of-fact and practical: "Basically you want to do the opposite of what Frederick's of Hollywood's cleavage bras do—instead of pushing the breasts up and together, you want to push them down and apart" (*Information*, 26). For this purpose the pamphlet recommends one of those "midriff bulge" wide elastic belts advertised in the back pages of Sunday supplements (mail-order address given in the text), which would be worn over the bust rather than the waist; larger-breasted women should get a trainer bra, take it apart and insert a strip of cloth between the cups, so that the breasts are pulled to either side of the chest, leaving the breastbone flat. This should be topped by a spandex elastic undershirt ("sold by many men's stores for potbelly control"), a T-shirt, and a shirt. While not comfortable, this will provide the desired masculine flat chest.

As for the crotch, close-fitting trousers mandate the use of padding. Two socks ("*dress socks*, that is . . . be realistic" [*Information*, 26]) can be inserted into an athletic supporter or, because they tend to shift around too much, into an athletic cup supporter, which has a pocket in front that snaps closed. Alternatively, the rolled-up socks could be pinned to the inside crotch of the underwear, so that no telltale straps and bands appear, facilitating the use of the restroom without major reorganizations of underclothing. The cross-dresser thus accoutered could remove her trousers, "showing the appropriate lump in your underwear (make sure the pins don't show)" (*Information*, 27). As it happens, in men's clothing parlance this bulge in the trousers is technically described as "dressing," and is taken into account by custom tailors, who will ask a man whether he "dresses right" or "dresses left," so that an allowance can be made in the cutting of the garment.

Information for the Female-to-Male Crossdresser and Transsexual is full of historical anecdotes and capsule case histories, described on the back cover as "dozens of true stories of females who crossed over": fascinating end-of-page-filling-paragraphs on the order of the "words-of-one-syllable department" in the *New Yorker* or the similar fillers found throughout the *Reader's Digest*. The anecdote at the bottom of the section on "The Crotch" describes a Phoenix woman who died in 1906, who dressed as a man throughout life, married twice, and "made careful arrangements to prevent detection of sex after death, but these were frustrated as he died in a hospital. He wore an elaborately-constructed imitation penis and testicles made of chamois skin and stuffed with down, suspended by a band around the waist."

Much recent work by literary and cultural critics focuses on the "construction of gender," and the constructedness (rather than the naturalness, literality, biology, or essence) of male and female as culturally marked categories. In cases like these (and in the lives of transvestites or transsexuals who find this pamphlet helpful) the "construction" itself becomes literalized and essentialized. We might think of such phallic cross-dressers—and, indeed, of all lifetime "passers"—as the Martin Guerres of gender. If they are taken for males (or, in the opposite case, females) throughout their lives, to what gender *do* they belong? Does the post mortem unmasking of the Phoenix cross-dresser (whose second wife, a chorus girl, wept on learning of his death and declared that the idea of his being a woman was "nonsense") make him finally a female? This is the conundrum magnificently explored in David Hwang's play *M. Butterfly*, to which we will return later.

What *is* gender, after all? What is a man or a woman? It is easy to be amused by the image of the female-to-male cross-dresser pinning dress socks to her/his underwear. (The concept of "dress socks" is itself conventionally gender-marked. No such category currently exists for women's hosiery, although women's stockings—not recommended in the pamphlet—would probably make the same size bulge in the pants.) But there is a sense in which this image defines the constructedness of gender identity in our culture. And, as Freud long ago pointed out, the laughter here is in part the laughter of unease. How big is big enough? How artificial are the "real" signs of gender? Do a man's tight pants reveal anything different from what these prostheses show?

The men's room is another potential Waterloo (like the locker room, and, indeed, the bedroom) for female-to-male cross-dressers. Here the pamphlet is its usually detailed and helpful self, advising, as we have already noted, that "there should be no problems using the men's room—just use the stall," and suggesting that you should "blow your nose in the toilet paper if you're paranoid that taking it sounds suspicious" (*Information*, 27). The cultural paranoia of being caught in the ultimately wrong place, which may be inseparable from the pleasure of "passing" in that same place, depends in part on the same cultural binarism, the idea that gender categories are sufficiently uncomplicated to permit self-assortment into one of the two "rooms" without deconstructive reading.

We should note that the women's room (or "powder room") is as challenging a site of testing and passing for male-to-female cross-dressers as is the men's room for the female-to-male. An article in *Tapestry*, a national journal for persons interested in cross-dressing and transsexualism, discusses the perils of putting on makeup in public. After visiting the cosmetic counter in a department store and thus joining "the language of women," "the next step is their clubhouse—the powder room. Being able to 'freshen your makeup' with the girls in the powder room, while highly dangerous for any except the most accomplished TV, is a rite of passage and for many a real goal of achievement."[11]

The male-to-female cross-dresser, whether transvestite, transsexual, or female impersonator, has a much easier access to how-to advice than the female-to-male does, as *Information* laments. Every "woman's magazine" contains at least one article on makeup, another on hairstyling, and several on the latest in fashions. But a male-to-female transvestite is not a woman, and specialized advice is sometimes necessary. Many shops catering to male-to-female cross-dressers advertise in transvestite and transsexual magazines: a recent selection in *Tapestry* included "Lydia's T.V. Fashions" of Sherman Oaks, California ("We can make you the lady you want to be"), the Versatile Fashion Boutique of Anaheim ("Dress Up in Sexy Things & Shoes & Boots"), Lee's Mardi Gras Boutique on West 14th Street in New York City ("We Have More of What You Want: Bras, Panties, Garterbelts, Braselettes, Corselettes, Waistcinchers, Girdles, Foundations, Teddies, Slips, Camisoles, Bodystockings, Gowns, Negligees, Peignoirs, Robes, Hosiery, Stockings, Pantyhose, Tights, Fishnet Stockings, Larger Sizes, Shoes, High Heels, Slings, Slides, Sandals, Strappies, Maids' Uniforms, Leather Accessories, Gloves, Prostheses, Padding, Wigs, Eyelashes, Nails, Cosmetics, Makeup"), and Cross-dresser's Delight, with a telephone area code in the Boston area, offering a Full Service Wardrobe, including "Medieval Accessories."

These shops advertise the availability of assistance from their fashion and makeup consultants. But there are also how-to articles available to the home cross-dresser. The SHAFT Newsletter, a transvestite publication in the U.K., recently published an article called "Woman to Woman" which was reprinted first by the Bulletin of the Beaumont Society, an organization for heterosexual transvestites in Great Britain, and then by *Tapestry*. In it the author outlines a "check list for those in the first stages of becoming a woman," noting that general suggestions like "develop a dress sense," offered by SHAFT's contributors, had been too vague to be of much use. The list of categories in "Woman to Woman" is telling, and compares interestingly to *Information*'s "How to Look 30 When You Are 30."

In a section on "Mirror Use," for example, the article recommends spending as much time as possible trying on all your clothes in front of a full-length mirror. Its recommendations on makeup include a cross-cultural comparison of American and British style that emphasizes the importance of vestimentary codes: "In the United States old ladies wear much more make up than they do here in this country; we tend to find that idea rather disgusting, so it is important if you want to pass as a British lady that you follow the rules." "I am not defending the rules," notes the author, "merely pointing them out."[12] Here words like "lady" (a class marker) and "rules" clearly identify the

"Woman to Woman" check list as another version of sumptuary legislation, while the telltale "pass" ("to pass as a British lady") marks the point of deliberate transgression.

A transvestite magazine is, in fact, a perfectly logical site for the dialectic of subversion and containment, and this piece articulates, with artless cogency, a program for co-optation and assimilation. So, for example, on the topic of "Nail Polish," the author notes that "Bright red nail varnish went out with the dodo and is now only associated with 'common women,' a dreadful analysis I know, but these are the mores that are prevalent today." On "Hair Style": "bouffant styles belong in the sixties, so choose a style that is up to date. . . . If you wear wigs choose them with care." On eye-makeup, a caution against overpenciling the eyebrows ("Bette Davis's heyday was a long, long time ago"). All of this wise counsel offers a warning against nostalgia and belatedness—against, that is to say, a fantasy ideal of woman that "went out with the dodo," and had, indeed, as much claim to natural reality.

On "Clothing," there is further sensible advice: "Never buy on impulse . . . . If you have a large frame, avoid frills and busy prints . . . . Choose clothes that are plenty big enough . . . . Do not wear long necklines unless you are prepared to ensure the exposed chest and neck area is completely hair free. This means shaving or using a depilatory nearly every day." Remember that this is advice for the *passing* male-to-female transvestite, not for the radical drag queen who *wants* the discontinuity of hairy chest or moustache to clash with a revealingly cut dress. But except for this specialized advice about depilatories, it is striking how closely this "check list," from the opening invitation to narcissism and mirror use through the injunction to wear sensible shoes, resembles advice given by "Woman to Woman" in popular magazines like *Cosmopolitan* and *Self*.

It is easy to say that the readership of *Tapestry* and *SHAFT* has bought into the concept of woman as artifact, assembled from a collection of parts: wig, painted nails, mascara and "blush." Gender is commodified and constructed in the pages of these journals, so that the article's title begs for double quotation marks: " 'Woman' to 'Woman.' " But so, we might say, have the woman's magazines. The anxiety of artifice that marks such a check list emphasizes the degree to which the " 'woman' " speaking, and the " 'woman' " listening, are unsure about the legibility of their desired social identities. But—and this is the key point here—so are the "women" who read "women's magazines"—or, for that matter, feminist journals. The mystery of "femininity" remains as mysterious to women as it did to Freud. The social critique performed by these transvestite magazines for readers who are not themselves cross-dressers is to point out the degree to which *all* women cross-dress as women when they produce themselves as artifacts. This is yet another way in which transvestism creates culture, produces and is produced by the Symbolic.

"Woman to Woman" ends with two rather charmingly self-deprecating sections on "Terminology" and "Behavior" that underscore this need to be contemporary rather than dated, to avoid exactly the kind of stereotyping male-to-female transvestites often invite. Here, *in toto*, is the section on "Terminology":

> Familiarize yourself with the current expressions to describe your clothes rather than those dredged up from your subconscious; they are probably your mother's! For example, sandals are never referred to as "strippies" or "strappies" these days, flat shoes are no longer called "flatties," and the use of such expressions sounds self conscious.
>
> Nor do we describe such items belonging to ourselves as little (a "little black dress" or "a little black number" went out years ago) and it can sound ludicrous when the nice "little strippies" being described are actually size nines, or the "little black number" is a size eighteen. Such outmoded expressions put the user in the category of "odd," the last category one would wish to be in. (70).

Here once again the desire to pass—not, above all, to be put in the category of "odd"—mandates conformity to prevailing vestimentary rhetoric, and a corresponding realism of expectation. To be "*outmoded*," a word that means literally "out of fashion," is the fear that haunts both language and dress.

Note that the "Terminology" section explicitly identifies "your mother's" expressions with "your subconscious." It has become a something of a cliché in the popular analysis of transvestism to attribute the desire to cross-dress to an overdependency on the mother, whether that overdependency is fueled by love or hate. The classic pop illustration is Hitchcock's film *Psycho* (1960), in which Anthony Perkins, as the psychotic murderer and recreational taxidermist Norman Bates, wears his mother's dress. Excessive closeness to the mother, a desire not only not to be separated from her but to *be* her, has been suggested as an explanation for the dowdy or dated appearance of some transvestites— for example, some of Divine's female characters—who seem to be dressing according to the styles of their mothers' generation.[13] But this "explanation" is resisted by cross-dressers who write about their own interest in clothes and makeup. We noted a warning against datedness in "Woman to Woman"'s advice on hair styles ("bouffant styles belong in the sixties") and nail varnish ("Bright red nail varnish went out with the dodo"). But the implication in such comments is not, or not primarily, that cross-dressers *want* to dress like their mothers, but rather that they need access to other arbiters of style and taste—and that they also need, like other "daughters," to separate themselves from the notion that "the mother" is somehow equal to "woman." The specter of "the mother" is raised here so that it can be confronted, rather than mimicked or parodied.

As for "Behavior," "Woman to Woman" is again right on the mark. In advice that Huck Finn would have found useful, the article points out that "sitting down wearing a skirt has an art to it. Never sit with the knees apart, particularly if the skirt is on the short side. The embarrassed looks on your companions' faces are likely to be there because they can see your knickers." Likewise, "If you are six-foot-two do not refer to the five-foot male in the doorway as a 'big strong man,' you are liable to be misunderstood." And finally, in a piece of wisdom that complements the female-to-males' concern with looking one's age: "If you are in your fifties and don't wish to behave and dress like a middle aged granny, choose models of the same age who do not. To dress and act like a young girl when you are not is a recipe for disaster" (70). Readers of *Lear's* and *Mirabella* may wish to consider the usefulness of this advice. The article also warns "TSs and TVs" against "standing in sculptured poses, chins at a certain angle, bags clutched under their arms." Transvestite "women," in other words, if they want to be believable as women, should not present themselves as statues or as mannequins, despite the long history of romantic imagery that insists on just such a role. Mannequins, models, dummies; these postures and identities are functional only in a frame, whether on the page of a glossy magazine or in a department store window. Once again the "imitation woman" is able to double-read the "real" one.

But where are the *female-to-male* cross-dressers? Not in the personals pages of the *Tapestry*. While male-to-female cross-dressers have access to both mainstream women's magazines and TV-TS journals like *Tapestry*, the pamphlet *Information for the Female-to-Male Crossdresser and Transsexual* notes the "lack of a crossgender peer group" for female-to-males. Although female-to-males frequently seek support from "the general male-to-female transvestite/transsexual community," often, the authors say, "trying to discuss female-to-male questions with the male-to-female may result in the female-to-male's feeling even more isolated and alone. The male-to-female is necessarily preoccupied with the very notions from which the female-to-male hopes to escape and it may be extremely hard for the male-to-female to empathize with someone who embraces the masculine."[14]

Here gender theory and lived experience coincide to explore the pitfalls of gender assignment, whether that assignment is "essential" (male-to-females still assert a kind of male privilege which is none the less hegemonic for being transvestite), "constructed" (male-to-females resist a valorization of the "masculine" even in female-to-males), or "performed" (male-to-females are interested in "sisterhood" and "sorority," female-to-males lack a sense of community and are often forced to go it alone, reinforcing the stereotype of the strong and independent man). "The major task of the female-to-male is to (all by himself) openly define his innermost feelings . . . he must be an exceptionally strong person" (*Information*, 42). Although a monthly newsletter (*Metamorphosis*) and at least one organization that holds weekly meetings for female-to-males serve this subsector of the cross-dressing community,[15] the dissymmetry between the two groups is striking. Is the greater visibility and organizational strength of male-to-females another sign of male power? Or of *female* power? And what does it have to do, finally, with clothing? *Do clothes, after all, in some sense make the man?*

Gender roles and categories are most vulnerable to critique when they are most valorized, when their rules, codes, and expectations are most ardently coveted and admired. If a "man" is someone who has a bulge in his pants, if a "woman" is someone whose makeup is impeccable, the social and political usefulness of such legibility is put under hard scrutiny. Cross-dressing for success is not the same as cross-dressing successfully, but in the context of self-help magazines and pamphlets—as in the history of dress codes and sumptuary legislation—the second goal can often help to expose the ideological preconceptions of the first.

TRANSVESTISM AND THE POWER ELITE

Sen. *Edward M. Kennedy* donned a blond wig, falsies and a miniskirt, playing *Fawn Hall* to nephew *Joseph P. Kennedy's* Col. *Oliver North* at an annual off-the-record staff Christmas party last week.

Boston Globe, December 20, 1987[16]

It couldn't have happened to a nicer guy and artist—the birthday greeting mounted by the San Francisco Symphony for Isaac Stern's 70th birthday in Stern Grove yesterday afternoon.

A high point was clearly the surprise appearance of the ballerina "Natasha Milanova Rostropovich"—a demure male figure costumed in tutu and tights, wig and all, who daintily curtseyed and tiptoed around the orchestra to the front of the stage, picked up a cello and began performing "The Swan" from Saint-Saens' Carnival of the Animals . . .

It was indeed revealed to be Mstislav Rostropovich, the great cellist and conductor of the National Symphony Orchestra, when he doffed his wig and tiara and blew kisses at Stern, who sat doubled up in laughter at the table of honor with his family.

San Francisco Chronicle, July 23, 1990[17]

Having sampled the self-help literature that promotes cross-dressing as a relatively marginalized and privatized expression of gender, I want now to turn to the ways in which cross-dressing also inhabits, surprisingly enough, the very heart of public, institutional, and mainstream structures.

Cross-dressing for success is obviously easier if you are already successful—successful, that is, not as a cross-dresser, but as a member of the power elite. Ted Kennedy in a blond wig and falsies, Mstislav Rostropovich in tutu and tights, are asserting a class privilege that permits them to dress down by dressing up: to carnivalize their political or cultural power. Kennedy's occasion for cross-dressing was archetypal carnival: not only a Christmas party, a traditional time for social inversion from the Middle Ages on, but an *off-the-record* Christmas party for his *staff*. This was the world-turned-upside-down in every particular, including the cross-dressed uncle's fake servility to his much younger nephew. Rostropovich, in his ballerina costume, played a selection from the "*Carnival* of the Animals," and then "doffed his wig and tiara" as he blew kisses toward the seventy-year-old birthday boy.

But these members of the power elite cross-dressed—in public at least—only after they had achieved a certain social and political standing. A riskier path was, apparently, chosen by Edward Hyde, Lord Cornbury, later Third Earl of Clarendon.

The portrait of Cornbury, Governor of the royal provinces of New York and New Jersey from 1702 to 1708, hangs today in the New-York Historical Society, where it has long been a subject of interest, and lately, of controversy. For the portrait shows Lord

Cornbury dressed as a woman. His political enemies reported his predilection for women's clothes, apparently as much in sorrow as in anger, as evidence of his poor judgment and failed governance. Robert Livingston observed that "His dressing himself in women's clothes was so unaccountable that if hundred[s] of spectators did not daily see him it would be incredible." [18] Lewis Morris wrote to the Secretary of State to complain of "his dressing publicly in woman's cloaths every day, and putting a stop to all publique business while he is pleasing himselfe with [that] peculiar but detestable magot"[19]. The clergyman Elias Neau noted in the same year that the Governor "continues to dress himself in Women's Cloths, but now 'tis after the Dutch manner,"[20] suggesting that this was a practice of long standing.

What reason did Cornbury, a married man who was noted for his devotion to his wife, give for his transvestism? He is said to have claimed that, as Queen Anne's relative and representative, he should represent her as literally as possible. When he opened the Assembly in women's dress, and "some of those about him remonstrated, his reply was, 'You are very stupid not to see the propriety of it. In this place and particularly on this occasion I represent a woman [Queen Anne] and ought in all respects to represent her as faithfully as I can.' "[21] But gossips also testified to his doing business in women's clothes, and "sitting at the open window so dressed, to the great amusement of the neighbors" (Glenbervie, 77).

The charge of transvestism, and the authenticity of the portrait, have lately been challenged by a historian who argues that the story of Cornbury's desire to look like Queen Anne was a derisory tale told by his colonial opposition, and that the portrait itself is not of Cornbury at all.[22] Art historians, it seems, agree that the painting is not a caricature but a serious representation, and that it is of English rather than colonial origin. Beyond that nothing is proven, and the portrait of a man in a low-necked blue dress and white gloves remains identified as that of Cornbury. Gay historian Jonathan Ned Katz describes it as "quite a sight," and notes with some satisfaction that Cornbury, "an utterly corrupt and despised colonial official, appears to have been entirely heterosexual!"[23]

If the Cornbury portrait is authentic, it represents the sitter's desire to be portrayed in this fashion. But such commissions would appear to be unusual. The portrayal of a man in a dress has, in fact, been a time-honored way of attempting to demean him in Western culture from Hercules (forced by the Lydian Queen Omphale to wear women's clothes and to spin) to Michael Dukakis. In today's largely homophobic mainstream America, to picture a heterosexual politician in full-scale drag is to accuse him of "unmanliness," and it often carries a tacit message of closet homosexuality, or, what amounts to the same thing in some eyes, support for gay rights and other liberal causes. We might recall the crack by columnist Mike Barnicle about the Presidential candidacy of Michael Dukakis, cited above as an epigraph: "Unless he's caught wearing one of Judy Garland's old dresses, he's going to be the next president of the United States." (Here

"Judy Garland" is an oblique placeholder or metonym for "homosexuality"; Garland, an entertainer very popular with gay men, has often been the object of stage impersonation by professional female illusionists like Jim Bailey. Garland herself frequently cross-dressed on stage, so that a man in one of Garland's *dresses* is in some indefinable way "less of a man" than she was.)

But a "comic" image of Dukakis in a dress was, as it happens, part of a more serious attack on his credentials by the political right. In an interview with the Reverend Jerry Falwell of the Moral Majority on ABC television's "Good Morning America," reporter Joan Lunden asked Falwell about "this comic book that you've been touting, the one that depicts Michael Dukakis as pro-sodomy and even pro-bestiality. Don't you think it's maybe a little too much, and maybe even a bit irresponsible?" "I mean, it shows him there in the wig and the dress and all that . . . . What surprises people the most is that we all remember when you sued a national magazine when they used a caricature in an ad."

"Yes, but that was a parody and it was absolutely false," Falwell replied equably. By contrast, the comic book distributed by his son Jonathan was written, he explained, by "a Christian cartoonist," and was "footnoted, documented, totally accurate." "It portrays the person in the context of what he is for or against." It portrayed, that is to say, Michael Dukakis in a wig and a dress—a Dukakis who was (*therefore?*) somehow responsible for, if not actively a participant in, sodomy, bestiality, and the spread of the AIDS epidemic. Columnist David Nyhan, reporting the story, added—apparently without conscious double entendre—that "Falwell later covered his rear by saying both Bush and Dukakis are 'really just men.' "[24]

The suggestion that a powerful *woman* is a secret cross-dresser has, in recent times, also been used as a political put-down. Comedian Whoopi Goldberg commented that she had no real quarrel with Vice President Dan Quayle, the butt of many media jokes: "What bothers me more is his holier-than-thou wife. She's probably a cross-dresser or something."[25] "Cross-dresser" is here, apparently, an all-purpose epithet for secret vice. It is unclear from this remark whether Goldberg intends some comment on Mrs. Quayle's sexuality. What does seem clear is the suggestion that it is *Marilyn* Quayle who "wears the pants" in the family.

Women who literally wear the pants in U.S. political life have, as might be expected, often been objects of ridicule. This appears to have been the case with Dr. Mary Walker, the founder of "The Mutual Dress Reform and Equal Rights Association" in the middle of the last century. Dr. Walker's career as a reformer was hindered rather than helped by her insistence on wearing men's clothes. She had been briefly married—for the ceremony she wore a short dress over her long "reform" trousers—and then divorced; she was commissioned as an assistant surgeon in the Union Army in 1864, was arrested as a spy, and was later exchanged for a Confederate officer. She claimed to have received the Congressional Medal of Honor from President Andrew Johnson for her service in the army, although the War Department reported in 1917 that its records contained no mention of the award, and removed her name from its rolls. Nonetheless, she wore the Medal prominently displayed on her lapel and became a familiar figure in Washington, dressed in full masculine apparel, from striped trousers and frock coat to high silk hat. Walker never tried to pass, never masqueraded as a man, but her sartorial style offended some, amused others, and tended to discredit rather than reinforce her campaign for hygienic dress reform.[26]

I find Walker's story of particular interest because it illustrates the way in which the wearing of military orders by women has been regarded as a curious reversion to "feminine" taste, a kind of jewelry. Does the sight of women wearing medals or "orders" attached to their lapels suggest that such "orders" can be *un*pinned, *de*tached, from *men*? The spectacle of women in men's clothes, or at least in men's *uniforms*, both military and lay, seems to lead back to the question of *male* cross-dressing and its relationship to structures of hierarchy and power.

Max Beerbohm tartly observed at the trial of Oscar Wilde that one of the men testifying for the Crown was "wearing Her Majesty's uniform, another form of female attire."[27] This felicitous phrase contains more than one witty turn, since it is almost possible for a fleeting moment to imagine Queen Victoria herself in military garb ("Her Majesty's uniform"), or, alternatively, to envisage the Crown's witness as dressed in Victoria's clothes. The assertion that an army officer's uniform is "another form of female attire," however, focuses attention on the "fancy dress" aspect of soldiering—an aspect that came under serious and sustained scrutiny by the man who coined the term "transvestite," the German homosexual rights advocate, Magnus Hirschfeld.

Hirschfeld was himself a homosexual and the founder of the first Institute of Sexual Science; he collected a library of more than 20,000 volumes and 35,000 pictures, most of which, together with sex questionnaires filled out by thousands of subjects, were destroyed by the Nazis. His ground-breaking study, *Die Transvestiten* (*Transvestites*), was published in 1910.[28] Among Hirschfeld's most intriguing observations were his remarks on transvestism and the military. He noted that both women and men in the armed services seemed to cross-dress in numbers disproportionate to the general population, the women *as* men—either literally, by passing, or metaphorically, through the wearing of uniforms and medals—the men by divesting themselves of their uniforms and dressing in women's clothes.[29]

Hirschfeld saw this "intense love of uniform" as itself a cause as well as an effect.[30] Women joined the army, he suggested, because they liked to dress up in uniforms. Men who wore uniforms did so in part because they unconsciously understood them to be "fancy dress." Whatever the specific semiotic relationship between military uniforms and erotic fantasies of sartorial gender, the history of cross-dressing within the armed services attests to a complicated interplay of forces, including male bonding, acknowledged and unacknowledged homosexual identity, carnivalized power relations, the erotics of same-sex communities, and the apparent safety afforded by theatrical representation.

As Allan Bérubé points out, American GIs in World War II put on all-male shows that frequently included female impersonation routines. The Army, in fact, found itself in the position of officially supporting soldier theatricals as what it described as "a necessity, not a frill."[31] Despite this description, frills were very much part of the picture; Bérubé notes that the soldier show handbook for the show *Hi, Yank!* included "more than eight pages of dress patterns and illustrations for soldier drag, including instructions for making a 'G.I. showgirl' gown out of a salvaged blanket and for making a bodice for a ballet tutu out of a GI 'T shirt dyed pink.' " Irving Berlin's *This Is the Army*, the most famous of all World War II soldier shows, included "the three basic wartime styles of GI drag . . . the comic routines, chorus lines or 'pony ballets' of husky men in dresses playing for laughs; the skilled 'female' dancers or singers; and the illusionists or caricaturists, who did artistic and convincing impersonations of female stars."[32]

This Is the Army sent different messages to different audiences; straight spectators saw reversals of gender roles and the comedy of men ludicrously dressed as women, as well as the skill of impersonation; gay members of the audience caught double entendres, often unintentional, "transforming every aspect of the performance into a homosexual subplot" (Bérubé, 72). Gay camp, unacknowledged by the popular press, was represented by all-male GI productions of Clare Booth's all-female play *The Women*, favorably reviewed by *Life* magazine, and by innumerable send-ups of the movie star Carmen Miranda and the Andrews Sisters. Occasionally—in fact, more than occasionally—gay GIs who performed as female impersonators were courted by members of the audience, even by officers. And the GI drag shows also provided an opportunity for gay men to befriend each other, whether or not they openly acknowledged that they were gay (Bérubé, 88–90).

Perhaps the most fascinating detail in Bérubé's account, at least to a literary critic, is the way in which "camouflage" became a term covering costume, set design, camouflage design for combat—and gay identity. Many of the camoufleurs had held civilian jobs as set designers, fashion designers, or window dressers; when the 4th Air Force Engineer Camouflage School performed a show called *You Bet Your Life,* they sang a song about camouflage that declared, "Though we're like mirages,/ We're all camouflages—/ Things Are Not What They Seem."[33]

That things are not always what they seem—or that seeming itself, the mirage or camouflage, was what there was to see—was a lesson taught to willing GIs stationed in England during World War II by the self-described "effeminate homosexual" Quentin Crisp. "Even when it was obvious that they had mistaken me for a woman," he writes in *The Naked Civil Servant*, "they allowed themselves to be enlightened with no display of disgust."

American: Can I walk you home, ma'am?

Me: You think I'm a woman, don't you?

American: You waggle your fanny like a woman.

Me: Oh, I should ignore that.

American: I'm trying to, but it's not that easy.[34]

"I and most of the homosexuals whom I knew best wanted 'something in a uniform,' " Crisp recalls. He especially liked sailors, whose profligacy with money was "an irresistible lure—especially when combined with the tightness of their uniforms, whose crowning aphrodisiac feature was the fly-front of their trousers. More than one of my friends has swayed about in ecstasy describing the pleasure of undoing this quaint sartorial device." On a trip to Portsmouth in 1937, when, he reminisces, "the whole town was like a vast carnival with, as its main attraction, a continuous performance of *H.M.S. Pinafore*," Crisp, strolling along the seafront, was instantly surrounded by sailors. "Our progress," he noted, "was like a production number in a Hollywood musical" (Crisp, 91, 92). (Crisp's choice of *Pinafore*, an operetta named after a fictional ship that is in turn named after a garment worn by small girls, seems characteristically—and charmingly—apt.)

"Sailors," according to the authors of a recent history of drag in Britain, "have always been more tolerant of queens than have the general public. Presumably this is because they like having sex with them."[35] As Bluebell, a "Sea Queen" for thirty-three years, remembers, "When I joined there were 257 liners and we used to do drag shows all the time. Sailors were far more used to queens than the people ashore were, and they loved the shows. Many of the sailors had a wife or girlfriend at home, but that didn't stop them from coming up to you at the beginning of a voyage and saying, 'You're mine for the trip' " (*Men in Frocks*, 32). Lorri Lee, who joined up in 1960, recalled that "The sea was an ideal life for the queens in those days. There were hundreds of us." "The Sea Queens were all drag Queens and we all had a frock tucked away, just in case. We did shows on a little stage on the ship: the crews got the dirty version, while the passengers got the cleaned-up one" (*Men in Frocks*, 31).

These nautical drag shows were relatively private affairs, but the association of sailors and cross-dressing seems to have struck a chord with a more popular and widespread audience. Quentin Crisp's amused description of himself and his sailor escorts making their way along the quayside "like a production number in a Hollywood musical" reflects the fact that several South Seas musical comedies of the 1940's actually featured some unlikely looking sailors in drag. In the 1941 *South of Tahiti*, for example, Andy Devine, Broderick Crawford, and Henry Wilcoxon as three hulking pearl divers caught in the act of theft were compelled to dance (in sarongs, sandals, and sailor caps) before a village audience; in *Song of the Islands* (1942) Jack Oakie, disguised as a woman, is in danger of becoming both the wife and the dinner of a cannibal chief until he is rescued by fellow sailor Victor Mature; in *Rainbow Island* (1944) Eddie Bracken, as one of three castaway sailors, cross-dresses as a native girl and takes the place of Dorothy Lamour while she dallies with one of his shipmates.[36]

To Americans brought up in the fifties, sixties, and even the seventies, however, the musical that instantly comes to mind in this connection is Rodgers and Hammerstein's *South Pacific*, with its memorable drag stage show, "Thanksgiving Follies," featuring a sailor in a skimpy grass skirt and Nurse Nellie Forbush in a baggy sailor suit.

The comic treatment of gender crossing in *South Pacific* is in part a displacement of anxieties about the transgressing of racial borderlines. The category crisis for which this carnival is an evident cover is that of mixed race and mixed nationality: the romantic mismatch in "Thanksgiving Follies" is bracketed by the ongoing "serious" love crises of Lieutenant Cable, who is engaged to a girl at home but has fallen in love with the young Tonkinese woman Liat, and of Nellie Forbush herself, who finds the Frenchman Emile, with his past marriage to a Polynesian woman and his half-Polynesian children, a far cry from the mores of her native Little Rock, Arkansas. (That Emile the Frenchman is played, in both stage and screen versions, by an Italian—Ezio Pinza, Rossano Brazzi—says something about American xenophobia and the fantasy of the all-purpose continental seducer in the postwar fifties.)

It is equally possible, however, to see the racial issues in the play as displacing a greater anxiety about gender, or about policing, or breaching, the borderline between gay and straight. As Bérubé notes, "Nellie" is gay male slang for an effeminate man, and "Butch" is lesbian slang for a masculine woman. (Bérubé, 88). When in the cross-dressed sailor skit Nellie Forbush plays a man whose name is Butch, an audience attuned to gay jokes would quickly get the point.

The song Nellie sings is "Honey-Bun" ("101 pounds of fun,/ That's my little Honey-Bun,/ Get a load of Honey-Bun tonight").[37] In the 1958 film version of *South Pacific* (starring Mitzi Gaynor, Brazzi, John Kerr, and Juanita Hall) the object of her serenade is Ray Walston as the Seabee Luther Billis in drag, wearing a grass skirt and a straw-like blond wig, with flowers in his hair, his "breasts" made of coconut shells and stuffed with packs of cigarettes. In the course of Luther's performance as Honey-Bun a sailor in the audience good-naturedly lobs a dart at his rear end, resplendent in red plaid shorts (Honey *Buns?*) underneath the grass skirt, but this joking version of anal penetration remains, on the surface, as unthreatening as does the whole representation of switched gender roles.

Throughout *South Pacific* Luther has been associated with rather fussy, "feminine" pursuits. Nurse Forbush praises his neat-handed ironing when he presents her with her laundry in a parcel. The opening scene shows him trying to sell sailor-manufactured grass skirts to the natives, and he wears floral garlands twined about him when (in his usual sailor clothes) he visits Bali Hai. When he puts these items of clothing on in the Thanksgiving Follies he is thus not so much carnivalized as interpreted, even exposed. His bare midriff (ostentatiously tattooed with a three-masted schooner) undulating expertly, he flaunts a large fig leaf on the underside of which is written, in large letters, the word "Spam." Walston, incidentally, would later appear as an effeminate cosmetician—and psychotic transvestite killer—in the 1967 film *Caprice*.[38] As we will see when we come to discuss the casting of transvestite and transsexual roles in films and plays, the subliminal association of a cross-dressed role in one film with an ostensibly "straight" role in another is one way in which transvestism functions as a social and political rhetoric.

South Pacific seems from the vantage point of the 1990's to be, even if inadvertently, the perfect camp musical, from the sailors' opening chorus of "There Is Nothing Like a Dame" and its litany of lack ("What ain't we got? You know damn well") to Nurse Forbush's theme song, "I'm in Love with a Wonderful Guy" in which she laments her susceptibility to believe "any fable I hear from a *person in pants*." The word "gay" appears incessantly, in song after song, always carrying a public message of Arkansas down home happiness, but often with the potential for a privately coded second meaning as well. (We might compare this double use of the term to Cary Grant's exasperated explanation, when caught dressed in a woman's frilly bathrobe in *Bringing Up Baby* [1938], that he "just went gay all of a sudden."[39])

The "Thanksgiving Follies," as the name implies, is a carnivalized occasion, and we should note that drag shows and cross-dressed impersonations in the context of the armed forces often seem related to the trope of the world-turned-upside-down. The enlisted men perform for the officers as well as for their peers. No (male) officers cross-dress on these occasions, although female officers—like nurses—occasionally do so. In David Lean's 1957 *The Bridge on the River Kwai*, British soldiers in grass skirts and halter tops put on a show for their comrades to celebrate the bridge's completion (and their impending move to a new prison camp); despite his preoccupation, Alec Guinness as Colonel Bogey feels required to attend and applaud. So that it is the "men"—that is, the enlisted men—who play "women," not the officers. But then it is the officers who are (already) in the fancy uniforms. Guinness, indeed, had himself already played Dame character roles, for example in the 1950 film *Kind Hearts and Coronets*.

FROCKS AND BONDS

> Dressing in drag ... won't help a chief executive who is cutting workers' salaries while raising his own no matter how good he looks in heels.
>
> *New York Times*, March 25, 1990[40]

To cross-dress on the stage in an all-male context like the army or the navy is a way of asserting the common privilege of maleness. Borderlines like officers/"men" or gay/straight are both put in question and redrawn or reaffirmed: "woman"—the artifact made of wig, makeup, coconut breasts, and grass skirt or sailor's "frock"—offers a space for fantasies that are at once erotic and misogynistic.

When we turn to the male-bonding rituals provided by institutionalized transvestite theaters in privileged spaces like universities and millionaires' clubs, we can see that cross-dressing for success is the mark of both the well-born and the self-made(up) man. Many Ivy League schools have long traditions of male drag shows, from Princeton's Triangle Club to the University of Pennsylvania's Mask and Wig. But the oldest of these, and probably the best known, is Harvard's Hasty Pudding.

The Hasty Pudding Theatricals at Harvard College developed as an offshoot of a secret society founded in 1795. Members of the Hasty Pudding Club met in dormitory rooms to declaim orations on serio-comic topics. After a few years the orations turned into mock trials and gradually became more and more theatrical; the first full-fledged Pudding Play, produced by Lemuel Hayward in December 1844, was called "Bombastes Furioso" and featured a cross-dressed heroine called Distaffina, attired in "a low neck and short sleeves," who provoked thunderous applause from the assembled undergraduates when she introduced "a fancy dance."[41]

Both Distaffina and her audience, of course, were male Harvard students, drawn from a certain privileged class of American society. Over the years, Pudding Shows featured such luminaries as Oliver Wendell Holmes (1860), William Randolph Hearst (1885), John Reed (1910) and George Santayana (as Lady Elfrida in *Robin Hood* [1886]). Henry Cabot Lodge wrote one Pudding Show (1871); Theodore Roosevelt was club secretary in 1879, and J.P. Morgan, manager ten years later. Under Morgan's leadership *The Duenna* precipitated the Club into (temporary) financial ruin.

Not only political, legal, and financial leaders but also future men of the theater got their start in Harvard's cross-dressed extravaganza. Arthur Sullivan wrote the operetta *Cox and Box* in 1875; Alistair Cooke directed *Hades, the Ladies!* in 1934; Alan Jay Lerner (later to co-author *My Fair Lady*) wrote the words and music for *Fair Enough* in 1939; and Jack Lemmon, starring in a drag role in *Proof of the Pudding* in 1945–46, anticipated his tour de force appearance as the cross-dressed Daphne in *Some Like It Hot*. As with today's equally exclusive and privileged all-male Tavern and Bohemian clubs, which cater largely to an older and perhaps more politically conservative crowd, Harvard's Pudding to a certain extent mainstreamed and "legitimized" female impersonation, establishing it as a class act to be acted out, and acted up, by the members of a certain class. Indeed, the Pudding shows, when they went on tour in the teens and twenties, traveling from Cambridge and Boston to Providence, New York, and Baltimore, served as mating dances for the debutante set; the traditional bare-legged kickline that ended every performance, rather like the revels of Renaissance court masques, led to a mingling of the (cross-dressed) actors and their (often female and upper-class) audiences, and thence to socially prominent marriages.

But this mainstream, ostensibly heterosexual, and socially privileged niche established for the Hasty Pudding Theatricals coexisted with, and was, we might want to argue, maintained and policed by, boundary transgressions of all kinds—transgressions that tested the limits of inside and outside, town and gown, male and female, "masculine" and "effeminate," gay and straight, through the figure of the transvestite actress, the spectacle of what one Club chronicler calls "Harvard's Hairy-Chested Heroines." In other words, the Theatricals, which gradually became independent of the secret society, externalized and acted out—in a psychoanalytic as well as a thespian sense—crises and conflicts displaced from, but closely adjacent to, the construction of a certain kind of "manhood" or "maleness" crucial to the maintenance of an intellectual and social hegemony whose American name, and sign, was "Harvard."

Let us see how this comes about. American academia was, together with the clergy, one of the last bastions of sumptuary regulation in the New World. (We can see vestiges of this today in private military schools like VMI and the Citadel, as well as in the fascinating phenomenon of a reimposition of dress codes in inner city schools, to prevent competitive and costly sartorial display among schoolchildren, from name-brand running shoes to gold tooth-caps.) The Laws of Harvard College from 1655 onward are quite explicit about codes of dress and ornament, as well as behavior, for undergraduates. And while sumptuary laws in the English Renaissance are largely directed at class rather than gender transgressions, the Harvard College Laws, dating from the mid-eighteenth century, are clearly concerned with gender. As we will see, however, it is not always so easy to tell what the opposite of "manliness" is deemed to be.

Thus, for example, long hair was deemed by the "Colledge" in 1650 to be particularly "uncivil and unmanly," but the long-haired models to be eschewed here are not women but "Ruffians and barbarous Indians."[42] Specific items of clothing (coat, gown, and cloak) were mandated by the "Chauncy Code" of 1655 and the "Mather Code" of 1692, and dandyism was proscribed (no locks or foretops, no curling, crisping, parting, or powdering the hair); the tone of these codes is highly reminiscent of earlier European sumptuary laws, rejecting "strange ruffianlike or Newfangled fashions" and "lavish Dresse, or excess of Apparell."[43]

Something strange, however, took place in 1712. George Hussey, an undergraduate, was publicly admonished and "degraded" for wearing women's apparel on the streets of Cambridge on Election Day. The aptly named Hussey (scion of a Nantucket Quaker family) was required to make a public confession; he paid a fine and left Harvard, marrying a Nantucket woman and settling down on the island.[44] In 1734, the college laws were revised, now explicitly forbidding students to wear women's apparel. To the requirement that a scholar wear coat, cloak, and gown whenever he left the College Yard was added the following:

And If any shall Presume to put on or wear Indecent Apparell, he shall be punished According to the Nature and degree of the Offence . . . but If he wears womens Apparell, he shall be liable to publick admonition, degradation, or Expulsion.[45]

In 1767 the College's "Holyoke Code" retained the injunction against women's apparel and added, for the first time, a specific prohibition of acting in "Stage Plays, Interludes, or Theatrical Entertainments" in the town of Cambridge or elsewhere, although theatrical performances as parts of "Academic Exercises" were exempted from this ban. Thus the two kinds of behavior most visibly offensive to the Puritan antitheatricalists in England were reproduced at Harvard: acting on the stage, and dressing like a woman, were alike regarded as morally suspect, even corrupting, and were forbidden—outside the confines of the University. This is not in itself particularly surprising, since Harvard was founded by American Puritans. What is of interest, however, is the way both infractions came together in the University's most celebrated and proudly produced show-for-export, the Hasty Pudding Theatricals.

The wearing of women's clothes continued to be explicitly forbidden through at least 1816; by 1825, with the list of infractions growing yearly longer, the prohibition in dress was characterized merely as "indecency in language, dress, or behaviour," and this phrase recurs in the regulations for 1848.

Conflict with the law, both university and civil, was probably inevitable for an undergraduate theater group whose increasing focus was on female impersonation. And, as we will see, in two specific instances the club's ambivalent attitude toward gender bending came to the fore.

As early as 1854 some members of the Hasty Pudding had begun to specialize in female impersonation; Horace Furness '54 was the club's first diva, "The unparalleled Signorina Furness" (Calnek, 29); Charles Eliot Furness '63 kept up the family tradition. The focus on female impersonation, sometimes "cod drag," sometimes glamorous, continues to the present day, with recent impersonators—like their predecessors—choosing punning names that rival those of drag queens in gay nightclubs: Sharon Sharalike (1966); Ophelia Heartbeat, Lady Marion Haste, and Sonya Vabitszch (1977); Giovanna Dance and Jemima Fysmoke (1978), Kitty Litter (1984). (Compare these, for example, to *Torch Song Trilogy*'s Virginia Hamm and Bertha Vanation—or to the "Pansy," "Daisy," and "Lily" aliases chosen by public [offstage] female impersonators in the New York underground of the 1890's.)[46]

Private theatricals developed in the 1850's, and were still raunchily popular in the early 1900's, when "Bumming in France," starring "Ivan E. Rexionne" and "Willy Cracker," played successfully at Harvard. But public touring, at least by slightly sanitized shows, had already begun, and the 1917 show, "Barnum Was Right" (by playwright Robert Sherwood), allegedly ran into trouble with the Boston censor—not because boys played the parts of women on the stage, but because the members of the kickline refused to wear silk stockings. A Boston law banned bare legs for chorus girls, and the male chorines were held to the same standard. Local newspapers were full of reports on the controversy (which may, it seems, have been a student publicity stunt).

One paper quipped that the young actors, many from wealthy New York families, had always been known as "silk stocking men" (from the nickname of the Fifth Avenue electoral district),[47] while several commentators, including the censor (in an article denying the planned interdiction), pointed out that Scotsmen went barelegged under their kilts.[48] As it happened, the bare-legged controversy shared newspaper space with the Russian Revolution, and two weeks later the U.S. entered World War I, whereupon the production was scrapped, and the entire cast enlisted. But the playful send-up of Boston's blue laws, and the interesting question of whether the ban on bare legs applied to men dressed as "girls" (the standard term of the period) or only to "real girls" (the distinction made by the *New York Sun* in its headline, March 15, 1917) suggest, among other things, an *absence* of anxiety. The desire to provoke the straight-laced authorities, and an insistence on *difference* that would, in fact, be highlighted by the press handling of the whole affair, are part of the prevailing spirit of boys-will-be-boys-by-being-girls. Wearing women's clothing was not, apparently, transgressive enough; the kickline aspired to dress—or *undress*— like transgressive women, women on the borderline.

A quite different spirit infused the Pudding's other tangle with the law, which was, significantly, an intra-university rather than a town-gown affair. It began not at Harvard but at Yale, where a Dean ruled in December 1915 that members of the Yale Dramatic Association could not impersonate female characters for more than one year in succession, because continued impersonation tended to make men effeminate.[49] Officials at Columbia, NYU, Washington University, Princeton, Brown, and the University of Pennsylvania all pooh-poohed this idea. Penn's Provost assured the *Times* that "the men who made our best girls were just as much men as ever after the shows were over." The Director of Physical Education at Brown remarked that "if [playing a female role] should tend to make [a man] effeminate, his daily association with other men would counteract it," and "female impersonators in the show squads at Columbia and New York Universities" reported that the best "actresses" in their shows were also among the best athletes. A 250-pound football tackle, known as "the All-American 'pony' ballet girl," puffed on a cigar and uttered "several expletives" as he told the *Times* reporter—in a phrase familiar from the annals of professional female impersonation—that "We do not try to be womanish." "We are only artificial women," he assured his interlocutor. "We don't shorten our strides, and we wear just enough women's clothing and paint and hair to make us look the part."[50]

Viewed from today's vantage point this whole question may seem as comic as the silk-stocking controversy, and the tone of both the *Times* article and the officials interviewed seems to border on the risible (one "chuckled," another "was amused," a third "treated the question as something of a joke"). But Harvard, perhaps predictably, was *not* amused.

The renowned drama professor George Pierce Baker said that he approved of undergraduates playing feminine roles, but not of men adopting those parts "steadily for a livelihood," while an Associate Professor of Public Speaking felt that men who chose to play women onstage were likely to be effeminate, and—more importantly—that impersonation put an undue strain upon the throat. A few months after Yale's action Harvard's faculty met to consider instituting a similar one-year limit, citing—according to a newspaper account—"psychological investigation which showed that the portrayal of feminine parts too often tended toward effeminacy."[51] But despite initial reports that it had done so, the faculty declined to take such action, allowing the "skirt" parts of the Pudding Show—and of the similarly cross-dressed Pi Eta—to be played by the original cast.

We may note in many of these responses a familiar conflation of "effeminacy"[52] and cross-dressing, and the defense or reply of "manliness" as exemplified in athletic prowess. Homosexuality is not overtly at issue here, though it surely lies not too far beneath the surface, as for example in the Public Speaking professor's concern about students "already inclin[ing] toward effeminacy"—and, for that matter, in the titles of shows like "Bumming in France." But that athletes might be homosexuals seems not to enter the (conscious) minds of the university spokesmen; hence the idea that Brown's female impersonators could counteract any incipient effeminacy by "daily association . . . with other men." Indeed, it is suggestive that a phys ed instructor should be interviewed at all on the question. We are a long way from David Kopay's memoirs on being gay in the professional football world.

But let us return for a moment to the cigar-puffing athlete's calm assurance, "We are only artificial women." Clearly one implication of this is that there are, somewhere, real women, but the emphasis here is on *not* being one of them, *not* being "womanish," but being, instead, a "real man." A cross-dressed "actress" from New York University, interviewed on the same occasion, testified to the versatility of one of his colleagues, a football player and female impersonator. "Put football togs on him and he looked like a bruiser, but primp him up with lingerie and chiffon, and he looked like the queen of the prom," said the male actress. "He couldn't balance a teacup on a saucer, and he couldn't take a piece of candy without using his whole fist. That's how effeminate he was. And there are four others, good female impersonators, all of them, but rough enough for dock hands."

"Effeminate" here is not the opposite of "manly" but of "crude," or, in the article's terms, "rough," a term now commonly applied to a kind of sexual acting out that mimics—or draws upon—lower-class behavior, "rough trade." The butch-femme binarism, in other words, is being summoned into play to describe the (apparent) gender effects of class: teacup-balancing and the queen of the prom versus bruisers and dockhands. "Artificial women" are men who down-class themselves as they camp it up.[53]

And what about "real women'? How has this bastion of privilege risen to the challenge of coeducation—and of contemporary feminism and gender-bending? The club went co-ed in 1973. The Pudding's "Woman of the Year" award, instituted to declare "its peculiar love for women" (Calnek, 93), has in recent years been presented to cross-dressed actresses, like Julie Andrews (who played a female impersonator of a female impersonator in *Victor/Victoria*) and Mary Tyler Moore (who played a gender-reversed role in *Whose Life Is It, Anyway?*). In 1973 a one-time only "Person of the Year" award went to Gloria Steinem, who commented, "I don't mind drag—women have been female impersonators for some time" (Calnek, 95). Asked to explain the phenomenon of the Pudding show, a woman who was co-producer of two of them shrugged and updated Andy Hardy: "We're just a bunch of kids putting on a drag show," she said (Calnek, 110). The Pudding's most recent and admiring historian notes that times have changed at Harvard, that restrictions on social life are not what they were, that "men may even wear feminine apparel if they so desire" (Calnek, 110). The borderline of transgressiveness has been redrawn. Onstage/offstage, Yard/world, upperclass/otherclass, male/female, butch/femme, straight/gay—one after another these boundaries have been breached.

The Hasty Pudding Theatricals are, of course, only one exemplar of a kind of boys-will-be-boys transvestite theater that remains alive and well in exclusive (and powerful) all-male circles today. Boston's almost-100-year-old Tavern Club recently sought an exemption from the city's regulation barring sexual discrimination in private clubs on the grounds that female members would undermine the club's all-male theatrical productions. A long-time member who is an editor of the *Boston Globe* gave it as his opinion that "there should be clubs for men, clubs for women, and, in this case, clubs for men who want to dress up as women." And a lyric from a recent Tavern Club show, performed by a chorus of men in drag, caroled, "We Love the Ladies .... But we'd rather have the place in embers, than see them as regular members."[54]

But the best known of transvestite refuges among the power elite in the U.S. today is probably the fabled Bohemian Club of San Francisco, "the most exclusive club in the United States, with 2,300 members drawn from the whole of the American establishment and a waiting list 33 years long."[55] The Bohemian Club conducts an annual retreat in a redwood forest some seventy miles north of the city where its own musical comedy show, *The Low Jinks*, is performed by an all-male cast for an all-male audience of the wealthy and the famous. When an undercover reporter from *Spy* magazine attended this gathering in the Bohemian Grove, he reported rampant "sexism and racism" in the Jinks. "The biggest crowd pleaser was Bubbles Boobenheim, a showgirl turned patroness who rubbed her prosthetic behind against the elevator doors at stage left" (Weiss, 72). Bubbles, like all the "women" in the show, was of course played by a man in drag. Prostheses seem to have been the order of the evening; "the most striking prop of The Low Jinks," according to Weiss, "was a sculpture of a female torso whose breasts and buttocks had been attached to the front, an improvement that looked vaguely hostile," while "pee-pee and penis jokes" abound, suggesting "that starkest of male nostalgias, the hankering for the punctual erections of boyhood" (Weiss, 72–73). Another Grove play, *Pompeii*, was advertised with a poster depicting a giant erection under a toga. The set for the play featured "a wall inscription in Latin meaning 'Always hard' " (Weiss, 73). And, according to Weiss—for he is my only, and clearly a somewhat biased, source, since uninvited visitors to the Grove are strictly forbidden, as, needless to say, are women—"Bohemian discourse is full of oblique organ worship as well," like the constant rhapsodic reference to the redwoods as upright and stately (Weiss, 73), and, of course, the constant and competitive urination-for-distance that preoccupies Grove denizens ("nearby a young member of the cast dressed as a woman pulled apart purplish gossamer robes to pee" [Weiss, 75]). Homoeroticism mixes with male-bonding; the annals of the Club contain 100-year-old references to "slender, young Bohemians, clad in economical bathing suits" (Weiss, 76). Whatever the specifics of the nostalgia gripping the members of the Bohemian Club, the ingredients of this spectacle—artifactuality of both male and female bodies, anxious phallicism, cross-dressing—seem to suggest not only a familiar pattern but a specific prescription of *un*dress-for-success. This is, after all, the club of Kissinger and Reagan, of political as well as financial and show-business power.

Far from undercutting the power of the ruling elite, male cross-dressing rituals here seem often to serve as confirmations and expressions of it. Indeed, what is fascinating about the study of transvestism is precisely that it can occupy such contradictory social sites: stigmatized and outlawed in some circumstances, appropriated as a sign of privilege in others. It is easy to see the drag performances of the Bohemian Club or the Tavern Club as undisguised instances of misogyny or homophobia, but it is nonetheless curious that the means chosen to neutralize the threat of femininity and homosexuality should involve using a version of the poison as its own remedy.

3

THE TRANSVESTITE'S PROGRESS

THE PROGRESS NARRATIVE

> He gave up everything. There were certain rules and regulations in those days if you were going to be a musician.
> Kitty Oakes, former wife of jazz musician Billy Tipton[1]

The case of Billy Tipton, the married jazz musician with three adopted sons who was discovered after his death to have been a woman, received prominent coverage early in 1989 in the *New York Times*, the *Boston Globe*, the *Spokane Spokesman-Review,* and scores of other newspapers across the country. Tipton's former wife and one of his sons were interviewed on television (the other two sons are apparently negotiating movie rights to the story); the son, in a quote picked up by the wire services, declared with what I think is an admirable sense of the constructed rather than essential nature of gender categories, "He'll always be Dad to me." It was the funeral director who broke the news of Tipton's "real" gender, intending to spare the son the awkwardness of finding out what was described as the "truth," the "secret" in public.

Yet the Billy Tipton story is remarkable only in the fact that it caught the fancy of the media and the public. Historians record dozens, probably hundreds, of such stories of lifelong cross-dressers whose "true" gender identities were disclosed only after death, from the celebrated (like the eighteenth-century Chevalier d'Eon and the British Colonial Medical Officer James Barry) to the obscure.

Lucy Ann Lobdell left her husband and became the Reverend Joseph Lobdell, living with Maria Perry for ten years as man and wife.[2] Murray Hall, a woman who dressed as a man, married two women, adopted a daughter, became an influential figure in the New York City Tammany Hall Democratic machine, and was noted for his hard-drinking, poker playing, and womanizing.[3] Dr. Eugene C. Perkins, a physician in La Jolla, California, had been married for 28 years when his wife died in 1936. When Perkins died six months later, there was apparently some consternation in the medical examiner's office, for on the death certificate "male" was crossed out after examination of the body and "female" written in red ink. Katherine Vosbaugh, also known as "Frenchy" and "Grandpa," spent sixty years as a man, working as a bank clerk, restaurateur, cook, and sheepherder, and was only revealed to be a woman in 1907 when "his secret was discovered in a hospital in Trinidad, Colo."[4]

Nor is this story limited to female-to-male cross-dressers. A Mrs. Nash at Fort Meade in the Dakota Territory married a soldier, and after he was transferred, she married another. After her death, she was discovered to be a man.[5] In England Colonel Victor Barker was married to Elfrida Haward in St. Peter's parish church, Brighton. Six years later, jailed on an unrelated bankruptcy charge, Colonel Barker was revealed by a prison doctor to be a woman, and she was charged with perjury because of her marriage. Elfrida Haward, testifying before the court, claimed that she had not known the Colonel was a woman "until [she] read about it in the newspapers."[6] Like Billy Tipton, Colonel Barker had convinced his wife that he had an abdominal injury, in his case one suffered in the war, that prevented him from having normal sexual relations. These are really rather typical cases of what is a relatively widespread phenomenon. In other words, the saga of Billy Tipton is just the tip of an iceberg.

Why, then, was his life story so intriguing to the popular imagination? Or, to put the question slightly differently, what cultural fears, anxieties, and fantasies are being read into, and out of, the accounts of Tipton's life and death? What is being displaced here—and why?

One thing especially notable about the Tipton story is the way it was "explained," or "interpreted." Tipton's former wife, Kitty Oakes, explained that their marital arrangement did not include sexual intercourse, and that Tipton had told her he suffered an injury which required the wearing of broad surgical bandages across the middle of his body for support. As his wife, she bought the bandages, and never—she says—saw him without them. As for his transvestic masquerade, it was to be explained by economic and cultural factors. Jazz musicians in the thirties, forties and fifties were almost all male. Thus Tipton began appearing as a man, according to the *Times*, "to improve her chances of success as a jazz musician." "He gave up everything," says his former wife. "There were certain rules and regulations in those days if you were going to be a musician" (*Times*, A18).

Notice the difference of pronoun here: "*her* chances of success"; "*he* gave up everything." To the *Times*—citing the *Spokane Spokesman-Review*—the funeral director's empirical observations about anatomy clinched the case: read backwards, Tipton was a woman. To the wife and the son ("He'll always be Dad") Tipton is male, and is remembered in the historical present: he *is*, he will *always be*. Billy Tipton as dead body; Billy Tipton as living memory. These are not trivial differences: they mark the distinction between a positivistic and a theoretically inflected understanding of transvestism and its discontents.

But whatever gender Tipton is assigned after the fact, the "explanation" of his (or her) transvestism is *normalized*, by interpreting it in the register of socio-economic necessity. A patriarchal culture had ordained that jazz musicians were, or ought to be, male; therefore, it is claimed, Billy Tipton cross-dressed: in order to get a job; in order to succeed in the profession of his choice; in order to support his family.

But just how persuasive *is* this normalization, this explanation that explains away, that banishes transvestism and replaces it with economic expedience? Surely the elaborate business with Tipton's wife and the surgical bandages, so reminiscent of Freud's patient's "athletic support-belt . . . [that] covered up the genitals entirely and concealed the distinction between them,"[7] was not required by the social politics of the jazz world, the "certain rules and regulations" laid down by the Jack Teagarden and Russ Carlyle bands, or the nightclub audiences of the fifties who danced to the music of the Billy Tipton trio. Even if it was "necessary" for Tipton to pretend *in public* to be male, why was it "necessary" for him to marry a woman, and raise his adoptive sons to know him as "Dad"? The drummer of the Billy Tipton trio, Dick O'Neil, who played with the group for ten years, recalls that some members of the audience would make jokes about Tipton's baby face and high singing voice, remarking that he looked too feminine to be a man. "But I would almost fight anybody who said that," O'Neil claims. "I never suspected a thing."

This normalization of the story of the transvestite is all too typical of the way in which cross-dressing is treated, explained, and explained away, sometimes in very sophisticated and theoretically ingenious ways. Whatever discomfort is felt by the reader or audience ("I would almost fight" [resistance]; "I never suspected" [denial]; "He gave up everything" [rationalization]) is smoothed over and narrativized by a story that recuperates social and sexual norms, not only reinstating the binary (male/female) but also retaining, and encoding, a progress narrative: s/he did this in order to a) get a job, b) find a place in a man's world, and c) realize or fulfill some deep but acceptable need in terms of personal destiny, in this case, by becoming a jazz musician.

We should note the avoidance of any mention of sexuality in this version of the "progress narrative." Another common "answer" to why people cross-dress has been the assumption that the cross-dresser must be gay. This is a complicated issue, and one which I will take up in detail in Chapter 6. But let me say here, briefly, that several recent studies—including some conducted by transvestite organizations—suggest that, although lifelong cross-dressers like Lucy/Joseph Lobdell may well have been lesbians, a majority of *intermittent* transvestites are straight or bisexual and married. Transsexuals, who may cross-dress as part of their therapeutic migration toward living permanently as a member of the "other" sex, are statistically more often self-identified as gay than are transvestites. (Here we encounter a subtle question of definition and of the timing of medico-legal transformation; a "straight" transsexual, for example, may be a biological male who identifies himself as a woman, and who is attracted to men, while a "gay" transsexual is a biological male attracted to women.) What does seem clear is that the question of cross-dressing as an intermittent or constant, public or private, historical or literary representation is neither equivalent to nor entirely separable from the question of sexual object choice, whether heterosexual, homosexual, or bisexual.[8]

A "progress narrative" similar to the one told about Billy Tipton underlies the interpretation of a great number of cross-dressing stories in literature and film: Tony Curtis and Jack Lemmon in *Some Like It Hot*, Dustin Hoffman in *Tootsie*, Julie Andrews in *Victor/Victoria*, Katharine Hepburn in *Sylvia Scarlett*, virtually all of Shakespeare's female-to-male cross-dressers. Each is "compelled" by social and economic forces to disguise himself or herself in order to get a job, escape repression, or gain artistic or political "freedom." Each, that is, is said to embrace transvestism unwillingly, as an instrumental strategy rather than an erotic pleasure and play space; in each of the instances I have cited, indeed, heterosexual desire is for a time apparently thwarted by the cross-dresser's assumed identity, so that it becomes necessary for him or her to unmask. The ideological implications of this pattern are clear: cross-dressing can be "fun" or "functional" so long as it occupies a liminal space and a temporary time period; after this carnivalization, however, whether it is called "Halloween" (in Provincetown) or "green world" (in Shakespeare), the cross-dresser is expected to resume life as he or she was, having, presumably, recognized the touch of "femininity" or "masculinity" in her or his otherwise "male" or "female" self.

The exceptions to this rule—the Billy Tiptons—fascinate by their aberrance. That Tipton could have preferred the life he lived, could have chosen it, with all of its logistical complications and multiple social deceptions, over all other options (like a merely public, professional transvestite identity that ended at the door of his house, or his bedroom door; or an explicitly lesbian relationship) seems, to many, unimaginable. So social and ideological forces are mobilized to maneuver him into the position of a subject with limited and circumscribed agency, and the story is given a certain poignant human-interest edge because of his status as an artist. "He did it for his art."

By now it should be clear that I regard such appropriations of transvestism in the service of a humanist "progress narrative" as both unconvincing and highly problematic. Unconvincing, because they ignore the complex and often unconscious eroticism of such self-transformations and masquerades (whether or not they are to be called versions of "fetishism") and because in doing so they rewrite the story of the transvestic subject as a cultural symptom. Problematic, because the consequent reinscription of "male" and "female," even if tempered (or impelled) by feminist consciousness, reaffirms the patriarchal binary and ignores what is staring us in the face: the existence of the transvestite, the figure that disrupts.

Not surprisingly, when the notion of social progress is conflated with a biologistic or "evolutionary" progress, the limits of this strategy become all the more striking—especially when the object of scrutiny itself is an analogue *for* Western culture. I am thinking here about certain "progress narrative" readings of transvestism in Shakespeare's plays: progress narratives that focus on the female-to-male cross-dresser as a) a social or economic role model for modern women, or as b) the sign of an emergent male or female homosexual subculture, or as c) an acknowledgment of homoerotic attraction between the boy actor and his male admirers, or as d) a stage that girls pass through on their way to becoming women, or as e) a stage that boys pass through on their way to becoming men.

All of these readings do important cultural, social, political, and psychological work. The insistence on the part of gay theorists, for example, on keeping separate the categories of misogyny and homophobia rather than conflating them is a crucial corrective to earlier, and misleading, elisions. The feminist reminder that "wearing the pants" is, or has been, one way of achieving equality and visibility in a man's world places the question of transvestism in an important social and historical frame. Yet such progress narrative readings, by their very nature, *existentialize aesthetic questions*—whereas, I want to suggest, the figure of the transvestite in fact *opens up the whole question of the relationship of the aesthetic to the existential*. This, indeed, is part of its considerable power to disturb, its transgressive force.

In recent years fascinating evidence from history and material culture has been brought to bear upon the question of transvestism in early modern Europe. King James I was known to be bisexual; there were actual female-to-male cross-dressers in the streets of Shakespeare's London; in the early modern period male and female genitals were regarded by some medical experts as essentially the same organs, differing only in that women's were inside the body, and men's outside; lesbianism was culturally invisible in this period, was or was not punished by the courts, was or was not considered the same kind of behavior as male homosexuality, buggery, sodomy.

Paradoxically, however, these arguments from history, from what "really" happened or was "really" believed, seem in their very groundedness, in the reassurance they derive from historical "fact," to be an attempt to evade or repress another, perhaps more unwelcome (because more uncanny) kind of fact: the extraordinary power of the transvestite as an aesthetic and psychological agent of destabilization, desire, and fantasy.

In what follows, therefore, I will try to suggest both the limits of "normalization" and of the mainstreaming of transvestism, and the theoretical benefit of acknowledging what such normalization occludes: the power of transgressive desire.

ROSALIND THE YESHIVA BOY

> Rosalind's transvestism . . . functions to allow Rosalind to live out a
> freer, more assertive and independent role than she could otherwise. . . .
> In male garb, Rosalind automatically becomes the dominant figure. . . . It
> is she who deals with the outside world, who can meet and converse with

men, speak and act assertively, even authoritatively. . . . In short, she can
be a person.

Marilyn French, *Shakespeare's Division of Experience* (1981)[9]

In a quintessential version of the transvestite progress narrative, Shakespeare's cross-dressed female characters were often seen in the early years of feminist criticism as role models for modern (and postmodern) women. Resourceful, ambitious, passionate, smart, looking good in pants, these women—Rosalind, Viola, Portia, Julia, Imogen—provided authority and reassurance. Even Beatrice and Katherina, without benefit of breeches, spoke out in protest against patriarchy, and both were rewarded with desirable marriages.

All the more striking were the transvestite heroines, whether dressed as pages, country boys, or clerks. Theirs was a recuperative pattern: however outspoken they were, however much they challenged authority in the form of wicked dukes or moneylenders, they took pains to let their femaleness show. Rosalind and Julia swoon at moments of stress, Viola, facing the prospect of a duel, laments "a little thing would make me tell them how much I lack of a man" (*TN* 3.4.307–9), and Portia remarks to Nerissa that in their male disguise "they shall think we are accomplished/ With that we lack" (*MV* 3.4.61–63). "They," and "them," are of course the onstage (and offstage) audience of men—who ostensibly "had" what the cross-dressed women "lack." And if, as materialist critics of the eighties were quick to point out, these double entendres were in fact triple, because the transvestite women who "lacked" were in fact always already men, boy actors, with the audience very much in on the joke—this did not mitigate, but rather confirmed, the remanding of women back to their proper places at the end of the play. Cross-dressing, as contrasted with "masculinity" (like that detected by some critics in Goneril, or Lady Macbeth, or Volumnia), was playful and liminal—and also ameliorative and educational, whether for the "women" in the plays (Rosalind *et al.*) or for the audience.

We are accustomed to Shakespeare's being fetishized in Western culture, made the touchstone of issues literary, philosophical, and social, the surety and verification of the issues of our—or any—time. But it is striking to note that of all Shakespeare's cross-dressed heroines it is Rosalind who is almost always chosen as the normative case by nineteenth- and twentieth-century authors. When, for example, Oscar Wilde's Dorian Gray falls in love, it is with an actress playing the part of Rosalind—or rather, the part of Ganymede: "You should have seen her! When she came on in her boy's clothes she was perfectly wonderful. She wore a moss-coloured velvet jerkin with cinnamon sleeves, slim brown cross-gartered hose, a dainty little green cap with a hawk's feather caught in a jewel, and a hooded cloak lined with dull red. She had never seemed to me more beautiful."[10]

"Rosalind" appears, in fact, in a surprising number of modern texts as a kind of shorthand for the cross-dressed woman, or the enigma that she represents. Why Rosalind rather than Viola, or Portia, or Julia, or Imogen? Why is it so often Rosalind who is singled out as the exemplary early modern cross-dresser, the Katharine Hepburn (if not the Marlene Dietrich or the Annie Lennox) of her time? To approach this question, which has some larger implications for the cultural construction of transvestism, let us look at a few diverse and fascinating examples.

Théophile Gautier's 1835 novel, *Mademoiselle de Maupin*, is a remarkable text about gender undecidability in which the sexually enigmatic Théodore de Serannes is beloved by both the narrator d'Albert and his mistress, Rosette. The dramatic and the psychological plots of *Mademoiselle de Maupin* turn on a production of *As You Like It* in which Théodore appears in the part of Rosalind.

D'Albert the narrator, it is almost needless to say, is cast as Orlando. When he first sees Théodore dressed as Rosalind, he is enchanted: this is the answer to his prayers. "You would think he had never worn any other costume in his life! He is not in the very least awkward in his movements, he walks very well and he doesn't get caught up in his train; he uses his eyes and his fan to admiration; and what a slim waist he has! . . . Oh, lovely Rosalind! Who would not want to be her Orlando?"[11] Bear in mind that d'Albert at least thinks of himself as heterosexual; his desire is for Théodore to turn out to *be* a woman, so that he can safely love her. Thus his consternation when, in the third act, Rosalind cross-dresses, and appears as Ganymede.

> I grew all sombre when Théodore reappeared in masculine dress, more sombre than I had been before; for happiness only serves to make one more aware of grief. . . .
>
> And yet he was dressed in a way which suggested that this masculine attire had a feminine lining; something broader about the hips and fuller in the chest, some sort of flow which materials don't have on a man's body, left little doubt of the person's sex. . . .
>
> My serenity began to return, and I persuaded myself again that it was quite definitely a woman. (Gautier, 249)

Playing out the scene, in which Orlando tries to persuade the "fair youth" that he is really in love, and "Ganymede" reproves him for this mode of address, saying, "Nay, you must call me Rosalind," d'Albert feels that the play has been written for the express purpose of verbalizing his own situation. "No doubt there is some important reason, which I cannot know, which obliges this beautiful woman to adopt this accursed disguise" (Gautier, 252).

As for his rival in love, his mistress Rosette, *she* is also—again, needless to say—a member of the play's cast. Having refused the part of Rosalind for herself because she was reluctant to dress up as a man (a fact that surprises the self-absorbed and narcissistic d'Albert: "prudery is hardly one of her failings. If I had not been sure of the contrary, I would have thought that she had ugly legs" [Gautier, 235]), Rosette has accepted the role of Phebe, who falls hopelessly and fruitlessly in love with the fictive "Ganymede." As d'Albert observes complacently, the history of Phebe is her own, as that of Orlando is mine with this difference, that everything ends happily for Orlando, and that Phebe, disappointed in love, is reduced to marrying Sylvius [sic] instead of the delightful ideal she wanted to embrace. Life is like that: one person's happiness is bound to be someone else's misfortune. It is very fortunate for me that Théodore is a woman; it is very unfortunate for Rosette that Théodore isn't a man, and that she now finds herself cast into the amorous impossibilities in which I went astray not long ago. (Gautier, 257)

There is much more in this vein. Shakespeare's play serves as a *mise en abîme* into which Gautier's characters avidly hurl themselves, and the conundrum of gender undecidability is given a local habitation and a name. D'Albert's assertion, "I have no proofs, and I cannot remain in this state of uncertainty any longer" (Gautier, 257), mirrors Orlando's decisive "I can live no longer by thinking" (*AYLI* 5.2.50) and is equally self-delusive about the possibility of "proof" in matters of gender, identity, and role. "Théodore—Rosalind— for I don't know what name to call you by" (Gautier, 294). "Rosalind, you who have so many prescriptions for curing the malady of love, cure me, for I am very ill. Play your part to the end, cast off the clothes of the beautiful page Ganymede, and hold out your white hand to the youngest son of the brave Sir Rowland de Boys" (Gautier, 301).

So ends d'Albert's narrative. But this is not the end of the novel. Théodore now picks up the narration (this is very near the end of the book, Chapter 14 of 17) and "explains" the subterfuge. "Her" plan is in fact a "real life" version of the story of *As You Like It*:

This was my plan. In my male attire I should make the acquaintance of some young man whose appearance pleased me; I should live familiarly with him; by skilful questions and by false confidences which elicited true ones, I should soon acquire a complete understanding of his feelings and his thoughts. . . . I should make a pretext of some journey, and . . . come back in my women's clothes . . . then I should so arrange things that he met me and wooed me. (Gautier, 315)

The mystery would seem to be solved. Théodore, like "Rosalind" in the play, is a woman. Yet in the next moment she puts that identification, and the binarism of gender, in question.

I was imperceptibly losing the idea of my sex, and I hardly remembered, at long intervals, that I was a woman; at the beginning, I'd often let slip some phrase or other which didn't fit in with the male attire that I was wearing. . . . If ever the fancy takes me to go and find my skirts again in the drawer where I left them, which I very much doubt, unless I fall in love with some young beau, I shall find it hard to lose this habit, and, instead of a woman disguised as a man, I shall look like a man disguised as a a woman. In truth, neither sex is really mine . . . I belong to a third sex, a sex apart, which has as yet no name. . . .

  My dream would be to have each sex in turn, and to satisfy my dual nature: man today, woman tomorrow. (Gautier 329–30)

At the close of the novel, however, even this certainty about transvestism and the third kind is undermined. A new narrative voice takes over in the sixteenth chapter, recording visits by Théodore to the rooms of d'Albert and Rosette, and Théodore's departure the next morning. The novel's last chapter takes the form of a letter from Théodore to d'Albert, offered as a substitute and an "explanation": a letter which establishes Théodore as the locus of desire. "Your unassuaged desire will still open its wings to fly to me; I shall always be for you something desirable, to which your fancy loves to return" (Gautier, 347).

The transvestite here articulates herself/himself as *that which escapes*, what Lacan describes in his essay on "The Signification of the Phallus" as "desire":

> desire is neither the appetite for satisfaction, nor the demand for love, but the difference that results from the subtraction of the first from the second, the phenomenon of their splitting (*Spaltung*).[12]

Thus desire is by definition that which cannot be satisfied: it is what is left of absolute demand when all possible satisfaction has been subtracted from it. And this is another definition of the transvestite, exemplified in Shakespeare as in Gautier. The transvestite is the space of desire.

In a way this space is denied by readings of Shakespearean transvestism like that of Stephen Greenblatt, who writes that "the unique qualities of [Rosalind's] identity—those that give Rosalind her independence, her sharply etched individuality—will not, as Shakespeare conceives the play, endure: they are bound up with exile, disguise, and freedom from ordinary constraint, and they will vanish, along with the playful chafing, when the play is done."[13] But "vanishing" here is the converse of escaping. Greenblatt describes this as "an improvisational self-fashioning that longs for self-effacement and reabsorption in the community," and attributes that "longing" to "a social system that marks out singularity, particularly in women, as prodigious." But whose longing is it, really, that is being described here under the cover of a social and cultural constraint? If Rosalind's "unique qualities"—which is to say, her capacity for becoming or constructing Ganymede—will not endure, will "vanish" when the play is done, so too will Rosalind and Orlando and all the rest of the dramatis personae who are part of how "Shakespeare conceives the play." But in fact what lingers, like the smile of the Cheshire Cat, is precisely that residue, that supplement: Ganymede.

The "longing" for self-effacement and reabsorption is a domesticated and, I would suggest, finally once again patriarchal or masculinist longing, which is transferred onto the figure of the transvestite in a gesture of denial or fending off. Not to endure, to vanish—these are the negative reformulations of desire, which instead *escapes*, goes everywhere rather than nowhere, for the transvestite is the space of desire.

Let us look now at another recent fictional appropriation of Rosalind, this time from the twentieth rather than the nineteenth century: Angela Carter's novel *The Passion of New Eve*. First published in 1977, Carter's postmodern novel tells the story of Evelyn, a young Englishman who undergoes transsexual surgery to become Eve, and the woman of his dreams, Tristessa, a former Hollywood star who turns out to be literally a phallic woman, a male-to-female transvestite. The plot is intricate and unnecessary to summarize here, but the wedding scene between Eve and Tristessa is one that finds both participants cross-dressed. Tristessa wears "the white satin bridal gown he'd last worn thirty years before in. . . . *Wuthering Heights*," and Eve appears in a costume once intended for an actor playing Frédéric Chopin in the story of George Sand. (Sand was herself a famous cross-dresser, and Chopin, her lover, was notoriously described by his critics not only as "effeminate" but also as "the only female musician,"[14] so that Carter's plot of inverted inversion has yet further refractions, a cultural ripple effect.)

Here is Eve—formerly Evelyn—reflecting on her own reflection in the mirror:

> the transformation that an endless series of reflections showed me was a double drag. This young buck, this Baudelairean dandy so elegant and trim in his evening clothes—it seemed at first glance, I had become my old self again in the inverted world of the mirrors. But this masquerade was more than skin deep. Under the mask of maleness I wore another mask of femaleness but a mask that now I never would be able to remove, no matter how hard I tried, although I was a boy disguised as a girl and now disguised as a boy again, like Rosalind in Elizabethan Arden.[15]

The evocation of Rosalind, so similar, in a way, to that of Gautier's Théodore, produces similar ruminations on the questions of constructed and essential gender identity. "Rosalind" becomes here a sign word for that reflecting mirror, that infinite regress of representation, of which the transvestite (*always*, in one sense, "in double drag") is a powerful and inescapable reminder.

Why, then, is Rosalind the favorite among Shakespeare's cross-dressers, the shorthand term for benign female-to-male cross-dressing in literature and culture?

Rosalind differs from Viola in a crucial way: she returns to the stage dressed as a woman. In the last scene of the play she leaves the stage as Ganymede and returns, led by Hymen, in a "sight and shape" so unmistakably female as to give joy to Orlando and consternation to Phebe. In the Epilogue that follows "she" deliberately breaks the frame to acknowledge the "real" gender of the actor ("If I were a woman, I would kiss as many of you as had beards that pleased me, complexions that liked me, and breaths that I defied not" [*AYLI* 5.4.214–17]), and by calling attention to her underlying male "identity" as an actor ("*If* I were a woman") Rosalind opens up the possibility of a male/male homoeroticism between male audience member and male actor that is the counterpart of the male/"male" homoeroticism animating Orlando's conversations with Ganymede, as well as the converse of the female/female homoeroticism figured in the play by Phebe's infatuation.

But in returning dressed as a woman she also allows for the possibility of a recuperative interpretation (of which Greenblatt's is a very subtle and powerful version) that suggests a transformed woman now "reabsorbed" into the community and thus capable of "vanishing." Rosalind, according to this recuperative fantasy, has finished her job of education and self-instruction (Greenblatt calls it "improvisation," but it is clearly very temporary indeed), and can now take up her wifely role. There is no more need for Ganymede, who would have been very inconvenient if he had stayed around. As for the male Rosalind of the Epilogue, he doesn't need or want Ganymede either, except as an Ovidian reminder that gods and boys often go well together. ("Ganymede" was also Elizabethan slang, usually pejorative in tone, for a male prostitute or a servant kept for sexual purposes.[16]) Neither ending—that of the onstage pairs in marital ranks, nor that of the Epilogue and its wink to certain members of the audience—acknowledges the "other" transvestite, the one who is *not* there in either final scene or Epilogue. Yet it is "Ganymede" who is the play's locus of desire, "Ganymede," not Rosalind, with whom Phebe falls so hopelessly in love, "Ganymede" who enchants the audience. How are we to account for "Ganymede"? For the erotic?

Here, then, is the paradox. Only by looking at the transvestite on the stage, in the literary text, can we see clearly that he or she is not there. Only by regarding Ganymede, and Cesario and Dorothy Michaels in *Tootsie* as instated presences—not as other versions of Rosalind, or Viola, or Michael Dorsey, or Dustin Hoffman, but as constructs that have a subjectivity and an agency—can we understand something of their relation to narcissism, desire, and possibility. To appropriate them to a social and historical discourse is to understand their politics and their history, but not their power. For that power resides elsewhere.

A TALE OF TWO SINGERS

What a strange power there is in clothing.
I.B. Singer, "Yentl the Yeshiva Boy"

The point is made remarkably in the contrast between I.B. Singer's short story, "Yentl the Yeshiva Boy," published in 1962, and the 1983 Barbra Streisand film, *Yentl*, adapted from Singer's work. For Streisand makes her film a classic progress narrative or role-model allegory for the eighties, the story of a woman's liberation from old world patriarchy, the emigration of a Jewish Princess to the new world of Hollywood. Singer's story, by contrast, insists not only upon the quasi-mystical otherness of his nineteenth-century old world setting, but also upon the transvestite as a subject rather than a "stage." The "Anshel" of his tale escapes, is not converted but dispersed and reborn.

In Streisand's film, jokingly described by Hollywood skeptics as *"Tootsie on the Roof*,"[17] Yentl is a young girl who is more interested in studying the Hebrew scriptures with her scholar father than in buying fish with the local housewives. When her father dies, she faces herself in the mirror (in an important narcissistic moment), cuts off her long hair, and, dressed as a boy, sets off to become a scholar and spend her life reading the Torah.

She takes the name "Anshel," which, since it was the name of her brother who died in childhood, represents her fantasied male self. (Compare this to Viola/Cesario's affecting little story in *Twelfth Night* about a mythical "sister" who never told her love, and pined away—or, equally pertinent, Viola's decision to dress herself, in her guise as "Cesario," exactly like her brother, Sebastian.)

Inevitably, Yentl/Anshel meets a young man, Avigdor (Mandy Patinkin), with whom she falls in love, though he himself is in love with Hadass (Amy Irving). When Avigdor's marriage is prevented (his brother had committed suicide, rendering the whole family outcast and unsuitable for alliance), he urges "Anshel" to marry Hadass. A comic series of episodes follows, including one rather pointed scene at the tailor's, where the terrified husband-to-be is being fitted for a wedding suit. In the course of a long, determinedly broad song-and-dance number the audience is invited to speculate on "Anshel"'s trousers, and on what the tailors see—and don't see—beneath them in the course of their work.

These tailors, like the tailors who intimidated Freud's Wolf-Man, are *Schneiders*, cutters—a word related, as Freud points out, to the verb *beschneiden*, "to circumcise."[18] Are Orthodox Jewish men, ritually circumcised, really any different from women?, the film seems, teasingly, to ask. Streisand/Yentl/"Anshel," reenacting in comic (and musical) terms the always-already of castration/circumcision, draws attention to her quandary—the heterosexual female transvestite facing the prospect of marriage to a woman—as incapacity. In the next scenes, of the wedding and its remarkably eroticized aftermath, she will triumph over that apparent obstacle.

On the wedding night, "Anshel" persuades Hadass that there is no rush to consummate their marriage—that Hadass should choose sex rather than having it forced upon her. In an extraordinarily tender and erotic scene of instruction, the forbidden sexual energy is deflected into a mutual reading of the Talmud, with Streisand (the woman playing a woman dressed as a man) teaching Irving how to understand the Law. This is one of the scenes that most reminds me of Rosalind in *As You Like It*, in her guise as "Ganymede" teaching Orlando how to show his love.

Streisand's film is at least on the surface normatively heterosexual, so that this dangerous liminal moment in which Hadass falls in love with Yentl/Anshel is flanked—so to speak—on the one side by an early, comic moment in which Yentl/Anshel has to share a bed with Avigdor (who of course thinks she's a boy, and doesn't therefore understand her reluctance to strip and get under the covers) and on the other side by the revelation scene, in which Yentl declares her "true" sexual identity to Avigdor, ultimately baring her breasts to resolve his doubt.

Yet the scene between Streisand and Amy Irving smoulders with repressed sexuality. Irving later declared that she was "pretty excited. I mean, I'm the first female to have a screen kiss with Barbra Streisand! She refused to rehearse, but after the first take she said, 'It's not so bad. It's like kissing an arm.' I was a little insulted, because I believed so much that she was a boy that I'd sort of fallen in love with her" (Considine, 344). In another interview she explained that Streisand "was like the male lead, and she gave me the feminine lead. No problems."[19] Is Irving's "like" a comparative, or eighties babble-speak punctuation for emphasis? *Was* Streisand the male lead—or just an impersonator? Her own response to "Anshel's" undecidable and undeniable eroticism was, predictably, a kind of appropriative denial. When Hollywood producer Howard Rosenman, attending a private screening of *Yentl*, told her, "You were fabulous as a boy. Anshel was very sexy," she replied, he says, "very cutelike, in that nasal voice, 'Howard! Anshel is taken' " (Considine, 351).

Mandy Patinkin, the ("other") male lead, remarked of Streisand's performance, "I never thought of her as a girl. She was a guy, period." On the other hand, he said Streisand-as-director was "demanding, yet flexible and compassionate, with the gentleness of a woman" (Considine, 344). On screen, Patinkin's Avigdor is at first horrified, then attracted, as is the norm in contemporary cross-dressing films (compare James Garner's King Marchand in *Victor/Victoria*). "I should have known," he says, as he admits his love for her. An active, learned, acceptably transgressive figure (as contrasted with the unliberated Hadass, who cooks, bakes, and smilingly serves the men their favorite dishes), Yentl is the "new woman" of the eighties, a fit partner for a scholar—if she will only renounce her ambitions.

But the mechanism of substitution that is almost always a textual or dramatic effect of the transvestite in literature is again in force. Streisand as Yentl declines to marry Avigdor because she wants to be a scholar more than she wants to be anyone's wife. Happily, however, Avigdor's first love Hadass is still around, now educated through her "romantic friendship" or homoerotic transferential reading experiences with "Anshel." As the film ends, the transvestite "vanishes" and is dispersed; Avigdor and Hadass will marry and have a better—i.e., more modern and more equal—marriage than they would have if both had not fallen in love with "Anshel"; Yentl herself, now dressed like a woman, is on a boat going to America, where she can presumably live the life of a scholar without disguising her gender identity.

Thus instead of *class* substituting for gender, *national culture* does so. The transvestite is a sign of the category crisis of the immigrant, between nations, forced out of one role that no longer fits (here, on the surface, because a woman can't be a scholar; but not very far beneath the surface, because of poverty, anti-Semitism, and pogrom, Jewish as well as female) and into another role, that of a stranger in a strange land. Streisand's own cultural identity as a Jewish musical star, with unWASPy looks, a big nose, and a reputation in the business for shrewdness (read, in the ethnic stereotype, "pushy"), redoubles this already doubled story. As a Jewish woman in a star category usually occupied by gentiles (despite—or because of—the fact that many male movie moguls were Jews) she is Yentl/Anshel in another sense as well, "masquerading" as a regular movie star when in fact she differs from them in an important way.

Critics of the film have wished that it could be more progressively feminist than it is, given its date. "It is not," writes one observer, "so much a film about women's right to an education as it is a personal statement by Streisand about her own determination to exert influence in a world still dominated by male power structures."[20] The glee in certain quarters when Streisand was "stiffed" in the Oscar nominations, nominated for neither Best Actress nor Best Director (though she had campaigned for the attention of both Jewish and women voters in the Motion Picture Academy, and had earlier been given the Golden Globe award for Best Director), seemed to reinforce this male ambivalence about her career path, and to emphasize her insider-outsider position. "The Oscar nominations are out and Barbra Streisand didn't get any," gloated Johnny Carson on the *Tonight Show*. "Today she found out the true meaning of *The Big Chill*."[21]

Yet this analysis leaves out her Jewishness, which, in a plot line chosen presumably for its at least glancing relevance to her personal situation, is extremely striking. The unusual spelling of Streisand's first name, "Barbra" without the conventional third "a," is a kind of marker of her implicitly defiant difference. Nor is it surprising that the expression of difference should manifest itself in a transvestite vehicle. In fact, that transvestism here should be not only a sign of itself, and its attendant anxieties, including pan-eroticism (both Avigdor and Hadass fall in love with "Anshel," the transferential object of desire, who then strategically and inevitably subtracts "himself"), but also of other contingent and contiguous category crises (oppression of Jews in Eastern Europe, and the need or desire to emigrate; oppression or at least a certain "attitude" about female Jewish artists in Hollywood, and about women in the producer's role—the role so often occupied by Jewish *men*) is a compelling illustration of what I take to be the power of the transvestite in literature and culture. Streisand, who displaces both WASP women and Jewish men in her dual roles as star and producer, lobbied long and hard to get this particular property to work as a film. Her first public appearance on behalf of the film took place, perhaps significantly, at the annual United Jewish Appeal dinner in New York, where she was designated the UJA Man of the Year.

Yet on the surface Streisand's *Yentl* presents itself not as a disruption but as a progress narrative, the story of a woman's quest for education—in fact, the story of two women's quests. For Hadass is another version of the "normalized" Yentl, a sympathetic figure who—like Celia in *As You Like It*—comes to conclusions about the gender dissymmetries of love and power very similar to those of the cross-dressed woman. According to this reading, Yentl learns something both *for* and *from* Hadass; just as Celia profits from Rosalind's cross-dressing, and Nerissa from Portia's. *Yentl* thus becomes a story of female bonding or sisterhood, as well as a story of heterosexual love in conflict with professional fulfillment. As we have noted, Streisand aggressively denied any *non*-heterosexual possibilities encrypted in her text ("It was like kissing an arm"; "Howard! Anshel is taken").

Although her film makes much of the threat of cutting implied in the tailor scene, Streisand herself refused the unkindest cut, the loss of her long hair. Despite the alacrity with which many film actresses shed their locks on the way to movie stardom (Bette

Davis and Glenda Jackson as the bald Elizabeth I, Meryl Streep in *Sophie's Choice*, Vanessa Redgrave with her scalp shaved as Fania Fenelon in *Playing for Time*), Streisand wore a wig, and cut *it*, not her own hair, when she transformed herself in the film's key scene into a boy. "As a boy," reported a makeup artist who was on the scene, "she wore a short wig throughout the entire movie. There was no way she was going to part with those Medusa curls of hers. She loved her long hair" (Considine, 361–62).

The barb in "Medusa curls" is clear, whatever the makeup artist's knowledge of Freud. Streisand was—in this view—a self-made phallic woman, and one who refused to decapitate or castrate herself. Freud, writing of "the *phallic* mother, of whom we are afraid," notes that "the mythological creation, Medusa's head, can be traced back to the same *motif* of fright at castration,"[22] and remarks upon the paradoxical empowerment of the terrifying spectacle:

> The sight of Medusa's head makes the spectator stiff with terror, turns him to stone. Observe that we have here once again the same origin from the castration complex and the same transformation of affect! For becoming stiff means an erection. Thus in the original situation it offers consolation to the spectator: he is still in possession of a penis, and the stiffening reassures him of the fact."[23]

Streisand herself offered a physiological interpretation of Orthodox Judaism's division of labor between men and women. "I think it has to do with erections," she said. "A man is so capable of feeling impotent that what makes him able to have an erection a lot of the time is the weakness of women" (Considine, 341). "It's not law," she said, "It's bullshit. Men have used these things to put women in their place." In view of these comments, it is perhaps not surprising that I.B. Singer failed to admire her interpretation of his tale.

Singer spoke out angrily in the "Arts and Leisure" section of the Sunday *New York Times*, lamenting the addition of music to his story and singling out the star for blame: "My story was in no way material for a musical, certainly not the kind Miss Streisand has given us. Let me say: one cannot cover up with songs the shortcomings of the direction and acting." Above all he criticized the ending, which differed sharply from the original.

"Was going to America Miss Streisand's idea of a happy ending for *Yentl*?" he asked with withering contempt. "What would Yentl have done in America? Worked in a sweatshop twelve hours a day when there is no time for learning? Would she try to marry a salesman in New York, move to the Bronx or Brooklyn and rent an apartment with an icebox and dumbwaiter?" "Weren't there enough yeshivas in Poland or in Lithuania where she could continue to study?"[24] The gravamen of his charge was that the film was too commercial—and that Streisand was no Yentl, lacking "her character, her ideals, her sacrifice, her great passion for spiritual achievement."

The Yentl of Singer's 1984 blast at Streisand was, then, apparently a nice Jewish girl with a passion for Talmud, who needed, above all, a time and place for study—not the spoiled and materialistic Jewish Princess that he (and Johnny Carson) perceived in Streisand. But the Yentl of Singer's 1962 story is something rather different: a figure of ambivalence, complex subjectivity, and erotic power, who resembles a scholarly version of Gautier's Théodore as Rosalind. In fact, Yentl as transvestite contravenes both Streisand's reading of the story and Singer's own. To see how that happens, and what its theoretical consequences may be for the progress narrative, it may be useful to return to the text of I.B. Singer's story, "Yentl the Yeshiva Boy."

In Singer's story, Yentl, the daughter of a Jewish scholar, longs to study the Torah. Forbidden to do so by Jewish law, she studies secretly with her father until he dies. "She had proved so apt a pupil that her father used to say: 'Yentl—you have the soul of a man.' 'So why was I born a woman?'" she asks, and he answers, "'Even heaven makes mistakes.'" "There was no doubt about it," says the narrator,

> Yentl was unlike any of the girls in Yanev—tall, thin, bony, with small breasts and narrow hips. On Sabbath afternoons, when her father slept, she would dress up in his trousers, his fringed garment, his silk coat, his skull-cap, his velvet hat, and study her reflection in the mirror. She looked like a dark, handsome young man. There was even a slight down on her upper lip.[25]

After her father's death Yentl cuts her hair, dresses herself in her father's clothes, and sets off for Lubin. She takes a new name, "Anshel," after an uncle who had died, and joins up with a group of young students. (The replacement of Singer's "uncle" with Streisand's "brother" adds pathos—since the brother would have to have died in childhood—and also allows for the possibility of a ghostly "double" on the model of Viola's brother Sebastian.) Befriended by Avigdor, who takes "Anshel" with him to his yeshiva and chooses "him" for a study partner, she soon finds herself in a characteristic and problematic predicament: secretly in love with Avigdor, she is urged by him to marry his former fiancée Hadass.

"Stripped of gaberdine and trousers she was once more Yentl, a girl of marriageable age, in love with a young man who was betrothed to another" (Singer, 169). In this situation Yentl/Anshel sounds once again a little like Rosalind—"Alas the day, what shall I do with my doublet and hose?" [*AYLI* 3.2.219]—and even more like Viola—"... and I (poor monster) fond as much on him" [*TN* 2.2.34]—but with a disconcerting psychosexual twist. For she dreams that "she had been at the same time a man and a woman, wearing both a woman's bodice and a man's fringed garment. . . . Only now did Yentl grasp the meaning of the Torah's prohibition against wearing the clothes of the other sex. By doing so one deceived not only others but also oneself" (Singer, 169–70). With consternation, Anshel (as Singer refers to the cross-dressed protagonist throughout his tale) finds herself/himself proposing to Hadass, and only afterward rationalizes the proposal as something that she (or he) is really doing for Avigdor.

After the wedding the bride's parents, according to custom, inspect the wedding sheets for signs that the marriage had been consummated, and discover traces of blood. As the narrative informs us, with an infuriating lack of specificity, "Anshel had found a way to deflower the bride." "Hadass in her innocence was unaware that things weren't quite as they should have been." This cool, almost detached tone is quite different from Streisand and Irving's highly eroticized scene of displaced instruction. Meanwhile "Anshel" and Avigdor continue to be study partners, taking up—all too pertinently—the study of the Tractate on Menstruous Women (Singer, 179).

But all is not perfect. Anshel begins to feel pain at deceiving Hadass, and, besides, "he" fears exposure: how long can he avoid going to the public baths? So Anshel stages a scene of self-revelation to Avigdor, proclaiming "I'm not a man but a woman," and then undressing in front of him. Avigdor, who at first doesn't believe a word of this story, and indeed begins to fear that the disrobing Anshel "might want to practice pederasty" (Singer, 183), is swiftly convinced by what he sees, though when Yentl resumes her men's clothing Avigdor thinks for a moment he has been dreaming. "I'm neither the one nor the other," declares Yentl/Anshel. (Compare this to Théodore's declaration, "In truth, neither sex is really mine.") "Only now did [Avigdor] realize that Anshel's cheeks were too smooth for a man's, the hair too abundant, the hands too small" (Singer, 185). "All Anshel's explanations seemed to point to one thing: she had the soul of a man and the body of a woman" (Singer, 187). "What a strange power there is in clothing," Avigdor thinks (Singer, 188). He, and later others, even suspect that Anshel is a demon.

In Singer's story, Anshel sends Hadass divorce papers by messenger, and disappears. Avigdor, who had been married to someone else (but that's another story), also obtains a divorce and, to the brief scandal of the town, he and Hadass are married. When their child is born, "those assembled at the circumcision could scarcely believe their ears when they heard the father name his son Anshel" (Singer, 192).

One crucial difference, then, between the story and the film is that in the film "Anshel" disappears and Yentl escapes, travels, traverses a boundary—in this case the ocean dividing Old World from New. In Singer's story, "Anshel" is reborn as the child of Avigdor and Hadass. In both cases, however, "Anshel" is an overdetermined site of desire. Both Amy Irving and Mandy Patinkin declare their love to Streisand; she is *not*, as was the original plan, merely a transferential object for Hadass, but is instead the chosen beloved. In Singer's account, both Avigdor and Hadass are full of sadness rather than joy on their wedding day. Speculation about why Anshel had left town and sent his wife divorce papers runs riot. "Truth itself," observes the narrator, in a Poe-like statement that reflects directly on cross-dressing in the text, "is often concealed in such a way that the harder you look for it, the harder it is to find" (Singer, 192).

But what of the child, "Anshel"—*this* Anshel demonstrably a boy, since his naming occurs at his circumcision? This boy, both addition and substitution, replaces and does not replace the absent Anshel who was brought into being by Yentl. Once again the transvestite escapes, and returns powerfully and uncannily as the "loved boy." What is the relation between this boy and the transvestite?

Let us call him the changeling boy.

THE CHANGELING BOY

> The Greekes call this figure [*Hipallage*] the Latins *Submutatio*, we in our vulgar may call him the [*underchange*] but I had rather have him called the [*Changeling*] nothing at all swerving from his originall, and much more aptly to the purpose, and pleasanter to beare in memory; specially for your Ladies and prettie mistresses in Court, for whose learning I write, because it is a terme often in their mouthes, and alluding to the opinion of Nurses, who are wont to say, that the Fayries use to steale the fairest children out of their cradles, and put other ill favoured in their places, which they called changelings, or Elfs; so, if ye mark, doeth our Poet, or maker play with his wordes, using a wrong construction for a right, and an absurd for a sensible, by manner of exchange.
> George Puttenham, *The Arte of English Poesie* (1589)[26]

> "Vegetable?" asked Hook.
> "No."
> "Mineral?"
> "No."
> "Animal?"
> "Yes."
> "Man?"
> "No!" This answer rang out scornfully.
> "Boy?"
> "Yes."
> "Ordinary boy?"
> "No!"
> "Wonderful boy?"
> J.M. Barrie, *Peter Pan*[27]

Why changeling? Not literally, in the sense in which the changeling is usually described—that is to say, a child secretly exchanged for another by the fairies. Shakespeare's Henry IV, it may be recalled, wanted to believe that his son Harry and Harry Percy were changelings, the wrong one left in the Plantagenet cradle by mistake (*1 Henry IV* 1.1.84–89). But the infant Anshel is a changeling in that he is substituted for (by being named for) a figure who herself/himself incarnated change, and was himself/herself exchanged. Yentl becomes "Anshel" who becomes—in some quite complicated way—Anshel. A memory, a promise, a replacement, and a substitution.

The changeling boy. In *A Midsummer Night's Dream* he is all of those things. The locus of desire between, and for, Titania and Oberon. Omnipresent in his absence, not represented, beyond—is it possible?—representation, even in a play in which there are fairies and monsters and Amazons—and actors. For the changeling boy is in one way a figure for the boy actor, for the anxieties that surround him—again, not only in Shakespeare's time, but, equally, in ours. Is it a boy or a girl? In *A Midsummer Night's Dream* this question proposes itself in terms of nurturance and education. Is he to be Titania's or Oberon's? Coded male or female? Crowned with flowers, and made all Titania's joy, or raised up by Oberon, knight of his train, to roam the forests wild, and be his "henchman," his page of honor? As we have already noticed, in Tudor and Stuart times—indeed, until fairly recently—young boys and girls were dressed identically until about the age of seven, when the boys were "breeched," or put in breeches. The "changeling" is in one sense, then, a child on its way to becoming gendered, despite—or because of—the appellation "boy." But at the same time this "boy" is the object of immediate as well as displaced desire—maternal, heterosexual, homoerotic, pederastic.

The changeling is the son of Titania's votaress, the child, it would seem, of an exclusively female social economy. Why does Oberon want him? It is never made wholly clear, but Oberon's desire, in its unmastered importunity, is shot through with the sexual, with the erotic: the desire for a boy. Here embodied is what critic René Girard calls "mimetic desire,"[28] desire fostered by desire. In a play so preoccupied with change (of costume, of love object, of mind, of physical appearance, of moon, of mood) the changeling boy is change itself.

The battle between Titania and Oberon for custody of this "changeling" might, not wholly fancifully, be compared to the two recent trends we have noted in Renaissance scholarship about transvestism, one valorizing the female-to-male cross-dresser as a figure for emergent womanhood, either in economic or in psychological and social terms, the other privileging the historical facts of the playhouse, and the special role of the boy actor or boy actress as a sign of specifically homosexual energies in the theater, energies of male desire. Who is to have the changeling? A contract can be made between Titania and Oberon, but that is for ownership, for possession. The changeling himself is never present—or, at least, he never speaks. His absence, his elusiveness, is part of what makes him desirable. I think it is reasonable to project some such identity upon Shakespeare's changeling, to understand him, expressly, as a "transvestite effect."

In pursuit of this transvestite effect, this locus of desire, let me now turn to another of Shakespeare's "boys." Consider, for instance, Jessica's uncharacteristically bashful description of the "exchange" through which she assumes "the lovely garnish of a boy":

> *Jessica:* For I am much asham'd of my exchange:
> But love is blind, and lovers cannot see
> The pretty follies that themselves commit,

> For if they could, Cupid himself would blush
> To see me thus transformed to a boy.
>
> *Lorenzo*: Descend, for you must be my torch-bearer.
>
> *Jessica*: What, must I hold a candle to my shames?—
> They in themselves (goodsooth) are too too light.
> Why, 'tis an office of discovery (love),
> And I should be obscur'd.
>
> *Lorenzo*: So are you (sweet)
> Even in the lovely garnish of a boy.
>
> *MV* 2.6.34–45

Recall the dramatic situation here. Jessica is eloping with Lorenzo, her Christian lover, from her father's house, taking with her a casket of jewels and money. She has good reason, pragmatically, to protest that she might better be hidden in darkness than illumined by torchlight. At the same time, her language of protest is both strong and personal, tinged with more than a hint of a sense of impropriety—and Jessica in general is not a character we associate with moral sensibility. Her later antics on the road, trading her mother's ring for a monkey, suggest rather a certain coldness or heedlessness. Why then protest so strongly against this transvestite masquerade?

For one thing, remember that the play is set in Venice. And Venice, in the sixteenth century, was a place in which transvestite costume was a common choice of courtesans. Public prostitutes, writes Cesare Vecellio, while they dress variously depending on their economic status, almost always wear "a somewhat masculine outfit; silk or cloth waistcoats adorned with conspicuous fringes and padded like young man's vests, especially those of Frenchmen. Next to their bodies they wear a man's shirt. . . . Many of them wear men's breeches, . . . and one instantly recognizes them for what they are because of these trousers and certain little round pieces of silver they use as ornaments."[29]

Men's clothing was favored, it appears, both by prostitutes and by courtesans. The courtesan's long, formal skirt was often worn over a pair of men's breeches, as is illustrated in an engraving dating from about 1590.[30] A courtesan in a tiara, ruff, and full-length gown stands on the shore of what is apparently a canal, since gondolas can be seen gliding by in the background. The front panel of her skirt can be raised, completely obscuring her face and upper body, and revealing breeches that emphasize the pelvic area and high clog shoes. When the skirt flap is lowered again, the courtesan stands revealed (or concealed) in her elegant dress with its low-cut bodice. No one seeing only the first stage would suspect the "secret" disclosed by the second.

It is noteworthy that a hovering figure of blind Cupid takes aim at the standing figure, his arrow pointed toward her body, or even her heart. When the skirt is raised, however, Cupid appears to be aiming directly at the genitals. Since the figure is identified as a courtesan, and since Cupid, being blind, is a figure of erotic desire, the latter may be closer to the truth.

One semiotic benefit, if we can call it that, of this transvestite outfit was that it presented the courtesan as both woman and boy—both sexually enticing. Some Venetian men—like some Englishmen—kept both male lovers and female courtesans; not only were pants for women fashionable, but so was anal intercourse. Pietro Aretino wrote to a courtesan from Pistoia that it had been his good fortune to encounter her twice recently, "the first time as a woman dressed like a man and the next time, as a man dressed like a woman. You are a man when you are chanced on from behind and a woman when seen from in front." "You talk like a fair lady and act like a pageboy," he observed with indulgent pleasure. "Even the clothes which you wear upon your back, and which you are always changing, leave it an open question whether my she-chatterbox is really a he-chatterbox, or whether my he-chatterbox is really a she-one."[31]

We can perhaps see a little more clearly why Jessica would have found her transvestite costume as a page a source of "shame." "Turning the page," as it were, from recto to verso, appears to have been a popular pastime in the Venetian book of love. In fact, if we come back to the passage in which she expresses that shame, we find Cupid—and blind Cupid—very much on the scene.

> love is blind, and lovers cannot see
> The pretty follies that themselves commit,
> For if they could, Cupid himself would blush
> To see me thus transformed to a boy.

Some years ago, Edgar Wind and Erwin Panofsky disagreed about the nature of the blindfolded Cupid, whether his blindness was, as Panofsky contended, indicative of a lesser and more carnal kind of love, or, as Wind claimed, citing Ficino, Pico della Mirandola, Lorenzo de' Medici, and Giordano Bruno, rather a particularly sacred blindness: "the supreme form of Neoplatonic love is blind."[32] Jessica's citation of the blind Cupid figure admits (as we might expect) of both interpretations (love is blind; if he were not, lovers would be chagrined to see their own follies; thus love is both high and low, exalted and foolish, pure and evocative of desire). We might recall, however, the hovering figure of blind Cupid taking aim at the courtesan (or her private parts), an image that does not immediately suggest "the supreme form of Neoplatonic love," unless we read (as perhaps we could do) the Venetian engraving as an allegory—a favorite way of wishing away unwelcome facts when they stare us in the face.

But we might also think of Jessica's mention of Cupid in a slightly different context, equally relevant. "Cupid himself would blush/ To see me thus transformed to a boy." Remember that—as many recent critics have properly insisted on reminding us—the part of Jessica, like that of Portia and of all other women on the English public stage, would have been played by a boy, by a boy actor. "Transformed to a boy" thus has all the usual tonalities of *frisson,* the secret-on-the-surface waiting to be detected, and (perhaps) particularly of interest to that part of the audience that saw the "boy" as a special object of desire. We might think again of the Venetian courtesan presenting herself as a woman—which, presumably, she was—hiding beneath her skirt male breeches, capable of being sexually entered from the rear as well as from the front, as a "boy" and as a woman. Jessica presents the opposite sequence of deceptions, a boy actor dressed as a woman now disguising herself as a boy. Jessica expresses the wish to be "obscured," and Lorenzo assures her appreciatively that she *is* obscured "in the lovely garnish of a boy." In both cases, concepts like "boy" and "woman" are put in question, put under erasure, demarcating not biological or anatomical certainty or identity but a space of desire and possibility, "leaving it," as Aretino says suggestively, "*an open question*" whether he is a she, or she is a he—or what those terms really mean in a theatrical or erotic space.

Moreover, we might also want to recall that Cupid himself, on a famous occasion, disguised himself as a boy. The occasion, of course, was Aeneas' arrival at Carthage, and his need to inspire passion—and political complicity—in Dido. The plan is that of Venus, Aeneas's mother, who had already accosted him in her own disguise—that of one of Diana's nymphs. Now she determines to disguise her other son, Cupid, as Iulus, the son of Aeneas, and to substitute the one boy for the other, the young god for the human Iulus, that he might better achieve his aims of seduction—for Cupid is not an erotic object but Eros, eroticism itself. Venus summons Amor, Cupid, Desire, and tells him her plan. Iulus, the human child, cannot learn the "trick" that is necessary to ensnare Dido. A substitution is necessary:

> "You counterfeit his figure for one night,
> No more, and make the boy's known face your mask,
> So that when Dido takes you on her lap
> Amid the banqueting and wine, in joy,
> When she embraces you and kisses you
> You'll breathe invisible fire into her
> And dupe her with your sorcery."
>
> Amor
> Agreed with his fond mother's plan of action,
> Put off his wings and gaily walked as Iulus. . . .
>
> And, more than anyone, the Phoenician queen,
> Luckless, already given over to ruin,
> Marveled and could not have enough; she burned
> With pleasure in the boy and in the gifts.[33]

Pleasure in the boy and in the gifts. In Jessica and her casket of valuables. The "boy" here is not only the young male object of homoerotic desire, nor yet the doting Dido's restaging of the pre-Oedipal mother-child dyad, but a figure for both of those, and for more.

Let us return now, with these things in mind, to the phenomenon of the boy actor on the English Renaissance stage.

Boy actor. The term is conventional, and problematic. We know that boys played the parts of women on the Renaissance English stage, and that on the Continent both women and boys played women's parts. In some quarters it has become more usual to say "boy actresses," savoring the anomaly. Robertson Davies in his book *Shakespeare's Boy Actors*, published in 1939, calls the Elizabethan boy apprentices "female impersonators."

For that matter, what is a "boy"? You might think this was a simple matter. A boy is a male child below the age of puberty. But the term "boy" was also used to designate a servant or slave (especially in colonial or post-colonial Africa, and India, and parts of China, as well as in southern parts of the United States); in other words, "boy" functions as a term of domination, a term to designate an inferior, to create a distinction between or among men—of any age.

Shakespeare's Coriolanus combines several senses of "boy"—as young child and pederastic object—in his protest to his mother against *acting* (that is, being a "boy") in the marketplace:

> Away my disposition, and possess me
> Some harlot's spirit! My throat of war be turn'd,
> Which choired with my drum, into a pipe
> Small as an eunuch, or the virgin voice
> That babies lull asleep! the smiles of knaves
> Tent in my cheeks, and schoolboys; tears take up
> The glasses of my sight! (*Cor.* 3.2.111–17)

Harlot, eunuch, virgin, baby, knave, schoolboy—boy. Boy actor. To "boy" on stage, on the public stage in England before the Restoration, was "to represent (a woman's part)." Boys apprenticed to the adult actors of the company performed as women from their teens (some scholars have thought as early as the age of ten) till young adulthood, perhaps until their voices changed—although even this is not a certain limit; it is conceivable, indeed, that the term "boy actor" by this time had come to mean, in the English Renaissance, one who plays a woman's role, regardless of his age.[34]

Every reader of Shakespeare will recall the protest of Cleopatra (played, of course, in the period by a boy actor) against being taken to Rome where she should see "some squeaking Cleopatra boy my greatness/ I' the posture of a whore" (*A&C* 5.2.218–220). So to "boy" is to be anything but a man. Her captor, the "scarce-bearded [Octavius] Caesar," is taunted by Antony as "the boy Caesar," a designation that Octavius takes, rightly, as an insult: "He calls me boy" (*A&C* 1.1.21; 3.13.17; 4.1.1.) And to "boy" was also to furnish or supply with boys—presumably for erotic purposes.

What, then, if the "boy" of "boy actor" fame, appropriated by some recent historicist critics as a sign of the homoerotic subtext of Renaissance theater, and by some feminist critics as a sign of female power and agency—what if that "boy" were to be taken seriously as what it most disturbingly represents: the figure of the transvestite? Rather than appropriated, erased, or wished away, rather than taken primarily as a role model for female empowerment or gay—male or female—homoerotic play, this "boy" is a provoker of category crises, a destabilizer of binarisms, a transgressor of boundaries, sexual, erotic, hierarchical, political, conceptual. The changeling boy.

The changeling boy—and notice how often it *is* a boy—is a placeholder for the fantasy child who is not there. This is a version of Freud's family romance, only instead of the child fantasizing grander and more perfect parents, the parents fantasize a perfect child—a dream child, theirs and not theirs at once.

That Shakespeare knew, or intuited, such a power in the "boy" who is not a boy is clear from *A Midsummer Night's Dream*, where a travesty of transvestite theater is enacted by Flute ("let me not play a woman; I have a beard coming" 1.2.44) and by the all too-aptly named Bottom, who is eager to take the woman's part ("and I may hide my face, let me play Thisbe too. I'll speak in a monstrous little voice" 46–47). Bottom here becomes for a moment a monstrously ill-equipped version of the "boy actor," the grotesque figuration of that changeling boy who is the cause of dissension between Titania and Oberon.

Consider now the following précis, a description of a play about a changeling boy (written in Broadway-speak, the hyperactive language of theatrical reviews):

> This dazzling work of gut-wrenching dark comedy presents perhaps the most memorable of married couples. .... in a searing night of dangerous fun and games with a pawnlike other couple who innocently become their weapons in the savaging of each other and of their life together. By the evening's end, a stunning, almost unbearable revelation provides a climactic shock of recognition at the bond and bondage of their love.

This is not in fact, as it might seem to be, a description of a recent production of *A Midsummer Night's Dream*, but rather the back-jacket copy for the paperback edition of Edward Albee's 1962 play, *Who's Afraid of Virginia Woolf?* But with very little alteration, mostly a splitting and doubling of parts (*two* pawnlike other couples, who are in a way versions of their older patrons or hosts), this could be a description of Shakespeare's *Dream*.

Once we conceive the parallel, the plays look oddly, if perversely, similar. In both the moon shines, insistently, erratically. There are intermittent references to forest noises, animals, and archery. Martha the virago is at least as Amazonian as Hippolyta, as queenly as Titania in a car coat. She is the daughter of the college president, and, as George says when she is out of the room changing her clothes, "She is his . . . right ball, you might say,"[35] the phallic woman par excellence. She wears the pants, as she points out wearily to George ("I'm loud, and I'm vulgar, and I wear the pants in this house because somebody's got to, but I am *not* a monster. I am not" [Albee, 157]). In the course of the increasingly dream-like, booze-filled evening, men and women separate (to the bathroom, to the kitchen) and then come together again, as in Shakespeare's *Dream*—and, as in the *Dream*, games are played (Humiliate the Host, Hump the Hostess, and Get the Guests, as well as the final agonizing round of Bringing Up Baby). Martha sadly stalks and seduces Nick, the sexy young biologist, whose name may perhaps now remind us of that other Nick, Nick Bottom, the weaver.

Nick's name is never mentioned in Albee's script, though it is given in the cast of characters. Like "George" and "Martha" (Washington; the "Father of our Country," another parent with a fantasy child) Nick's name suggests a private joke. Like Bottom he is the animal lover who has a brief sexual interlude with the powerful woman, before she is returned, in some humiliation, to her husband.[36] It is unclear whether George sets up Martha and Nick the way Oberon sets up Titania and Bottom. What is quite clear is that the "bond and bondage of their love," as the jacket copy rather melodramatically calls it, is animated by a shared fantasy: the fantasy of a child.

Martha, warned by George against mentioning "the kid," begins at once to talk about their "son," whose life is then narrated at length. How Martha had wanted a child, how he was born, how he kept a bow and arrow under his bed. It is now the eve of his twenty-first birthday (in the film, his sixteenth), and he is expected home. So she says—but George has determined to kill off the fantasy child whose existence Martha has betrayed. "You broke our rule, baby," he says to her. "You mentioned him to someone else."

George is a professor of history; Nick teaches biology. The tension between history and biology, between historical narrative and culture on the one hand and genetic engineering on the other surrounds this fantasy of the absent child: a role for which both Nick and Honey are auditioned and finally rejected.

Why should we consider Albee's play with regard to the question of transvestism, the transvestite function, and the connection between the transvestite and the changeling boy? Despite Albee's denials, the rumor persists that *Who's Afraid of Virginia Woolf?* was originally written for an all-male cast—that it was a play for two gay male couples, which underwent a re-gendering for the Broadway stage, where it originally starred Uta Hagen and Arthur Hill. "What a dump!" the signature Bette Davis line stagily cited by Martha at the very beginning of the play, is a staple of female impersonators, a classic of the genre, readily recognizable and readable as camp. "Bringing Up Baby," the name George gleefully gives to the endgame of his plan, is, as we have noted, famous as the film in which Cary Grant, dressed in a fluffy nightgown, declares that he "just went gay all of a sudden."

The film version of Albee's play, stunningly directed by Mike Nichols, presented

Richard Burton and Elizabeth Taylor (in an Academy Award-winning performance) as the quintessential feuding academic couple, stuck in a town called New Carthage, a name that is probably a glance at college towns like Ithaca, but that also reminds us of that other Carthage, Dido's, and that other fantasy child who was not just an object of desire, but Desire himself. But if the original script of Albee's play had been written for men, for a transvestite, gay theater, the fantasy of the boy child would be even more poignant, even more explicable, even more ironic as the play's petty deceptions unfolded.

What I would like to suggest is that the fantasy child of Albee's play and the unseen, much desired changeling boy of *A Midsummer Night's Dream*, are versions of the same fantasy, the same mechanism of dream and desire. The same could be said, perhaps, about the seven frozen embryos at issue in a 1989 custody battle in Tennessee[37]—or, perhaps, even about all the fetuses sanctified by the right-to-life movement, only *until* the moment of their birth. The changeling boy, like the boy actor, points to the impossibility of realizing that fantasy—and the necessity of the fantasy *as opposed to* any realization. The phrase "changeling boy" reminds us that boys, and boy actors, *are* changelings, are not only in process of change but are significations of change, and *ex*change, in and of themselves. An actor is a changeling; a boy, in Shakespeare's culture as—somewhat differently, but still pertinently—in ours, is a medium, and a counter, of exchange. The fantasy child is the ultimate "transvestite effect," the figure that comes between demand and desire, the signifier that plays its role only when veiled. Both the boy actor and the changeling boy are figures for something that is not there. For if it were there, it would not be what is desired.

But the changeling boy whom Titania and Oberon both desire, whose possession inspires their mutual anger, their "dissension," and the fallen state of the fairy world— this Indian page boy, as he is also described, is most notable by his absence. Sometimes, misguidedly in my opinion, a director will cast the part, will provide a tyke in a turban who cannot be the object, the motivator, of all of that desire. As Albee's play makes clear, the whole point of the changeling boy is that he is *not* there, that he is an idea that can never be realized or possessed. Like the transvestite marking the space of representation itself, the changeling boy is that which, by definition, can never be present. For the minute he comes to be embodied, it is clear that he cannot be that which is so desperately sought.

4

SPARE PARTS: THE SURGICAL CONSTRUCTION OF GENDER

> The Maserati I picked up in Modena was a reconditioned model. Previously owned, the car had been lovingly rebuilt by the craftsman who had originally made it. The guarantee was the same as if it had been new. My automobile seemed a perfect reflection of my personal state. I too was reconditioned or at least on the way to being so.
>
> Renée Richards, *Second Serve*

"MALE SUBJECTIVITY"

Consider the dissymmetry in the following rhetorical matter. Long before critics wrote so eloquently about the constructedness (rather than the innateness) of gender, writers and ordinary citizens spoke readily about experiences that would "make a man" of some (male) candidate: war, perhaps, or sexual initiation, or some Hemingwayesque test of hunting or shooting or a battle one-on-one with nature. These things would, it used to be said, "make a man" of the hapless boy, test his mettle; hence a whole literature of male sexual and martial initiation, from—say—Coriolanus to Norman Mailer. Businessmen boasted of being "self-made men," and (in a slightly different spirit) Stephen Greenblatt writes of "Renaissance self-fashioning" in a book that, without regarding the fact as odd, treats only of men. Mafiosi, we are told by popular fiction and film, speak of "making one's bones"—of the first murder, which makes a boy a man. Teenage boys in my adolescence spoke, presumably, still speak, of "making it" with a girl, of "making out," of "making" her; my dictionary gives as definition 26 under "make" "*Slang*. To persuade to have sexual intercourse." The dictionary does not give a gender to the implied speaker, but I have never heard a woman speak of "making" a man in this way. To "make" a man is to test him; to "make" a woman is to have intercourse with her. Like the dissymmetry of reference in Spanish between a "public man" (a statesman) and a "public woman" (a whore), "making a man" and "making a woman" mean two very different things, culturally speaking.

When we refer to maturation for a girl, we speak, usually, of a passive process:

"becoming a woman," a process at the mercy of biology and custom. To "become a woman" is to get one's period, to develop rounded hips, full breasts—and, concurrently, to put away childish things. In my adolescence this meant, generally, male sports and games, which gave way to eye makeup and the junior prom. Happily we now live in a more enlightened age, an age that can produce a Florence Griffith Joyner (as well as a Martina Navratilova and, indeed, a Renée Richards). But the sociology of gender construction—as distinguished from its theorization—still encodes a dissymmetry. If sexual initiation can mean "becoming a woman"—and it can—this is still not the same, not entirely the equivalent, of "making a woman" of oneself, or of being taken to a place of initiation, like a brothel, by some kindly older relative or more experienced friend, to be "made a woman." The concept of "male subjectivity" to many custodians of Western culture—whether literary critics, psychoanalysts, or rock musicians, should they ever have recourse to the term—is in a sense redundant. To be a subject is to *be* a man— to be male literally or empowered "as" male in culture and society.

In short, I suspect that any discussion of "male subjectivity" (as a counterpart to "female subjectivity") is a recuperative cultural fantasy, a theoretical back formation *from* "female subjectivity," where the latter evolved as a politically necessary critique of the presumably *universal* subjectivity, the humanist concept of "man." Does "male subjectivity," conceptualized, represent anything more than a wishful logic of equality, which springs from a feminist desire to make "man" part rather than whole? Is "male subjectivity" not, in fact, like "female fetishism," a theoretical tit-for-tat which finally demonstrates the limits of theorization when it comes to matters of gender construction?

In what follows, I will propose the cultural discourses of transvestism and transsexualism as limit cases for "male subjectivity," places where the very concept of "male subjectivity" is stretched to the vanishing point—perhaps. My intent is to test the "differences" between theory and praxis on the question of gender construction, by noting a number of curious and compelling dissymmetries between "male" and "female" subjectivity as they are read backward from the borderlines of gender. What does a male transvestite theorize about his subjectivity? How is it inscribed in his dress, behavior, sexual object choice, core gender identity? What about a male-to-female transsexual? Is she culturally, politically, sexually the mirror image of her male counterpart, the former woman who has undergone hormone treatment and phalloplasty (the surgical construction of a penis) to become a man? What does, or might, the concept of "male subjectivity" mean to a transsexual, whether male-to-female or female-to-male?

THE ABSOLUTE INSIGNIA OF MALENESS

> Can you imagine the effect you will have on your partner as you enter
> a room dressed in the most elegant of feminine attire right down to these

European stretch pantless pantyhose! These "surprise pantyhose" will
complete your web of intrigue as you slowly raise your skirt to that
delectable area where "lo & behold" your male member will be anxiously
awaiting introduction.

ad for Surprise Pantyhose, *Crossdressers' Forum*

Let me begin this inquiry by returning to the views of an expert, one of the most
widely respected interpreters of gender identity today. Dr. Robert Stoller, a psychoanalyst
and professor of psychiatry at UCLA, is the author of numerous books and articles on
gender dysphoria, including *Sex and Gender* Volumes I and II (1968; 1975), *Splitting* (1973),
Perversion (1975), *Sexual Excitement* (1979), and *Observing the Erotic Imagination* (1985). Here,
from the influential first volume of *Sex and Gender,* is a passage widely quoted in both
medical articles and TV-TS (transvestite-transsexual) journals, describing the mechanism
of transvestite behavior:

> The whole complex psychological system that we call transvestism is a rather efficient method of
> handling very strong feminine identifications without the patient having to succumb to the feeling
> that his sense of masculinity is being submerged by feminine wishes. The transvestite fights this
> battle against being destroyed by his feminine desires, first by alternating his masculinity with the
> feminine behavior, and thus reassuring himself that it isn't permanent; and second, by being always
> aware even at the height of the feminine behavior—when he is fully dressed in women's clothes—
> that he has the absolute insignia of maleness, a penis. And there is no more acute awareness of its
> presence than when he is reassuringly experiencing it with an erection.[1]

Almost twenty years later, Stoller repeated this assertion—in much the same language:

> [T]he transvestite states the question, "When I am like a female, dressed in her clothes and appearing
> to be like her, have I nonetheless escaped the danger? Am I still male, or did the women succeed
> in ruining me?" And the perversion—with its exposed thighs, ladies' underwear, and coyly covered
> crotch—answers, "No. You are still intact. You are a male. No matter how many feminine clothes
> you put on, you did not lose that ultimate insignia of your maleness, your penis." And the transvestite
> gets excited. What can be more reassuringly penile than a full and hearty erection?[2]

Stoller's narrative style is both sympathetic and empathetic, adopting the affective
subject position of the transvestite ("*reassuringly* experiencing it with an erection"; "*reassuringly* penile"; "a *full and hearty* erection"). In the earlier passage, the phrase "absolute
insignia of maleness" is implicitly ventriloquized, the transvestite's-eye-view given in
indirect discourse; the later passage puts the equivalent phrase, "that ultimate insignia of
your maleness," firmly in quotes, as "the perversion," an allegorized voice of Transvestism,
is permitted to speak for itself. In both, however, and thus over a span of two decades,
Stoller points to the primacy of the penis as the fetishized self-object of transvestite
subjectivity. "The transvestite needs his penis as an insignia of maleness," he writes

elsewhere in *Sex and Gender*. "One cannot be a male transvestite without *knowing, loving, and magnificently expanding* the importance of one's own phallus" (Stoller, 1968, 188; emphasis added).

I have used Stoller as my chief evidence here because he is the most frequently cited of gender identity specialists. But he is far from alone. A vast medical literature exists on this question, overwhelmingly confirming the phallessentialist description of male transvestism and transsexualism.[3] Nor do we have to have recourse to doctors to test this hypothesis. Any pornographic bookstore or magazine stand will attest to the same facts: on page after page of magazines for male transvestites like *Great Pretenders*, *Transvestite Key Club*, *Petticoat Power* ("Like Father, Like Son"), *Meet-a-Mimic* ("Gorgeous Fun Loving Guys"), and *Crossdressers' Forum* photographs, both illustrations and "personals ads," depict transvestites in panties, garter belts, maids' uniforms, boots and chains, each with naked, erect, and prominently displayed cock and balls. The Stoller scenario of reassurance as potency—which is clearly indebted to the Freudian scenario of fetishistic display[4]—is visible or readable in every chapter of *Mario in Makeup* and *Bobby's New Panties*. What is the gendered subjectivity of these representations?

It is not clear to me who reads these novels and magazines, but some statistics suggest that male transvestites are largely middle-class, heterosexual, and married.[5] Their wives frequently belong to TV support groups, and join them on cross-dressed weekends in Provincetown and other, less obvious locales. Transvestites, cross-dressed, choose women's names, which they use in their personals ads, and also in their daily or episodic cross-dressing activities. Their wives will address them as "Donna" or "Jeanne" or whatever, when they are wearing women's clothes. Yet this is clearly not "female subjectivity," even though it goes by women's names. It is a man's idea of what "a woman" is; it is male subjectivity in drag. The discourse of reassurance is the manifestation of what the psychoanalyst Alfred Adler called "masculine protest"[6]: *despite* the female clothing and nomenclature, the male transvestite asserts his masculinity. As Stoller puts it in the passage quoted above, "[t]he transvestite fights this battle against being destroyed by his feminine desires, first by alternating his masculinity with the feminine behavior, and thus reassuring himself that it isn't permanent; and second, by being always aware even at the height of the feminine behavior—when he is fully dressed in women's clothes—that he has the absolute insignia of maleness, a penis." Paradoxically, then, the male transvestite represents the extreme limit case of "male subjectivity," "proving" that he is male against the most extraordinary odds. Dressed in fishnet stockings, garter belt, and high heels, or in a housedress, the male transvestite is the paradoxical embodiment of male subjectivity. For it is his anxiety *about* his gendered subjectivity that engenders the masquerade.

And what of the transsexual male? By the same reasoning, the male transsexual—the person who believes that he is a "woman trapped in a man's body"—marks the other pole of male subjectivity. For him "[t]he insignia of maleness is what causes his despair. He does not wish to be a phallic 'woman'; he wishes to be a biologically normal woman"

(Stoller, *Sex* l, 1968, 188). But in this case too the "insignia of maleness," present or absent, desired or despised, is the outward sign of gendered subjectivity. Erections, says Stoller, "force a sense of maleness" upon the transsexual; "the more intensely excited the organ is the more his need to be rid of it" (Stoller, 1968, 188).

The desire "to be rid of" the penis, by surgical or less permanent and costly means, has led to some ingenious arrangements. Thus in his youthful cross-dressing forays, the transsexual Richard Raskind, later to become Renée Richards, regularly stretched his penis backward between his legs to hide it, binding it with heavy adhesive tape, and used the same tape to tuck his testicles up into his abdomen. Over the years, Richards writes,

> I became more and more strict in this regard, increasing the strains and inventing new ways to eliminate the hated body parts. Sometimes I would knot a piece of fishing line or strong twine around the head of my penis and use that to pull it backward between my legs. The other end would be secured to a piece of rope cinched tightly around my waist . . . I could pass the string between the cheeks of my ass and up under the rope. Then I would pull the string taut causing my penis to be stretched brutally around the curve of my torso. Believe me, I have great respect for the resiliency of the human penis.[7]

The male-to-female transsexual's obsessive concern with "the absolute insignia of maleness" as a mistaken sign or a false signal of gender identity is based on the same conviction instrumental to the male transvestite: the conviction that masculine identity, male subjectivity, is determined and signified by the penis. Interestingly, this is the case even after sex change surgery has removed the unwanted organ. Thus Jan (formerly James) Morris, the travel writer whose autobiography, *Conundrum*, is subtitled *An Extraordinary Narrative of Transsexualism*, offers her account of her own transformation from the penile point of view:

> A neurotic condition common among women is called penis envy, its victims supposing that there is inherent to the very fact of the male organs some potent energy of spirit. There is something to this fancy. It is not merely the loss of androgens that has made me more retiring, more ready to be led, more passive: the removal of the organs themselves has contributed, for there was to the presence of the penis something positive, thrusting, and muscular. My body then was made to push and initiate, and it is made now to yield and accept, and the outside change has had its inner consequences.[8]

Seldom has "function follows form" been more ardently argued in gender terms. Whatever we may think of the politics (or psychology) of this statement, it unmistakably gives rise to the same overestimation of the penis that has characterized both the male transvestite and the male-to-female transsexual in the examples I have considered. In fact, the transsexual male represents the *other* extreme limit case of "male subjectivity" as it is constructed in Western culture. For the phallus is the insignia not only of maleness but of sexuality as such. Rather than regarding the penis (or the phallus) as incidental equipment contributory toward a general sense of "male subjectivity" that transcends the merely anatomical, both male transvestites and transsexuals radically and dramatically *essentialize* their genitalia. "The absolute insignia of maleness" *is* for them the index of male identity. Male subjectivity in this case is objectivity. And what I am suggesting is that these apparently marginal or aberrant cases, that of the transvestite and the transsexual, both define and problematize the entire concept of "male subjectivity." It is by looking at them, and at the cultural gaze that both constructs and regards them, that we can best test out the viability of the term.

"A REAL ONE"

They call it easing the Spring; it is perfectly easy
If you have any strength in your thumb: like the bolt,
And the breech, and the cocking-piece, and the point of balance,
Which in our case we have not got. . . .
        —Henry Reed, "Lessons of the War: Naming of Parts"[9]

What then of the wish—perfectly "natural," in cultural if not political terms (that is to say, in a phallocentric culture, dominated by male discourses in medicine, law, psychology, however traversed by feminism) to "be" a man? What do *female* transvestites and *female-to-male* transsexuals have to do with "male subjectivity"?

In 1968 Stoller maintained, as we have seen, that there was no such thing as a transvestite *woman*, a woman who would become erotically excited by the wearing of male clothing. Such women, he suggested, were really transsexuals, who really wanted to be men—which meant, to have a penis. In the cultural milieu of the mid-to-late sixties, with a new wave of feminism only beginning to manifest itself as a vital political movement, the mainstream expectation that the desire to be a man was "natural" seems to underlie Stoller's (and other clinicians') theories. The "perversion gap," the implication that women have neuroses (like hysteria) and only men have psychoses, perversions, and "paraphilias" (like fetishism and transvestism), grows out of this same dissymmetrical expectation. Psychiatrists and psychoanalysts might not subscribe to the Orthodox Jewish man's creed, thanking God daily for not making him a woman, but the assumptions on which they posited their canons of "normality" reflected a temporal cultural bias. Women who habitually cross-dressed were not psychotic (Stoller, *Sex* 1, 1968, 196); they merely wanted to be men, which in their society was a highly reasonable, indeed healthy, desire. "I have never seen or heard of a woman who is a biologically normal female and does not question that she was properly assigned as a female, who is an intermittent, fetishistic cross-dresser," Stoller wrote in 1968 (195). Women who cross-dressed were really *transsexuals*, who thought of themselves as men trapped in the bodies of women.

> If—imagine for a moment—in dead seriousness we should ever offer a penis to any of our women patients who are not transsexual, we would see that she would be horrified. But not the transsexual female. She would be most grateful indeed. (Stoller, 1968, 197)

The "absolute insignia of maleness" becomes the *sine qua non* of the "male subjectivity" of the transsexual woman. To "offer [her] a penis," "in dead seriousness," became the ambivalent task of the specialist in gender dysphoria, the "sex change doctor."

Some years later, returning to the question of "Female Transvestism," Stoller was willing to revise his absolute pronouncement against it. Clinical data, he explained, remains at a mimimum—he discusses only three cases, and still maintains that "fetishistic cross-dressing—in women" is "so rare it is almost nonexistent,"[10] but he was now ready to acknowledge that specific items of clothing, like "blue denim Levi's" (Stoller, *Observing*, 142), "engineer boots" (147) or a false moustache (140) can produce erotic and orgasmic sensations in women. This problem—that of female fetishism in general and fetishistic cross-dressing by women in particular—is a fascinating one, which deserves and has received interesting treatment recently by a number of feminist theorists, and I will address it directly in Chapter 5.[11] But I do want to point out that Stoller, in comparing and contrasting transvestite women to women with other "disorders," distinguishes them from transsexuals, butch homosexuals, and "women with 'penises'," whom he characterizes as "biologically intact women [who] feel and openly state that they are anatomically equipped with an intraabdominal or intravaginal penis, truly physically present." One of his transvestite cases was a "woman with a 'penis'," two were not, and the other two "women with 'penises' " he has treated were not erotically stimulated by wearing male clothing.[12] The transvestite "woman with a 'penis' " testifies that she wore pants to school at a time when it was not customary for girls to do so: "I was thin and I protruded in the front as though I had a penis. . . . Even when I wore a straight skirt (rather than a gathered full skirt) there would be a swelling, or my pubic area protruded" (Stoller, *Observing*, 148–50).

In another case history, this one describing a female transsexual, Stoller describes a young woman who had always thought of herself as a boy. All her childhood pictures showed her in boys' clothes, especially cowboy suits. She and her mother engage in a lively conversation about the guns she used to play with that fairly bristles with *double entendre*.

> *Patient*: I have always wanted—in fact, I still do—a good holster, because I like to shoot. I can't shoot a pistol very well, but I can shoot a rifle.

Mother: When you were small you always had guns strapped around you
. . . On summer vacation, she had a gun—some kind of pistol. What
kind was it?

Patient: Was that a real one?

Mother: Sure it was real.

Patient: A thirty-eight.

Mother: She slept with it under her pillow.

Patient: I slept with it because I felt it was real good. I didn't need it, but
I liked it a lot; it was real; it was a real gun and lots of kids didn't
have them. (Stoller, 1968, 198–99)

No gloss is offered, or needed, for this testimony to the importance of having a "real
one." ("Lots of kids didn't have them.") This patient managed to attend an all-girl's school
in the daytime and, cross-dressed as a boy, dated some of her unsuspecting classmates at
night. Stoller, who calls this impersonation "brilliant," comments that "he [the female-
to-male transsexual] was able to disguise his physical sexual characteristics by inventing
and manufacturing for himself a camisole for his chest and an artificial penis which would
give the right bulge to his pants. At one point, he was so successful (and had constructed
such an excellent 'penis') that he had 'intercourse' with a girl. For several months she
failed to have a period and was fearful that he had gotten her pregnant" (203–204).

The word "constructed" in Stoller's account is of interest, for here, indeed, is a self-
made man. Although both the word "penis" and the word "intercourse" are in quotation
marks, indicating that from Stoller's point of view they are not the real thing, the patient's
girlfriend plainly disagreed. Is it possible to think of "penis" and "intercourse" here as
concepts under erasure, "barred" words? Does "male subjectivity" in fact require the
putting of the "absolute insignia" in question in this way? This quest for the "real one"
led ultimately to surgical intervention. Was *this* patient's subjectivity "male"? What would
"male subjectivity" mean in such a case?

Notice that in this case the actual gender identification precedes the surgical makeover
by many years; one of the interviewing doctors even told the patient's mother that in
talking about her child as "she" she was "making a mistake," and the case history regularly
refers to the patient as "he." Pronomial confusion (pronomial dysphoria) is a constant
pitfall in discussions of the transsexual phenomenon, and is, again, an indicator of the
boundary-crossing that makes gendered subjectivity so problematic in such cases.[13]

Many "pre-op" transsexuals have chosen to halt their progress toward surgery, retaining
both male and female attributes induced by hormone treatment, and "passing" for the
chosen sex in dress and manner (a stage still mandated by doctors who treat transsexual
patients) but declining (for reasons variously economic, philosophical, pragmatic, and
social) to undergo the final surgical translation into the "other" gender. What this means
is that male-to-female transsexuals may, and increasingly do, retain "the absolute insignia

of maleness" together with their hormone-enhanced breasts, their women's clothes, and their new female names. Their "core gender identity," according to doctors, is that of the gender toward which they are crossing. But is their gendered subjectivity mimicry, or a "real one"? What would "real" and "mimic" mean in the cultural milieu in which all gender roles are constructed?

And what happens when technology catches up with cultural fantasy? When it becomes possible, in the context of a culture in which maleness is normative, to "make" a man?

"A POSSIBLE ARTIFACT": EVE'S RIB, ADAM'S APPLE

> Snips and snails and puppy dogs' tails . . .
> "What Are Little Boys Made Of?"

After years in which transsexualism was viewed as a largely male phenomenon, the situation of female transsexuals has lately come in for more direct scrutiny. The reasons for the emphasis on males (that is to say, persons who feel that they are women trapped in a man's body) are concisely outlined by Dr. Leslie Martin Lothstein, the co-director of the Case Western Reserve Gender Identity Clinic: 1) most gender clinics were set up to provide services for only the male transsexual; 2) the majority of transsexuals applying for sex reassignment surgery (SRS) were male (as Dr. Lothstein—a man—points out, this is "a possible artifact," since female transsexual surgery was not possible until fairly recently); 3) most transsexual researchers were males, and may have exhibited a bias toward male patients, together with a "homocentric" or "patricentric" discouragement of women who inquire about clinical treatment; 4) social pressures made it easier for female transsexuals to acclimate themselves to society in their unchanged status (a characteristic double bind for women: they often are not considered psychotic enough or distressed enough for treatment, since wishing to be or act like a man is considered "normal" or "natural" in this culture); and, finally, 5) men have traditionally had more latitude to express concern about sexual dysfunction than have women—or, put slightly differently, men have been allowed to have sex lives and to place importance upon sexual performance and response, while women have—until recently—been acculturated to deny, repress, or veil sexual feeling.[14]

Each of these "reasons" for the clinical neglect of female-to-male transsexuals, then, is based at least in part on the dissymmetry between the cultural status of males and of females. While much has been said about the "construction of women" in Western culture, women considered as an artifact of patriarchy, Petrarchism, primogeniture, and the necessities of domestic economy,[15] we hear much less about the "construction of men." That process is more usually, and more optimistically, called "self-fashioning," and, while queried as a realizable goal by even its strongest advocates, it persists as a male ideal of intentionality and control. There remains some desire to see men as not constructed but "natural," or essential—hence, again, the "naturalness" of women's desire to be more like men.

Transsexualism, manifestly, puts in question this very essentialism of gender identity, offering both surgical and hormonal—as well as psychological—"solutions" to gender undecidability. If a "man trapped in a woman's body" or a "woman trapped in a man's body" is claiming what doctors call a "core gender identity," and what literary and psychoanalytic theorists describe as female or male subjectivity, then the task (or art) of the surgeon is to refashion the body to suit the subjectivity. Again, it is instructive to note that this refashioning, or reconstruction, is far more readily and easily done with male-to-female than with female-to-male transsexuals. Indeed, the terms of reference here are themselves highly revealing; men who wish to become biological woman are generally referred to, in medical terminology, as "*male* transsexuals." Although their "core gender identity" is female, the culture still designates them male. In fact, the terms "transsexual" and "transvestite" are themselves normatively male in general usage; recent work on the early modern period, for example, has begun to speak of the visibility of "female transvestites" in London, while "transvestite" without a gender qualification is usually taken to refer to men in women's clothing.

What lies behind some of the resistance to or neglect of the female-to-male transsexual is, I think, a sneaking feeling that it should not be so easy to "construct" a "man"— which is to say, a male body. Psychoanalysts since Freud have paid lip-service, at least, to the maxim that "what constitutes masculinity or femininity is an unknown characteristic which anatomy cannot lay hold of,"[16] but it seems clear, as we have already seen, that there is one aspect of gender identity that can be laid hold of: the penis. Yet the surgical construction of the penis, what is technically known as *phalloplasty*, is consistently referred to in the medical literature as "not accomplished easily," "fraught with rather serious hazards," "still quite primitive and experimental," and likely to produce "poor cosmetic results" (which, as Lothstein notes, is "surgical jargon for a rather grotesque appearance" [293]).

The first "total reconstruction" of the penis (on a biological male) was performed in 1936,[17] but fifty years later "few, if any, surgeons, can construct a phallus that is aesthetically and surgically acceptable" (Lothstein, 299). Among the complaints of female-to-male post-operative patients have been: scarring of the abdominal area; a penis that was too small (not a complaint only of transsexuals); an inability to urinate; a dysfunctional penis that could not become erect except with the insertion of a rod. One doctor reported having seen a female transsexual's newly constructed penis fall off, which, he said "caus[ed] the patient to become extremely anxious" (Lothstein, 300). The penis had to be totally reconstructed. Another patient had to have reconstructive surgery after a tissue graft failed to take. "Both patients," their psychiatrist records, "developed massive castration anxiety" (Lothstein, 300).

Here is a new aspect of penis envy. The female-to-male transsexual (note that the doctor calls him/her a "female transsexual," although the patient, having endured all this reconstructive surgery, would doubtless prefer to be described as a "man") gets more than he (or she) bargained for: together with the penis, he/she (how meaningful that slash mark becomes) gets not only castration *anxiety* but something that sounds very much like *castration*: his (or her) penis falls off, and has to be replaced (again). To become an anatomical male in this case is to become a caricature of the psychological male, essentialized, literalized, made into a grotesque cartoon: the penis *does* fall off, as had always been threatened. And it *doesn't* become hard, as had always been feared. So the transsexual gets the name, but not the game. In early procedures for phalloplasty the surgeon sometimes used a piece of the patient's rib to stiffen the new penis permanently; this New Eve is reconstructed as Adam, the first-made "man," begotten from her *own* rib. (The role for which the surgeon is cast in this transformation needs no comment.)

Female-to-male breast surgery, the flattening of the chest by mastectomy, has likewise been described as often yielding "poor cosmetic results." In fact, patients are warned against surgeons who are hostile to the idea of transsexualism. Some surgeons have strong reactions to transsexual patients, and often, if the surgery is done in a teaching hospital, the surgeon turns out to be a resident or staff member who is offended by the procedure. "In one case, with which I am familiar," writes a doctor, "the patient's massive scars were probably the result of the surgeon's unconscious sadism and wish to scar the patient for " 'going against nature' " (Lothstein, 293). In spite of such unaesthetic results transsexual patients often go barechested, displaying what doctors call a "poor reality" sense along with their flattened chests. Another way of describing this, and a less condemnatory one, might be to say that the patient is regarding his new body *theoretically*; it is, he is, *male*, however attractive or unattractive the appearance.

Nonetheless, fears about gross physical scarring, an "unaesthetic neo-phallus" (Lothstein, 301), and an incapacity for erection and ejaculation make sexual reassignment surgery for female-to-males less common, and less clinically "satisfactory," than the converse procedure for male-to-females. I regard this as a political as much as a medical fact. Research money and scientific discovery have historically been tied to a strong desire within the culture for medical progress, whether in the development of vaccines to combat infectious disease or in the great advances in, say, plastic surgery as a result of disfiguring and disabling injuries suffered in wartime. The example of AIDS and its (mis)treatment by the Reagan and Bush administrations points out the opposite dynamic; a refusal to acknowledge, and therefore to make effective progress against, a major disease whose victims, and etiology, the dominant culture wants to wish (or throw) away. In sex reassignment surgery there remains an implicit privileging of the phallus, a sense that a "real one" can't be made, but only born. The (predominantly male) surgeons who do such reconstructive surgery have made individual advances in technique, but the culture does not yet strongly support the construction of "real men" by this route, preferring cold baths, rugged physical labor, and male-bonding rituals from fraternity beer bashes to the Skull and Bones society and the Fly Club, depending on the economic and cultural context.

We might note, as eloquent testimony to the (ambivalent) faith placed in the creative powers of the surgeon, the number and nature of surgical operations undergone by one transsexual subject, Renée Richards. Richards comments in her autobiography that the name she chose as her fantasy cross-dressed other quite early in her childhood suddenly occurred to her, on the operating table, to carry a special meaning: "Renée. Reborn." She does not mention the emblematic meaning of the name by which she was known to family and friends throughout her early life when *not* cross-dressed as Renée: that name, of course, was *Dick*. It is the cutting off, by surgery, of the name and identity of "Dick," in effect the quintessential penectomy, the amputation of male subjectivity, that enables the rebirth of Renée.

Dick Raskind took female hormones (in both injection and suppository form) to round his hips, thighs, and breasts, and, after a brief period when he grew a beard at a psychiatrist's suggestion ("if the thought of Renée came to mind, I needed only to stroke my chin and her specter was banished"; Richards, 140), he underwent electrolysis to remove his beard growth forever. These procedures, like the penectomy and the construction of a vagina, are standard for most male-to-female transsexuals. While hardly trivial, they fall within a new surgical "norm." But Richards also had what I like to think of as a "pomectomy"—that is, an operation to remove his Adam's apple, the "one aspect of his outward apparance that displeased" him (211). The surgeon, using a device like a dentist's drill, let his hand slip, and broke through the delicate larynx, leaving Richards with a permanently gravelly voice. (Disguised as an exotic dancer, rather than "out" in the doctor's office as a fellow physician, Richards felt doubly disempowered, unable to claim his subjectivity as a mainstream professional. Thinking him a gay female impersonator, the doctors and nurses treated him, in the hospital, without the deference he had come to expect as "professional courtesy"; here, hardly for the first time, presumptions about gender and class conspire to make the patient an object rather than a subject.)

After the Adam's apple operation Richards went to Casablanca, but had doubts about the ultimate surgical step, and returned to New York ("Dick's back!") and married a woman. His feminized breasts became a "continuing source of embarrassment" (263) and so he underwent breast reduction surgery ("This time I could go in as a doctor and be given due respect" [264]), not without some sense of irony: "I was probably the only person in the world who had ever had breast reduction under such bizarre circumstances" (266). In his "newly created silhouette" he was soon back on the tennis court, and, barechested, on the beach. But three years later his marriage ended, and he began the whole cycle all over again. In 1975, six years after first inquiring into the possibility of transsexual surgery, and 72 hours after locating a sex change doctor in New York who would accord him professional courtesy, Dick Raskind was surgically transformed into Renée Richards. Dick was gone. Or was he? Is the subjectivity exhibited in Richards's autobiography "female," or "male"?

As a college student Dick Raskind had attended Yale, where he apparently received a suitable education in canonical English literature, for his autobiography is filled with references to Milton. As many recent studies have pointed out, Milton had some interesting ideas about subjectivity, gender identity, and the construction of womanhood, and those ideas come into fascinating play in *Second Serve*. Before undergoing surgery, but after her body had been modified by female hormones and electrolysis, Renée reflects en route to Casablanca, "I was like one of Milton's spirits in *Paradise Lost*: 'for spirits when they like can either sex assume or both' " (228). After the sex change operation, when she is briefly permitted to play tennis on the women's circuit, she remembers, "I was like Eve in the Garden of Eden but with a tennis ball instead of an apple" (313). The Adam's apple surgery itself does not seem to have reminded her of Milton, however, and it is difficult to tell whether the book's most Miltonic moment is at all ironized for her—the moment when, like Eve, she gazes into a mirror and falls in love with what she sees. It is, for Renée Richards, the post-operative moment, when the surgeon holds up a mirror that reflects her newly constructed vagina. And even—or especially—here, the question of male vs. female subjectivity is far from simple: "What I saw was essentially what I had seen so many times between the legs of the women with whom I'd been intimate—a normal looking introitus but incredibly distinctive because it was mine" (284). The "I" of this statement is, at least in part, Dick, however much the "mine" belongs to Renée.

CHANGING THE SUBJECT

> *Dr. Paul Walker:* I think it's important not to call it sex change because these people felt this way from day one. It's not that they felt like little girls and one day decided, "gee, maybe I'm a boy."
> *Phil Donahue:* It's not what, doctor?
> *Dr. Paul Walker:* It's not a sex change. They've always felt this way.
> *Donahue* show, 1982

But what *is* a transsexual? Is he or she a member of one sex "trapped" in the other's body? Or someone who has taken hormones and undergone other somatic changes to more closely resemble the gender into which he (or she) was not born? Most pertinent to this inquiry, does a transsexual *change subjects*? Or just bodies—or body parts?

"Transexuals," writes Dr. John Money of the Johns Hopkins University Gender Identity Clinic, a respected expert in the field,

undergo hormonal reassignment so that their body-sex will be more congruous with their self-perceived mental sex. Mentally, masculine has already metamorphosed into feminine (or vice versa) before the taking of hormones. Thus the transexual condition does not provide information on the effect of sex hormones, if any, on bringing about the metamorphosis. . . . the time for such a hormonal metamorphosis, if ever, is during prenatal life, with a possible short extension into neonatal life.[18]

Money is sure, then, medically speaking, that "transsexualism" (his preferred spelling)[19] is mental rather than hormonal. Yet, interestingly, Money also describes transsexuals in terms of semiology—and while some of his "insignia" are biological or anatomical, others are the products of custom or culture:

Forfeiture of the insignia of the sex of birth is the defining characteristic of transexualism as compared with other manifestations of gender crosscoding. For female-to-male transexuals, it means having a man's haircut, flattening or amputation of the breasts, having no menstrual periods, having nothing insertable into the vagina, and modulating the pitch and intonation of the voice to be more baritone and mannish. For male-to-female transexuals, forfeiture means becoming a eunuch with no testicles, penis, or scrotum, losing facial or body hair, not cutting the head hair, and modulating the pitch and intonation of the voice to a feminine-sounding husky falsetto. (Money, 89)

Having no menstrual periods and losing body hair are medically produced effects; castration and "having nothing insertable into the vagina" are surgical alterations; and short (or long) haircuts are clearly social choices or erotic styles without medical consequence or pertinence. The lowering or raising of the voice in pitch and intonation falls somewhere in between, since its effect is that of style but its achievement is dependent upon hormones. Yet all of these attributes are linked together as "insignia" of gendered subjectivity. Precisely where we might wish to turn to medical discourses for specificity and distinction, we find, instead, a blurring of categories and boundaries.

The term "transsexual" is used to describe persons who are either "pre-op" or "post-op"—that is, whether or not they have undergone penectomy, hysterectomy, phallo- or vaginoplasty. Transsexualism is not a surgical product but a social, cultural, and psychological zone. Gender identity clinics administer a battery of tests to candidates for sexual reassignment, including Wechsler Adult Intelligence Scale, House-Tree-Person, Rorschach, Drawing of Self-Concept, Thematic Apperception, MMPI, and the Jenkins test. It is possible to "fail" these tests for transsexualism, as well as to "pass" them.

Here is how Jan (formerly James) Morris describes another such "test"—a moment in which her subjectivity (and her body) deconstructs the binary. Prior to surgery, her body transformed by hormones, and equipped thus with both female breasts and a penis, Morris approached the security check at Kennedy airport after an international flight:

> Dressed as I am in jeans and a sweater, I have no idea to which sex the policemen will suppose me to belong, and must prepare my responses for either decision. I feel their silent appraisal down the corridor as I approach them, and as they search my sling bag I listen hard for a "Sir" or a "Ma'am" to decide my course of conduct. Beyond the corridor, I know, the line divides, men to the male frisker, women to the female, and so far I have no notion which to take. . . . An awful moment passes. Everyone seems to be looking at me. Then "Move along there lady, please, don't hold up the traffic"—and instantly I join the female queue, am gently and (as it proves) not all that skillfully frisked by a girl who thanks me for my co-operation, and emerge from another small crisis pleased (for of course I have hoped for this conclusion all along) but shaken too. (Morris, 110)

But the transsexual surgery itself brought to a close Morris's halcyon if confusing days of biological multivalence. In a characteristically self-dramatizing moment on the eve of his sex change surgery, Morris writes, "I went to say good-bye to myself in the mirror. We would never meet again, and I wanted to give that other self a long last look in the eye and a wink of luck" (140). Nora Ephron, reviewing the book for *Esquire* in 1974 when it was first published, adds her tart gloss: "The wink of luck did that other self no good at all; the next morning it was lopped off, and James Morris woke up to find himself as much a woman as hormones and surgery could make him."[20] Ephron's response exhibits both a feminist consternation about this medical construction of "woman" and a residual sense that gender identity inevitably involves loss or partialness. For Ephron this is still "James Morris," however bizarrely altered by surgery. She objects to Morris's girlishness, her pleasure in "feminine" helplessness when there are willing males about to put cars in reverse and open bottles, her eagerness to spend her day in gossip sessions with village ladies. To Ephron this self-image made Morris not a "woman" but "a forty-seven-year-old *Cosmopolitan* girl" (Ephron, 204), whose consciousness needs raising whatever the gender of her subjectivity (or her sexual organs).

Yet in point of fact even for a feminist like Ephron the "absolute insignia of maleness" remains the prime indicator of gender, whether or not it happens to remain attached to the subject's body. She reads Morris's subjectivity, his/her "self," as precisely a reference to male anatomy. "The wink of luck did that other self no good at all; next morning it was lopped off." Metonymically, the penis becomes the "subject" both of the sentence and of *Conundrum*. Despite the fact that Morris considers her subjectivity to be conditioned by nurture as well as surgery ("the more I was treated as a woman, the more woman I became. If I was assumed to be incompetent . . . oddly, incompetent I found myself becoming"), for Ephron "it"—the "it" that was unceremoniously "lopped off"—is still the determinative sign of gender.

In reviewing Morris's book at all Ephron underscores a central cultural fact about the surgical discourse of gender: transsexualism as depicted in films, novels, and memoirs, paradoxically, amounted in effect to a *new essentialism*, while it focused attention on the twin anxieties of technology and gender. The body was again the focus of gender determination. The boundary lines of gender and of subjectivity, never clear or precise, their very uncertainty the motivation behind the anxious desire to define, to delimit, to *know*, are not only being constantly redrawn, but also are receding inward, *toward* the mysterious locale of "subjectivity," away from the visible body and its artifacts. To see how this has happened, it may be useful to return briefly to the tribulations of Renée Richards, the transsexual ophthalmologist and tennis player, to see how "transsexualism" is itself undergoing a kind of reconstructive surgery.

When Dick became Renée through surgery, some tournament players protested that because of her superior muscle development and larger frame Renée was really a man playing women's tennis. The proof of gender, they claimed, was not in sex organs at all, but rather in chromosomes. X—or Y—still marked the spot. It was not the phallus or the penis ("lopped off" by surgery) nor the reconstructed vagina lined with penile skin that identified Renée Richards's true gender, but rather the apparently unalterable pattern of genes and chromosomes with which Richards had been born. The U.S. Open Committee declared that Renée could play if she could pass the so-called Barrbody test, in which some cells are scraped from the mucous membranes lining the cheek and placed under a microscope; certain bodies that indicate femaleness, called Barrbodies, are counted, and their presence in appropriate numbers indicates that the subject is female. The ground of the medical argument, in other words, had shifted from surgery to genetics. A new essentialism stood ready to take the place of the old. Although, as Richards herself explains, "even normal women occasionally fail it because the number of Barrbodies is not consistent from one day to the next," and despite the fact that she had done the test on herself previously and had "achieved borderline results" (Richards, 355), the United States Tennis Association insisted that this test was the necessary, and determinant, indicator of gender.

In the case of Renée Richards, this argument failed. Barred from the Open for a deficiency in Barrbodies, Richards was later invited to compete professionally by a promoter who had been the main force in the development of the Virginia Slims Circuit— a sponsor whose cigarette slogan, appropriately enough, was "You've come a long way, baby." After playing exhibition matches with Billy Jean King (who was later pilloried in the press for an extramarital lesbian relationship) and Bobby Riggs (who had been known to play tennis in a dress), Richards filed suit with the help of lawyer Roy Cohn and won. She was permitted to play tournament tennis on the women's circuit.

But the replacement of the surgical by the medical, of the seen by the unseen borderline, is omnipresent in competitive sports today, in the controversy about the use of steroids. A recent political cartoon by *Atlanta Constitution* artist Doug Marlette showed a huge, hairy, lantern-jawed athlete in a singlet, being told in the first frame by a tiny coach, "You're disqualified. You failed the test for steroids." In the second frame the coach comments, as a tear rolls down the athlete's cheek, "I hate to see a woman cry." In the last several Olympics U.S. media commentators have pointed out the solidity of body mass on Eastern European female athletes, with the clear implication that their training is augmented by steroid use. Dan Duchaine, a former body builder and self-styled "steroid consultant," contends in his 1980 pamphlet "The Underground Steroid Handbook" that steroids should be regarded as a technological advancement "like the creation of better running shoes." Commenting on the steroid drug Maxibolan, he writes, "Maxibolan is used by a lot of women body builders as it is not very androgenic [that is, it doesn't produce major male characteristics, unlike some other steroids], and of course, doesn't leave needle marks that the girls in the locker room can gossip about."[21]

This shift in the grounds of medical definition raises further and important questions. After the boom in transsexual surgery in the seventies, there is some evidence that those who once looked toward surgery for the solution to the conundrum of sexual identity are considering other options. As Renée Richards points out wryly at the end of her autobiography, "the flood of transsexuals" predicted by the U.S.T.A. (males who would presumably undergo sex change operations in order to make a fortune on the women's tennis circuit) failed to materialize (Richards, 344, 365). And in the meantime the medical proving grounds of gender identity has moved inward away from anatomy and toward boundary lines invisible to the naked eye (chromosomes, Barrbodies, body chemistries, as well as body shapes altered by steroids). This further invalidation of the test of anatomical gender identity, whether "natural" or surgically wrought, has translated the anxieties of gender to a new register, a new kind of uncertainty and artifactuality.

Jan Morris writes in a 1986 postscript to *Conundrum*,

> I have a feeling ... that the specifically transsexual urge is less common now than it was in 1974; perhaps the slow overlapping of the genders has weakened it, certainly homosexuals have been spared their agonized and misguided search for physical escape. In recent years I have had few requests for Dr. B's address in Casablanca; more and more my correspondents recognize that this book is not really about sex at all. (Morris, 176).

But if the story of transsexualism is not about sex at all, is it about subjectivity, specifically, "male subjectivity"? Does subjectivity follow the knife, or guide it? If a "woman trapped in a man's body" is "really" a woman, and a "man trapped in a woman's body" is "really" a man, what is the force of that "really"?

The phenomenon of transsexualism is both a confirmation of the constructedness of gender and a secondary recourse to essentialism—or, to put it a slightly different way, transsexualism demonstrates that essentialism *is* cultural construction. Nora Ephron accuses Jan Morris of essentializing stereotypes (believing in an essentializing stereotype as what a woman is). But according to what principle does she argue? That anatomy is destiny? That subjectivity follows the sign of the genitals? Or rather is she arguing that there is a difference between social construction and surgical construction, that to be a woman one needs to have been socialized as one? But if that is the case, is social construction "natural," and surgical construction "artificial"?[22]

The transsexual body is not an absolute insignia of anything. Yet it makes the referent ("man" or "woman") seem knowable. Paradoxically, it is to transsexuals and transvestites that we need to look if we want to understand what gender categories mean. For transsexuals and transvestites are *more* concerned with maleness and femaleness than persons who are neither transvestite nor transsexual. They are emphatically not interested in "unisex" or "androgyny" as erotic styles, but rather in gender-marked and gender-coded identity structures.

Those who problematize the binary are those who have a great deal invested in it. In putting in question the age-old boundary between "male" and "female" they also put in question a newer binarism which has become something of a theoretical commonplace, and which now begs to be deconstructed, if we are to come to terms with "subjectivity" as a category to be linked with gender identification in the nineties: that between "constructed" and "essential."

POSTSCRIPT: THE TRANSSEXUAL ON THE CUTTING-ROOM FLOOR

> Now you can look like a perfect lady . . . wearing nothing more than panties and these beautiful . . . Realistic Breasts. Look and feel like the complete woman in these fantastically realistic latex breasts. They are soft and flexible as the real thing. Whether you're nude or wearing your loveliest gown, these light, comfortable breasts will make you vibrantly feminine. . . . If you want to become the perfect female the amazingly life-like TREASURE CHEST is a must!
>
> ad for TREASURE CHEST, *Transvestite Key Club*

It is probably not an accident that several male-to-female transsexuals (Jan Morris, Renée Richards, Christine Jorgensen) have achieved some social and professional celebrity *as* transsexuals, while no example comes to mind of a female-to-male who has "come out" into the public eye. At least while he was *alive*. One of the most striking dissymmetries between "male" and "female" subjectivities today is the public's fascination with men who have been surgically transformed to women when they are alive, and with women who have lived their whole lives as men, only after they are *dead*.[23] This cultural fascination with women as *either* dead *or* culturally constructed, already artifactual, is a tradition in Western literature and art at least as old as Petrarch.[24]

In order to frame a discussion of transsexualism in the media, literature, and film, I want to look briefly at an unlikely precursor for the depiction of the anxieties attendant upon the breaking of the taboo against surgically constructing a *man*: Mary Shelley's *Frankenstein*.

Frankenstein has been read as an allegory of woman and as an inspired and terrifying preview of technologies of reproduction. But it can also be read as an uncanny anticipation of transsexual surgery and, perhaps, specifically female-to-male transsexual surgery. It will be appropriate to begin with a literary moment that marks the place of technological intervention.

> When I found so astonishing a power placed within my hands, I hesitated a long time concerning the manner in which I should employ it. Although I possessed the capacity of bestowing animation, yet to prepare a frame for the reception of it, with all its intricacies of fibres, muscles, and veins, still remained a work of inconceivable difficulty and labour. I doubted at first whether I should attempt the creation of a being like myself, or one of simpler organization; but my imagination was too much exalted by my first success to permit me to doubt of my ability to give life to an animal as complex and wonderful as man. The materials at present within my command hardly appeared adequate to so arduous an undertaking, but I doubted not that I should ultimately succeed. I prepared myself for a multitude of reverses; my operations might be incessantly baffled, and at last my work be imperfect, yet when I considered the improvement which every day takes place in science and mechanics, I was encouraged to hope my present attempts would at least lay the foundations of future success. Nor could I consider the magnitude and complexity of my plan as any argument of its impracticability. It was with these feelings that I began the creation of a human being.[25]

The association of the Frankenstein story with transsexualism is not as far-fetched as it may at first appear, given the recent history of film. In fact, *The Rocky Horror Picture Show* (1975) turns the tables on the dynamic of doctor and transsexual patient, presenting the erotically pansexual Tim Curry in red lace corset, black garter belt and stockings as Dr. Frank-N-Furter, the "sweet transvestite from Transsexual Transylvania," who is not the monster but the mad scientist. Frank (whose name and costume both make him the symbolic realization of the "phallic woman") officiates in his lab over the making of a man: the blond, muscle-bound, not-too-bright Rocky Horror (Peter Hinwood).

The success of *Rocky Horror* as a cult film has been attributed at least in part to its anything-goes attitude toward gay, straight, bi and incestuous sex. Thus an admiring critic reports that "one Frankie fan underwent a sex change operation, the better to conform to the mad Transsexual's transvestite role. (Whether he became a she, or she became a he, my informant could not say)."[26] But even more indicative may be the fact that the role of Frank-N-Furter has attracted women. "The one thing I wanted," says a woman who played the part of the transsexual scientist,

> was to get to the point where people would not be sure which I was. I am intrigued by the fact that there is a masculine element in me, and I enjoy being able to bring it out. Women's lib aside, we still believe that femininity is soft and passive. As Frank, I have a chance to be on top of things, to

be a faggot Clint Eastwood. Frank-N-Furter may wear Joan Crawford makeup and high heels, but he's still so masculine there's no way you could mistake him for a woman.[27]

At least in 1982, when this remark was recorded, a man—even, or especially, a cross-dressed man—was necessary as a role model for a woman who wanted to be "on top of things." Only as a female female impersonator, playing a character (not an actor but a character, Frank-N-Furter) so masculine he could never be taken for a woman could she realize her own fantasy of power, the "masculine element" in her. Women's lib aside.

How has the development of transsexual surgery affected cultural representations of gender?

Surgical techniques developed as early as the 1920s inflamed the imagination—and the anxieties—of authors, readers, and audiences in the ostensibly quiet fifties. Thus in 1951 the seventeen year old Richard Raskind, already living a double fantasy life as "Dick" and "Renée," came by accident—in a West Point bookstall—upon a paperback copy of *Man into Woman*, the story of a Danish painter named Einar Wegener, who had undergone surgery to have a woman's ovaries transplanted into his body. "Einar Wegener had died within a year after this surgery. Yet he had been a woman."

For Dick it was a realization full of dire overtones. Renée had been up to this time, only a persistent yet unattainable fantasy. She had thrust herself into the outskirts of reality, but that was as far as she could come. Now I could feel Renée strengthen. She had glimpsed a possible way. (Richards, 54)

Renée's rhetorical phallicism, "strengthen[ing]" and "thrust[ing]" herself into the "out*skirts* of reality," contrasts here tellingly with the dire news for Dick.

It was, however, the Christine Jorgensen case, in 1952, that most titillated and unsettled the fifties' public complacency about the absoluteness of gender roles. When Christine Jorgensen's story first appeared in the newspapers, it opened up the media possibilities of what her friend Dr. Harry Benjamin would later describe as "the transsexual phenomenon."[28] Jorgensen herself was inundated not only with questions (did she sleep in pajamas or a nightgown?) but also with offers of employment from such diverse sources as Warner Brothers Studio, the 46th Street Theater in New York City, the Copa Club in Pittsburgh, Pennsylvania, the New York Press Photographers' Association and the Kappa Delta Kappa fraternity of the University of Houston ("Congratulations Your Selection As Sweetheart of Fraternity, Would Appreciate Visit and Autographed Picture").[29]

A film of the Jorgensen story (starring John Hansen in the title role) was not made until 1970. But in 1953, in the same year in which the surgery took place, a remarkable film called *Glen or Glenda* was produced on a shoestring budget by Edward D. Wood, Jr., himself described as "a well known authentic Hollywood transvestite,"[30] who also played, under a pseudonym, the starring role of Glen (or Glenda). Bela Lugosi appears in the film as a kind of Alistair Cooke figure *avant la lettre*, darkly muttering gibberish about snips and snails and puppy dogs' tails, a recurrent motif that not only introduces the theme of castration in an unforgettable way, but also, again uncannily, offers a citation of *Frankenstein*: "like a Frankenstein monster ... " Lugosi gloats, as around him lightning strikes and thunder rolls.

Glen or Glenda is clearly haunted by the Jorgensen case. It begins with a quick montage of newspaper articles about sex change surgery, and with the death of Patrick/Patricia, who commits suicide, leaving a note saying that society will not let him wear the clothes he wants, and that he cannot go on living without doing so. A concerned, avuncular policeman, discovering the body, goes to consult an eminent psychiatrist, who tells him two stories.

The psychiatrist's first story is that of Glen (or Glenda), a closet transvestite who is engaged to a woman named Barbara, and can't figure out a way to tell her his secret. Glen suffers the tortures of the damned (almost literally, since he is haunted in his dream thoughts by the figure of a devil who turns out, later in the film, to be his father in waking life). Finally Glen tells Barbara the truth, and she accepts it. The doctor tells the engaged couple that Glenda can disappear if Glen makes Barbara into his mother, his wife, his sister, and so on—thus she will be all the women he needs, and Glenda will have no role. Pointing to some medical charts on the wall, the doctor assures them that Glen is physically all male, not a hermaphrodite or pseudo-hermaphrodite. Biology, in other words, is on his (or, rather, Barbara's) side.

In the second story, we hear of Alan, who will become Ann—a more advanced case of transvestism. Alan is not described as a transsexual, and, in fact, that term is not used anywhere in the film. Alan's mother wanted a girl, and his father didn't care. He grew up liking girls' things, went into the army and served well, but carried with him a suitcase full of women's clothes (we may note that Renée Richards, at Yale as Richard Raskind, did the same). When Alan completed his military service, he sought medical help. Alan, the psychiatrist tells the attentive policeman, was a pseudo-hermaphrodite. He was born with the organs of both sexes, one set perfect, the other imperfect. Alan therefore underwent a course of hormone treatments and sex reassignment surgery. He was taught the woman's role in sex, and, according to his doctor, lived happily ever after.

Notice that in both of these cases biology turns out to be right. Glen was not a hermaphrodite, and becomes a heterosexual non-cross-dressing husband; Alan, who had a biological reason for his transvestism, is surgically changed into a woman. The theme of technology is strong throughout the film. A chorus of scoffers (clearly embodying middle America's most small-minded and conservative elements) periodically make such pronouncements as "if God had wanted men to fly he would have given them wings," and that "if God had wanted men to have automobiles he would have given them wheels"; likewise (say these scoffers), "if God had wanted men to be women he would have made them women." (And given them what? The scoffers don't say.) But this view is discounted both by the film and by the psychiatrist, who is the instated figure of authority and knowledge. The law of binaries is at work in *Glen or Glenda*, too, since there are two kinds of transvestites, a mild case and an advanced case—*not* an opposition between transvestites and transsexuals, as in the medical discussions of Stoller and others some ten years later. The film's videocassette copy dismisses it as "a camp classic, full of stiff acting, nonsensical dialogue, [and] shameless use of stock footage." Certainly there is no denying the considerable (and delicious) element of camp, especially in Lugosi's scenes and the softcore porn sequence with Barbara. But to consign *Glen or Glenda* completely to the realm of camp seems like phobic overreaction on the part of the promoters; the film itself, while clearly low-budget, is a fascinating narrative, full of unexpectedly perceptive readings of character and detail, and often quite moving in its attempt—through the observer-figure of the nonplussed but gamely compassionate policeman—to come to terms with this new technological fact of life.

Perhaps predictably, as the possibility of "sex change operations" became better known, public fascination with this new technology (which offered a glimpse of a surgical primal scene while putting gender identity in question in a particularly vivid way) led to the creation of figures like Myra Breckinridge and Roberta, the transsexual in John Irving's *The World According to Garp*. In a short story called "Self-Experiment: Appendix to a Report," German writer Christa Wolf examines the complexity of postmodern gender (and political) identity through the account of an experimental subject given a sex-changing drug. The female-to-male transsexual here is unnamed as a woman, but is given, as a man, the name "Anders"—literally, "other."[31] The transsexual in fiction and film was a reified figure for blurred gender, and could be also readily appropriated to problematize sexual stereotypes. Thus the dildo rape in *Myra Breckinridge* (1970) drew attention to Myron/Myra's voluntary castration, while Raquel Welch's breasts called equal attention to what s/he had traded the phallus in *for*. "Where are my tits?," cries Myron, grabbing at his chest as he awakens from the operation. Gore Vidal told *Variety* magazine during the casting of *Myra Breckinridge* that " 'not one' actor so far had come forward for the part of the young man,"[32] which was ultimately played by Rex Reed, but Rebecca Bell-Metereau points out that "Even if a female impersonator had appeared for the part, he would have needed breasts to play the role convincingly."[33] Breasts here become in effect items of costume, body clothing requisite for the part.

Dog Day Afternoon (1975), a film directed by Sidney Lumet and starring Al Pacino as Sonny and Chris Sarandon, in an Oscar-winning performance, as his "wife," is based on an actual incident in which a man tried to rob a bank to get enough money for his "wife's" sex change operation. Sarandon, as Leon, tells the police that a psychiatrist advised him he was a "woman trapped in a man's body." A newscaster on a TV broadcast reports that Sonny and Leon were married in an official ceremony by a priest, attended by seven bridesmaids (all male), Sonny's mother, and 70 wedding guests. "We have been able to obtain a still photograph of Leon in his gown," says the newsanchor, as the photo of Sarandon in a wedding veil and sprigs of stephanotis is flashed across the airwaves. "Leon has confirmed that the gowns for him and his bridesmaids cost $700. We have not been able to confirm the story with the priest who performed the ceremony," the anchorman continues, and then, in what I hope is a deliberate *mot* on the part of screenplay writer Frank Pierson, he adds, "however, we are told that he was subsequently defrocked."

In Robert Altman's *Come Back to the Five and Dime, Jimmy Dean, Jimmy Dean* (1982), Karen Black plays Joanne, a transsexual who was formerly Joe, the only male member of the Jimmy Dean fan club that is now having its reunion in a dime store in rural Texas. In *Jimmy Dean, Jimmy Dean*, the audience's curiosity about the primal scene of sex change is voiced on-screen by Sissie, the flirtatious and sexually experienced hometown girl played by Cher, and this curiosity is then taken up by all the other characters. But the sex change operation itself, the act of Joe's castration as his entry into the forbidden world of women, is not, it turns out, this film's real surgical secret. We learn, as the fan club does, relatively early about "Joanne's" former identity. Only much later do we discover that Sissie's breasts, the "knockers" to which she attributes her sexual success, have been replaced by prostheses as a result of a mastectomy. The loss of the real breasts has led to the loss of her boyfriend, Buck; the image of bodily loss in this case has been displaced upward, so that Sissie's mastectomy, not Joe's transsexual surgery, becomes the real castration. The separation of Buck from Sissie (again, the names are not, presumably, random choices) follows as an inevitable social concomitant, yet another version of the same story told by the body.

Welch's Myra Breckinridge is a sadistic figure who announces that her "goal is the destruction of the traditional man." Like Bobbi, the female half of Michael Caine's persona in *Dressed to Kill* (1981), Myra thus marks transsexualism as a site of cultural anxiety so profound that it manifests itself in psychosis—the psychosis of the character absorbing and displacing, if it does, the public's fears about crossing these forbidden boundaries.

In *Dressed to Kill* Bobbi is explicitly described as a "pre-op transsexual." It is his/her desire to have the operation, and the resistance to surgery on the part of her other half, the therapist Dr. Robert Elliott, that leads to the homicidal outbreaks. Dr. Elliott finds himself sexually aroused by women; Bobbi finds such male arousal intolerable, since it denies the new gender identity Bobbi/Robert desires (here the film follows the received views of orthodox psychoanalytic opinion). By locating Bobbi/Robert specifically and medically on the borderline ("pre-op transsexual") Brian De Palma's film capitalizes on the increased anxiety that the possibility of surgical transformation permits. In this the film shows its difference from Hitchcock's cross-dressing landmark *Psycho* (1960), to which it is greatly indebted, by moving the focus of attention from the mind to the body.

Similar scenes of instruction are found in both films. In *Dressed to Kill* Nancy Allen (De Palma's then-wife) as Linda, the prostitute with the heart of gold, gives a little lecture on transsexual surgery (male-to-female penectomy) as young Peter (well named, again) and the audience hang on her words, fascinated and horrified. This is a rewriting or restaging of the psychiatrist's authoritative explanation of split personality disorders in *Psycho*: Norman Bates as both mother and son. Here again the element of *physical* and *surgical possibility* heightens the fascination, ups the stakes.

Not surprisingly, the transsexuals presented in these novels and films are all male-to-female transsexuals. Clearly it made a difference whether the transsexual was played by a man or a woman, and also what attempts were made to indicate a blurring of gender. As Bobbi/Robert Elliott, Michael Caine, though he is described as "pre-op," shows none of the external bodily changes that a course of pre-operative hormone treatments would have produced: breasts, or a softening of the contours of the face, or a rounding of the hips. Karen Black's transsexual Joanne looks nothing like a man, and indeed, nothing like the young man (Mark Patton) cast in the part of Joe, her former self. John Hansen played Christine Jorgensen in a blond wig; John Lithgow, in a much-praised performance, played Roberta (the former Philadelphia Eagles tight end, Robert Muldoon) in *The World According to Garp*, and reported that "sitting alone in my trailer, all dressed up in drag, I would run my hands over the strange, artificial curves of my body, look at myself in the mirror, smile and wink. Boy-John and girl-John were sharing a secret, a sexy joke that no one else was in on."[34] (A few years later Lithgow would become the butt of such a "secret, sexy joke," as the French diplomat René in David Hwang's *M. Butterfly*—who had an affair with a cross-dressed man and believed him to be a woman.)

Perhaps significantly, in fiction as well as in film sexual identity and sexual change are marked not only by changes in the body but by changes in dress, often by a kind of double-cross-dressing. The most extreme version that I know of, and one that declares its anxieties about transvestism and transsexualism in astonishingly overt ways, is Thomas Harris's 1988 novel, *The Silence of the Lambs*, now transformed into a sensational film. Harris tells the story of a serial killer, known by the police-coined pseudonym of Buffalo Bill, who stalks his female victims in order to skin and flay them, and literally to wear their skin. Buffalo Bill, it transpires, is a psychopath who believes—wrongly—that he is a transsexual. Repeatedly rejected by gender clinics, since he has failed the psychological tests by which transsexuals are diagnosed, he takes hormones to change the shape of his body, undergoes electrolysis, and, trained as a tailor, sets about "making himself a girl suit out of real girls."[35]

"What does he want her for?" asks the female detective, paraphrasing Freud. "He wants a vest with tits on it," explains the police informant, a brilliant psychiatrist and sociopathic killer imprisoned in a state hospital for the criminally insane, who alone seems to understand Buffalo Bill's motives. As these brief excerpts will suggest, Harris's book manifests its cultural anxiety through a kind of baroque bravado of plot. In one sense determinedly politically correct—Buffalo Bill is *not* a transsexual, and both transsexuals and gender clinics are exonerated from even associative blame—*The Silence of the Lambs* is nonetheless a fable of gender dysphoria gone spectacularly awry. The allegorically dislocated, self-diagnosed "woman trapped in a man's body," denied the palliative of surgical transformation, now settles for flaying, tanning, and stitching together a chamois shirt of human skin.

One final question. Why does a "nose job" or "breast job" or "eye job" pass as mere self-improvement, all—as the word "job" implies—in a day's work for a surgeon (or an actress), while a sex change (could we imagine it called a "penis job"?) represents the dislocation of everything we conventionally "know" or believe about gender identities and gender roles, "male" and "female" subjectivities?

In my discussion of *Come Back to the Five and Dime, Jimmy Dean, Jimmy Dean,* for example, I noted that in that film Sissy's loss of her natural breasts—her signature attribute—to cancer, and their replacement by prostheses, constituted both the film's surgical secret and also one of its real moments of pathos. The part of Sissy—as we also noted—was played by Cher, a versatile actress with an equally versatile, and apparently ageless, body, who has been often described in newspapers and fanzines as herself the embodiment of "spare parts": at various times her nose, breasts, thighs and buttocks have each been singled out for attention, and attributed to the plastic surgeon's skill. (The body changes achieved by exercise and diet, both staples of the actress's profession, do not for Cher— any more than for Madonna—catch the imagination of the larger public. We expect miracles, not self-discipline, from our culture heroes.) Is *Jimmy Dean* then to be taken as an intertextual reference to Cher's own constructedness, or relentless self-construction?

If, as I have been arguing, transsexual surgery literalizes the constructedness of gender, it is worth asking why this culture so relentlessly fetishizes sexual difference. How are the pleasures and anxieties of crossing this particular boundary related to shifting definitions of subjectivity? Why do we not think that Cher becomes "another person" when she changes her figure by surgical means, while we do regard Renée Richards as someone different from, though uncannily similar to, Dick Raskin? Is it the change of pronoun, finally, as much as surgical intervention, that makes so profound a difference?

5

FETISH ENVY

Whose underwear is under there? "Fruit of the Loom." 'Cause it fits.
advertising jingle for "Fruit of the Loom" underwear, 1989

A fetish is a story masquerading as an object.
Robert J. Stoller, M.D., *Observing the Erotic Imagination*[1]

Few women are ready to go to a party dressed in a skimpy white toga
that reveals a pair of shorts embellished with a large drawing of a phallus.
San Francisco Examiner, October 22, 1989[2]

A fetish gave my patient the power to ignore a man and deny his penis.
Her bitter resentment against men for her lack of a penis and for her
great need of them, stemming from oedipal sexual disappointment, was
expressed in an attachment to fetishes. This was especially notable when
she lavished attention on her denim jacket and turned away from the
analyst.
David A. Raphling, M.D., "Fetishism in a Woman"[3]

The concept of "male subjectivity," as I have been suggesting, is a back-formation designed to reconstruct "man" as part rather than whole, partial and limited rather than universal and representative. If there are really two genders, then there ought to be both a "male subjectivity" and a "female subjectivity." But, as we have seen, "male subjectivity" has been so long taken as subjectivity *itself* that the distinction is in constant danger of collapsing. In a similar vein, fetishism has been seen as exclusively male. As Stoller put it, women who wear men's clothes "have no clothing fetish": they suffer from the perfectly understandable desire to *be* men. For Freud, indeed, penis envy is the very cornerstone of female subjectivity. If, therefore, feminist critics have attempted to claim the "right to fetishize" for women, might this not be merely another version of penis envy?

At the end of her provocative essay on female fetishism Naomi Schor raises this point directly, confessing to "a persistent doubt that nags at [her] as [she] attempt[s] to think through the notion of female fetishism. What if the appropriation of fetishism . . . were in fact only the latest and most subtle form of 'penis-envy'?"[4]

What I am going to suggest here, using examples from Shakespeare's plays, from modern theatrical productions, from psychoanalysis, from evolutionary biology, and from pop music videos, is that this question, though highly pertinent, is wrongly posed, because it is, finally, tautologous. Penis envy *is* phallus envy, phallus envy *is* fetish envy. It is not clear that it is possible to go "beyond ideology" here; the ideology of the fetish is the ideology of phallocentrism, the ideology of heterosexuality.

"If the penis was the phallus," writes Eugénie Lemoine-Luccioni, "men would have no need of feathers or ties or medals."[5] The penis is an organ; the phallus is a structure. What does it mean to say that envy for the one is envy for the other? Here we might remind ourselves of what Freud has to say directly about "penis envy" : that it marks the castration complex of the young girl; that she wishes to be able to exhibit the penis she does not have (as, for example, by urinating while standing up)[6]; that a "successful" maturation toward adulthood will convert this female wish for the penis into a wish for a baby, and that the "ultimate outcome of the infantile wish for a penis . . . in women in whom the determinants of a neurosis in later life are absent [is that] it changes into the wish for a *man*, and thus puts up with the man as an appendage to the penis."[7]

Why is fixation on the penis (and by extension, the phallus) not called a fetish when it is attached to a man? The concept of "normal" sexuality, that is to say, of heterosexuality, is founded on the naturalizing of the fetish. And this in turn is dependent upon an economics of display intrinsic both to fetishism and to theatrical representation.

In general, according to Freud, men have perversions, women have neuroses. Perversions have to do with having something, and neuroses, with lacking something. Thus, when Freud articulated for psychoanalysis both the idea of "penis envy" and the psychoanalytic concept of the fetish as "a substitute for the woman's (the mother's) penis that the little boy once believed in and . . . does not want to give up," he privileged the "man's penis" as the "normal prototype of fetishes."[8] The "woman's real small penis, the clitoris," was, he claimed in the same essay, "the normal prototype of inferior organs," where "organ-inferiority" became the basis of all neuroses. Men had the penis; men had the fetish.

Lacan, in moving from penis to phallus, from the level of anatomy or "nature" to that of the unconscious and of representation, addressed the question of fetishism in relation to the phallus as the mark of desire. Thus, commenting on "the absence in women of fetishism," Lacan notes (after Freud) that the "imaginary motive for most male perversions is the desire to preserve the phallus which involved the subject in the mother." Since fetishism represents "the virtually manifest case of this desire," he concludes that "this desire," the desire to preserve the maternal phallus, "has a different fate in the perversions which she [i.e., woman] presents."[9] Again following Freud and Ernest Jones, Lacan locates both this desire and this perversion in "the homosexual woman," who exemplifies the patterns of "courtly love" in that she "excels in relation to what is lacking to her." So it is the lesbian, and not the straight woman, who follows the path of something analogous to fetishism. Lacan notes "the naturalness with which such women appeal to their quality of being men, as opposed to the delirious style of the transsexual male," and takes this as a sign of the path leading from feminine sexuality to desire. It is the trajectory of desire which is at issue here—the position of "the homosexual woman" as not the object but the subject of desire.

In the woman who lacks the penis but "has" the phallus (that is, who "has" it by becoming aware of its lack), it is phallus envy, the desire for desire, that motors and motivates her actions. "Having" the phallus, having the fetish, became therefore a matter of one's position in the symbolic register and in the economy of desire. "Men" have the phallus; "men" have the fetish. What is at stake, once again, is the ownership of desire.

What I will be arguing is that fetishism is a kind of theater of display—and, indeed, that theater represents an enactment of the fetishistic scenario. Thus Freud's "penis," the anatomical object, though understood through Lacan's "phallus," the structuring mark of desire, becomes re-literalized as a stage prop, a detachable object. No one has the phallus.

In contrast to other animals, sexual visibility in humans is marked in the male rather than the female. In most mammals, readiness for sex (and for reproduction) is displayed by estrus, a regularly recurrent period of ovulation and excitement—what is also called "being in heat." The human animal substitutes erection for estrus, the overt, signalized sexual readiness of *man* for the overt, signalized sexual readiness of woman. It is no accident, I think, that the invention by humans of recreational sex (sex not for reproductive purposes but for fun) is coextensive with this shift from female to male display. Since the theory of fetishism employs a developmental narrative that implies loss, here is another version: phallocentrism is *loss* of estrus. So that the loss or lack that is described in the Freudian fetishistic economy as castration is itself a substitution for another loss or lack. Phallic fetishism—which is to say, fetishism—is already a substitution and displacement. And Freud's attempt to make the fetish part of the *female* body is both denial and displacement.

As Naomi Schor notes, "it is an article of faith with Freud and Freudians that *fetishism is the male perversion par excellence*. The traditional psychoanalytic literature on the subject states over and over again that there are no female fetishists; female fetishism is, in the rhetoric of psychoanalysis, an oxymoron" (Schor, 365). For the same reason, there have traditionally been in psychoanalytic literature no female transvestites, although, as we have seen, the fantasies collected by Nancy Friday in *My Secret Garden* (for example, a woman admiring herself in the mirror wearing jockey shorts with a tampax protruding from them), self-help manuals for female-to-male passing transvestites (for example, how to pin rolled-up socks to the inside crotch of your underwear to enable you to pass in the men's room), recent medical acknowledgments (for example, that items like "blue denim Levis," "engineer boots," or a false moustache have in fact produced orgasmic sensations in women),[10] and a wealth of historical research from the medieval and early modern periods have turned up innumerable cases of women who were, or are, fetishizing cross-dressers.

Freud describes the fetishist as someone who both believes in the "reality" of castration and refuses to believe it. "*Je sais bien, . . . mais quand même . . .*" says the little boy in Mannoni's example; "I know, but still. . . . "[11] As Sarah Kofman argues, "since there can be no fetishism without a compromise between castration and its denial and because the fetishist split—this is what distinguishes it from psychosis—always preserves the two positions, the fetish can in no sense be a simple *Ersatz* of the penis; if there were really a *decision* in favor of one of the two positions, there would no longer be any need to construct a fetish."[12] And Derrida, reading Freud, observes that it may be possible "to reconstruct from Freud's generalization a 'concept' of fetish that can no longer be contained within the traditional opposition *Ersatz/non Ersatz*, or even within opposition at all."[13] An example of an "undecidable" fetish is in fact given by Freud, in his description of a garment that rendered the wearer's gender unknowable:

> the case of a man whose fetish was an athletic support-belt which could also be worn as bathing drawers. This piece of clothing covered up the genitals entirely and concealed the distinction between them. Analysis showed that it signified that women were castrated and that they were not castrated; and it also allowed of the hypothesis that men were castrated, for all of these possibilities could equally well be concealed under the belt. ("Fetishism," 156–57)

Whose underwear is under there?

This is where the transvestite comes in, not as a mask or masquerade, or male *or* female, but as a theoretical intervention. For the transvestite is the equivalent of Lacan's third term, not "having," or "being," the phallus, but "seeming," or "appearing": "the intervention of a 'to seem' that replaces the 'to have,' in order to protect it on the one side, and mask its lack in the other."[14]

That the fetishistic patient is sometimes *in fact* a transvestite renders more complex but also more plausible the argument that the transvestite on stage or in culture is himself/ herself a fetishization. The fetish is a metonymic structure, but it is also a metaphor, a figure *for* the undecidability of castration, which is to say, a figure of nostalgia for originary "wholeness"—in the mother, in the child. Thus the fetish, like the transvestite—or the transvestite, like the fetish—is a sign at once of lack and its covering over, as in the case of Freud's patient's athletic support-belt—a garment very similiar to devices worn, as it happens, by some present-day female-to-male transvestites.

The history of the fetish in representation (and this is not just, as the anthropological nature of the term implies, in non-Western cultures) indicates that the fetish *is* the phallus, the phallus *is* the fetish. Let us look at some examples. I will be concentrating here, at least initially, on the plays of Shakespeare, in part because Shakespeare has virtually come to define theatrical representation in Western culture, and also because there has been so much recent attention to cross-dressing in his plays, though it has tended to focus on social and political, rather than theoretical, issues.

Shakespeare's plays are famously full of moments in which characters express castration anxiety—or threaten castration. Iago to Brabantio: "Look to your house, your daughter, and your bags" (*Oth.* 1.1.80); Solario, mocking Shylock's loss, ventriloquizing his imagined voice: "two stones, two rich and precious stones, /Stol'n by my daughter! Justice! find the girl,/She hath the stones upon her, and the ducats" (*MV* 2.8.20–22)—*Jessica* as phallic woman; Malvolio, caught in his erotic daydream, a masturbatory fantasy: "having come from a day-bed, where I have left Olivia sleeping. . . . perchance wind up my watch, or play with my—some rich jewel" (*TN* 2.5.48–60); Viola, in a double entendre clearly aimed by the playwright at the audience: "A little thing would make me tell them how much I lack of a man" (*TN* 3.4.302–303).

To best make an argument about fetishism in the plays, though, I select an obvious example from Renaissance theatrical representation: that of the codpiece, itself, bizarrely, a sign of gender undecidability, since it is the quintessential gender mark of "seeming," Lacan's third term interposed between "having" and "being" the phallus: the space, as I have argued, occupied by the transvestite. The codpiece is the thinking man's (or woman's) bauble, the ultimate detachable part.

It may seem curious to choose the codpiece to demonstrate something about "*female* fetishism," but in fact it is perfectly logical to do so. For the codpiece, like Freud's undecidable underpants, is a sign of what might—or might not—be "under there." A woman with a codpiece—what in Middleton and Dekker's play *The Roaring Girl* (1611) is called with fear and titillation a "codpiece daughter"—is the figure of the phallic woman, the ultimate fantasy of male transvestite scenarios (if the psychoanalysts are to be believed). At the same time the woman with the codpiece is the onstage simulacrum of the female transvestite, a crossover figure who, whether or not she exists in psychoanalytic theory, has a substantial claim to existence in history and in representation.

More importantly—and less intuitively—the codpiece confounds the question of gender, since it can signify yes or no, full or empty, lack or lack of lack. It is the stage equivalent of Freud's equivocal underpants. The codpiece is therefore a theatrical figure for castration—which is to say, a theatrical figure for transvestism itself. We might call it a foundation garment.

One thing that sticks out about the codpiece in all of Shakespeare's direct references to it is its explicitly (and precariously) artifactual nature. For example, when Julia and her waiting-woman Lucetta in *The Two Gentlemen of Verona* discuss Julia's transvestic disguise (in terms that anticipate a similar conversation between Portia and Nerissa), the *pièce de résistance* of her male costume is clearly the codpiece:

Lucetta: What fashion, madam, shall I make your breeches?

Julia: That fits as well as, "Tell me, good my lord,
What compass will you wear your farthingale?"
Why, ev'n what fashion thou best likes, Lucetta.

Lucetta: You must needs have them with a codpiece, madam.

Julia: Out, out, Lucetta, that will be ill-favour'd.

Lucetta: A round hose, madam, now's not worth a pin,
Unless you have a codpiece to stick pins on.

TGV 2.7.49–56

Like Portia's comment that she and Nerissa, once cross-dressed, will appear "accomplished/ With that we lack" (*MV* 3.4.61–62), this exchange draws attention to what is absent, to what seems. Since the original "actresses" in their parts were boys, they in fact "have" what they seem to "lack"—or do they? That the codpiece is to be ornamented by sticking pins in it is not entirely comforting—and in the case of Julia the whole codpiece itself will be an ornament, pinned on, rather like the socks in the jockstrap of the passing female-to-male transvestite. It is a detachable part.

But Julia, of course, is a woman in disguise. (Although "she" is also a boy in disguise as a woman in disguise.) Surely there are "real men" in the plays, with real contents in their codpieces? It's not so clear.

In *Much Ado About Nothing* the scoundrel Borachio refers to "the shaven Hercules in the smirch'd worm-eaten tapestry, where his codpiece seems as massy as his club" (3.3.136–7). The Riverside editors, like others, suggest that this "shaven Hercules" is a representation of the hero as subjugated by the Eastern Queen Omphale, dressed as a woman and put to work spinning among her maids.[15] An earlier reference to Hercules in the same play (2.1.253) cites this incident. But A.R. Humphries in the Arden edition finds an allusion to the cross-dressed Hercules unlikely (although he has no satisfactory alternative to suggest) because "Borachio's Hercules is in man's dress with a club."[16]

The "man's dress" to which Humphries refers, however, is a hypothetical metonymic expansion of the codpiece, the only item of clothing specifically mentioned. The whole malappropriate discussion comes in the context of a description of "fashion," a "deformed thief" who "giddily . . . turns about all the hot bloods between fourteen and five-and-thirty" (3.3.121–9), so that we might expect some connection between male erotic energy and this item of self-advertising sartorial style that "puts the goods in the shopwindow," as used to be said of low-cut blouses for women. Indeed, both editors characterize the "codpiece" in determinedly non-anatomical terms, as if it were itself a totally whimsical deformation of fashion with no reference to the body: "the bag-like flap at the front of men's breeches" (Riverside); "projecting forepiece of men's breeches" (Arden). Whose underwear is under there?

So the "codpiece" of *Two Gentlemen* is pinned to the pants of a cross-dressed woman, and the "codpiece" of *Much Ado* marks the representation of a hero who may well be wearing the classical version of drag. In neither situation does there seem to be a phallus in the case—or rather, what is represented is the transvestite fantasy, the phallic woman. The anxiety of male artifactuality seems already much in evidence. And things are not made more reassuring by the "codpiece" references in *The Winter's Tale*, *Love's Labour's Lost*, and *King Lear*.

In *The Winter's Tale* Autolycus boasts that it is easy to "geld a codpiece of a purse" (*WT* 4.4.610–11). In *Love's Labour's Lost* Berowne, decrying the power of Cupid, calls him "king of codpieces," using "codpieces" as the metonymic equivalent for "men," and the Fool in *Lear* does the same: "The codpiece that will house/ Before the head has any" (*Lr.* 3.2.27–28). In both cases the part is detached by metonymy. And the Fool, of course, also refers to *himself* as a codpiece ("Marry, here's grace and a codpiece—that's a wise man and a fool" [3.1.184–85]), alluding to the common wisdom that fools had extra-large genital equipment to compensate, so to speak, for their lack of brain-power—the celebrated "fool's bauble."

In a recent one-man show in San Francisco called "Feast of Fools," actor-mime Geoff Hoyle presented the history of the fool in Western culture in a series of vignettes. In sequence after sequence the Fool was defined by his comic interactions with a detachable phallus, from the medieval "bauble" to Pantalone's money bag to modern sight gags involving a third leg or a large, red, preternaturally sensitive nose.

The New York-based Mabou Mines troupe has been performing an experimental version of *King Lear* in which *all* the roles are cross-dressed ("a kind of homage to Charles Ludlam," says the director). As a result, many of the Fool's lines play like phallic jokes, especially his advice to Lear, "delivered," wrote one reviewer, "with a reference to his own anatomy—'have more than thou showest.' "[17]

And what about men dressed as women?

The Dame of English Panto had, we might say, an early incarnation in the figure of the cross-dressed Falstaff in *The Merry Wives of Windsor*. As it happens, the cultural production of *The Merry Wives* is linked to a famous "historical" incident of cross-dressing, the founding of the Order of the Garter, when, supposedly, King Edward III picked up a garter dropped by the Countess of Salisbury at a dance, and rebuked his critics with the words that became the Order's motto, "*Honi soit qui mal y pense*." Editors following Leslie Hotson have suggested that the play was written for the Garter Feast of 1597, and several scenes take place at the Garter Inn; an extended passage in Act 5 describes the festivities that attend the installation of a knight (5.5.57–74). Criticism of *Merry Wives* has stressed the historical and cultural links among the Order of the Garter, Queen Elizabeth, and courtly forms,[18] but in emphasizing a female ruler's association with a male order, critics have occluded—or repressed—the fantasy of the founding scenario, which imagines a transvestism of the opposite (gender) kind, the king wearing the countess's garter.

The presence of male-to-female cross-dressing in the play—from Falstaff to the boys costumed as (and substituted for) Anne Page in the comic denouement—is related, I would suggest, on the one hand to this "foundational" subtext, and on the other, to the omnipresent pun on "page" as a surname, a male-to-female disguise, and a code word for male homosexual love object.

Yet Falstaff is not often discussed in the context of Shakespearean cross-dressing; he's not much of role model for women *or* for men, dressed as he is like an old woman, carried onto the stage in a basket, his motive seduction, his cause both ludicrous and offensive. He thus satisfies neither the feminist role-model progress narrative of the early 1970s nor the recuperative image of the Shakespearean "sensitive man." If the Falstaff of the history plays is these days often compared to the stage of the pre-Oedipal, and even to the pre-Oedipal mother—and he is—the Falstaff of *Merry Wives*, always carefully kept separate from the history Falstaff, is something of an embarrassment, not even a glamorous drag queen like Antony in Cleopatra's tires and mantle, but rather the quintessence of what is known in transvestite circles as "cod drag."

"Cod"—as in codpiece. *Eric Partridge's Dictionary of Slang and Unconventional English*[19] defines "cod" as "the scrotum," or in plural, "the testicles." Since 1690 (that is, after Shakespeare) "cod" has also meant "a fool." In its verbal form, "to cod" is "to chaff, hoax, humbug; to play the fool." Adjectivally, it connotes "burlesque; especially *cod acting*, as in acting a Victorian melodrama as though it were a post-1918 farce or burlesque." Since 1965, Partridge adds, "it has been used colloquially for 'pretence, or mock'—e.g., *cod German, cod Russian.*"

So "cod" means both scrotum or testicles, and hoax, fool, pretence or mock.[20] The anxiety of male artifactuality is summed up, as it were, in a nutshell.

What is particularly important to note here is that, traditionally, transvestism on the Western stage and in clubs and drag acts has turned on the artifactuality of *women*'s bodies—balloon breasts, fluffy wigs, makeup. Is it possible that this overt acknowledgment of artifice—often a source of consternation to women and to feminists—masks another (I hesitate to say, a deeper) concern about the artifactuality and the detachability of maleness? What if it should turn out that female fetishism is invisible, or untheorizable, because it coincides with what has been established as *natural* or *normal*—for women to fetishize the phallus *on men*? Lacan, in fact, says as much when he asserts that "[woman] finds the signifier of her own desire in the body of him to whom she addresses her demand for love. Perhaps it should not be forgotten that the organ that assumes this signifying function takes on the value of a fetish" ("Signification," 290).

To deny female fetishism is to establish a female desire for the phallus on the male body as *natural*. Heterosexuality here—as so often—equals nature. Female fetishism is the *norm* of human sexuality. That is why it is invisible.

We might note that when the English stage ceases, after the Restoration, to be a transvestite theater—when actresses appear on the public stage in roles previously reserved for men—their appearance coincides with the redesign of the playhouse to include the Italian innovation of the front curtain. The curtain is a veil that marks off the "not real" from the "real." The work done by transvestism in putting the phallus under erasure is now done by a different kind of theatrical punctuation. The one substitutes for the other—the curtain for the transvestite troupe, both marking theatrical difference. The phallus only does its work when veiled: veiled by the difference of not knowing whether there is difference or not (since "having" and "lacking" can both be kinds of "seeming"); veiled by the curtain that says, "this (and only this?) is theater." Or, to put it another way, the substitution of female actresses for boy actors is not a naturalizing move that returns theater to its desired condition of mimesis, replacing the false boy with the real woman. It is, instead, a double substitution—a re-recognition of artifice—something tacitly acknowledged by Restoration critics when they praised the women for playing female roles almost as well as the boy actresses did, just as later critics would praise nineteenth-century actresses playing Hamlet, Othello, or Iago, for their fidelity in representation—*not* for being dogs walking on their hind legs. "Mrs. Waller's Iago, last night, was truly great," "worthy of being ranked with the best Iago we have ever seen" "the best 'Iago' which has been produced on our stage since the days of the elder Booth."[21]

And here it will be useful to look briefly, and in conclusion, at yet another contemporary instance, which could be compared to Emma Waller's celebrated moustachioed Iago, or to the cross-dressing of Viola in the style of her "lost" brother Sebastian—an impersonation which turns on Viola's (supposed) "lack." Here my example is drawn not from a Shakespearean production but from the cross-dressing and fetishization which has become so noticeable a part of contemporary rock and pop music in performance—specifically, the theatrical relationship of influence and parody between Michael Jackson and Madonna.

In some of Madonna's most recent theatrical self-representations she has made herself deliberately into a figure that seems to echo the onstage moves of Michael Jackson. Here I have in mind, in particular, a music video called "Express Yourself" and the moment she chose to perform from that video at a recent Music Video Awards Show.[22] Appearing in a men's double-breasted suit (the mammary description of this garment almost surely a kind of unexpressed pun), as she does periodically throughout the longer version of "Express Yourself," she danced before the audience in a style directly imitative of Jackson, mimicking many of his moves, and wearing his signature look of white socks and shiny black men's shoes. Flanked by two female back-up singers in pinstripes, she assertively claimed all possible gender space, at one point stripping off her jacket to reveal a lacy teddy beneath, so that she became a kind of sartorial centaur.

But the moment that scandalized critics was a moment of sheer quotation from Michael Jackson, when Madonna danced toward the audience and squeezed her crotch. Now, in video and in live dance performance Michael Jackson often makes this kind of theatrical gesture, and no one ever complains—quite the contrary. But Madonna, squeezing what she hadn't got (or *had* she?), emblematized the Lacanian triad of having, being, and seeming. Squeezing the crotch of her pants became for her, onstage, the moment of the claim to *empowered transvestism*, to seem rather than merely to have or to be—*not* (and this distinction is important) just a claim to empowered womanhood. In this moment, and in the very fact that she chose the cross-dressed costume from her longer video to present at the opening of the awards show, Madonna became transvestism itself, the more so since she was, apparently, so deliberately troping off Michael Jackson.

"Good *madonna*, give me leave to prove you a fool." (*TN* 1.5.57) The speaker is Feste the clown, who surely knows if anyone does about the fool's bauble which is the codpiece.

Madonna is a famous female star who is impersonating a famous male star who is celebrated for his androgynous looks and his dancing style. Why is it shocking when she grabs her crotch, repeating as she does so a gesture familiar to anyone who has watched a two-year-old male child reassuring himself of his intactness? Not because it is unseemly for a woman to do this—although it may be, to some people—but because what she is saying, in doing so, is: I'm not intact, he's not intact; I *am* intact, this is what intact is.

Theater elicits, produces, and panders to *fetish envy*, in both its male and its female spectators. Female fetishism, fetish envy, is indeed possible in a theatrical space where the symbolic nature of the maternal phallus makes it the only phallus that is real. Thus the transvestite in Shakespeare—both the boy actor and the cross-dressed woman— becomes not an accident of historical contingency but the necessary intervention that makes fetishism not only possible but foundational to theater itself.

6

BREAKING THE CODE:
TRANSVESTISM AND GAY IDENTITY

> In the long run, it's not breaking the code that matters—it's where
> you go from there. That's the real problem.
>
> Hugh Whitemore, *Breaking the Code*[1]

A COMPLEX ARTICULATION

In the spring of 1990 the following fairly typical letter appeared in the pages of a nationally syndicated advice column for adolescents:

> Dear Beth: Several times you have mentioned transvestism in your columns. I am about to let my girlfriend, who I hope will eventually be my fiancée, know that there are times when I would rather wear her panties and pantyhose than my own underwear.
>
> Can you tell me what percentage of men enjoy this? Maybe it will help me convince her that I'm not really off the wall. I and others like me lack the acceptance that gays now generally enjoy. —Lewis

The columnist, Beth Winship, replied

> I have never seen a statistic on the percentage of transvestites, but I know there are quite a number because I get a steady stream of letters from them. Most people assume that cross-dressing is a sign of homosexuality. It is not. Some gay men like to dress in women's clothes, but not all, and most transvestites are not gay. Many have happy and contented wives. I hope this persuades your girlfriend.
> —"Ask Beth" column, April 29, 1990[2]

Out of the dozens of such letters I could quote here, I choose this one because of the writer's plaintive concern that "I and others like me lack the acceptance that gays now generally enjoy." Lewis regards himself as a member of a misunderstood and misread minority, less adequately represented in public discourse than gays and lesbians, and *distinct from them*; Beth, in her reply to him, concurs. But clinical, psychological, and medicalized distinctions notwithstanding, the confusion between—or conflation of—transvestism and gay identity becomes evident virtually whenever transvestism becomes a topic for public debate, whether in the popular media, in transvestite journals, or at academic conferences. In each case vested interests are very much at stake. Thus, for example, in a series of *Donahue* programs on female impersonators in a Chicago club (1984), on cross-dressed fashion (featuring host Phil Donahue in an unbecoming skirt, also in 1984) and on cross-dressers and their wives (1987), the chief question raised by audience members—after the question of which bathroom cross-dressers used—was whether or not men who wore women's clothes were gay. Or *looked* gay. "You think it makes me look gay?" asked Phil about his skirt. "It sure does," responded an audience member, and others agreed.[3]

Donahue asked the female impersonators who performed at the Chicago club if they were gay (most were; one now had a female lover, but described himself as "bisexual": "I was [gay], but now I'm not. I do this as a profession now"); on this show, as on others on similar subjects, Donahue went out of his way to assert, in a way meant to be sympathetic to gays and lesbians, that "we are in a homophobic culture. We are scared of gay people." As for the impersonators themselves, they testified to a persistent tension within the gay community about female impersonation and drag: "Some people don't like it at all. They are very prejudice[d] towards it because we are the effeminate side of the gay personality."[4]

Presenting a group of male cross-dressers and their wives to an audience in 1987, Donahue cited some clinical facts about transvestism: "Most cross-dressers are not, repeat, not gay. Most cross-dressers are male, not all, but most. Cross-dressers come from all walks of life and all economic strata of our society. The guy next to you in the board room may be wearing women's underwear." He also stressed a basic distinction between transvestism and transsexualism: "Cross-dressers have no interest in changing their bodies."

Despite these repeated clarifications, audience members and callers raised questions about child molestation (statistically a crime perpetrated far more often by straight men than by gays, though the callers didn't seem to think so) and the influence of a man's cross-dressing on his children. The wives who appeared onstage were supportive, explaining that the disclosure of this secret had made their husbands feel closer to them, and distinguishing between the cross-dresser's "femme" persona and his other identity as a heterosexual man. Bonnie's husband, "Rhonda," said he "like[d] simple acrylic nightgowns and usually wears pantyhose," and Bonnie interposed that "Rhonda" was not the person she had sex with. "I sleep with Rhonda but I make love to my husband and my husband does not wear negligees to bed, if you make the distinction."[5] Many, both in the audience and beyond it, find this a distinction difficult to make. But cross-dressers don't, or say they don't, and neither do their wives. (And looking *at* rather than *through* the transvestite means listening *to* rather than merely around or beneath what cross-dressers have to say about their own relationships and identities.)

A program virtually identical to this last *Donahue* was aired by Donahue's chief media rival, Geraldo Rivera, in February of 1989. Like Donahue, Geraldo began by informing his audience that "experts will vouch for this, the cross-dressers are not gay, they're not homosexual, they're not transsexual either."[6] The usual audience questions—which restroom do you use when cross-dressed (the women's room), what do your children think (they see it as a kind of hobby), do you want to change your sex (no, but I want to change my gender)—were asked and answered, and Geraldo made the same joke Donahue had made about cross-dressers *literally* coming out of the closet (*Geraldo*, 6; *Donahue* 1987, 3).

A similar conflation between cross-dressing and homosexuality tends to occur in our culture when the starting point is homosexuality rather than cross-dressing. Here is one brief but symptomatic example: to illustrate a (favorable) review of Allan Bérubé's book, *Coming Out Under Fire: The History of Gay Men and Women in World War Two*, the *New York Times Book Review* chose a photograph of a WAC putting makeup on a male soldier who wears false eyelashes and a flowered hat. The caption read, "A WAC lieutenant teaches a soldier how to impersonate a woman for a soldier show during World War II."[7] The concept "gay man" in this illustration is completely subsumed, and taken over, by the image of cross-dressing. Although Bérubé's book does contain a chapter on "GI Drag," the element of transvestism or travesty in gay army life is a very small part of his argument. The cover of his book shows two photographs quite different from that of the soldier-actor in makeup: one of a man in ordinary men's clothes leaning on a truck, the other of a woman in a skirted uniform seated on the fender of a car. Neither is in drag. But the *Times* book review editors chose the photograph they did, presumably seeking a shorthand vestimentary code for "gay soldier" that would be instantly recognizable and legible, however partial or false.

In mainstream culture it thus appears just as unlikely that a gay man will be pictured in non-transvestite terms as it is that a transvestite man will be pictured in non-gay terms. It is as though the hegemonic cultural imaginary is saying to itself: if there is a difference (between gay and straight), we want to be able to *see* it, and if we see a difference (a man in women's clothes), we want to be able to *interpret* it. In both cases, the conflation is fueled by a desire to *tell the difference*, to guard against a difference that might otherwise put the identity of one's own position in question. (If people who dress like me might be gay, then someone might think I'm gay, or I might get too close to someone I don't recognize as gay; if someone who is heterosexual like me dresses in women's clothes, what is heterosexuality? etc.) Both the energies of conflation and the energies of clarification and differentiation between transvestism and homosexuality thus mobilize and problematize, under the twin anxieties of *visibility* and *difference*, all of the culture's assumptions about normative sex and gender roles.

In a homophobic and norm-obsessed culture, then, does "transvestite" really after all become a code word for "gay and lesbian"? The conflation of transvestism and gay identity has become a political factor for both of the populations most directly concerned; for strategic as well as descriptive reasons both gays and transvestites, as well as "straights" on both the right and the left, at times conflate, and at other times strenuously resist the conflation, of the two categories.

Alan Bray, in his book *Homosexuality in Renaissance England*, offers a warning against the projection of one period's assumptions onto another's representations when he contrasts Thomas Middleton's description of an encounter with a transvestite in *Micro-Cynicon* (1599) with the transvestite practices of eighteenth-century "molly houses." "Middleton's tale," writes Bray, "is not concerned with homosexuality." Male-to-female transvestites in the streets of Elizabethan London wanted to be mistaken for women, probably for mercenary reasons.

> The transvestism of the eighteenth-century molly house was in this respect the very opposite. It was about homosexuality; it was not intended to deceive and, as the molly houses themselves, was wisely kept as unobtrusive as possible. Effeminacy and transvestism with specifically homosexual connotations were a crucial part of what gave the molly houses their identity.[8]

The conflation of "transvestite" with "gay and lesbian" is itself a matter of historical contingency, a matter of the moment in which we—or some of us—now find ourselves. There have been historical moments in the West, as well as the Far East, the Near East, Africa, and elsewhere, in which the matter of sexual orientation has had little or nothing to do with transvestite representation, and vice versa. Indeed, as Foucault and others have argued, the very concept of "sexual orientation" as a self-definition is itself of relatively recent, and local, vintage. Nevertheless, the history of transvestism and the history of homosexuality constantly intersect and intertwine, both willingly and unwillingly. They cannot simply be disentangled. But what is also clear is that neither can simply be transhistorically "decoded" as a sign for the other.

CATEGORY CRISES

The term "transvestite" was invented by the German sexologist and homosexual rights activist Magnus Hirschfeld (1868–1935) in the early part of the twentieth century. Hirschfeld observed in *Die Transvestiten*, on the basis of his own research among (and friendship with) hundreds of cross-dressers, that transvestism was not in itself a sign of underlying homosexuality and in fact occurred most frequently in heterosexuals. Hirschfeld saw a relationship between androgynes and transvestites; where androgynes were concerned with the *physical* marks of gender (beard, breasts, genitals), transvestites concerned themselves instead with *psychical* or psychological gender signs, like dress and names. Male transvestites, he thought, were resistant to being called or thought of as homosexuals, and hated "sissies"; female transvestites were more likely to be homosexual, although some fell in love with feminine men. But he argued strongly that transvestism was a "thing in itself," quite distinct from sexual orientation.[9]

In later years researchers and clinicians have tended to reconfirm this judgment, even as they acknowledge a broad spectrum of cross-dressing behaviors from transvestophilia (or transvestic fetishism) to transsexualism to the non-fetishistic cross-dressing that is commonly known as transvestism. Richard F. Docter identifies "five heterosexual behavior patterns involving cross dressing: fetishism, fetishistic transvestism, marginal transvestism, transgenderism, and secondary transsexualism (TV type)" and "four homosexual behavior patterns involving cross dressing: primary transsexualism, secondary transsexualism, so-called drag queens, and female impersonators."[10] In Docter's terms, "drag queens" are cross-dressed prostitutes, including "she-males" (men who wear flamboyantly feminine costumes, makeup, and hairstyles while they signal an unmistakably male body beneath their female clothes), while "female impersonators" are professional entertainers. The term "female impersonator" at the turn of the century also meant male homosexual cross-dresser, while "drag queen" does not by any means always connote prostitution in general slang usage, but itself sometimes crosses over into entertainment or recreational self-display.[11] As this multiplication of categories and shifting of connotations indicates, slippage and confusion seem to be constitutive rather than accidental features of the attempt to define transvestism.

"Transvestism alone," gender researcher John Money stresses, "is not a *syndrome* of cross dressing. Instead it is a *manifestation of the act* of cross dressing. Since dressing is traditionally gender-coded almost everywhere on earth, cross dressing is one highly specific act of gender crosscoding" (emphasis added).[12]

One source of confusion over the relation between transvestism and homosexuality has to do with the difference between gender construction and sexual attraction. In response to an inquiry about whether male cross-dressers could be "lesbians trapped in male bodies," a male sex educator and counselor who was himself a cross-dresser testified on the *Geraldo* show in February 1989 to the "confusion that the public has between sex-role preference and expression, and gender-role preference, which is what we see here" (*Geraldo*, 10–11). The question, offered as an earnest attempt to understand, came from someone who confessed having "a difficult time classifying these men as heterosexual men," despite their evident attraction to—and in some cases marriage to—women. One of the married cross-dressers explained, kindly, that "You're confused about the reason we dress. We're not dressing for a sexual reason, to attract anyone. We're expressing a femininity that we have within" (*Geraldo*, 10).

This "confusion," of gender versus sex or sexuality, is in fact one of the key misunderstandings that has produced the issue under debate. But, as we will see, the distinction is not always an easy one to make; the borderline between gender and sexuality so important to much recent feminist and gender theory is one of the many boundaries tested and queried by the transvestite. The cultural effect of transvestism is to destabilize all such binaries: not only "male" and "female," but also "gay" and "straight," and "sex" and "gender." This is the sense—the radical sense—in which transvestism is a "third."

At the close of his program on married cross-dressers, Phil Donahue offered the television audience the address of an organization called Tri-Ess, the initials of which stand for "Society for the Second Self." Tri-Ess, which is sometimes described as a "sorority" and calls its cross-dressed members "sisters," has been at the center of a controversy among cross-dressers that again underscores the tensions around transvestism and gay identity, because Tri-Ess restricts its membership to heterosexual, male cross-dressers. In a published debate in a journal called *Gender Expressions*, Eileen McCleary, a Tri-Ess member, and Joann Roberts, a founder of the Renaissance Educational Association and the author of a book called *Art and Illusion—A Guide for Crossdressers*, disputed the merits of Tri-Ess's exclusionary policy.

Roberts accused Tri-Ess of discrimination and homophobia, reading the Tri-Ess claim of offering a "comfortable environment" for cross-dressers as a confirmation of "the homophobic nature of their closed membership policy," and dismissing as "machismo" and disrespectful of women the idea that Tri-Ess excludes gays and transsexuals because to include them would upset members' wives. "The Tri-Ess Philosophy has become the Fundamentalism of the crossdressing community," she concludes. "Why are they so afraid to admit gay TVs? Because they know that almost all crossdressing has erotic, sexual roots and that the 'hobby' line is only a ploy to defuse the issue with the general public. If they are seen to associate with gay TVs, then somehow that is an admission that transvestism is sexual."[13] The question was also raised as to whether cross-dressing groups did, or should, serve as dating agencies for members; some wives apparently fear that if gays were admitted, their husbands might take up new relationships that excluded them. This fear again speaks to the ambivalence about the gay/TV axis, even among sympathetic spouses.

The alternative to Tri-Ess is the "open" group, and in many cities such groups exist side-by-side with "closed" (male hetero) gender societies. McCleary argued that choice within cross-dressing lifestyles as well as the choice to cross-dress was essential for the community, and cited some statistics from a national TV-TS journal to support the fact that sexual orientation is in fact on the minds of cross-dressers when they identify themselves as such. (For example, she reports that 19% of those placing personals ads noted that they were members of Tri-Ess, while an additional 16% described themselves as "hetero.") The personals ad, which solicits companionship and—often—sex, seems a loaded indicator for determining whether cross-dressing and gay and lesbian lifestyles coincide, but what is quite clear from both the Tri-Ess controversy and even fragmentary data like these is that the *question* of such an overlap is very much on the minds of cross-dressers, as of the general public.

A male transvestite's cross-gender identity as a "woman," or a female transvestite's identity as a "man," is not, or not always, what some psychologists call a "core gender identity," for the word "core" here insists on a *ground*, an identifiable "real" gender identity, rather than on the complex interplay, slippage, and parodic recontextualization of gender markers and gender categories that characterize transvestic fantasy. The transsexual may wish to literalize that fantasy through an alteration in the body; the transvestite keeps the fantasy in play, though often in a ritualized way, by deploying a rhetoric of *clothing*, *naming*, and *performance* or *acting out*. This is not at all the same as saying that transvestism is a game, an act, or a wholly discretionary, optional, and playful set of behaviors. Quite to the contrary, it is, for many transvestites, both a profoundly serious and also a lonely business—as can be seen in both the personals ads and the self-help journals of the TV community today, and in the landmark fiction of the early years of this century, where sexual and sartorial borderlines were increasingly explored and crossed.

SCENES OF CONSTRUCTION

In a famous episode in Oscar Wilde's *Picture of Dorian Gray*, the beautiful Dorian fatally entices the painter Basil Hallward to the attic where his telltale picture hangs, describing it as a text, "a diary of my life from day to day."[14] Looking at the portrait, reading the diary, Dorian recognizes his other self (or, in Tri-Ess terms, his "second self")—and kills the man who shares that guilty knowledge. Greta Garbo, it is said, once hoped to play the part of Dorian Gray in a film—with Marilyn Monroe cast in the part of Sybil Vane.[15]

Many literary works produced during the period of Krafft-Ebing and Havelock Ellis tend to exhibit similar signs of anxiety or curiosity about sexual self-difference, often situated as episodes of reading: in a book, in a portrait, in a mirror.

First, let us look briefly at Virginia Woolf's *Orlando*, an upper-class fairy tale *à clef*, which reports its protagonist's transformation from a man to a woman as a transsexual procedure "accomplished painlessly and completely"[16] without the necessity of surgical intervention, through what is in effect a pronoun transplant:

> Orlando had become a woman—there is no denying it. But in every other respect, Orlando remained precisely as he had been. . . . His memory—but in future we must, for convention's sake, say "her" for "his" and "she" for "he"—her memory, then, went back through all the events of her past life without encountering any obstacle. (Woolf, 97)

Having "looked himself up and down in a long looking-glass, without showing any signs of discomposure," Orlando moves on to a whole new set of costumes and roles; for her, as Gilbert and Gubar point out, "costumes are selves and thus easily, fluidly, interchangeable."[17] Gender here resides in the imaginary, and the symbolic, like Orlando's Turkish trousers, follows the sign. The novel's confident assertion that "Clothes are but a symbol of something hid deep beneath. It was a change in Orlando herself that dictated her choice of a woman's dress and a woman's sex" (Woolf, 133) suggests a privileged sphere of choice and self-determination, even the self-determination to be a "mixture . . . of man and woman" that seems, on the one hand, to belong to the realm of fantasy, and, on the other, to that of the wealthy and the worldly. Whatever Orlando *is*, her clothing reflects it: the crossing between male and female may be a mixture (a synthesis), but it is not a confusion, a transgression. The inside always corresponds to the outside. Just as there is no contradiction between the clothes and the "something hid deep beneath," there seems to be no contradiction between saying "it was a change in Orlando herself" and "Orlando remained precisely as he had been." There are no vested interests patrolling that borderline in Woolf's fantasy.

For medical and political authorities, however, a woman dressed in a man's clothes (a *non*-coincidence between inside and outside) is what is disturbing. As Carroll Smith-Rosenberg has noted, Richard von Krafft-Ebing's *Psychopathia Sexualis* "made dress analogous to gender. Only the abnormal woman would challenge conventional gender distinctions—and by her dress you would know her."[18] Women "with a strong preference for male garments," women who "cropped [their] hair short,"[19] who hated dolls and needlework, liked cigars, and wanted to marry women, were, so Krafft-Ebing asserted, easy to spot and diagnose. "These women," says Smith-Rosenberg, were for Krafft-Ebing "the female analogy of effeminate men" (Smith-Rosenberg, 270). This conflation of economic, professional, and political desires with sartorial and sexual ones, a conflation that marked the early years of Victorian feminism and continues in some quarters today, was a way of stigmatizing lesbians, female cross-dressers, the poor, and the unconventional by rendering medical judgment upon them.

Probably the most famous—and paradigmatic—primal scene of reading is the one in Radclyffe Hall's *Well of Loneliness* (1928), in which the physical and especially the *sartorial* stigmata of "inversion" were available to be read—in which, that is to say, *clothing* seems to be a determinant signifier of sexuality. *The Well*, published in the same year as *Orlando* (and defended by Virginia Woolf in court after it was banned in England), is, like *Orlando*, a "lesbian novel"; but where Woolf fantasizes a fluid and optional transmigration of body and clothing to suit the inner needs or whims of the moment, Radclyffe Hall, and her protagonist Stephen Gordon, see "choice" in a much more restricted frame.

In Hall's novel, the "invert" Stephen Gordon comes upon a copy of Krafft-Ebing in her dead father's study.

Krafft-Ebing—she had never heard of that author before. All the same she opened the battered old book, then she looked more closely, for there on its margins were notes in her father's small, scholarly hand and she saw that her own name appeared in those notes. She began to read, sitting down rather abruptly. For a long time she read; then went back to the book-case and got out another of those volumes, and another. . . .[20]

Stephen's visit to Sir Philip's study has been occasioned by her mother's horrified discovery of her sexual passion for another woman, and Stephen's consequent eviction from the Edenic estate of Morton upon which she had been born and reared. Soon Stephen is talking to the phantom of her father ("You knew! All the time you knew this thing, but because of your pity you wouldn't tell me" [Hall, 204]) and, shortly after that, she appeals to yet a higher authority for solace, turning from the *Psychopathia Sexualis* to her father's Bible, which opens, unerringly, to the passage describing the mark of Cain. Krafft-Ebing, the dead father, the Bible: from these textualizations she maps her own story.

But even before this momentous recognition Stephen had begun to buy her suits, shoes, and neckties from a men's bespoke tailor (Hall, 136). When she leaves Morton for London (and becomes, instantly, a celebrated novelist), she has her hair cropped like a man's ("mightily did this fashion become her . . . Sir Philip also had been proud of his hair in the days of his youthful manhood" [Hall, 210]). Later, when war comes and she joins the ambulance corps with a group of similarly "less orthodox" women ("bombs do not trouble the nerves of the invert" [Hall, 271]), she finds that they share a passion for the wearing of military uniforms. Her body, as well as her clothes, marks her out as different. Her French fencing master, "pass[ing] his hand down her thighs and across her strong loins," murmurs in professional admiration that she has "the man's muscles" (Hall, 256), while, in a mirror scene that recalls at once Lacan, Narcissus, and Dorian Gray, Stephen confronts her naked body:

That night she stared at herself in the glass; and even as she did so she hated her body with its muscular shoulders, its small compact breasts, and its slender flanks of an athlete. All her life she must drag this body of hers like a monstrous fetter imposed on her spirit. . . . Oh, poor and most desolate body! (Hall, 187)

This second reading scene, like the first, is both a recognition and a misrecognition. Yet re-read from the perspective of the 1990's, Stephen Gordon's anguished glance in the mirror offers an object lesson in historical relativism, for the monstrous body of 1928 is the ideal female body of the fitness generation. Cropped hair, menswear suits, thin flanks—these are not only the signature characteristics of "cross-dressed" entertainment figures like Annie Lennox or k.d. lang or Madonna, but also the high-style looks of the mainstream fashion magazines since the sixties. Stephen Gordon's tragic difference has crossed over into heterosexual style.

TRANSVESTITE PANIC

In an eloquent and important book articulating an agenda for gay theory, Eve Kosofsky Sedgwick expands Dr. Edward J. Kempf's phrase "homosexual panic," first coined in 1920 to describe the fear, fostered by same-sex contiguity in army camps, prisons, monasteries, boarding schools, and the like, that one might be homosexual, might be having homosexual "cravings," or might be thought of as being homosexual.[21] The theories of sexologists like Krafft-Ebing and Havelock Ellis contributed to this cultural visibility of the homosexual or the "invert" as a kind of person, often genetically determined and thus "doomed," whose physiological characteristics were unmistakable: "effeminate" men or "mannish" women. It is not surprising that, at the time that such categories were being theorized, they were also being increasingly actualized both in literature and in historical culture: the novels of Proust and Woolf and Barnes; the lesbian culture of Paris, the "decadence" of Berlin.

Sedgwick's use of "homosexual panic" has given the term a powerful currency in today's critical discussions. It may be useful here to speculate on the correlative existence of what could be termed "transvestite panic": the fear on the part of some gay men today and some male homosexuals earlier in the century that they themselves will be coded, and dismissed, as effeminate—or worse, as "women" —and the correlative fear on the part of some lesbians that they will be coded as "masculine," as "drill sergeants," as a recent letter to the *New York Times* euphemistically put it. This transvestophobia from within gay culture reflects a division between "macho" or "butch" and "effeminate," "nelly" or "femme" that sometimes includes an uneasy intolerance of otherness within gay identity. Thus a paradox: transvestism is said to be "about" gay identity and gay erotic style, but gay identity is not "about" transvestism, not "about" men mimicking women or women mimicking men.

While on the one hand the political energies of radical drag, post-Stonewall, are admired and valorized, this kind of drag is itself somehow "macho"; in contrast, the overt self-advertisement of a Quentin Crisp, who could write that "blind with mascara and dumb with lipstick, I paraded the dim streets of Pimlico with my overcoat wrapped around me as though it were a tailless ermine cape,"[22] is a cause of awkwardness and embarrassment. In a culture that, struggling with all its energies against the AIDS virus and the massive bureaucratic indifference to this tragic epidemic, increasingly presents images of gay male health in T-shirt, tank top, and close-cropped hair and beard, such flaming creatures of the past, with hennaed hair and painted fingernails, may seem anachronistic and even self-hating.

But Quentin Crisp was, in fact, deploying the old, conservative government tactic of the sumptuary laws to new, subversive and powerful effect. He wanted to be *seen* and *read* as who and what he was; he wanted not to be mistaken or obliterated from view. "I went to school, as one might say, in mufti, but my hair and my fingernails were long enough to cause comment from strangers on the way there and back" (Crisp, 31). Like Oscar Wilde and Stephen Tennant (the "great sissy" of whose finger waves, pancake makeup and dyed hair dusted with gold John Waters has recently written, with admiration, that he made Aubrey Beardsley and Ronald Firbank seem butch[23]), Quentin Crisp made dress a statement of his difference, and of his cultural visibility.

It is interesting that after one escapade in which he wore a black silk dress to the Regent Palace Hotel (his escort wore a dinner jacket) Crisp eschewed drag, noting that its only effect on him was to make him look less feminine, by calling attention to his Adam's apple and his bony insteps. Of his evening at the Regent Palace, he remarked, "the evening was a triumph, in that it was boring; nothing happened," and his opinion of transvestite dances and drag parties—which he says he never attends—is that they are likewise dull in the extreme (Crisp, 76–77). His interest was not in passing as a woman (which produced the scenario in which "nothing happened") but in "presenting to the world . . . a brand image of homosexuality that was outrageously effeminate." Among those who took the greatest offense at this, Crisp says, were homosexuals "who were effeminate but did not think of themselves as outrageous" (Crisp, 79).

Crisp's memoirs, witty, tart-tongued, and full of acute cultural observations, note that in the twenties the "boyish" look was high fashion for *women*:

> The short skirts, bobbed hair, and flat chests that were in fashion were in fact symbols of immaturity. . . . The word "boyish" was used to describe the girls of that era. This epithet they accepted graciously. They knew that they looked nothing like boys. They also realized that it was meant to be a compliment. Manliness was all the rage.
>
> The men of the twenties searched themselves for vestiges of effeminacy as though for lice. (Crisp, 21)

Now, Quentin Crisp is writing, of course, of the 1920's and 1930's. He "wore makeup at a time when even on women eye-shadow was sinful" (Crisp, 1). His book, *The Naked Civil Servant*, was published in London in 1968, a year after the Wolfenden Report on Homosexual Offenses and Prostitution, and two years before the Stonewall riots. So the picture he presents of the life of a self-advertising effeminate homosexual may seem in many ways completely out of date. Today, for example, even the most conservative straight politicians now wear makeup on camera—and sometimes off. Senator Strom Thurmond of South Carolina dyes his hair and applies eyeliner to his hairline; Senator John Warner of Virginia, the former spouse of Elizabeth Taylor, insists on doing his own makeup for television.[24]

But what is so interesting about Crisp's autobiographical memoir, beyond its witty frankness and its lively prose style, is the way in which it points to a polarization about dress and demeanor *within* the gay male society of which he was a part. For this polarization, this incipient transvestophobia, is represented in many of the classic texts of emergent gay identity from the end of the last century on.

"The men of the twenties," Crisp noted drily, "searched themselves for vestiges of effeminacy as though for lice." The word "effeminate," as it has come to be used in recent years, implies some kind of loss, or lack, but the OED charts a fascinating progress—or regress—of the word. "That has become like a woman: womanish, unmanly, enervated, feeble; self-indulgent, voluptuous; unbecomingly delicate or over-refined." This (sense 1.a) is the usual modern understanding of "effeminacy," covering a whole range of types and behaviors from the dandy to the fop to the "sissy boy" and the "nelly." But the idea that effeminates are "self-indulgent, voluptuous," appears to derive—as does a pseudo-etymology of the word itself—from the notion of men excessively "devoted to women." This, at least, is a common Renaissance sense—that effeminacy is generated by sexual voluptuousness directed toward *women*, not toward men. Historically, then, "effeminacy" is misogynistic as well as homophobic—no surprise, really, since, once again, what is being protected here is a notion of manhood or manliness as social norm. On the other hand, there also exist meanings for "effeminate," albeit now marked "obsolete" in the OED, that use the word "without implying reproach: gentle, tender, compassionate" (sense 1.c) This is the sense in which, as we shall shortly see, Sarah Ponsonby, the "softer" or more "domestic" partner of the two cross-dressing Ladies of Llangollen, is called "effeminate"—a sense we have lost entirely in our contemporary stigmatization of the word.[25]

So "effeminate" can mean a condition *caused by* women (by excessive sexual interest in them) or the condition of being *turned into* a "woman" (with the implication that the "effeminate" man is not at all sexually interested in women). "Woman" is, in either case, a stigmatized and fantasized *agent*. In expressing condemnation of various types of men, it is always *women* who are scapegoated.

One might think that therefore it would be men who would be blamed for what is wrong with some kinds of women, but instead we find, in parallel discussions of what is to be condemned in "masculine" women, that it is not men but women, again, who are to blame. Underlying the history of what Krafft-Ebing called "the Mannish Lesbian" is a lingering presumption that male *is* better, that, once again, to wish to be a man is perfectly "normal," and indeed, culturally speaking, perfectly logical. It was Havelock Ellis, the champion of the *male* homosexual as distinctly *not* effeminate but "brave and honorable" (that is to say, "male" rather than "female"),[26] who divided *female* homosexuals into two groups: the "congenital invert" who belonged to an "intermediate sex" and the potentially "healthy" heterosexual who was prey to the advances of the invert. Since, according to Ellis, the congenital female invert was often, alas, a woman "of high intelligence" who could be found in the workplace, the boarding school, or the women's college, the statistically small group of genetically anomalous "inverts" could, and did, corrupt the much larger population of female "homosexuals" who, while not themselves "inverts," were genetically predisposed to seduction by women. And the result was degeneracy—an increase in feminine criminality, feminine insanity, and a disinclination to marry and bear children. This description of politically and intellectually independent women as corrupting agents, this illogical "logic" that read transvestism as a sign of "mannishness," and "mannishness" in women as coextensive with the women's movement and with the feminist politics of the early twentieth century, has set the agenda even for today's debates about butch-femme and its relation to class, politics, sexual behavior, and the signifying code of "male" dress.

When Quentin Crisp defiantly declares himself an "outrageously effeminate homosexual," he is attempting, with considerable bravado, to recuperate "effeminacy" as descriptive of a male social and erotic and political style rather than as an *effect*. But notice that Crisp distinguished between "drag," in which he has no interest, finding it unprovocative, dull, and boring, and "effeminacy," signified for him by a deliberately disconcerting mélange of stylistic tropes (hair, makeup, jewelry, walk, gesture). Where should we situate "transvestism" or "cross-dressing" in this continuum? Crisp selects from among the complex sartorial vocabulary of cross-dressing in order to declare himself as a certain kind of person, at a certain time and place. His self-presentation is deliberately hyperbolic, parodic—and, in being so, simultaneously confrontational and self-protective. What is crucial to him is that he should be read, visually and sartorially, as who and what he is— that he should be unmistakable, should avoid becoming the cause of mistakes in others.

Contrast Crisp with the transsexual Jan Morris, who sets out quite deliberately to turn herself, in both dress and demeanor, into an ordinary Englishwoman in a twin set (what Americans call a sweater set—a pullover and matching cardigan) and tweeds. Where Morris becomes sartorially *invisible*, by transforming herself into a woman, Crisp remains defiantly visible as an effeminate man.

This need to read and be read is itself, within gay and lesbian culture, a double-edged sword. The social semiotics of butch-femme, like that of Quentin Crisp's camp, has often provoked homophobia, and thus periodically stirs apologists within the gay and lesbian community to call for moderation. The recent wave of homophobic sentiment connected with the AIDS epidemic prompted some gay activists to urge sartorial and behavioral caution. More than thirty years ago playwright Lorraine Hansberry, writing in the lesbian journal the *Ladder*, made the same kind of claim for prudent invisibility.

> Someday I expect the "discrete" [sic] lesbian will not turn her head on the streets at the sight of the "butch" strolling hand in hand with her friend in their trousers and definitive haircuts. But for the moment it still disturbs. It creates an impossible area for discussion with one's most enlightened (to use a hopeful term) heterosexual friends.[27]

But it is precisely this kind of "cultural visibility"[28] that marks sartorial display in the lesbian community—a modern version of the kind of sartorial transgression that provoked the sumptuary laws and dress codes of earlier times. When the lesbian activist and critic

Joan Nestle was living in New York in the fifties, she was careful, when preparing for a night out, to heed the warning of older lesbians. "Always wear three pieces of women's clothing," they counseled, "so the vice squad can't bust you for transvestism" (Nestle, 162). The slippage between "lesbian" and "transvestite" here played into the hands of the law: by defining or reading the one as the other the vice squad could prosecute lesbians, not for making love with women, but for walking through the park.

Is butch-femme transvestite? Yes—and no. Cross-dressing, as Nestle notes, signals women's break with the traditional social and erotic terrain assigned them, so that some prostitutes, for example, were required to wear items of men's clothing as a badge of their profession.[29] So too with lesbians, or at least, according to Nestle, lesbians (like her) from the fifties: "Dress was a part of it: the erotic signal of her hair at the nape of her neck, touching the shirt collar; how she held a cigarette; the symbolic pinky ring flashing as she waved her hand" (Nestle, 104). And also this challenging paradox, thrown down like a gauntlet: "Lesbians have always opposed the patriarchy; in the past, perhaps most when we looked most like men" (Nestle, 106).

LONGTIME COMPANIONS

The pleasures—and the sometimes deconstructive, sometimes assimilationist effects—of playing with patriarchal structures and gender roles is nowhere more in evidence than in the conjunction of homosexuality, transvestism, and that cornerstone of normatively heterosexual institutions: marriage. For it is in the discussion of "marriage" that the necessary questioning of the idea of the "original" and the "copy" has taken its most effective form.

How does cross-dressing or transvestism inflect the "marriage model"? A measure of the cultural overdetermination of this question can be found in the prevalence, and persistence, of what might be called "transvestite weddings"—and in their imaginative variety. The custom of mock-marriage, with one or perhaps *both* partners in transvestite garb, was well known in the gay male molly house subculture of the eighteenth century. The act of having sexual relations was referred to as "marrying" or as a "wedding night," and it took place in a room called a "chapel"; the term for sexual partner was "husband."[30] The so-called "womanless wedding" is still a feature of men's club revels in parts of the American South, and doubtless elsewhere as well. Interviewing a heterosexual couple in which the husband was a cross-dresser, Geraldo Rivera offered as a fantasy-contrary-to-fact his image of "two brides walking down the aisle," and was startled to learn that the couple in question had, indeed, been married in a pair of wedding dresses (Geraldo, 1989, 6). Sally Jessy Raphael presented her audience with a similar spectacle on the air ("Donna says she knew that the only way she could get Bob to walk down the aisle today was if he could do it wearing a wedding dress"[31]).

Freud once imagined himself as a bride in a wedding dress,[32] and a feminist friend told me that she had bought her own wedding gown at a transvestite clothing shop in Philadelphia.[33] It might indeed be argued that in a way all marriages, even heterosexual marriages, are "mock marriages," in their dependence upon certain aspects of sartorial tradition and ceremony. Consider the following entirely typical report from the society page of the Nantucket *Inquirer and Mirror*:

> The bride, given in marriage by her father, wore a gown of tissue taffeta with a sabrina neckline. The bodice of lyonlace had a dropped waist. The skirt and cathedral train were edged with Schiffili lace. Her cathedral length veil and blusher were attached to a headpiece of silk rosebuds and pearls. The bride carried a garden clutch bouquet of champagne roses, French lilac, pale pink grandiflora roses, and old fashioned stock accented with glacier ivy.[34]

What gets married *is* a dress. As Judith Butler convincingly suggests, "The replication of heterosexual constructs in non-heterosexual frames brings into relief the utterly constructed status of the so-called heterosexual original. Thus, gay is to straight *not* as copy is to original, but, rather, as copy is to copy. The parodic repetition of 'the original,'. . .reveals the original to be nothing other than a parody of the *idea* of the natural and the original."[35]

This may be one reason why the wedding dress has featured so prominently, from time to time, in "non-traditional" accounts of dressing up by gay men—and female impersonators. In the 1989 film about gay men in the 1980s, *Longtime Companion*, David (Bruce Davison) tells a funny story about trying on his sister's wedding dress, tripping on its train, and tumbling down a flight of stairs, to be discovered some time later by appalled family members. British female impersonator Bunny of the group Bunny and the Wabbits confided to an interviewer that "The first dress I ever wore was my sister's wedding dress, and I have never looked back."[36] The female impersonator Divine appears in an elegant wedding dress and veil in John Waters's transvestite comedy *Female Trouble* (1975). A century ago the American Sarah Grand's novel *The Heavenly Twins* (1893) featured cross-dressed wedding attendants, the girl outfitted as a page, the boy dressed as a bridesmaid. As we have already noted, a transvestite wedding with seven male bridesmaids was a key romantic memory for one of the bank robbers in *Dog Day Afternoon*, while Angela Carter's post-modern novel *The Passion of New Eve* describes a wedding "in double drag," between Eve, a male-to-female transsexual dressed in a formal suit, and Tristessa, the actress with a phallus, in the wedding dress she wore for *Wuthering Heights*.

A recent inquiry to etiquette columnist Miss Manners from a woman who had been asked by a future bridegroom to act as his "best person" noted that "some of the other women in the bridal party are apprehensive about my role in the wedding, which will be a formal church ceremony." Miss Manners (correctly, it seems to me) read this "apprehensiveness" as having to do with cross-dressing and with gendered behavior: "Do they imagine that one of them will have to dance with you at the reception? Do they think of the recessional as a parade of pseudo-romantic couples? . . . Of course you will dress as a lady and dance with gentlemen."[37]

But "marriage" as contrasted with "wedding" is really what is at issue for gay theorists; "marriage" as the normative form of the sexual-social dyad. One of the ways in which straight culture tries to "read" gay lifestyles is through the "normative" model of heterosexual marriage, which is one reason why gay and lesbian theorists—and activists— have so energetically sought to define gay relationships in other terms.[38] "The 'presence' of so-called heterosexual conventions within homosexual contexts," writes Judith Butler, "as well as the proliferation of specifically gay discourses of sexual difference, as in the case of 'butch' and 'femme' as historical identities of sexual style, cannot be explained as chimerical representations of originally heterosexual identities. And neither can they be understood as the pernicious insistence of heterosexist constructs within gay sexuality and identity. The repetition of heterosexual constructs within sexual cultures both gay and straight may well be the inevitable site of the denaturalization and mobilization of gender categories" (Butler, 31).

To resist the inevitability of the model of heterosexual marriage, of heterosexism itself as prior and normative and gay culture as a presumptive copy, imitation, or parody of that original, is thus a crucial project for some gay and lesbian theorists.[39] Yet despite the strong theoretical and political representations of some of its most articulate spokespersons, the gay and lesbian community is not united on the question of marriage, as witness a recent letter to *Out/Look* that describes "the debate about gay marriage vs. domestic partnership" as a debate about assimilation versus separation. "If the majority of gays prefer assimilation," the writer asks, "what is the gay rights movement doing for them if it does not promote gay marriage? Does the gay rights movement exist to promote the agenda of a radical anti-marriage minority of gays who claim to know what's best for all of us. . .?"[40]

Historically the marriage model seems to have been enabling to many same-sex couples, as well as to individual persons trying to find a language for the kinds of lives they envisage with their lovers. For some of those "marriages" vestimentary codes played a key part in defining or demarcating difference: difference not only from heterosexual structures but also within the homosexual relationship, in the allocation of domestic roles and tasks. As will be clear from these examples, vestimentary *invention*, not just imitation or even parody, seems to have been at play; as will be equally clear, cross-dressing seems often to have been itself an enabling element in contextualizing and realizing gay marriage.

Consider the case of the celebrated "Ladies of Llangollen," a pair of aristocratic Irish ladies who eloped together to a cottage in North Wales at the end of the eighteenth century. Eleanor Butler (later Lady Eleanor) and Sarah Ponsonby, despite the infuriated objections of their families, set up housekeeping in the Vale of Llangollen. A dozen years after the elopement an article entitled "Extraordinary Female Affection" in the *General Evening Post* reported their story matter-of-factly to the public, observing that

> Miss Butler is tall and masculine, she wears always a riding habit, hangs her hat with the air of a sportsman in the hall, and appears in all respects as a young man if we except the petticoats which she still retains.
>
> Miss Ponsonby, on the contrary, is polite and effeminate, fair and beautiful.[41]

This division into the "male" and the "female," or the "masculine" and the "effeminate" partners, seems partially generated by the choices of the two ladies, and partially imposed from outside. "Miss Ponsonby does the duties and honours of the house, while Miss Butler superintends the gardens and the rest of the grounds," announced the *General Evening Post*. Lady Eleanor kept a daily journal, while Sarah Ponsonby kept an account book full of recipes. The word "elopement," which the paper uses to describe their removal together to Wales, is the standard term employed by all modern biographers (e.g., Mavor, ll). The *Post* noted that "Miss Butler . . . had several offers of marriage, all of which she rejected," and that "Miss Ponsonby, her particular friend and companion, was supposed to be the bar to all matrimonial union."

Over the years the ladies were visited by such admiring luminaries as the playwright Sheridan, the poet Wordsworth, the novelist Sir Walter Scott, and the orator and philosopher Edmund Burke. Scott's son-in-law commented with affectionate if patronizing indulgence on their powdered hair (a style at the time affected by *men*) and their eccentric dress: "heavy blue riding habits, enormous shoes, and men's hats, with their petticoats so tucked up that at the first glance of them, fussing and tottering about their porch in the agony of expectation, we took them for a couple of hazy or crazy old sailors."[42]

The actor Charles Mathews, describing "the dear old gentlemen called Lady Butler and Miss Ponsonby" as he first glimpsed them in the theater audience, likewise commented on their male attire when viewed from the waist up: "As they are seated, there is not one point to distinguish them from men: the dressing and powdering of the hair, their well-starched neckclothes; the upper part of their habits, which they always wear, even at a dinner-party made precisely like men's coats; and regular black beaver men's hats. They looked exactly like two respectable superannuated old clergymen."[43] Mathews found them both charming and ridiculous; he could hardly keep his eyes off them for the first ten minutes of the performance, and he took their presence as a high compliment, since they seldom went to the theater at all. A few weeks later, on invitation, he paid a call, discovering "the dear antediluvian darlings attired for dinner in the same manified dress, with the Croix St. Louis, and other orders, and myriads of large brooches, with stones large enough for snuff-boxes, stuck into their starched neckcloths."[44] He longed, he said, to "put Lady Eleanor under a bell-glass" and bring her home for his wife to look at.

Another distinguished visitor, Prince Puckler Muskaus, recording in a letter the "singularity" of the two ladies, noted the same collection of military medals, and the same striking combination of male (and occasionally female) items of apparel: "Both wore their hair, which is quite full yet combed down straight and powdered, a gentlemen's round hat, a gentleman's cravat and waistcoat, instead of the 'inexpressibles' however, a short *Jupon* and gentlemens' boots. The whole was covered by an overdress of blue cloth of a quite peculiar cut, keeping the middle between a gentleman's overcoat and a lady's riding habit."[45]

"Keeping the middle": the ladies' dress—from their lack of wigs ("both wore their hair") to this "peculiar" overdress, "between a gentleman's overcoat and a lady's riding habit"—declared the "singularity" of their situation. That they cared fiercely about their clothes, and did not merely put on the nearest available or most convenient costume, is attested to by a prolonged negotiation with their tailor, who sends the wrong colored coats ("a Vulgar ordinary Snuff Colour like a Farmer's Coat") with the wrong ornamentation ("a paltry, devlish, Tawdry three-colour'd thing like a Fairing"). "Just looked at them obsessed with fury," writes Lady Eleanor, "the total Mistake of our orders—pack'd them up, and return'd them to him by the Same Coach in which they came" (*Journal*, October 7, 1785; Mavor, 182). Several more returns were necessary before the order was properly filled.

These descriptions date from the ladies' last years, when they had become comfortable caricatures of themselves. Clearly, they were protected by their class and their distinguished acquaintance from the obloquy that might have greeted a less socially acceptable *ménage*, and their dress and appearance, while in some sense "male," were also sufficiently "singular" to make them legible as "keeping the middle," as identifiable cross-dressers rather than women passing for men.

The French novelist Colette, who herself sometimes cross-dressed and had a number of lesbian relationships, was fascinated by the "ladies" and their *Journal*, describing them as "two women who, refusing to be the parody of a couple, pass through, leave out the stage of spurious nuptials and attain the refuge of sleeping together."[46] Colette was especially intrigued by a single reference in the *Journal* to "*the* bedroom and *the* bed where," she wrote, "repose two sweet, foolish creatures, so intensely loyal to a delusion" (127). Notice her choice of phrase: "loyal to a delusion" and "refusing to be the parody of a couple." But parody and parity here are in equipoise; when Colette says the Llangollen ladies refused to be the parody of a couple she means both that they *were* a couple and that they refused to be taken as a (mere) imitation of one. "You were the prudent warden—the masculine element," Colette apostrophizes "stout-hearted Eleanor," while Sarah is described as "the weaker one" who "tightens her arms round the neck of the elder" and "permits herself neither to sob nor to whimper" (Colette, 126–27). But what is most arresting about Colette's transference onto this long-ago relationship is her sense of its demystification and indeed impossibility in the present day.

> Eighteen hundred and thirty one . . . Exactly a century has passed since the death of [Sarah Ponsonby]. Can we possibly, without apprehension, imagine two Ladies of Llangollen in this year of 1930? They would own a car, wear dungarees, smoke cigarettes, have short hair, and there would be a liquor bar in their apartment. Would Sarah Ponsonby still know how to remain silent? Perhaps, with the aid of crossword puzzles. Eleanor Butler would curse as she jacked up the car, and would have her breasts amputated. (Colette, 130–131)

We might contrast the irony and disillusionment of Colette's fantasy of modernity and loss with the almost exactly contemporaneous fantasy of Woolf, whose Orlando, transported to "the present moment" of 1928, "lit a cigarette, puffed for a moment or two in silence" and hopped into her motorcar, only to "change her skirt for a pair of whipcord breeches and leather jacket . . . in less than three minutes" (Woolf, 217–22). But even among the avant-garde in the twenties and the thirties the idealization of "marriage" had a compelling force for lesbians—as it had for Hall's Stephen Gordon.

As has often been noted, Gertrude Stein's sexual attitudes were in a way as Victorian as her prose style was modernist; her relationship with Alice Toklas *was* a "marriage," a bond of exclusivity, fidelity, and domestic partnership in which Stein was the "male" partner (the term is Shari Benstock's[47]). Yet Stein's distinctive mode of dress—the large overcoat, Greek sandals, loose skirts, and (from 1927, when she was 53 years old) cropped hair—should not be confused with the masculine dress assumed by lesbians like Radclyffe Hall, whose alter ego as "John" represented another, and preferred, persona. Toklas's flowered dresses and feminine hats marked her out as "feminine" (whether or not she was "femme" in her private sexual relations), but this model, of the lesbian "marriage" troped on heterosexual "norms," was itself far from the "norm" of lesbian life in the Paris of these years. The flowing Greek robes worn by habituées of Natalie Barney's Temple à l'Amitié, and the cult of Sappho and all things Greek fostered by Barney's set, offered an alternative sartorial mode, a mode of "feminine" elegance that declared itself as artistic, aristocratic, and sexually free-spirited (rather than monogamous). The lesbianism of Paris, in short, was neither exclusively "male" nor exclusively "female" (to use terms that overwhelmingly proclaim their own inadequacy). Nor—and this is important to say— did choice of dress necessarily signal anything like active or passive roles in courtship or in lovemaking. The fiction that the "butch" or the female-to-male cross-dresser is always the seducer was no more true then than it is now.

SIGN, CO-SIGN, TANGENT

> Gender is one of my favorite erotic playgrounds. So you can't assume
> that just because I'm in a dress I left my dick at home.
> Anonymous (a lesbian), "S/M Aesthetic"[48]

If transvestism offers a critique of binary sex and gender distinctions, it is not because it simply makes such distinctions reversible but because it denaturalizes, destabilizes, and defamiliarizes sex and gender *signs*. When a homosexual relation seems to trope off a heterosexual relation, what is revealed is that the signs by which heterosexuality had encoded and recognized itself have been detached from a referent with which those signs are thereby revealed to have had a conventional rather than natural connection.[49] Thus Joan Nestle strongly defends butch-femme relationships against the claim by lesbian-feminists that butch-femme merely reproduces heterosexual models. "Butch-femme relationships, as I experienced them," she writes, "were complex erotic statements, not phony heterosexual replicas. . . . None of the butch women I was with, and this included a passing woman, ever presented themselves to me as men" (100).

In a brief and powerful essay that she says took her forty years to write (she was about forty when she wrote it), Nestle deconstructs the term *Lesbian-feminist* as itself a butch-femme relationship, "butch-femme," that is, "as it has been judged, not as it was." *Lesbian*, she says, bears "the emotional weight that butch does in modern judgment," and *feminist* becomes "the emotional equivalent of the stereotyped femme, the image that can stand the light of day."[50] Many feminists of the 1970's were chary of calling themselves lesbians without the hyphenated adjunct. Nestle critiques the term *role-playing* as it is used to describe butch-femme relationships, since for her the names came after, not before, the roles; "as a femme," she insists, "I did what was natural for me . . . I did not learn a part."

Sue-Ellen Case argues in "Toward a Butch-Femme Aesthetic" for the importance of the lesbian roles of butch and femme as strong models for the theorization of a feminist subject "endowed with the agency for political change, located among women, outside the ideology of sexual difference, and thus the social institution of heterosexuality."[51] Case protests against the aestheticization and appropriation of camp, "the style, the discourse, the *mise en scène* of butch-femme roles" (Case, 286) by avant-garde critics like Susan Sontag, and also against "the critical maneuvers of heterosexual feminist critics who metaphorize butch-femme roles, transvestites and campy dressers into a 'subject who masquerades' " or cross-dresses (Case, 289).

What I want to stress here, from Case's essay, is both the way in which she insists on the suppression of the butch in favor of the femme in film theories of spectatorship like that of Mary Ann Doane, and the close connection Case makes between classism and the feminist critique of butch-femme. (Joan Nestle also makes this last point forcefully in *A*

Restricted Country: upper-class butch-femme figures, like Natalie Barney, Renée Vivien, Vita Sackville-West, and Radclyffe Hall are regarded as style setters and role models; but the butch-femme style of the working-class lesbian, especially the passing female-to-male transvestite, the bull dyke, the bulldagger, makes heterosexual feminists uncomfortable.[52])

"What would you say butch/femme is about?" lesbian columnist Lee Lynch asked a lesbian friend. "Butch," replied the friend, "is knowing how to stand on a streetcorner and catch a femme's eye." "And femme?" "Is spotting the butch and knowing how to get her clothes off." Laughingly, Lynch asked what had happened to the rhetoric of equality. "Are you saying the femme is the active partner?" And her friend laughed back. "Don't you *know* that by now?"[53]

Here it is *difference* that is erotic; difference within sameness, a difference discerned, descried, achieved rather than given. But the mechanism of dislocation, of the detachable part, what I have throughout been calling the anxiety of artifice, becomes the sartorial signature of gay and lesbian dress—and undress. A leather jacket with a plenitude of zippers; a close-cropped haircut; makeup on a man; the absence of makeup on a woman. Taken separately—taken apart—these are signals, like the earring on the proper ear, the pinky ring, the bunch of keys. But the conundrum remains. If one piece, or a couple, of these sartorial signs are present we call it fashion; mainstreamed, it may not even any longer signify erotic style or sexual preference ("Fancy dress has become national costume," notes Quentin Crisp [Crisp, 77]).

Nor is it always easy to "read" butch-femme on the street. "Since at times femmes dressed similarly to their butch lovers," Nestle notes, "the aping of heterosexual roles was not always visually apparent, yet the sight of us was enraging" (102). Onlookers shouted at them, as they walked hand in hand, "Which one of you is the man?" A butch woman was stoned in Washington Square Park for wearing men's clothes. A group of straight people in the 1950s, encountering Nestle as she walked through Central Park, inquired cheerfully of one another, as if she weren't there, "What shall we feed it?" "*It*" is the word that stings, the third category, dehumanized and dehumanizing. Radclyffe Hall describes a similar scenario in *The Well of Loneliness* when Stephen Gordon visits a Bond Street jewelers in search of a ring for the woman she loves:

> People stared at the masculine-looking girl who seemed so intent upon feminine adornments. And someone, a man, laughed and nudged his companion: "Look at that! What is it?"
> "My God! What indeed?"[54]

Times change, styles change, eroticisms reconfigure and resignify. The 1987 edition of a San Francisco guidebook advises tourists visiting the Castro (the city's gay scene) to "Cast aside stereotypes for your trip to San Francisco. Fathers now worry if a son's hair is too short, if his dress is too macho, or his muscles too well-developed, since these are the trademarks of the new breed of San Francisco gay man."[55] One stereotype or "trademark" is here being substituted for another. Likewise, "Eighties butch-femme," declares an article in the gay-lesbian journal *Out/Look*, "—if it accurately can be termed as such—is a self-conscious aesthetic that plays with style and power, rather than an embrace of one's 'true' nature against the constraints of straight society. . . There is no longer a clear one-to-one correspondence between fashion and identity. For many, clothes are transient, interchangeable; you can dress as a femme one day and a butch the next. You can wear a crew-cut along with a skirt. Wearing high heels during the day does not mean you're a femme at night, passive in bed, or closeted on the job."[56]

Nor—is it needless to say?—can this assumption be made about a *man* in a dress, about men in drag. The politics of drag are complicated by persistent divisions within gay male culture about the relationship of "dressing up" to gay male identity. Is the drag queen a misogynistic put-down of women, a self-hating parody, or a complex cultural sign that defies any simple translation into "meaning"?

As Oscar Montero has argued, although "drag may become so incorporated into the fabric of a culture . . . may answer so precisely that culture's own desire that it ceases to provoke and becomes entertainment," as in the case of female impersonators Danny La Rue or Charles Pierce, drag can also be an important destabilizing element that, in performance, "questions the limits of representation." "The imperfection of her imitation is what makes her appealing, what makes her eminently readable. Foolproof imitations of women by men, or men by women, are curious, but not interesting. There has to be some telltale, not the gross five o'clock shadow or the limp wrist of the amateur, but something readable, a foot that is too big, a subtle gesture or the peculiar grain of the voice."[57] Thus "illusionist" Jim Bailey, in his one-man show as Judy Garland, was "unmistakably a man in a dress," according to one critic ("he's no Garland, but he's prettier"),[58] while another noted that "everyone had time to become acquainted with all the ways Bailey does not resemble Garland. Then he moved—a few of her familiar, jerky, offhand motions, her tender way of embracing herself" so that ultimately "he reversed the impressionist's illusion: the longer he was onstage the more he resembled her."[59]

Colette testifies to the same technique of double-reading in her account of cross-dressing in the lesbian Paris of the twenties:

> How timid I was, at that period when I was trying to look like a boy, and how feminine I was beneath my disguise of cropped hair. "Who would take us to be women? Why, women." They alone were not fooled. With such distinguishing marks as pleated shirt front, hard collar, sometimes a waistcoat, and always a silk pocket handkerchief, I frequented a society perishing on the margin of all societies. (Colette, 67)

This emphasis on *reading* and *being read*, and on the deconstructive nature of the transvestite performance, always undoing itself as part of its process of self-enactment, is what makes transvestism theoretically as well as politically and erotically interesting—

at least to me. No critic has made this point more forcefully than the Cuban writer Severo Sarduy, formerly a writer with the journal *Tel Quel*, and author of a series of postmodern novels in which the figure of the transvestite serves as the hinge of a postmodern culture in the process of political and social rupture.[60]

In an essay called "Writing/Transvestism" Sarduy makes explicit the fascination of transvestism as inversion carried to its limits. Citing Lacan (the unconscious is structured like a language subject to its own codes and transgressions; signifiers produce an *effect* that is their sense) and Barthes (metaphor is a sign without content; the symbolic process is one that designates a distance from meaning), Sarduy locates the crux of this new or renewed understanding about the signifier and its displacements in transvestism:

> Transvestism . . . is probably the best metaphor for what writing really is: . . . not a woman *under whose outward appearance* a man must be hiding, a cosmetic mask which, when it falls, will reveal a beard, a rough hard face, but rather *the very fact of transvestism itself*. . . . the coexistence, in a single body, of masculine and feminine signifiers: the tension, the repulsion, the antagonism which is created between them. . . .
> Painted eyebrows and beard; that mask would enmask its being a mask.[61]

Not something beneath the mask, but *the very fact of transvestism* itself. This is the directive to look *at* rather than through the transvestite once again; and it is worth noting that Sarduy does not need to disarticulate his fictive transvestites from their homosexuality in order to do so. He does not read or write transvestism as a figure for something else; for Sarduy, transvestism, like those other, supposedly "exterior" elements—the page, the blank spaces, the horizontality of writing, the writing itself—are the alternative signifiers waiting to be read. "These are the things that a persistent prejudice has considered the exterior face, the obverse of something which must be what that face *expresses*" (Sarduy, 32). But, for Sarduy, what that face expresses, and what transvestism expresses, is *itself*—figure rather than ground, figure as ground, and as the calling into question of the possibility of ground. "Those planes of intersexuality are analogous to the planes of intertextuality . . . planes which communicate on the same exterior." And "that interaction of linguistic textures, of discourses, that dance, that parody, is writing" (Sarduy, 33).

THE REVERSE OF THE MEDAL

That transvestism might be thought to be, in Severo Sarduy's phrase, an *obverse* of something is strikingly represented in gay and lesbian writing from the turn of the century. The erotic novel *Teleny* (1893) by "Oscar Wilde and others"—a novel in which both low- and high-class transvestism play an important part in the plot—has as a subtitle the phrase "The Reverse of the Medal." The British painter Gluck (born Hannah Gluckstein), who dressed throughout her life in men's clothes, depicted, in a painting entitled

"Medallion" (which she liked to call the "YouWe" picture), the profiles of herself and her lover Nesta Obermer as two sides of a coin. In Radclyffe Hall's *The Well of Loneliness*, the elegant patroness of a lesbian salon, Valerie Seymour (a figure clearly modeled after American heiress Natalie Barney), tells the "invert" Stephen Gordon that she has two sides to her "abnormal" nature: "you're appallingly over-sensitive, Stephen—well, and then we get le revers de la médaille; you've all the respectable county instincts of the man who cultivates children and acres" (Hall, 407). The phrase "the reverse of the medal," meaning "the other side of the question" (OED medal 3.b), implies both an alternative and, in some cases, a hidden underside—sometimes a sleazy or questionable one (the "picture of Dorian Gray" is in a way the realization of this image). As such it serves effectively as a figure for transvestism and its secrets.

The figure of speech is brought startlingly and literally to life in Greta Garbo's celebrated transvestite film *Queen Christina* (1933). Riding—astride, in male clothing—through the snowy Swedish woods, Christina comes upon a carriage that has foundered in the drifts. She is taken for a boy by the Spanish nobleman within, who tosses her a coin as a reward for her assistance. It is only when Christina looks at the coin in her hand—a coin that contains her own female image as Queen of Sweden—that she realizes that she has successfully passed as male; the reverse of the medal. Emboldened, she rides on to an inn where she is again read as a young man, and, through a series of comic and erotic misadventures, finds herself sharing a bed with her recent acquaintance on the road. The reverse of the medal—the other side of the coin, we would say—shows her her gender, and her complex sexuality, through the looking glass.[62]

But the reverse of the medal is not just its obverse; it is also the fact of reversibility and artifactuality as such, the dissociation of signs from their purportedly "natural" referents.

WORKING WITH PIECES

Looked at sartorially, and in terms of gender, this description of doubling, mimicry, impropriety, and undecidability fits remarkably well as an account of the theatrical performance mode known as *drag*. Drag is the theoretical and deconstructive social practice that analyzes these structures from within, by putting in question the "naturalness" of gender roles through the discourse of clothing and body parts.

Anthropologist Esther Newton has offered a useful structuralist analysis of drag that turns on such oppositions as inside/outside (or underneath/outside), back/front (or face/ass), claiming that "the gay world, via drag, says that sex-role behavior is an appearance; it is 'outside.' It can be manipulated at will." Drag is thus another way of reversing the medal.

Newton describes two fundamental levels on which the sartorial system can be manipulated by drag performers and other gender benders. *Within* the system, "inside" clothes (underwear, lingerie) can be feminine while "outside" clothes are masculine; this method, as she points out, is more commonly used by heterosexual transvestites than by drag artists. Or sex-role referents within the sartorial system may be deliberately mixed or self-contradictory: an earring, lipstick, high heels, and so on, worn with traditionally "masculine" clothing. Onstage, this method is called, significantly, "working with (feminine) pieces"—so that the artifactuality of the "feminine" (or the "feminine piece") is overtly acknowledged and brought to consciousness.

The second level on which drag functions theatrically involves an exploitation of the opposition between construction and essence. Here too detachable parts come into play: the wig, the "breast," the falsetto voice are, one by one, exposed as artifice and (at least temporarily) discarded. Clearly this is in one sense a mode of corporeal and gender reassurance: "I (still) have a man's voice, a penis, a flat chest," though I can play at having—and therefore in a sense "really" have—what women have, *as well*. As Newton points out, this assertion that "appearance is an illusion" works in two simultaneously contradictory ways, by declaring that the outside (the performer's clothing) is feminine and his inside (the body inside the clothing) is masculine, and, at the same time, that the outside (the performer's body) is masculine and his inside (his "essence" or "self") is feminine.[63]

As part of its mechanism as a political theater, drag institutionalizes the destabilizing gesture—as in the traditional doffing of the wig, at the close of *Victor/Victoria* or of Ben Jonson's *Epicoene*. It is a reading technique—a technique for double-reading gender on and off the stage. But drag is preeminently a male-to-female art, as the author of "The Anguished Cry of an 80's Fem: 'I Want to Be a Drag Queen,' " complained: "When lesbians sponsor strip shows, or other fem erotic performances, it is very difficult to 'code' it as lesbian, to make it feel queer. The result looks just like a heterosexual performance, and lesbian audiences don't respond to it as subversively sexual, specifically ours."[64] Can lesbians—and "male impersonators," and straight or bisexual women interested in destabilizing sex- and gender-roles—"work with pieces"? And which "pieces"?

Two "pieces" of the vestimentary puzzle have been of special interest, both to gays and to straights, as powerful—and powerfully ambivalent—floating signifiers of erotic style in the period since the First World War. They are not articles of clothing, *per se*, but rather what a department store would call "accessories"—in this case, accessories both before and after the "fact" of lesbianism: the monocle, and the cigarette, cigarette holder, or cigar.

LE MONOCLE DE MA TANTE

Both the elegance and the pathos of lesbian Paris in the twenties were evoked by the painter Romaine Brooks, whose extraordinary portraits of herself, the Duchesse de Clermont-Tonnerre (Elizabeth de Gramont), the artist Gluck (as "Peter, a Young English

Girl"), and Una Troubridge in male attire, offer perhaps the best visual icons of transvestite high style in the period. The tuxedo, the cigarette, the cropped haircut, and the monocle are the most recognizable and readable signs of the lesbian culture of Paris.

The high-fashion clothing of women like Radclyffe Hall, the Marquise de Belbeuf (Colette's lover), Romaine Brooks, and Una Troubridge was in part an extension of the costume of the male dandy. It declared at once its difference from, and its alliance with, masculine social and economic power; it was for these women also a privileged marker of class, the more so because female-to-male cross-dressing was explicitly forbidden by an ordinance of 1800, strictly enforced a century later by the Paris prefect of police (Benstock, 48). Upper-class women could travel by private coach in their tuxedos and cravats; women of the middle and lower classes for whom conformity to prevailing standards meant cross-dressing only covertly and in the evening had to conceal themselves in long wraps en route to lesbian bars. As for those who cross-dressed to pass rather than as an intermittent pleasure, their transvestism was of yet a different order. Radclyffe Hall as "John" (and, in London, Vita Sackville-West as "Julian," wearing men's clothes and smoking a cigarette as she strolled with her female lover through the streets of Mayfair[65]) represented choice and privilege, however infused with a rhetoric of pathos. "Missy," the Marquise de Belbeuf, "lived in the Passy quarter," writes Janet Flanner, "always as a man." "She always wore men's clothes, indeed she wore quite a lot of them, which made her look plump."[66] When she attended a family funeral in a mourning veil and a black dress, her young relations complained that she "looked like a man dressed as a woman," and begged her to resume her usual male attire. In *The Pure and the Impure* Colette gives "Missy" the interesting pseudonym of La Chevalière, which suggests not only horsemanship but also the most famous of all French transvestites, the eighteenth-century Chevalier d'Eon.[67]

"Some of them wore a monocle," Colette writes affectionately of these "mannish women," a "white carnation in the buttonhole, took the name of God in vain, and discussed horses competently" (Colette, 73). What she is describing is not only a sartorial, but also an erotic, style.

As for Brooks and Troubridge, their images linger not so much in words as in Brooks's own compelling portraits, where, once again, the detachable part as floating signifier of gender is on display. For Brooks, the top hat; for Una Troubridge, the monocle, the sign of the upper-class dandy. In a learned exposition on "Eyeglasses" that traces the history of eyewear from the Renaissance to the contact lens, the *Encyclopaedia Britannica* observes succinctly in the penultimate paragraph that "The monocle is an affectation."[68] Dorothy Sayers's Lord Peter Wimsey, Djuna Barnes's Baron Felix Volkbein: the squinting, monocled aristocrat declares his class (and, in some eyes, his decadence). He also declares his gender. Is it possible that this extravagantly beribboned piece of eyewear represents yet another displacement upward of the single and singular male organ—so frequently itself called "one-eyed" in contemporary macho fiction of the Mailer-Roth variety?

Shari Benstock describes Brooks's portrait of Una Troubridge as "angry and self-tortured"; "her right eye enlarged and made unreal by a monocle, producing an asymmetrical and frightening gaze" (Benstock, 304–5). Radclyffe Hall, too, wore a monocle and carried a cigarette holder (Benstock, 35). Whatever the symbolism consciously intended by the wearers and bearers of these social and sexual props, the effect was a complicated combination of class and gender; just as a man with a monocle was coming to be thought of as effete, a woman with a monocle was regarded as a sign of defiant pathos. Through this addition both declared, indeed flaunted, both what they "had" and what they lacked.

This outfit—monocle, male attire, (and, often, a cigar)—became a kind of signature in film as well as society: Lil Dagover as the German cabaret performer in Fritz Lang's *Doctor Mabuse* (1922); Sandra Shawn in *Blood Money* (1933), even Betty Grable singing "Burlington Bertie" in the 1947 musical *Mother Wore Tights* in tux, top hat—and the by now inevitable monocle.[69]

But the monocle is also an ideal instance of the denaturalizing of the sign in the context of gender and (homo)sexuality. This is an apt occasion to note the way in which what Lacan calls "the phallus" differs from the anatomical penis. The monocle looks nothing like a penis (or a phallus). It can be put on (inserted in the eye socket) or taken off, left to dangle, propped up imperiously as a sign of attentiveness. An indication at once of supplement and lack, both instrumental and ornamental, connoting weakness (in the eye) and strength (social position, as well as class and style), the monocle both *reflects* and *peers into* or *through*. Simultaneously a signifier of castration (detachable, artifactual, made to be put on and taken off) and of empowerment, the monocle when worn by a *woman* emphasizes, indeed parodies, the contingent nature of the power conferred by this instrumental "affectation."

Freud's essay on "The Psychogenesis of a Case of Homosexuality in a Woman" (1920) contains a curious image, interpolated by the analyst, of the patient's apparent indifference to his exposition: "Once when I expounded to her a specially important part of the theory, one touching her nearly, she replied in an inimitable tone, 'How very interesting,' as though she were a *grande dame* being taken over a museum and glancing through her lorgnon at objects to which she was completely indifferent."[70] A lorgnon is not a monocle, but a pair of spectacles on a stick, the "femininized" version of the peering instrument. It is perhaps significant that Freud imagines her *not* as cross-dressed but as coldly ladylike, *not* as masculine but as feminine. But—or and—we should note that the monocle—and, indeed, the lorgnon—is a preeminently detachable part.

Perhaps even more relevant to the question of the monocle squint is Lacan's discussion of anamorphosis and the scopic field. An anamorphosis in optics is an image distorted so that it can be viewed without distortion only from a special angle or with a special instrument. Anamorphic art thus puts the stability of the viewer's position in question—there is no sure *ground* on which to stand to view "correctly." Instead all seeing, and everything seen, is revealed as radically contingent, depending upon the angle from which we look, the instrument through which we gaze. And Lacan's name for this is *travesty*.

> Generally speaking, the relation between the gaze and what one wishes to see involves a lure. The subject is presented as other than he is, and what one shows him is not what he wishes to see.
>
> The lure plays an essential function. . . . It is not something else that seizes us at the very level of clinical experience, when, in relation to what one might imagine of the attraction to the other pole as conjoining masculine and feminine, we apprehend the prevalence of that which is presented as *travesty*. It is no doubt through the mediation of masks that the masculine and the feminine meet in the most acute, most intense way. . . .
>
> Only the subject—the human subject, the subject of the desire that is the essence of man. . . . knows how to play with the mask as that beyond which there is the gaze.[71]

It should come as no surprise, then, to find the pop star Madonna, ever acute to the power of travesty, desire, and the duplicitous masks of gender, sporting a monocle (as well as a pinstriped suit strategically slashed to let her peach satin brassiere poke through, another literalization of the "double-breasted suit") in her 1990 "Blond Ambition" tour. The pun on blond-blind reinforces the point; in the country of the blind, the one-eyed man is king. Once again Madonna, unerringly, puts her finger on the detachable part. The very ludicrousness of the monocle assured its high visibility as a status symbol, here a retro-symbol of a fantasized and dated patriarchy assumed and transumed by the pansexual material girl. But in mimicking and appropriating effete male power Madonna also reincarnates an earlier moment in this century when women wore monocles to assert sexual difference *within*. "The monocled women in tuxedos," the generation "that had been 'liberated' to dress, talk, smoke and act like men" (Benstock, 307) —a generation that included not only Radclyffe Hall, Una Troubridge, and Romaine Brooks but the cross-dressing Dolly Wilde (niece of Oscar), Janet Flanner, Elizabeth de Gramont, and Lucie Delarue-Mardrus—ironically reinscribed the "male" (or the pseudo-male) as the position of power. Terry Castle has brilliantly suggested that Janet Flanner in a monocle is the model of, and for, the signature portrait of Eustace Tilley on the cover of the *New Yorker*, so that the *New Yorker* is in some sense "originally" a lesbian magazine, however that identity was masked.[72]

THIS IS NOT A PIPE

Havelock Ellis's survey of "Sexual Inversion in Women," published in 1895, noted that sexually inverted women had not only a "pronounced tendency to adopt male attire" and a "capacity for athletics" but also a "pronounced taste for smoking." [73] Even if we leave aside for the moment the interesting inversion here of cause and effect (do propensities for male attire and smoking "cause" sexual inversion, or are they merely cultural symptoms and signposts?), we can readily see the way in which Ellis (and others) uneasily read the crossover between social and sexual liberation.

The cigar as a theatrical or cinematic prop became, not very subtly, the test of "manhood"—a test failed by Julie Andrews in her disguise as "Victor," the supposed "female impersonator" of *Victor/Victoria*, while in the uproarious black-made film *Boy! What a Girl!* (1947) Tim Moore, also cast as a female impersonator, is constantly in search of a cigar. Doubtless, even in the movies, a cigar was sometimes only a cigar. But a cigarette in the mouth of a woman in pants was nonetheless enough to give some pause. Freud, himself a roller of big cigars, saw smoking (in males) as a sign of "constitutional intensification of the erotogenic significance of the labial region" in the proto-narcissistic, auto-erotic child. " 'It's a pity I can't kiss myself,' [the aggressively sucking child] seems to be saying."[74] Studio portraits of Dietrich as the nightclub singer in *Morocco* (1930) stress the completeness of the ensemble: top hat, tails, cigarette, and ironic stare. Colette describes herself in the same regalia, again caught by the camera's eye: "photographs show me wearing a stiff mannish collar, necktie, short jacket over a straight skirt, a lighted cigarette between two fingers."[75]

The cigarette in this period is a sign of sophistication and glamor; thus was a whole generation seduced. It is fascinating to see this tacit juxtaposition of "mannishness" and smoking recapitulated in a recent tobacco company advertising campaign that was to have been aimed at "virile females"—by which was meant not urban intellectuals but blue-collar women aged 18 to 24. The R.J. Reynolds company's plans to market Dakota cigarettes to these women were outlined in a proposal called "Project V.F.," for virile female. And what is, or was, a V.F.? "A woman with no education beyond high school, whose favorite television roles are 'Roseanne' and 'evening soap opera (bitches),' and whose chief aspiration is 'to get married in her early 20's and spend her free time 'with her boyfriend doing whatever he is doing.' "[76] Not, then, overtly, a cigarette for lesbians.

William Safire's column "On Language" in the *New York Times* explored, with mingled delight and consternation, the notion of the "virile female." As Safire noted, the intended smoker of Dakota was the opposite of the "feminists attracted to Philip Morris' Virginia Slims, with its slogan 'You've Come a Long Way, Baby.' "[77] The Dakota smoker would be someone who "enjoys events like tractor pulls and rodeos, fiercely but tenderly stands by her man, dresses like Dolly Parton on a fine day in the country and smokes Marlboro" (Safire, 18). In what sense, he asks, is such a woman accurately described as *virile*? And he answers his own question without ever using the l-word, describing "the critical issue" as a syntactical one:

[C]an you use *virile woman* without committing an oxymoronic act? do adjective and noun absurdly conflict?

No. *Masculine woman* is an acceptable phrase, as is *effeminate man*; what is meant here, however, is different from a female who acts like a man. A *virile woman*, as I interpret the promotional message, is "a woman who associates herself with activities and images formerly considered of primarily male interest." (Safire, 18)

And as for the male of the species:

> What is the equivalent modifier to apply to men? If you can call a woman *virile* without impeaching her femininity, what is a non-effeminate word for a man who has the attributes of womanliness? *Sensitive*. (Safire, 19)

The (hetero)sexual politics of this linguistic analysis are striking—the implication, for example, that to "call a woman *virile* without impeaching her femininity" is a universally (and commercially) desirable feat. *Masculine* (for women) and *effeminate* (for men) are advertising and journalistic negatives, but *virile* and *sensitive* are somehow acceptable. (Is it imaginable that either Safire or R.J. Reynolds has done field research on this question? I would like to see figures on the number of non-lesbian 18- to 24-year old women who were happy with the designation *virile*.) Safire's analysis also occludes, even as it glancingly notes, the issue of class: the *virile woman*, tractor pull and all, is clearly lower or lower-middle class. To what class can the *sensitive man* belong, if not to the yuppie-baby-boomer? And what cigarette, if any, does he smoke? Presumably neither Marlboro nor Virginia Slims.

Furthermore, just as Dakota was being prepared for—and subsequently withdrawn from—test-marketing, the fashion pages of the high style magazines like *Taxi* and *Details* began to feature women smokers—not at tractor pulls but on the streets of Paris and New York. Actress Daryl Hannah was pictured in *Interview* wearing a black teddy and thigh-high boots, and smoking a cigar. An advertisement for designer Donna Karan's DKNY line featured a model with shoulder length hair and dark glasses, wearing a pants suit, and smoking a long cigar. "Smoking," notes Mark Crispin Miller, "has a strong erotic connotation. ... A cigaret is a sign of sophistication and power."[78] The femme fatale of forties and fifties films, from Joan Crawford to Lauren Bacall, glamorized smoking for women—for *straight* women. "A man's expectations are harder than ever to satisfy," says Miller. "It's not just the pressure of the job, but the unprecedented difficulty of having an erotic life that makes women smoke." But what happened to the *butch*-femme fatale? The high-style lesbian with the cigarette holder has become a quotation, or a citation, of an earlier time safely "glamorized" by nostalgia. Between the *virile female* who fiercely but tenderly stands by her man and the fashion model flaunting her cigar, the bifurcation of class (upper/lower) has subsumed and made invisible the question of sexual orientation and erotic style.

Transvestism *is* a vestimentary code, in Barthes's sense, a rhetorical system of significa-tion. But it is also a code in the sense invoked by Hugh Whitemore's play about the gay mathematician and cryptographer Alan Turing: a secret or private language that must keep changing in order to avoid being broken, or broken into, by those whom it seeks to elude or escape. Once a code is cracked or broken, it is defunct; it no longer functions as a code. Gay transvestism, transvestism in gay subcultures, from the New Orleans drag show to the Parisian salon, encodes not only identity, but also eroticism and desire. It speaks from the borderline, a borderline that is always shifting, as the parameters of Turing's code kept shifting to avoid detection.

One of the most visible displacements of gay transvestism, in fact, is the vestimentary code that we call "fashion," both high and low, from the designs of Jean-Paul Gaultier, incorporating the corset as an item of outerwear for Madonna's onstage costumes and for the season's couturier coats ("She loves the corset, and I love it, too," Gaultier told the *New York Times*. "Her look is so 'me' "), to the whole concept of "punk," once a term for a male homosexual lover, now a sartorial style for men *and* women, by no means all of them gay or lesbian: close-cropped or spiky hair, leather, black, and chains. Ironically, the relationship between transvestism and gay identity, the articulation of gay and lesbian personhood through the vehicle of cross-dressing, has in a way come full circle from the molly houses of the eighteenth century—where men went to dress and gossip like women, and to make love to one another—and the sartorial self-proclamation of "inverts," male and female, at the turn of the present century. In fashion the migration can be traced from gay to straight at least as readily as from straight to gay. Lesbian styles of the twenties—men's formal dress, top hats and tails—popularized onstage by entertainers like Marlene Dietrich and Judy Garland, became high-fashion statements, menswear for women re-sexualized as straight (as well as gay) style.

"Voguing," the dance craze of the 1980's, celebrated in Madonna's top-of-the-charts song and video, originated in gay fashion houses in Harlem, and in the exaggerated poses of models and mannequins. "Until now it has been performed mostly by male transvestites," reported *Time* magazine, describing it as "an attitudinal affectation that mixes model-like poses with the athleticism of break dancing and the wry sophistication of gay humor." "Voguing began in the 1960's in Harlem, where transvestites parodied Seventh Avenue by calling their social clubs houses and holding annual balls that featured the dance style."[79]

A film made about these fashion "houses," *Paris is Burning*, a lively and perspicacious documentary about gay black and Latino men who compete in drag balls, was the hit of the art cinema world in 1991. Jennie Livingston's extraordinary film shows drag performers in a wide variety of stage roles, from Patti LaBelle to cardiganed college students, runway models, and aristocrats. Performer Pepper Labeija, who is first seen in ballroom drag, all gold and flounces, is then interviewed at home in his men's clothes. Asked to describe himself, he says with weary bravura, "I am Pepper Labeija, the Legendary Mother of the house of Labeija." The ball subculture divides its members into "children" (younger performers), "legends" (experienced drag artists who have won trophies), and a "mother" and "father"; the older generation in general is more flamboyant than the young, who have in some cases had breast implants or sex change surgery; Terence Rafferty, in an enthusiastic review in the *New Yorker* (appropriately titled "Realness"), calls them "Method actors of drag."

Where Pepper Labeija declares, pointedly, "I've been a man, and I've been a man who emulated a woman. I've never been a woman," some of the younger generation seem determined to cross over the line. As one young performer asserts, "I would like to be a spoiled rich white girl." "Realness" is indeed the issue here; realness not only in the drag world, but also in the world it mirrors and critiques. As Rafferty suggests, "The most self-aware of the gay men we see here revel in the ironies of their social and sexual identities." "Virtually every aspect of this community of underdogs imitates some perceived value of the white middle-class heterosexual society from which they feel excluded."[80]

We might note that in fashion the "original" is often the vision and handiwork of gay designers. It is the "copy" that often makes its way down the chain of style and fashion signifiers. *Crossover* style, the mainstreaming of pants for women, bright colors and makeup for men, women wearing men's cologne and men wearing bikini underpants—above all, style as self-conscious *parody*, not only in drag clubs but in fashion magazines and rock groups, has rendered gay sartorial difference again almost invisible. So the borderline again shifts; as outsiders become insiders, a new inside, a new code, is designed for use.

But this emphasis on the mainstreaming of gay style and the influence of gays and lesbians in the worlds of fashion, art, and society should not obscure the fact that men and women who are read as gay, and as gay cross-dressers—drag queens, transvestites, butches, nellies, dykes on bikes—are often subjected to cultural oppression, stigmatization, discrimination, and vilification, all the behaviors that have come to be grouped under the term "homophobia." When the word "homophobia" appears in a major headline on the front page of the "Living Arts" section of the *New York Times*, it is clear that even the mainstream is becoming aware of "hostile actions against homosexuals" and "anti-gay bias."[81] There are still penalties imposed on those who question boundaries when there are vested interests at stake—especially, perhaps, sexual and erotic boundaries. Thus Marshall Kirk and Hunter Madsen's book *After the Ball: How America Will Conquer Its Fear and Hatred of Gays in the 90s* angered many in the gay and lesbian community by proposing that gay people alter their behavior and lifestyle to make themselves less threatening to straights. Kirk and Madsen, both of whom are gay, were widely perceived as policing a boundary, promulgating a new code of behavior and assimilation.[82]

Yet, as Whitemore's Alan Turing remarks, "In the long run, it's not breaking the code that matters—it's where you go from there. That's the real problem." A problem, and an opportunity. Looking back over the more than twenty years since the 1969 Stonewall Rebellion, we sometimes tend to forget that that rebellion, which ushered in a new era in gay life, was led by transvestites and drag queens. The transvestites involved in the Stonewall Riots and radical drag groups like the Sisters of Perpetual Indulgence have demonstrated that there is real political energy to be obtained from reversing—rather than disseminating—gender signs. And transvestism has been the site of activism in part because it is activism in sight. The proud self-assertion of sartorial and erotic difference has produced conflict both within the gay and lesbian community and between gays and straights, but it has also made visible not only overly anti-gay prejudice but also the masked and gentrified homophobia that sometimes passes for tolerance. Some years ago Esther Newton asked pertinently in "The Myth of the Mannish Lesbian," "Why should we as feminists deplore or deny the existence of masculine women or effeminate men? Are we not against assigning specific psychological or social traits to a particular biology? And should we not support those among us, butches and queens, who still bear the brunt of homophobia?"[83] These questions, posed in 1984, have more urgency than ever today.

Are "lipstick lesbians" abandoning a long and important commitment to political visibility, or are they rather indulging the freedoms gained by an earlier generation of "out" dykes in short hair and leather? Questions like these divide the lesbian community, as terms like "lifestyle lesbianism" replace, for the moment at least, the "lesbian-feminism" of the early seventies and eighties. "Even the *Wall Street Journal*," writes Arlene Stein in *Out/Look*, "reports that 'lipstick' lesbians are clashing with flannel-shirted 'crunchies' in the hallowed halls of Yale" (Stein, 38). The doubly privileged site of this "clash" (both Yale and the *Wall Street Journal*) seems to make the need for some difference within more imperative.

As the idea of "lesbianism" becomes more visible and indeed—however temporarily—more fashionable, from the playful clowning of Madonna and Sandra Bernhard ("are they or aren't they?") and the practiced evasiveness of k.d. lang ("You can analyze me to death, but it's just that I grew up as a tomboy and I prefer my hair being short and I love Nudie suits") to the frankness of Martina Navratilova (who recuperates for lesbians in tennis, to some degree, the Billy Jean King lesbian scandal of some years ago), questions about "political correctness," erotic style, and responsibility to the lesbian community continue to be asked. Is k.d. lang, with her "legions of dyke-devotees," copping out when she avoids coming out? "When she calls herself a tomboy, and says that she doesn't care whether men or women are attracted to her, is it simply a ploy to maintain her cover?" (Stein, 40). What are the politics of cross-dressing in a fashion-conscious era where you are what you wear?

As Colette noted, "The seduction emanating from a person of uncertain or dissimulated sex is powerful" (Colette, 76). But what is seductive for Colette, or for rock fans, or for the readers of *Out/Look* or *On Our Backs* is offensive and threatening to people like Senator Jesse Helms. Thus, among the showpieces of the Robert Mapplethorpe exhibit excoriated by Helms and others for its images of gay male sexuality was an arresting self-portrait of the photographer in which he appears as a transvestite. On the cover of his book *Certain People: A Book of Portraits* is a self-portrait of Mapplethorpe in a black leather jacket and a dark shirt, with a cigarette dangling from his mouth; on the back cover is a second self-portrait. "This time Mapplethorpe's hair is teased into a woman's hairdo; his eyes are open and his lips parted in an unspeakable expression of softness, imploring, and—perhaps—fear. His upper torso is bare and strikingly resembles a woman's breasts. These photographs are repeated, in reversed order, near the center of *Certain People*. . . . It is as though Mapplethorpe tells us that every portrait in the book is some combination, some special alloy, of the two 'pure' sexual postures that make up its covers, the two ends of his spectrum."[84]

Mapplethorpe compared his own art to that of Warhol and Duchamp, two significant influences on his career: "Certainly Warhol comes from Duchamp, which is the opening up of a way of thinking, of possibilities."[85] One of the most famous and influential creations of Duchamp was his female alter ego Rrose Sélavy, who was Duchamp himself in drag—her name a multiple pun in French on art, eros and life. The portrait of Rrose Sélavy appeared on perfume bottles designed by Duchamp, bearing the ironic legend "Eau de Voilette" [veil water], and her name was signed to other Duchamp-made artifacts; a wonderful portrait of Rrose Sélavy by Man Ray shows the artist in a wig, makeup, necklaces and a high-style ruffled dress and hat.[86] The famous Chris Makos photograph of Warhol, "Altered Image," in a blond wig, makeup, jeans and a necktie, his hands coyly hiding his crotch, is in fact Warhol dressed in homage to Rrose Sélavy. For Duchamp, Warhol and Mapplethorpe it was in part the figure of the transvestite—of the artist as transvestite—which made for "the opening up of a way of thinking, of possibilities." Possibilities for rupture and for the reconfiguration of the cultural Imaginary, but not without cost. It was Mapplethorpe's vision of the instability of the boundary that threatened. "The message that Mapplethorpe delivers," wrote David Joselit in the exhibition catalogue, "is that the experience of any masculine or feminine identity is the sensation of an unstable, constantly readjusted succession of poses. In his work, the crossing of boundaries between aggression—or phallic drive—and submission is not simplistically developed as an opposition between masculinity and femininity, it is experienced as a drama that takes place within the entire range of sexual identities—in man and woman, and in homosexual and heterosexual alike" (Joselit, 21). The portrait of Mapplethorpe as a transvestite—which confronted the spectator as she or he entered the gallery,[87] stood on—and stood for—that borderline, that boundary being questioned as it was crossed.

Vestimentary codes, clothing as a system of signification, speak in a number of registers: class, gender, sexuality, erotic style. Part of the problem—and part of the pleasure and danger of decoding—is in determining which set of referents is in play in each scenario. For decoding itself is an erotics—in fact, one of the most powerful we know. But any erotics is also anxiety producing, and this kind of cultural and political anxiety often has real and adverse consequences for those who are testing the boundaries. The difficulty, the challenge, and the interest posed by the complex interrelationship between transvestism and gay identity lie in simultaneously tracking the dissemination of the signifiers of sex and gender and in combating the oppressive effects of institutionalized binarity. For in political and social terms, in the lives of real people, male and female, straight and gay, there is finally no "free play of the signifier." There is play, plenty of play, but ultimately nothing—and especially not sexual lifestyles—is free.

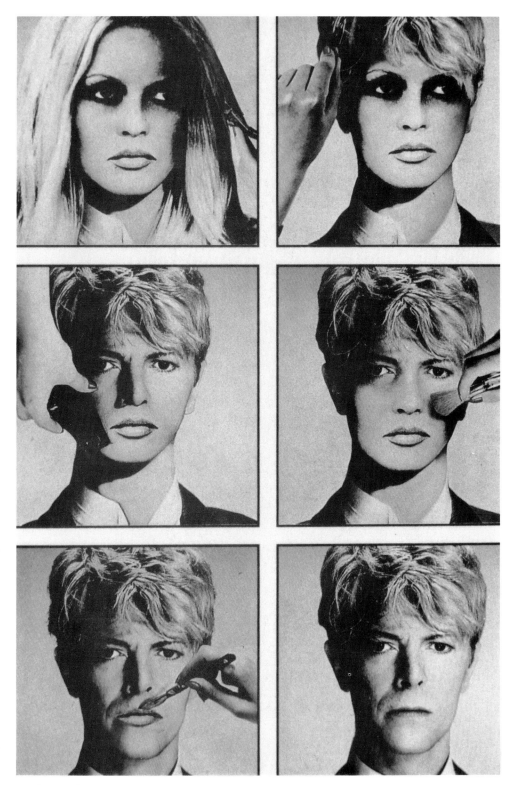

Make-Up for Beginners: Brigitte Bardot to David Bowie.

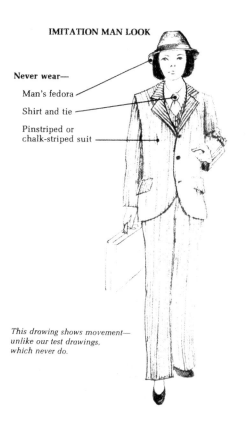

An early diatribe against gender confusion. *Hic Muller: or, The Man-Woman,* pamphlet published in London, 1620.

IMITATION MAN LOOK

Never wear—

Man's fedora

Shirt and tie

Pinstriped or chalk-striped suit

This drawing shows movement—unlike our test drawings, which never do.

Sartorial pitfalls for the woman executive. From John T. Molloy, *The Woman's Dress for Success Book,* 1977.

Opposite page: A Venetian lady of fashion with skirt covering her breeches. Breeches were a common costume for courtesans of the period. Engraving, c. 1590.

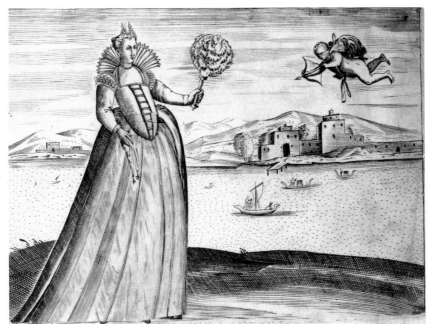

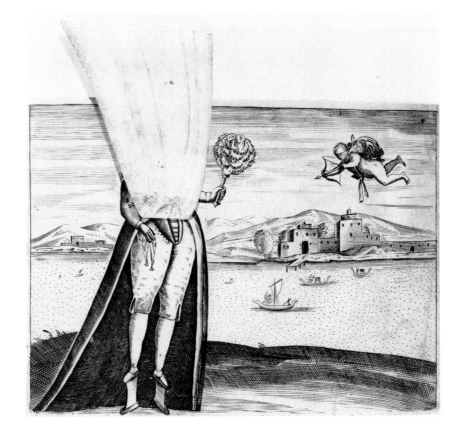

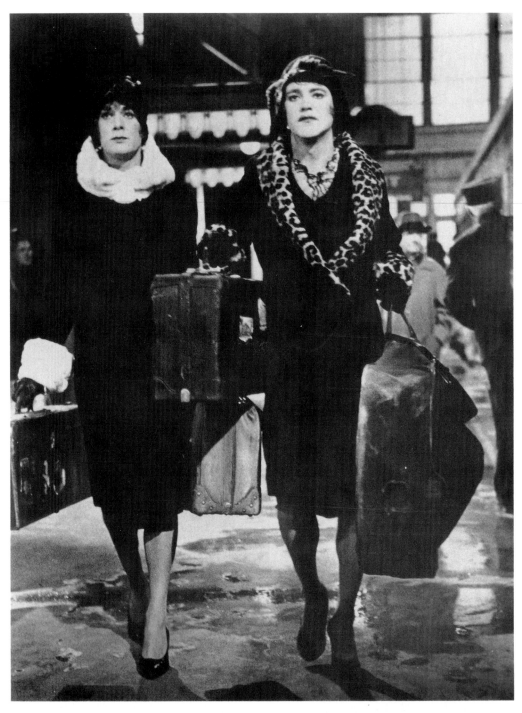

Hot to trot. Tony Curtis and Jack Lemmon as Josephine and Daphne in *Some Like It Hot* (1959).

Star-crossed cinema.

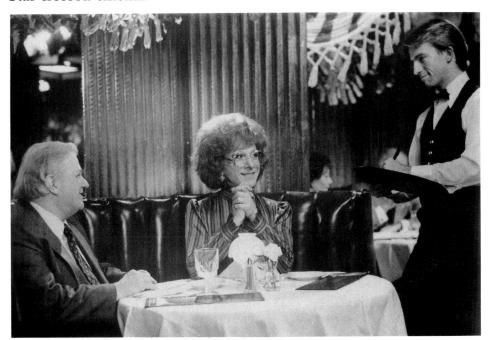

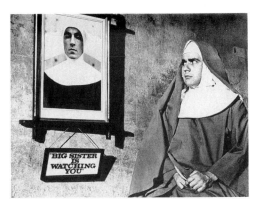

Clockwise from top: Dustin Hoffman, *Tootsie* (1982); Cary Grant, *Bringing Up Baby* (1938); Barbra Streisand, *Yentl* (1983); Peter Cook and Dudley Moore, *Bedazzled* (1967).

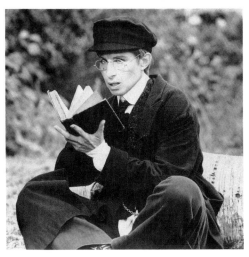

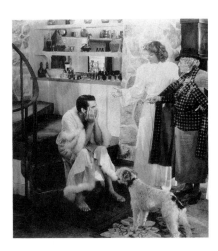

ress up
ur Shakespeare.

rah Bernhardt as
mlet.

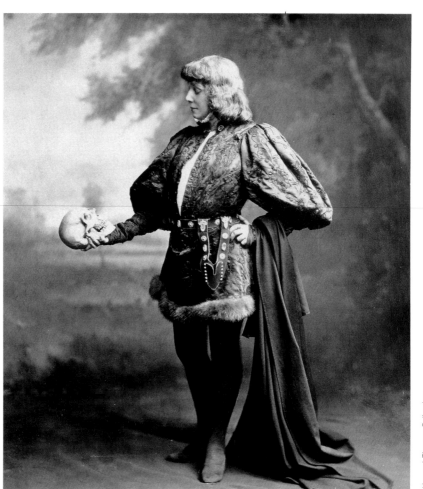

: Charlotte
hman as Ro-
; right: Cather-
Macready as
ock.

osite page: The
ng Laurence
ier as Katherina
he Taming of the
w.

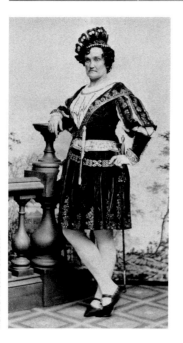

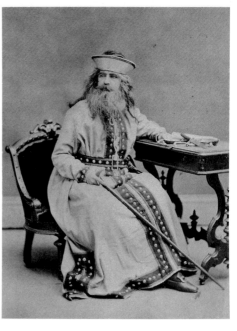

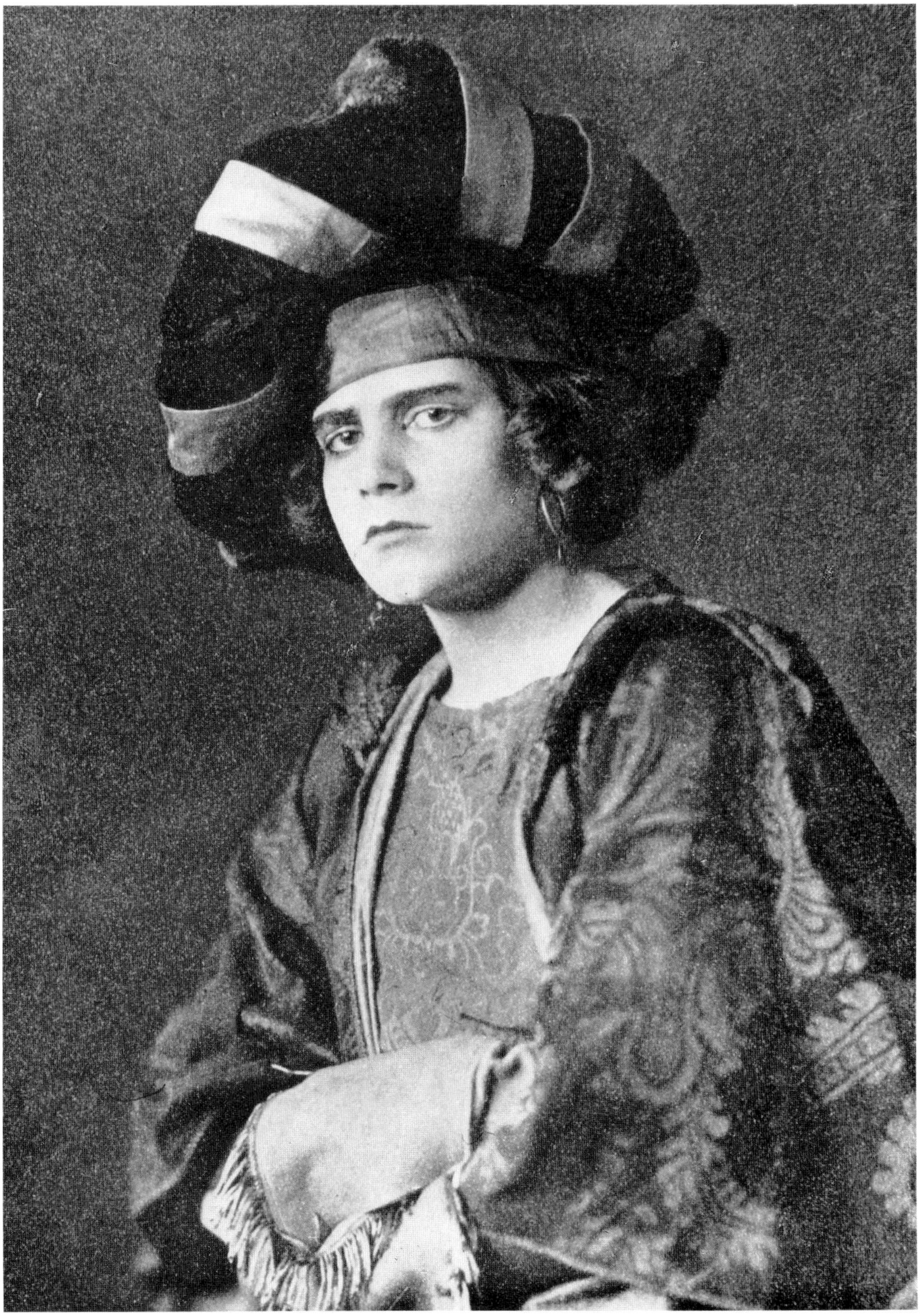

Hasty Pudding Theatricals, Harvard College.

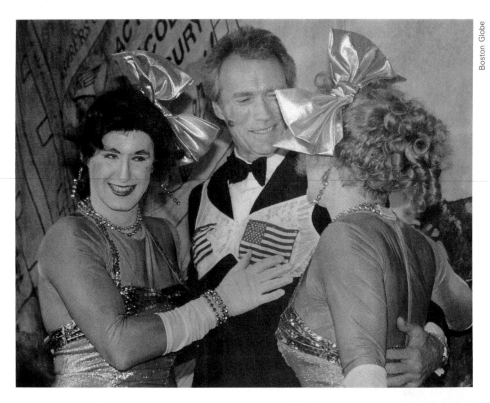

Clint Eastwood, receiving his award as Hasty Pudding Man of the Year, with cast members of the 1991 show, *Safari Sagoodi*.

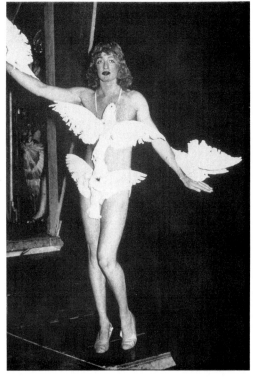

George H. Earle, IV, as the Dove Queen, *Come Across*, 1937.

Opposite page, clockwise from top left: John Warren, Amos Mason, and George Shattuck as ballerinas, 1862; Warren, Mason, and Shattuck thirty years later; "Creepy Twins," date unknown.

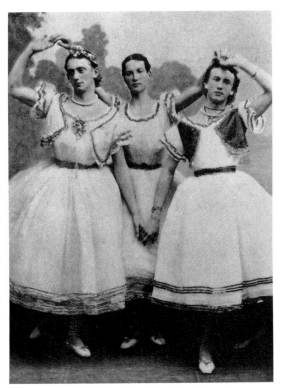

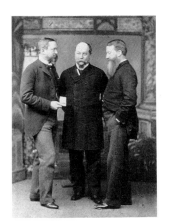

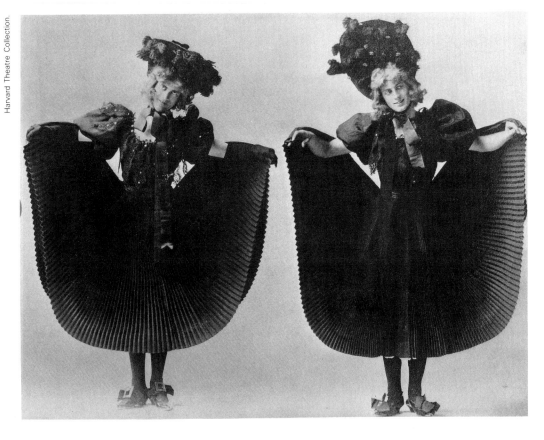

Detachable parts.

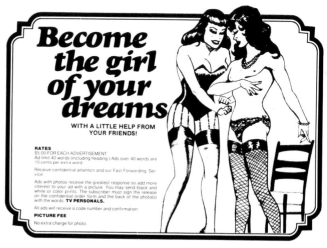

Mary Martin and Myron McCormick, *South Pacific.*

Young man getting dressed for the Hasty Pudding show.

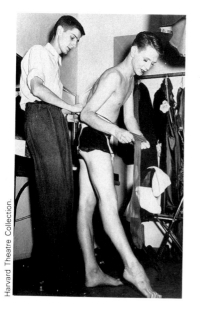

Ad from transvestite magazine.

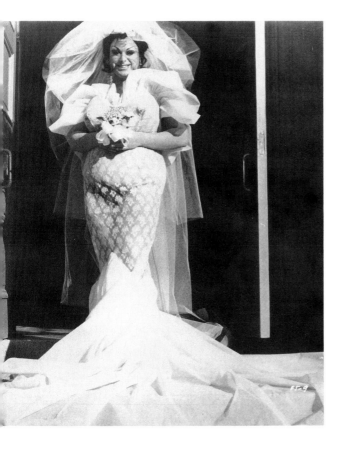

Divine in a wedding dress, from *Female Trouble*.

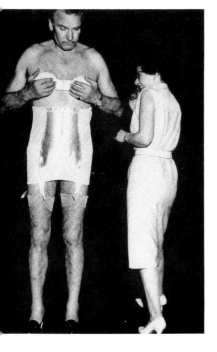

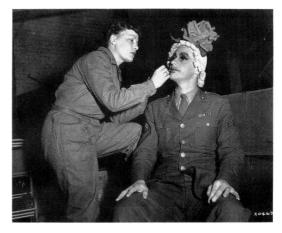

Above: A WAC lieutenant demonstrating "how to create a female soldier for a show" to an audience of soldiers in London during World War II.

Left: Laurence Olivier being fitted for a drag role.

Women of fashion.

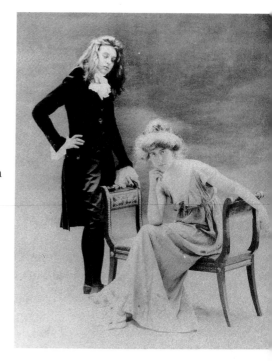

Renée Vivien dressed as a page, with Natalie Barney.

Katharine Hepburn on the set of *Sylvia Scarlett* (1935).

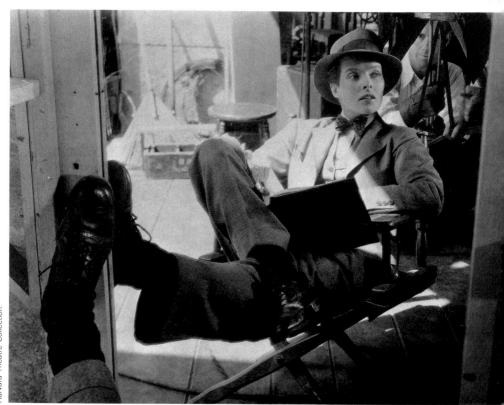

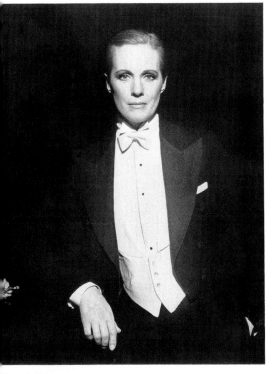

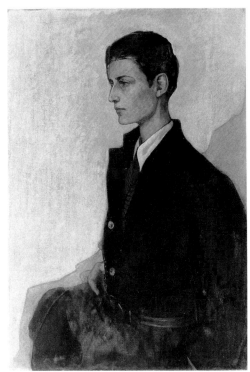

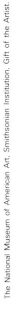

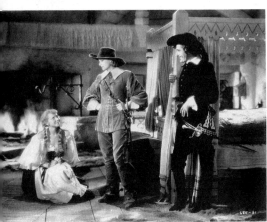

Clockwise from top left: Julie Andrews in *Victor/Victoria:* the artist Gluck as *Peter (A Young English Girl)*, by Romaine Brooks; Greta Garbo in the title role of *Queen Christina* (1933).

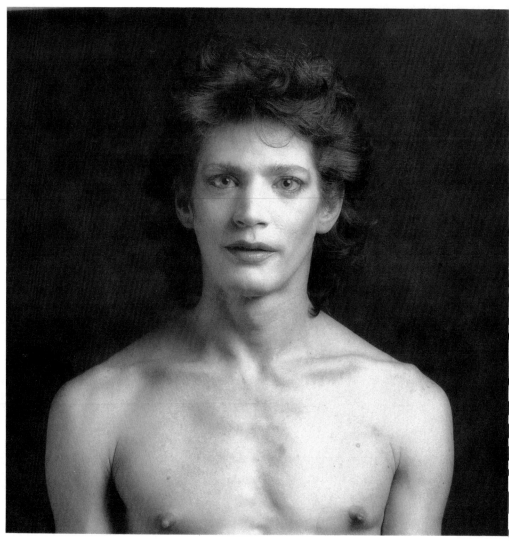

Above: Robert Mapplethorpe, *Self Portrait,* 1980.

Opposite page: Surrealist cross-dressing: Rrose Sélavy, alias Marcel Duchamp, by Man Ray.

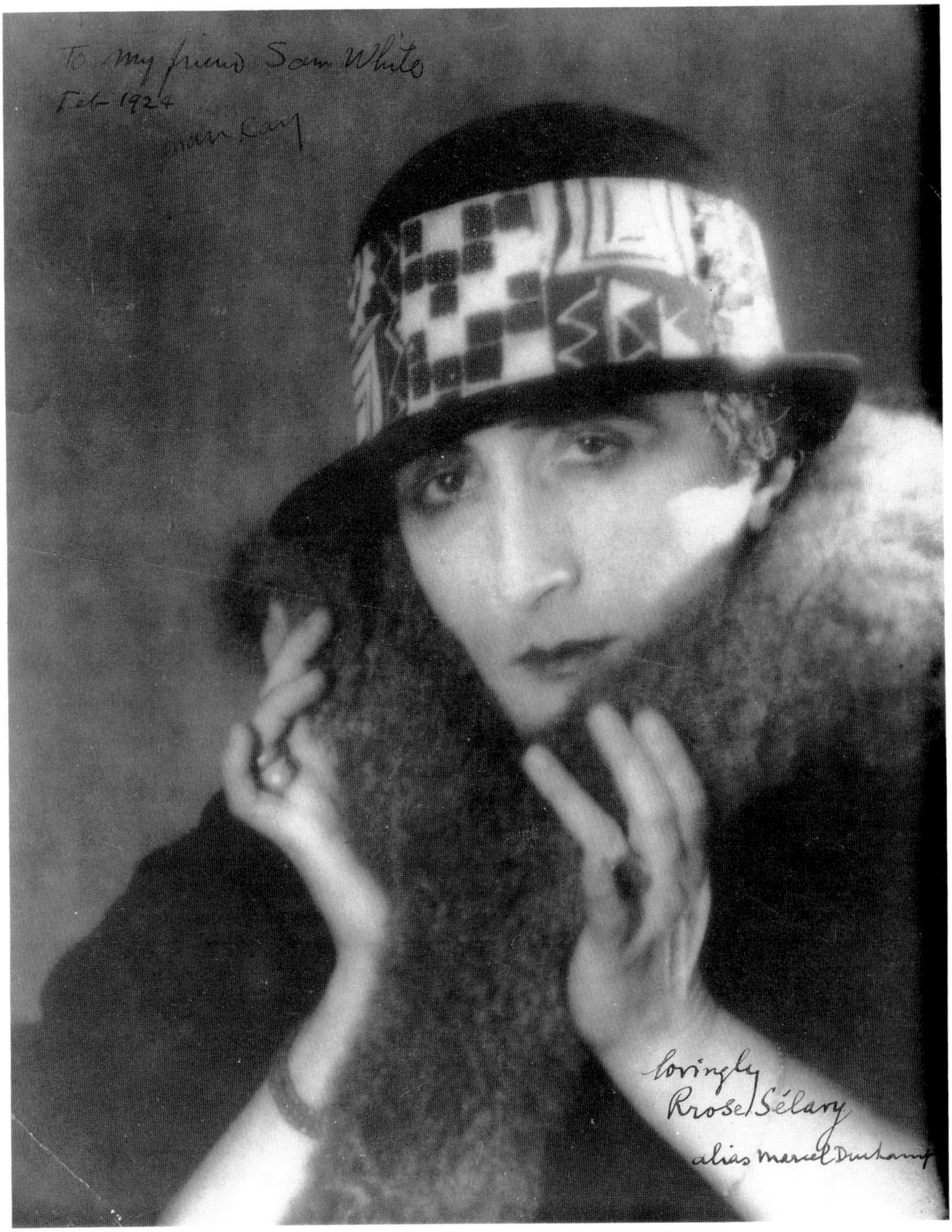
To my friend Sam White
Feb 1924
man Ray
lovingly
Rrose Sélavy
alias Marcel Duchamp

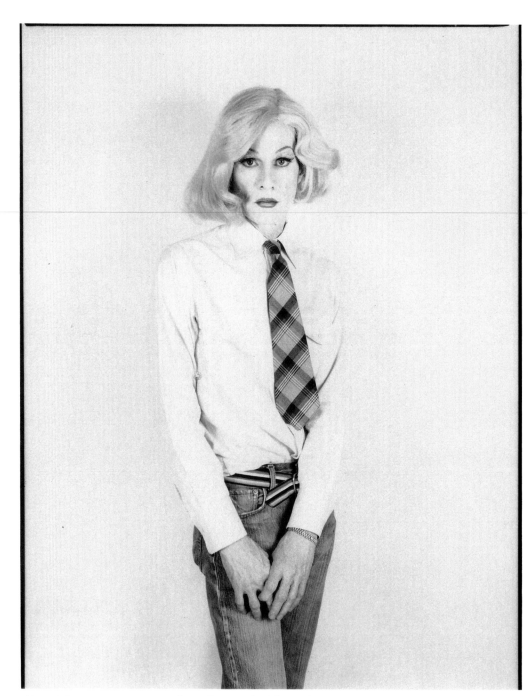

Altered Image, a portrait of Andy Warhol by Chris Makos.

II

TRANSVESTITE EFFECTS

7

FEAR OF FLYING,
OR
WHY IS PETER PAN A WOMAN?

Lord Robert Baden-Powell, founder of the Boy Scouts, was so struck by J.M. Barrie's *Peter Pan* when it first appeared on the London stage that he returned immediately to see it again—alone—on the following day. He wrote to friends urging them to do the same, and he began to entertain the actress who played the part of Mrs. Darling. A few years later he wrote to another young actress friend, telling her that he thought of her as "a sort of Pete—(h'm, that's odd; there is no feminine for Peter) a sort of girl Peter Pan, the boy who couldn't grow up. And long may you be so."[1] When, despite this invitation, she did grow up, he discontinued their correspondence.

"Peter Pan," as one chronicler has observed, "is the ultimate ambition of all actresses, just as Hamlet is of all actors."[2] There is a curious absence of symmetry in this apparently symmetrical assertion, since Peter, as well as Hamlet, is nominally gendered male. Moreover, as we have already noted, Hamlet has in fact been played many times by actresses, some of them, indeed, the greatest actresses of their time.

Peter Pan, however, has been from the first played by a woman: Nina Boucicault, Maude Adams, Pauline Chase, Joan Greenwood, Mary Martin, Cathy Rigby—the list goes on and on, since the play quickly became an annual Christmas fixture both in London and in New York. It was not until the 1982 production by the Royal Shakespeare Company at the Barbican that a major professional company cast a man in the role. This move was seen as "mak[ing] the play a tragedy"[3] and "elevating it from the ghetto of children's theatre into a national masterpiece,"[4] as well as restoring the author's putative intention. In other words, the presence of a female lead in the title role relegated the play to the marginal backwaters of kids' stuff, and, at the same time, to the carefree playing fields of comedy. Like *Hamlet*, *Peter Pan* could be a national masterpiece of tragic drama; all it needed was the RSC and a star with a phallus. It was a matter of putting the "peter" back in Peter Pan.

Like Peter's shadow, however—or, for that matter, Captain Hook's right hand—this "peter" proved to be a detachable part. The overdetermined name of "Peter Pan" covers over a story that is both complex and instructive. If it is in part the rather moving story of James Barrie, twitted by cruel humorists for his putative impotence as "the boy who couldn't go up,"[5] a man who devoted a lifetime to caring for the five sons of Arthur and Sylvia Llewelyn Davies, and whose plays and novels dwelt constantly on the desire to be boy eternal, it is also the story of transvestism as and in power. For to look at Peter Pan is to see transvestism embodied, and disembodied. Only the RSC production, which purported to "restore" Barrie's "original intention,"[6] was in fact in drag.

"A PLAY FOR CHILDREN"

> My dear Maudie,
> I have written a play for children, which I don't suppose would be much use in America. . . . I should like you to be the boy and the girl and most of the children and the pirate captain."

So wrote J.M. Barrie to the actress Maude Adams, on April 8, 1904. Partly at the behest of the shrewd American producer Charles Frohman, "Maudie" was cast in the play's first American production, not as "the girl" (Wendy) but as "the boy" (Peter Pan). Frohman saw clearly that Peter was the star part (he had been instrumental in changing the play's title from "The Great White Father," Barrie's choice, to "Peter Pan"); he also foresaw the difficulty involved in casting the other parts if Peter were really to be played by a boy, since the other children would have to be even younger, and English law at the time prohibited the use of minors under fourteen on stage after 9 p.m.[7]

In the London production that preceded it by half a year, in time for the Christmas season, Nina Boucicault played Peter, and was remembered more than thirty years later as "the best" of all the Peters, by a reviewer who was twelve years old at the time : "Others will be more boyish, or more principal-boyish, or gayer and prettier, or more sinister and inhuman, or more ingeniously and painstakingly elfin," wrote Denis Mackail, "but Miss Boucicault was the Peter of all Peters . . . She was unearthly but she was real. She obtruded neither sex nor sexlessness. . . ."[8] Boucicault (1904–5) was followed by a number of other actresses over the course of the next several decades. Until 1928, all the Lost Boys but Slightly, the "most conceited"[9] of them, were likewise cross-dressed, played by actresses rather than actors.

Pauline Chase, Barrie's goddaughter, was the most famous of the early London Peters, despite (or, perhaps, because of) the fact that, as Eva Le Gallienne (who would later play the part in America) complained, she "didn't look like a boy or even make any attempt to look like one" (Green, 124). Photographs of Chase show her as—to quote one theater historian—"frank and boyish, but by no means sexless—[an actress] who might equally well be playing Rosalind" (Green, 124). Children in the audience occasionally demanded to be reassured about "Peter's" real gender, and Chase reports one incident in which a diminutive doubting Thomas appeared in her dressing-room.

A young gentleman of about six was brought to see me, and I gathered from his introductory remarks that his big brother had made him uneasy about my sex. He put two cunning test questions to me (probably suggested by the brother). The first was, "Can you whistle?" By great good luck I could whistle that day. Then, "What do you think of kissing?" he asked anxiously. "Rotten," I said. He was immensely relieved. Then I knew I was all right . . .[10]

Barrie, instructing a newly cast Peter (Edna Best) for the part in 1923, offered a binarism of his own that is somewhat reminiscent of recent feminist work on the "butch-femme" aesthetic, though Peter was neither precisely butch nor absolutely femme. "Either he must be the whimsical, fairy creature that Nina Boucicault made him, or he must be the lovable tomboy of Pauline Chase. There is no other way" (Green, 126). So much for the "original intention" of the author to cast a man in the role. And so much, also, for the crisis of indeterminacy. Peter was to be either a "tomboy" or a "fairy." And the Lost Boys, patterned not only on the Davies children but also on young Etonians eager to "scout" for their elders, were, in effect, Peter's "fags."

PETER AND WENDY

But what does it mean that Peter Pan has (almost) always been played by an actress?

Does it mean that Peter is a woman? In a way, we might say so—or say at least that Peter is Wendy's ego-ideal. Barrie, as many critics have pointed out, wrote at the same time as Freud, and was as good an instinctive Freudian as he was a classic candidate for Freudian analysis. Early in *Peter and Wendy*, the 1911 novel that followed the play, Mrs. Darling is described as sorting through the odds and ends in her children's minds,

and of these quite the most perplexing was the word Peter. She knew of no Peter, and yet he was here and there in John's and Michael's minds, while Wendy's began to be scrawled all over with him. The name stood out in bolder letters than any of the other words, and as Mrs. Darling gazed she felt that it had an oddly cocky appearance.

"Yes, he is rather cocky," Wendy admitted with regret.[11]

Mrs. Darling, finding this mental graffiti "scrawled all over," begins to interrogate her daughter and learns that "he" is Peter Pan, someone she dimly remembers believing in herself a long time ago. Now, however, she doubts whether there is any such person, and besides, "he would be grown up by this time."

"Oh, no, he isn't grown up," Wendy assured her confidently, "and he is just my size." She meant that he was her size in both mind and body; she didn't know how she knew it, she just knew it. (*PW*, 20)

That Peter is a kind of Wendy Unbound, a regendered, not-quite-degendered alternative persona who can have adventures, fight pirates, smoke pipes, and cavort with redskins is certainly one feasible way of understanding him—and her. Peter can do all kinds of things that Wendy, Victorian girl-child that she is, is forbidden. The critic's observation that Pauline Chase looked like Rosalind fits in well enough with this perception, since as we have seen Rosalind is the very type of the cross-dressed woman, appropriated over and over again as a legitimation of temporary and transitional crossover status, returning to marriage and her wifely role (and clothes) at play's end, just as Wendy returns to the nursery and is married- and mothered-off in the coda Barrie wrote as an "Afterthought" to his play. The grown-up Wendy cannot fly, and her dress of leaves is too short to wear; she doffs it the way Rosalind doffs her doublet and hose. And the last scene shows her married and with a child of her own. In fact, Peter's disinclination to romantic love (he infuriates Wendy, Tinker Bell, and Tiger Lily by refusing to understand what they might want to be to him, if not his mother) might be "explained" along the same lines by reading Peter as a cross-dressed version of Wendy—and Wendy as an unambivalent heterosexual. This reading would be a kind of progress narrative, in which the stage of believing in Peter became, in Neverland (or Freud's dream-work) the same as the stage of *being* him—while retaining the dreamer's prerogative of being herself at the same time.[12]

But to rest on this interpretation would be to write out, to erase, the transvestite and his/her power to destabilize and disturb. If Peter Pan is played by a woman because he *is* a woman, or rather, because he is a little girl's fantasy other, the play and the novel become safely recontextualized parts of the Victorian scene, and words like "tomboy" become labels for life-stages we all grow out of. Let us try again.

Why is Peter Pan played by a woman? Because a woman will never grow up to be a man.

TO BE BOY ETERNAL

"I don't want ever to be a man," he said with passion. "I want always to be a little boy and to have fun. So I ran away to Kensington Gardens and lived a long long time among the fairies." (*PW*, 43)

"I don't want to be a man. O Wendy's mother, if I was to wake up and feel there was a beard!"
"Peter!" said Wendy the comforter, "I should love you in a beard"; and Mrs Darling stretched out her arms to him, but he repulsed her.
"Keep back, lady, no one is going to catch me and make me a man."
(*PW*, 206)

The playbill for the first London production at the Duke of York's Theatre clearly proclaimed the play's subtitle, "Peter Pan or, The Boy Who Wouldn't Grow Up."

To base an argument about Peter Pan—or *Peter Pan*—on an allegorical reading of James Barrie's life is both to underestimate and to overestimate the power of the biographical Imaginary. But it would be pointless to ignore the evidence of pathos and nostalgia in his writings, both public and personal: Barrie, like Polixenes and Leontes, longed for a boyhood that never was—a boyhood that could only be staged in Neverland. This is, after all, one of the functions that pastoral performs: it offers a scenario of cultural nostalgia, under which both the personal and the political may be conveniently if temporarily subsumed. And this nostalgia is never wholly separable from the fear of death, or from the erotic. Freud's two drives meet in pastoral, which is one reason why there is so much overlap—I would not call it coincidence—between the dreamworld of the unconscious and the landscape of Fairyland or Neverland.

For Barrie, boyhood begins with loss, with not being the right boy, the boy who *should* have been the boy eternal. His older brother David, the apple of his mother's eye, was killed in a skating accident on the eve of his fourteenth birthday. His mother apparently never fully recovered from this blow—nor, it seems, did Barrie himself. Then aged six, already runty, as he was to be all his life, he was urged by his sister to go into his mother's darkened room and remind her that she still had another boy. From the dark his mother called out, "Is that you?," and, as Barrie remembers, he "thought it was the dead boy she was speaking to, and I said in a lonely little voice, 'No, it's no' him, it's just me.' "[13] In a pathetic attempt to please his mother he learned how to whistle and stick his hands in his pockets like David, doubtless inflicting more pain as he made himself into the ghost— or the shadow—of the lost golden child. And David had—would always have—his revenge: "When I became a man . . . he was still a boy of thirteen" (*Margaret Ogilvy*, 15– 16).

The specter of "David" in fact haunts Barrie throughout his lifetime. In his novel *The Little White Bird* (1902), the first narrative appearance of Peter Pan, the story of Peter in Kensington Gardens is an encapsulated tale within the plot, a story told by a lonely bachelor to his child friend, David, to whom he becomes a secret benefactor. "There never was a cockier boy." At one point he takes David home with him overnight, undresses him for the bath with trembling hands, and accedes to David's request to crawl into his bed. The last play of Barrie's life was called *The Boy David* and was ostensibly about the young King David of the Bible, though it is clearly also related to the boy David of *The Little White Bird* and the dead David Barrie. And this heroic boy was, equally clearly, another incarnation of Peter Pan. The "boy David" was, significantly, played onstage by a woman, Elisabeth Bergner (who also played Rosalind to Olivier's Orlando). In his will Barrie praised Bergner's performance as David as "the best performance ever given in a play by me" (Birkin, 299).

In fact the loss of David replays itself in Barrie's life and work in three forms: 1) in his passionate devotion to the five Llewelyn Davies boys; 2) in the recurrent motif of the "dead child," the return of the repressed in his works; and 3) in the valorization of the concept of the "boy." The cross-dressing of Peter Pan in the theater is thus—like the cross-dressed Yentl and the cross-dressed Jessica—a version of what I have called the changeling boy, the fantasy child who personates change, and *exchange*. In the case of Peter, of course, the changeling himself is also the agent of exchange, taking the Darling children from their nursery. Let us see how this came about, and how it makes the portrayal of Peter by an actress in a way inevitable, not because Peter is a woman, but because Peter is, theoretically and culturally, a transvestite.

"BOYS CANNOT LOVE"

Barrie befriended the five Davies boys in Kensington Gardens, moved his residence in order to be able to see and play with them daily, took them on holidays, narrativized them as Peter and the Lost Boys, and ultimately adopted them, only to have the two most precious to him (George and Michael) die tragically young. The youngest of the sons, Nicholas (Nico), argued strenuously, years after the fact, that Barrie was neither a pedophile nor a homosexual, at least in practice: "I'm 200% certain that there was never a desire to kiss (other than the cheek!), though things obviously went through his mind—often producing magic—which never go through the more ordinary minds of such as myself . . . All I can say for certain is that I . . . never heard one word or saw one glimmer of anything approaching homosexuality or paedophilia; had he had either of these leanings in however slight a symptom I would have been aware. He was an innocent—which is why he could write *Peter Pan*" (Birkin, 130). It is tempting to suggest that Barrie is not the only innocent here, though the difference between acts and "leanings" is obviously crucial, and was clearly so to Barrie himself.

We might compare Barrie's situation with that of his great admirer, the "boy-man," Lord Robert Baden-Powell, who, like Barrie, made a highly successful career out of his idealization of boys and boyhood. Baden-Powell was famous for his "skirt dancing" and female impersonations both at school and throughout his long career in the British army. "In the army," writes his biographer, "he would make a speciality of female roles."[14] He and his "best friend in the world," Kenneth McLaren, whom he called "the Boy," shared a bungalow at Muttra in India, and made sure that they were assigned a shared residence every time the regiment moved to a new location. Baden-Powell later wrote concerning the institution of marriage that he was convinced two men could live as happily together as a man and a woman (Jeal, 74).

Baden-Powell met McLaren in 1881 and "the Boy" costarred with him—as the female lead—in two theatrical productions; in one of them Baden-Powell played the lady's lover, in the other, her father. McLaren was described by a subaltern as having "made a very pretty girl," and Baden-Powell concurred that he "made a wonderfully good lady" (Jeal,

66). About twenty years later McLaren married; Baden-Powell himself would not do so until 1912, when he was 55.

As we have already noticed, Baden-Powell was fascinated all his life with the figure of Peter Pan; he was obsessed with keeping the body "clean" (an adjective he applied to boys and men but not to women); and he expressed a strong interest in nude figure studies of young boys. Biographer Tim Jeal takes note of recent suggestions that Baden-Powell "may have been a homosexual," and offers instead what he calls a broader view: "Whether a man acts upon a homosexual inclination or not (or even acknowledges his tendency) is not more significant than the effect such a tendency will have upon his life if it is denied. Indeed, a repressed instinct may well affect behaviour and thoughts more dramatically than a proclivity actively pursued" (Jeal, 75).

This medicalizing vocabulary ("repressed instinct," "proclivity," "homosexual inclination") should not obscure a valuable insight here: that the category "repressed homosexual" itself represents a kind of appropriation and reading *through* that puts the interpreter in the position of the subject who knows—knows somehow "better" than the person whose life is under scrutiny. Baden-Powell cross-dressed, admired photographs of nude boys, and lived with a male fellow-officer in a relationship he himself compared to marriage. He also founded the Boy Scouts, an organization that promoted homosocial male bonding as the best way to build character. This may add up to a diagnosis of "repressed homosexuality," but that label is not itself an "answer." Baden-Powell's life, which also included a heterosexual marriage and family, is both more peculiar and more complex. Cross-dressing and a male-male "marriage" here skirt, so to speak, the question of homosexuality; to claim that Baden-Powell was a homosexual, whether or not he actually had sex with men, is a psychological and political move: a part of the story, but not its defining "secret."

The case of Barrie, while different in many of its particulars from that of the robust soldier Baden-Powell, likewise resists easy categorization. It too is more fascinating, and more paradoxical, than any single retrospective diagnosis will support. Barrie's own marriage to the actress Mary Astell deteriorated rapidly after he began to attach himself to the young Davieses and their mother, Sylvia; but from the beginning his sexual self-esteem was blighted, and he saw himself as a "boy" trying to play a man's part. A Notebook entry two days before the wedding, on July 9, 1894, read as follows:

—Our love has brought me nothing but misery.
—Boy all nerves. "You are very ignorant."
—How? Must we instruct you in the mysteries of love-making? (Birkin, 29)

The two transparently autobiographical novels that Barrie wrote during this period, *Sentimental Tommy* and *Tommy and Grizel*, return again and again to the image of the boy who couldn't grow up.

He was a boy only. She [his wife] knew that, despite all he had gone through, he was still a boy. And boys cannot love. Oh, is it not cruel to ask a boy to love? . . . He was a boy who could not grow up . . . He gave her all his affection, but his passion, like an outlaw, had ever to hunt alone.

Poor Tommy! he was still a boy, he was ever a boy, trying sometimes, as now, to be a man, [but] always when he looked round he ran back to his boyhood as if he saw it holding out its arms to him, and inviting him to come back and play. He was so fond of being a boy that he could not grow up. In a younger world, where there were only boys and girls, he might have been a gallant figure . . . .

"I am his slave myself," writes the narrator, "I see that all that was wrong with Tommy was that he could not always be a boy."[15]

The "boy" figure is split in *Tommy and Grizel*; by this strategy the narrator distances himself from the "boy's" dilemma, and grants him permission to be the way he is; disavowal and splitting thus constitute a regime for the management of fantasy and desire. But the identity of the "boy" is not so stable as it may at first appear. After he met Sylvia Llewelyn Davies, Barrie revised the figure of "Grizel" in his novel so that she resembled Sylvia rather than his wife Mary, and added this telling detail: "There were times when she looked like a boy."[16] So that the "boy" could be George Llewelyn Davies—or his mother Sylvia. The male child—or the grown woman. Where is Barrie, the missing "boy" of this complex erotic exchange?

The same transparent defensive splitting marks the narrative structure of *The Little White Bird*, the thinly veiled story of Barrie's friendship with the young George Davies. Captain W—, "a gentle, whimsical, lonely old bachelor" who is also a writer, becomes involved with a young married couple. When the couple's son David is born he pretends that he too has just had a child, whom he calls "Timothy." Shortly thereafter he discovers that David's mother is pawning her possessions in order to buy clothing for her son, whereupon he announces to the couple that "Timothy" has died, leaving behind a whole wardrobe of clothing for which he now has no use, and which can be given to David. Captain W—elegizes his fantasy child in an extraordinary chapter called "The Last of Timothy":

. . . the reader must have seen at once that I made away with Timothy in order to give his little vests and pinafores and shoes to David . . . .

Timothy's hold on life, as you may have apprehended, was ever of the slightest, and I suppose I always knew that he must soon revert to the obscure. He could never have penetrated into the open. It was no life for a boy.[17]

Two years after the publication of *The Little White Bird*, Sylvia Llewelyn Davies gave birth to her fifth son, and it was rumored among the family that he would be named Timothy. But her husband Arthur Davies, perhaps understandably, given the oppressive omnipresence of Barrie in his family circle, preferred another—perhaps any other— name, and the infant was called Nicholas instead (Birkin, 101). So that "the phantasy of Timothy" remained just that—another fantasy child displaced by a real one, a boy like other boys, a boy who *would*, inevitably, grow up to be a man.

"Timothy," of course, coexists in *The Little White Bird* not only with David, the adoptive child ("the little boy who calls me father," as he is characterized in the book's opening sentence) who flourishes as a result of Timothy's "death" and is dressed in his clothes, but also with Peter Pan, first described in print in this novel, whose role as genius loci of Kensington Gardens is to dig graves for the human children who fall out of their perambulators and perish there after lock-out time. So that Peter Pan himself is, from the first, associated with dead children, as well as with the boy eternal. The Peter of the novel prolongs his idyll with the fairies in the garden so long that, when he does finally attempt to return to his mother, he finds her sleeping "with her arm round another little boy," and the iron bars of the window shut against him (Barrie, *LWB* 166-67). This scenario rewrites the story of Barrie, his mother, and his dead brother David, while inverting the ages of the two boys; the returning Peter is too late, as young J.M. Barrie was too late, to break into the mother-child dyad. Belatedness is his defining condition.

In later incarnations, both in *Peter and Wendy* and in the play version of *Peter Pan*, Peter himself becomes, not the excluded, but the pan-erotic object of desire, the one who can take the kiss from Mrs. Darling's mouth when neither Wendy nor Mr. Darling can; in this therapeutic revision, Peter Pan *is* the changeling boy, who replaces those Lost Boys who have fallen out of perambulators. Yet he is also, inevitably, a marker of loss as well as of desire. In an autograph addition to the second draft of the 1908 ending of the play, Peter is explicitly identified as both dead baby and fantasy child:

I think now—that Peter is only a sort of dead baby—he is the baby of all the people who never had one.[18]

In *Peter and Wendy* Mrs. Darling sees Peter in the faces of all the women who never had children (*PW*, 22-24).

The fantasy child, the child who is not there, haunts text after text for Barrie. In *Dear Brutus*, written in the same year, the lonely Will Dearth is granted a magic wish, and given a dream-child, Margaret; daughters, he tells her, are better than sons, because you can tell them how you feel about them. But in the third act Dearth "comes to" and realizes that he has lost the dream-child.

Yet how can the "Margaret" of *Dear Brutus* be a "boy," especially when Barrie goes out of his way to distinguish between daughters and sons? Consider this: much earlier in his life Barrie befriended a young girl, the daughter of the poet W.E. Henley, whose name was Margaret. She called him, we are told, "my Friendy"—but, since she couldn't pronounce her r's properly, he became instead "my Wendy." And the name "Wendy," which had not existed before, was chosen by Barrie for Peter's special companion. "Wendy," then, was Barrie himself; Barrie was Wendy, Margaret was—Peter Pan. And Margaret Henley died at the age of six. Her cloak was later copied for Wendy's onstage costume, but she is herself a prototype of the dead child, and that child was always, in whatever guise he or she appeared, Peter Pan, "the boy who wouldn't grow up." (Notice that "wouldn't" here has shifted its meaning, from "was unable to" to "refused to"; thus does the playwright take control of his fiction.) Margaret Henley was, in effect, the first cross-dressed incarnation of Peter Pan. Or, to put it another way, Peter Pan was always already female. Or was s/he?

Barrie himself, at least in his later life, played with the idea of gender-bending. The sentiment of Will Dearth (daughters are better than sons because you can tell them how you really feel about them) had its epistolary precursor in two letters the playwright wrote to George Davies at the front. "I had hardly finished reading and re-reading [your letter]," he writes, "(quite as if I was a young lady)" (February 28, 1915[19]), and, "more and more wishing you were a girl of 21 instead of a boy, so that I could say the things to you that are now always in my heart" (March 11, 1915).[20] This would seem to be his way of smoothing out or justifying an intensity of feeling, of reinscribing his own emotions in a way that puts them in quotation marks, and makes them utterable.

Likewise, resisting the idea of pedophilia, at least two of his biographers have preferred to call him maternal; thus Andrew Birkin describes "his own profound yearnings for fatherhood—or, perhaps, motherhood" (Birkin, 157), and Peter Davies, commenting on Barrie's feelings for his brothers George and Michael, says that their characteristic form included "a dash of the paternal, a lot of the maternal, and much, too, of the lover—at this stage Sylvia's lover still imperfectly merged into the lover of her son."[21] This move, while sympathetic and understandable, is rather like that of those feminists who appropriate—too quickly—the position of the cross-dresser for "woman." If Barrie is not behaving "like a man," it does not follow that the only other choice is for him to be a woman—or a mother. It is perfectly possible that Barrie *was* a pedophile, whether or not he performed sexual acts with children. The "boy who couldn't go up" story suggests that his marital sex life was dormant or non-existent. He may quite plausibly have felt both "maternal" emotion and desire for the young Davies. But whatever *Barrie*'s gender subjectivity, *Peter*'s is textually diagnosed quite early in his career, by the wise old bird Solomon Caw, the resident psychologist of Kensington Gardens. Peter, according to Solomon, was suffering from a kind of species dysphoria, caught between being a bird and being a human child:

"Then I sha'n't be exactly a human?" Peter asked.
"No."
"Nor exactly a bird?"
"No."
"What shall I be?"
"You will be a Betwixt-and-Between," Solomon said, and certainly he was a wise old fellow, for that is exactly how it turned out.

LWB, 134

"A Betwixt-and-Between." This is the "third sex" in yet another guise, transparently displaced onto the antithesis between bird and human, but representing as well the dichotomies that both consciously and unconsciously obsess Barrie and his works. Man/woman, father/mother, man/boy. That these are Victorian dichotomies, and dichotomies of Barrie's own life, does not fully account for the power of their dissemination. *Peter Pan* quickly became the best loved of all Christmas entertainments, a figure of new mythology, beatified by Walt Disney and alliteratively commodified as peanut butter. The peanut butter jars of my childhood were adorned with the image of Maude Adams, the first great American Peter. What the middle-class children of America—and of Britain—saw, when they looked at Peter Pan, was, then, an adult woman, who was also a little boy.[22] And what I want to suggest here is that this split vision is precisely what entranced, what held spellbound: the power of transvestism in and as the cultural Imaginary.

"OF WHOM HE IS NOT ONE"

"Children know something they can't tell," observes Nora Flood in a famous moment in Djuna Barnes's *Nightwood*, when she is confronted with the specter of the transvestite Dr. O'Connor. "They like Red Riding Hood and the wolf in bed!" And they also like Peter Pan. The real question to be answered here may not be, Why is Peter Pan played by a woman?, but, Why is that fact not culturally disturbing or threatening? For while both his intimates and his observers clucked about Barrie's overinvestment in the Davies boys, they also cooed at his brilliant inventions, and at his instant rapport with children. His play was regarded as the essence of benign fantasy, as witness its later transmogrification by the Disney studio. *Peter Pan* is nowhere condemned as a drag show. Yet when the audience is asked, in one of the dramatic climaxes of the play, whether it believes in fairies, it has already given its assent to another suspension of disbelief: that Peter can be a "boy" and a woman at once. The stage directions always call him "he," as they do at this climactic moment, when he appeals to the audience to save Tinker Bell: "He rises and throws out his arms he knows not to whom, perhaps to the boys and girls of whom he is not one" (*PP*, 119).

Is the reason that audiences are not made anxious by Peter Pan as a woman because the play, by making the woman the answer to the riddle rather than herself the enigma, defuses the anxiety about women's secret "masculinity" and castrating power?

If "Peter is a woman" is the answer, it can cease to be the question. Rather than detecting "masculinity" behind the woman, the audience of *Peter Pan* detects "femininity" behind the boy. This discontinuity, oddly, produces not consternation but reassurance. Love for—or cathexis onto—a "boy" turns out to be love for or cathexis onto a woman, after all.

We might note that throughout his life James Barrie developed crushes on actresses, as well as boys. His wife, Mary Astell, was featured in one of his early plays, and she was only one in a series of leading women who occupied his conscious daydreams, and for whom he wrote specific parts, and even entire theatrical vehicles. But while his passionate relationships with boys were defused through strategies of displacement (writing, storytelling, gift-giving, adoption), his relationships with women caused much more acute overt anxiety. The therapeutic work that *Peter Pan* is doing is not only to rewrite a relationship with boys (or children) as a story about men and women, Peter as a kind of closet Rosalind, but also to do the opposite: to recast (literally) the problematic perception of "masculinity" and dominance in women as a contest between a boyish woman hero and a feminized male villain, both of whom are crossover figures, repeatedly twinned in the text: Peter Pan and Captain Hook, a dream and a nightmare of transvestism.

THE PRINCIPLED BOY

A surprising amount of critical disavowal has gone into distinguishing *Peter Pan* from the traditional transvestite Christmas pantomime, partly on the basis of audience (for children; by children) and dramatic structure. Its homologies with pantomime—the woman as Principal Boy, Hook as the logical extension of the Panto Dame—are repeatedly denied or minimized by critics who want to claim a different, less popular, theatrical status for Barrie's play.[23] Yet *Peter Pan* is in a way a theoretical deconstruction of Panto, an exposure of its underlying fable.

As it evolved in the latter part of the nineteenth century from its roots in *commedia dell'arte* and the harlequinade, the pantomime was a traditional Christmas entertainment in which an actress, designated the Principal Boy, played the hero's part, and an actor (the Dame) played the comic female character, usually an old and/or ugly woman. Fairy tales often provided the foundation for the plot: Cinderella, Dick Whittington and His Cat, Mother Goose, the Babes in the Wood. The first Principal Boy may have been Madame Vestris; dressed on the standard outfit of blond wig, short tunic, fleshings and high heels, the early Principal Boys were ample of figure. As the twentieth century wore on the Principal Boys became slimmer, more "boyish." The Ugly Sisters of Cinderella, the Cook in Dick Whittington, Mother Goose, and the Queen of Hearts are all classic Dame parts, played by such renowned actors as Dan Leno, George Robey, and Malcolm Scott ("the Woman Who Knows").

"The dame," writes Peter Ackroyd, "is never merely a drag artist, since she always retains her male identity. The performer is clearly a man dressed as an absurd and ugly woman, and much of the comedy is derived from the fact that he is burlesquing himself as a male actor."[24] By contrast the "male impersonator, the actress in trousers, lacks depth and resonance"; she "is never anything more than what she pretends to be: a feminine, noble mind in a boy's body." The sexual politics of this contrast are disturbing, since they at once elevate the female impersonator as a finer artist and establish a ground of the "real" in the class of absurd and ugly women—women who are, even in their absurdity and ugliness, better played by men. But read as a critique of the relationship between Peter Pan and Captain Hook, this view of the politics of Panto is inadvertently suggestive. For Hook becomes a Dame in double drag, while Peter—again escaping judgment—"is never anything more than what [he] pretends to be."

The existence of the "Principal Boy" as a theatrical type offers a historical explanation for the fact that Peter Pan has always been an actress's part, an explanation that runs parallel to what might be called the psychobiographical evidence from Barrie's life. Leaving aside the tantalizing question of why Victorians might have wanted to see women as "boys," even—or especially—women with considerable embonpoint, the tradition of the Principal Boy suggests that casting a woman for Peter might have been more "natural" than it seems from the viewpoint of the later twentieth century. But the key question still remains: why, long after pantomime faded as a theatrical vehicle, did the boy Peter remain a woman in Britain; and why, in the U.S., which lacks any analogous mainstream transvestite theater,[25] did this tradition take hold? In other words, what unconscious work is being done by *Peter Pan*? In order to see this more clearly, we need to take note of attempts to dismiss or repress the play's transvestism in favor of allegorical readings (both from the left and from the right) that recast the transvestite as a figure for something *else*.

One of the forerunners of Barrie's play was a pantomime he wrote for the Davies children and their friends called "The Greedy Dwarf," starring Sylvia Llewelyn Davies (under her maiden name of du Maurier) and her brother Gerald, an actor who would later double the parts of Mr. Darling and Captain Hook. In the playbill for "The Greedy Dwarf" Sylvia Davies was described as "The Principled Boy." Jacqueline Rose, noting the connection between *Peter Pan* and the pantomime, claims that the difference between them is that the play more than the pantomime gives the audience "the right to look at the child." She thus directs attention *away* from the transvestite and toward the child. Where Gilbert and Gubar look at transvestism and see powerful modernist women (and wimpy modernist men), where Stephen Greenblatt looks at transvestism and sees the boy actor constructing female subjectivity, Rose looks at transvestism and sees a cultural myth of childhood. But this trajectory might as readily be reversed. If, as she asserts, "Peter Pan is, of course, both child and woman," something very peculiar is going on here both in cultural and in political terms—not only in the purported Victorian conflation of child and woman, but in the denial of cultural presence to the transvestite. Rose's subtle and powerful reading of *Peter Pan* effectively performs the erasure—yet again—of the transvestite as subject. It is in fact a measure of transvestism's own power that such powerful critics, thinking that they are coming "face to face" (Rose, 112) with the deconstruction of cultural mythology, actually, again and again, look away.[26]

Rose describes *Peter Pan* as "the ultimate fetish of childhood," marked by a disavowal of both sexuality and sexual difference.[27] Its fetishistic quality is precisely inextricable from its anxieties about sexual difference, its constant reenactment of the fantasy of castration, together with a tacit recognition of how castration makes and marks culture. Peter's shadow, Hook's hand, John's hat—these detachable parts organize the whole of the story. The crocodile who hungers after the rest of Hook is a kind of ambulatory vagina dentata, overtly gendered female: "we shall see for whom she is looking presently" (*PP*, 75). Her quest for gustatory satisfaction is the only thing that terrifies the Captain, and Peter makes sure that she gets him in the end. Peter's shadow is likewise seized upon by a predatory female animal, the dog-nurse Nana, who holds it in her mouth (*PP*, 25). It is in search of the shadow that Peter returns to the nursery, and his failure to stick it on with soap leads Wendy to sew it on for him. Naturally he finds her essential to his self-image. Here is the scene in the nursery, right after the two are introduced:

> Wendy: No wonder you were crying.
>
> Peter: I wasn't crying. But I can't get my shadow to stick on.
>
> Wendy: It has come off! How awful. (*Looking at the spot where he had lain.*) Peter, you have been trying to stick it on with soap!
>
> Peter: (*snappily*) Well then?
>
> Wendy: It must be sewn on.
>
> Peter: What is "sewn?"
>
> Wendy: You are dreadfully ignorant.
>
> Peter: No, I'm not.
>
> Wendy: I will sew it on for you, my little man. . . . I dare say it will hurt a little.
>
> Peter: (*a recent remark of hers rankling*) I never cry. (*She seems to attach the shadow. He tests the combination.*) It isn't quite itself yet.
>
> Wendy: Perhaps I should have ironed it. (*It awakes and is as glad to be back with him as he to have it. He and his shadow dance together. He is showing off now. He crows like a cock. He would fly in order to impress Wendy further if he knew that there is anything unusual in that.*)
>
> Peter: Wendy, look, look; oh, the cleverness of me! (*PP*, 79–80)

That this is a scenario of castration anxiety and subsequent phallic display seems, to me, at least, strikingly self-evident. And it is repeated on the level of the social when the two children introduce themselves.

> Peter: What is your name?
>
> Wendy: (*well satisfied*) Wendy Moira Angela Darling. What is yours?
>
> Peter: (*finding it lamentably brief*) Peter Pan.
>
> Wendy: Is that all?
>
> Peter: (*biting his lip*) Yes.
>
> Wendy: (*politely*) I am so sorry. (*PP*, 28)

Even from the moment of introduction Peter feels cut down to size. This incident also appears in *Peter and Wendy*, where Wendy reflects to herself that "it did seem a comparatively short name," and Peter feels "for the first time that it was a shortish name" (*PW*, 39). What has this drama of castration to do with transvestism, and with the casting of actresses rather than actors in the role of Peter and the Lost Boys?

GETTING OFF (ON) THE HOOK

Peter Pan is not, of course, the only potential figure for transvestism in the play. Let us consider the other obvious cross-dresser onstage, Captain James Hook. "In [his] dark nature there was a touch of the feminine, as in all the great pirates," says the unnamed narrator of the novel (*PW*, 115). Novel and play agree on Hook's physical appearance:

> cadaverous and blackavized, his hair dressed in long curls, which looked like black candles about to melt, his eyes blue as the forget-me-not. . . . In dress he somewhat aped the attire associated with Charles II, having heard it said in some earlier period of his career that he bore a strange resemblance to the ill-fated Stuarts. A holder of his own contrivance is in his mouth enabling him to smoke two cigars at once. Those, however, who have seen him in the flesh, agree that the grimmest part of him is his iron claw. (*PP*, 199)

The exaggerated—and therefore anxious—"phallicism" of the well-named Hook (*two* cigars, a hook, and sausage curls) is both emphasized and undercut by his traditional stage presentation; the frilled jabot and cuffs, and the x-shaped beauty mark or scar that adorns his cheek.[28] The Hook of my own childhood was Cyril Ritchard, a veteran of the English Pantomime, celebrated for his performance of such stock Panto roles as the Ugly Sisters in *Cinderella*, and thus clearly recognizable as a Dame as well as a Pirate Captain, the Panto figure emerging artfully through the use of feminized makeup and occasional swishy gestures.

Whatever the period of Charles II meant to Barrie—and this was, of course, the historical period in which English pirates were most notable for their exploits in the Caribbean West Indies—the "dandiacal" Hook, in original context a send-up of Etonian style, reads onstage from the latter part of the twentieth century as—dare we say it in the context of *Peter Pan*?—something of what, in the fifties at least, would have been called a fairy. He thus functions as an antitype to Peter, reinscribing the cross-dressed Panto dyad of Dame and Principal Boy. Indeed, there is a way in which *Peter Pan* seems to be the unconscious of Panto, the dark dream narrative behind the seasonal festival that, after all, commemorates the birth of the most Principal Boy of all time.

The roles of Hook and Mr. Darling are frequently doubled in performance, and have been since the first production, when Sylvia Davies's brother Gerald du Maurier played the two parts. In a way, then, Hook *is* Mr. Darling; both are clearly figures of and for castration (Hook with his missing hand; Mr. Darling in the doghouse). But, more interestingly, Hook is also Peter—or Peter is Hook. Peter hoodwinks Hook by assuming a voice that pretends to *be* him ("If you are Hook . . . tell me, who am I?" asks Hook, plaintively [*PW*, 115]). In the play the stage directions warn against raising the curtain one time too often: "*the curtain rises to show PETER a very Napoleon on his ship. It must not rise again lest we see him on the poop in HOOK'S hat and cigars, and with a small iron claw*" (*PP*, 145). This is what it would mean—or what it might mean—for Peter to "grow up and be a man."

Dandyism and "effeminacy," which are often, as we have noted, confused or conflated with homosexuality in moral diatribes from William Prynne to Jerry Falwell, are also read as cultural class markers, and Hook's Etonian past (he worries constantly about "good form," and his last words before being swallowed by the crocodile are "Floreat Etona") sets him up as an obvious target. But his specificity as a pirate is more interesting than his identity as a dandy, especially in light of the drag elements that have over the years crept into Hook's stage representation.

"A touch of the feminine, as in all the great pirates," writes Barrie. What do we know about the social life of pirates? It has been claimed—in a highly problematic study—that the English pirates of Charles II's time were largely "homosexual buccaneers," who chose the alternate lifestyle of piracy in the Caribbean as a way of securing a homosocial and homoerotic world in which sodomy and male bonding fostered a self-sufficient, psychically healthy society apart from European constraints.[29] The study's author, who presents a fairly utopian vision of "sodomy and the pirate tradition," is at pains to combat allegations of effeminacy among the pirates. Gold earrings, he claims, were "clearly a part of their fashion rather than distinctly effeminate," and most pirates dressed rather plainly, "aside from a few captains noted for their ornate dress," like "Calico Jack" Rackham, known for his taste in bright waistcoats, ribbons, and breeches.[30] Those recorded incidents that show pirates dressing up are "obviously playfulness and celebration rather than a longing for effeminate trappings" (Burg, 168). Leaving aside the pejorative term "effeminate," let us look at a couple of such incidents.

An eighteenth-century English sea captain seized by pirates reported that his captors, searching his cabin, "met with a Leather Powder Bag and Puff, with which they had powder'd themselves from head to Foot, walk'd the Decks with their Hats under their Arms, minced their Oaths, and affected all the Airs of a Beau."[31] Another contemporary observer describes a group of pirates who captured a hoard of clothing and presented "a comical sight as they strutted about the island in feathered hats, wigs, silk stockings, ribbons, and other garments."[32] Dressing up seems to have been *noticed* as pirate behavior, whatever it may imply (or have implied) about pirate sexuality. The way in which certain pirate trademarks, like the gold earrings, have been appropriated (or reinvented) by both gay and straight male subcultures, suggests that the stage pirates of *Peter Pan*, or at least the ornately got-up Captain Hook, could be seen as verging on the edge of drag. Panto plus pirate (plus public school).

Pedophilia among pirates, claims this same study, was known and tolerated, especially among ship's captains, whose isolation at the helm might lead them to seek young companions in preference to age-mates who could not be coequals in rank. (Here we might compare Jacqueline Rose's description of "Hook's desire for Peter, which in the earliest versions [of the play] brings him hot on Peter Pan's tail and right into Kensington Gardens" [Rose, 37].) Again, whatever the truth about social tolerance, it seems clear from numerous sources that a large number of boys served aboard the pirate ships, as cabin boys or "powder monkeys." In fact, a look at the records of pirate voyages discovers clear cases of transvestism not among male, but among female, pirates.

Anne Bonny, the wife of Calico Jack Rackham, dressed as an ordinary seaman and fought alongside other members of the ship's crew, keeping her gender a secret, until she fell in love with a blond young Dutchman, who—to her consternation, it is said—also turned out to be a woman in disguise, an Englishwoman named Mary Read. Read and Bonny became friends; both had been dressed as boys by their parents since childhood, and had in fact themselves been changelings of a sort; Bonny's father, embarrassed by having an illegitimate daughter, had her put into breeches and pretended she was a relation's son; Read's mother substituted her for an older child, a son, who died. It might be possible to say that the borderline life of a pirate, sailing on the windy side of the law, marks a crossover occupation that suits their gender histories—or at least the desire to narrativize them. "The figure of the pirate is the figure of interruption," as Jacques Lezra has observed.[33]

A contemporary woodcut print marking their conviction for piracy on November 28, 1720, shows both women ready for battle, with swords in one hand and hatchets in the other (Defoe, 155). It is the woodcut as much as anything else that tells the tale, for the story of Bonny and Read became extremely popular, and Read was celebrated as "the notorious Female Pirate,"[34] heading the (rather extensive) list of cross-dressed female sailors, soldiers, warriors, and cabin boys that were celebrated in ballad, broadside, and folksong.[35] In the eighteenth century, pirate costumes were popular wear for women in the transvestite masquerades that were a conspicuous feature of English upper-class social life.[36]

The travesty costume of Captain Hook thus arguably partakes of both male and female cross-dressing elements. In his way he is as much a figure for (as well as of) cross-dressing as Peter. (Several rock figures of the seventies and eighties, notably Adam Ant and the cross-dressing Annie Lennox, affected pirate costume.) The hints that Peter is himself a version of Hook, or that he might become so, contribute to the sense that cross-gender representation is itself at stake in *Peter Pan*. We might note that when Barrie played Peter Pan games with the Davies boys at Black Lake Cottage in Surrey, he cast himself as Captain Hook (Birkin, 140).

THE CULT OF THE BOY

The appearance of the transvestite in a cultural representation signals a category crisis, and in *Peter Pan* category crises are everywhere. As we have already noted, Barrie's preferred title for his play was "The Great White Father," and what seems today like incredibly naive racial politics are inscribed in its plot (this is presumably one reason why Disney, no racial progressive, was attracted to the story). Tiger Lily is a redskin, but also a member of the "Piccaninny tribe." She is also, apparently, an Amazon of sorts, since she greets the sexual advances of men with bloody hostility: "She is the most beautiful of dusky Dianas and the belle of the Piccaninnies, coquettish, cold and amorous by turns; there is not a brave who would not have the wayward thing to wife, but she staves off the altar with a hatchet" (*PW*, 73–75). Colonialist readings of the play, with the Neverland as the New World and Peter Pan leading the children of the Old World to leave their musty nurseries and seek freedom in America, were, not surprisingly, popular in the U.S. (that mythologizer of American youth, Mark Twain, was a great fan), while white Southerners in Selma, Alabama, perhaps noting the name of the Indian tribe, took exception to Peter's relationship with Tiger Lily (Birkin, 126–27).

But the most obvious crisis signaled in *Peter Pan*, one so obvious as to seem banal, is that between youth and age, or time and timelessness—the boy who wouldn't grow up.

So obvious and *so* banal is this connection that it has been the focus of a best-selling work of pop psychology, *The Peter Pan Syndrome*. Subtitled "Men Who Have Never Grown Up," this 1983 paean to narcissism seems as if it ought to be reproving the "man-child" who suffers from the six symptoms of "PPS": Irresponsibility, Anxiety, Loneliness, Sex Role Conflict, Narcissism, and Chauvinism, but in fact it artfully winds up blaming the woman, specifically the Wendy who indulges the "victim" (for so he is always described) rather than healthily repudiating him like the Tinker Bell. What makes Peter choose Wendy over Tinker Bell is, according to the author, Dr. Dan Kiley, the sex role conflict, and this in turn can be blamed on feminism, which allows girls to be more aggressive and competitive, and thus scares little boys. "Girls have a license to actualize both the masculine and the feminine sides of their personality," Dr. Dan tells us. Indeed, "girls are no longer considered 'butches' or 'dykes' if they want to participate in bodybuilding or basketball. Boys don't have this same license."

The "sex role conflict" makes little boys phobic about "crossing into traditional feminine territory," while girls "are given a script that permits them to cross into traditional masculine territory" (Kiley, 116). The rhetoric of "crossing" here seems subliminally to remind Dr. Dan that "Peter Pan is usually played by a female in theatrical productions of the play" (Kiley, 119). The balance of the book gives specific advice for parents, wives, lovers, friends and siblings—and the "PPS victim" himself—on how to help overcome the syndrome, together with case studies that record the doctor's therapeutic successes.

"Larry overcame the Peter Pan Syndrome and returned from Never Never Land. If he could do it, anybody can" (288).

Dr. Dan finds it "ironic and sad that there is considerable political support for the feminist and gay rights movements, but nothing to boost the morale of the man who wants permission to cry in the arms of the woman he loves."[37] In other words, the story this psychologist has to tell is all about white male self-pity. (Yet another version of "The Great White Father.") Notice that here the allegorical valence of Peter Pan's youth has shifted radically, from a spiritual asset to a psychological liability.

Where Peter Pan differed from the Lost Boys was in his *perpetual* youthfulness, at least while he resisted the blandishments of Mrs. Darling. The Boys, by contrast, were young only because Peter regularly purged their ranks of pubescence. "When they seem to be growing up, which is against the rules, Peter thins them out" (*PW*, 69). This same thinning-out process was used on the children who played the Boys onstage. The actress Pauline Chase described the day of reckoning for the cast in rather Barrie-like prose: "Every December a terrifying ceremony takes place before *Peter Pan* is produced, and this is the measuring of the children who play in it. They are all measured to see whether they have grown too tall, and they can all squeeze down into about two inches less than they really are, but this does not deceive the management. . . . 'It won't do, my lad. . . . We are sorry for you, but—farewell!' Measuring day is one of the many tragedies of *Peter Pan*."[38]

A strikingly similar process was used to thin out the members of a contemporary late eighties pop group, Menudo, whose name in Spanish means "small change." Menudo, a group that appealed to predominantly pre-teen female audiences, was made up of young boys who were regularly replaced when they got too big or their voices changed. Thus, like the Lost Boys, the group remained forever young, at the cost of expelling some of its members.

Peter Pan's emphasis on youth made Peter himself, as Andrew Birkin remarks, "the first of the pre-teen heroes; girls wanted to mother him, boys wanted to fight by his side, while the ambiguity of his sex stimulated a confusion of emotional responses. The play soon began to attract a hard-core following of matinee fanatics who occupied the front row of the stalls to hurl thimbles at Peter and abuse at Hook" (Birkin, 118). (At a key moment in the play Peter, with Wendy as his language tutor, confuses "thimble" with "kiss.")

It is not surprising that the figure of the transvestite should mark this particular crisis, since cross-dressing, both for theatrical performance and to pass, often traverses age boundaries—in both directions. Indeed, one ancillary effect of the youth cult is its implication in cross-dressing. Innumerable pop, rock, and heavy metal groups have incorporated drag elements for the titillation of youthful audiences (David Bowie, Boy George, Tiny Tim, the New York Dolls, Twisted Sister, Motley Crue, and so on). Androgyny is, it might be said, a cultural effect of adolescence, which is one reason for the emergence as a cultural form of what British rock critic Simon Frith has called "The cult of the Boy."[39]

But what has happened to the extraordinary popularity of Peter Pan today? Where is Peter Pan now in the cultural Imaginary? Gymnast Cathy Rigby has taken up the part—and the guy-wires—and is touring the country as the current female incumbent in the role of Peter in Barrie's play. Her performance is stalwart and touching, or so at least it was the evening that I saw her. Rigby is much more conventionally "boyish" than the angular Mary Martin, and much more athletic and lithe. With her hair in a blond mop, her hands on her hips and her chin jutting forward, she looked uncannily like Barrie's photographs of George Llewelyn Davies. And when she flew into the audience for her curtain call, the three feminist critics with whom I shared a section of the balcony all, involuntarily, cheered.

Yet for us—and for many in the audience (at least those over the age of ten)—the Victorian nursery set and its casement windows opened onto nostalgia, rather than the kind of singleminded passion for the play and its hero that drove Lord Robert Baden-Powell to write, in his fifties to his bride-to-be, asking her whether she was "perhaps Wendy?" and inviting her to go with him to a performance of *Peter Pan*. (The future Lady Baden-Powell, for her part, imagined herself as a "Lady Scoutmaster," wearing not the Girl Guides' but the Boy Scouts' uniform—so perhaps they were well matched, after all.[40]) But Baden-Powell's fixation on Peter Pan was compelled by his belief that such a passion was innocent and ideal.

Transgression without guilt, pain, penalty, conflict, or cost: this is what Peter Pan—and *Peter Pan*—is all about. The boy who is really a woman; the woman who is really a boy; the child who will never grow up; the colony that is only a country of the mind. A contemporary version of that fantasy cannot afford to tie itself, any longer, to the plot of Barrie's *Peter Pan*, with its not-so-buried stories of race, gender, and class inequality—not only because the underplot is morally culpable, but also because in a multicultural society such a fantasy no longer really works. The embarrassing and invidious racial subtext of "The Great White Father" in *Peter Pan* is thus another repressed that returns. And its return discloses a new identity for Peter Pan.

For the real energy of the Peter Pan cult does not, at this moment in theatrical history, lie any longer with Barrie's play. The quintessential incarnation of Peter Pan today is not Cathy Rigby but rather the pop entertainer *Vanity Fair* called the decade's biggest star and the "ultimate crossover artist"—Michael Jackson.

"Crossover" here is a technical term from the world of popular music, denoting the success of black artists with white (as well as black) audiences—a phenomenon that scholars of the field date to the mid-to-late eighties.[41] In 1987 *Billboard* magazine began to list a Hot Crossover 30 Chart. And the two artists that above all seem to have made crossover "hot" were Prince and Michael Jackson. "Maybe it started with [Jackson's] *Thriller*," writes one critic, with admiration (Perry, 51).

Constructed from the first as a child star, Jackson seems to have sensed from the beginning that to grow up would be to put an end to his magic. "Michael Jackson really does not want to grow up," comments one observer. "He's said so many times."[42] "I would like to think that I'm an inspiration for the children I meet," Jackson writes in his autobiography, *Moonwalker*. "It was kids who never let me down."[43] He identifies explicitly with other performers who entered the limelight as children. "I love Elizabeth Taylor," he says, "I identify with her very strongly because of our experiences as child stars" (Jackson, 281). Explaining "the nose job I freely admitted I had, like many performers and film stars," he draws an analogy between himself and Judy Garland (Jackson, 38-39). (Thus the child stars with whom he compares himself are, interestingly, women.) Michael Jackson is certainly not a cross-dresser. His appeal is androgynous, and ageless. When he dances, he flies; in some of his videos he literally scatters fairy- or pixie-dust. "We Are the World, We Are the Children," he sings, stressing the fact that, from the moment he wrote it, "I had thought that song should be sung by children. When I first heard children singing it . . . I almost cried" (Jackson, 262).

Michael Jackson as a cultural figure, Michael Jackson in performance, erases and de-traumatizes not only the boundaries between male and female, youth and age, but also that between black and white. For Jackson—in performance—enacts the fantasy of transcendence. In the video of "Moonwalker" he flies above all boundaries as if conflict, and mortality itself, could simply be transcended. In his private life he befriended and identified with Ryan White, the young AIDS patient who was for tragic reasons a boy who would never grow up.

The power of Michael Jackson as an entertainer is that he seems to internalize these cultural category crises, and, in internalizing them, to make possible a new fantasy of transcendence—a fantasy that is, perhaps, as close to innocence as the age allows. "The Legend Continues," declares another of his albums and videos. Appropriately, *Life* magazine described Michael Jackson in its special issue on the eighties not only as "the highest-impact rock star this side of Presley" and "the most fluid dancer this side of Astaire," but also as "the most androgynous folk hero this side of Peter Pan."[44] Indeed, it comes as no surprise to find that he lives on a 2,700-acre estate near Santa Barbara—featuring a zoo, and a private amusement park—that is called Never Land Ranch.[45]

8

CHERCHEZ LA FEMME:
CROSS-DRESSING IN DETECTIVE FICTION

He'd taken a wig out of the bag he carried, donning it, looking up at
me with a curious light in his eyes.
I was looking at the blonde who'd killed Daggett.

Sue Grafton, *"D" is for Deadbeat*[1]

THE CASE OF THE MISSING TRANSVESTITE

Cross-dressing is a classic strategy of disappearance in detective fiction. The lady
vanishes by turning into a man—or the man by turning into a woman. In P.D. James's
Devices and Desires[2] (1989) the woman dressed in trousers, a beret, and a trench coat who
lures victims into the bushes turns out to be a man in disguise; in Charlotte McLeod's
The Corpse in Oozak's Pond (1987) Professor Peter Shandy, an amateur detective, spies on
the cross-dressed murderer through a keyhole in a parody of the primal scene, gaining
by this vantage point "a clear view of the hands that had always been kept covered and
. . . the head that wasn't wearing a wig."[3] In Sue Grafton's *"D" is for Deadbeat* a young
boy whose family has been killed by a drunk driver masquerades as a woman to lure him
to his death. In the film *La Cage aux Folles* (1978) the strait-laced Chairman of the League
of Decency finds himself trapped by investigative reporters in an apartment above a
transvestite nightclub, and escapes detection by putting on makeup, a wig, and an off-
the-shoulder dress. And in Ellery Queen's 1970 novel *The Last Woman in His Life*[4] the
murderer is a closeted gay transvestite whose overprotective mother had kept him in
dresses and whose library shelves are crowded with telltale works by Melville, Proust,
Wilde, and Christopher Marlowe. Employing every homophobic cliché imaginable,
Queen's novel (the name of the author, a pseudonym for a pair of presumably straight
male collaborators, seems almost like self-parody here) culminates in a dénouement in
which the killer, dressed in a sequined gown, a green "fun" wig, and a pair of long white
gloves, is rejected by the object of his affections and murders him in a cataclysm of self-
hating rage.

At the close of literally dozens of English Renaissance plays the cross-dressed page doffs her doublet and hose and reveals herself to be a woman—usually a well-born and marriageable woman. This "blank page" is inscribed with a double story, a double "reality." But in detective stories the woman, instead of materializing, often disappears: into thin air, down a conjectural rabbit hole, or, as I will suggest in a moment, into what Sigmund Freud described as the navel of the dream. In *The Last Woman in His Life*, for example, the word "home," the clue whispered by the dying man, which turns out on the novel's last page to have been—according to detective Queen—a failed attempt to communicate the word "homosexual," asserts as well the uncanny or *unheimlich* nature of the murderer: familiar and strange, alien and known, male and female, for the cross-dressed culprit was a longtime friend whose transvestism, like his homosexuality, had been concealed from the victim.

What are the implications here for narrative? The novel of detection plays at and with rational structures, with logic, with an accretion of detail that slowly and carefully builds up a picture of the criminal—what these days is called a "profile," what medicine—or psychology—calls a syndrome, what Freud and Sherlock Holmes would agree to call a case. The profile is read, the syndrome is diagnosed, the case is conjecturally "solved"— and then the whole picture dissolves.

The cross-dresser plays a crucial narrative role as that which is mistaken, misread, overlooked—or looked *through*. In order for the mystery to play itself out, for the suspense to be prolonged, it is crucial for both the reader and the detective to fail, at first, to recognize the existence of a transvestite in the plot. The (false) assumption that a person wearing a dress and long blonde hair is a woman, or that a slim figure in pants is a boy, is a necessary stage in the unraveling of the plot. In fact, the habit of looking *through* rather than *at* the cross-dresser, which—I have been arguing—constitutes a major obstacle to an understanding of how transvestism works as an intervention in literature and culture, is in the detective story an absolutely foundational move. In other words, writers of detective fiction deliberately make use of the erasure (or appropriation) of the cross-dresser; only belatedly does the transvestite phantom assume an independent conceptual reality as the clue that has been (in)visible all along. The "Purloined Letter" strategy, to hide something in plain view, is never better exemplified than in the case of the missing transvestite. When he or she is "found," or discovered, the mystery is solved. Thus the remarkable number of recent detective stories that have included cross-dressers as hinges of plot development and disclosure testify, not only to a general social and cultural interest in the ambiguities of gender boundaries, but also to the function of such over-looking as part of what makes detective fiction—and narrative structures—work.

I want to look closely and in some detail at a few detective novels and short stories, all by prominent practitioners of the craft (Dorothy Sayers, Arthur Conan Doyle, Josephine Tey, Ruth Rendell), for each reveals something telling—we may as well call it a clue— about the conjunction of sartorial gender and the un-knowability of essences or identities, the ways in which clothes can, quite calculatingly, make the man (or woman). It will be immediately clear that these detective plots have many congruences with the genre of the horror film, with films like Hitchcock's *Psycho* and De Palma's *Dressed to Kill*. But one thing that is especially fascinating about the way cross-dressing works in detective fiction is the way in which it concerns itself with language, and with the written and spoken word printed on a page—in dialogue, in narrative, in encapsulated letters, or other inset clues—as a hieroglyph of transvestic impersonation.

Let me give two brief illustrations of this kind of hieroglyph, one from Conan Doyle's *Study in Scarlet*, the other from a police procedural novel by mystery writer Ruth Rendell.

A Study in Scarlet contains one overt scene of cross-dressing and disappearance, in which a cab supposed to be conveying an old woman whom Holmes is trailing to her lodgings proves, on arrival, to be empty. "You don't mean to say," exclaims Watson, "that that tottering, feeble old woman was able to get out of the cab while it was in motion, without either you or the driver seeing her?"

> "Old woman be d———d!" said Sherlock Holmes, sharply. "We were the old women, to be so taken in. It must have been a young man, and an active one, too, besides being an incomparable actor. The get-up was inimitable. He saw that he was followed, no doubt, and used this means of giving me the slip."[5]

This is the classic instance, a maneuver borrowed, as Holmes is quick to see, from the stage. But elsewhere in Conan Doyle's novel there occurs, in effect, a different kind of occasion for cross-dressing, an occasion which is specifically *linguistic* rather than sartorial, but in which, once again, the lady vanishes. It occurs in the "dark, grimy apartment" in London where Holmes, Watson, and the self-important police detectives Lestrade and Gregson discover a clue written on the wall: "Across this bare space there was scrawled in blood red letters a single word—RACHE" (*Scarlet*, 25). Lestrade exults in the discovery "with the air of a showman exhibiting his show," and to his colleague's depreciatory question "What does it mean?" he replies, triumphantly:

> "Mean? Why, it means that the writer was going to put the female name Rachel, but was disturbed before he or she had time to finish. You mark my words, when this case comes to be cleared up, you will find that a woman named Rachel has something to do with it. It's all very well for you to laugh, Mr. Sherlock Holmes. You may be very smart and clever, but the old hound is the best, when all is said and done." (*Scarlet*, 25)

Holmes, who had indeed burst into laughter, bides his time until they prepare to leave, at which point he delivers what the narrator describes accurately enough as a "Parthian shot": "One . . . thing, Lestrade . . . 'Rache' is the German for 'revenge': so don't lose your time looking for Miss Rachel." And the lady vanishes.

Here is another brief but telling example, from Ruth Rendell's 1978 cross-dressing mystery, *A Sleeping Life*.[6] Inspector Wexford is seeking to learn the answers to a series of related questions: Who killed the "biggish and gaunt" (Rendell, 6) Rhoda Comfrey, found wearing heavy makeup and stiletto heels? What is her relationship to the elusive author Grenville West, deemed "almost certainly homosexual" by Wexford's prudish partner, since West is unmarried, likes France, and writes historical novels (Rendell, 126)? One of West's books is dedicated to "Rhoda Comfrey, without whom this book could never have been written."

But the ultimate clue for Wexford turns out to be a matter of orthography, a diphthong: the "*ae*" he hears, mistakenly, at the beginning of the word "eonism," when it is spoken by his disaffected married daughter. (A woman would " 'just have to practice aeonism,' observed the daughter, bitterly, 'if she really wanted to have a man's position in the world' " [Rendell, 128].) The diphthong is entirely Wexford's aural invention (his daughter speaks, and does not write, the word), and it consequently takes him several pages and several forays through the dictionary to realize that the word that haunts him is not related to "transcending time" (Rendell, 149) but rather to the Chevalier d'Eon (and, since Wexford does his homework, to Isabelle Eberhardt, James Miranda Barry, and Martha Jane Burke—better known as Calamity Jane—all famous lifelong transvestites).

Rhoda Comfrey, it turns out, is a cross-dresser with a double life; she is also Grenville West, and her death occurred when a young woman infatuated with "West" came face to face with her on a bus queue: "What [the murderer] saw when they confronted each other must have been enough to cause a temporary loss of reason. . . . She saw, in fact, a travesty in the true meaning of the word, and she stabbed to death an abomination" (Rendell, 180).

In this case, instead of disappearing into her other identity and escaping from the text, as for a while she seems to do, Rhoda Comfrey reassumes her "real" gender and the rather exaggerated feminine garb that marks her as a figure of pathos, a failure as a woman who finds comfort as well as material success in her existence as a man. It is this appearance that marks her as a "travesty" and an "abomination." For her "dressing as a woman was very much what it would be like for a normal man to be forced into drag" (Rendell, 174). Somehow the cross-dressed woman is herself to blame.

Does the telltale diphthong indicate something extra, or something missing? The *ae* in "aeonism" is in fact a misspelling of the term for transvestite, not an alternative form of the word. It is detected through an analogy with "mediaeval," where two spellings are accepted—but that period seems "aeons" away, and the historicity of cross-dressing, although attested to by the obligatory list of famous transvestites, is regarded throughout as a kink; the murderess, a rather pitiful and wistful figure, is treated with compassion both by the detective and by the author. But the diphthong itself becomes the orthographic mark of cross-dressing: two-in-one, two-as-one, inaudible as difference—passing. A diphthong, we might remember, is a literally a "double voice," a "double sound"—a phonetic equivalent of the question of identity. In detecting the diphthong Inspector Wexford, a very literary policeman, detects a whole invisible history of representation.

As we will see, these linguistic, orthographic, or grammatical clues appear time after time as counterparts to literal acts of cross-dressing within detective texts. My next example, from Dorothy Sayers, may further clarify this point.

INDEFINITE ARTICLES

In one of Dorothy Sayers's several short stories featuring her aristocratic detective Lord Peter Wimsey, a young French thief is apprehended by the urbane and bilingual Wimsey through a gender error in language.[7] The thief is a "slim, shingled creature with the face of a Paris *gamin*," whom Wimsey finds attractive on first glance, although he "was forced to admit to himself that her ankles were a trifle on the thick side" (Sayers, 26). In the stepped-up pace of the short story format, where every phrase counts, this is already a clue to gender ambiguity. The young woman is overheard in a heated argument with her male traveling companion about which of them has the tickets for the Channel crossing; a helpful porter suggests that the missing tickets may be in the man's trousers pocket, as indeed they turn out to be. But in the meantime, listening to the long exchange among travelers and their porter in French, Lord Peter has heard the young woman say something curious: "Me prends-tu pour un imbecile?" His suspicions are immediately aroused, he tracks down the young lady and finds that she is working as a lady's maid to a wealthy Duchess, and ultimately he unmasks "her" as a female impersonator.

The title of Sayers's story is "The Entertaining Episode of the Article in Question," and Lord Peter's disquisition on the crime makes the identity of the "article" clear. It is perhaps worth taking note of *his* language as he does so. "I have mentioned to you before, Charles," he says to his friend the police inspector,

> the unwisdom of falling into habits of speech. They give you away. Now, in France, every male child is brought up to use masculine adjectives about himself. He says: Que je suis beau! But a little girl has it rammed home to her that she is female: she must say: Que je suis belle! It must make it beastly hard to be a female impersonator. When I am at a station and I hear an excited young woman say to her companion, "Me prends-tu pour *un* imbecile"—the masculine article arouses curiosity. And that's that!

At this point the chastened thief bows in the direction of the detective and compliments him on his command of the French language. "I will," he says, "pay great attention in future to the article in question" (Sayers, 34).

But there is more than one article in question here. Notice that Wimsey's own "habits of speech" clothe gender in sexuality; the French girl "has it rammed home to her that she is female." We discover that the thief's real name is "Jacques Lerouge, known as Sans-culotte"—the man without breeches, his name taken from the French revolutionaries who wore pantaloons instead of the knee-breeches favored by the upper classes. And the missing "billet" had been found in the "pantalon" of the supposed young woman's companion.

Furthermore, the pseudonym of Jacques Sans-culotte in his role as a lady's maid is "Célestine Berger" ("Nobody off the stage is called Célestine," says the ever-acute Wimsey. "You should say 'under the name of Célestine Berger' "). This too is a learned gender joke, for *La Celestina* is a famous Spanish Golden Age text about a hymen-mender, one who sews up the hymens of girls and women who have lost their virginity.[8] At once inside and outside, the "in-between" that erases the distinction between, the hymen concealed inside "Célestine's" name—a name immediately perceived as false, as itself a restitching of what has been opened—re-signifies in yet another romance language the question of gender, anatomical, sartorial, grammatical.

GOODNIGHT, IRENE

"To Sherlock Holmes she is always *the* woman." So begins one of the earliest of the Holmes stories, "A Scandal in Bohemia." And who is "she"? Irene Adler, who bests him at his own game, who eludes his capture (and her own humiliating display as quarry to Holmes's client, the King of Bohemia)—who escapes his trap as she escapes his notice, by cross-dressing as "a slim youth in an ulster." In this case *the* woman of detective fiction is the cross-dressed woman, the place where X marks the spot of something that is not there.

The faithful Doctor Watson had, by his own account, he says, drifted apart from Holmes because of his own recent marriage and "complete happiness." Actually, what he writes is "my marriage had drifted us away from each other," as if the marriage were the agent, he and Holmes the passive recipients of its agency. Watson's wife (at this point, 1888, his first wife, Mary Morstan) is not mentioned; it is the institution, not the woman-as-wife (or the wife-as-woman), that acts, while Holmes, "who loathed every form of society with his whole Bohemian soul," continues his detective investigations, "alternating from week to week between cocaine and ambition."

To Sherlock Holmes she is always *the* woman. I have seldom heard him mention her under any other name. In his eyes she eclipses and predominates the whole of her sex. It was not that he felt any emotion akin to love for Irene Adler. All emotions, and that one particularly, were abhorrent to his cold, precise but admirably balanced mind. He was, I take it, the most perfect reasoning and observing machine that the world has seen, but as a lover he would have placed himself in a false position. He never spoke of the softer passions, save with a gibe and a sneer. . . . And yet there was but one woman to him, and that woman was the late Irene Adler, of dubious and questionable memory.[9]

The "late" Irene Adler. So she is dead—she has not escaped, after all. Watson seems eager to pin her down, to be finished with her story, even as he acknowledges her fascination for Holmes, and perhaps because of that fascination. Apparently Watson does not share Holmes's unambivalent admiration; in this opening paragraph, which ends so like an obituary, he describes Irene as "of dubious and questionable memory." By "memory," Watson means, presumably, moral reputation. Indeed, no woman could be less like the docile, daughterly Mary Morstan, Watson's wife, than Irene Adler, who outwits Holmes by penetrating his disguise and turns the tables on him by cross-dressing as a man, calling out cheekily on the street "Good-night, Mister Sherlock Holmes," before departing England forever. Irene's "dubious and questionable" behavior, in Watson's disapproving phrase, most probably includes both her sexual affairs, including the one with the King of Bohemia that threatens to culminate in the "scandal" of the title, and her stage career. As she writes to Holmes in taking her leave of him, "you know, I have been trained as an actress myself. Male costume is nothing new to me. I often take advantage of the freedom which it gives" (Doyle, 228).

But let us linger for a moment on Watson's words of disapprobation: "the late Irene Adler, of dubious and questionable memory."

When Holmes asks Watson to look Irene up in his index, he finds a suggestive biographical summary:

Born in New Jersey in the year 1858. Contralto—hum! La Scala, hum! Prima donna Imperial Opera of Warsaw—yes! Retired from operatic stage—ha! Living in London—quite so! (Doyle, 215)

This biographical note contains all the clues needed to unravel the mystery, such as it is, of Doyle's story, if not of Irene's identity. A career in European opera was for American women of the period often both professionally lucrative and socially liminal. Liaisons between opera singers and titled figures were not unusual, and "retired from operatic stage" is a plausible euphemism for "kept woman." Operatic "trouser roles" had achieved a considerable popularity, so that women were often seen on the stage playing and singing the parts of young men, in operas like *Faust* and *The Marriage of Figaro*. The male "freedom" that such cross-dressed women exhibited on the stage itself contributed to their erotic appeal, to the scandalousness of their untenable promise. Irene's voice is low for a woman; contralto is the lowest female voice part, intermediate between mezzo-soprano and tenor, and thus a sign of her capacity for crossing gender boundaries. Thus when she calls out to him in the street, Irene's voice will not give her away, even though Holmes will remember that he has heard it somewhere before.

Why is she said to be born in New Jersey? Perhaps as an oblique reference to that other king's mistress from the other Jersey, Lillie Langtry, who was born in 1853, and whose stage career—in theater rather than opera—culminated in a famous portrayal of Rosalind, the cross-dressed heroine of Shakespeare's *As You Like It*. But in any case Irene's American nationality is yet another indication of her liminal status. Her "freedom," on which she comments in her farewell letter, is suggested at the outset by her international career, her rootlessness: New Jersey, Milan, Warsaw, London. When last heard of she is heading for "the Continent"—last heard of, we should say, until the news comes from Watson in his report of the case that she is dead. What a relief such news must have been to him.

"A Scandal in Bohemia" is, at least in part, a rewriting of Poe's "Purloined Letter," and a comparison between these two classics of detection reveals some telling similarities and equally telling differences. In Doyle's "Scandal" the King is not, as he is in Poe, an obliquely mentioned "personage," but Wilhelm Gottsreich Sigismond von Ormstein, Grand Duke of Cassel-Falstein, and hereditary King of Bohemia. And in Doyle it is the King, and not, as in Poe, the Queen, who is the "illustrious personage whose honor and peace are . . . jeopardized."[10] In fact the gender reversals, in a story that will culminate in a moment of cross-dressing, are not without significance. The King himself arrives at Baker Street in a costume that, in its non-Englishness, seems almost like a masquerade costume, and in some details feminized, despite his 6' 6" height. As Watson records,

His dress was rich with a richness which would, in England, be looked upon as akin to bad taste. Heavy bands of astrakhan were slashed across the sleeves and fronts of his double-breasted coat, while the deep blue cloak which was thrown over his shoulders was lined with flame-coloured silk and secured at the neck with a brooch which consisted of a single flaming beryl. (Doyle, 213)

Like Poe's Queen, the King of Bohemia has been guilty of indiscretion, in this case an entanglement with Irene Adler. Instead of a letter, the incriminating evidence is a photograph. The King is now about to be married to the second daughter of the King of Scandinavia, Clotilde Lothman von Saxe-Meningen (again the name is ostentatiously given rather than, as in Poe, occluded and effaced), and since the Scandinavian royal family have "strict [moral] principles" and the lady herself is "the very soul of delicacy" (Doyle, 216), revelation of the King's affair would be catastrophic. Irene has threatened to send the photograph to the Scandinavian royals on the day that the Bohemian King's betrothal is publicly proclaimed, and the King is convinced that she will do it: "she has a soul of steel. She has the face of the most beautiful of women, and the mind of the most resolute of men" (Doyle, 216).

Holmes's job is to retrieve the photograph. As did the police in "The Purloined Letter," so the King's agents have tried, without success, to retrieve the incriminating document by searching Irene's house. Poe's Prefect of Police reports that the Minister's apartment has been minutely examined, and the Minister himself "has been twice waylaid, as if by footpads, and his person rigorously searched" (Poe, 11), and the King likewise describes previous attempts to find the photograph: "Twice burglars in my pay ransacked her house. Once we diverted her luggage when she travelled. Twice she has been waylaid. There has been no result" (Doyle, 216). Just as Dupin staged a distracting outcry in the street that enabled him to effect the substitution of his letter for the Queen's in the Minister's card rack, so Holmes hires accomplices to lurk in the street outside Irene's house and, disguised as a Non-conformist clergyman, himself feigns injury in a street brawl in order to be carried into the house. Having instructed Watson to set off a smoke rocket and raise a cry of fire, he is able to watch Irene's actions when she thinks her possessions are threatened, and notes the probable location of the photograph ("in a recess behind a sliding panel just above the right bell-pull") just as Dupin, on his first visit to the Minister, noted the probable location of the letter in the card rack hanging on the mantlepiece. And just as Dupin returned the next day to perform the act of theft and substitution, so Holmes intends to do the same, bringing, for his own gratification, the King and Watson with him. "It might be a satifaction to his Majesty to regain it [the photograph] with his own hands" (Doyle, 226).

Only something goes wrong. When Holmes and his party return to Irene's house, they find that she has departed, taking the incriminating photograph of the two lovers with her, and leaving behind another photograph of herself alone, in evening dress, and a letter explaining her own detective activities. When Holmes and Watson returned to Baker Street the previous evening, they were greeted by a passerby, who called out, "Good-night, Mister Sherlock Holmes." "There were several people on the pavement at the time, but the greeting appeared to come from a slim youth in an ulster who had hurried by. 'I've heard that voice before,' said Holmes, staring down the dimly lit street. 'Now, I wonder who the deuce that could have been" (Doyle, 227).

"Who the deuce." The "slim youth" is of course a double figure, the cross-dressed Irene, whose dual nature has already been described by that least subtle of observers, the self-important King: "she has the face of the most beautiful of women, and the mind of the most resolute of men." In the letter she leaves for Holmes she describes her penetration of his clergyman's disguise and her response in kind:

> But, you know, I have been trained as an actress myself. Male costume is nothing new to me. I often take advantage of the freedom which it gives. I sent John, the coachman, to watch you, ran upstairs, got into my walking-clothes, as I call them, and came down just as you departed.
>
> Well, I followed you to your door, and so made sure that I was really an object of interest to the celebrated Mr. Sherlock Holmes. Then I, rather imprudently, wished you good-night, and started for the Temple to see my husband. (Doyle, 228)

The fact that Irene leaves a letter behind her is another revision of Poe; where Dupin had the last word in his battle of wits and revenge with the Minister, Irene, in the position of the Minister, gets her own last word in as she departs. And the substitution, too, is hers rather than the detective's, here the replacement of one photograph (rather than one letter) for another.

For Holmes the first picture occupies the place of the primal scene, depicting the lovers together ("We were both in the photograph." "Oh, dear! That is very bad! Your Majesty has indeed committed an indiscretion" [Doyle, 216]), while he himself, as is common for fictional detectives, is in the position of the fascinated and excluded child onlooker. ("He never spoke of the softer passions, save with a gibe and a sneer. They were admirable things for the observer—excellent for drawing the veil from men's motives and actions. But for the trained reasoner to admit such intrusions into his own delicate and finely adjusted temperament was to introduce a distracting factor which might throw a doubt upon all his mental results" [Doyle, 209].) The unimaginable liaison between King and actress remains untouchable, unable to be recovered; Irene has taken away the double photograph, as she has taken herself away, leaving England "never to return" (Doyle, 228) with her husband, the lawyer Godfrey Norton.

Indeed Irene Adler's marriage, a match which she substitutes for and prefers to the originally desired marriage with the King ("I love and am loved by a better man than he," she writes to Holmes), is an occasion at which Holmes—once more in disguise—is pressed into service as an official witness. His recompense for this service, appropriately enough in terms of the story's logic of substitution, is a "sovereign," a gold coin which he tells Watson he will wear on his watch chain in memory of the event. But his real reward, the payment he requests from the King (as a substitute for the ring the King offers from his own finger), is the photograph, that is, the second photograph, the photograph of Irene alone, in evening dress. He will possess her simulacrum, and will take that simulacrum from the King, as his by right. But the other Irene, the Irene of the walking-clothes who beats him at his own game, escapes—escapes the story, escapes England, escapes both the King and Holmes. Her absence, his inability to possess her, confirms his vocation and his quest. Like Spenser's Prince Arthur, following the trace of pressed grass that is his only sign of the vanished Faerie Queene, Holmes undergoes his series of "Adventures" as displacements of the quest for *the* woman. But we might say that what is "pressed" in *The Faerie Queene* is *re*-pressed in "The Adventures of Sherlock Holmes." Indeed, the only other figure who likewise eludes his grasp, at least for a while, is the master criminal, the Napoleon of crime, Professor Moriarty.

So Holmes does not see what he desires to see, the photograph of Irene and the King. He is compelled to witness (that is, to see officially) Irene's marriage to Norton. Violating one of his own key precepts, he sees but he does not observe when he glances at the slim youth in the ulster who calls out his name. "Good-night, Mister Sherlock Holmes." In the text the word "Mister" is written out, not abbreviated, although the more usual abbreviated form appears elsewhere in the same story, as for example in Watson's closing paragraph ("how the best plans of Mr. Sherlock Holmes were beaten by a women's wit"

[Doyle, 229], or even in Irene's letter to him). I will hazard the guess that "Mister" written out fully in Irene's single transvestite line carries an undertone of mockery, a false honorific quality: "I call you 'Mister' in recognition of your status as a great detective; but 'Mister' as a title of respect, like 'Mister' as a sign of gender, can be mis-leading, mis-taken, myster-ious." Watson's final sentence, the last sentence of the story, returns to this question of title and address:

> He used to make merry over the cleverness of women, but I have not heard him do it of late. And when he speaks of Irene Adler, or when he refers to her photograph, it is always under the honourable title of *the* woman. (Doyle, 229)

IF THE SHOE FITS

In Josephine Tey's mystery novel, *To Love and Be Wise*, a beautiful young man appears at a publisher's book party, captivates the residents of an artist's colony in the "discovered" village of Salcott St. Mary, and, shortly thereafter, disappears, leaving behind him the suspicion that he has met with foul play.

From his first appearance in the novel, Leslie Searle is described not only as beautiful but as "disconcerting" and "uncanny," evoking a sense of "wrongness," a "pricking excitement."[11] The seasoned and sophisticated London detective Alan Grant is described three times as being "disconcerted" (Tey, 6,8,13) when, in the crush at the publisher's party, Searle presses close to him and looks up at him, laughing. Walter Whitmore, the beloved British radio personality whom Searle has come to the party to meet, notes a "strangeness" about him, an "unplaceable quality. Something not quite of the world of men" (Tey, 50). Emma Garrowby, who dislikes Searle, thinks of him as "the creature" (Tey, 30, 55), and, shying away from the word "beauty," speaks of his "personableness" instead (Tey, 23). Lavinia Fitch, whose romance novel is being honored at the party, thinks that he is "uncanny," "there is no other word" (Tey, 58), and remarks, in a kind of paraphrase of Freud on the narcissistic woman, that she gets "the same 'kick' out of being in a room with him that I would get out of being in a room with a famous *criminal*. Only nicer, of course. But the same feeling of—of *wrongness*" (Tey, 59, emphasis added).[12]

The reader will not be surprised, under the circumstances, and given these plain hints, to learn that Leslie Searle is a woman masquerading as a man. Her intent is, in fact, criminal; Walter Whitmore had been engaged to her beloved cousin, the actress Marguerite Merriam, and Searle blames Walter—wrongly, as it turns out—for Marguerite's suicide. She has arrived at Salcott St. Mary in her (perfectly legitimate and public) persona as Leslie Searle, the famous American photographer of movie stars, his identity attested to by a photographic self-portrait in the magazine *Screen Bulletin*. Her plan is to win

Whitmore's friendship and trust, convince him to collaborate on a co-authored travel book, and, at the first opportunity, do away with him.

I have used the third person singular feminine pronoun here for clarity's sake, but to call Searle "she" is in fact quite misleading, in terms both of the narrative exposition of the plot and—as I hope to convince you—of the point of cross-dressing in this, as in other, mystery fiction. "Leslie Searle" is how he is described, and in the masculine throughout, until his disappearance. Only later does Detective Grant discover that the Miss Lee Searle who lives in Hampstead and paints for a living, the woman whom he has taken for Searle's cousin, is in fact Leslie Searle himself—or rather, herself.

But we are getting ahead of the story here. Clues as to Searle's "true" gender abound in the text, from Walter's typically sentimental (and obtuse) perception that he is not of the world of men, to the observation of two percipient women that Searle gossiped with an elderly spinster film buff "as though he had been a woman himself and interested in the small talk of the film world" (Tey, 62), "like a couple of housewives swapping recipes" (63). Searle has "skin like a baby" and a "nice gentle voice," is "extraordinarily graceful for a man" ; "his attractions," Lavinia thinks, "don't add up to Leslie Searle." "The—the *exciting*—thing is left out. *What* is it that makes him different?" (Tey, 59). The "thing" that makes him exciting, of course, is *that* "the thing is left out"—without the phallus, Leslie Searle arouses excitement, pleasurable or unpleasurable, in everyone he meets. Emma Garrowby worries that "the creature" will make her daughter Liz, now engaged to Walter, fall in love with him. Liz Garrowby herself wonders at her own "attraction" to Searle, which she distinguishes, with relief, from being "in love" (Tey, 57). In a deftly plotted "nothing up my sleeve" moment very early in the book Liz is asked to pack Searle's clothing when he comes to Salcott as a houseguest, so that she, and the reader, can see that his wardrobe is unexceptionably male: "custom-made of the best materials," although his expensive shoes, which buckle rather than tying, are deemed regrettable— a sign of showy, American taste. And "nothing up my sleeve" marks a whole kind of rhetoric in the detective's mind, at least. When Searle disappears Inspector Grant remarks that the case "smell[s] strongly of sleight-of-hand. Now you see it, now you don't. The old conjurer's trick of the distracted attention. Ever seen a lady sawn in half?" he asks his Sergeant. "There's a strong aroma of sawn lady about this" (Tey, 80).

Sawn lady, indeed. For Searle *has* disappeared, after publicly picking a fight with Walter Whitmore in the sight of the patrons of the local inn. He was "provocative," reports the plummy Whitmore, ever the straight man. "I think that is the word" (Tey, 83). Inevitably, and according to Searle's plan, suspicion falls on Whitmore—has he murdered the young photographer and thrown him in the river? Without the body, nothing can be proven— but suspicion, to a revered and pompous public figure, is almost as bad as an actual charge of murder.

The vicar of Salcott St. Mary, an ardent adept of demonology, is ironically described by a chi-chi writer-in-residence as having "the perfect solution." He "believes that Searle was never really here at all. He holds that Searle was merely a demon who took human shape for a little, and disappeared when the joke grew stale or the—the juice ran dry, so to speak" (Tey, 114). Earlier, the intuitive Lavinia Fitch had recorded the same anticipatory fantasy: "If he were to disappear tonight, and someone told me that he was just a beautiful demon and not a human being at all, I would believe them. So help me, I would" (Tey, 59). What is really ironic about the vicar's (and Lavinia's) reading of Leslie Searle is its truth; this "perfect solution" in fact describes the perfect crime, in which the narcissistic woman cross-dresser, with her "self-sufficiency and inaccessibility" like that of "great criminals" and "humorists" (Freud, "Narcissism," 70), deconstructs her constructed identity and disappears down the rabbit hole, or into the navel of the dream.

The hole into which Leslie Searle disappears is elaborately described by the Inspector and the police. It is "an oblong of empty space" in a tin paint-box containing Searle's photographic equipment, from which "something roughly 10 inches by 3½ by 4 had been taken out" (Tey, 86–7). Because the box had not been disturbed since the disappearance, the space remained clearly defined; it had not been filled in by the tumbling about of other objects, and therefore remained as a tantalizing clue to Searle's identity. "What had lain in that oblong gap?" (Tey, 90) The guesses of various officials and others connected with the case assume the form of a psychological test: Sergeant Williams thinks it could have been a bar of soap or a revolver, the local garage man suggests a spanner, a famous actress proposes a hair brush. But the space in the photographic box remains the sign of Searle's disappearance—and of his identity, until its contents are at last revealed when Inspector Grant comes face to face with Miss Lee Searle of Hampstead. "No run-of-the-mill hard-working one-of-a-bundle detective would think up anything so outré as a parcel containing one pair of women's shoes and a coloured silk head-square" (Tey, 196). "You forgot my lipstick . . . in the little parcel," she returns with perfect good humor (Tey, 201).

So the parcel contained, in effect, materials for the construction of a woman—the shoes, the scarf, the lipstick—*even though* the person who assumed this disguise was herself *already* a woman. In other words, to disguise herself as a woman this woman has to cross-dress, to put on the external signs or accoutrements of "femaleness" or "femininity," in much the same way that male-to-female transvestites do.

That cross-dressing as a man for Leslie Searle is "natural," and femininity "constructed," is suggested by her own biographical narrative. Orphaned as a child in America, she wanted to travel and to photograph the world, so she took a car and "went West."

> I wore pants in those days just because they were comfortable and cheap, and because when you are five feet ten you don't look your best in girlish things. I hadn't thought of using them as—as camouflage until one day when I was leaning over the engine of the car a man stopped and said: "Got a match, bud?" and I gave him a light; and he looked at me and nodded and said: "Thanks, bud," and went away without a second glance. That made me think. A girl alone is always having

trouble—at least in the States she is—even a girl of five feet ten. And a girl has a more difficult time getting an "in" in a racket. So I tried it out for a little. And it worked. It worked like a dream. I began to make money on the Coast. (Tey, 200)

Here are the classic socio-economic reasons for a woman's cross-dressing: safety, economic success, entry into a man's world of easy camaraderie and acceptance. Readers of the novel are given an anticipatory clue about the existence of some such concealed narrative in Inspector Grant's encounter, shortly after Searle's disappearance, with Dora Siggins.[13]

He picked up Dora in the long straight of dull hedged lanes that ran for a mile or more parallel to the river just outside the town. In the distance he had taken the plodding figure to be a youth carrying a kit of tools, but as he came nearer and slowed in answer to the raised thumb, he found that it was a girl in dungarees carrying a shopping bag. She grinned cheekily at him and said:
"Saved my life, you have! I missed the bus because I was buying slippers for the dance tonight."
"Oh," said Grant, looking at the parcel that had evidently refused to go into the overflowing bag. "Glass ones?"
"Not me," she said. . . . "None of that home-by-midnight stuff about me. 'Sides, it wasn't a glass slipper at all, you know. It was fur. French, or something. We learned that at school." (Tey, 122)[14]

Despite her unisex clothes, which make her look like a young man with a tool kit, Dora is marked in the text as reassuringly heterosexual. Not only does she have dancing shoes, she also has a boyfriend who works in a garage, and whom she is engaged to marry as soon as he gets a pay raise. The boyfriend has the tools, she has the overflowing shopping bag. Long afterwards Grant remembers Dora Siggins's parcel containing dancing shoes, figures out by analogy what was in the "gap" in Searle's box, and sends Dora, anonymously, a box of chocolates, hoping "that it would lead to no misunderstanding with the boy friend" (123). But the box of chocolates as the sign of male-to-female courtship has already led to misunderstanding in the text, when Walter Whitmore brings home a "little packet" of chocolate dragées for his fiancée Liz Garrowby, congratulating himself on his unusual thoughtfulness, and finds that Leslie Searle has bought her "a great flat box of candy from the most expensive confectioners in Crome. Four pounds weight at the very least. . . . So like an American to buy something large and showy. It made him quite sick to look at it" (Tey, 55).

Notice "so like an American." "American" throughout the novel marks an ambivalent and liminal place as regards not only courtship customs but also dress and social behavior— much as it did with Conan Doyle's Irene Adler. Leslie Searle's "regrettable" shoes (Tey, 21) with buckles instead of ties are distinctly "American," and when Sergeant Williams, hearing from Grant that Searle was "a very good-looking young man indeed," jumps to a certain conclusion about his sexual object choices, Grant corrects him, obliquely, by displacing his answer from sexuality to geography:

"What was he like, sir?"

"A very good-looking young man indeed."

"Oh," Williams said, in a thoughtful way.

"No," said Grant.

"No?"

"American," Grant said, irrelevantly. And then, remembering that party, added: "He seemed to be interested in Liz Garrowby, now that I remember." (Tey, 74)

Within this relatively stable world, bounded by the indigenous residents of Salcott St. Mary on the one hand, and the "Salcott aliens" (Tey, 33) who have settled in this artist's colony on the other, Leslie Searle, American, like Leslie Searle, cross-dresser, is a liminal and disturbing presence, who becomes even more disturbing when he disappears. The phrase "artist's *colony*" is a fair enough political description: Marta Hallard the famous actress, Toby Tullis and Silas Weekley, temperamental best-selling novelists, Serge Ratoff the once-famous dancer now on the skids, Miss Easton-Dixon who writes a lucrative annual Christmas book, Lavinia Fitch and Walter Whitmore—these are colonizers whose invasion of sleepy Salcott St. Mary has transformed its economy as well as its politics. That Tullis and Ratoff are gay—and feuding former lovers—is of no consequence to the village, which accepts these marks of otherness as readily as it accepts Walter's plangent glorification of the pleasures of country life.

But Searle is "other" in a different way, and his presence puts in question the fairly stabilized binaries of country/city, artisan/artist, straight/gay, obscure/famous, that have enabled this "colony" within England to function. When Searle disappears, erasing the constructed fiction of his presence, leaving behind the gap in the box that is a figure for his identity, he performs an action which is, I want to suggest, highly characteristic of the role of the cross-dresser, and especially of the cross-dressed woman, in detective fiction. Searle opens the gap and slips through it. Cherchez la femme, but the woman, the cross-dressed woman, always escapes, because she was never really there.

Was—or in the historical present with which we tend to discuss novels—*is* Leslie Searle "actually" or "really" a woman? To say this is to miss the whole point, to reduce or appropriate to one side of a comforting binarism something that cannot be so readily reduced or appropriated. The vicar and the intuitive Lavinia Fitch are closer when they call Searle a demon, someone who was never really there. Consider the way in which Inspector Grant "proves" his case (to himself, for there is never really any expectation of prosecution, since there is no crime; the crime, like "Searle" and the "oblong gap," exist only as defined by the space that demarcates their absence). Grant has cabled to America, and asked the police of Jobling, Connecticut, to look up a birth certificate.

The infant that Mr. and Mrs. Durfey Searle took with them when they left Jobling for points south, was, they reported, female. (Tey, 203)

The structure of deferral and displacement in this statement is significant. When the Searle parents *left*, they *took with them* an infant who *was*, *they reported*, female. Like Leslie Searle's disappearance from Salcott St. Mary, this is a trace, or, rather, the record of a trace. Female infant Searle disappears from Jobling, Connecticut, and is "identified" by Grant as Miss Lee Searle of Hampstead, who had engineered a "slick exit from a masquerade" in place of "a planned get-out to murder." But like Searle's English lawyer, "an old man in a funny little office called Bing, Parry, Parry, and Bing, but I don't think he is any of them, actually" (Tey, 205), Lee/Leslie Searle (needless to say, the androgynous name, more common in England than in America, assists the uncanny affect from the beginning) is not so easy to identify. Like the murder plot itself, undertaken to avenge the death of Searle's beloved cousin, Marguerite Merriam, and abandoned because, as Grant points out, "You found out the person you loved never existed" (198), Searle's presence in and subsequent departure from Salcott St. Mary is a construction based upon a misapprehension. And it is through this loophole that the woman escapes, for she was never, in that sense, really there.

Grant confronts Lee Searle with a disquisition on transvestism that summarizes popular wisdom on the subject: a woman recently died in Gloucestershire who had worked for twenty years hauling coal; no one knew she was not a man, not even the doctor who attended her last illness. A "normal popular young man," who played billiards, belonged to a men's club, and was "walking out with one of the local beauties," was discovered to be "a normal young woman." "It happens somewhere or other every year or two. Glasgow [Tey's home town]. Chicago. Dundee." "Some are genuinely happier in men's things; but a great many do it from love of adventure, and a few from economic necessity. And some because it is the only way in which they can work out their schemes" (Tey, 194).

Here is the rational and comforting, because "medical" and "historicizing," account of the female transvestite. Like the psychiatrist's explanation of split personality in *Psycho*, and the detailed account of transsexual surgery offered at the end of *Dressed to Kill*, this explanation finally cannot describe the particularity or the affect of the present instance. Lee Searle lives part of her life in London as a woman painter, the other part in Hollywood as a famous male photographer. Even her "real" name is in some question: "My name actually is Leslie, but mostly they called me Lee. *She* always called me Lee." "So your passport is a woman's one?" Grant asks. "Oh, yes. It is only in the States that I am Leslie Searle. And not all the time there" (Tey, 200).

Furthermore, having "solved" the case, and contextualized it as "normal" transvestism, warning Lee Searle against the consequences of masquerade, Inspector Grant indulges himself in a final fantasy, a "lovely, mad notion" (Tey, 206). He will call up his actress friend from Salcott St. Mary, for whom he has often been a social escort, and ask if she wants another woman for her dinner party, "and she would say yes bring anyone you like, and he would bring them Lee Searle" (Tey, 206). Of course he can't do this, it would be "frivolous," "not . . . quite grown up," "sadly unbecoming an officer of the Criminal Investigation Department" (Tey, 206–7). He will have to solace himself with reporting the success of his detective efforts. So that what remains here, the residue, is desire. The "oblong of empty space where something had been taken out," the gap of the box of the cross-dressed woman, the space which has been identified only through the chance encounter with Dora Siggins has become a kind of Pan-Dora's box, and what is left is not evil but desire. As with Sherlock Holmes and Irene Adler, the trace left by the woman in man's clothes, by the construct of cross-dressing, becomes the impetus for detection, the path of displacement, one quest (for truth? for justice? for the answer to the puzzle or the riddle?) replacing another, which remains unsatisfied.

The presence in these *written* texts of an overdetermined linguistic or grammatical or even orthographic element acts out, as it were, the supplementarity of the transvestite—his or her presence as a necessary extra, an addition that was always there. In other kinds of narrative structures, like film, or drama, or biography, or psychoanalysis, the scene of discovery and reversal is played out somewhat differently, but in each of these structures, considered *as* narrative, the transvestite—and the cultural habit of translating or looking through the transvestite—plays a major role.

In the remainder of this chapter I will turn briefly to strategies of detection as they are manifested in some of these other narrative genres. The scene of discovery—the particular locus in which the "crime" of impersonation is revealed—is, as will be clear in a moment—highly suggestive for the cultural anxieties surrounding cross-dressing. In films, plays, and biographies the discovery space is very often the bed, the place of sexual unmasking; in psychoanalysis, it is the mirror.

BED CLOTHES

"Truths" about gender and sexuality in cross-dressing narratives are likely to be revealed in bed, which is one reason why bed scenes occur so frequently as moments of discovery—or near-discovery. In a way such scenarios of revelation are the obverse of the famous episode in *Nightwood* when Nora Flood finds Doctor O'Connor in bed in drag. Where Nora has known the doctor as a male-identified man and is startled to discover him wearing a dress, blond wig, rouge, and mascara, most bedtime "discoveries" pair two similarly dressed figures, supposedly of the same gender, whom exigencies of plot—some version of "no room in the inn"—have required to share a bed.

Famous bed scenes of sexual discovery in films like *Sylvia Scarlett, Queen Christina, Tootsie,* and *Some Like It Hot*—as well as in plays like Simone Benmussa's *Singular Life of Albert Nobbs* (1977)—confront both "male" and "female" cross-dressers with this test, which is, in dramatic or cinematic terms, a familiar discovery device from the vocabulary of farce. In fact the etymology of "farce," from "stuffed," suggests the logistical problem; the bed is overstuffed with too many personae: 1) the naive or innocent partner; 2) the cross-dresser in his or her assumed persona, and 3) the man or woman inside the cross-dressed disguise, who both fears and desires exposure, both fears to express, and expresses, desire. Which of these personae (the cross-dresser *in* costume, or the cross-dresser *within* the costume) is really the *third* here, the intrusive, disruptive, and deliciously destabilizing presence? The answer to this question, or rather, the question itself, is part of the conundrum of suspense and discovery.

But it is the doctor or mortician as the ultimate agent of discovery, the bed as a deathbed rather than a place of sexuality and procreation, that is a recurrent feature of the cross-dressing story as it is told, not in film or detective fiction, but in biography and newspaper reports. We have seen that Billy Tipton's lifelong transvestism was reported, not by his wife or his three adopted sons but by the funeral director. Likewise, as we will see in more detail below (Chapter 10), the Chevalier d'Eon's "real" identity as a man was revealed at his death to the astonishment of the gentlewoman who had been "her" companion for years.

One of the most compelling versions of this oft-told tale is that of Dr. James Miranda Barry, the Inspector General of the Medical Department of the British Army, who served for forty-six years as a physician and surgeon, and then was, as the Registrar General of Somerset House announced succinctly, "after his death found to be a Female."[15]

Throughout Barry's life rumors were spread about his gender: "Many surmises were in circulation relating to him," wrote a patient from his earliest days in Cape Town, "from the awkwardness of his gait and the shape of his person it was the prevailing opinion that he was a female,"[16] and another commented that "The grave doctor who was presented to me was a boy of 18, *with the form, the manners and the voice of a woman. . . .* ".[17] When Barry became the protegé of Lord Charles Somerset it was scandalously bruited about that Somerset was "Dr. Barry's little wife" (Rose, 70), a characterization intended to demean both parties by implying the existence of a homosexual liaison between them, especially since it was Barry, and not Lord Charles, who was frequently described as looking like a woman. Barry was scrupulously careful about hygiene, and famous for his unwillingness to submit to physical examinations.

Rumors, accusations, and "revelations" pursued him from South Africa to England to the Windward and Leeward Islands; many of those who met Dr. Barry in the 1850s— and wrote about the fact forty years later—took it for granted that he was a woman. Florence Nightingale, who took him at face value as a man, heartily disliked him because he had unforgivably scolded her in front of a crowd of soldiers. "After she was dead I was told she was a woman," Nightingale wrote. "I should say she was the most hardened creature I ever met throughout the army."[18]

Nightingale's account switches pronouns at the moment when she comes to describe Barry after death; before that she describes him sitting on "*his* horse," and writes that "*he* kept me standing" and "*he* behaved like a brute." Barry's biographer June Rose replaces these "he"s with bracketed "she"s, maintaining a consistent use of feminine pronouns throughout the book. Since Rose's biography is called *The Perfect Gentleman* we might suspect some irony in the juxtaposition, but Rose—like Barry's other biographers— insists on solving the mystery by emphasizing Barry's identification as a woman, suggesting a variety of motives for "her masquerade."[19]

When the Registrar General of Somerset House, the British records office, wrote— as he was bound by duty to do—to inquire about Barry's death, he received a reply from a staff surgeon who said he had known Barry for years in the West Indies and in England, and had never suspected that he was a woman. It was the charwoman who laid out the body who had brought certain physical anomalies to his attention. The charwoman had claimed that the body was that of a woman, and, moreover, that it bore stretch marks indicating that Barry had once borne a child. The doctor told her, rather shortly, that "whether Dr. Barry was a male or a female" was none of his business, much less of hers, but that he himself "thought he might be neither, viz., an imperfectly developed man," a "hermaphrodite."[20] This account is superbly melodramatized as a detective scenario of reversal and discovery in an 1881 novel about Barry, *The Modern Sphinx*, in which, at the crucial moment, an Assistant Surgeon "exclaim[ed] as he flung back the bed-clothes, 'See Barry is a woman!' "[21]

We may be amused by the dramatic style of *The Modern Sphinx*, but "See Barry is a woman!" is effectively the denouement of the historical biographies as well as the acknowledged fictionalizations of James Barry's life. Yet the question here remains: what does it mean to say that "he" was *really* "she"? If a person lives his or her life consistently under a gender identity different from that revealed by anatomical inspection after death, what is the force of that "reality"?

Correspondents to *The Lancet*, the British medical journal, reopened the question in a spirited correspondence in 1895 that suggests the detective story structure that lies not far below the surface of the Barry story—if terms like surface can be used at all reliably in a narrative that is, so to speak, all about the question of the surface. A Navy doctor wrote to ask whether "this story [of an Army doctor who turned out to be, post mortem, a woman] rests upon any credible foundation or is the mere figment of an idle brain?"[22] "James Barry is no figment, and the story of her sex is undoubted," replied a reader who had lived near Barry in Piccadilly.[23] The author of *A Modern Sphinx*, "E. Rogers, Lieutenant Colonel," wrote *The Lancet* several times to confirm the "truth" of the story (and to make readers aware that his book, though out-of-print, could still be obtained. In his fourth letter he included prices and a mailing address for interested buyers, indicating either considerable public interest or his desire to create some).[24]

What is perhaps most interesting in this correspondence, however, are the "clues": "in contradistinction to the shooting-coats which all the other students [at Edinburgh] wore, he invariably appeared in a long surtout," wrote one respondent. "Dr. Barry was afraid to go home by himself through a rather rough part of town" and could not be taught to box, since "he never would strike out, but kept his arms over his chest to protect it from blows." Yet despite noticing "the above-mentioned womanly traits," a doctor who had been a fellow student never had "the slightest suspicion of her sex."[25] A correspondent who wrote directly to Rogers (and whom Rogers sees fit to quote at length) mentions "a queer fondness for animals, keeping several cats and dogs very happily; rather bombastic in speech and repellent in manner, but kind and anxious to do good," adding that he feels he "must retain the feminine gender, for I believe that is only too true."[26]

But this is the investigative spirit of a London already familiar with the detective skills (and female impersonations) of Sherlock Holmes. Another article, published thirty years earlier in *The Medical Times and Gazette*, had noted that "the physique, the absence of hair, the voice, all pointed one way, and the petulance of temper, the unreasoning impulsiveness, the fondness for pets, were in the same direction," yet the author chose (at least in some sentences) to retain the masculine pronoun: "His declining years were comforted by the cat, dog, and parrot, so dear to elderly women, especially single ones."[27] And a stern and repressive letter from the Deputy-Inspector-General of Hospitals at Sandhurst tried to put all the nonsense aside once and for all: "The stories which have been circulated about him since his death are too absurd to be gravely refuted," he wrote.

> There can be no doubt among those who knew him that his real physical condition was that of a male in whom sexual development had been arrested about the sixth month of fetal life. It is greatly to be regretted that the opportunity of his death was allowed to pass without exact observation of his real condition by a skilled person.
>
> The real marvel of his history is, that being of a frame so feeble, without domestic resources, with a temper so irritable and even mischievous, in spite of frequent severe sickness in tropical climates, and constantly at variance with authority, [he] should have attained the highest rank in the Medical Department, and have lived to the age of 65 years.[28]

THE MIRROR CRACK'D

To pursue this question, it will be useful to look at yet another narrative paradigm that depends upon the reading of clues, suspense, hidden motives, and disguise: the detective story of psychoanalysis. From among the numerous possible examples of psychoanalysis as a mode of detective fiction that turns upon a problematics of gender, let me choose two: the first, one of Freud's most important case studies, actually (and importantly) an exercise in *textual* analysis, and the second, a brief but fascinating description of a fetishistic cross-dresser from Joan Riviere's essay, "Womanliness as a Masquerade." Both of these cases turn, in a way that is striking and suggestive, upon a scene of gender "discovery" that takes place before a mirror.

Senatspräsident Daniel Paul Schreber suffered from the delusion that he had to be transformed into a woman in order to redeem the world.[29] Schreber's case is a unique one for Freud in that what was analyzed was not the patient but his *Memoirs*, which were published in 1903. As Freud notes in his Introduction, he never met Schreber, but because of the particular nature of his illness a textual analysis of the *Memoirs* served as well, or better, than would psychoanalytic sessions:

> Since paranoics cannot be compelled to overcome their internal resistances, and since in any case they only say what they choose to say, it follows that this is precisely a disorder in which a written report or a printed case history can take the place of personal acquaintance with the patient. For this reason I think it is legitimate to base analytic interpretations upon the case history of a patient suffering from paranoia (or, more precisely, from dementia paranoides) whom I have never seen, but who has written his own case history and brought it before the public in print. (Freud, *Case of Paranoia*, 9)

Freud thus takes upon himself the role of textual critic, as Schreber has taken upon himself the role of doctor. The real doctor in the case, the doctor who attended Schreber, was the neuro-anatomist Paul Emil Flechsig, and it was to Flechsig that Schreber initially assigned the part of persecutor, the "person in question" to whom Schreber, once he has been transformed into a female body, was supposed, according to his *Memoirs*, to be surrendered for the purposes of sexual abuse. (Freud, *Case of Paranoia*, 19; Schreber, 56).

Cross-dressing figures prominently in Schreber's delusional fantasy. He tells us that he shaves his face clean of moustache and beard, and takes pleasure in "feminine toilet articles, in small feminine occupations, in the tendency to undress more or less and to look at himself in the mirror, to decorate himself with gay ribbons and bows" (Schreber, 388; Macalpine and Hunter, 273). Indeed, he protests that

> The *only thing* which could appear unreasonable in the eyes of other people is the fact, already touched on in the expert's report, that I am sometimes to be found standing before the mirror or elsewhere, with the upper portion of my body bared, and wearing sundry feminine adornments, such as ribbons, false necklaces, and the like. This only occurs, I might add, when I am *by myself*, and never, at least so far as I am able to avoid it, in the presence of other people. (Schreber, 429; Freud, 21)

And, again, he says that he is

> bold enough to assert that anyone who should happen to see me before the mirror with the upper portion of my torso bared—especially if the illusion is assisted by my wearing a little feminine finery—would receive an unmistakable impression of a *female bust*." (Schreber, 280; Freud, 33)

The "rays" or "voices" that tortured the Senatspräsident mocked his femininity, calling him, derisively, "Miss Schreber," in English (Schreber, 127; Freud, 20). From a very different place Freud joins this chorus, diagnosing Schreber's condition culturally as well as clinically as illness, as the desire for a loss (e-masculate), at the same time that he understands part of Schreber's delusion to be based upon his own childlessness, his desire to give birth, and thus to become the phallic mother, the self-sufficient bisexual. Why "*Miss* Schreber" in English? Because of the fear/desire that something would shortly be "missing"? (It is surprising, in a way, that Freud does not comment on this, since he is usually quick to note the importance of a foreign word or term in the dream-work.)

In one of the most ingenious and compelling passages of his analysis, Freud explores the various unconscious permutations of the (supposedly) unacceptable statement, "*I* (a man) *love him* (a man)," which he finds to underlie paranoia among males. This "homosexual wishful fantasy of *loving a man*" is translated, Freud suggests, into a variety of more "acceptable" manifest thoughts: "I do not *love* him—I *hate* him" (because he hates me; delusions of persecution); "I do not love *him*—I love *her*" (erotomania); "It is not *I* who love the man—*she* loves him"; or, "It is not *I* who love the women—*he* loves them" (jealousy); or, finally, "*I do not love at all—I do not love any one*" ("I love only myself"; megalomania, the sexual overvaluation of the ego) (Freud, *Case of Paranoia*, 62–65). As he did in his essay on "Fetishism," Freud here discovers that a striking behavioral disorder that manifests itself in a man's dressing up in women's clothes (and, in the case of Schreber, fantasied female body parts) is a clever defense against the acknowledgment of homosexuality.

Significantly, Freud describes this "transformation" as an "emasculation fantasy." Something is to be taken away from, not given or added to, Schreber in his metamorphosis into a woman. Schreber himself uses the term "unmanned" (*Entmannung*), which he glosses as "transformed into a woman," and describes in precise anatomical detail.[30] There is no question but that he considers this a degradation, since he couples it with the fantasy of being sexually "misused" by Flechsig and left to rot. But the degradation is conceptual rather than perceptual. Regarding himself as a powerless victim, rather than an instigator or desirer of these changes, Schreber uses in his description of the physical body he thinks himself to possess quite the opposite kind of language: phrases like "female nerves of voluptuousness," especially in the region of the breasts, and skin with "a softness peculiar to the female sex" (Schreber, 87; Freud, 32). In fact, he describes his assumption of female anatomical characteristics in terms of a kind of dressing, a putting or "drawing" on, rather than a taking off or un-sexing. As so often in descriptions of male-to-female cross-dressing, the cross-dresser puts *on* stereotypical attributes, bodily characteristics, or decorations (jewelry, makeup, wigs) rather than taking them off. Here again is woman as artifice and construct. Thus Schreber writes, in a remarkable passage,

It has become so much a habit with me to draw female buttocks on to my body—*honi soit qui mal y pense*—that I do it almost involuntarily every time I stoop. (Schreber, 233; Freud, 32-33)[31]

Honi soit qui mal y pense. The Old French warning, "evil to him that thinks evil," is, as it happens, the Motto of the Order of the Garter, an astonishing example, in this cross-dressing story, of the unconscious at work.

If Schreber were a patient in the 1980's, his doctor might have referred him to a gender identity clinic, and diagnosed him as a male transsexual. Indeed, that is, in effect, what two contemporary analysts do in their critique of Freud. "Schreber was not a transvestite," write Ida Macalpine and Richard Hunter. "Not uncommonly female patients complain of having a male mind in a female body, and male patients that they have a female mind: and request their body be altered accordingly, by surgery and hormones. When supported by physicians, especially endocrinologists, and surgeons, it accounts for the cases of change of sex reported in the newspapers" (Macalpine and Hunter, 404–405).

Thus one detective, Freud, looking *through* the transvestite, sees Schreber's fantasy of becoming a woman as a paranoid delusion, based upon an unsatisfactory relationship with his masterful father, an unsuccessful political career, a barren marriage, and repressed homosexual desires. For him the sex change fantasy is central to his interpretation, and the second delusion, that of redeeming the world, is dependent upon the first. Macalpine and Hunter, looking *at* the transvestite, reverse the importance of these two delusions, and suggest that Schreber would have benefited from an acceptance of his gender confusion. They refute Freud's clinical diagnosis of this symptom. "The answer may be simply that it is not unconscious homosexuality which makes him ill . . . to confront a patient with his anxiety and depression in terms of uncertainty in his own identity, to try and understand and trace out such body fantasies with him, often leads to amelioration of symptoms, sometimes surprisingly quickly." (Macalpine and Hunter, 410–411)

Since Schreber, by the time these analyses took place, was himself already a narrative, no definitive "solution" seems forthcoming, even if one were thought to be desirable. In any case, even after he had recovered from his most debilitating symptoms, Schreber apparently continued to cross-dress before the mirror, his upper body bared, wearing "sundry feminine adornments." "The Herr Senätspresident," wrote Freud, with what appear to be mixed emotions, "confesses to this frivolity at a date . . . at which he was already in a position to express very aptly the completeness of his recovery in the region of practical life" (Freud, *Case of Paranoia*, 21). Perhaps in this case the lady did not, entirely, vanish; she was still visible through the looking-glass.

Let me come, finally, to my other psychoanalytic example, that of the "manifest homosexual" man in Joan Riviere's "Masquerade" essay. I will have much more to say about Riviere's theory of masquerade elsewhere in this volume, especially below (Chapter 13) in my discussion of star-quality and theatrical display. What I want to point out here is simply the way in which this little fetishistic scenario—virtually a parenthetical remark in an essay largely devoted to the situation of *women* who assume a "mask of femininity"—

plays out the story of narration, detection, revelation, and disguise. Here, in full, is Riviere's account:

> In one such man with severe inhibition and anxiety, homosexual activities really took second place, the course of greatest sexual gratification being actually masturbation under special conditions, namely, while looking at himself in the mirror dressed in a particular way. The excitation was produced by the sight of himself with hair parted in the centre, wearing a bow tie. These extraordinary "fetishes" turned out to represent a *disguise of himself* as his sister: the hair and bow were taken from her. His conscious attitude was a desire to *be* a woman, but his manifest relations with men had never been stable. Unconsciously the homosexual relation proved to be entirely sadistic and based on masculine rivalry. Phantasies of sadism and *"possession of a penis"* could be indulged only while reassurance against anxiety was being obtained from the mirror that he was safely "disguised as a woman."[32] (emphasis in the original)

Here the paradigm of detection is deployed by the analyst to discover the true identity of the cross-dresser. We might notice that where according to Robert Stoller "reassurance" comes for transvestites in the possession of a penis and its capacity for erection, for Riviere's fetishist the possession of the penis is itself grounds for anxiety—an anxiety that can only be allayed by the "reassurance" that he is now in disguise. "Safely 'disguised as a woman' " the man with the bow tie was also vouchsafed a *disguise of himself*—himself, that is, as a reflection of his sister. He did not, in other words, see his sister in the mirror, but himself disguised as his sister. He saw, apparently, both the "woman" and "himself."

Who is in the place of the detective here? Riviere, who sees that the fetishist is imitating his sister, or the fetishist himself, who looks in the mirror and sees what he needs to see? If, in Stoller's felicitous phrase, "a fetish is a story masquerading as an object,"[33] then it can only function erotically while it is in masquerade. "If the text becomes conscious, the fetish no longer in itself causes excitement, is no longer a fetish" (Stoller, 155–56). Within the dynamics of fetishism, then, the deferral of detection, the deferral of the denouement, is part of the story. "Cherchez la femme" may seem to be the watchword of the genre of detection, a call to action for both detective and reader; for the psychoanalytic subject whose story is being told, however—as for Holmes in his pursuit of "the woman"—to seek for the woman is to find the cross-dresser, the transvestite, the phantom, the (reversed) image in the mirror, the embodiment of desire: that which must always elude a final capture.

9

RELIGIOUS HABITS

As the French say, there are three sexes—men, women, and clergymen.
Sydney Smith, *Lady Holland's Memoir* (1855)[1]

In early 1980 a retired American Bishop sent four ecclesiastical vestments—an alb, cincture, stole, and amice—out to be cleaned. When they were returned to him, according to the publication *Christian Century*, the cleaner's slip indicated that the Rev. John Baumgartner had been charged for "one dress, long; one scarf; one rope; and one apron."[2] This difficulty of classifying items of religious dress, not only according to their ecclesiastical names and functions, but also in accordance with the conventions of sartorial *gender*, is emblematic of a kind of crossover in vested interests that has over the years taken on a complex significance.

The deliberate cultural misreading of priests' garments as women's clothing was perhaps most memorably, if irreverently, expressed by Tallulah Bankhead, when she encountered a robed thurifer swinging his incense vessel in an Anglican church: "Love the drag, darling," Tallulah is said to have remarked, "but your purse is on fire." Boy George, the pop icon of male-to-female cross-dressing, who once referred to himself as a drag queen, offered a different perspective on his attire when interviewed by the authors of *Men in Frocks*, an oral history of female impersonators on the London club scene: "I dress in a similar way to a priest or an archbishop," George wrote in answer to their inquiries. "I wear robes, not dresses, and to be a transvestite you must wear women's undergarments. I don't."[3]

Boy George's first real professional success—a harbinger of things to come—took place when he appeared onstage in the late 1970's dressed in a nun's habit. Yet some of his most startling outfits—smocks covered with Hebrew lettering, worn with a wide-brimmed black hat and braided artificial earlocks—were designed to echo and parody another kind of religious "cross-dressing," the costume of the observant Hasidic Jew.[4] Since, as we will shortly see, the feminization of the Jewish male was a common pejorative trope of nineteenth-century social theory, the appearance of Boy George, the most defiantly transvestic figure of the seventies and eighties, *both* in women's clothes *and* in mock-Hasidic garb made the associative link between Jews and women—a staple of anti-Semitic pseudoscience—all too clear. In the context of George's pop group, Culture

Club, this was apparently intended as a send-up, a parody of prejudice as well as of belief. But the use of Western religious costume as part of a lexicon of gender-bending, whether intended as serious social commentary or as a pop throwaway, is a striking manifestation of cultural anxiety.

Madonna, the pop figure who perhaps more than any other has read the temper of the times, artfully manipulates these categories in many of her music videos, whose conflation of religious and erotic themes has sometimes scandalized her critics. The resonances of her given name (in full, Madonna Louise Veronica Ciccone) and reminiscences of her own Catholic upbringing inflect the tone of songs like "Papa Don't Preach" and "Like a Prayer."[5] In a restaging of the latter for her "Blond Ambition" tour Madonna, like Boy George, uncannily evoked Hasidic as well as Catholic images when she and her back-up singers, dressed in long black caftans, waved their hands above their heads as they danced in a "church" lit with votive candles.

Jews and Catholics—especially Jewish men and Catholic nuns—have borne the main brunt of this gender critique. But even Protestants have been targets of transvestic mimicry, in the persistent portrayal of "mannish" or "unfeminine" women as old maids or "church hens" who channel their sexual frustration into crushes on the rector or repressive social morality. Consider the success of male comedian Dana Carvey's character, "the Church Lady," for years a featured comic turn on the television show "Saturday Night Live." The Church Lady, her stockings drooping around her ankles above her sensible shoes, her mouth pursed in sanctimonious certainty, deplores, with relentless good cheer, those who, like "your Gary Harts" and "your Jimmy Swaggarts," have their "bulbous knotty parts" caught between Beelzebub and a hard place. Carvey's Church Lady dispenses "Church Chat" to sinners in a parody of repressive prurience: the spinster as both male- and female-manquée. The persistent popularity of this character (portrayed by a comic who also does a respectfully swishy George Bush imitation and a character called "Lyle, the effeminate heterosexual") suggests something of urban America's unease with religious fundamentalism—and also something of its abiding suspicion that religion itself is somehow "unmanly." We might recall as well the popular distrust, in the sixties, of long-haired and sandaled "Jesus freaks"—young men who were often, against much evidence to the contrary, described as "effeminate" or as "looking like girls." Things have changed since the time of muscular Christianity, both in the U.S. and in Britain.

As the example of Bishop Baumgartner's cleaning bill suggests, one thing that has certainly changed over time is the way in which religious costume is *read*. Western ecclesiastical dress today shares with the academic robe and the military uniform the distinction of representing one of the few remaining "legible" dress codes. Where once sumptuary laws tried to ensure that class, rank, occupation, and (to a certain extent) gender were immediately readable in and through details of costume, by the close of the twentieth century only the likes of cardinals, monks, nuns (in habits), uniformed police officers and lieutenant colonels can be decoded with certainty, by rank and hierarchy, according to established items of signifying dress: collars, stoles, surplices, soutanes, birettas, liturgical or academic colors, stripes, medals, and epaulets.

This is not to say that signifying styles do not exist in other social realms: a punk teenager today may wear a Mohawk haircut dyed pink, as well as a black leather jacket and multiple earrings, as a sign of the group to which he (or she) belongs; a gay man might signify his specific sexual interests by the placement of a ring of keys at his hip; a bride in the U.S. or Western Europe is still identifiable by her long white gown and veil. But religious costume, like military uniform, aims at making the appearance of the wearer literally "uniform" in *professional* terms: an archbishop, a Carmelite nun, or a Hasidic rabbi—like a Green Beret, or (on commencement day) a professor with a degree in Forestry from Yale—can be identified, at least in context, by those who know the vestimentary signifying code. Individual style is supposedly screened out as professional uniformity takes over: hence the army haircut, the wimple, the mortarboards for academic women as well as men.

But the case of ecclesiastical or religious dress is particularly fascinating because of the ways in which particular items of clothing have tended to cross *over* gender lines, not through uniformity *per se*—although, as we will see, there have been attempts to make women's and men's costumes the same within specific orders or denominations—but rather by the migration of styles over time from one gender to another. In eighteenth-century England, for example, parasols were popular for ladies, but umbrellas became items of daily use for clergymen who officiated at burial services—at least fifty years before fashionable gentlemen began to carry them (Mayo, 83).

Terms like "defrocking" or "unfrocking," to describe the dismissal of priests, seem quaint and slightly precious today, but the word "frock" began as a term for a monk's garment, and has only fairly recently become a word for female as opposed to male attire; the frock was the monk's, friar's, and then the clergyman's identifying costume, and a man's "frock coat" had skirts like a "frock"; so too, with "gown," which in its original Latin form meant a furred garment for elderly or infirm monks. Trousers were viewed by the ancient Romans as the costume of barbarians, and were thus eschewed by churches and monasteries in favor of the gown (Mayo, 22).

Wigs, an extravagant French court style for men, were, perhaps surprisingly, taken over with enthusiasm by the English clergy as well as by lawyers from the time of Charles II. At first the clergy spoke out against them, since the Fathers of the early Church had denounced the wearing of wigs *by women* as vanity, and, indeed, as mortal sin, the instrument of the devil. For *men*, however, wigs became and remained fashionable, despite the traditional Pauline belief that "if a man have long hair it is a shame to him" (I Cor. 11:14–15). Soon "the clergy were all to be found in wigs,"[6] which were regarded as a badge of respectability.

"It was observed that a periwig procured many persons a respect, and even veneration, which they were strangers to before, and to which they had not the least claim from their personal merit. The judges and physicians, who thoroughly understood this magic of the wig, gave it all the advantage of length as well as size."[7] Gentlemen, including clergy, who wore wigs were invariably clean-shaven; the wig thus not only augmented the phallus but replaced the beard. Puritans, however, protested against the fashion, and by 1770 the wig had again gone out of style. Five years previously periwig makers had petitioned the King, reporting with dismay "that men will wear their own hair."[8] Anglican clergy and some Non-conformists, however, continued to wear wigs for another fifty years, and the legal profession in the U.K., still apparently relying on the "magic of the wig," retains it to this day, although among laypersons the wig now counts as an item of female rather than male adornment—becoming in some quarters the very sign of female impersonation. (Thus, for example, the Lord Chamberlain in England has insisted that drag shows end with the obligatory removal of wigs,[9] a convention that, as we have noted, appears in theatrical and cinematic representations of cross-dressing from Ben Jonson's *Epicoene* to *Some Like It Hot*, *Victor/ Victoria* and *Tootsie*.)

The role of religion in Western culture as itself an oppositional structure that depends upon discriminating between insiders and outsiders and upon sharply delineated male and female spheres leads to a construction of both Christianity and Judaism that almost inevitably invites both gender parody and gender crossover. The male nun, the female monk, the feminized Jewish man are recurrent figures of fantasy as well as of history and propaganda. They too are "third kinds," figures who put in question received beliefs— in this case, the very kinds of signifying practices (like, for example, celibacy and circumcision) that create and police religious faith. Moreover, since ecstatic religion depends to a certain extent upon the existence of exceptions, chosen persons who explicitly violate the very tenets that faith and custom ordain for the ordinary practitioner, the presence of transvestite figures, or of the phantom of the transvestite in the representation of holy personages (saints, virgin martyrs, rabbinical leaders) is in a way, oddly, to be expected: these are the exceptions that prove the rule.

TRANSVESTITE SAINTS

The transvestite female saints of the Middle Ages were legion as well as legend, despite the Deuteronomic prohibition against wearing the clothes of the opposite sex. Pelagia, the archetype of the transvestite saint, is said to have been a dancing girl and prostitute; when she changed her ways, and converted to Christianity, she also changed her name and her clothes, wearing a hair shirt beneath her male outer garments, and taking the name of Pelagius. Only after her death was she revealed to have been a woman. St. Eugenia, who cross-dressed in order to join an all-male religious community and shortly became an abbot, was accused of rape by a rich lady who desired her; to disprove this charge she disrobed to prove that she was a woman. Thecla, a wealthy and beautiful virgin, became a follower of St. Paul and cut her hair, assuming for a while the garments of a man.

Saint Anna entered a monastery dressed as a man and was thought to be a eunuch; a monk who had been told that "brother Euphemius" might really be a woman pushed her down a cliff. The list of these female transvestites is long, and their stories follow a familiar pattern: Saints Perpetua, Anthanasia, Apollinaris or Dorotheus, Euphroysne, Anastasia Patricia, and others all don male clothing at a time of personal crisis—marking a break with a former existence—and in doing so fulfill the words of St. Jerome, that a woman who "wishes to serve Christ more than the world . . . will cease to be a woman and will be called man."[10]

Perhaps the most striking attribute of some of these female transvestite saints was that they are said to have been *bearded*. St. Wilgefortis, also known as Uncumber, wanted to remain a virgin and devote herself to the contemplative life, but her father insisted on marrying her off to the King of Sicily. Wilgefortis prayed for deliverance, and was answered by the sudden growth of a long moustache and a curling beard. When the King glimpsed this feature of his bride through her veil (which she had artfully contrived to push aside), he rejected her; her father then had her crucified. The names by which Wilgefortis is known in various languages—based on roots meaning "deliverer" or "(un)trouble"[11]—suggest the extremity of her plight and the irony of her father's "solu-tion." In England Uncumber became the patron of married women who wanted to get rid of their husbands. (St. Galla and St. Paula were other bearded female saints who also attempted to avoid marriage through this miraculous stratagem.)[12]

Stories of pious women dressed as men to avoid becoming the source of sexual temptation are over and over again conjoined with tales of their "fathering" children. John Anson provides a persuasive psychoanalytic reading, noting that the chroniclers of these tales were male celibate clerics, and that therefore the question for interpreters of the saints' legends is not one of female psychology (why would a woman dress as a man in this situation?) but rather of "monastic fantasy":

> what finally comes into view with these lives is the guilty desire that underlies the whole dreamwork; for instead of an overture rejected, a sexual act is committed and laid to the blame of the saint, who undergoes the punishment as a kind of surrogate. Thus, quite simply, the secret longing for a woman in a monastery is brilliantly concealed by disguising the woman as a man and making her appear guilty of the very temptation to which the monks are most subject; finally, after she has been punished for their desires, their guilt is compensated by turning her into a saint with universal remorse and sanctimonious worship.[13]

But this fantasy of the cross-dressed woman fathering a child has implications for the religious culture as well as for the individual. Here psychoanalysis crosses with social and political tensions in a time of institutional change. The transvestite effect, the overdetermined appearance of the transvestite, reflects what might in this case be called a genealogical anxiety—an anxiety about the question of *paternity* which, in the case of the Catholic Church, is in fact a foundational mystery. For twelfth-century monasticism the story of the cross-dressed "father" might well, as Anson suggests, bear the brunt of a celibate clerisy's repressed and conflicted desires, but it also points toward other kinds of conflict, social and theological as well as sexual. The identity of the Father was the mystery—and the certainty—on which the faith was based. These "local" stories of other mysterious paternities, with their transvestite under- and overtones, reanimate the conundrum of divine fatherhood in the context of a world-turned-upside-down. A crisis of belief is here displaced onto the axis of gender.

The social dissymmetry we have noticed again and again—that to wish to be a man is regarded as somehow "natural" or of higher status, whereas to wish to be a woman is perverse—presumably influences the fact that, whereas there are many female transvestite saints, there are no male transvestites who are similarly revered. (As the authors of *Men in Frocks* point out, succinctly, "she cross-dresses because she wants to be taken seriously; he generally cross-dresses because he doesn't" [Kirk and Heath, 9].) There was even a female transvestite pope, the legendary Pope Joan, in the ninth century, who was said to have fallen in love with a monk who was her teacher and cross-dressed to join him in a life of scholarship; after his death, she was chosen as pope, only to be undone by her own sexuality: she became pregnant by a Benedictine monk who resembled her dead lover, and her gender was supposedly revealed when, in the middle of a papal procession, she went into labor and gave birth to a child. Throughout the thirteenth, fourteenth, and fifteenth centuries the truth of this story was largely accepted; a statue of Pope Joan was installed in the Cathedral of Siena, and at the Council of Constance in 1415 John Hus denounced the delegates for permitting a woman to be pope. Only later did Joan's story become reassigned to legend rather than to fact. (We might note that in this account, whether legendary or factual, "female" failings are what get Pope Joan into trouble, quite literally; but her heterosexuality is confirmed by the story of both her initial love affair and her pregnancy, so that even in this particular she is finally unthreatening to established norms and hierarchies.)

The most famous of all cross-dressed saints, of course, was St. Joan, whose transvestism was viewed as itself a mark of abomination. The transvestite female saints of the Christian monastic tradition were among Joan's models. Like them she broke with her parents, refused to marry the husband they had chosen for her, and rejected male domination even as she assumed male privilege. Yet unlike these women she did not choose the costume, or the life, of a monk; instead, crossing class as well as gender lines, she maintained herself as a knight.

It was in fact for transvestism, not for heresy, that Joan was put on trial by the Inquisition. No less than five charges against her detailed her transvestism as emblematic of her presumption: she was unwomanly and immodest, ran the charges, she wore sumptuous clothing to which she was not entitled by rank, and she carried arms.

> The said Jeanne put off and entirely abandoned woman's clothes, with her hair cropped short and round in the fashion of young men, she wore shirt, breeches, doublet, with hose joined together. . . .

> And in general, having cast aside all womanly decency not only to the scorn of feminine modesty, but also of well instructed men, she had worn the apparel and garments of most dissolute men, and, in addition, had some weapons of defence.[14]

Her questioners at the trial repeatedly asked why she had assumed male garb, and repeatedly she insisted that she had done so at the command of God and his angels—not for convenience in the field. "The dress is a small, nay the least thing," she is famously reported to have said at the fourth public session (Barrett, 70), but nonetheless she would not exchange her men's clothes for women's, even when bribed with the promise of the right to hear Mass.

The final draft of the charges against her makes clear her determined obstinacy: "The said Catherine and Mary [Joan's 'voices'] instituted this woman in the name of God, to take and wear a man's clothes; and she had worn them and still wears them, stubbornly obeying the said command, to such an extent that this woman had declared she would rather die than relinquish these clothes" (Barrett, 227–28). Marina Warner points out that Joan throughout the trial identified herself as a woman in man's clothes, that she never tried to pass as a man—that, in fact, the paradox or singularity of her transvestism, her identity as, precisely, a woman who chose—or was directed—to dress as a man, was a source of her subversive strength. "She was usurping a man's function but shaking off the trammels of his sex altogether to occupy a different, third order, neither male nor female, like the angels."[15]

Her defenders were deeply concerned about the transvestite issue, and before her capture learned arguments were propounded, claiming that the victory at Orléans proved the rightness of her condition and her cause, and arguing as well that the Deuteronomic prohibition had been overturned by the new dispensation of which she was a sign. Warner effectively posits Joan's transvestism as itself a structure of *language*: "a figure of speech to lay claim to greatness beyond the expected potential of her sex"; for the virgin martyrs "transvestism becomes the transitive verb in a sentence of self-obliteration" (Warner 149, 157). Yet the clothing she chose, and the trial itself, declare not invisibility or annihilation but rather a special and unmistakable visibility or legibility.

The French analyst Catherine Clément notes the case of an anorexic girl who wanted not to have periods so as "to be neither boy nor girl." As Clément comments, she wanted "to play the disorder of androgyny against the order of the female cycle [called *règles*, or rules, in French], to be neither one thing nor the other, *neuter*."[16] Many accounts of Joan suggest that she was amenorrheic, and that because she did not menstruate she occupied a physiological position that was neither male nor female.[17] This desire to see Joan as somehow beyond gender—"neither boy nor girl"—reflects not only a contemporary religious fantasy, but also a peculiar modern anxiety about the entrapment of gender and gender roles.

Thus, for example, feminist Andrea Dworkin reads Joan's case as one of the triumphant avoidance of heterosexual intercourse; when, after her recantation, she was returned to her prison cell dressed in women's clothes, she became vulnerable, in Dworkin's view, to rape or attempted rape by her captors.[18] Dworkin, who regards heterosexual intercourse as an instrument for the enslavement of women, needs her Joan to be a woman, *not* a transvestite. For her, Joan's male clothing must be a polemical and rhetorical signifier *against* men, rather than a signifier of maleness. She therefore makes short work of those who would romanticize and aestheticize Joan's cross-dressing, the "scholars and artists" by whom she is "[e]ssentially seen as a transvestite."[19] Joan, according to Dworkin, became "an exile from gender with a male vocation and male clothes" (Dworkin, 100).

By contrast actresses cast as Joan in G.B. Shaw's play have interpreted her transvestism as a reflection of "normative" culture. Jane Alexander, for example, offers a classic version of the progress narrative. "It's very much like Calamity Jane," she explains:

> Calamity simply dressed in men's clothes because she had to do men's work. Riding a horse was the primary mode of transportation for Joan and for Calamity, and it doesn't make a lot of sense if you want to get somewhere fast to be doing it with a skirt and sidesaddle. That was all. It was utilitarian.[20]

Alexander's emphatic dismissal of homosexuality as a factor ("I didn't see her at all butch or dyke") retains the notion of a Joan who is both transcendent and "normal": "I don't think that she had a crush on anybody except maybe the saints, and so everything was projected out. It was just a young sexuality that was substituting for what might have grown up later with the love of a good man." Two other recent Joans, Sarah Miles and Lee Grant, both draw an analogy with Peter Pan (Hill, 103, 144), while Janet Suzman offers a provocative argument about the transformative agency of clothing: "what happens when you wear pants or chain mail is that you naturally change. . . . when you wear that sort of clothes it just happens. They dictate what you do" (Hill, 157). Suzman's intuition—very much that of an actress—unwittingly echoes the fears of the Puritan antitheatricalists who objected to cross-dressing on the Renaissance stage: that wearing the clothing of the other gender might change the wearer, that a disquieting power—a power at once sexual and political—did somehow inhere in clothes.

THE EROTICS OF THE CLOTH

> Rows and rows and rows of old white men in lace dresses were watching the cardinals make their entry.
> former nun Patricia Hussey, describing the Conclave of Cardinals in the Vatican[21]

Priests, noted Henry Adams, were in many ways equated with women in medieval society—both, for example, were exempt from military service.[22] Natalie Davis points out that in the England of Henry VIII, during the carnivalized reign of the Boy bishop, young male children taken from house to house could be dressed *either* as females *or* as priests—another indication that they were equatable. In the Feast of Fools celebrated in French cathedrals in the fifteenth and sixteenth centuries, young clerics dressed as women, and made "wanton and loose gestures."[23] This "feminization" of the priest or monk (beardless, wearing a cassock that could be thought to resemble a woman's skirt, devoid of political power, living in quiet obedience, and performing domestic chores) was an idea that could coexist with the opposite stereotype as represented by Chaucer, the "virile" monk whose sexual exploits matched his magnificent clothing. Both kinds of stories about monks suggest a fascination with what they "really" do, with how they wear their difference. Hyper-maleness and feminization, hardly for the first time, are produced as effects of institutionalized male bonding.

The erotic potential of this scenario when allied to anti-Catholicism and specific Protestant fantasies found a particularly congenial home within the conventions of the Gothic: a literary development which, not at all surprisingly, encoded transvestism as the figure of erotic and religious transgression. Thus Matthew Lewis's Gothic novel *The Monk* (1796) offered, early in its pages, the revelation that the young novice "Rosario" was actually a beautiful young woman named Matilda.[24] When, after a series of suspenseful delays, Rosario confesses his real gender identity to the Monk, Ambrosio (" 'Father!' continued he in faltering accents, 'I am a Woman!' "[25]), the pronouns shift, and with them Ambrosio's passions. By the end of Chapter 2 the Monk has forgotten his vows and "clasped her rapturously in his arms" (*Monk*, 90).

The Monk's notorious deployment of gender travesty in a religious context provided not only titillating shock value but also a "reading" of Catholicism as hypocritical and erotic, something to be unmasked. The specificity of ecclesiastical cross-dressing here functions overtly as propaganda. As so often when transvestism is subject to scrutiny, its subtext is unbridled sexuality. Yet like so many Gothic conventions, the trope of the female monk—like that of the male nun—has the uncanny effect of bodying forth repetition through a kind of emptying out. The permeable boundary of the cowl or veil becomes a borderline between denial or repression on the one hand and sexual fantasy on the other, projecting both desire and its interdiction in the same figure. As Eve Sedgwick observes, "The veil is the place of any voided expectation."[26]

A good example is the case of the mysterious Black Friar in Byron's *Don Juan*. When Juan, a houseguest at an estate in rural England, peers out of his "Gothic chamber" and sees to his astonishment "a monk arrayed/ In cowl and beads and dusky garb" (Canto 16:15, 21), he is intrigued and disconcerted ("did he see this? Or was it a vapour?" [16:527]).[27] He descends to breakfast, where his hosts discern the reason for his distress, and tell him the legend of the Black Friar who has haunted the property since Henry

VIII's dissolution of the monasteries. The ghostly Friar first appeared at a moment of rupture, the moment of the displacement of Catholicism by Henry's new Church of England. What rupture for Juan is signified by this apparition, that "makes him as silent as a ghost"?

Retiring to his bed the following evening Juan waits, expectant of a repetition—for, as we already noted, the monk's cowl is itself a figure for repetition as well as for substitution and displacement. And the "sable Friar," when he appears, is of course a woman: in the dark Juan thrusts out his arm to encounter "a hard but glowing bust" as he descries "a dimpled chin, a neck of ivory":

> Back fell the sable frock and dreary cowl
> And they revealed, alas, that ere they should,
> In full, voluptuous, but not o'ergrown bulk,
> The phantom of her frolic Grace—Fitz-Fulke!
> (16:123)

This denouement, like that in *The Monk*, is not entirely unexpected. At the breakfast table the Duchess of Fitz-Fulke had "played with her veil/And looked at Juan hard, but nothing uttered" (16:31) when he admitted to his spectral visitation of the night before; the Duchess's "veil" here marks a place of simultaneous revelation and disclosure. Juan's own state of undress—"Completely *sans-culotte* and without vest;/ In short, he hardly could be clothed with less" (16:111)—puts him in a position that is vulnerably "feminized," the more so since the Duchess apparently permits herself to be the sexual aggressor. Yet the Duchess's disguise does not merely signal either a convenient device for seduction or Juan's own insecure "masculinity": rather it manifests itself as a transvestite effect, an uncanny third: indeed it is never certain that the Friar/Duchess of the second night was the same figure that appeared on the first. As we will see when we come to a very similar figure, the transvestite "nun" in Charlotte Brontë's *Villette*, that which is disclosed is not always the same as that which is clothed. Or—to cite the medieval proverb that makes clear the fact that a monk or friar was regarded, in some quarters, as already in disguise—*cucullus non facit monachum*: the cowl doesn't make the monk.

In eighteenth-century masquerades ecclesiastical dress was a favorite kind of travesty, charged with erotic significance: men dressed as nuns, women as priests and cardinals; the clothing of the higher Catholic clergy (abbesses, cardinals, even the pope) afforded opportunities for the luxurious display of jewels, robes, and furs. Some Protestant sects, like Quakers and Methodists, offered sartorial models that were also inviting to parody, but Catholic costume was by far the most popular.[28] The pretense of celibacy offered the most titillating opportunity for inversion: the scandal of cross-dressing and the scandal of religious impersonation, when present in the same transvestic figure, intensified the libertinism of the masquerade.

The sartorial fantasy of Catholic crossover goes in both gender directions, male to female as well as female to male. Underneath the cowl and flowing robes the body of the celibate is itself an object of suspicion. In the wedding scene that concludes the film *La Cage aux Folles*, for example, the female impersonator Albin (Michel Serrault), seated in the front pew of the church in his white pantsuit and jewelry, glances knowingly at the priest celebrating mass, who is also dressed in flowing white robes richly ornamented with jewels and gold. From close-cropped hair to extravagant theatrical gesture, the two men mirror one another, and both, in the camera's eye, upstage the bride.

For reasons that may have as much to do with the Catholic-school education of screenwriters and filmmakers as with any more theoretical considerations of gender, many recent British and American films have tended to show more male "nuns" than "feminized" priests. In *The Magic Christian* (1969-70), characterized by Vito Russo as "a viciously homophobic film,"[29] Peter Sellers donned a series of disguises including that of a "disco nun." Dudley Moore and Peter Cook are dressed as nuns for a comic episode in *Bedazzled* (1967), and Burt Reynolds and Jack Weston, a pair of Boston detectives chasing a rapist, likewise costume themselves as nuns—Reynolds still wearing his moustache—in *Fuzz* (1972).

The recent British comedy film *Nuns on the Run* (1989) depicts two burly male bankrobbers, Brian (Eric Idle) and Charlie (Robbie Coltrane), who take refuge in a convent and in desperation outfit themselves as nuns, with wimples, robes, and (underneath them) sturdy white brassieres, all pilfered from the linen supply room. They even change their names: Charlie becomes Sister Inviolata of the Immaculate Conception, and Brian, Sister Euphemia of the Five Wounds. Fearing exposure, the hapless thieves rush to a local pharmacy to buy razors and face-makeup, and spend the balance of the film avoiding the advances of a randy priest and demonstrating to an attractive young woman that they are in fact men, not women—or nuns. One comic scene features Coltrane in full nun's drag in the women's shower room, surrounded by naked students, his face a study in desire and consternation.

Reviewers who admired the film were generally also admiring of its affectionate attitude toward nuns; thus Vincent Canby in the *New York Times* remarks at the outset that "if nuns weren't so intimidating (for whatever reasons) the sight of bogus nuns cutting up in most un-nunlike ways, could not have remained as good for the sustained guilty giggle as it still is."[30] It would be interesting to probe Canby's unspoken, parenthetical "reasons," which suggest not only the specter of boyhood memories, but also a leftover Gothic sensibility of the kind that made the phantom nun a favorite of nineteenth-century fiction.

But the "drag nun" as a radical transvestite figure—*pace* Boy George—offered a political intervention within the context of street theater in the 1970's and 80's quite different from this nostalgic and comfortable glance backward. In London, drag performer Howard Wakeling dressed as the Virgin Mary for a Gay Liberation Front dance in one of London's town halls in the early seventies.[31] Jack Fertig, better known as Sister Boom Boom, wore a nun's habit, large foam-rubber breasts, false eyelashes, and stiletto heels on the streets of San Francisco, leading the troupe called the Sisters of Perpetual Indulgence, and garnering 23,000 votes in a 1982 vote for city supervisor as "Sister Boom Boom, nun of the above."

At the 1984 Democratic National Convention in San Francisco Fertig and the sisters performed a piece of street theater in which they stripped the pants off an actor representing Jerry Falwell, revealing a black corset and fishnet stockings.[32] And when Sister Boom Boom and friends, dressed in their version of religious garb, visited an exhibit of Vatican art at a San Francisco museum, the spectacle arrested even staid art-lovers piously listening to their rented cassettes.[33] Why nuns? Why nuns and, or as, transvestites?

This anti-Catholic fantasy, that religious costume cloaks and conceals disguised persons of the opposite sex who offer unlimited sexual pleasure to lustful and hypocritical "celibates" sequestered in orders, has become over time almost a cliché. Its permutations can be found not only in explicitly proselytizing anti-Catholic literature but also, quite regularly, in pornography, and indeed, in pop singer Madonna's "Like a Prayer" video. As in certain anecdotes about eunuchs and castrati, the surprise of the contrast between dress and undress adds spice to the encounter.

One particularly effective and complex deployment of this fantasy, both *as* a fantasy and as a series of interpretative codes, can be found in Charlotte Brontë's novel *Villette*, in which Lucy Snowe several times sees the spectral figure of a nun. Informed by Gothic convention, and by the agitated rhetoric of Lucy herself, this spectacle becomes in effect an hysterical symptom, accompanied as it is by specific erotic and repressive details. Although only Lucy speaks in hysterical capitals ("the very NUN herself!")[34] the "lay Jesuit" Paul Emanuel shares her vision of what he calls "the mystery."

In the event, the mystery is "solved" in what appears to be a very prosaic way. The "nun" has been a man in disguise, Ginevra Fanshawe's secret suitor Count Alfred de Hamal, to whom the carefree Ginevra had told the school's legend of the nun who haunts the grounds. Ginevra herself explodes the fiction in a spectacular fashion, by arranging the nun's costume on Lucy's bed so that she discovers it in the middle of the night: "by the faint night lamp I saw stretched on my bed the old phantom—the NUN" (*Villette*, 467). The phantom, half-perceived, is expressly phallic, male, and threatening: "what dark, usurping shape, supine, long, and strange? Is it a robber who has made his way through the open street-door, and lies there in wait? it looks very black" (*Villette*, 466). Overwrought, Lucy tears the habit to shreds and discovers that "the long nun proved a long bolster dressed in a long black stole, and artfully invested with a white veil. The garments in very truth, strange as it may seem, were genuine nun's garments, and by some hand they had been disposed with a view to illusion. Whence came these vestments? Who contrived this artifice?" (*Villette*, 467).

What and who, then, *was* the nun who haunted Lucy Snowe? Sandra Gilbert and Susan Gubar interpret the nun in *Villette* as a sign of woman's oppression rather than as a transvestic apparition: for them "the nun's way is . . . symbolic for Lucy of the only socially acceptable life available to single women—a life of service, self-abnegation, and chastity."[35] Eve Sedgwick argues that she is "a personification of the fact of doublenessness, rather than just *a* double."[36] Mary Jacobus identifies the nun as "the joker in the pack, the alien, ex-centric self which no image can mirror—only the structure of language,"[37] so that the nun, like the purloined letter in Lacan's reading of Poe, becomes a signifier of signification itself, and of its displacements.

But this elegant invocation of both deconstructive and feminist subtexts within the novel turns away from the displacement of gender and sexuality. Although these critics have rightly pointed toward *Villette*, and in particular toward the incident of the nun and the buried letters, as crucial texts for Brontë and for feminism, they have oddly neglected the two things about this "nun" that seem to me most striking: her "maleness" and her "Catholicism." What would happen if we were to take those particulars, which distinguish this "nun" from a variety of other phantoms, not in the direction of the deconstruction of language but in the direction of the deconstruction of gender?

It is surely not enough to say that the nun in *Villette* "turns out to have been" Alfred de Hamal, a man in woman's disguise, the sexual partner not of Lucy but of the self-assured and transgressive Ginevra. De Hamal himself is produced in the text as a gesture of demystification, as it were after the fact; Lucy herself half-guesses that it must be a man ("not a woman of my acquaintance . . . she was not of female height" [*Villette*, 467]). We may notice that the novel contains other cameo scenes of cross-dressing and cross-gendering that bear upon this one: Mrs. Bretton drapes her sleeping son in her own sky blue turban; John Bretton's beloved remembers him in his younger days as being "more like a girl" (*Villette*, 274); Bretton tells Lucy that "if you had been a boy, Lucy, instead of a girl . . . we should have been good friends" (*Villette*, 312); and, most strikingly, Lucy refuses to dress like a man when she takes a male role in a school play: "To be dressed like a man did not please, and would not suit me" (*Villette*, 134).

Lucy's resistance to looking like a man is very strong: her voice is "unsteady" as she expresses her disavowal of the role, and calm returns only when she is able to craft for herself a costume that keeps the middle, retaining her "woman's garb" and adding to it a few signs of maleness. Is this because she is afraid she will really be read as, be taken for, be unmasked as a man? Reading this passage against the description of the cross-dressed male "nun" who represents Ginevra's freedom to choose both sex and marriage (a freedom itself indissolubly linked to her own wealth and station) we can see identification as well as fear in Lucy's repeated sightings of the nun, who is in so many ways expressly her double, her veiled other: a man costumed as a nun.

As we have noted, the apparition of the nun can be read—and is indeed read within the novel—as an hysterical symptom; this is certainly what Dr. John suspects, although

M. Paul, the believing Catholic, is willing to credit the "reality" of the figure since he has seen it himself.

Freud and his French Catholic mentor Jean-Martin Charcot regarded the nun as the very type of the repressed hysteric, as Freud notes often in his early writings:

> If a hysterical subject seeks intentionally to forget an experience or forcibly repudiates, inhibits and suppresses an intention or an idea, these psychical acts, as a consequence, enter the second state of consciousness; from there they produce their permanent effects and the memory of them returns as a hysterical attack. (Cf. hysteria in nuns, continent women, well-brought-up boys, people with a hankering after art or the stage, etc.)[emphasis in the original][38]

"It is owing to no chance coincidence," adds Freud, "that the hysterical deliria of nuns during the epidemics of the Middle Ages took the form of violent blasphemies and unbridled erotic language."[39] The nun—who, according to this description, represses and repudiates the sexual desires she has literally dis-avowed—is the quintessential figure of the hysteric. The *transvestite* nun in Brontë's novel acts out Lucy's inhibited and suppressed desires—desires that even on "the stage" (in the vaudeville drama where she is forced to play a man) are angrily denied: "To be dressed like a man did not please, and would not suit me."

Where for Freud—and Charcot—the repressed nun *embodied* hysteria, for Brontë the nun is a *sign* of that repressed hysteria—the more so because there is no nun, only "her" clothes, which are themselves subjected by Lucy to such violent attack. "I tore her up—the incubus!" she says (*Villette*, 467). Incubus, not succubus. Male, not female demon. Yet the category crisis here is as much England/France and Protestant/Catholic as it is male/female: the phantom appearance of the transvestite, once again, marks a category crisis *elsewhere*. The Protestant calumny about cross-dressed "nuns" and "monks" is here a symptom of a peculiarly *literary* disorder or syndrome, the "Gothic." But *this* symptom, in Lacan's phrase, speaks—speaks even though, and perhaps because, the "nun of the attic" (*Villette*, 467) never utters a word.

"Nun of the above"—Sister Boom Boom's flippant political slogan—in fact describes quite well the psychogenesis of this haunting figure of the transvestite nun. The third space—the space of thirdness—is simultaneously demarcated, filled, and emptied out by the phantom nun—the nun (or "none") that calls into question categories of male and female, Catholic and Protestant, English and French, gay and straight: in Wallace Stevens's words, "nothing that is not there, and the nothing that is." That the story of the transvestite nun is so often tinged with a suspicion of hysteria indicates not only the subtextual misogyny and/or homophobia that marks these particular instances, but also a more general and pervasive fear of transvestism *as* a powerful agent of destabilization and change, the sign of the *ungroundedness* of identities on which social structures and hierarchies depend.

JEW, WOMAN, HOMOSEXUAL

"Blessed art Thou, O Lord our God, King of the Universe, who hast
not made me a woman."
Morning service for Orthodox Jews, preliminary blessings [40]

The German actor Curt Bois, perhaps best known to modern audiences as the
pickpocket in *Casablanca*, appeared in a 1927 film, *Der Furst von Pappenheim,* as a vaudeville
entertainer who performs in drag. In the film Bois's character consents to a rendezvous
after the show with a rich man (Hans Junkermann) who doesn't know he's a man. The
results are predictably comic, the same old story of cross-dressed mistaken identity and
double-take. But there was one complicating factor, not within the film itself but
subsequent to its release. For Bois was a Jew. After he fled Germany during the Nazi
regime, the Nazis excerpted clips from this film to "prove" that Jewish men "minced
about in women's clothes."[41]

Historically Jews in Europe—both men and women—had long been subject to
sumptuary laws of a stigmatizing kind. Yellow circles made of cord at least an inch thick
had to be worn on the chests of Venetian Jews by an order of 1430; Pisa a century earlier
had required an "O of red cloth"; and Rome insisted that male Jews wear red tabards
and Jewish women red overskirts.[42] Red or yellow clothing signs continued to be required
of Jews in Italian city-states throughout the Renaissance, prefiguring the equally infamous
yellow stars-of-David imposed by Nazi law. Other distinguishing signs, notably the earring,
were traditional among Jews and also among prostitutes, so that the supposed "connection
between Jews and prostitutes" could be enforced by sartorial fiat, as well as by a social
and political rhetoric of pollution (Hughes, 37). By a deliberate and powerful campaign
of degradation and re-marking, prostitutes and Jewish money-lenders, both construed as
somehow necessary for the service of the state, were conflated into a single class: "loose
women and Jews formed a single sumptuary category" (Hughes, 47).

Not only sartorially, but also "scientifically" and "theoretically," the idea of the Jewish
man as "effeminate" as well as "degenerate" has a long and unlovely history in European
culture. Otto Weininger's *Sex and Character*, perhaps the most influential work of pseudoscience written on the topic in the nineteenth century, was published after the suicide of
the author, himself a Jew, in 1903. Weininger set out to prove that all Jews were,
essentially, women. "Those who have no soul can have no craving for immortality, and
so it is with the woman and the Jew," wrote Weininger.[43] "As there is no real dignity
in women, so what is meant by the word 'gentleman' does not exist amongst the Jews"
(Weininger, 308). "Jews and women are devoid of humour, but addicted to mockery"
(Weininger, 319). "Judaism is saturated with femininity," he declared (Weininger, 306).
And, yet again, "The true conception of the State is foreign to the Jew, because he, like
the woman, is wanting in personality; his failure to grasp the idea of true society is due

to his lack of a free intelligible ego. Like women, Jews tend to adhere together" (Weininger, 307–8).

Before we dismiss this as the social psychology of a singular crackpot, of interest only to bigots and the morally deranged, we should note that, at the time that it appeared, Weininger's book impressed Freud, a Jew—and Charlotte Perkins Gilman, a feminist—as a major contribution to the understanding of human psychology.[44] It is even clear why this might be so. Freud and Breuer are singled out for praise in Weininger's discussion of hysteria (Weininger, 267–77), and indeed Weininger's explanation of what he means by Jewishness ("I do not refer to a nation or to a race, to a creed or to a scripture . . . but mankind in general, in so far as it has a share in the platonic idea of Judaism"; Weininger, 306) sounds very like Freud's own conflicted credo as expressed in the Preface to the Hebrew translation of *Totem and Taboo*, where Freud refers to himself as "an author who is ignorant of the language of holy writ, who is completely estranged from the religion of his fathers—as well as from every other religion—and who cannot take a share in nationalist ideals, but who has yet never repudiated his people, who feels that he is in his essential nature a Jew and who has no desire to alter that nature".[45]

Charcot, the Paris physician and theorist of hysteria after whom Freud was to name his eldest son, drew attention to "the especially marked predisposition of the Jewish race for hysteria"[46] and other kinds of mental illness—due, he thought, to inbreeding. Charcot had identified and charted an iconography of hysteria—a series of ritualized, dance-like gestures and grimaces—to which, once again, could be compared the "gesticulation" of the Jew.[47] Here, too, was a model *against* which Freud was anxious to define himself; he would be like the French doctor, whom he so much admired, not the (female or Jewish) patients.

As for Gilman, she would have found in Weininger's book an entire chapter of praise for "Emanicipated Women," with specific mention of Sappho, George Sand, Madame de Staël, George Eliot, and Rosa Bonheur, among others, as individuals who had transcended their debilitating condition of womanhood: "the degree of emancipation and the proportion of maleness in the composition of a woman are practically identical," he wrote. "Homo-sexuality in a woman is the outcome of her masculinity and presupposes a higher degree of development" (Weininger, 66). Where emancipation movements in the mass are doomed to self-obliteration, individual women had it within their power to become like men.

"Manliness," not gender, is Weininger's chief concern. Like Freud's friend Fliess he believed in the importance of periodicity, and noted that the nineteenth and twentieth centuries, like (he thought) the tenth, fifteenth and sixteenth, were marked by "an increased production of male women, and by a similar increase in female men." The "enormous recent increase in a kind of dandified homo-sexuality" was a sign of the "increasing effeminacy of the age" (Weininger, 73)—of which, once again, the Jew-as-woman was also a preeminent sign.

Furthermore, the *way* Jews supposedly spoke, with a break in the voice and a sing-song manner, set Jewish men apart, and linked them with feminized males or castrates. The Jewish "break in the voice," like the "soft weakness of form," "femininity," and "Orientalism" of the Jewish man, were attributed by Walter Rathenau to inbreeding and separateness: "In the midst of a German life, a separate, strange race ... an Asiatic horde."[48] (Rathenau—another German Jew, who like Weininger sought to establish his own difference within Jewishness—was later to become the foreign minister of the Weimar Republic, thus repositioning himself as a quintessential insider rather than a "foreign" Jewish outsider.) "The change of voice signaled the masculinization of the male; its absence signaled the breaking of the voice, the male's inability to assume anything but a 'perverted' sexual identity" (Gilman, *Sexuality*, 266).

Indeed, the curious quality of the Jew's voice was also one of the identifying stigmata of the *homosexual* according to nineteenth-century typologies, so that the connection between Jewishness and "perversion" was further "demonstrated" or "proven" by this alleged symptom. Like the "masquerade squeak" deliberately adopted by participants in eighteenth-century English masquerades, obscuring gender identities and "suggesting comic emasculation,"[49] this auditory sign was taken as both an index of corruption and a sign of infantilism and bestiality. The voice became itself an indication of unmanliness, a kind of aural clothing that linked Jew and "woman," Jew and emasculated man, Jew and degenerate male homosexual.

Marcel Proust, a homosexual and a half-Jew, explicitly compared the two conditions: each—homosexuality and Judaism—was in his view "an incurable disease."[50] Homosexuals, like Jews, were described by their enemies as discernibly members of a race, and each recognized fellow members of the "brotherhood" instinctively. Proust's Charles Swann is a Jew in love with a courtesan; his homosexual Baron de Charlus is a gossip as well as an aesthete, an effeminate dandy and a snob. Proust himself exemplified the tendency of the persecuted to ally themselves with their persecutors, depicting his homosexual characters as both degenerate and feminine, and—at the same time—fighting a duel with another homosexual who had put Proust's own manliness in question.

How does this feminization of the Jewish man—the voice, the shrug, the small hands, the extravagant gestures, the "Oriental" aspect—manifest itself in the lexicon of cross-dressing? In part by the crossing of the dandy and the aesthete—in Proust; in *Nightwood*'s Baron Felix Volkbein ("still spatted, still wearing his cutaway," moving "with a humble hysteria among the decaying brocades and laces of the *Carnavalet*" [9, 11]); in Radclyffe Hall's figure of the artist Adolphe Blanc, who designed ballets and ladies' gowns for a living, a homosexual and a "gentle and learned Jew" (*The Well of Loneliness*, 352)—with the Hasid.

The traditional long gown (Shylock's "Jewish gaberdine") and uncut hair, the lively gesticulation (and wild, ecstatic dancing) of the Hasidic sect—all these could be regarded as woman-like or "feminine," as well as simply foreign or alien. Adolf Hitler in *Mein Kampf*

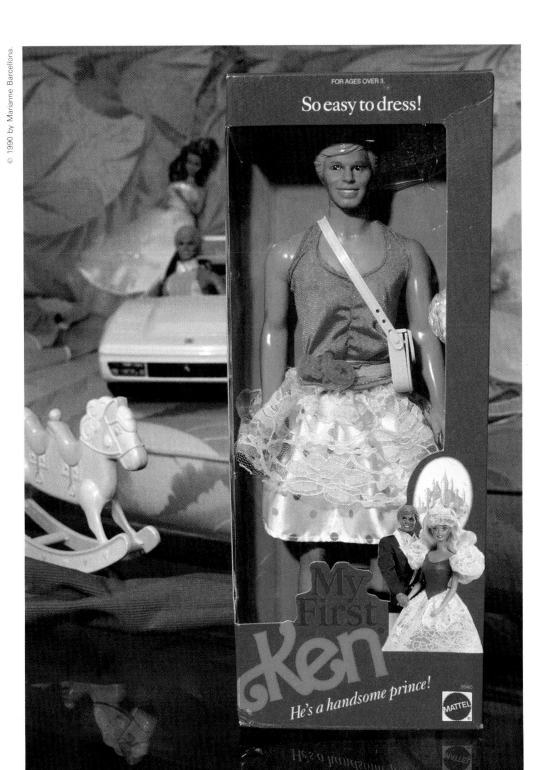

Cross-dressed Ken.

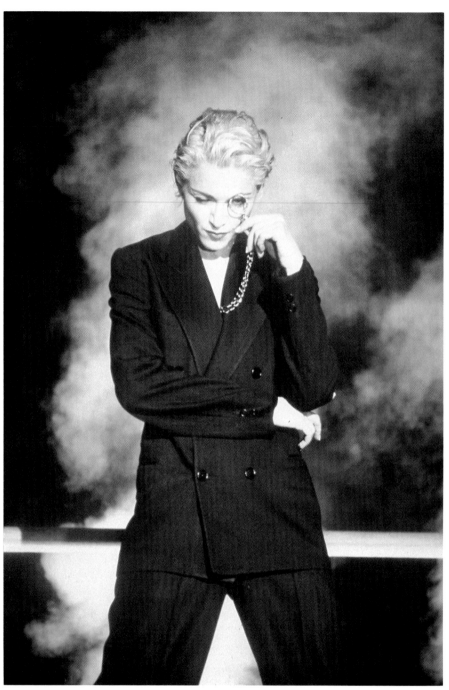

Madonna, *Express Yourself*.

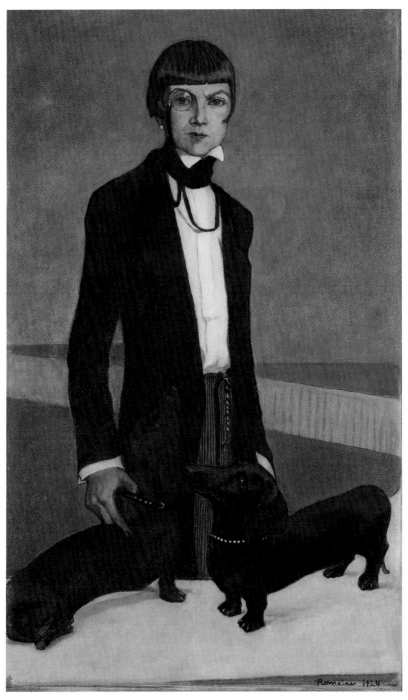

Una, Lady Troubridge, by Romaine Brooks.

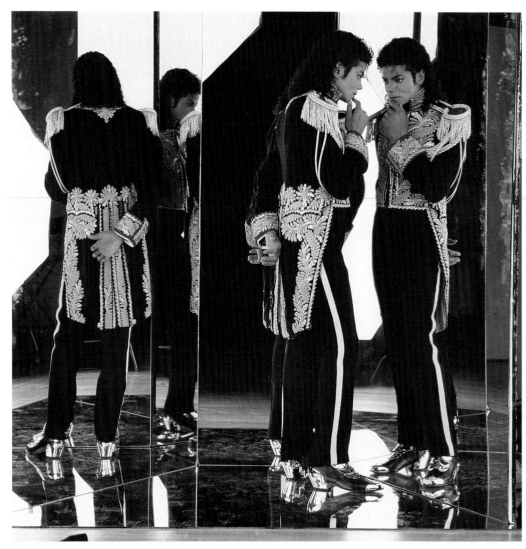

Above: Michael Jackson. Photo by Annie Leibovitz.

Right: Elvis Presley in a gold lamé suit.

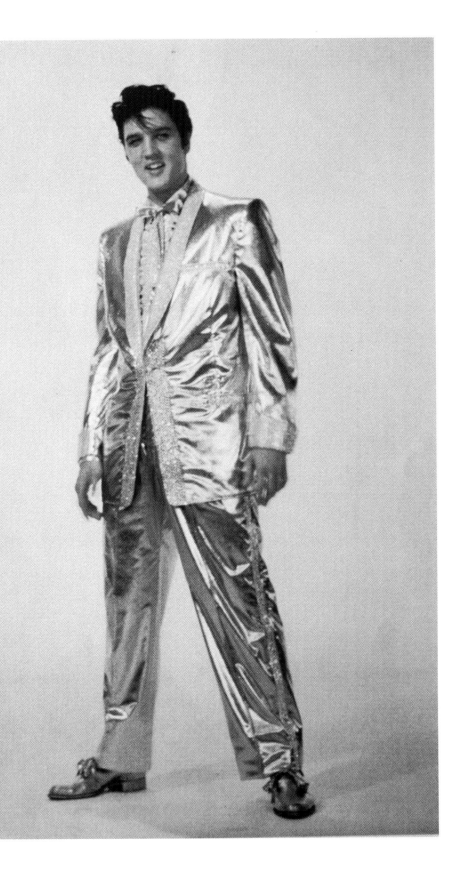

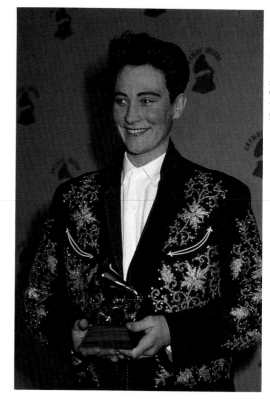

Vinnie Zuffante, Star File, Inc.

k.d. lang.

Boy George.

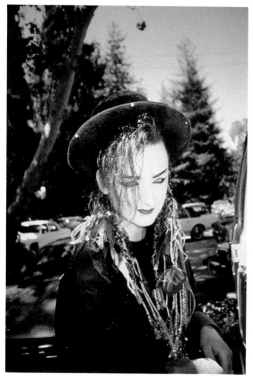

Opposite page: Frida Kahlo, *Self-portrait with Cropped Hair*, 1940. The inscription, from a popular song lyric, reads, "Look, if I used to love you, it was because of your hair; now that you're shorn I don't love you anymore."

D. Elkouby, Star File, Inc.

Mira que si te quise, fué por el pelo,
Ahora que estás pelona, ya no te quiero.

1940 Frida Kahlo.

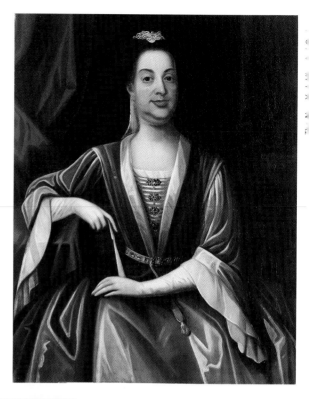

Edward Hyde, Lord Cornbury, colonial Governor of New York and New Jersey. Cornbury is believed to have dressed in women's clothes in deference to the monarch, Queen Anne, whose relation he was, and whom he desired, he said, to "represent as faithfully as I can."

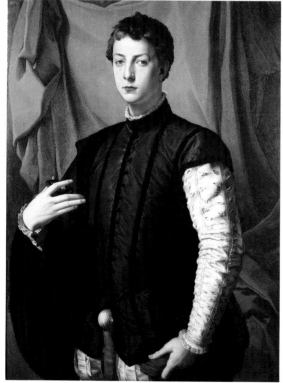

Clothes make the man. An elegant young man with a codpiece (*Lodovico Capponi*) by Bronzino.

dramatically describes his encounter with the phantom of Jewishness in the streets of Vienna—the same city where Freud was attempting to erase the visible signs of "Jewish effeminacy": "Once, as I was strolling through the Inner City," Hitler writes, "I suddenly encountered an apparition in a black caftan and black hair locks. Is this a Jew? was my first thought."[51] And the longer he "stared at this foreign face, scrutinizing feature for feature, the more my first question assumed a new form: Is this a German?" The "unclean dress and . . . generally unheroic appearance of the Jews," "these caftan-wearers," convince Hitler that he is face to face with otherness—with the not-self (which is to say, the self he fears). When he contemplates "their activity in the press, art, literature, and the theater," he concludes that Jews have been "chosen" to spread "literary filth, artistic trash, and theatrical idiocy." The chapter in which he sets out this conversion experience is called, straightforwardly, "Transformation into an Anti-Semite."

As we have seen, *Yentl*—both the Streisand film and the Singer short story—allegorizes this subtext of the Jew as always-already a woman in a spirit diametrically opposed to the vituperative claims of anti-Semitism. Yet the secret—open to the audience and the reader—of "Anshel"'s gender tells a double-edged story about the "manliness" of Torah study and scholarship. In Jewish tradition there is no higher calling for a man; as witness, for example, the tension in the film *Hester Street* (1975) between the assimilated husband, eager for commercial success, and the retiring scholar whom the heroine finally marries. Which is the "real man" here? And in the case of Yentl, is the "real" story one of a woman who needs to "become a man" in order to study Torah—or the story of a Torah scholar who is "revealed" to be a woman? When at the Second Zionist Congress in 1898 Max Nordau called for all Jews to become "muscle Jews" rather than pale, thin-chested "coffeehouse Jews,"[52] he was responding in part to this uncomfortable schism within Jewish identity, as well as to the racialist cult of "manliness" then rampant in Germany.

One mode of Jewish "manliness" mandated a life of study; another accepted a definition of "manhood" based upon martial values and physical perfectionism. Here, too, definitions of "homosexuality" cross with stereotypes of Jewish male identity, for the "homosexual" could be either super-male, especially manly and virile, and therefore associating only with other men (rather than with polluting and "effeminizing" women), or, on the other hand, a "degenerate" "aesthete," blurring the boundaries of male and female—Carpenter's *Intermediate Sex,* Symonds' and others' "Uranians." Thus the popular English writer Hector Hugh Munroe, better known as Saki—himself a homosexual—endorsed prevailing social prejudices against Jews and effeminate men, and spoke enthusiastically about male-bonding in wartime; he enlisted in the British Army during World War I, although he was forty years old, and was killed at the front.[53] Meanwhile yet another German Jew, Benedict Friedländer, wrote *against* Jews in *defense of* homosexuals, claiming that it was Jews who falsely impugned the manliness of homosexuals as a way of defaming Aryan virility.[54]

Friedländer's animus was at least in part a reaction against the followers of Magnus

Hirschfeld, the homosexual rights reformer who was also a Jew. Yet the strategy of pitting one minority against another, even (or especially) when one might be thought of as a member of *both* groups, is a familiar device for self-exoneration. "Self-hatred," an attitude all too easily ascribed to both homosexuals and Jews, is often claimed as the underlying rationale for figures like Friedländer, Rathenau, and especially Weininger, whose suicide is read as proof of his internal struggle. Whatever the psychological truth of this claim, the desire to move from outsider to insider status, to resolve category crises by displacing blame onto a minority group from which one can distance oneself, seems to have operated with uncanny effectiveness in the recoding of the Jew as a "woman," the ostensible opposite of the "manly" Aryan—and the "manly" homosexual.

That Jews were "fantastic," "Oriental," and "especially female"[55]—that they were, in fact, whether by social oppression or biological inheritance, "no more than degenerate, masturbating women" (Gilman, *Sexuality*, 267)—was a common charge in the early years of the twentieth century, against which Freud and others struggled by attempting to articulate universal, as opposed to racially separate, human characteristics. As I have pointed out elsewhere, "Jew" and "woman" are both entities of difference for Freud, against which he defines himself.[56] This desire, not to be categorized and stigmatized as a feminized Jew, is one factor that motivates Freud's typologies of sexuality and his desire *for* the universal.

For example, as Sander Gilman notes, it was alleged by some in the Early Church that Jewish men menstruated; Freud and his friend Wilhelm Fliess theorized a male as well as a female periodicity that was universal, and not specific to Jews. Fliess became—briefly—celebrated as the theorist of the nose as a site of primary sexual neurosis; a "suspicious shape to the nose" was thought (by Fliess, at least) to be the result of masturbation, and he frequently performed operations on the noses of patients to relieve neurotic symptoms.[57] It is almost surely no accident that the nose was a legible marker of Jewishness—especially for Jewish *men*. Moreover, the most obvious "sign" of Jewish "feminization" was the practice of circumcision, the ritual practice that most directly and visibly offered a threat to "manhood." As Gilman points out, "the late nineteenth-century view associated the act of religious circumcision with the act of castration, the feminizing of the Jew in the act of making him a Jew" (Gilman, *Sexuality*, 265). Fliess's obsession with nasal surgery—and Freud's enthusiastic endorsement of it—might be regarded as a displacement upward, as well as a displacement away from the Jewish-specific and toward the medical-universal. That some of Fliess's most troubled cases were the cases of *women* whose noses were said to evince neurotic signs suggests the lengths to which this mechanism of displacement could go, to distance the male Jewish physician from the specter of Jewish effeminacy, and from the haunting fear of the Jew-as-woman.

Stanley Cavell locates the shadow of this fear in *The Merchant of Venice*, in the possibility that Shylock, bargaining for the pound of flesh to be "cut off and taken, in which part of your body pleaseth me" (*MV* 1.3.146-147), might be intending "to do to him what circumcision, in certain frames of mind, is imagined to do, i.e., to castrate,"[58] and thus to perpetrate on the body of his double the marking of his own difference. We might, indeed, suspect that representations of Shylock over the years would have touched on this slippage between "Jew" and "woman," from the "Jewish gaberdine" to the constant taunt of questionable manhood (Shylock "gelded" of his daughter and his ducats, his "two stones, two rich and precious stones" taken by Jessica so that she becomes, in his unwary phrase, and at his cost, the phallic woman: "she hath the stones upon her, and the ducats" [*MV* 2.8.22]). (Here it is not without interest that it is the *Jewish woman* who gelds or castrates her own father; as with James Joyce's Bella Cohen—or indeed with the stereotypical "Jewish American Princesses" of macho-Jewish writers like Roth and Mailer—the fantasized Jewish woman crosses over into the space of "masculinity" which is put in question by the ambivalent cultural status of the Jewish man.)

The stage Jew's false nose and wig as well as his skirt-like "gaberdine" (a garment, incidentally, worn elsewhere in Shakespeare only by Caliban) offer a panoply of "detachable parts," of which the circumcised penis is the invisible but nonetheless dominant sign, the index of anxiety—and consequently of a certain recurrent risibility. The *nose* fixation is much more overtly played out in Marlowe's *Jew of Malta* than in Shakespeare's *Merchant*, for Barabas, the Maltese Jew, keeps a Turkish servant who revels in the length of his own nose, and declares that it is sure to please his master.

The *wig* question, however, has preoccupied some chroniclers of *Merchant* onstage to what seems a surprising degree: did Burbage wear a red wig—and a long nose—when the play was first performed by Shakespeare's company? Why was Edmund Kean the first to wear a black wig after so many others had—perhaps in imitation of the traditional iconography of Judas Iscariot—worn red ones? (Because he was poor, and probably had only a black and a gray wig in his collection of stage props, runs the accepted answer.)[59] The wig, in other contexts a shorthand sign of male-to-female gender impersonation, here attaches itself to the question of signatory Jewishness. Attaches, and detaches, for the wig is a quintessentially detachable part, yet another index of the displacement upward of anxieties of loss. In a way the Shylock wig might be compared to the beards of the female transvestite saints: as simultaneously superfluous and necessary, defining and putting in question identities of gender, religion, and belief.

Moreover, we might note that in the Orthodox Jewish tradition it is *women*, and not men, who wear wigs after marriage, as a way of concealing their looks, a sign of modesty and domesticity like the veil. The Orthodox Jewish woman of Eastern Europe cut her hair off after marriage so that she would no longer be attractive to men (other than her husband). Over her shorn hair she wore a wig, called a *sheitl*—a device that could still be seen on immigrant women in New York's Lower East Side in the early part of this century. The *sheitl* looked like a wig; that was part of its function, since an attractive and deceptively "natural" hairdo would defeat the purpose.

This emphasis placed upon Shylock's wig by nineteenth-century theater historians—and by the actors themselves—may thus reflect a displacement from a stereotype of the Jewish woman—at least the "Oriental" or Eastern European variety, very "foreign" in appearance to Western European eyes—onto the stigmatized Jewish man, who is once again coded "as" a woman by this preoccupation with the style and type of his wig.

In terms of stage history, although representations of Shylock have ranged from comic to tragic, from racist to sympathetic, from red-wigged to black- and gray-bearded, Shakespeare's Jew has not been overtly "feminized," despite the standard shrugs and the occasional lisp affected by actors in search of "authenticity." Twentieth-century productions have tended to be wary of Shylock's dignity; Olivier played the part as if he were Disraeli, in frock coat and top hat. In light of the connection between the cross-dressed woman and the Jew, it seems to me significant that the two most notable stage Shylocks in recent years, Antony Sher and Dustin Hoffman, have both achieved success in cross-dressed roles: Hoffman as "Dorothy Michaels" in *Tootsie*, Sher as the transsexual hero of the 1987 film *Shadey*.

There was also quite a vogue for *female* Shylocks, that is to say, actresses playing the part of Shylock, in the nineteenth and early twentieth centuries. In the 1820's Clara Fisher was praised in both England and America for her interpretation of the role. The celebrated American Charlotte Cushman, who had played Portia to the Shylocks of William Macready and Edwin Booth, achieved considerable success in the part of the Jew in the 1860's. As with Cushman's other male Shakespearean roles—as Romeo, Hamlet, and Iago—her performance was assessed on its own terms, not as a curiosity, and this seems also to have been the case with the Shylock of Mrs. Catherine Macready, the eminent Shakespearean's wife.

A few years later, however, the oddness of a woman playing Shylock dominated at least some of the reviews; when Lucille La Verne played the role in London in 1929 the *London Times* critic commented that "this Shylock occasionally left the Rialto; never the Contralto."[60] Appearing as it did on the eve of the U.S. stock market crash, this glib dismissal of the female Shylock among the money-changers has its own ironic and defensive tone.

Female *children* also played Shylock in the middle of the nineteenth century: Jean M. Davenport, Lora Gordon Boon (with her sister Anna Isabella playing Portia), and the infant prodigies Kate and Ellen Bateman; at four years of age, Ellen's Shylock and her six-year-old sister's Portia played to first-run theaters as well as to lecture halls. The nineteenth century's penchant for both child actors and male impersonators makes these Shylocks less anomalous than they might seem at first (Ellen Bateman, for example, also played Richard III and Lady Macbeth), but the phenomenon is nonetheless worthy of mention.

The theme of castration that could be readily discerned beneath the surface of the play also led to at least one pertinent drag production of *Merchant* by Harvard's all-male Hasty Pudding Theatricals, a 1915 show entitled *The Fattest Calf*, in which the intactness of Antonio's padded, outsize, elaborately measured lower leg is preserved against Shylock's designs by a double-cross-dressed Portia, a male student playing a woman playing a boy.

It is, in fact, this particular mechanism of displacement which gives such force to the transvestite transformation of Leopold Bloom in the Nighttown section of Joyce's *Ulysses*. Gilbert and Gubar, in discussing Bloom in Nighttown, never mention his Jewishness; for them the fantasy of Bloom in corsets, petticoats, and fringes suggests that "to become a female or to be like a female is not only figuratively but literally to be de-graded, to lose one's place in the preordained hierarchy that patriarchal culture associates with gender."[61]

Yet the key passages in this phantasmagoric section of *Ulysses* point to a relationship between Bloom's Jewish identity and his role as "the new womanly man."[62] Diagnosed by "Dr Malachi Mulligan, sex specialist," as "bisexually abnormal," with "hereditary epilepsy . . . the result of unbridled lust," showing "marked symptoms of chronic exhibitionism" and "prematurely bald from selfabuse" (*Ulysses*, 493), he is endowed with many of the "symptoms" of supposed Jewish degeneration. In the next sequence he becomes not only a woman but a mother, giving birth to "eight male yellow and white children" who "are immediately appointed to positions of high public trust" and high finance (*Ulysses*, 494), as Bloom is asked whether he is "the Messiah ben Joseph or ben David."

The domination sequence with Bella/Bello Cohen in which Bloom turns into a "soubrette" who will be dressed in lace, frills, and corsets is likewise cross-cut with anti-Semitic stereotypes; Bella herself, "a massive whoremistress," has "a sprouting moustache" and an "olive face, heavy, slightly sweated, and fullnosed, with orange-tainted nostrils" (*Ulysses*, 527)—all parodic traits of the "Jewess." Her transformation into Bello, "with bobbed hair, purple gills, fat moustache rings round his shaven mouth, in mountaineer's puttees, green silverbuttoned coat, sport skirt and alpine hat with moorcock's feather" (*Ulysses*, 531), is not so much the portrait of a man, despite the male pronouns that now describe "him," as it is the caricature of a mannish lesbian.

As for Bloom, now "a charming soubrette with dauby cheeks, mustard hair and large male hands and nose, leering mouth" (*Ulysses*, 536), the nose is, once again, the giveaway— the nose and the gesticulating hands. It is "with hands and features working" that he offers his exculpatory "confession": "It was Gerald converted me to be a true corsetlover when I was female impersonator in the High School play *Vice Versa*. It was dear Gerald. He got that kink, fascinated by sister's stays. Now dearest Gerald uses pinky greasepaint and gilds his eyelids" (*Ulysses*, 536).

Bello, poking under Bloom's skirts, compares his "limp" penis to Boylan's "fullgrown . . . weapon," and suggests that he take up the style of the effeminate cross-dresser: "the scanty, daringly short skirt, riding up at the knee to show a peep of white pantalette, is a potent weapon. . . . Learn the smooth mincing walk on four inch Louis XV heels, the

Grecian bend with provoking croup, the thighs fluescent, knees modestly kissing . . . Pander to their Gomorrahan vices . . . What else are you good for, an impotent thing like you?" (*Ulysses*, 540). And Bloom, as he "simpers with forefinger in mouth," performs the specific act of sensual finger sucking that Freud, citing the Hungarian pediatrician Lindner, read as the pathological, masturbatory, and auto-erotic "image of the female as child."[63]

In other words, Leopold Bloom's transformation into a "woman," and, moreover, into a pathological, infantile, and perverse figure who is also a "female impersonator" capable of "Gomorrahan vices," is not a sign that he is "a 'new womanly man' whose secret manliness may ultimately seduce and subdue insubordinate New Women," as Gilbert and Gubar would have it (*Sexchanges*, 336), but rather a sign of the interimplication of the Jew, the homosexual, and the "woman" in late nineteenth- and early twentieth-century culture.

These examples of gender crossover have focused on the feminization of the Jewish male, a common, even an obsessive concomitant to anti-Semitic thought and to the gesture of disavowal ("that is not me"; "that is the not-me") exemplified in Hitler's "recognition" of the Jew in *Mein Kampf*—a "recognition" that, in effect, codes the Jew as the *unheimlich*, the uncanny, the repressed that will always return—the very essence of the Wandering Jew. I want to close this section, however, by briefly considering a couple of examples of anti-Semitic gender critique that work slightly differently, and then glancing at one theatrical strategy that repositions the cross-dressed Jewish man.

Jean-Paul Sartre's novella, "The Childhood of a Leader" ("L'Enfance d'un chef"), tells the story of a young boy, unsure about his own gender role, who fantasizes about his mother's masculinity. "What would happen if they took away Mama's dress, and if she put on Papa's pants?" "Perhaps it would make her grow a black moustache—just like that."[64] As Alice Kaplan points out, the moustache is "a clear cultural signifier, by 1939, of Hitler" and "a complex ideological sign in this novel," since it marks an imaginary or fantasized projection by the boy, Lucien, onto his mother's face, and thus onto the face of the French motherland. The transitional object for Lucien is not only the moustache—the novella ends with his looking in the mirror and deciding to grow one of his own—but also anti-Semitism. He reads Barrès's *Les Déracinés*, and determines on an identification for himself that involves the exclusion of "non-French" Jews. Lucien's early experience with homosexuality contributes to his resolution to seek a renewed "masculinity" for himself. Treated in childhood by his mother's friends like a "little girl," he reinvents maleness, through the fantasized phallic French mother, by defining it against the Jews—and the Jew (homosexual; "little girl"; child) in himself. "Only anti-Semitism," as Kaplan shrewdly notes, "succeeds in giving him the gift of masculinity he has sought since the first scene of the novel."[65]

My second example comes from *Cabaret*, the film about decadent Berlin in which—as we have already noticed—transvestism plays a key role. The transvestite "women"

(Elke, Inge) encountered by the protagonist in the men's room and the nightclub are not, so far as we know it, Jews: they are identified as male Germans in drag. But in the cabaret act performed by Joel Grey as the demonic master of ceremonies there *is* a representation of Jewishness, coyly disclosed in the scurrilous final line of a song apparently bathetic and empty. The act involves a female figure in a gorilla suit and frilly pink costume, about whom the m.c. croons, "If You Could See Her With My Eyes." The song, apparently a lament for star-crossed love, describes the cruelty of the outside world in failing to acknowledge his beloved's qualities; throughout, the gorilla twirls on his arm, bats her eyelashes, and generally makes herself ludicrous, until the close, when the refrain "If you could see her with my eyes . . ." concludes with a conspiratorial hiss: ". . . she wouldn't look Jewish at all."

The band's ironic fanfare underscores the point; the contrast with the film's shy and beautiful Jewish heroine could hardly be greater. Here cross-species representation marks the Jewish woman as dark, animal, hairy, and witless; the "feminized" m.c. with his painted lips and the male-to-female transvestites in the chorus usurp and co-opt both all "male" and all "female" space onstage, leaving "the Jew" to be represented by a gorilla in a tutu.

As a final footnote to this we might take note of the anti-Semitic vaudeville act in Joseph Losey's 1976 film about Nazism and identity in wartime France, *Mr. Klein*. Modeled on the infamous Nazi propaganda film *Jew Süss* (1941), the act features a street singer whose jewelry is stolen by a sneaky caricature of a Jew, while the club audience roars with delight. The singer is played by a "female impersonator, dressed and made up in dark expressionistic style."[66] As with Joel Grey and his fellow vaudevillians in *Cabaret*, here "female impersonator" itself becomes a privileged category, endorsing a certain kind of decadence and crossover while denying and stigmatizing the Jew as outside that aesthetic economy. Female impersonation, while on the one hand a sign of decadence, was thus also a prerogative of power. Jews could be "feminized," but that was not at all the same as choosing to play a female role.

It would remain, some years later, for a Borscht Belt comedian like Milton Berle, whose routines so often included a drag act, to cross-dress for success, recuperating, however unconsciously, this "feminization" of the Jewish man, and deploying gender parody as an empowering strategy. For Berle, a Jewish comic nicknamed "Mr. Television" because of the popularity of his Texaco Star Theater when it appeared on NBC in 1948, was in some ways the premier video entertainer of the post-war era. "He was a man who wasn't afraid of a dress," wrote the *New York Times* in fond retrospect, "and for four years he owned Saturday night."[67]

10

PHANTOMS OF THE OPERA: ACTOR, DIPLOMAT, TRANSVESTITE, SPY

TURNCOATS

Most transvestites are not spies. Indeed, recent statistics in Massachusetts suggest that most transvestites in that state, for example, are married heterosexual truck drivers or computer engineers.[1] But some of the most famous transvestites in history have been "actresses," diplomats, and spies. Why should this be?

Perhaps the most celebrated brief description of treason is the terse little epigram ascribed to Elizabeth I's godson, Sir John Harington:

> Treason doth never prosper, what's the reason?
> For if it prosper, none dare call it treason.
> Harington, *Epigrams*

What is being described here is a hermeneutic of *passing* or *crossover*. If treason *works*, it gets mainstreamed or translated into another, non-oppositional category, a new political orthodoxy. This will come as no surprise to any reader of George Orwell—or of history. But the mechanism that is here being described is also the mechanism of gender impersonation, transvestic passing. If we were to take Harington's epigram about treason and replace "treason" with some metrically equivalent word—like "passing"—we would be characterizing a social and sartorial inscription that encodes (as treason does) its own erasure.

Successful treason is not "treason," but governance, or diplomacy. Is successful cross-dressing, when undertaken as a constant rather than an episodic activity, and when undetected, still cross-dressing? Let us consider a few striking examples, from both "history" and "literature"—examples that themselves cross over generic boundaries of the factual and the fictive. For reasons that are perhaps worth exploring, the site of several such examples has been the opera house: in Rome, in France—and in China.

THE OCCIDENTAL TOURIST

> A former French diplomat and a Chinese opera singer have been
> sentenced to six years in jail for spying for China after a two-day trial that
> traced a story of clandestine love and mistaken sexual identity. . . .
>   M. Boursicot was accused of passing information to China after he fell
> in love with Mr. Shi, whom he believed for twenty years to be a woman.
>   —*New York Times*, May 11, 1986

This story, which scandalized and titillated Western journalists and readers, was—perhaps predictably—received slightly differently in different parts of the West. The British press treated it as another homosexual spy scandal, analogous to those involving gay men like John Vassall, Kim Philby, Donald Maclean, Guy Burgess, and Anthony Blunt. Boursicot's explanation for his gender "mistake," that the couple had always had sexual relations in the dark, was dismissed as a thin cover for something else. According to one British chronicler of spy activities, "the likeliest explanation" for this unlikely story was "that Boursicot knew the truth and was hopelessly entangled in a web of lies begun to hide his homosexuality, which he continued to deny."[2] In other words, the "secret" here was homosexuality, the denial of which became so important for Boursicot that he was willing to be branded a fool and a traitor.

The French, not surprisingly, had a slightly different view as to where the shameful secret of this story really lay. A panel of French judges sentenced both Boursicot and his lover to six years in prison. Their treason in itself was not considered very serious—only minor documents were leaked. But at least one French judge seemed less appalled by the evidence of treachery than by the apparent fact that a Frenchman was unable to tell the difference between a man and a woman.[3]

As for the American press, its attitude may perhaps be exemplified by the spectacular coverage afforded the incident by *People* magazine. *People* arranged for interviews with the two principals in the scandal—a coup it trumpeted with understandable self-congratulation ("until now" neither man had been willing to discuss their relationship; "finally last week they agreed to talk"; "theirs is a story of East meeting West, and of political upheaval, sexual ambiguity and betrayal"; "it is a conundrum, finally, that will never be solved") and so on and on. But underneath this veneer of wide-eyed openness *People*, too, offered a social critique of sorts. And *People*'s contempt, unlike that of the British or the French, was directed not at Boursicot, the now openly gay Frenchman, but at Shi, the Asian "woman" in the story, now living, like Boursicot, in Paris. "A delicate man of 50 whose most striking features are his tiny hands," writes *People*,

> he leads his life like an exiled, impoverished princess, living in apartments provided by friends whom
> he calls "protectors," carrying himself like a faded diva.
>   "My life has been *très triste, très triste*, don't you agree?" he asks, in the dramatic French he favors.

"But one cannot fall into *une vie de désespoir*." With a sigh, catching his middle-aged reflection in the mirror, he adds, "I used to fascinate both men and women. What I was and what they were didn't matter."[4]

What *does* matter to *People*'s readers, of course, is the question that underlies every account of this story: what did they *do*? And how could Boursicot possibly *not have known*? The British accounts imply that he did know, and was ashamed to admit it; the French judge exhibited consternation at an ignorance that seemed to reflect badly on a prized national trait, heterosexual connoisseurship. The American press, at least as represented by the voice of the *People*, applies a characteristic investigative technique: American know-how.

Shi says he kept himself covered with a blanket in a darkened room and never allowed Boursicot to touch his crotch. He hid his genitalia by squeezing them tightly between his thighs. Even today [Boursicot] still cannot explain why sex with Shi seemed "just like being with a woman." He does not believe he had anal intercourse with Shi; he thinks his lover might have "put cream between his thighs," and that he penetrated Shi's closed legs. In any case, Boursicot stresses, they had sex only rarely. (*People*, 96–97)

Thus to the British, the answer to the "conundrum" was that Boursicot was gay; to the French, the answer—shameful to admit—was that he was a nerd; to the Americans, he was merely a dupe, misled by the tactics of a "faded diva" with a tube of K-Y jelly.

What is particularly interesting to me in all of these readings is that none of these accounts is willing to recognize the role of the central figure in the story, the transvestite. Attention focuses on sexual object choice (gay or straight) and on erotic style (dominant, submissive) rather than on the cultural "fact" at the center of the fantasy: the fact of transvestism as both a personal and a political, as well as an aesthetic and theatrical, mode of self-construction. Once again, as so often, the transvestite is looked through or away from, appropriated to tell another kind of story, a story less disturbing and dangerous, because less problematic and undecidable.

That Boursicot could fall in love with a man, or be duped by a spy—these are tales for which we have cultural contexts and cultural stereotypes. But that Shi could be—professionally, as an actor and a spy, and personally, as Boursicot's lover—a transvestite, whose entire persona put in question the cultural representation of gender—this was a "truth" too disturbing not to be explained away. And the masterstroke of *M. Butterfly*, the play based upon this affair, is that it puts in doubt, in question, the identity *of* "the transvestite." For by the end of the play it is the Western diplomat, and not the Chinese spy, who wears the wig, kimono, and face-paint of the (deliberately ambiguous) "*M.*" Butterfly.[5]

Both the original casting and the playbill of *M. Butterfly* drew attention, in different ways, to gender undecidability. The part of the diplomat, René Gallimard, was played by

John Lithgow, who had appeared in a celebrated performance as the transsexual Roberta Muldoon (formerly a pro football player called Robert) in the film version of *The World According to Garp*. As for the Asian actor/spy, that part was taken by a newcomer, B.D. Wong, whose gender was concealed by a playbill bio that carefully avoided all gendered pronouns. Until B.D. removed his briefs onstage at the end of Act 2—the spy's final debriefing—it was not possible to know unless one had read the play, or the news stories what his gender "really" was.[6]

When playwright David Henry Hwang heard about the Boursicot-Shi story, he was determined to write a play about it. He was equally determined not to find out any of the (disputed) details, since to him the events suggested a particular, and familiar, story about nationalism and sexuality—a story that he thought of as a "deconstructivist *Madame Butterfly*." Over dinner one evening, he reports, a friend asked him if he had heard about "the French diplomat who'd fallen in love with a Chinese actress, who subsequently turned out to be not only a spy, but a man." He then found a two-paragraph account in the *New York Times* that quoted the diplomat, Boursicot, as explaining that he had never seen his "girlfriend" naked because "I thought she was very modest. I thought it was a Chinese custom" (Hwang, 94).

Hwang, a Chinese-American, was well aware that this was *not* a Chinese custom—that Asian women were no more shy with their lovers than are women of the West. He concluded that Boursicot had fallen in love with a stereotype, the image of the "Oriental woman as demure and submissive" (the word "Oriental" itself, he explains, is an imperialistic term imposed by Western discourse; "in general. . . . we prefer the term 'Asian' " [Hwang, 94]). Hwang had never seen or heard Puccini's opera, but he was familiar with the derogatory remark frequently made about Asian women who deliberately presented themselves to men as obedient and submissive: "she's pulling a Butterfly." He was also familiar with the personals ads that run in magazines and on cable TV advertising "traditional Oriental women" as mail-order brides, and with the gay stereotype of the "Rice Queen," a gay Caucasian man primarily attracted to Asians, who always plays the "man" in cultural and sexual terms, while the Asian partner plays the "woman."

When Hwang consulted the libretto to Puccini's opera, therefore, he was gratified to find it a repository of sexist and racist clichés. From his point of view, he notes, the " 'impossible' story of a Frenchman duped by a Chinese man masquerading as a woman always seemed perfectly explicable; given the degree of misunderstanding between men and women and also between East and West, it seemed inevitable that a mistake of this magnitude would one day take place" (Hwang, 98). Inevitable, that is, that racism and sexism should intersect with one another, and with imperialist and colonialist fantasies. The idea that good natives are feminized—submissive and grateful—and that the passive, exotic, and feminized East is eager to submit to the domination of the masculine West—this is a story so old that, in Hwang's play, it became new.

Perhaps significantly, this fantasy of the "Orient" was conjoined, for European and

Anglo-American modernists, with an infatuation for Oriental theater, likewise conceived as symbolic and mystical rather than psychological and mimetic. In the thirties Antonin Artaud responded rapturously to the Paris visit of a Balinese theater troupe, declaring that its "pure theater" heralded the supercession of the playwright in favor of "what we would call, in our Occidental theatrical jargon, the director; but a director who has become a kind of manager of magic," whose actors became living hieroglyphs, their gestures "mysterious signs which correspond to some unknown, fabulous, and obscure reality, which we here in the Occident have completely repressed."[7] "There is an absolute in these constructed perspectives," wrote Artaud, "a real physical absolute which only Orientals are capable of envisioning" (Artaud, 67).

The idealization of theater here reflects, once again, an idealization of the "Orient"— and, not coincidentally, of "woman." Thus Artaud muses on "the women's stratified, lunar eyes: eyes of dreams which seem to absorb our own, eyes before which we ourselves appear to be *fantome*" (Artaud, 65).

In 1955 the Peking Opera came to the Théâtre des Nations, to be greeted by the press with hyperbolic praise.[8] (In fact, had he wished to, the model for *M. Butterfly*'s Gallimard, Bernard Boursicot, could have seen this cultural event during this visit, or on subsequent occasions when the troupe returned to Paris, in 1958 and 1964. As it happens, he did not.) One of the Chinese opera's most important works is a traditional piece called *The Butterfly Dream*, or *The Story of the Butterfly*: a folktale about a beautiful girl who impersonates her lazy brother so that she can get an education. Like Shakespeare's Viola, or I.B. Singer's Yentl, the girl in the opera falls in love with a young man who thinks she is a boy.

It was this part, in fact, that made Shi Pei Pu a star in China. And at least according to one account it was looking at a scrapbook containing pictures of Shi in his cross-dressed *Butterfly* role that led the French diplomat Boursicot to believe he was really a woman, when the two men first met at a party at the French embassy. Although Shi was dressed in men's clothes at the time, the photographs of him in women's costume apparently persuaded Boursicot that he had detected his "real" gender.

(The two men's stories differ slightly on this point. Boursicot says that Shi took him aside after they had become friends and confided that he was actually a woman, just like the character in *The Story of the Butterfly*—that his mother, having borne two daughters, was afraid to tell his father the third child was also a girl. Shi contends that he was showing Boursicot the scrapbook and that Boursicot—rather like d'Albert in Gautier's *Mademoiselle de Maupin*—leapt to the conclusion that he was really a woman, with expressions of relief and delight.)

Now, what I want to argue here is that the figure of the cross-dressed "woman," the transvestite figure borrowed from *both* the Chinese and Japanese stage traditions, the Peking Opera and the Kabuki and Noh theaters, functions simultaneously as a mark of gender undecidability and as an indication of category crisis. Man/woman, or male/female, is the most obvious and central of the border crossings in *M. Butterfly*, but the fact that the border is crossed *twice*, once when Song Liling becomes a "woman," and the second time when René Gallimard does so, indicates the play's preoccupation with the transvestite as a figure not only for the conundrum of gender and erotic style, but also for other kinds of border-crossing, like *acting* and *spying*, both of which are appropriations of alternative and socially constructed subject positions for cultural and political ends. "Actor" and "spy" both become, like "transvestite," "third terms," or, more accurately, terms from within the third space of possibility, the cultural Symbolic, the place of signification. And that space of "thirdness" is marked, tagged, signaled, by the presence (or, as explicitly in this play, the construction) of the transvestite.

In order to make this argument, I will briefly summarize the action of *M. Butterfly*, and then take up a number of key and related issues: specific category crises within Hwang's play—crises of nationalism and sexuality troped on the transvestite figure; the concept of "saving face" and the overestimation of the phallus; and the formal and theoretical interrelationships among acting, spying, diplomacy, and transvestism.

For reasons both political and theoretical, I will be using the pronouns "she" and "her" to describe the Chinese actor when dressed as a woman, and the pronouns "he" and "him" when the actor is dressed as a man. This may at first seem confusing, but that is, of course, part of the point.

Hwang's play begins with the diplomat, René Gallimard, in his French prison cell, and proceeds by flashback to tell the story of his love affair with Song Liling, the Chinese opera star he calls "Butterfly." His first encounter with "her," at an ambassador's residence in Peking where "she" performed the death scene from Puccini's opera, had convinced him that "she" was a woman. She quickly perceives both his ignorance and his fascination, and invites him to attend performances of the Chinese opera. As their relationship develops, René becomes more successful in his diplomatic career as well, and is promoted to Vice Consul. Always shy and inept in his relationships with Western women, and now fearing that his relationship with a Chinese will expose him to ridicule, he finds himself instead—because he has a "native mistress"—the envy of the consular office. He discovers that he can treat Song Liling with cavalier neglect, and this further strengthens his sense of masculinity. Briefly he engages in another affair, this one with a young Danish woman student whose name is the feminine twin of his: Renée. (Denmark here is presumably chosen for its connotations of sexual freedom, and "Renée"—as with "Renée Richards"—in part because it means "reborn.")

But Renée, who is eager to parade naked before him, and whose language is as frank as her sexual behavior, strikes him as paradoxically "*too* uninhibited, *too* willing . . . almost too . . . masculine." In other words, the play provides Gallimard with *two* narcissistic "female" doubles: the "masculine" Danish woman with the beautiful body, and the "feminine" Asian woman who turns out to be a transvestic man.

When Song Liling writes him an imploring note, saying "I have already given you my shame," René knows he is in command. "Are you my Butterfly?" he demands, requiring her to acknowledge the scenario of cultural domination and submission. When she assents ("I am your Butterfly"), he takes her to bed—in the dark, and clothed, for she protests that she is "a modest Chinese woman." In this first section of the play, then, Gallimard becomes—as he tells the audience—the Pinkerton of Puccini's opera, exploiting and abandoning his Oriental mistress.

In the second half of the play, the roles will be reversed. René is sent back to France; none of his predictions about the war in Indochina have come true. The Cultural Revolution comes to China, and the actor Song Liling is sent by the Mao government to Paris, to resume his work as a spy, by resuming his women's clothes, and his relationship to Gallimard. At "Butterfly"'s urging, René becomes a courier, photographing secret documents which Song passes on to the Chinese embassy. Then comes the trial. In front of the audience the Chinese actor removes his kimono, wig, and makeup, and appears before René and the audience as a man in an Armani suit.

The French judge asks the question the audience has wanted to ask all along: "Did Monsieur Gallimard know you were a man?" And Song Liling answers with two rules. Rule One: "Men always believe what they want to hear." And Rule Two: "The West has sort of an international rape mentality towards the East." And he defines "rape mentality" this way: "Her mouth says no, but her eyes say yes."

> The West thinks of itself as masculine—big guns, big industry, big money—so the East is feminine—weak, delicate, poor . . . but good at art, and full of inscrutable wisdom—the feminine mystique.
>
> Her mouth says no, but her eyes say yes. The West believes the East, deep down, *wants* to be dominated—because a woman can't think for herself. . . .
>
> You expect Oriental countries to submit to your guns, and you expect Oriental women to be submissive to your men. That's why you say they make the best wives. (3.1)

But why, the judge asks, would that make it possible for Song Liling to fool Gallimard?

> One, because when he finally met his fantasy woman he wanted more than anything to believe that she was, in fact, a woman. And second, I am an Oriental. And being an Oriental, I could never be completely a man.

Yet there is another power reversal to come. Before Act 3 is over, and before René can stop him, he has completely removed his clothes, and stands naked, revealed as—in René's words—"just a man"—"as real as hamburger" (3.2). And René chooses "fantasy" over "reality." If his "Butterfly" is not the Perfect Woman he has thought her to be, he will become that perfect Oriental woman himself. Song Liling—revealed at last to be a man—becomes the Pinkerton figure, and Gallimard literally transforms himself into "Madame Butterfly," dressing himself in the kimono and wig Song has discarded, making up his face in the traditional Japanese fashion, and ultimately committing ritual suicide—*seppuku*—plunging a knife into his body as the music from the "Love Duet" blares over the speakers. The final stage picture is a reversal of the first: Song, dressed as a man, stares at a "woman" dressed in Oriental robes, and calls out, "Butterfly? Butterfly?"

BORDER-CROSSINGS

M. Butterfly itself stands at the crossroads of nationalism and sexuality, since the axis along which it plots its dramatic movement is that of West/East and male/female. These two principal binarisms are brought immediately into both question and crisis, for one cultural fact of which René and his wife Helga—a diplomatic couple stationed in China— are blissfully ignorant is that the Peking Opera is a transvestite theater: all women's roles are played by men. After his first encounter with Song Liling, Gallimard reports that he met "the Chinese equivalent of a diva. She's a singer at the Chinese opera." In other words, he is convinced that the performer he met was a woman. His wife is surprised to hear that the Chinese even *have* an opera.

Undoubtedly, much of the Broadway audience shares this cultural indifference, which will be René's downfall. ("I asked around," he says. "No one knew anything about the Chinese opera.") Only much later does the play offer enlightenment, in a conversation between Song Liling and her female confidant-superior in the Chinese Communist Party:

> *Song:* Miss Chin? Why, in the Peking Opera, are women's roles played by men?
>
> *Chin:* I don't know. Maybe, a reactionary remnant of male—
>
> *Song:* No. (*Beat*) Because only a man knows how a woman is supposed to act.
> (2.7)

One category crisis leads to another, as Gallimard, voicing the indifference of the West to distinctions of national and cultural tradition in a region romanticized simply as "the Orient" or "the East," conflates China and Japan. Captivated by Song Liling's performance as Cio-Cio San, the heroine of *Madame Butterfly*, he assumes that what he is seeing is "authentic," and that an Oriental actress can bring Puccini's character to life in a way no Western diva could. After the performance, he seeks out Song Liling to tell her so:

> *Gallimard:* I usually don't like *Butterfly*.
>
> *Song:* I can't blame you in the least.
>
> *Gallimard:* I mean, the story—
>
> *Song:* Ridiculous.
>
> *Gallimard:* I like the story, but. . . . I've always seen it played by huge women in so much bad makeup.

Song: Bad makeup is not unique to the West.

Gallimard: But who can believe them?

Song: And you believe me?

Gallimard: Absolutely, You were utterly convincing. [. . .]

Song: Convincing? As a Japanese woman? The Japanese used hundreds of our people for medical experiments during the war, you know. But I gather such an irony is lost on you.

Gallimard: No! I was about to say, it's the first time I've seen the beauty of the story.

Song: Really?

Gallimard: Of her death. It's a . . . a pure sacrifice. He's unworthy, but what can she do? She loves him . . . so much. It's a very beautiful story.

Song: Well, yes, to a Westerner.

Gallimard: Excuse me?

Song: It's one of your favorite fantasies, isn't it? The submissive Oriental woman and the cruel white man.

Gallimard: Well, I didn't quite mean . . .

Song: Consider it this way: what would you say if a blond homecoming queen fell in love with a short Japanese businessman? He treats her cruelly, then goes home for three years, during which time she prays to his picture and turns down marriage from a young Kennedy. Then, when she learns he has remarried, she kills herself. Now, I believe you would consider this girl to be a deranged idiot, correct? But because it's an Oriental who kills herself for a Westerner—ah!—you find it beautiful.
Silence.

Gallimard: Yes . . . well . . . I see your point . . .

Song: I will never do Butterfly again, M. Gallimard. If you wish to see some real theatre, come to the Peking Opera sometime. Expand your mind. (1.6)

Notice that even though Gallimard knows nothing at all about the Peking Opera—clearly he has no idea that its women's parts are all played by men—he assumes that "the Orient" can be represented in a single, and conventional, way. He conflates China and Japan, much in the way that Artaud fantasized a pure and symbolic "Oriental theater" from the visit of a single Balinese troupe.

But if *M. Butterfly* deliberately challenges the conflation of China and *Japan* as some mystical element called "the Orient," it also offers up another, less obvious conflation of national qualities between China and *France.* "What was waiting for me back in Paris?" Gallimard asks, rhetorically. "Well, better Chinese food than I'd eaten in China . . . And the indignity of students shouting the slogans of Chairman Mao at me—in French" (2.11).

Like the exchange of roles between Song and Gallimard, between culturally constructed "woman" and culturally constructed "man," this apparent paradox is presented as not really a paradox at all. In a global cultural economy all constructions are exportable and importable: recipes, slogans, and gender roles are all reproduced as intrinsically theatrical significations.

The crossover from China to France, as from "female" to "male," is underscored theatrically by the presence onstage, during the scene of Song Liling's testimony and confession in the French court, of the actor who had played the French consul in China, and who now "enters as a judge, wearing the appropriate wig and robes" (3.1). Moments before in this same scene Song Liling had removed "her" wig and robes, the formal black headdress and embroidered kimono of Butterfly, and appeared for the first time onstage as a man, in a "well-cut Armani suit." In the courtroom scene "wig and robes" take on a new set of vestimentary significations, now the accoutrements of Western (specifically French) maleness as power and authority, the traditional costume of the judge. In the scene that follows, to the blaring music of the "Death Scene" from *Butterfly*, Gallimard will enter, "crawling toward Song's wig and kimono," while "Song remains a man, in the witness box, delivering a testimony we do not hear."

SAVING FACE

Makeup, costume, gesture, symbols, and stylization are the key elements of the "Oriental theater" (whether Chinese, Japanese, or Balinese) that captivated Europe. Significantly, they are also the key elements of female impersonation as it is practiced in the West. What David Henry Hwang did, in writing his play about the seduction of a Western diplomat by a Peking Opera star, was to demystify, and then remystify, the material basis of female impersonation. In so doing he recast the roles, allowing Gallimard to see that it was he, and not Song Liling, who was playing the woman in the piece, and thus revealing the mechanism of female impersonation as a political and cultural act.

One of the faults Gallimard found with Puccini's opera, as we have noted, was that the part of Butterfly was always played by "huge women in bad makeup." At the end of *M. Butterfly*, Gallimard seats himself at the same dressing table where Song Liling had unmasked himself, and smears his face with white face-paint. The whiteness of the makeup is traditional in Japanese theater as a sign of the ideal white complexion of the noble, who can afford to keep out of the sun, and the pallor of the protected young woman (or trained geisha) even today.[9] We might note that in *Chinese* opera face-painting participates in an entirely different sign system, in which white on an actor's face symbolizes treachery, as red does loyalty, yellow, piety, and gold, the supernatural.[10] In this story of spies and treason the Chinese and Japanese significations are at odds with one another, and Song has already warned Gallimard not to conflate the two.

For Gallimard himself, of course, the white makeup has yet another significance, since he is continually described as a "white man" throughout the play, even in France, where "There're white men all around." When he covers his face with dead white paint Gallimard demonstrates the inexactness of this cultural shorthand. His already pale face takes on a dramatic sharpness, as he continues his painting. A red slash of mouth, dark black lines of eyebrows—this is not the careful and seductive adornment of acculturated woman or trained actor, but something that verges on tragic parody. He lifts the wig—which has remained onstage on a wig stand since Song's unmasking—onto his head, and slips his arms into the kimono. And as he makes up his face, he talks to himself, and to the audience:

> *Gallimard*: Love warped my judgment, blinded my eyes, rearranged the very lines in my face . . . until I could look in the mirror and see nothing but . . . a woman.
> *Dancers help him put on the Butterfly wig.*
>
> *Gallimard*: I have a vision. Of the Orient. That, deep within its almond eyes, there are still women. Women willing to sacrifice themselves for the love of a man. Even a man whose love is completely without worth.
> *Dancers assist Gallimard in donning the kimono. They hand him a knife.*
>
> *Gallimard*: Death with honor is better than life . . . life with dishonor. . . . [. . .] And I have found her at last. In a prison on the outskirts of Paris. My name is René Gallimard—also known as Madame Butterfly. (3.3)

"Death with honor is better than life with dishonor." These lines from Puccini's opera have been quoted throughout the play. When juxtaposed to Gallimard's transformation, they underscore the fact that the dramatic use of face makeup in *M. Butterfly* is a remarkably literalized commentary on the concept of "saving face" in Chinese culture. It should come as no surprise to learn that this term, "saving face," is an invention of the English community in China, and not, strictly speaking, a Chinese phrase at all—although, equally significantly, it is common enough in Chinese to speak of "losing face" or doing something "for the sake of one's face." To "save face" in *M. Butterfly* it is necessary to "lose face." Song Liling in the character of Butterfly signals this in her letter to Gallimard: "I have already given you my shame." When Song Liling goes to a mirror at the end of Act 2 and starts to remove her makeup—and when Gallimard reverses this procedure in Act 3, sitting at the same mirror to make up his face—the figure of face is laid bare. And of course "figure" means "face."

Let me again emphasize that it is the omnipresent question of transvestism that makes this translation possible. Nationalisms and sexualities here are in flux, indeed in crisis, but what precipitates the crisis is the conflicting intertextual relationship between a transvestite theater that traditionally presents "woman" as a cultural artifact of male stagecraft (in the Chinese opera; in Kabuki theater) and a Western tradition of female impersonation that defiantly inverts the criteria for assertive individual "masculinity."

To Western audiences the all-male Kabuki tradition in Japan is perhaps the best known of the Asian transvestite theaters.[11] The tradition of the *onnagata*, the male actor of female roles in the Japanese Kabuki theater, is an honored position passed down from one generation to another, and Tomasaburo IV, the present *onnagata*, has become a major celebrity both in Japan and in Europe and the U.S.

Yet even here things are not quite what they seem—or rather, what they seem always to have been. For the earliest form of Kabuki was in fact the so-called Women's Kabuki (*onna-kabuki*) of the late sixteenth century. But women were prohibited from the stage in 1629 because of allegations of immorality, political as well as sexual; many were prostitutes, and actors were by edict officially to be segregated from the general populace. After a brief interlude in which Kabuki actresses attempted to evade this regulation by reversing the theater's previous practice, and having men play men's roles and women, women's roles, women disappeared from the stage altogether, and did not reappear as performers in Japan until after 1868.

The women were succeeded on the stage by long-haired, handsome boys, in what was known as Young Men's Kabuki (*wakashu-kabuki*), but these boys proved, apparently, too attractive to some of the samurai in the audience, and in 1652 Young Men's Kabuki was also forbidden. The present form of all-male theater therefore derives from the "Male" Kabuki (*yaro-kabuki*) of the seventeenth century, in which boys and young men were required to cut off their forelocks and shave their foreheads in order to appear less seductive.[12]

As for the Chinese opera, its *tan*, or female impersonator, wears a mask corresponding to the class of woman he is portraying: *chingyin*, the elegant lady, *huatan*, a woman of the lower classes, or *taomatan*, an Amazon or militant—but in these cases, too, it is "types" or idealizations at which he aims.[13] The emphasis in the male-to-female transvestism of the Peking Opera, as in Kabuki and in *M. Butterfly*, is on "ideal" and transcendent womanhood, an abstraction politically inflected and sexually aestheticized so that it can only be conceptualized and embodied by men.

Thus the celebrated eighteenth-century *onnagata* Yoshizawa Ayame declared that "if an actress were to appear on the stage she could not express ideal feminine beauty, for she could only rely on the exploitation of her physical characteristics, and therefore not express the synthetic ideal. The ideal woman," said Ayame, "can be expressed only by an actor."[14] Consequently, "were a woman to attempt to play a Kabuki female role," as one Western scholar of Japanese theater contends, "she would have to imitate the men who have so subtly and beautifully incarnated woman before her" (Pronko, 195). Only the *onnagata*, the female impersonator, is the real or true stage woman.

This is a view of the mimetic power of female impersonation long held by some admirers of Western male transvestite theater. Thus, for example, when the English traveler Thomas Coryate visited the theater in Venice in 1611 he was amazed to see "women acte, a thing that I never saw before," and to do so "with as good a grace, action, gesture . . . as ever I saw any masculine Actor."[15] Likewise, as we have already seen, the Restoration actor Edward Kynaston, who specialized in female roles at a time when the tradition of the "boy actor" was going out of style, was praised by one critic as a "Compleat Female Stage Beauty," more affecting than any woman.[16] Not too long ago Kenneth Tynan remarked about Shakespearean theater that Lady Macbeth was "basically a man's role," and that "it is probably a mistake to cast a woman [in the part] at all."[17] And in modern Japan, where Shakespeare is much admired, we are told that audiences "enjoy seeing Lady Macbeth played by a famous [male] Kabuki star, precisely because it is more artificial, thus more skilful, in a word, more beautiful."[18]

Commenting on Jean Genet's play *The Maids*, Jean-Paul Sartre makes a similar observation about what he calls Genet's "de-realization" of women, and of femininity. Genet had envisaged, in *Our Lady of the Flowers*, a play in which women's roles were played by adolescent boys, with a placard nailed to the stage to declare this fact to the audience. "Appearance," writes Sartre, "which is constantly on the point of passing itself off as reality, must constantly reveal its profound unreality."

> Everything must be so false that it sets our teeth on edge. But by virtue of being false, the woman acquires a poetic density. Shorn of its texture and purified, femininity becomes a heraldic sign, a cipher. As long as it was natural, the feminine blazon remained embedded in woman. Spiritualized, it becomes a category of the imagination, a device for generating reveries. Anything can be a woman: a flower, an animal, an inkwell.[19]

Anything, that is, except a woman. "Genet is trying to present to us femininity without woman." (Sartre, 11)

> In order to achieve this absolute state of artifice, the first thing to do is to eliminate nature. The roughness of a breaking voice, the dry hardness of male muscles and the bluish luster of a budding beard will make the de-feminized and spiritualized female appear as an invention of man . . . as the impossible dream of man in a world without women. (Sartre, 9)

Indeed, David Hwang himself is far from immune to this kind of sentiment. "What interested me most from the start," he reflected in an interview, "was the idea of the perfect woman. A real woman can only be herself, but a man, because he is presenting an idealization, can aspire to the idea of the perfect woman. I never had the least doubt that a man could play a woman convincingly on the stage." And he added, "I also knew it would not hurt in commercial or career terms to be able to create a great part for a white male." As for "real" women, Hwang is less interested in their "perfection," or, indeed, in their subjectivity: "Pleasure in giving pain to a woman is not that far removed,

I think, from a lot of male experiences," he says. "As an Asian, I identify with Song," but "as a man, I identify with Gallimard."[20]

Hwang's play establishes Gallimard clearly as a man unsure of his own sexual attractiveness, a man who is easily discomfited by his forthright Danish mistress's theory of warfare as a displacement of phallic inadequacy. ("I think the reason we fight wars is because we wear clothes. Because no one knows—between the men, I mean—who has the bigger . . . weenie." [2.6]) It is striking that transvestite theater in England and the United States, both Shakespeare's theater of "boy actors" and the more recent manifestations like the Hasty Pudding Show or the chorus of hula-skirted sailors in *South Pacific* (another East-West borderline marked by rampant cross-dressing), so often turns on a stage rhetoric of phallic reassurance. For phallic reassurance, and its theatrically "comic" underside, the anxiety of phallic insufficiency, is the Western transvestite theater's equivalent of saving—or losing—face. By a familiar mechanism of displacement (upward or downward), which is in fact the logic behind Freud's reading of the Medusa, "face" and "penis" become symbolic alternatives for one another. And this, in turn, suggests a reason for the presence, throughout *M. Butterfly*, of an insistent and anxious language of phallic jokes—jokes about phallic inadequacy.

For example René, remembering himself as a boy of twelve having discovered his uncle's cache of girlie magazines, imagines a pinup girl in a sexy negligee stripping in front of him: "My skin is hot, but my penis is soft. Why?" *Girl*: You can do whatever you want. *Gallimard*: I can't do a thing. Why?" (1.5) He reflects that when a woman calls a man "friend" she's calling him "a eunuch or a homosexual" (1.11), and his friend Marc jokes about having had to set up René's first sexual encounter. The one relationship that makes him feel like "a man" is that with Song Liling, and the more he neglects her, the more male and potent he feels. We may recall that his affair with the Danish girl Renée was predicated on her difference from "Butterfly": "It was exciting to be with someone who wasn't afraid to be seen completely naked. But is it possible for a woman to be *too* uninhibited, *too* willing, so as to seem almost too . . . masculine?"

Renée's exhibitionism is directly contrasted with Butterfly's modesty. When Gallimard, stung by humiliation at work (his political prophecies have not come true), decides to return to Butterfly and displace his humiliation onto *her*, he demands that she do the one thing she has consistently refused him: to strip. But before she can comply, he withdraws his request: "Did I not undress her because I knew, somewhere deep down, what I would find? Perhaps" (2.6). The phallus can play its role only when veiled.

At one point in the play Song Liling, determined to keep Gallimard's affections from straying, tells him she is pregnant, and then produces a child she says is his son (following, as it happens, the scenario of the Boursicot-Shi relationship).[21] She announces that she will name the child "Peepee." And to Gallimard's appalled remonstrance she offers the reproach of cultural difference:

> *Gallimard:* You can't be serious. Can you imagine the time this child will have in school?
>
> *Song:* In the West, yes.
>
> *Gallimard:* It's worse than naming him Ping Pong or Long Dong or—
>
> *Song:* But he's never going to live in the West, is he? (2.9)

We may recall that the Chinese actor-spy on whom Song Liling's part was based was named Shi Pei Pu. The name Pei Pu may have suggested to the playwright the joke on "Peepee." But in any case little "Peepee," the detachable phallus (who may someday grow up to be Long Dong), is the "proof" of Gallimard's "masculinity."

In an earlier scene, his wife had urged him to see a doctor to find out why they were unable to have children. "You men of the West," said Song Liling to him on that occasion, "you're obsessed by your odd desire for equality. Your wife can't give you a child, and *you're* going to the doctor?" "Promise me . . . you won't go to this doctor. Who is this Western quack to set himself as judge over the man I love? I know who is a man, and who is not" (2.5). There could be no better example of the translation of "saving face" into phallic terms. "Of course I didn't go," Gallimard comments to the audience. "What man would?"

WHAT PASSES FOR A WOMAN IN MODERN CHINA

Was Bernard Boursicot wrong to believe that Shi Pei Pu was a woman? If we are serious about describing gender as constructed rather than essential or innate, the lifelong transvestite puts this binarism (constructed/essential)—like so many others—to the test.

The most direct revelation of Song Liling's activities as a spy in *M. Butterfly* comes, significantly, in a conversation that also addresses the question of cross-dressing and the essence—or construction—of womanhood. The scene is the flat shared by the lovers in Beijing, 1961. Gallimard has left for the evening, and Comrade Chin, Song Liling's female government contact, is interviewing Song about American plans for increased troop strength in Vietnam—all information passed through the French embassy. Chin, writing as fast as she can, can hardly keep up with the numbers of soldiers, militia, and advisors. "How do you remember so much?" she asks. "I'm an actor." "Is that how come you dress like that?" "Like what . . . ?" "You're wearing a dress. And every time I come here, you're wearing a dress. Is that because you're an actor? Or what?" "It helps me in my assignment," says Song.

"Remember," cautions Comrade Chin, "when working for the Great Proletarian State, you represent our Chairman Mao in every position you take." "I'll try to imagine the Chairman taking my positions," replies Song, with an irony entirely lost on her interlocutor. "Don't forget," says Chin as she is leaving, "there is no homosexuality in China."

And Song answers, "Yes, I've heard." And then to the audience, after the departing Miss Chin in her Mao suit, he comments, "What passes for a woman in modern China" (2.4). What *passes* for a woman—this is the real question. And, in René's horrified recognition that "the man I loved was a cad, a bounder," what passes for a man.

Song's ironic and disparaging aside, "What passes for a woman in modern China," marks a crucial dissymmetry in the playtext. Focusing on male pathos and male self-pity, *M. Butterfly* is intermittently antifeminist and homophobic, ridiculing the *female* cross-dresser, Miss Chin, while it elevates Gallimard's plight to the plane of high drama. The other women in the play, like Renée and Helga, are likewise presented in caricature rather than in sympathetic depth. This is a critique frequently made of contemporary male transvestite theater, that it occludes or erases women, implying that a man may be (or rather, make) a more successful "woman" than a woman can. In Hwang's play cross-dressed men are emblematic of cultural crisis (or even of the "human condition"), but the cross-dressed woman is a risible sign of failed "femininity."

Here too, though, it is worth recalling that the "women," like the "men" in Hwang's play, are gendered *in representation* rather than in "reality." Making Miss Chin the butt of broad jokes about uniforms, bureaucratic dress-for-success, and the totalitarian erasure of difference offers a sharp contrast between the impossibility of androgyny by sartorial fiat and the subversive power of transvestism both to undermine and to exemplify cultural constructions. Nonetheless, the easy laugh elicited by Song's put-down on "passing for a woman" is too anti-butch not to let the fear of women, and women's difference, come through. What is really at stake here, it seems to me, is a subconscious recognition that "woman" in patriarchal society is conceived of as an artifact—and that the logical next step is the recognition that "man" is likewise not fact but artifact, himself constructed, made of detachable parts. This is the anxiety that lies beneath the laughter; and it is on this anxiety of artifactuality that the aesthetic claims of transvestite theater are, paradoxically, based.

That acting, espionage, and, indeed, diplomacy should be formally or structurally cognate with transvestism is not really surprising. Using the language of vestimentary codes, actors, spies, and transvestites could be characterized as potential or actual *turncoats*. Another suggestive sartorial term popularly in use to describe espionage activities is *cloak and dagger*—again, pointing to the element of disguise, but also of theatricality virtually for its own sake, and of displacement onto clothing—away from the body. Artaud's praise of Oriental theater was in fact literally a praise of cloak and dagger—of "those who confer upon each man in his robes a double made of clothes—those who pierce these illusory or secondary clothes with a saber, giving them the look of huge *butterflies* pinned to the air" (Artaud, 62). What these activities have in common, however, is more than metaphorical or literal change of costume. It is an ideology of construction.

"The woman of Fashion," says Roland Barthes in *The Fashion System*, is a collection of tiny, separate essences rather analogous to the character parts played by actors in classical theater; the analogy is not arbitrary, since Fashion presents the woman as a representation, in such a way that a simple attribute of the person, spoken in the form of an adjective, actually absorbs this person's entire being; . . . the paradox consists then of maintaining the generality of the characteristics (which alone is compatible with the institution of Fashion) in a strictly analytical state: it is a generality of accumulation, not of synthesis: in Fashion, the *person* is thus simultaneously impossible and yet entirely known.[22]

"Personality" is something that is acquired from the outside, not the inside, from accumulation, not synthesis. We might compare this to what Diderot says about the paradox of acting: that the actor, the great actor, must not feel.

At the very moment when he touches your heart he is listening to his own voice; his talent depends not, as you think, upon feeling, but upon rendering so exactly the outward signs of feeling, that you fall into the trap. He has rehearsed to himself every note of his passion . . . The broken voice, the half-uttered words, the stifled or prolonged notes of agony, the trembling limbs, the faintings, the bursts of fury—all this is pure mimicry, lessons carefully learned, the grimacing of sorrow, the magnificent aping which the actor remembers long after his first study of it, of which he was perfectly conscious when he first put it before the public, and which leaves him, luckily for the poet, the spectator, and himself, a full freedom of mind. . . . He feels neither trouble, nor sorrow, nor depression, nor weariness of soul. All these emotions he has given to you.[23]

This (de)construction or (de)composition of the fantasy of "character" is precisely what is at work and on display in *M. Butterfly*. Barthes's description of the fashion system suggests that "personality" in the discourse of clothing is an illusion, made up of an accumulation of signifying "essences": "in Fashion, the *person* is thus simultaneously impossible and yet entirely known." In David Henry Hwang's play the vestimentary codes of stage, gender, nation, and race conspire together to make the person of the play's title, the *dramatis persona*, likewise, in Barthes' terms, both "impossible" and "entirely known." As Song Liling changes costume, from the "traditional Chinese garb" of the opening tableau to the "Anna May Wong" black gown from the twenties and the chong sam in which "she" appears at home to Gallimard (1.10) to the Armani slacks and gold neck chain in which "he" reveals "his" true gender in the courtroom in France, s/he also changes "character," becomes, as s/he has always been, unknowable, unknown.

"What passes for a woman." And what passes for a man. *Passing* is what *acting* is, and what *treason* is. Recall that the French diplomat Boursicot was accused of *passing* information to his Chinese contacts. In espionage, in theater, in "modern China," in contemporary culture, embedded in the very phrase "gender roles," there is, this play suggests, *only* passing. Trespassing. Border-crossing and border raids. Gender, here, exists only in representation—or performance.

This is the scandal of transvestism—that transvestism tells the truth about gender.

Which is why—which is one reason why—like René Gallimard, we cannot look it in the face.

WHEN IN ROME

"The title raises a question: *What is Sarrasine?* a noun? A name? A thing? A man? A woman? This question will not be answered until much later . . ."
Roland Barthes, *S/Z*

It is instructive to juxtapose *M. Butterfly* to another extraordinary tale of gender confusion in the opera house, Balzac's *Sarrasine*, the story of a young sculptor who becomes infatuated with a Roman opera singer, La Zambinella. Here the cross-cultural divide lies between France, specifically Paris, and the Rome of the Papal States. Sarrasine, like Gallimard, is something of a late-starter and a sexual naif: "He had no other mistress but sculpture, and Clothilde, one of the luminaries of the Opera. And even this affair did not last." He had been "kept, as a matter of principle, in total ignorance of the facts of life."[24]

Sarrasine travels to Italy, and arrives in Rome, intoxicated by the foreignness of the city. One evening he goes to the opera at the Teatro Argentina and is overwhelmed by the voice and beauty of the star, La Zambinella. "With his eyes, Sarrasine devoured Pygmalion's statue, come down from its pedestal. When La Zambinella sang, the effect was delirium" (Balzac, 238). The next day he sends his valet to rent a season box, and

in a week he lived a lifetime, spending the mornings kneading the clay by which he would copy La Zambinella, despite the veils, skirts, corsets, and ribbons which concealed her from him. In the evenings, installed in his box early, alone, lying on a sofa like a Turk under the influence of opium, he created for himself a pleasure as rich and varied as he wished it to be. (Balzac, 240)

The figure of the recumbent Turk marks the cross-cultural move of the text just as it marks Sarrasine's own passion not only as narcissistic, but also as passive, receptive, "feminine." In the morning Sarrasine is active, in the evening, passive; in the morning he is French, in the evening, Turkish. The axis of cultural difference is crucial to the possibility of misreading. And Rome for him is, as the text will establish, as foreign and "Eastern" a world as Turkey—or ancient Greece. Before his journey, he seeks perfection in one "unworthy model" after another, "without having encountered under the cold Parisian sky the rich, sweet creations of ancient Greece" (Balzac, 238). Since this will be a story of mistaken gender identity, based upon an error of cultural misconstruction just like Gallimard's, the transposition of gender and culture (male West vs. female East) again literally dis-locates or dis-places the site of Sarrasine's anxiety.

It is remarkable how similar Sarrasine's "adventure" is to Gallimard's. Night after night he visits the opera, becoming a familiar foreign figure among the indigenous audience, and begins to be persuaded that the diva returns his feelings. He catches La Zambinella's eye when she appears onstage, and, generalizing on his (meager) experience of women, understands his opportunity: "She gave Sarrasine one of those eloquent glances which often reveal much more than women intend them to. . . . Sarrasine was loved!" (Balzac, 241). When invited to meet her one night after the theater, he "adorn[s] himself like a girl about to appear before her first love" (Balzac, 242) and presents himself to his beloved.

Significantly, what he notices are her *clothes*: her coquettish and voluptuous slippers, her well-fitting white stockings. As with Gallimard and Song Liling, what he sees is concealment, deflection:

> She had removed her costume and was wearing a bodice that accentuated her narrow waist and set off the satin panniers of her dress, which was embroidered with blue flowers. Her bosom, *the treasures of which were concealed*, in an excess of coquetry, by a *covering* of lace, was dazzlingly white. Her hair arranged something like that of Mme du Barry, her face, though it was *partially hidden* under a full bonnet, appeared only the more delicate, and *powder* suited her. (Balzac, 243, emphasis added)

He admires her weakness; she shudders at the sudden popping of a champagne cork, and he glows, "How much is protective in a man's love!" (Balzac, 244). Without even Gallimard's self-irony ("So much for sheltering her in my strong Western arms!") he exults, "My strength your shield!" He admires her modesty: "she had begun by pressing his foot and teasing him with the flirtatiousness of a woman in love and free to show it; but she suddenly wrapped herself in the modesty of a young girl" (Balzac, 244). It is in fact this "modesty" that makes him think seriously about the future.

> "And if I were not a woman?" La Zambinella asked in a soft silvery voice.
> "What a joke!" Sarrasine cried. "Do you think you can deceive an artist's eye? Haven't I spent ten days devouring, scrutinizing, admiring your perfection? Only a woman could have this round, soft arm, these elegant curves." (Balzac, 247)

When La Zambinella is frightened by a garden snake, and Sarrasine crushes it under his heel in good biblical fashion, he is emboldened to a further pleasantry: "Now do you dare deny you are a woman?" (Balzac, 248).

Sarrasine's enlightenment, or demystification, will unfold in a scene which is, actually, more reminiscent of Gautier's *Mademoiselle de Maupin* than of *M. Butterfly*, for it occurs when he sees his beloved cross-dressed, as d'Albert sees Théodore in the part of Rosalind/Ganymede in *As You Like It*. But where d'Albert takes hope (his love may be a woman after all) Sarrasine loses it. Notice that, as with Gallimard and Song Liling, the meeting takes place at the home of an ambassador. The subtext of diplomacy constructs the ambassadorial residence or diplomatic community as a "third place" analogous to the "third sex" of actor or performer.

"Is it out of consideration for the cardinals, bishops, and abbés present," Sarrasine asked, "that she is dressed as a man, that she is wearing a snood, kinky hair, and a sword?"

"She? What she?" asked the old nobleman to whom Sarrasine had been speaking. "La Zambinella."

"La Zambinella!" the Roman prince replied. "Are you joking? Where are you from? Has there ever been a woman on the Roman stage? And don't you know about the creatures who sing female roles in the Papal States?" (Balzac, 250)

The open secret here, like the open secret about the Chinese opera, is that there are no female performers on the Roman stage. Sarrasine, like Gallimard, is the victim (or the beneficiary) of cultural ignorance and cultural difference. His beloved, as the reader has suspected for some time, is a castrato. And it turns out that the very Roman prince who tells Sarrasine this story is the one "who gave Zambinella his voice"—that is to say, who castrated him. The economy of give and take is nicely balanced; what Sarrasine construes as irremediable loss the prince understands as gain: "if he makes a fortune, he will owe it all to me" (Balzac, 250).

The castrato Zambinella sings *en garçon* in front of an audience of men in skirts (cardinals, bishops, and abbés). Somewhere in the background lurks the old adage about what to do "when in Rome." The celibate, skirted princes of the Church are more "men" than he, because they *know*. Certainty and decidability are coded masculine, doubt and undecidability, feminine. The native is masculine, the foreign, feminine. And the expected response, from Sarrasine as from Gallimard, is shame: "they will make a fool of you" (Balzac, 249). "I only agreed to trick you to please my friends, who wanted to laugh," explains Zambinella (Balzac, 251).

But what Sarrasine cannot bear is not so much shame as it is ambiguity and undecidability, which he reads as absence and therefore as lack of value. "You are nothing. If you were a man or a woman, I would kill you." The fear of castration is here terrifyingly literalized. "Monster. You who can give life to nothing" (Balzac, 252). Recall that Song Liling's ultimate triumph over Gallimard was to appear to bear him a child, something his European wife could not do. The revelation of her pregnancy kept him from renewing his demand that she strip, that he see her naked. It was the ultimate "proof" of her identity as a woman—and therefore of *his* identity as a *man*. "If La Zambinella had had children," comments Barthes, "(a paradox indicative of the deficiency which makes her what she is), they would have been . . . delicately feminine creatures . . . as though in La Zambinella there had been a dream of normality, a teleological essence from which the castrato had been excluded, and this essence was femininity itself" (Barthes, 38). Her "deficiency" makes her what she is. As Barbara Johnson points out, "in [Sarrasine's] narcissistic system, the difference between the sexes is based on symmetry, and it is precisely the castrato that Sarrasine does indeed love—the image of the lack of what he thereby thinks he himself possesses." "The castrato," in Johnson's lucid formulation, "is simultaneously outside the difference between the sexes as well as representing the literalization of its illusory symmetry. He subverts the desire for symmetrical, binary difference by fulfilling it."[25]

Castrati, or *evirati* ("emasculated men"), played the theatrical and social roles of both "men" and "women." The castrato embodied paradox: his body was changed so that his voice would not. One kind of "performance" was denied him so that success in another could be achieved. Even the origin of this art remained shrouded in shame, and also in mystery. One of the most famous stories told about the castrati is that of Charles Burney, an eighteenth-century English traveler, who reported that it was impossible to discover *where* such surgical operations were performed.

> I enquired throughout Italy at what place boys were chiefly qualified for singing by castration, but could get no certain intelligence. I was told at Milan that it was at Venice; at Venice that it was at Bologna; but at Bologna the fact was denied, and I was referred to Florence; from Florence to Rome; and from Rome I was sent to Naples. The operation is most certainly against the law in all these places, as well as against nature; and all the Italians are so much ashamed of it, that in every province they transfer it to some other.[26]

Like a phantom or a ghost, the place of castration—on the map, on the body—itself became undecidable.

The practice of castrating young boys to preserve their singing voices was a "solution" offered by the medieval Church to get around the regulation that women were not to sing in churches (thus taking literally Saint Paul's instruction, "Let your women keep silent in the churches" [1 Cor.14:34]). Since aesthetic considerations required high singing voices, something had to give, or go; in the event, castration was apparently thought of as less morally problematic than the presence of women, and an art form was born.

The legal strictures against castration were ambivalent, to say the least. Although anyone who participated in any way in such an operation was excommunicated, there was no punishment imposed upon the castrate, and the money was good: poor families thus sometimes found the castration of a son financially expedient. A body of Church music for castrati became important in the fifteenth century, and three centuries later, when European opera had evolved as a major art form, a star system for castrati developed in Italy and Germany.

At first castrati sang male roles (like the title role of Monteverdi's *Orfeo*), but because of a bias against female singers on the stage—and, in Rome, an actual papal prohibition—the castrati began increasingly to appear in the opera as women. In the eighteenth century it is estimated that seventy percent of *all* opera singers in Italy were castrati.[27]

Some castrati took wives, or were said to have had affairs with their female admirers. Casanova reported that at Covent Garden "the *castrato* Tenducci surprised me by introducing me to his wife, by whom he had two children. He laughed at people who said that a *castrato* could not procreate."[28] But Tenducci's marriage was later declared null and void,[29] and recent medical experts have doubted that castrati could consummate heterosexual love affairs (Peschel and Peschel, 31–33). Other castrati apparently lived the lives of women offstage as well as on. Many had male patrons, as well as female admirers.

Musically, over time, the castrati became "changelings" in more than one sense. Not only did "trouser roles" or "breeches parts" in opera (male roles written for the female voice, like Octavian in *Der Rosenkavalier*, Oscar in *Un ballo in maschera*, Nicklausse in *Les contes d'Hoffmann*) derive from the earlier use of castrati, but so too did *bel canto* singing as performed by both men and women, in operas by Rossini, Bellini, and Donizetti (Peschel and Peschel, 36). When the female singer playing Count Octavian cross-dresses as a woman, some of the gender ambiguities of operatic roles are subject to scrutiny, if not critique, from within. The castrati were gone, but their legacy—marked in the place of their absence—remained.

In his *Memoirs*, Casanova comments on the popularity and flirtatiousness of two of Rome's best-known castrati. One he mistook for a woman when he met him in a café in women's clothes; of the other he remarks that, "though one knew the negative nature of this unfortunate," one could not help being charmed. "One glance at his chest . . . [and] you were madly in love." As for the Roman infatuation with the castrati, Casanova observes drily, "Rome, the holy city which in this way forces every man to become a pederast, will not admit it, nor believe in the effects of an illusion which it does its best to arouse."[30]

This is a reasonable description of the paradoxical act of bad faith which characterizes the spectators at many theatrical displays of female impersonation. The overheated atmosphere of the Roman opera, which could provoke Sarrasine's "mistake," was unique in Europe at the time; neither the French nor the English showed a real appreciation of the castrati, though not necessarily for the same reasons. The singing of La Zambinella precisely arouses the effects of an illusion in which Sarrasine is not permitted to believe, just as the refusal to permit such an illusion to exist was the ultimate repression against which René Gallimard felt the need to protest, both by becoming the cross-dressed woman and by killing her.

DIPLOMATIC IMMUNITY

> All men have been of his occupation: and indeed, what *he* doth feignedly,
> that do *others* essentially.
> Sir Thomas Overbury, "Of an Excellent Actor"[31]

Actor, diplomat, transvestite, spy. Treason is often associated with "acting ability," the ability to delude others and, on occasion, oneself. Anthony Blunt, discussing his double life and the ease with which he was able to fool even his own brother, remarked, "You must admit, I'm a very good actor."[32] The wife of George Blake (a KGB spy who had infiltrated British intelligence) claimed that she had never really been married to him because he turned out to be someone entirely different from the person she thought he was.[33] The word "spy" itself, in its associations with the gaze and with voyeurism, suggests a more fundamental (and theoretically interesting) similarity between secret seeing and exhibitionism, being seen. During the U.S. Civil War several cross-dressing women apparently served as spies.[34] In fact, as I have already noted, some of the most celebrated (or notorious) transvestites in history have been diplomats or spies. I would like now to look at two such cases in greater detail.

In the careers and writings of the seventeenth-century Abbé de Choisy and the eighteenth-century Chevalier d'Eon questions of transvestism, gender undecidability, cultural, national and racial stereotypes, and even the opera as a scene of revelation and discovery intersect with diplomacy and espionage, suggesting that the juxtaposition of these details in Hwang's play and Balzac's story is less extraordinary, and more uncanny, than it may at first appear. The life of Choisy is fascinating in the ways in which it manipulates and calls in question the stability of categories like audience and actor, politics and theater, male and female. And the story of the Chevalier d'Eon, as will shortly be clear, was a perfect example of the legerdemain of diplomacy as theater, as well as the perhaps tragic tale of an actor imprisoned by his role.

François Timoléon (later Abbé) de Choisy, the French courtier, historian, and one-time deputy Ambassador to Siam, is today perhaps best known for his two sets of *Memoirs*, one on the life and times of Louis XIV, and the other a set of autobiographical *Fragments* chronicling his own life as a cross-dresser. His *History of the Church*, described as his most monumental work, was written when he was dressed as a woman. As d'Alembert observes, "to appreciate the literary value of these ecclesiastical annals it will perhaps suffice to call to mind the picture of an old priest, more than seventy years of age, dressed in a costume unsuited to his age, sex and condition, working on a history of martyrs and anchorites."[35]

In youth and middle age Choisy, who cross-dressed in women's clothes from his earliest childhood, had a highly successful career on the stage (and off) as an actress in a Bordeaux theater. Indefatigably heterosexual, he dressed himself in a gown and his mistress as a boy and attended the opera with her, attracting more attention to the spectacle in the audience than to the performance on the stage. Sent to Rome to attend the election of the Pope, he dressed as a woman at the coronation ball—and continued to do so for the next several years while he lived in Italy. When he visited Siam in the entourage of Louis XIV's ambassador, we are told, he "went gorgeously arrayed in a feminine evening gown, make-up and jewelry. The Siamese thought it was a European custom of some sort" (Ackroyd, 9). Here we have the inverse of the East/West stereotype we saw in *M. Butterfly*; instead of the West feminizing the East, the East feminizes the West, or naturalizes the "feminine" it sees.

Choisy was the third son of a strong-willed mother, who gave birth to him in her middle age, and dressed him in women's clothes throughout his childhood. In his adolescence she applied a depilatory lotion to his face so that his beard would not grow. After his mother's death he continued to cross-dress, and appeared regularly as a woman both in Paris and in the provinces, attending church, receiving the attentions of curés and chevaliers, and adopting beautiful young girls as his bedfellows.[36]

In Paris he was well known as a cross-dresser, and though his relatives were occasionally mortified by his appearance, most of his acquaintance were charmed. With deliberation he set about acclimating them to his appearance. Dressed modestly and conservatively, as he says, "only" in a black *robe de chambre* with a long train held by a lackey, a "small" peruke, "quite simple earrings" and two face patches, he called upon the local curé in the faubourg Saint-Germain, and was told that his costume was more attractive than that of the little abbés with their *just-au-corps* and "little cloaks that commanded no respect" (Choisy, 38). He made similar calls on the churchwardens and on all his female neighbors, and wore the same dress for a month, while faithfully attending High Mass every Sunday and visiting the poor once a week.

Gradually in this manner he increased the daring of his costume; at the end of a month he unfastened three or four buttons at the top of his robe, wore diamond earrings, a powdered peruke, and three or four patches around his mouth and on his forehead; as he had expected, people became accustomed to this, and after another month he felt confident enough to unbutton the bottom of his gown. He stopped wearing trunk-hose ("to me it was hardly becoming to a woman") and exposed his shoulders, kept soft and white by a nightly wash with veal water and sheep's foot grease. When the curé came to call on a supper party, one of his lady neighbors asked whether he was not a "lovely woman," and when the curé replied that "she is in masquerade," Choisy corrected him: "No, monsieur, no; in the future I shall not dress otherwise" (Choisy, 29). As far as his extravagant tastes allowed—for he was an inveterate gambler and in money troubles periodically throughout his life—Choisy kept this promise.

Among his numerous and influential acquaintance, Madame de la Fayette and Monsieur de la Rochefoucauld urged him to dress exclusively as a woman rather than as a man with pendants and patches (Choisy, 63). One of his great admirers was Monsieur, the King's famously bisexual brother, who according to Choisy longed to dress as a woman himself, and made an appearance thus dressed at a masked ball.

"I went everywhere," he writes, "calling, to church, to a sermon, to the Opera, to the theatre, and I believed everyone had become accustomed to it; I made my lackeys call me 'Madame de Sancy.'" But it was the opera, in fact, that was to prove his social downfall.

Always attracted to young girls, Choisy had formed an early liaison with a young woman whom he dressed at his own expense *en garçon*, in a complete man's costume and peruke, gloves, cravat, and hat. He called her Monsieur de Maulny, and went through a form of marriage with her, he dressed *en femme*, she *en garçon*. One day he "risked" going to the opera with his cross-dressed mistress, "M. de Maulny," but everyone stared, and though some complimented him on his beauty, he stayed away for some time after that. "I had," he says, "to avoid scandal." He began to receive anonymous letters, one of which he quotes because of its "sensitive and intelligent" opinions:

> I concede that you are beautiful, and I am not surprised that you like women's attire, which greatly becomes you; but I cannot forgive you the *alliance*, I dare to call it scandalous, which you have made openly and before the world with a young girl who is our neighbour and whom you make dress as a man to add a spice to her. It would be one thing if you dissembled your weakness, but you flaunt it; you are seen in your carriage in the *promenades publiques* with your "husband," and I almost expect that one day you will pretend you are carrying a child. Think of this, my dear lady, and search your heart. (Choisy, 47)

The "dear lady" did think, and took heed. The error of Choisy's ways, we may notice, is not so much his own cross-dressing (the letter writer scruples to address him as a "lady") as it is the *alliance* with his cross-dressed "husband." The problem is one of propriety and display, and it is at the opera, above all, that such things are judged. When on another occasion the young Dauphin, aged about twelve, found him "lovely as an angel" and paid him compliments at the opera, his preceptor looked him up and down and voiced his disapproval:

> I admit, madame, or mademoiselle, I do not know what to call you, I admit that you are beautiful, but have you no shame at wearing such clothing and acting as a woman, seeing that you are fortunate enough not to be one? Go, go and hide yourself; Monsieur le Dauphin finds you very ill as you are. (Choisy, 65)

Although the little Prince ardently expressed his disagreement, Choisy was upset and angry. "I left the Opera without returning to my box, determined to abandon all the finery which had incurred such an untoward rebuke. But I found it impossible to make up my mind and I decided to live three or four years in a province where no one would know me, and where I could make myself pretty as I wished until I tired of it" (Choisy, 65).

With a blond peruke covering his black hair he set out for Bourges, and established himself as a "Comtesse" in the village of Crespon. There he took as his mistress a young actress whom he trained for the stage (demonstrating his own skill at women's parts) and installed in a company. As he had done earlier, he dressed his lady *en garçon*. Called "the little Comte," she rode by his side in peruke and riding habit, until her pregnancy obliged him to dress her again in women's clothes. The prophecy of his anonymous correspondent had obliquely come true, although it was the "Comte" and not the "Comtesse," the "husband" and not the "wife," who was with child.

In contrast to his deportment in the city, Choisy did not cross-dress in the provinces only for show, on the occasion of masked balls or theatrical performances. His neighbors believed that he was a woman, and under cover of this female persona he was able to take on as protegées young women of the neighborhood, whom he taught to dress and do their hair, and also deflowered. Cross-dressed, his hair in curling-papers, he presided at the *petite ruelle* and made love to his bedmate, while pretending to his neighbors that nothing unusual was going on. "The spectators increased the delight even more; it is sweet to deceive the eyes of the public" (Choisy, 86). In bed, as on the stage at Bordeaux, he was again acting the woman, while sexually "performing" as a man. And as at Bordeaux, to be "deceiving" everyone was still sweet.

Choisy's theatrical metaphors are neither inadvertent nor unconscious. His *Memoirs* are full of the language of acting. "I have taken the part of a girl for five months in the theatre of a large town," he boasts. "Everyone was deceived" (Choisy, 27). "I was a good actress, it was my first occupation" (Choisy, 78). For him the opera, in particular, was a testing ground, a place to see and be seen, a "scene" of instruction and deception in which the interrogating gaze traveled not only between the audience and the performers but also from one audience member to another. Even in a religious dialogue (written penitently after a spell of illness in which he hallucinated that hell was full of "ne'er do wells dressed as women") he later "proved" the immortality of the soul by comparing it to the singing of the leading soprano at the opera.

But Choisy the "actress" was also Choisy the diplomat. Exiled to Italy by disapproving relatives, he gambled away his money and came back to France to enlist himself in the service of the Church. Intrigued by the idea of the planned embassy to Siam, he persuaded the King to appoint him coadjutor or deputy. Just before his departure for Siam he married a woman who bore him a child; on the journey he was made a priest by the Bishop *in partibus* in Siam. No social role, it appears, was foreign to him—male or female, priest or husband. Despite his nightmares about cross-dressed wastrels in hell, he seems to have suffered relatively little anxiety about his own gender roles. The *Memoirs* tell a story of occasional social gaffes and mild rebukes, but they also describe a man who delighted in clothes, in exhibiting himself in public arrayed in costly robes and patches, and who was quite comfortable proffering "substantial pleasures" to his mistress in bed while wearing curling-papers in his hair.[37]

If Choisy was an actress who became a diplomat, the Chevalier d'Eon, the most famous transvestite in Western history, was a diplomat who became an actress. This extraordinary personage, after whom Havelock Ellis wished to name the transvestic syndrome *eonism*, was the Chevalier d'Eon de Beaumont.[38]

Born in France in 1728, d'Eon was short and plump, with a soft face and voice. Some speculation persists that he was physically hermaphroditic, or, at least, sexually indeterminate in external appearance, with large hips and a full chest. Although he apparently dressed like a man at school, he was sent to Russia in 1755 to act as a spy in the court of the Empress Elizabeth at St. Peterburg, and it is alleged by some biographers that he there dressed like a woman for the purposes of espionage—though others claim this rumor has no foundation in fact. Whether d'Eon actually impersonated a woman in Russia or not seems in a way less important than the desire—the persistent cultural desire of historians, biographers, and readers—to think that he might have done so.[39] The desire, the fantasy, expresses an unconscious wish—as well as an unconscious fear, and an unconscious recognition.

Sent to London in 1762 as a Minister Plenipotentiary for the French Foreign Service, d'Eon served there for fifteen years and became the subject and object of controversy. The London *Public Advertiser* for March 21, 1774, reported that

> There is as great a singularity in the character of the Chevalier d'Eon, as *in our ignorance of his sex.* The rule of his life is peculiar to himself; no other man or woman would, in the same position, write and behave as he does. (emphasis in the original)[40]

This undecidability—"no other man or woman"—was to continue throughout his life. The French Ambassador complained to Louis XV about d'Eon's behavior and he was recalled to France, but refused to go. The Count de Broglio wrote to the King that

> This singular being (because the Sieur d'Eon is a female), is, more so than many others, a compound of good qualities and of faults, and he carries the one and the other to extremes. . . . he occasionally signs his letters "William Wolff."[41]

Notice again the rhetorical situating of d'Eon between binaries; his disputed gender and his other ambivalences ("a compound of good qualities and of faults") seem to reinforce one another. His male English alias, "William Wolff," raises the ante further. Was d'Eon male or female, French or English, good or bad, mad (several modern commentators diagnose "paranoia") or sane?

The London Stock Exchange took bets on his gender. Gambling policies of insurance were taken for very large amounts of money at Brooks's, White's, and other clubs, and the *Public Advertiser* reported that

> the Chevalier d'Eon with justice complains of our public prints . . . they lately made a woman of him, when not one of his enemies dared to put his manhood to the proof. He makes no complaint of the English ladies.[42]

Betting was so heavy that d'Eon feared that he would be kidnapped by those who "had heavy stakes on his sex, and were pressing for having the question resolved offhand" (Telfer, 214).

A few years later the new king, Louis XVI, sent his envoy Beaumarchais to England to persuade the Chevalier to return. Instead, according to some accounts, d'Eon persuaded Beaumarchais that he was in fact a woman, trapped in male clothes for political purposes; others claim that Beaumarchais (himself the Rabelaisian author of *The Barber of Seville* and *The Marriage of Figaro*, whose own connection with the opera is worth a passing comment) knew perfectly well what the "facts" were, but saw a chance to help out his fellow Frenchman and also win some money.[43] In any case, as a condition for returning home, d'Eon was required by Beaumarchais to sign a Covenant.

"I require absolutely," declared this remarkable document,

> that the ambiguity of her sex, which has afforded inexhaustible material for gossip, indecent betting, and idle jesting liable to be renewed, especially in France, which his pride would not tolerate, and which would give rise to fresh quarrels that could only serve, perhaps, to palliate and renew former ones; I require absolutely, I say, in the name of the King, that the phantom Chevalier d'Eon shall entirely disappear, and that the public mind shall for ever be set at rest by a distinct, precise, and unambiguous declaration, publicly made, of the true sex of Charles-Geneviève-Louise–Auguste–Andrée-Timothée d'Eon de Beaumont before she returns to France—her resumption of female attire settling for ever the public mind with regard to her; with all of which she should the more readily comply just now, considering how interesting she will appear to both sexes. (Telfer, 245–46)

To this d'Eon inserted in his own hand in the margin further "proof": "Seeing that his/her sex (*son sexe*) has been proved by witnesses, physicians, surgeons, matrons and legal documents." Beaumarchais's desperate desire to "know," and to get rid of all undecidability ("I require absolutely"—repeated twice, for emphasis, in the document; "the phantom . . . shall entirely disappear"; "a distinct, precise, and unambiguous declaration, publicly made") is thus contravened by the very ambivalence and undecidability of language: *son sexe*, his or her sex. *What* has been proven? The attestations of the physicians, surgeons, matrons, and legal documents attest to a sentiment which (like that contained in the Queen's correspondence in Poe's "Purloined Letter") the public is never permitted to read. D'Eon's marginal gloss, which seems to reinforce Beaumarchais's Covenant, in fact undermines it—as his career would continue to do throughout his life.

In 1775 d'Eon, still in England amidst renewed betting on his gender identity (bets ran seven to four that the Chevalier was a woman rather than a man[44]), wrote to the papers to ask that gambling policies be discontinued.

> He is convinced that there are amongst the great in France some that abuse the perfect knowledge they have of his sex, so as to engage certain bankers in Paris to correspond with certain bankers in London . . . He declares that he will never manifest his sex till such time as all [gambling] policies shall be at an end.[45]

The personal pronouns of this announcement seem to declare his gender as male, despite the air of mystery (note again the recognition of a desire for certainty in the phrase "the perfect knowledge . . . of his sex"), but within a month he was writing to his friend the Count de Broglio with the opposite information:

> It is time to undeceive you. For a captain of dragoons, and aide-de-camp in wars and politics, you have had but the semblance of a man. I am only a maiden who would have perfectly well sustained my part until death, had not politics and your enemies rendered me the most unfortunate of women. . . . [46]

For all that he claims, repeatedly and earnestly, to want these inquiries to cease, it is d'Eon who continuously provokes them, enjoying, or so it seems, the very ambivalence that wrought epistemological havoc among his acquaintance, both in France and in England. He exists, in effect, on that borderline between genders, as between countries. He occupies, and defines by his own indefinition, the locus of diplomat as actor, transvestite as conundrum, the personification of a dilemma about the very question of certainty that will not go away.

A young English girl wrote him—in French, since she had been educated in a French convent—with the forthrightness of youth:

> Miss Wilkes presents her compliments to Monsieur the Chevalier d'Eon, and is very anxious to know if he is really a woman as everybody asserts, or a man. It would be very kind of Monsieur the Chevalier d'Eon to communicate the truth to Miss Wilkes, who entreats, with all her heart, to be informed of it. It would be still more kind of him if he would come and dine with her and her papa, to-day or to-morrow, or, in fact, as soon as he is able to do so. (Gaillardet, 196)

But the courts, predictably, required more proof, since a great deal of gambling money was involved. A suit was filed in London, the settlement of which was contingent on the establishment beyond a doubt of d'Eon's real gender. A surgeon was called, who testified that he had seen d'Eon in a professional capacity and could therefore depose on her true sex, and also another witness, who had been shown, by d'Eon, both her female wardrobe and her bosom. The courts declared that d'Eon was a woman, but the defendant found a loophole that invalidated the gambling policies, so that "the decision at once and for ever deprived all insurers in the 'd'Eon policies' of the golden harvest they so long and patiently expected."[47]

Again d'Eon was up to the challenge. Shortly after the verdict was declared she appeared in London in "her real character as a female, for the first time on August 6, being dressed in an elegant sack, her head-dress adorned with diamonds, and bedecked in all the other elegant paraphernalia of her sex."[48] But in order to dissociate herself from either side in the gambling suit, when the time finally came for her to depart England for France, she drove off in a post-chaise in military uniform, wearing the cross of St. Louis. She left behind a public protest, in the *Morning Post and Daily Advertiser,* &c., against any claims that she was financially or in any other way interested in the "policies respecting my sex," and declaring that, in consequence of the "judgment in the Court of King's Bench, July 1, to determine my sex," "I quit with grief my dear England."[49]

What is so striking here is that exile, or repatriation—geographical displacement—is so directly linked to gender "determination," the erasure of ambiguity. Declared to be a woman by the English courts, she departed for France—where the same phobic response awaited her. "In the King's Name" she was commanded to obey the terms of the Covenant with Beaumarchais, and desist from wearing the uniform of a dragoon. She was "forbidden to appear in any part of the kingdom in any other garments than those suitable to females."[50] The French, like the English, preferred certainty to uncertainty. In fact, uncertainty—gender undecidability—was what they could not tolerate, what they had to erase, or, at least, put under erasure.

Now styled "Chevalière," d'Eon was given a substantial female wardrobe and presented at Court, from which she wrote,

> I cannot express my repugnance, my grief, my pain, my troubled state, my vexation, and my shame, at having to appear thus publicly at Court in the dress and position of a female; but the King's council considered such a change indispensable. . . . In being stripped of man's estate and of my uniform, I am divested of every vice and of every danger incidental to such a condition; and being invested with the character of a female, am forced, in spite of myself, to adopt the vocations and virtues incumbent thereon.[51]

Various observers comment on d'Eon's awkwardness and oddness in women's clothes. She herself complained that

> Since leaving off my uniform and my sword, I am foolish as a fox who has lost his tail! I am trying to walk in pointed shoes with high heels, and have nearly broken my neck more than once; it has happened that, instead of making a courtesy, I have taken off my wig and three tiered headdress, taking them for my hat or my helmet.[52]

But what seems most frustrating are the forced inactivity and the trivial pursuits to which Court ladies were restricted. It seems likely that the King and his ministers saw this "fixing" of d'Eon's gender identity as a way of containing his/her anarchic impulses, and also of humbling or humiliating this volatile personality. Like Hercules enslaved by Omphale, or Spenser's Artegal subjugated to Radigund, d'Eon was compelled into a gender role (and a wardrobe) that seemed to render him (or her) safely a member of the second sex from a political and martial point of view. Thus Voltaire, on receiving a mezzo-tint representing d'Eon as Minerva, commented,

> Here is a nice problem for history. Some Academy of Inscriptions will prove the case to be most authentic. D'Eon will be a Maid of Orleans who will not have been burnt. It will be seen how we have improved in our customs.[53]

D'Eon complained in letters of feeling constrained by petticoats, that "This very sedentary life is completely ruining the elasticity of my body and mind." "You must be aware that to play the part of a maid at Court is one of the most stupid imaginable, so long as I am still able to play that of a lion in the army. . . . "[54]

Debarred from fulfilling this ambition, d'Eon returned to England and took up late in life the career of a female fencer, in part to pay off her always considerable debts, but also as a kind of theatricalization of the desired role of soldier in the King's forces. A female fencer could perform in "play" what a court lady could not do in earnest—that is to say, fight. By taking up the profession of fencer (in contradistinction to the "profession of that [female] sex" of which she complained[55]) d'Eon could separate gender identity from gender role. Even as a woman, she could "play [the part of] a lion," if not in the army, then at least in Carlton House, as a contemporary newspaper account testified:

> The most remarkable occurrence of the fencing match at Carlton House was the assault between Monsieur de Saint-George [a celebrated mulatto fencer] and Mademoiselle d'Eon, the latter though encumbered, as she humorously declared herself, with three petticoats, that suited her sex much better than her spirit, not only parried skillfully all the thrusts of her powerful antagonist, but even touched him by what is termed a *coup de temps*, which all his dexterity could not ward off. . . . A gentlemen present assures us that nothing could equal the quickness of the repartee, especially considering that the modern Pallas is nearly in her sixtieth year, and had to cope with a young man equally skillful and vigorous.[56]

The image of Pallas Athena is not inadvertent here; on another occasion, appearing before the Prince of Wales at the King's Theatre, d'Eon was dressed in armor, with a casque and feather, representing Athena (or, indeed, the Maid of Orleans). Still another newspaper reports Mademoiselle d'Eon playing chess against an expert, again for prize money, at the Chess Club in St. James' Street. The game of kings, queens, rooks, and pawns offered an apt if tacit commentary on d'Eon's life as man and woman, diplomat, soldier, captive woman, and stage performer.

One critic attributes the Chevalier d'Eon's "anxieties" to the "ambiguous reputation concerning his sexuality," noting that d'Eon was notoriously extravagant, insecure, and aggressive.[57] But whose anxiety is it that provokes the wild betting, the King's Covenant defining his envoy's gender, the forced rustication to Court in women's clothes? Whatever d'Eon's state of mind, it was his observers who were most profoundly unnerved, who wished most ardently and passionately for a resolution of this enigma, an end to undecidability, the fixing of gender identity once and for all.

Here is d'Eon on the subject, writing to a friend, in cipher, at the height of the London betting mania:

> I am sufficiently mortified at being what nature has made me, and that the dispassion of my natural temperament should induce my friends to imagine, in their innocence, and this in France, in Russia, and in England, that I am of the female sex. . . . I am what the hands of God have made me.[58]

This indirect assertion (of maleness? of hermaphroditism? of sexual indeterminacy?) appears in the same letter in which d'Eon notes that no one has dared to wager publicly on the nature of his/her sex since d'Eon "stamped virile proofs on the faces of two insolent fellows." Yet, on the other hand, we are told that all the references in d'Eon's journal, kept during the last years of life and presumably for d'Eon's eyes alone, are written in the feminine gender.[59] Which is the more potent signifier here: the pronoun or the phallus?

And what about d'Eon's sex life? The Abbé de Choisy, although he was not above granting some "small favors" to his admirers when he appeared as a woman on the stage, was, at least in his *Memoirs*, a man rampantly and triumphantly attracted to women. The Chevalier d'Eon was never known to have engaged in love affairs or sexual intrigues, either in the Court or in the military camp. His cold temperament was as celebrated as his cross-dressing. When he refers to "what nature has made me" he may be describing some physical infirmity. Was he then "compensating," in psychoanalytic jargon, or "acting out," for sexual inadequacy, actual or fancied? Whatever psychodrama was played out inside him, the very elusiveness of his sexual nature made him the source of mystery, not only for the curious of his own time (whether wagerers or politicians), but also for the sexologists of the early twentieth century. When Havelock Ellis coined the term *eonism* his act of naming was the same kind of fixing or labeling gesture as the King's Covenant requiring d'Eon to declare himself a woman "by a distinct, precise, and unambiguous declaration," so that the "phantom" of indefinition would disappear. Ellis's coinage created a category, but what it could not do was to resist successfully the powerful cultural desire to binarize.

When d'Eon died in 1810 her companion, Mrs. Cole, with whom she had lived for many years, was astounded to learn that she was a man. So was the surgeon who attended her last illness, and who had attended d'Eon for the last year of her life. A surgeon and a notary public inspected the corpse. The surgeon "found the male organs in every respect perfectly formed"; his certification, being presumably of public interest, was published in the *Times* on May 25, 1810. The notary declared that, having been "permitted to inspect the corpse," he could "assure" his correspondent "that the late Chevalier, called, when living, Mademoiselle d'Eon, had the visible organs of generation of a male, and was a very man."[60]

With his death, we seem to have reached the bottom line. Charles-Geneviève-Louis–Auguste-André-Timothée d'Eon de Beaumont was registered at birth and certified at death as a male—a "very man." If any of the insurance policies betting on his sex were still extant and valid, the payoff would seem to be assured. But here is the question I would like to pose: does the fact that he was born a male infant and died "with the male organs perfectly formed" mean that he was, in the years between, a man? A "very man"?

At d'Eon's death, according to some calculations, he had lived 49 years as a man and 34 years as a woman.[61] The English court, and the French king, "proved" he was a woman.

And the autopsy "proved" he was a man. Clearly one thing put in question here is the relativity of "proof." According to what canons? Dictated by what exigencies? With what ideological concerns in view: medical, political, social, sexual, erotic? The questions raised by d'Eon's story are very similar to those explored in *M. Butterfly*—and, indeed, in the case of jazz musician Billy Tipton. As all of these stories demonstrate, the definition of the grounds of human gender will always involve more, and less, than any clearly decidable "bottom line."

11

BLACK AND WHITE TV: CROSS-DRESSING THE COLOR LINE

[Frances E.W. Harper] was so articulate and engaging as a public speaker, audiences concluded that she couldn't possibly be a black woman. Some even speculated that she must be a man, while others reasoned that she was painted to look black.

Hazel V. Carby, Introduction to *Iola Leroy*[1]

"What she doin' coming back here in dem overhalls? Can't she find no dress to put on?"

Zora Neale Hurston, *Their Eyes Were Watching God*[2]

[H]e come to visit me while I was sewing and ast me what was so special bout my pants.

Anybody can wear them, I said.

Men and women not suppose to wear the same thing, he said. Men spose to wear the pants.

So I said, You ought to tell that to the mens in Africa. . . . men and women both preshate a nice dress.

Robe you said before, he say.

Robe, dress. Not pants, anyhow. . . . Here, help me stitch in these pockets.

But I don't know how, he say.

I'll show you, I said. And I did.

Now us sit sewing and talking and smoking our pipes.

Alice Walker, *The Color Purple*[3]

In "The Last Supper at Uncle Tom's Cabin/ The Promised Land," a compelling work of dance and theater produced by the Bill T. Jones/Arnie Zane & Co. dance troupe, black choreographer Bill T. Jones closed a section based on Sojourner Truth's "Ain't I a woman" speech with the vision of an extraordinary figure. "The last person onstage," reported one reviewer, "is a tall, glamorous, black male dancer who sashays briefly in a tight white miniskirt and white high heels. He doesn't look masculine, feminine, androgynous, gay or straight; he doesn't even look like a parody. He looks like sex, only more so."[4]

The transvestite as a recurrent, disturbing, and often repressed or unacknowledged figure haunts images of African-Americans in literature and culture, from slave narratives and minstrel shows to *Uncle Tom's Cabin* and *Pudd'nhead Wilson*. At first, in effect, another mode of involuntary servitude, appearing almost obsessively in texts written, or performances staged, by white artists and producers, sometimes poignantly, at other times as a mode of caricature and ridicule, the cultural masquerade of transvestism has been appropriated with enormous energy, perception and wit by black performers, writers, and filmmakers as a vehicle for social and political empowerment, and has in recent years achieved a palpable material success in the mainstreaming of "crossover" artists and arts, from jazz to rock and roll and rap music, from Flip Wilson to Little Richard.

These transvestic representations often appear, significantly, within a context that includes "crossing" (or "passing") simultaneously as an element of gender and of race. In fact, the overdetermined presence of cross-dressing in so many Western figurations of black culture suggests some useful ways to interrogate notions of "stereotype" and "cliché". For the immensely evocative concept of the "invisible man" coined by Ralph Ellison fits the description of the transvestite as that which is looked *through*, rather than *at*, in contemporary criticism and culture. The recurrent thematic of transvestism in and as an aspect of black American culture—and, equally, as a device deployed to subvert or disempower that culture—is seldom noticed. Yet, as we will see, it is one of the master's tools that does, in fact, help to dismantle the master's house.

"MIRTH AND GIRTH"

In November of 1987 Mayor Harold Washington of Chicago died unexpectedly in office. Six months later, in an uproar that divided the city, a delegation of black Chicago aldermen descended upon the School of the city's Art Institute and forcibly removed from the wall a portrait, submitted to a private competition, depicting the late mayor variously described by the newspapers as "dressed in frilly white lingerie,"[5] "wearing filmy lingerie"[6] and "depicted in women's frilly underwear."[7] The title of this controversial work, by art student David K. Nelson, was "Mirth and Girth."

The reason I cite these largely overlapping verbal descriptions in such detail is because the portrait itself almost immediately disappeared from public view, and existed subsequently only in its various characterizations. It became in effect a phantom or a ghost— yet another of transvestism's powerful avatars. After a brief sensation on the first day, when local TV stations showed it on the evening news, representations of the portrait vanished, as if by common consent among the media.[8] *Chicago Tribune* columnist Bob Greene, noting that a flood of calls had come into the newspaper decrying what was described as "censorship," retorted that "I was very proud of this paper for not running a picture showing the now notorious painting." Failure to reprint the painted image of the nearly naked mayor was not, he said, a cover-up. "The news stories about the controversy described, in accurate detail, what the painting looked like. The newspaper ran a photo of the painting (its front not visible) being removed from the Art Institute. That was the news."[9]

This detail—of the painting seen only from the back—again uncannily calls to mind Poe's purloined letter, which became a signifier rather than a signified, something that produces certain effects rather than a unit of meaning, by a similar repression of its content. But the fact that what was being repressed—or rather, suppressed, or censored, or withheld, depending upon one's point of view—was a portrait of a heavyset middle-aged black man in women's underwear, is itself not without significance. David K. Nelson's portrait struck a nerve in the black community because it touched on a painfully familiar stereotype—that of the feminized black man, disempowered and made ridiculous, the object of the (white majority) gaze.

Nelson claimed that his motivation was "iconoclasm," and a defense of his First Amendment right to free expression was undertaken by the American Civil Liberties Union. But the particular icon that was here placed on display, in substitution for an idealized image of the mayor—the spectacle of a cross-dressed black man—told an uncomfortable, indeed intolerable, story. It is not surprising that before it was returned to the artist the portrait itself was physically attacked—or that, in this chain of ironic substitutions, the metonymic gesture of hostility toward the painter was transformed into violence done to the painted body of the dead mayor: "a 5-inch gash from the chin to the chest of the depiction of Mayor Washington."[10] Clad only in bra, bikini pants, garter belt, and stockings, the figure of Mayor Washington—"Mirth and Girth"—was the nightmare realization of a long-held fear: that the black man in power, in public office, in a business suit and tie, was not only an emperor without clothes, his self-delusion penetrable to the clear-eyed glance of a child (or a student), but also—what was incomparably worse—a "woman." Which is to say, a transvestite. Not even a "real" woman, but some unsexed third sex. Someone who "passed." Or tried to.

The element of "passing" here had a multiple resonance, for privately it had been rumored among Chicagoans for some time that Mayor Washington was gay. He kept his private life reasonably private; he was not "out." So the portrait's outrage was compounded, for the display of it was itself a forcible "outing," a revelation of something that the mayor, when alive, had chosen not to reveal, and that his friends, supporters, and mourners, chose—for reasons of loyalty, and perhaps also for homophobic reasons—to deny or to keep to themselves.

The political furor was immediate and passionate. The aldermen, alleging that the portrait was an "incitement to riot," had it removed by police, and demanded a public apology from the Art Institute and full-page ads to that effect in Chicago newspapers. To make things even worse, the public dialogue became infused with anti-Semitism. Alderman Alan Streeter asserted that "the fellow that drew that picture is Jewish"[11]; the firing of mayoral aide Steve Cokely the previous week after he made anti-Semitic remarks was condemned as a "double standard" by Alderman Bobby Rush, a veteran of the Black Panther movement of the sixties[12]; and Alderman Robert Shaw publicly accused the ACLU—whose legal director was a Jew, Harvey Grossman—of always taking "the white side" in black-white disputes.[13]

The displacement of prejudicial commentary from one embattled minority onto another, the desire to scapegoat another vulnerable group so as to assuage one's own pain and vulnerability, is a familiar and dismaying move; it is also, self-evidently, a sign of what we have been calling "category crisis" at its rawest and most disturbing. And once again transvestite representation is located at the site of crisis: black-white, black-Jewish, male-female, gay-straight. No wonder the media turned its collective face away. No newspaper, no newsmagazine reproduced the image. *Time* did not cover the story; *Newsweek* carried about three paragraphs, with no illustration; *Jet* had several pages without a picture. Only the art journals published Nelson's "Mirth and Girth," together with an article describing the aldermen as the real iconoclasts, belonging to "an iconoclastic tradition that includes the National Socialists' infamous attacks on the 'degenerate art' of modern Germany," who "spoke of burning Nelson's painting—and in fact managed to slash it before it left the school in the hands of the police."[14]

The shock and disgust of the aldermen (and many others) at this "reprehensible" exhibit ("the unspeakably offensive nature of the perverse caricature of a much-beloved and only recently dead black mayor" as it was described in a *Tribune* editorial[15]), the cry of "censorship," the immediate protest of the artists over the threat to their First Amendment rights, the apology issued by the Art Institute, the removal of the offensive object—all of these things call to mind the recent controversy over the exhibit of photographer Robert Mapplethorpe's work at the Corcoran Gallery in Washington, D.C., and the related flap over a photograph by Andrès Serrano of a crucifix in what was said to be a vial of urine. Fueled by the moral indignation of right-wing Senator Jesse Helms, the U.S. Congress in 1989 passed legislation denying funds to galleries and artists who "promote, disseminate, or reproduce materials considered obscene, including sadomasochism, homoeroticism, [and] the sexual exploitation of children or individuals engaged in sex acts." The Helms Amendment also specifically prohibits support of arts projects "which, when taken as a whole, do not have serious literary, artistic, political or scientific value."[16]

Although Chicago's black aldermen and Senator Helms might seem to make strange bedfellows, the repressive sentiments of both are similar, in that both would deny the validity of certain kinds of representation. But while Helms—and Congress—spoke out against federal funding, the aldermen and police of Chicago went further, removing the offensive object from the wall, failing to protect it against physical assault and disfigurement. What happened to the portrait of Mayor Washington in frilly underwear was, in fact, a kind of symbolic rape, and, at the same time, a kind of symbolic castration. Where once—and not all that long ago—black men had been kidnapped, strung up on trees, hanged by the neck, and quite literally emasculated with knives or razor blades, the aldermen, responding to a portrait that seemed to do the same to the image and memory of Harold Washington—a portrait *hanging* on the Art Institute wall—performed (or sanctioned, or failed to protect against) a similar act of violence upon the offensive representation. To put it another way: the portrait's attackers, perceiving it to enact castration, "castrated" it as an act of revenge, slitting it open. And after the physical damage was done, the portrait itself disappeared from sight, although the artist is said to have rejected an offer of $15,000 for it (Taylor, 37).

This nightmare vision, of the American black man as always already feminized and humiliated, was in fact exactly what had to be repressed—and what (therefore) keeps returning. It is no accident, I think, that this image should coexist with another, apparently contradictory image, that of the black man who wields power—in this case political, in other cases more explicitly sexual, power.

Why was it that the portrait of Mayor Washington in frilly lingerie aroused such violent emotions in the black community? Because—I want to suggest—it tells a story that has been put under erasure, blacked out, blotted: the story of the transvestite as the figure of crossover itself, of that which is both fantasized and feared. The black male transvestite marks the place of that which is bracketed, the paradox of the black man in America as simultaneously a sign of sexual potency and a sign of emasculation or castration.

Paradoxically, the black American male has been constructed by majority culture as *both* sexually threatening *and* feminized, as both super-potent and impotent. The easy "equation" between castration and feminization, offensive alike to men and to women—as if the violent mutilation of the black male body somehow made it equivalent in power and social status to that of a woman—is an all-too-clear demonstration of the ways in which categories like "gender" and "race" have been made to intersect and cross over one another in the service of political rhetoric and cultural domination. To change sex is to slide along a power differential. To change power is to change sex.

But the figure of the transvestite specifically *as rupture or disruption* here enters the discourse of gender and power with an unsettling force. The forcible cross-dressing of Mayor Washington's image "downward" toward a ludicrous "femininity" (which has nothing to do with femininity as it would be understood by and through women; which has nothing to do with the—again paradoxically—*empowered* images of Marlene Dietrich, or Madonna, in garter belt and bustier, much less with comparable political figures like Dianne Feinstein, Geraldine Ferraro, or Margaret Thatcher, unimaginable in comparable undress; which has nothing to do with gay power or gay rights) is a sign at once of the denigration of blacks *and* of women. As Myra Jehlen has noted, "One stereotype of the black man threatens violence and uncontrollable sex. The other has him contemptibly effeminate. Black men are seen simultaneously as excessively male and insufficiently masculine."[17] Yet it is not a foregone conclusion that black transvestism is always *dis*empowering, nor is it easy to tell when the intervention of the transvestite figure is empowered, and when it is disempowered.

To make this point more vividly, I want to juxtapose to the degrading and now-absent painting of Harold Washington another visual image of a black man in what might be described as a version of drag, this one proudly produced and everywhere displayed, the joint effort of establishment politics and narcissistic macho self-commodification. I am referring to a photograph of the black celebrity Mr. T.

Mr. T. is a television and film star, best known for his appearances on the hit TV series "The A-Team" (NBC 1983-87), who combines the aggressive physicality and muscular maleness of the black athlete with the ostentatious wearing of ornate gold jewelry. I am not sure whether or not it was in fact black professional athletes, football and basketball stars, who legitimized gold necklaces, rings, and bracelets as on- as well as off-the-field (or -court) wear for all Western sports figures. It may be that the crosses and Christophers worn by white Catholic players set this fashion, which was then taken up by black players. But in any case Mr. T., festooned with gold at the neck, wrists, fingers, and ears, became a remarkable as well as an exemplary figure. For what he wore were *chains*. *Gold* chains, draped around his neck in careless profusion. Chains signifying not enslavement but freedom, the freedom of the marketplace as well as of the ballot box.

Sometime in the mid-eighties a remarkable photograph, taken by Mary Anne Fackelman at the White House, circulated in major newspapers and magazines around the world. (In the fall of 1989, the year after the Reagans vacated the White House, it appeared in *Newsweek* as an illustration to a review of several books about the Reagan years; the review was entitled, with some pertinence, "The Faking of the President."[18]) In the photograph, Nancy Reagan, dressed in a demure schoolgirl frock of black and red stripes with a red collar and black tie, sat on the lap of Mr. T., dressed as Santa Claus, under a Christmas tree adorned with white angels and candles. In her hand Nancy held the box from a Mr. T. toy. Mr. T. himself, in red tights and sleeveless shirt trimmed with furry white, his muscled arms bare, his athletic socks rolled up over his calves, his black beard and mohawk haircut unaltered for the occasion, stares impassively out at the camera as Nancy-the-schoolgirl kisses his (Santa's) brow, presumably in gratitude for the gift. Around his neck Mr. T. wears a thick collar of gold chains, too many to count; his wrist and fingers are encrusted in gold jewelry, as is his left ear. Across the page in *Newsweek* is an inset photo of former Interior Secretary James Watt in face-makeup and a babushka.

Reportedly, Nancy Reagan requested both Mr. T.'s presence at the White House Christmas party, and his appearance as Santa Claus.[19] What does this tell us about black super-maleness, the fantasies of powerful WASP women, and the strategic appropriation of transvestism as a gesture of defiance and defense?

In *The Signifying Monkey* Henry Louis Gates, Jr. offers a powerful reading of the magnificent "royal chain, a chain of gold that signified his cultural heritage" worn in

Africa by the freed slave James Albert Ukawsaw Gronniosaw as a "link" between Gronniosaw's royal past as an African prince and the captivity into which he was taken. As Gates notes, "Gronniosaw's signifying gold chain is an ironic prefigurement of Brother Tarp's link to *his* cultural heritage, a prison gang, in *Invisible Man*."[20] But Mr. T is no invisible man. His autobiography, we might note, was called *Mr. T.: The Man With the Gold.* The expensive chains hanging in such profusion around his neck are indeed the ironic antitypes of those iron chains that bound African-American slaves.[21] But it is Mr. T. who wields the power in this photograph, Mr. T. who holds the onlooker with his gaze.

BLACK TRANSVESTISM: SOME PRELIMINARY OBSERVATIONS

It has become a commonplace, following the black poet and critic Sterling Brown, to identify six kinds of black character types in American literature: the contented slave; the wretched freeman; the brute Negro; the tragic mulatto; the local color Negro; and the exotic primitive.[22] Donald Bogle rendered some of these in less elegant, more offensive and vernacular terms as *Toms, Coons, Mulattoes, Mammies, & Bucks* in a book on blacks in American films.[23] But the black transvestite—male or female—is conspicuously missing from these lists, though he or she is readable, below the surface, in all of them. I am speaking here, of course, of images initially imposed upon black characters by white authors—although, as we will see, the fantasy of the black transvestite became so recognizable, haunted representations of black culture so consistently, that black writers and artists have been able to turn it to their own account.

In undertaking a reading of these images, it seems crucial here, therefore, to make two preliminary observations: first, that the presumed audience for representations of black transvestism in American literature, history, and popular culture is almost always a predominantly *white* audience, even when the author or artist himself or herself is African-American. Richard Wright's radio play "Man of All Work," for example, was originally commissioned by a radio station in Hamburg, Germany.[24]

The term "crossover," as we have noted, is frequently applied to figures from the music world who traverse the territory from one audience to another, from, let us say, the black audience of Motown to the white audience of major nightclubs, videocasettes, or the old Ed Sullivan Show, or from country to rock to pop. We have already seen the way in which "voguing," a dance style that began as a "campy, stylized version of runway modeling"[25] among transvestites in Harlem in the sixties, became part of mainstream popular culture for white U.S. teenagers in the late eighties and nineties.

The phenomenon of racial "crossover" in the music world—the popularity of black artists and black sound with white audiences—has led some outspoken commentators, like the black singer Terence Trent D'Arby, to charge angrily that "any black act in the States who has been [a] massive quote-unquote crossover success has had to emasculate himself to some degree. Prince has had to play the bisexual image, cast aspersions as to his dominant heterosexuality, Jackson's had to be asexual, Vandross couldn't possibly offend anybody, George Benson . . . it's like in the contract, it certifies them to a free plastic surgeon visitation, guarantees them a makeup artist at all times to lighten 'em up for photographs if you sell more than two million albums, and these guys wouldn't do or say anything which would lose them one record sale."[26] Black saxophonist and activist Morris Wilson quipped sardonically, in what he called "a kind of joke that I did in the black community," that "Prince was the top white act out there right now!"[27]

To note the importance of the white media and of white readers and audiences in the success of a book, the making of a star or the popularity of a dance craze is not to deny the considerable cultural or economic power of the market in the black community for black-produced art, but rather to frame a discussion of "black transvestism" as an intervention startlingly powerful and effective, whether the images produced are engaging (and generated by the performer himself or herself, like Flip Wilson's "Geraldine") or dismaying (and imposed from without, like the portrait of Mayor Washington). It is precisely because this transgressive figure receives and transmutes the volatile racial and sexual attitudes of white American majority culture that it has had such a remarkable—and dangerous—history of representation. *The issue of who manipulates the image and whose pleasure or power it serves is, in the specter of black transvestism, brought to a state of crisis.*

My second preliminary observation is that the figure of the "black transvestite" here includes apparently quite incommensurate "male" and "female" representations. If—as I have just suggested—we are dealing here with a power differential on a sliding scale, a cultural rhetoric of difference as doubly inflected by race and gender, so that "passing" becomes the key word to describe the ways in which each crosses over into the terrain of the other (black to white or white to black; male to female or female to male), then we should expect that the political valence of male-to-female transvestism in African-American culture might contrast even more vividly with that of female-to-male transvestism than it does when racial inequality is not a complicating factor.

Yet what I will suggest here is that, although the contextual representation of black male-to-female and female-to-male transvestites indeed differs greatly the one from the other, the *effect* of their disruption is, in both cases, to unsettle expectations and bring them to crisis—in other words, that both do similar kinds of cultural work in and for white majority audiences. But the most extraordinary cultural work done by the transvestite in the context of American "race-relations" is to foreground the impossibility of taxonomy, the fatal limitation of classification *as* segregation, the inevitability of "miscegenation" as misnomer. The possibility of crossing racial boundaries stirs fears of the possibility of crossing the boundaries of gender, and vice versa. What the "black transvestite" does is to realize the latent dream thoughts—or nightmares—of American cultural mythology as the manifest content of American life.

The pattern of subjection and subjugation imposed upon African-American cultural representations in the U.S. and in Western Europe through the figure of transvestism (both male-to-female and female-to-male) has been in recent decades strategically appropriated by black artists, with the result that transvestism has become a powerful rhetorical force for intervention *by* blacks in formerly white-dominated cultural arenas like literature, film, and television. By "transvestism" I mean here to designate not only full gender-masquerade, as in the case of Ellen Craft, or Stowe's Eliza Harris, or the white female impersonators playing black women in the antebellum minstrel show, or the black transvestite call "girl" in the 1983 film *Risky Business*, but also the synecdochic quotation of transvestism, as in the wearing of earrings or gold necklaces by black men, like Mr. T., coded as he-men and heterosexual objects of desire. For such quotations deliberately flaunt what had been previously seen as demeaning. They turn inside-out the valuation of cross-dressing, male-to-female and female-to-male, producing it not as an imposed and enslaving act of castration or ungendering, but rather as a language of reassignment, empowerment, and critique.

The appropriative gestures of black artists toward the specter of black transvestism, however conscious or unconscious, do not always, of course, succeed in vanquishing the unregenerate racism of stereotypes, nor are they always to be found in a political alliance with pro-feminist, anti-sexist attitudes. Some images of black transvestism are racist, some are sexist, some are both, and it is not necessary to try to see Mr. T. as a feminist (much less a woman) in order to see his cultural effect on crossover images of gender and race.

Furthermore, the degree to which such appropriation is deliberate, "intentional," or designed will vary from case to case, and is, I think, always at best a matter of hypothetical speculation. (Even if we possess documentary "evidence" that an artist has a certain "meaning" in mind, the unconscious of the text—novel, play, film, historical event—may be in conflict with the conscious purpose of its maker. In other words, the unconscious, as well as the conscious, may have "intentions," and the two sets of intentions might well be expected to come into conflict with one another.) But in the scenario of black transvestism, a double "dark continent" for motive-hunters, the pressure of cultural context upon individual creative design seems exacerbated. Simply, the stakes are higher, since what is at issue are the fundamental categories of American presumptions of hierarchy, identity, and destiny.

THE CULTURAL RHETORIC OF MINSTRELSY

Ralph Ellison noted that the minstrel show was a "ritual of exorcism," in which the minstrel mask, by reducing the African in America to a "negative sign," managed both "to veil the humanity of Negroes thus reduced to a sign, and to repress the white audience's awareness of its moral identification with its own acts and with the human ambiguities pushed behind the mask."[28]

In view of this observation, it is worth bearing in mind that the minstrel show of nineteenth-century America was for all intents and purposes a transvestite theater. Although some white female troupes played in blackface, most of the troupes were all-male, men who blacked their faces with burnt cork to sing, dance, and tell jokes in "Negro" dialect. But the audiences of these minstrel shows did see female figures on the stage—female impersonators, usually well dressed and elegant, portraying "plantation yellow girls"—the tragic mulattoes of transvestism. The female impersonators were double crossover figures, men playing women, whites playing blacks. In fact Julian Eltinge, the most celebrated female impersonator of his time, began his career in George M. Cohan's touring minstrel shows.[29] As with the English Pantomime (or indeed with the "mammy" and the "tragic mulatto") the black female subject of minstrelsy was split into two visions, or versions, of "woman": the low comedy "Funny Old Gal" (the Charley's Aunt or Dame role) and the romantic "prima donna" or "wench."

The female impersonators were the best paid performers in the minstrel company. The actress Olive Logan noted that "some of the men who undertake this business are marvellously well-fitted by nature for it, having well-defined soprano voices, plump shoulders, beardless faces, and tiny hands and feet." The impersonator's art required a careful judgment of "where fun stops and bad taste begins." Thus the "Funny Old Gal" had more license than the elegant balladist; "clad in some tawdry old gown of loud, crude colors, whose shortness and scantiness display long frilled 'panties' and No. 12 valise shoes," she took part in the traditional "walk-around," from which more elegantly dressed impersonators were barred, "since no lady dances with plantation negroes."[30]

Among the men "marvellously well fitted by nature" for the romantic female role was the most famous of the minstrel prima donnas, Francis Leon, known simply as "Leon" or "The Only Leon," who began his career as a female impersonator at age 14 in 1858, starred in burlesque minstrel show operas, and was by 1882 the highest paid of all minstrel performers, and one of the most highly praised.[31] Leon's reviewers praised him in terms closely analogous to those used to describe the most popular boy actors during the Restoration, when women as well as men played female parts—that is, they compared him favorably to "real" women. "He is more womanly in his by-play and mannerisms than the most charming female imaginable," wrote one, and another commented that some spectators refused to credit the fact that he was a man. "Heaps of boys in my locality," the reviewer wrote from Rochester, New York, "don't believe yet it's a man in spite of my saying it was." This ambiguity in Leon's charms could in fact "make a fool of a man if he wasn't sure."[32] The "boy"-"man" dichotomy, always pertinent to the discourse of race and (as we have seen) the discourse of transvestism, is here deployed with a beguiling insouciance.

Leon was the superstar of minstrelsy's female impersonators, the "best male female actor known to the stage" (New York *Clipper*, May 28, 1870). Visited in his dressing room by an admiring reporter, he confided "with real feminine pride" that he wore only genuine women's clothing, not "costumes." His wardrobe included some 300 dresses and a great deal of jewelry; his dressing room was full of "powder, paint, and perfume." He prided himself on his good taste, and on avoiding cheapness and vulgarity. But "The Only Leon" was only the best known of the impersonators, many of whom were apparently attractive to male and female spectators alike, their clothing described by reviewers in detail.[33]

It has been speculated that women liked to watch the minstrel "prima donnas" because of an interest in the latest fashions, and because they supposedly offered no sexual competition, while men—it is alleged—liked them because their deceptive appearance was titillating, and their stagy giddiness put women back in their places at a time when the women's movement had begun to question the appropriateness of that place (Toll, 144). Whatever we may think of these rather familiar-sounding speculations about the purpose and effect of cross-dressing in and on a culture, it is important to see that the element of "blackness"—or "blackface"—skews the equation, especially since women's rights was, together with abolition, one of the white minstrel shows' most consistently lampooned targets. They ridiculed bloomers in particular, and women's desire to wear pants in general:

> When woman's rights is stirred a bit
> De first reform she bitches on
> Is how she can wid least delay
> Just draw a pair ob britches on.[34]

As Robert Toll points out, "Women, like Negroes, provided one of the few stable 'inferiors' that assured white men of their status." Thus it was probably predictable that "throughout the nineteenth century, minstrels never varied from their complete condemnation of women's rights" (Toll, 163).

Putting these two pieces together—the popularity of male-to-female transvestite performers playing "plantation yellow girls," and the fierce resistance to women's rights—we can see that "The Only Leon" in his real dresses might indeed seem more desirably like a "woman" (at least, an idealized and tamed woman) than the politicized "bitch" in "britches" of the minstrels' doggerel. "Black" (or "Negro") was as much in quotation and under erasure as "woman" in the white minstrel show: a black-impersonating female impersonator summed up and disempowered (or emasculated) two threatening forces at once.

During World War II vestiges of the minstrel show reappeared as part of the all-male soldier theater touring the armed forces. The smash hit *This Is the Army* featured a minstrel number, "Mandy," in which white soldiers in blackface played both men and women. The U.S. armed services at the time were still racially segregated, despite the fact that the cast of *This Is the Army* included black soldiers as well as white, so that the minstrel convention thus sidestepped the pitfall of interracial courtship, even in representation. An all-black soldier show called *Uncle Sambo* was planned, and it was not until near the end of the War—when WACs were also beginning to play the parts of women in GI shows—that black and white female impersonators in drag shared the stage.[35]

And what about women in blackface? Hollywood films from the twenties to the fifties periodically featured women in blackface drag. In 1928 silent film star Madge Bellamy appeared in the film *Mother Knows Best* as Al Jolson, the blackface star, singing his signature tune "Mammy."[36] Judy Garland played a minstrel boy in blackface in *Babes on Broadway* (1941), in which she co-starred with Mickey Rooney similarly dressed and made-up (Dickens, 182), and Doris Day appeared in blackface in *I'll See You in My Dreams* (1951) (Dickens, 190). In all of these representations cross-cross-dressing conflated women and blacks as "boys," social children, high-spirited but not wholly grown up. Bellamy, who played the part of a white Jewish man, Jolson, whose career was based on the success of a minstrel number, rings the changes on cultural and gender crossover without really commenting upon it.

Social commentary, however, was forthcoming from another quarter. Black blues singer Gertrude "Ma" Rainey's song, "Prove It On Me Blues"—originally merchandised in 1928 as a "race record" sold to black people—cast her rhetorically in the first-person role of a cross-dressing lesbian who has no use for men. "Went out last night," the song says,

> With a crowd of my friends,
> They must bin womens
> Cause I don't like no mens.
> It's true I wear a collar and a tie . . .
> You all say I do it,
> Ain't nobody caught me,
> You sure got to prove it on me.

I "wear my clothes just like a man," declares the singer. Whether or not Ma Rainey was herself a lesbian—and jazz historian Chris Albertson thinks she may have been—this anthem to transgression, sung with the accompaniment of a tub-and-washboard band, powerfully establishes a rhetoric of self-assertion and resistance through the crossing over of white and middle-class norms.[37] Even more powerful was a figure like Gladys Bentley, a black lesbian who performed in men's attire, attracting other lesbians and male homosexuals to the nightclub scene. Bentley, a "tough-talking, masculine acting, cross-dressing, and sexually worldly 'bull dagger' "[38] who was the headlined entertainer at The Clam House in Harlem—where she appeared in a white tuxedo and top hat—wore men's clothes on and off the stage for most of her life. When she appeared at a nightclub in Los Angeles in 1940, the club had to get a special police permit "to allow Gladys Bentley, 250-pound colored entertainer, to wear trousers instead of skirts, during her act" (E. Garber, 59). The vilified bitch in britches—surely imagined by the minstrel writers as a white suffragist, not a black lesbian—here speaks in her own voice.

Meanwhile, in France, another powerful and original black woman artist took up the figure of transvestism and turned it to her own ends. It is instructive, in fact, to compare the career and artistry of "The Only Leon," a white man who depicted black womanhood to white audiences in a long-running theatrical revue, with that of another international star: the black American woman Josephine Baker, a major crossover figure of the twenties who began her career in the famous Revue Nègre in Paris, and then moved to the Folies-Bergère. In making this comparison, and in reading Baker as a transvestite, I want again to underscore the cultural work done by the hidden trope of transvestism in the recent history of African-American art.

Josephine Baker's first appearance with the Revue Nègre in November 1925, when she came onstage clowning, her body contorted, her face screwed up, and her cheeks puffed out, astounded the audience. Her rear end, moving "at incredible speeds," "seemed to take on a life of its own."[39] She did the split; she shook and shimmied; she left the stage on all fours, and immediately returned. "Is it a man? Is it a woman?," asked a reviewer in the journal *Candide*.[40]

When she danced the Charleston onstage, Baker "sang in a man's voice." She described herself as having "pointed knees and the breasts of a seventeen-year-old boy."[41] Her famous banana skirt, worn at the Folies-Bergère, is unforgettably described by Phyllis Rose as looking, when she danced, "like perky, good-natured phalluses" in "jiggling motion" (Rose, 97); later, when she appeared with the Ziegfield Follies, the bananas had transmuted into tusks.

Baker's associations with transvestism are ubiquitous. At a wild party in Berlin she danced with a woman in a tuxedo, and provoked in an impresario fleeting notions of an interracial, same-sex ballet; she sometimes appeared onstage, Dietrich-like, in white tie and tails; her Folies-Bergère shows often involved cross-dressing skits and tableaux; on one occasion, at a costume ball aboard ship, she encountered the architect Le Corbusier dressed as "Josephine Baker," his skin blacked, his hips circled with a waistband of feathers. She seems to have found herself—or to have been found—almost constantly in contiguity with cross-dressing.[42] Nor is this really cause for surprise. Josephine Baker was, often deliberately but sometimes in response to others' cultural agendas, an occasion for the theatricalization of scandal and transgressiveness. In 1970, near the end of her career, she gave away a collection of her 1950's Paris gowns (enough Diors and Balenciagas to fill three taxicabs) to a white female impersonator, Lynne Carter.

Carter was a New York celebrity who had appeared in at least one important role as a black woman, performing as Pearl Bailey at the Apollo Theater in 1965. Disdaining makeup, he played the part without blackface and in a blond wig, relying on gesture, voice, and mannerism to evoke Bailey's distinctive character. Like many other theatrical impersonators (some prefer the term "illusionist") Carter drew a distinction between his onstage and offstage personae, wearing two pairs of stockings rather than shaving his legs. His comments on women sound like lay, intuitive versions of the "masquerade" theories of Riviere and Lacan: "I have found," he is quoted as saying, "that women always wear a mask. It's made of cosmetics and fashion. Women consider it a masculine trait simply to be yourself. But they end up being caricatures of themselves, which makes them easy to mimic."[43]

Commenting on the ironic appropriateness of the Carter-Baker connection, Phyllis Rose observes that "In the overdressed years which succeeded her underdressed years, Baker was a sister of Lynne Carter, speaking to fantasies of the defeat by artfulness of biological imperatives like age and gender, finding a new audience among men who made similar icons of the artifice of femininity out of Marlene Dietrich and Mae West. She was a female impersonator who happened to be a woman" (Rose, 253).

The "female female impersonator" has become an important subject of recent feminist analysis, a sign of the constructedness of "woman" and of women's interimplication with the male "gaze" and with contingent categories like social class. Yet it seems curious that Rose should focus on "biological imperatives like age and gender" rather than the obvious differential of race as a factor in Baker's "female impersonation." Rose's whole biography, as she herself makes clear in her preface, is structured on similarities rather than differences between the biographer and her subject.[44] But Josephine Baker was not merely a "female impersonator" in her *later*, "overdressed" years, nor was her "impersonation" itself ordained by the artifactuality of women, "made of cosmetics and fashion," in Lynne Carter's words. Baker's identity as a transvestite begins with race as well as with class and gender, and it takes its shape from material culture, from the very nature of the theater in which she performed.

The Revue Nègre, the place of Baker's Paris debut, was, in its structure, very like the old minstrel shows. An opening act of black jazz musicians gave way to a production number, black men and women in colorful costumes against a backdrop of steamboats on the Mississippi, and this was succeeded by a series of other tableaux. Baker's first appearance—the one that called forth the "Is it a man? Is it a woman?" review—had her dressed in torn shirt and shorts, her lips painted oversize in the style of blackface.

In New York, as in Paris, the fashion for blackface in the sophisticated theatrical world meant that both white and black performers, when playing black parts, painted their faces with burnt cork and made up their lips and eyes in a caricature of "blackness." Appearing in New York City in a show called *The Chocolate Dandies* in the early twenties, Baker, significantly, played a part that recalled *both* the prima donna or wench, *and* the Funny Old Gal of the minstrel shows. For the latter, the Funny Old Gal, she wore bright cotton dresses, oversize shoes, and blackface, crossing her eyes in her signature fashion; for the "wench" role she changed into an elegant white satin dress with a slit up the side. Bear in mind that these terms are borrowed from minstrelsy, specifically from white minstrelsy, to describe female impersonators, not women. They were not part of the black revue *per se*. Or were they?

An extraordinary controversy developed in the black American press as a result of the use of the word "wench" to describe Baker in an article in *Time* magazine. "In sex appeal to jaded Europeans of the jazz-loving type," wrote *Time,* "a Negro wench always has a head start."[45] In angry response, the black Chicago newspaper *The Defender* ran an editorial to protest the use of "wench," which it called "a vile word" associated with sadism and disturbed sexual fantasies, to characterize Baker.

But "wench," as we have seen, was also a stock role in white minstrelsy for a female impersonator, like the enchanting Francis Leon, "more womanly in his by-play and mannerisms that the most charming female imaginable," according to the New York *Clipper* in 1872.[46] If Leon sounds like Lynne Carter doing Pearl Bailey *without* the help of blackface, that is not, perhaps, altogether a surprise. But Josephine Baker herself is also a performer in the tradition of "The Only Leon." And Baker's tour de force as singer, dancer, and crosser of boundaries is marked not only by the anomaly of the black face in blackface, but also by the phenomenon of the black female entertainer taking on the dual roles of the wench and the Funny Old Gal. Josephine Baker's stage persona becomes a witty and knowledgeable appropriation of minstrelsy—and of minstrelsy's construction of both blackness and women. But the appropriation was not without cost.

Just as in some contexts black men "became" "women" in and for white Western culture (physically, through the violence of lynching and castration; socially, through their relegation to domestic service, subservience, and comic inconsequence), so in this case a black woman "became" a "man."

Barbara Fields has recently and powerfully pointed out the flaws in a racial reasoning that can admit that a black child can be born to a white parent, but deny that a black parent could ever give birth to a child who is white.[47] Racialists of the early part of this century were certain of their definitions, and of the dangers of racial crossing; thus, for example, Madison Grant, in a book called *The Passing of the Great Race,* wrote with certainty in 1916 that "the cross between a white man and an Indian is an Indian; the cross between a white man and a Negro is a Negro; the cross between any of the three European races and a Jew is a Jew."[48] The "cross" is the "cross" borne by crossover figures in the arts, in politics, and in social history. It is also the "cross" of the cross-dresser, the transvestite.

Baker, the American version of Baudelaire's black mistress Jeanne Duval, curiously became at the same time "a phallic symbol," a figure of "compelling potency." Like her banana skirt and its "perky phalluses" her entire body was readable, or misreadable, as a sign of maleness—of *black* maleness. A sign, that is, of the menace—and the consequent eroticism—of the black *man* in Western culture. But in this case a black man in captivity, as it were: on the stage.

PASSING TO FREEDOM:
THE ART OF THE CRAFTS

In one of the best known of the slave narratives, William and Ellen Craft's *Running a Thousand Miles for Freedom,* the authors describe their dramatic escape from Macon, Georgia, in 1848, the light-skinned wife disguised as a white man, her darker-skinned husband as her slave attendant. Thus the wife became the "man," and the husband the "boy."

The Crafts' account begins with a figure that we have seen, uncannily, to attach to cross-dressing stories over and over again, so as to form part of those stories' unconscious: the figure of the changeling.

> Notwithstanding my wife being of African extraction on her mother's side, she is almost white— in fact she is so nearly so that the tyrannical old lady to whom she first belonged became so annoyed, at finding her frequently mistaken for a child of the family, that she gave her when eleven years of age to a daughter, as a wedding present. . . . [49]

Ellen Craft's "crime," in the eyes of the white family, is to look as if she belongs— a kind of "passing" which is not deliberate but inadvertent, based upon similarity and contiguity: passing as metonymy. To keep her in chains, it becomes necessary to break the chain of signification: in order that she not be "mistaken for a child of the family" (a particularly ironic observation, since her father was in fact her master, and her mother one of his slaves), Ellen is removed from her surroundings, separated from her mother and her friends. This forced separation, however, has a benefit as well as a cost, for it removed her at the same time from the harsh old mistress, whose cruelty was such that, William Craft records, she did not much grieve at her loss. The story thus has built into it a wicked stepmother as well as a good (lost) mother, and is, in fact, a classic nightmare version of the family romance.

Even without the superadded element of cross-dressing, then, the normative condition of the child-slave is thus that of the changeling. Transvestism, deployed strategically as disguise, uncovers as it covers, reveals the masquerade that is already in place. Seeking to explain this to a sympathetic audience of putatively white readers, Craft begins with the instance of a *white* child "wrongly" (since he or she is not black) sold into slavery:

> . . . as the evidence of a slave is not admitted in court against a free white person, it is almost impossible for a white child, after having been kidnapped and sold or reduced to slavery, in a part of the country where it is not known (as often is the case) ever to recover its freedom.
>
> I have myself conversed with several slaves who told me that their parents were white and free, but that they were stolen away from them and sold when quite young. As they could not tell their address, and also as the parents did not know what had become of their lost and dear little ones, of course all traces of each other were gone. (Craft, 271–2)

As a rhetorical writing strategy, this is remarkably effective, since it puts a white reader of *Running a Thousand Miles* in a condition of imagined jeopardy, voiceless and placeless, caught in the same double bind as the Crafts themselves. William Craft continues with the extended tale of "the long-lost Salomé Muller," a white German immigrant girl, orphaned soon after her arrival in New Orleans, who was sold as a slave and worked as a field hand for twenty-five years before she was accidentally recognized by a woman who had come over in the same ship ("There was no trace of African descent in any feature of Salomé Muller," Craft, 273); and with "the case of a white boy who, at the age of seven, was stolen from his home in Ohio, tanned and stained in such a way that he could not be distinguished from a person of color, and then sold as a slave in Virginia" (Craft, 274). Like Salomé Muller's, this boy's story has a happy ending; he succeeds in escaping and in rejoining his parents. This is the frame in which William Craft presents his own tale of transformation and escape: as these white children are taken for black, and then taken because they are black, so he and his wife, employing and controlling a correlative mode of "passing," pass from slavery to freedom by crossing another boundary, the boundary of gender.

It is significant here that it is the wife who dresses as a man and not the husband who dresses a woman. As so often in the political economy of cross-dressing, traversing the boundary from female-to-male also involves tres-passing onto the terrain of another class. The trajectory female-to-male is not always correlated with upward mobility, obviously; the butch aesthetic focuses attention on working-class clothing and style, and in any case such transhistorical, cross-cultural assertions are of limited use. But Ellen Craft's whiteness did permit her to pass "up" into the class of slave owner—male slave owner. "Knowing," writes her husband,

> that slaveholders have the privilege of taking their slaves to any part of the country they think proper, it occurred to me that, as my wife was nearly white, I might get her to disguise herself as an invalid gentleman, and assume to be my master, while I could attend as his slave, and that in this manner we might effect our escape. (Craft, 286)

He accordingly purchased articles of clothing "piece by piece (except the trousers which she found necessary to make)" (Craft, 287) and his wife, a ladies' maid, hid them in a locked chest of drawers. Once she was dressed in her disguise, writes William Craft, "I found that she made a most respectable looking gentleman" (Craft, 290).

Many of the details of the disguise were invented by Ellen Craft herself. Yet one critic, retelling the story of the Craft's escape, attributes all of these stratagems to the husband, and not the wife: "William bought Ellen a suit of clothes and dark glasses, cut her hair, and bandaged her to hide her beardless chin . . . knowing that in her role as traveling slaveholder the illiterate Ellen would be expected to sign hotel registers, he bandaged her right arm."[50] Of all these assertions, the only one that is corroborated in the text is that

William cut his wife's hair; on all the other points, he is quite clear that the specific details of the disguise were her idea. He conceived of the plan, and persuaded her to go along—that much is true. But it was Ellen Craft who invented the persona of the young invalid gentleman that was to prove so effective.

When the couple fell into temporary despair about their telltale illiteracy, which would reveal their imposture, it was Ellen who "all at once . . . raised her head . . . and said 'I think I have it! . . . I think I can make a poultice and bind up my right hand in a sling, and with propriety ask the officers to register my name for me!' " (Craft, 289). Similarly, William's narrative says explicitly that it was Ellen who thought "that she could get on better if she had something to go over the eyes; so I went to a shop and bought a pair of green spectacles" (Craft, 289); it was Ellen who conceived the device of the handkerchief and the second poultice to hide her beardless face, since "it . . . occurred to her that the smoothness of her face might betray her" (Craft, 289).

In her disguise "she made a most respectable looking gentleman." Making and respectability are alike stressed here. If a gentleman can be made as well as born, why not make one from even the most unpromising material: a female Negro slave? The balance of the narrative demonstrates over and over how artificial a term "gentleman" can be, not only in terms of manners but in terms of gender—at one point, for example, two ladies in a railroad car in Virginia appear to have fallen in love with the "very nice young gentleman." "Oh, dear me," said one wistfully to her father, "I never felt so much for a gentleman in my life!" "To use an American expression," comments the now Anglicized Craft, "they fell in love with the wrong chap" (Craft, 303). The threat of erotic race-mixing, the besetting fear of miscegenation that dominates so much of the period's rhetoric of race hatred, is here cast in a comic mode, at the cost of repressing any untoward thoughts about same-sex, as opposed to mixed-race, border-crossing.

As for respectability, this is clearly very much on William Craft's mind, as he assures his readers:

> My wife had no ambition whatever to assume this disguise, and would not have done so had it been possible to have obtained our liberty by more simple means; but we knew it was not customary in the South for ladies to travel with male servants; and therefore, notwithstanding my wife's fair complexion, it would have been a very difficult task for her to have come off as a free white lady, with me as her slave. (Craft, 290)

Cross-dressing was a necessity, not a pleasure, and though it called for improvisation, it was not in itself "liberating" for the woman in disguise. The first thing Ellen Craft did once the couple reached Philadelphia was to throw off her disguise and "assume her own apparel" (Craft, 315). Throughout the journey William Craft describes his feigned "master" as declining to join a young officer in "something to drink and a cigar," "as he had not these accomplishments" (Craft, 302), feigning illness to avoid conversation, pretending deafness to preclude the obligation to socialize, retiring to bed so as to be able to remove the cumbersome poultices. But notice William Craft's choice of pronoun in these descriptions: "as *he* had not these accomplishments." From the moment they set out for the railway station in disguise Craft describes his wife as a man. "My *master* (as I will now call my wife) took a longer way around. . . . He obtained a ticket for himself and one for his slave. . . . My master then had the luggage stowed away . . . The cabinetmaker [for whom William Craft had worked] looked into my master's carriage, but did not know him in his new attire" (Craft, 294). It is as if the constant vigilance against slips and detection enforced on the journey to freedom were still required, or had become second-nature, in the retelling. Looking around in the carriage, "my master" was terrified to see on the same seat "an old friend of my wife's master, who dined with the family the day before, and knew my wife from childhood" (Craft, 294). The split and self-divided subject here takes on further complexities, new shades of meaning.

Ellen Craft became a master; William Craft became her boy. "Boy, do you belong to that gentleman?" asked a ticket agent. "I quickly replied 'Yes, sir' (which was quite correct)" (Craft, 301). A railway guard accosts him to ask "Boy, what did your master want?" prompting an explanatory footnote in which Craft tells his readers that "every man slave is called boy till he is very old," and when an obnoxious old lady mistakes Craft for her own runaway slave, he reports, "My master said, 'No; that is my boy' " (Craft, 304). This curious cross-dressed version of the Greek man-boy pair is an *in*version, in which the dominant role is played by the woman in disguise.

Ironically, though, it is the husband and not the wife who is accused of cross-dressing. "For the purpose of somewhat disguising myself," William Craft recounts, "I bought and wore a very good second-hand white beaver, an article which I had never indulged in before." An uncouth planter, envying him the hat ("just look at the quality on it; the President couldn't wear a better") complains that the "d———d nigger [is] dressed like a white man" (Craft, 307). The displacement of social anxiety from one category to another (race, class, gender) through the appearance of a transvestite marker in the text is here clearly in evidence. The wife's transvestism and the husband's sartorial class-jumping (read as race-jumping: "dressed like a white man") occupy the same discursive space, act out the same aggressions and repressions. And this chain of substitutions takes on an extra poignancy when the figure of crossing is literally traversing a border, when the crosser, and the cross-dresser, is a runaway slave.

REDRESSING UNCLE TOM

What was narrative autobiography for the Crafts, the runaway slave woman disguised as a man, became exemplary fiction in the work of at least two major white authors, Harriet Beecher Stowe and Mark Twain. In Chapter 37 of *Uncle Tom's Cabin,* entitled

"Liberty," Eliza Harris cross-dresses as a young man, "adapting to her slender and pretty form the articles of man's attire, in which it was deemed safest she should make her escape," and cutting off her "silky abundance of black curly hair."[51] Eliza, like Ellen Craft, is very light-skinned. ("You would scarcely know the woman from a white one," remarks one of her hunters.) She is thus, like Ellen Craft, easily able to "pass" both as male and as white. "There, an't I a pretty young fellow?" she asks her husband George, and George, though concerned for her safety, is captivated by her transformation. " 'Well, indeed,' said he, holding her off at arm's length, and looking admiringly at her, 'You *are* a pretty little fellow. That crop of short curls is quite becoming. Put on your cap. So,—a little to one side. I never saw you look quite so pretty.' " At this point their son Harry, henceforth to be called "Harriet," is brought in, dressed in girl's clothes.

Eliza's sexual appeal for her husband is enhanced in this moment by her male disguise, as well as by the danger in which escape will put them both. It is notable that George must instruct her on how to wear her adopted clothing—the cap and the cloak; they are still his province and not hers. She is not a "man," but some medial construction—yet another permutation of the elastic and gender-conflicted concept of the "boy." As for little Harry, he is not only disguised but neutralized. In his case the boy becomes a "girl." And what are we to make of the fact that the name he is now given, "Harriet," is the name of the novel's author? It is almost as if Stowe places herself within the narrative as the wide-eyed, "peeping," and disbelieving child of the primal scene—the primal scene, here, of American cultural intercourse, the imagined and unimaginable coupling of race and gender:

> "What a pretty girl he makes," said Eliza, turning him round. "We call him Harriet, you see;— don't the name come nicely?"
> The child stood gravely regarding his mother in her new and strange attire, observing a profound silence, and occasionally drawing deep sighs, and peeping at her from under his dark curls.
> "Does Harry know mamma?" asked Eliza, stretching her hands toward him. (Stowe, 411)

But if Eliza is a black woman disguised as a white man, some commentators have seen in Stowe's Uncle Tom a black man who looks like a white woman. Thus John William Ward, commenting on the dramatic necessity of Eliza's race- and gender-crossover, finds in it an implicit critique of Tom's passivity: "We cannot say," he writes, "whether Mrs. Stowe was aware of the implications of her decision to put Eliza in the disguise of a man to make good the last step in her escape, but the implications for the meaning of what the woman stands for in *Uncle Tom's Cabin* are immense. The patient, submissive character, ennobled by feeling, and symbolized most by the good woman, is simply ineffective. . . . This is why 'Uncle Tom' remains an epithet, a term of raging scorn, in the mouth of the Negro ever since Mrs. Stowe wrote her book."[52] Ward's comments date from 1966, the height of the Black Power movement in American race relations. For him, the novel's "real" woman is not Eliza but Tom, the "patient, submissive" believer in non-violence and compliance. This says much about Ward's views of women, as well as about his unhappiness with Stowe's views of blacks. Once again oppressed or disempowered categories are set over against one another. Ward does not imagine the possibility of power accruing to medial figures who are not "women" or "men," yet it is precisely the disruptive power of transvestism in *both* Eliza *and* Tom that here enables social—and literary—critique.

A number of years later Leslie Fiedler made an observation similar to Ward's when he commented that "Uncle Tom is really a white mother in blackface and drag," and that he constitutes "a secret self-portrait of the author." "Merely by having been born a woman in her time and place," said Fiedler, "Mrs. Stowe had been born in her deepest self-consciousness a slave."[53] But in alluding to the artifice of transvestism and minstrelsy, "blackface and drag," Fiedler not only reiterates the social critique of Uncle Tomism but also, if inadvertently, hints at the ways in which theatrical representation can embody such a critique, and deploy it for political ends.

Nowhere in modern theater history does the function of transvestite theater as the enactment of cultural fears and beliefs stand out more clearly than in Jean Genet's 1959 play, *Les Nègres,* where the actors are black and the blackface is whiteface, and in which the figure of the integrationist clergyman Diouf, perhaps the ultimate political portrait of Uncle Tom in drag, offers a grotesque conflation of mime and mammy. Translated as *The Blacks,* and subtitled *A Clown Show,* the play was first produced in the U.S. in 1961 with a cast that included such major black actors as Roscoe Lee Browne, James Earl Jones, Louis Gossett, Cicely Tyson, Godfrey Cambridge, Maya Angelou Make, and Raymond St. Jacques, all of whom would go on to have distinguished careers. As an adolescent newly awakened to both the civil rights movement and my own sexuality, I saw *The Blacks* at the St. Mark's Playhouse in New York. From that time to this it has defined for me what "theater"—and "political theater"—means; only David Hwang's *M. Butterfly* has had a comparable effect on me, and perhaps for similar reasons. Let me try to give some sense of this by describing a climactic moment in the play.

Mr. Samba Graham Diouf (Godfrey Cambridge) is grotesquely dressed as a white woman in a blond wig, a laughing carnival mask with big cheeks and white gloves. He is to take the part of the dead white woman in the ceremonial reenactment of a ritual murder—a murder which, as it turns out, is itself only a blind for the real action of subversion to be carried out. Diouf is the weakling of the group, frightened, unsure of himself, a "poor trembling Negro" "behind the mask of a cornered White." In short, he is already feminized, even before they dress him up, even before he is forced to slip on a woman's skirt, even before they mime a series of mock-births, reaching under his skirt to pull out a series of dolls symbolically representing the "white" authority figures (all masked blacks) in the play: the Governor, the Judge, the Queen. In his hand Diouf holds a pair of knitting needles and some pink wool. "She" has all the parody Christian female virtues: she knits helmets for little chimney sweeps, she does watercolors, she sings in church. But in order to play (an invisible) piano, as instructed, "she" must hand the knitting to someone else—someone sitting in the audience, a spectator. As I sat in the front row of the St. Mark's Playhouse with my high school boyfriend in the spring of 1962, I hoped, desperately, that the someone would not be me.

As it happened, it wasn't. It was the man to my left. But as Godfrey Cambridge in his skirt and wig came toward us, toward me, holding out the knitting—which, all too clearly, would have to be returned later on, requiring the recipient to take part in, to be implicated in, the play—as all of this became unmistakably evident in the very act of an actor crossing over (crossing over the invisible line between actor and audience, as he simultaneously crossed over from black to "white," from male to "female"), I began to catch some glimpse of why it was that neither politics nor sexuality was, or could be, a safe spectator sport.

The black man Diouf, like Fiedler's Uncle Tom, becomes a mother, elevated in the play's last ironic reversal to a position of adoration and respect. "Tomorrow, and in the ceremonies to come, you'll represent the Worthy Mother of the heroes who died thinking they'd killed us, but who were devoured by our fury and our black ants."[54] Genet's epigraph to the play is frequently quoted by analysts of race and culture:

> One evening an actor asked me to write a play for an all-black cast. But what exactly is a black? First of all, what's his color?

It seems plausible in light of the present discussion (and in view of Genet's other writings) to rework this conundrum in terms of gender: "What exactly is a man (or a woman)? First of all, what's his/her gender?"

IN TWAIN

Among white American authors, Mark Twain is probably the best known for his repeated, almost obsessive, interest in the twin problems of race and gender as realized in the figure of the transvestite.

Twain's fascination with historical cross-dressers led him to write the *Personal Recollections of Joan of Arc* (1896). He was also intrigued by the real-life story of Dr. James Barry, the famous lifelong female-to-male transvestite who became British Colonial Medical Officer in 1822. The story of Dr. Barry is told by Twain as a kind of postscript to his two-volume travel book *Following the Equator* (1897)—a book intermittently concerned with the interimplications of race and gender. Volume 2 of that work, which ends with a portrait of Dr. Barry, begins with an account—almost a reverie—about a young black male Singhalese servant:

beautiful black hair combed back like a woman's, and knotted at the back of the head—tortoise-shell comb in it . . . ; slender, shapely form; jacket; under it a beltless and flowing white cotton gown—from neck straight to heel; he and his outfit quite unmasculine. It was an embarrassment to undress before him.[55]

Twain was also the author of a series of little-known "transvestite tales," written over a long period from the 1860's to the early 1900's. His continuing interest in this phenomenon was manifested in burlesque stories like "1,002nd Arabian Night" (1883), about babies switched at birth, and "Hellfire Hotchkiss" (1897), about a "genuwyne male" woman and a "genuwyne female" man in a Missouri town,[56] and in a series of tales that center on cross-dressing women put on trial as putative fathers in paternity suits—tales that sometimes eventuate in the birth of infants who fit the description we have been evolving of the "changeling boy"—the fantasy child of transvestism.[57]

But the most literal changeling boy in Twain is Tom Driscoll in *Pudd'nhead Wilson,* who is exchanged in the cradle for a white baby born on the same day. The exchange is performed by Tom's mother Roxana, and the substitution is made easier—indeed, made possible—by the fact that Tom, like his mother, looks white.

He had blue eyes and flaxen curls like his white comrade, but even the father of the white child was able to tell the children apart—little as he had commerce with them—by their clothes; for the white babe wore ruffled soft muslin and a coral necklace, while the other wore merely a coarse tow-linen shirt which barely reached to its knees, and no jewelry.[58]

The question of *clothing* and of the *exchange* of clothing is thus from the beginning part of the story. When "Tom" (whose actual name, appropriately enough, is Valet de Chambre, later shortened to "Chambers") grows up and becomes a gambler and a thief, he disguises himself in women's clothes in order to carry out his robberies in the neighborhood. As for his mother, Roxy, she too becomes a cross-dresser, disguising herself in a man's clothes and hat in order to escape from a cruel slavemaster (to whom her son, now installed as the young master of the house, has secretly sold her).

Roxana changes not only her clothes but also her complexion, described as "very fair, with the rosy glow of vigorous health in the cheeks" (*PW,* 29): "I blacked my face," she says (*PW,* 135). In order to look black—the color that defines her social and legal condition—she must put on blackface, like the end men of the minstrel show. *Pudd'nhead Wilson* is in fact an exemplary instance of the category crisis, the slippage from one borderline to another, in this case race to gender, or gender to race, marked by the appearance of the transvestite. Or of two transvestites, mother and son.

For "Tom," too, blacks his face. (Can it be only a coincidence that his name is the same as that of Stowe's legendary "contented slave"?) Determining on the murder of his stepfather and benefactor, "He unlocked his trunk and got his suit of girl's clothes out from under the male attire in it, and laid it by. Then he blacked his face with burnt cork"

(*PW,* 142). Once the deed is done, he "put on his coat, buttoned his hat under it, threw on his suit of girl's clothes, dropped the veil" (*PW* 142), and effects his escape by the simple act of vanishing into another gender, taking off his "girl-clothes" the minute he reaches his room. "A woman who doesn't exist any longer, and the clothes that gave her her sex burnt up and the ashes thrown away" (*PW* 150–51).

The invisible man is here invisible because he is a "woman"— a woman wearing a *veil.*

Here it will be useful to look at W.E.B. Du Bois's image of the "veil" in *The Souls of Black Folk,* a text written in the same years—perhaps the most famous single description of the black American as split subject.

> The Negro is a sort of seventh son, born with a veil, and gifted with second sight in this American world. . . . It is a peculiar sensation, this double-consciousness, this sense of always looking at one's self through the eyes of others. . . . One ever feels his twoness,—an American, a Negro; two souls, two thoughts, two unreconciled strivings; two warring ideals in one dark body, whose dogged strength alone keeps it from being torn asunder.
>
> The history of the American Negro is the history of this strife,—this longing to attain self-conscious manhood, to merge his double self into a better and truer self.[59]

Barbara Johnson has observed that this passage "assume[s] without question that the black subject is male," that it renders the black woman totally invisible.[60] What it also does is to valorize the numbers one and two, as if they were the only options for the making of the subject—or of history. But when read against, or across, for example, the "history" of the Crafts, Du Bois's "veil" suggests still further implications for the veiled figure which we have seen to be linked to the transvestite. William and Ellen; slave and master; husband and wife; black and white. Double authorship, marriage, the split subject, the color line, the binary of gender. In between each and every one of these pairings, these couples, comes the disruptive figure of the transvestite. Not one, but three; the third is the cross-dressed figure of Ellen Craft, so vividly, multiply veiled in her kerchief, her poultice, her dark glasses.

"The veil" for Du Bois is a figure for the existence of blacks in American culture. In a passage from *The Souls of Black Folk* less well known than the one just quoted, Du Bois meditates movingly on color and the crossing of boundaries in the birth of his own baby son:

> Why was his hair tinted with gold? An evil omen was golden hair in my life. Why had not the brown of his eyes crushed out and killed the blue?—for brown were his father's eyes, and his father's father's. And thus in the land of the Color-line I saw, as it fell across my baby, the shadow of the Veil. (Du Bois, 1947)

Tragically, the child died in infancy, and Du Bois, reflecting on what his dead son had been spared by not living "within the Veil," or under the burden of blackness, makes of

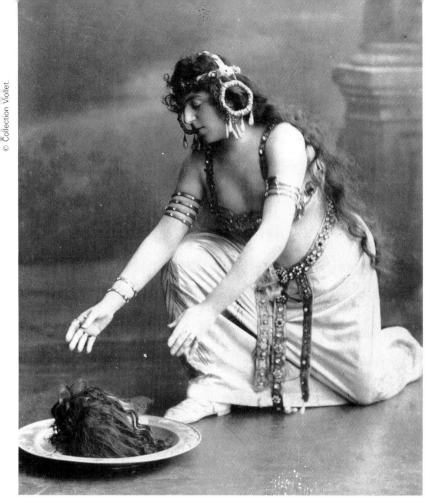

Oscar Wilde as Salome.

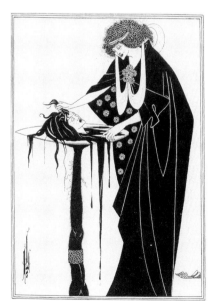

Salome by Aubrey Beardsley.

Transvestite pirates—two eighteenth-century women and Captain Hook.

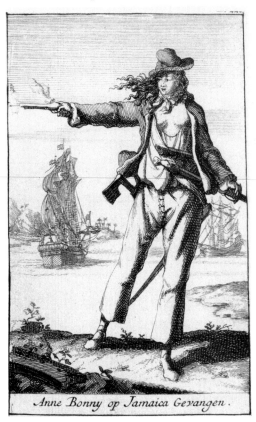

Anne Bonny op Jamaica Gevangen.

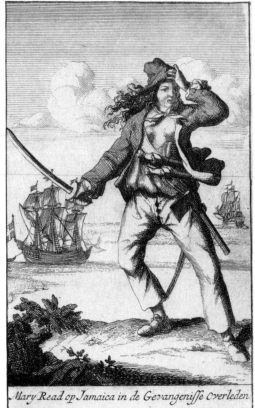

Mary Read op Jamaica in de Gevangeniſſe Overleden

Anne Bonny and Mary Read, two eigh-teenth-century pirates who dressed as men.

Ernest Torrence as Captain Hook.

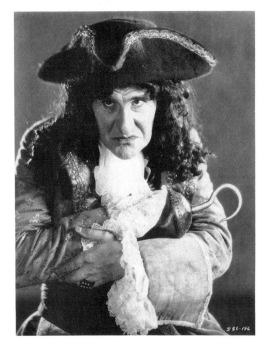

Peter Pan, the eternal boy, always a woman.

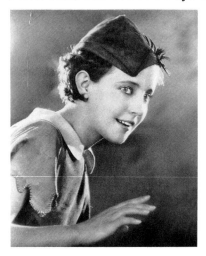

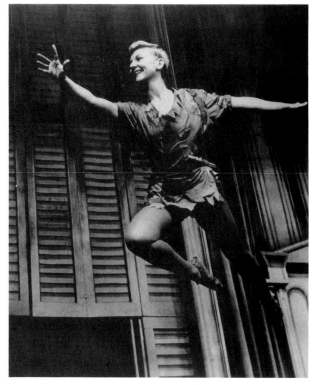

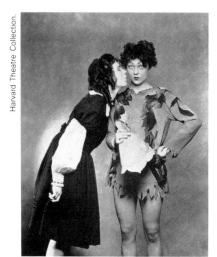

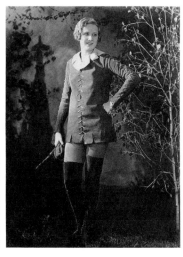

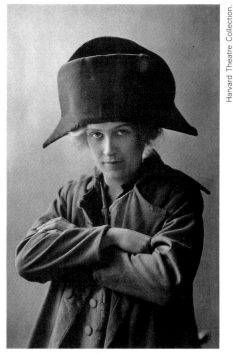

Clockwise from top left: Betty Bronson; Mary Martin; Pauline Chase; Marilyn Miller; Eva Le Gallienne.

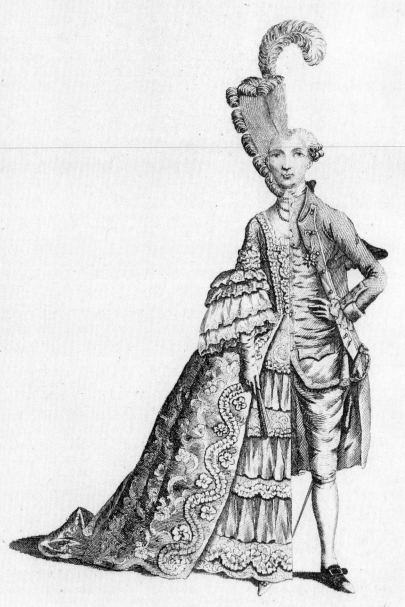

MADEMOISELLE de BEAUMONT, or the
CHEVALIER D'EON.
Female Minister Plenipo. Capt. of Dragoons &c. &c.

The Chevalier d'Eon,
Charles Geneviève Louis Auguste André Timothée de Beaumont.

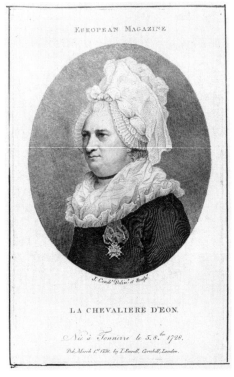

EUROPEAN MAGAZINE

LA CHEVALIERE D'EON.

Née à Tonnerre le 5.8.e 1728.

Pub. March 1st 1791. by T. Sewell, Cornhill, London.

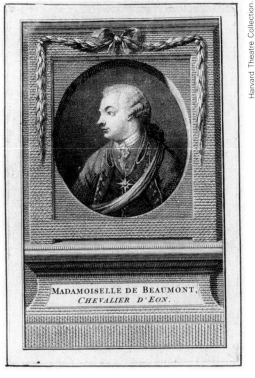

MADAMOISELLE DE BEAUMONT,
CHEVALIER D'EON.

Clockwise from top left: D'Eon as an old woman; as a young man (but identified as ''Madamoiselle de Beaumont''); as a young woman in a low-cut gown.

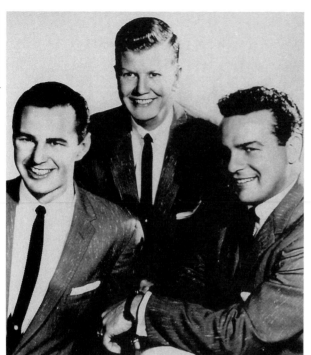

Gender benders.

The Billy Tipton Trio: Billy Tipton (center) with Ron Kilde and Dick O'Neil. To the surprise of his colleagues, wife, and adopted sons, jazz musician Tipton was discovered upon his death to be a woman.

Dr. James Barry, Inspector General of the Medical Department of the British Army, who served for more than forty years as a physician and surgeon, and was "after his death found to be a Female."

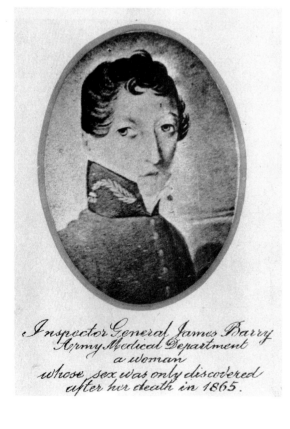

Inspector General James Barry Army Medical Department a woman whose sex was only discovered after her death in 1865.

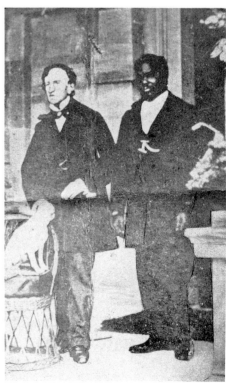

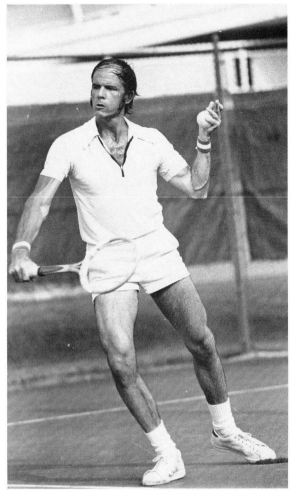

Dr. Richard Raskind

Renée Richards.

Tennis star Renée Richards, formerly Dr. Richard Raskind, whose transsexual surgery was the subject of a bestselling autobiography and a TV movie.

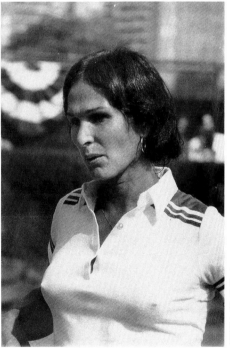

Minstrelsy as double-cross-dressing. White male minstrels performed as both black and white women on the minstrel stage.

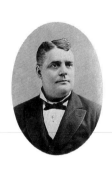
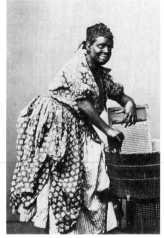
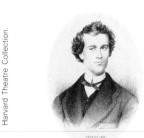

Above: Chas. Wilson; *right:* Francis Leon, "The Only Leon."

Below: Tony Hart (on left, with Mrs. Tony Hart, right).

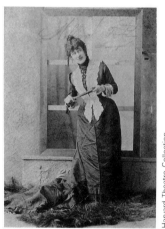

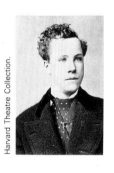
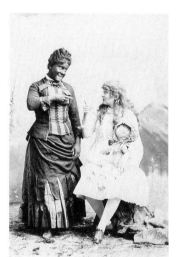

Right: Julian Eltinge, among the most successful female impersonators of his day, began his career in George M. Cohan's touring minstrel show.

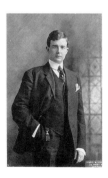
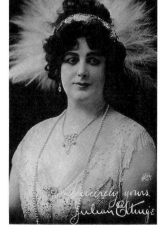

Three twentieth-century black entertainers.

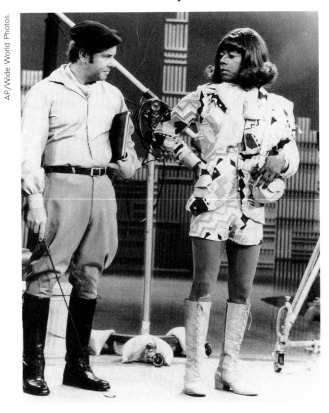

Left: Flip Wilson as Geraldine. *Below:* Little Richard; Nancy Reagan and Mr. T.

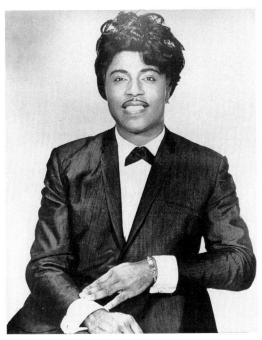

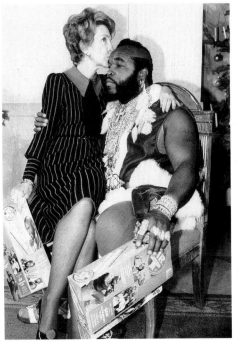

Clockwise from top: Marlene Dietrich, *The Blue Angel* (1930); Betty Grable, *Mother Wore Tights* (1947); Helmut Berger, *The Damned* (1969); *The New Yorker* cover drawing by Rea Irvin.

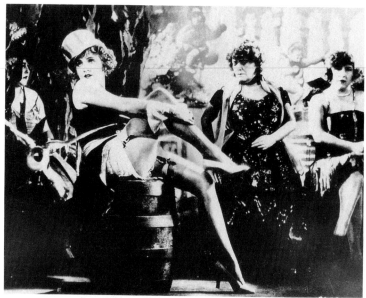

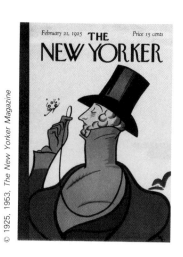

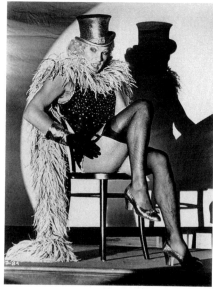

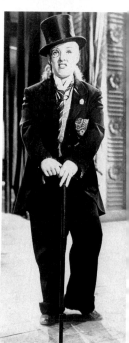

Class acts.

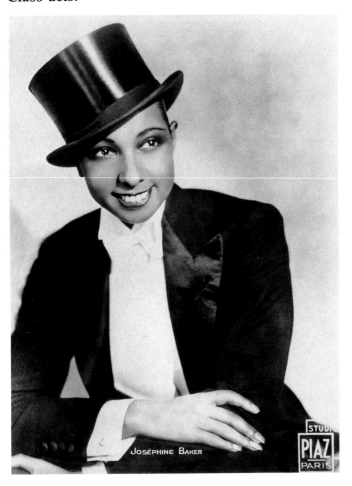

Josephine Baker.

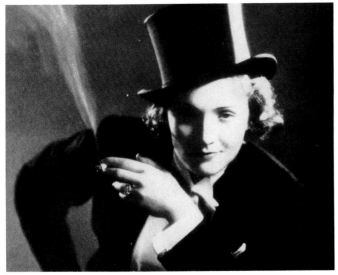

Marlene Dietrich.

The chic of Araby.

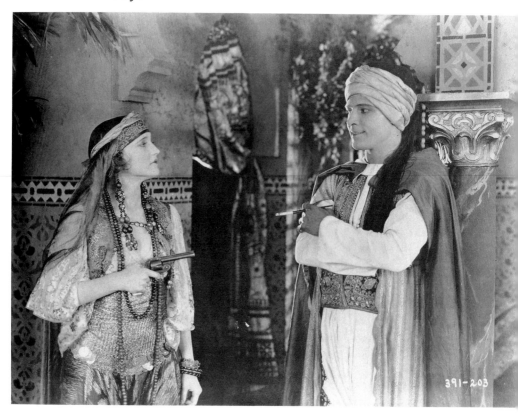

Rudolph Valentino brandishes his cigarette, Agnes Ayres cocks a pistol in *The
Sheik* (1921).

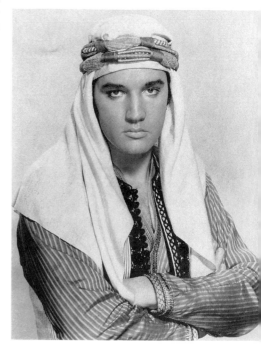

Elvis Presley, *Harum Scarum* (1965).

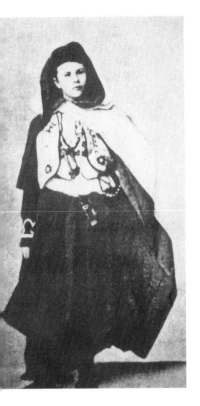

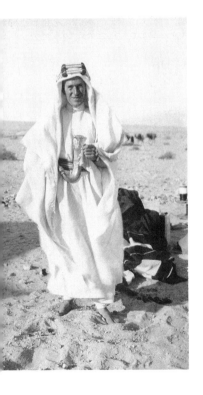

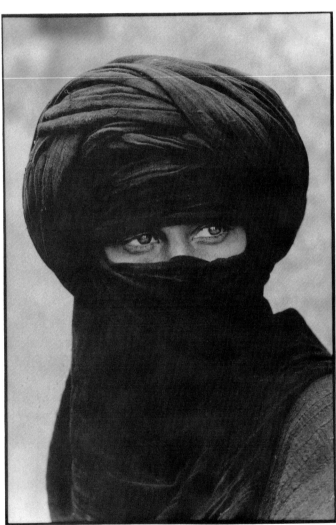

Top left: Isabelle Eberhardt as a young Arab, in clothes from a French photographer's studio trunk. *Above:* Debra Winger as a Tuareg boy, *The Sheltering Sky* (1991). *Left:* T.E. Lawrence.

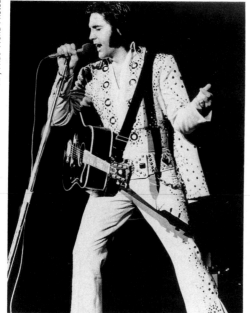

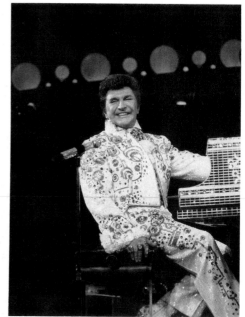

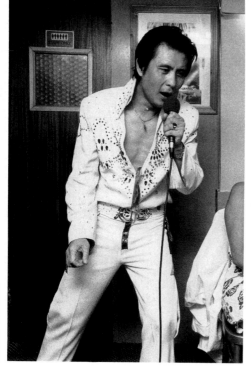

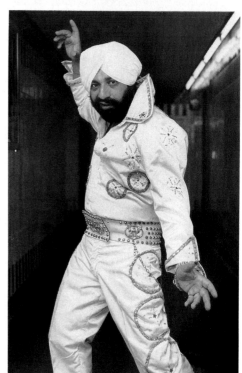

Elvises and Liberaces.

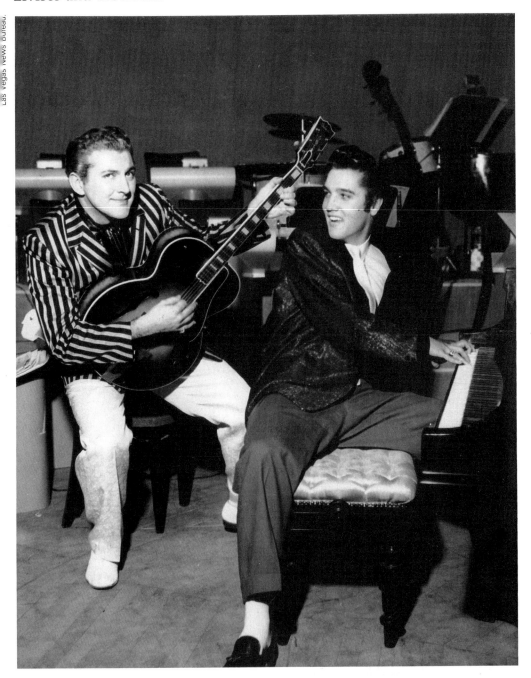

Above: In a famous publicity shot, Liberace and Elvis trade jackets and instruments.

Opposite page, clockwise from top left: Elvis, "The King"; Liberace, "Mr. Showmanship"; Peter Singh, "The Rocking Sikh"; Hong Kong born Paul Chan, "The First Chinese Elvis."

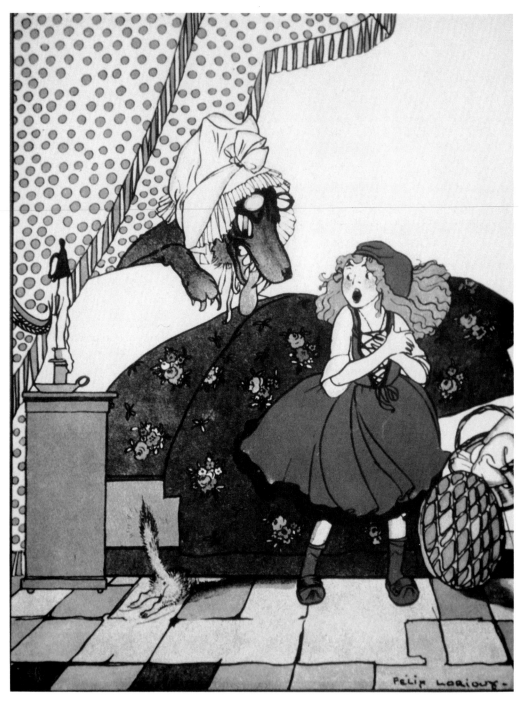

''O grandmother! What a big . . . nose you have!'' Red Riding Hood sizes up the wolf. Illustration from a French edition of the tale.

him a double changeling, a changeling who crosses both the line dividing black from white and—as if it were somehow the same thing—the line dividing life from death.

But Twain's veil, Tom Driscoll's veil, the veil of another "tragic mulatto" crossing a forbidden boundary, marks the radical indeterminacy of gender—gender as an *effect of race*. The mechanism here is that of displacement as psychic defense. For when Tom dresses as a woman, he disguises his *gender* because he is ashamed of his *race*. To "drop the veil" is to pull it over his face, to voluntarily veil himself. Inadvertently, then, read backwards through Du Bois's compelling image, Tom's disguise, the woman's veil, becomes a signifier of that very blackness he is so anxious to conceal. The irony of Tom's desperate ploy—to pass as a woman because he has been passing as white, and then to obliterate the damning evidence, burning both male *and* female clothes—is that it marks him unmistakably, if only for a moment, as a black transvestite, the true son of the mother he despises and sells down the river.[61]

MAID SERVICE

A number of recent films and television programs have featured a curious new stereotype, the black (male) maid, in what looks like the latest permutation of Uncle/Auntie Tom. Let me give three brief examples. Jacob, the barefoot black male maid of *La Cage aux Folles,* has a voice like Butterfly McQueen and likes to parade around the apartment in an apron and a wig. When forced into the "cross-dressed" role of butler, as part of the grand plan to deceive the strait-laced Deputy about the nature of the relationship between Renato and the female impersonator Albin, Jacob breaks into occasional giggles. He is as much a queen as Albin, and as little a success as a "man."

In the film *Longtime Companion* (1989), the story of several gay male couples—gay *white* male couples—and the AIDS epidemic, the black "maid" is Henry, the home attendant who comes in daily to help the wealthy David care for his dying lover, Sean. Henry is as swish as they come; he is also reliable, resourceful and tactful, clearing up David's breakfast dishes although that is not part of his job, helping to wash Sean and make him comfortable, then taking himself off when David wants to be alone. The only black man in the film, as well as the campiest, Henry raises through his characterization serious questions about the class- and race-consciousness of the filmmakers in their determination to dramatize the heroic ordinariness of gay .(white) men.

Television regularly takes fewer risks than film, and the manifestation of the black male maid that appeared briefly in one episode of the television show *Designing Women* was hedged about with disavowals and disclaimers. Anthony (Meshach Taylor) is persuaded against his will to dress as an Hispanic maid in order to fool the Immigration and Naturalization Service; one of the women with whom he works fears that her maid will be deported if she does not apply for citizenship. Interviewed by a black male bureaucrat at INS headquarters, Anthony, in false breasts, long peasant skirt and headscarf, is so successful that the bureaucrat flirts with him throughout the subsequent swearing-in ceremony—to which Anthony wears a stylish dress and jewelry, and looks, in consequence, like a woman of the upper-middle rather than the lower class. He first resists the role, then triumphs in it; he is a hero to his upscale (white) female friends, who urge him to undertake the masquerade and are of course never deceived by it. Nonetheless, the trope of the black-man-as-maid is again, albeit briefly, invoked.

But the figure of the black male maid has never been more effectively or seriously explored than it was by black novelist Richard Wright. In an extraordinary short story called "Man of All Work," originally written in the mid-fifties as a radio play and later published in his book *Eight Men,* Wright describes the circumstances of a black man who goes to work, dressed in his wife's clothes, as a maid. Carl is an out-of-work professional cook with a family to support. The story opens with his waking in the dark to feed his infant daughter a bottle, displacing his wife Lucy, who has been told by her doctor to rest. His young son is eager to watch: "Papa," he says, "I want to see you feed her," and Carl complies. "Now watch, I lift her head up a bit, then put the nipple in her mouth. See? She's stopped crying."[62] Carl's nurturance—and his profession—thus make him from the first a "mother" as well as a father, a "woman" as well as a man. But this femininity is, in the context of the family, supplement rather than lack. It is only when he ventures into the white world of domestic employment that gender roles become a trap for him. In the house of Mr. and Mrs. Fairchild, and their even-more-symbolically-named daughter, Lily, Carl becomes "Lucy," taking on his wife's name as well as her clothing.

Carl's transvestism is occasioned by the most conventional of motives, the need for work—the same motivation that triggers the comic cross-dressing story lines of films like *Tootsie* and *Victor/Victoria.* But "Man of All Work" is from the first fraught with danger and discomfort, as well as with dissonant notes of what can only be called black comedy. Thus Carl, scanning the morning papers, finds no ad for a cook under "Male Help Wanted," but the perfect situation for him is described—in the *wrong* gender column: "cook and housekeeper wanted. Take care of one child and small modern household. All late appliances. Colored cook preferred" (Wright, 122). Although the ad does not say so, Carl knows that "they want a woman," and determines to do something about it.

Remember that this is a radio play. Carl is therefore an invisible man in even more than the usual sense of the term, and his wife's consternation when he tells her to turn on the light and look at him is fully shared by the listening—as well as the reading—audience. "OHHHHHH! Who are you . . . Oh, God! I thought you were somebody else. Oh, Carl, what are you doing? Those are my clothes you got on. You almost scared me to death" (Wright, 123). Like the absent picture of Mayor Washington, visible only from the back in the newspaper photo, then completely dropping out of sight, the spectacle of Carl Owens in his wife's dress is withheld from the audience, and becomes, in consequence, a double scandal. Throughout the scene that follows Lucy Owens continues to implore him to "TAKE OFF MY DRESS!" "GET OUT OF MY DRESS!" "PULL OFF MY DRESS!" while Carl explores, without conscious irony, the ironic appropriateness of his disguise. To her protest that people can look at him and see that he's a man, he has an unanswerable answer:

> Ha, ha. No, Lucy, I just looked at myself in the bathroom mirror. I've got on a dress and I look just like a million black woman cooks. Who looks that close at us colored people anyhow? We all look alike to white people. Suppose you'd never seen me before? You'd take one look at me and take me for a woman because I'm wearing a dress. And the others'll do that too. Lucy, colored men are now wearing their hair long, like mine. Isn't that true? Look at Sugar Ray Robinson's hair. Look at Nat King Cole's hair. Look at all the colored men in the Black Belt. They straighten their hair. It's the style. . . .
>
> I'm just about your size. Your dresses fit me. I'll take your purse. I'll wear low-heeled shoes. What's more I don't need any make-up. A cook isn't supposed to be powdered and rouged. I've shaved very, very closely. I'm taking my razor with me; if my beard starts to grow, I'll sneak a quick shave, see? All I have to do is say 'Yessum, No'm,' and keep my mouth shut. Do my work. My voice is tenor; nobody'll notice it. I'll get the money we need and we're saved. . . .
>
> There isn't much difference between a man's walk and a woman's. . . . Nobody'll know but you. (Wright, 124)

In short,

> "I put on your dress, I looked in the mirror. *I can pass.* I want that job—" (Wright, 123, emphasis added)

"Passing" here itself passes from the category of race or color to the category of gender; a black man sees that he can pass as a woman because he is, in white eyes, always already a woman: "We all look alike to white people." "Nobody'll know but you." The connection between gender-passing and racial-passing is made clearer by what seems an intertextual link with Fanny Hurst's *Imitation of Life* and the 1934 film version directed by John Stahl.[63] For Carl the professional cook, arriving like Hurst's Delilah early in the morning to apply for the job, wins over his prospective employer, just as Delilah does, by making pancakes. This talent immediately establishes the transvestite "Lucy" as an authentic black woman. Not that Mrs. Fairchild has ever had any doubts: "I just look at a person and something tells me that they ought to be all right" (Wright, 130). This is a good example of what I have described as looking *through* rather than *at* the transvestite. Mrs. Fairchild sees just what she wants to see—or does she? How are we to construe the serio-comic scene that follows, in which she insists that "Lucy" scrub her back while she is naked in the bath?

But there is another spectator on the scene, one with big eyes: the young daughter of the house, Lily Fairchild, whose telltale name sets up the sad joke of the plot. "Mama," Lily asks, "does Lucy know about Little Red Riding Hood?" and the cross-dressed "Lucy" replies, "Miss Lily, I know all about her" (Wright, 131). The power of the Red Riding Hood figure in the sexual mythology of transvestism extends from Freud's Wolf-Man to Djuna Barnes's Nora. Here it is reinforced by Lily's seemingly endless litany of questions: why are "Lucy's" arms so big, and so hairy, and so muscular? Why is her voice "heavy, like a man's"? Why is her face hard and rough? Why does she hold her cigarette in her mouth "like Papa holds his, with one end dropping down"? (Wright, 134;140).

Lily alone sees "Lucy" as a transvestite, and this dangerous knowledge must be explained away, so the child will be told that "Lucy" looks like a man not because she is one but because she works so hard: "Lucy, don't you ever wear lipstick, like Mama?" (Wright, 141). The difference between Carl Owens and Lucy Owens is no greater—in fact may be much less—than the difference between Lucy Owens and Anne Fairchild.

"How will anybody know?" Carl had teased his wife. "Lift up my dress?" (Wright, 125). This is of course exactly what happens when, almost as soon as he is hired as a "colored woman" by the Fairchild family, the wife asks him to scrub her back in the bathtub, the husband makes a pass at him (so that "passing" leads to becoming the object of a "pass"), and the family doctor, summoned when the wife in a panic shoots him, asks, gingerly, "Did you, for some reason, *make him wear that dress?*". The doctor who pronounces a transvestite's true gender after the fact is a familiar figure from such "real-life" cases as Billy Tipton and the Chevalier d'Eon. In "Man of All Work" the doctor's knowledge is juxtaposed to the Fairchilds' ignorance, as they repeatedly use female gender pronouns and the doctor as repeatedly avoids or evades them: "Is *she* living? Will *she* pull through?" "I shot *her*," and "Er . . . *The patient* has a chance." "I put *the patient* on your living-room couch," and "Where did you find *this servant?*" (Wright, 152–53, emphasis added). "Your female servant is a man wearing a woman's dress." "How is that possible? Aren't you mistaken . . . ?" "Look. I'm a doctor. The most elementary thing I know is the difference between a man and a woman" (Wright, 154).

But Carl Owens in Lucy's dress *is* in a way "the difference between a man and a woman." Since the reader (and the radio audience) already knows the transvestite secret here, the force of these discrepant awarenesses, and of the doctor's scientific certainty, is to enforce the Fairchilds' incredulity—and Mr. Fairchild's opportunism. A moment before he had been culpable of making a pass at a black woman servant; now he imagines a scenario in which he (not his wife) shot the male interloper, since he must "logically" be a rapist: "that's our answer! I was protecting white womanhood from a nigger rapist impersonating a woman! A rapist who wears a dress is the worst sort!" (Wright, 154–55).

So what, precisely, *would* anyone *know,* if they did what Carl mockingly suggests to Lucy, and "lift[ed] up [his] dress?" What would they see? "A flesh wound in the thigh," says the doctor, "A great loss of blood" (Wright, 153). Paradoxically, both castration *and* erection, the black man in women's clothes performing domestic service, the black man as imaginary rapist performing sexual service. That the black man in the Western cultural

Imaginary has so often been portrayed as simultaneously a figure of power and of disempowerment makes this figure of the male-to-female transvestite both an ironic commentary and a knowledgeably deployed cliché. For Wright's story knows all about the black man in the dress, and does not discover but rather reworks the old caricature, the old charade. "Now, I've talked to this boy," says the doctor. "He seems straight, if a man wearing a dress can be described as straight . . . He says if you'll pay his doctor's bill and give him two hundred dollars, he'll forget it. . . . But he insists on borrowing a suit of your clothes to go home in. . . . His suit is hidden in his coal house." "O.K.," replies Fairchild, "give 'im something from my clothes closet. But get 'im out of here quick" (Wright, 157–58). From the coal house to the closet. From the closet to the bank.

"I've talked to this boy. He seems straight, if a man wearing a dress can be described as straight." How does a "boy" become a "man" in the eyes of these white men? By putting on a dress.

TURNING TRICKSTER

In his autobiography, *Moonwalker,* Michael Jackson tells the story of an early appearance he and his brothers made at the famed Apollo Theater in Harlem. Waiting their turn to perform, they stood in the wings and watched another act:

> [W]hen we did the Apollo Theater in New York, I saw something that really blew me away because I didn't know things like that existed. I had seen quite a few strippers, but that night this one girl with gorgeous eyelashes and long hair came out and did her routine. She put on a *great* performance. All of a sudden, at the end, she took off her wig, pulled a pair of oranges out of her bra, and revealed that she was a hard-faced guy under all that makeup. That blew me away. I was only a child and couldn't even conceive of anything like that. But I looked out at the theater audience and they were *going* for it, applauding wildly and cheering. I'm just a little kid, standing in the wings, watching this crazy stuff.
> I was blown away.[64]

What the young Michael Jackson here instinctively realizes and responds to, what the adult Michael Jackson chooses to narrate as an exemplum, is the power of theater and theatricality, the way in which gender-bending and gender parody, the creation of an illusion, plays upon the energies of an audience. The "*great* performance" of the stripper is both her dance as a "woman" and her subsequent self-revelation as a "guy under all that makeup." The performance is in Harlem; the time is the sixties. The anecdote, as described in *Moonwalker,* has something about it of the primal scene of show business.

In the management of his own exceptionally successful career Jackson, who does not cross-dress, has deftly manipulated the stage vocabulary of gender. He is lithe, athletic, dazzling as a dancer, compelling as a singer. He deploys the aesthetics of androgyny with skill and grace. His face, since plastic surgery altered his nose (he later added a chin cleft), has been compared to the faces of Elizabeth Taylor and Diana Ross.[65] His signature white socks, single glove, and sequined clothing are readily identifiable—and often imitated—marks of his personal style. Why is he the "most famous entertainer in the world"?[66] Why does the fact that he looks and dresses the way he does enhance his popularity?

Vanity Fair's photograph of Michael Jackson, by the brilliant *Rolling Stone* portraitist Annie Leibovitz, shows him in a familiar Jackson uniform of epaulets, gold braid, and black tailcoat with red cuffs that is somehow reminiscent both of a mythical middle European dynasty and of a matador's costume. His long hair curling down his neck, his eyes made up, his shoes high-heeled and gleaming, he stands before a mirror rapt in thought. ("For all his famous friends," writes *VF,* "the only one who really knows him is the man in the mirror" [*Vanity Fair,* 170]). But *which* man, in *which* mirror? The photograph shows *three* full length Michaels and a fraction of a fourth, with the implication that an infinite series of reflections might be visible, and that no one is the "original"—all are simulacra, whether viewed, as in the photograph, from the left, the right, or the rear, with hand curling toward the viewer.

The Leibovitz photograph of Michael Jackson, in short, may be the ultimate illustration of the argument for and against "the third" which was set forth in the introduction to this book. *Three* here marks a space of possibility, clearly indicated as a beginning rather than a limit, because of the teasing presence of the fourth just moving out of the viewer's sight. It is a portrait of a man—and an entertainer—who controls how he is read and seen.

Michael Jackson began his stage career as a child star, but other black male child stars, especially those of an earlier time, have not had the cultural—and material—power to craft their stage and screen images. Consider, for example, the screen careers of the black male children of early films, specifically in America's cinematic fantasy about childhood as presented in the long-running series of two-reelers, silent and sound, called "Our Gang."

The "Our Gang" comedies of the 1920's, 1930's and 1940's starred not one but two black children about whose sexual identity there was—at the time—considerable speculation. Farina, played by Allen Hoskins, was usually dressed in gingham, with a head of curly pigtails tied up in ribbons; when Farina became excited or frightened, the pigtails stood on end.

In "Saturday Morning" (1922) Farina is called "Maple" and seems to be a girl; in "Seein' Things" (1924) gangs repeatedly threaten to capture "her," but when Farina has a dream in the same film he identifies with a dapper male character seen earlier in the film flirting with a pretty girl. In "It's a Bear" (1924) Farina is scolded by an older child, who tells "her" to "Quit chasin' things—be a lady." Film historians Leonard Maltin and Richard Bann describe this as the "curious Julian Eltinge aspect of *Our Gang,*"[67] noting that the same thing happened a decade later with Buckwheat. The studio was apparently deluged with letters inquiring about Farina's "real" gender, and *Our Gang* founder Hal Roach capitalized on the public's curiosity, putting out press releases that artfully avoided the use of gender pronouns or the actor's name.

Buckwheat, played by Billie Thomas, appeared in Hal Roach's "Our Gang" series from 1934 to 1944. He too wore gingham and had pigtails that stood erect at times of stress. Buckwheat, like his predecessor Farina, stirred speculations about gender—and with some reason, since the part had originally been played in three episodes by a little girl, Willie Mae Taylor, and in another episode by Carlena Beard. In fact, when Billie Thomas was cast in the role he was at first supposed to be playing a girl, though his gender later "evolved into the male category" (Maltin, 175). In "Anniversary Trouble" (1935) the "female" Buckwheat, then imagined as the daughter of a maid played by Hattie McDaniel, is impersonated by Spanky in order to fool the gang; this disguise makes Spanky a "female impersonator" of a "female impersonator," junior style (Maltin, 170; 175; Bogle, *Blacks,* 405, 470).

It is worth wondering why only the *black* children of this series, specifically the black *boys,* were presented in such a way as to foreground their gender indeterminacy. (In some episodes white members of the gang appeared comically dressed as "ladies" for stage shows or plays-within-the-play, but this was clearly a quite different kind of "fancy dress," in which their gender identities were never put in question.) As a counterpart to the feminization—or emasculation—of adult black men in literature and culture, this tendency is striking. We might note further that both Hoskins and Thomas were dark-skinned, not the preferred color tone for African-Americans in the U.S. entertainment industry. Unlike Stowe's fictional Harry/Harriet they were not racially indeterminate. Dark-skinned blacks got roles as servants or comics, while only light-skinned or yellow actors and actresses could be considered for serious roles. "Passing" as a girl here emphatically did not mean "passing" as white, and the comic aspect of "Farina" and "Buckwheat" (both light or white grain products) was enhanced, so to speak, by the blackness of the young actors playing these parts.

Roach's media campaign deliberately positioned Farina and Buckwheat—or Hoskins and Thomas—in some third gender category. Playing upon racial attitudes prevalent in the early part of the century—and not eradicated today—he made them, simultaneously, figures of fun and figures who could not provoke sexual fear.

But Buckwheat and Farina are not self-designated "transvestites" in the most obvious theatrical sense of the term. From a host of examples of deliberate, adult male-to-female cross-dressing in recent popular culture, let us consider three: Flip Wilson's character "Geraldine," "Jackie," a transvestite call "girl" in the 1983 mainstream film *Risky Business,* and "Madame Deborah," a stylish grande dame in a 1947 black film, *Boy! What a Girl!,* before we return to the question of the racial and sexual politics of "transvestism" as a cultural strategy in the mainstreaming of black pop and rock.

Geraldine Jones, who appeared on "The Flip Wilson Show" from 1970 to 1974, was TV's most overt, and best-loved, TV. Clerow ("Flip") Wilson, black television's first major star, was more popular at the time than Bill Cosby, and his choice of a transvestite alter ego for black male identity is not without significance. Many of Geraldine's stock retorts carried with them more than a hint of double entendre or, at the very least, sexual doubletalk: "don't touch me! Don't you ever touch me!," she warned, and "When you're hot, you're hot. When you're not, you're not," and, most memorably from the perspective of the transvestite, *What you see is what you get.*" Sometimes criticized as merely a reprise of the hen-pecking Sapphire on "Amos 'n' Andy," and thus as a stereotyped racial portrait of the dominating black woman, Geraldine, immensely appealing to the viewing public at a time of political militancy among blacks, seems to be at once an advance and a throwback. Wilson was careful to keep Geraldine well dressed, in Pucci prints and colored stockings; he acceded to studio requests that he reduce the size of her bust. Her voice was the voice of Butterfly McQueen, who played the role of a slave in *Gone With the Wind.* But she had a mind of her own. As with Carl Owens in Richard Wright's short story, Flip Wilson achieved "success" by turning himself into a woman. ("Wasn't . . . Geraldine just a ghetto caricature?" Donald Bogle asks, rhetorically, "A transvestite's dream?" [Bogle, *Blacks,* 487–88].)[68]

It is striking that all of Wilson's show business breaks came at moments when he was cross-dressed, starting with his stage debut at the age of nine, when he stepped in as understudy for a girl who was to play Clara Barton in the school play. The turning point in his career was his appearance on the *Tonight Show* with Johnny Carson in 1965; he broke up the audience with a sketch about a black woman buying a wig, who asks the salesperson for reassurance: "You sure it don't make me look too Polish?" After the first attempt at a Wilson TV special flopped in 1968, he introduced Geraldine as an airline stewardess on his 1969 NBC special, playing in tandem with white comedian Jonathan Winters, wearing a gray wig, as "Maude Frickert." And one of his most popular sketches involved Columbus's discovery of America—a sketch in which he plays both Queen Isabella (a.k.a. Queen Isabel Johnson), eager to fund the voyage once she learns that America is the place to find Ray Charles, and a "West Indian maiden" who informs the hapless "Chris Columbus" that the natives don't want to be discovered.[69]

"Geraldine is an attitude," Wilson told an interviewer. "Flip Wilson might hold back on saying something but Geraldine will jump down your throat" (*Ebony,* 182). In effect the black male comedian was here empowered by his female double. "Geraldine" could speak when "Flip Wilson" deemed it prudent to remain silent; she could get away with things that were still transgressive for him.

Yet the implications for both women and blacks were complex and disturbing. Wilson may have believed, as he said, that Geraldine's success indicated his rapport with both sexes (and, by implication, both races), but the kind of "success" involved in a black male comedian's impersonation of an assertive and flamboyant black woman as a vehicle for his own professional and economic liberation repeated as many patterns as it reversed. Nonetheless, Wilson's success as a television star was indubitable, and a breakthrough for black comedians; one of the minor ironies of *Time* magazine's 1972 cover story on him was a quotation from Bill Cosby, described as someone "whose own show on NBC never achieved high ratings and lasted only two seasons" (*Time,* 57). "Geraldine," the transvestite in her wig and Puccis, opened the door for blacks to mainstream TV comedy.

But this was television. In the movies, the figure of the black female transvestite or female impersonator is still highly charged, and, in white-produced films, the charge is almost always negative. Everything that Geraldine is not: marginal, promiscuous, larcenous, physically threatening—marks the place of the transvestite in middle-class, middle-of-the-road movie theaters. Thus, for example, in *Risky Business* (1983), a film produced by whites for largely white audiences about privileged high school students in an all-white suburb, the specter of black transvestism disrupts, if only for a moment, the hero's adolescent fantasy of sexual initiation. Tom Cruise plays Joel *Goodson* (the name is indicative of the role), a teenager in Glencoe, a wealthy lakeside suburb of Chicago. When his parents leave him home alone while they go off on a vacation, Joel's friend dials the number of a call girl, "Jackie."

We see Jackie getting out of the taxi in Joel's driveway; only her long legs, their taut calves encased in pink tights, and her stiletto heels are visible. Cruise comes down the staircase when the doorbell rings—first pausing to check his hair in a mirror—and opens the door, revealing Jackie, in a blond wig and low cut dress. She is, in fact, a black male transvestite.

The credits list a male actor, Bruce A. Young, in the role, but the screenplay never explicitly identifies her as a man in drag, so that Joel's consternation becomes all the funnier because it is never verbalized. Jackie—whose own name now takes on an ambivalent resonance somewhere between "Robinson" and "Onassis"—offers a clue about her gender as well as her race. Agreeing amiably to accept a financial settlement rather than the expected sexual encounter, she endorses the view that you should get what you pay for. "When you buy a *TV,* you don't buy a Sony when you want RCA." Jackie, the black "TV," is the antithesis of the white teenager's dream.

A comic figure but at the same time a figure of pathos, Jackie marks out the film's self-chosen limits of gender, class, and race. In *Risky Business* the presence of the black transvestite in what is essentially a "cameo" role both destabilizes and frames the classic American fantasy tale of the white youth coming to manhood. Without a clear consciousness of doing so, this mainstream film records—and attempts to set aside—a cultural fear so deeply ingrained that it can only be presented in the form of a joke.

This image of the black man in drag as a figure of sexual excess, however comically deployed in a mainstream comedy like *Risky Business,* recalls the racialist eugenics of the turn of the century, when drag balls for blacks (often attended by curious white audiences) were cited by physicians as a sign of degeneracy and biological "erotomania." In an essay describing "An Organization of Colored Erotopaths" a St. Louis nerve and mental disease specialist described in 1893 a "sable performance of sexual perversion" in which all the men "are lasciviously dressed in womanly attire . . . and deport themselves as women," and in which "the naked queen (a male)" stood or sat on a pedestal, "his phallic member, decorated with a ribbon, . . . subject to the gaze and osculations in turn of all the members of this lecherous gang of sexual perverts and phallic fornicators."[70] Even though the author of this study later acknowledged that "white degenerates" as well as blacks could be found at such occasions, and that, in fact, blacks were *less* likely ("in [his] own personal observation") to be homosexual than "white males or white females," the allegations of "perversion" stood.[71]

Here once again the double bind of the black man as excessively (hetero)sexually active and feminized or homosexual is represented as some version of cultural "fact." What seems also to be revealed in this rather prurient "scientific" account is the overdetermination of the phallus, both as a signifier for the fantasy hypersexuality of black men in the eyes and minds of white observers, and as the demystifying gesture, the familiar punch line, of a certain genre of transvestite theater. When this gesture of reassurance, which has a certain context within the semiotics of drag, was conflated with white sexual fantasies about black men's bodies and appetites, the result was "proof" of erotomania.

For black men in Hollywood films explicit drag roles have been proliferating, a reflection both of the ambivalence about gays and lesbians in black culture and of the ambivalence about black males in white culture. As critic David Frechette noted in *Black Film Review,* "Hollywood has consistently treated the Black gay character as a mammie/buddy, an almost always finger-snapping queen whose entire presence is defined by hilarity."[72] "Auntie Tom" roles conflate misogyny and homophobia in what is, in some circles, a sure-fire comic formula.

In some circles, but not in others. When we compare *Risky Business* with a "race movie" made by blacks for black audiences, we find that the female impersonator, far from being a threatening impediment to the adolescent love plot, is in fact instrumental to it. In *Boy! What a Girl!* (1947) the false "Madame Deborah," played with verve by Tim Moore, "Amos 'n' Andy" 's Kingfish, becomes the principal, if improbable, object of both romance and sexual desire.

In *Boy! What a Girl!* two handsome young men in Harlem scheme to get investment money from a wealthy Chicago investor so that they can marry his two daughters and pursue their own careers as theater entrepreneurs. A key player in the investment scheme is to be Madame Deborah, who lives in Paris and whom the young men have never met. When Madame Deborah wires that she is delayed, a member of the theater company who specializes in female impersonation is dragooned into playing the part.

Predictably, the Chicago businessman falls in love with "her." When the real Madame Deborah appears, incognito, the plot reaches a crisis which is resolved by the female impersonator's self-revelation, and the real Deborah's rather improbable engagement to the businessman.

The detachable floating signifiers of transvestism and gender impersonation carry much of the comic action. We first meet the false "Madame Deborah," whose name is "Buggsy," when he has yet to don his impersonator's regalia. He is bald, and smokes a cigar. His ample false bosom is the place where he stores both his money and his cigars. As we might expect, in fact, the cigar becomes a comic crux. Does a lady smoke cigars? "Madame Deborah" surprises her suitor by asking for one. The real Madame Deborah, informed airily by her false counterpart that cigars are all the rage for ladies in "gay Paree," chokes when she tries to puff on one. (Like the Princess and the Pea, the "real" woman here reveals her "delicacy.") The unmasking or unveiling of Buggsy as "Madame Deborah" comes when he oversteps his bounds in an excess of artistic zeal and performs a dance in a gauzy tutu and toe shoes. Our last glimpse of him shows him still in his tutu, but having doffed his wig, about to put on a pair of trousers and resume his "male" identity.

Boy! What a Girl! presents a black female impersonator who is clearly an actor. Despite his false bosom and wig, Buggsy's "manliness" is never in question, or indeed at issue, although the presence in the plot of a foppish and ineffectual Frenchman (one of Madame Deborah's other suitors) displaces the theme of "effeminacy" onto an adjacent national stereotype. The tutu and dancing shoes are a cultural quotation of the "wench" in the minstrel show, here played in the manner of the Funny Old Gal, for both knowing and innocent laughs.

But this "race movie" tells the story of the paradoxical and temporary empowerment of the black-man-as-woman *and* of the black-woman-as-man, the story of *both* Madame Deborahs, one in drag, the other, despite her failure of the cigar test, the financial power behind the scenes. The companionable scene in which the two Deborahs sit side-by-side on a couch and have a sisterly chat (and a smoke) is one of the most attractive moments in the film. In a sense the two are one: the false "Madame Deborah," homely, comic, resourceful, and male, is the flip side of the "real" Madame Deborah, rich, shrewd, and beautiful, who nonetheless responds to the last-minute marriage proposal of the crude and comic businessman in a way a modern audience can only find dismaying. The engagement is *her* unmasking, the revelation that this self-assured and witty woman somehow needs a man, virtually any man. Both Deborahs lack something, or rather, think they do: the film's deliberate equation of what they lack with the ubiquitous cigar says less about putatively "phallic" women than it does about the power of impersonation, and its limits.

Black-owned and black-produced art has come a long way since *Boy! What a Girl!,* but the political implications of this particular story about the transvestite as at once parodic and empowered are no less relevant now than they were in 1947. Transvestism in black popular culture has crossed over into the mainstream. By 1984 formerly "feminine" or gay fashions, like the pierced ear with a single earring, had been mainstreamed for black men enough to be featured on an episode of "The Cosby Show," where Cliff Huxtable's son Theo sports an earring in order to attract a girlfriend. (This is also a matter of the wheel coming full circle, of a much earlier male style dating from the Renaissance crossing back over from women to men.) The gender-bending of white pop and rock stars in the seventies and eighties was greatly indebted to earlier black gender crossover, like the falsetto voice which characterized some black male singing styles in the fifties, and which was itself impersonated, with enormous success (artistic and financial) by Elvis Presley.

But the theatrical self-construction of contemporary superstars, black and white, owes a particular debt to one remarkable entertainer, Richard Penniman, "Little Richard," who became as famous for his extravagant clothing, makeup and pompadour—and for his gay and bisexual lifestyle—as for his unsurpassed contribution to rock and roll music. Billed as the "King of the Blues" and later as the "King of Rock 'n' Roll," he added, remembers arranger Johnny Otis, "and the Queen, too!"[73] (White, 36). In the early fifties, when Little Richard began performing, makeup and glitter were alike unknown for mainstream performers, and gay assertiveness would normally have seemed a barrier to stardom. But, as Richard is careful to point out, his gay persona was an effective distraction from his race. "We were breaking through the racial barrier," he observes.

> The white kids had to hide my records cos they daren't let their parents know they had them in the house. We decided that my image should be crazy and way-out so that the adults would think I was harmless. I'd appear in one show dressed as the Queen of England and in the next as the pope. (White, 66)

This is an unusually clear exposition of how anxiety can be displaced from one category crisis to another. A corollary of this strategy (which may be hindsight, but was nonetheless effective) was the impersonation by *white* performers, some of them gay, of the transvestic display that Richard had made his own. Elton John, for example, performing as a blues guitarist called Reggie Wright in an act that opened for Richard's band on an English tour, changed his name and his wardrobe virtually on the spot, and decided to make a career playing rock and roll (White, 133).

When Little Richard played Las Vegas in 1968 he was "coming on as 'the bronze Liberace' " (White, 140) promoting his gay image. Elvis Presley stopped by the Aladdin Hotel to catch his act, and the Elvis of the Las Vegas years, as we will see below (Chapter 13), was as influenced by Richard's costumes and makeup as by his musical style and energy. "Covers" of his signature songs, like "Tutti Frutti" and "Long Tall Sally," were recorded by white singers like Pat Boone who made millions on them, but Richard had an enormous following among white audiences; his music was rock and roll, not rhythm and blues. In general the press was so busy discussing his style that race was to a certain extent relegated to second place among his detractors' concerns, at a time in history in which segregation was still a fact of life in many southern towns.

Little Richard's transvestism was more than just an adventitious posture or a publicity stunt in these cultural transactions. His own vitality as a performer derived in part from the outrageousness of his outfits, the capes, the blouse shirts, the sequins, the mascara, the conked, oiled pompadour. When he gave up the stage for the pulpit, and began to denounce homosexuality as the devil's work, he declared that he had "cut off [his] crown of hair for a crown of life" (White, 206).

A decade later the pop and rock star Prince, whose most recent biographer sees Little Richard, piled-up hair and all, as "an obvious role-model" for him,[74] became in *Purple Rain* (1984) an eroticized "crossover god/goddess, part black, part white, part male, part female," a "self-indulgent, lost little boy vamp" (Bogle, 171), whose mascara and eyeliner inspired imitation by straight as well as gay young black men.

"Prince," writes Dave Hill, "is a boy who quite likes to be one of the girls." He "rearranged himself into a kind of universal hybrid," with "a knack of delighting the ladies, by rolling [James] Brown's machismo and Richard's effeminacy up together, . . . skittering from one part of the sexual spectrum to the other, with plenty of stops in between." "From Little Richard to David Bowie to Boy George, straight, white record buyers had fallen hopelessly in love with distant, fragile pop icons who broke the gender rules," and Prince was in a position to reap the profits (Hill, 128, 130, 14). Racial stereotyping has here become race-and-gender send-up, controlled by the artist, and deliberately deployed to cross both boundaries and markets.

Manifestly, the characterization of the black transvestite signifies differently in different cases and contexts. Transvestism can be a trickster strategy for outsmarting white oppression, a declaration of difference, a gay affirmative or a homophobic representation. This crossover in gender style is not, of course, limited to African-American culture, but rather, as we have seen, typifies patterns that can be found in Western culture from the medieval period on. But in the representation of black people in novels or films or television or music videos, whether produced by whites or blacks, such gender crossover is especially highly charged, because it represents a kind of "double-cross."[75] "Passing" in African-American culture has, too often, been a matter of life and death. The use of elements of transvestism by black performers and artists as a strategy for economic, political, and cultural achievement—from Richard Wright's "Man of All Work" to Prince, from Ellen Craft, an involuntary actor, to Grace (and Geraldine) Jones, from Farina, the highest paid member of the "Our Gang" company, to Little Richard and Prince—marks the translation of a mode of oppression and stigmatization into a supple medium for social commentary and aesthetic power.

12

THE CHIC OF ARABY: TRANSVESTISM AND THE EROTICS OF CULTURAL APPROPRIATION

In a startling dramatic moment in David Lean's *Lawrence of Arabia* (1962) an Arab chieftain loyal to the old ways confiscates and smashes the camera of an American reporter because he thinks the reporter has captured his image. This incident, which may feel assaultive to the audience imagining itself behind the *other* camera, the movie camera, testifies not only to differences in religious belief, East and West, but also to a historical moment of technological intervention: the moment when the image of T.E. Lawrence, dressed in the flowing skirts of an Arab prince, captured the imagination of the newspaper-reading public.

The photograph is in its material form a "negative," a phantom or ghost, an inverse or inverted image of what it will, when "developed," come to represent. The photograph, in other words, is a "film" that presents itself in order for the viewer to believe that some reality lies *behind* it. Here, indeed, is its specific if figural relevance to Middle Eastern representation: for the photograph is, in these particulars, very like the veil. And it is the veil, a garment that simultaneously conceals and reveals, the material embodiment of the literal striptease, that is the most characteristic adornment of the transvestite of "Araby."

Lawrence once wrote that he adopted the costume of the desert Arabs—skirt, headdress and sandals—at the invitation of his chosen Arab leader, Emir Sherif Feisal, whose regal good looks reminded him of his childhood hero, Richard I, the Lionhearted.[1] "Suddenly Feisal asked me if I would wear Arab clothes like his own while in the camp. I should find it better for my own part, since it was a comfortable dress in which to live Arab-fashion as we must do. Besides, the tribesmen would then understand how to take me."[2]

The robes in which he was originally dressed by his Arab friends were "splendid white and gold-embroidered wedding garments which had been sent to Feisal lately (was it a hint?) by his great-aunt in Mecca" (*Seven Pillars*, 129).[3] In David Lean's superb film, Peter O'Toole, in the title role, cavorts with increasing delight in these white and gold garments, bowing to his shadow in the sun like an Arabian Malvolio, while the troops look on in amused pleasure. Feisal's wedding garments are the costume of a bridegroom, but in

Western translation, as in O'Toole's inspired promenade through the sands, they are emblematically transformed into the white dress and veil of an Occidental bride. Indeed, Lawrence himself returns again, offhandedly but with a characteristic self-irony, to this figure of the wedding dress and its cross-cultural cross-gendering; on the Roman road to Damascus, he reports, "Rain came and soaked me, and then it blew fine and freezing till I crackled in armour of white silk, like a theatre knight; or like a bridal cake, hard iced" (*Seven Pillars*, 508).

Throughout *Seven Pillars of Wisdom* Lawrence reports, again not without a certain pleasure, that British army officers repeatedly either snickered or sneered at his costume, finding it not only offensively "Oriental" but (what may have seemed the same thing) feminizing. Arriving at Suez with the astounding news of the capture of Akaba, he was first given the cold shoulder at the Sinai Hotel because of his dress, and challenged as to his military and national identity: "they looked at my bare feet, white silk robes, and gold head–rope and dagger. Impossible!" (*Seven Pillars*, 327)

In his account of his first encounter with General Allenby, Lawrence reports with amused self-regard that the General, although adapting rapidly to less traditional modes of warfare, "was hardly prepared for anything so odd as myself—a little barefooted silk-skirted man" (*Seven Pillars*, 33). Later, as he is supervising the long-overdue cleansing of the fetid Turkish hospital at Damascus, "a medical major strode up and asked me shortly if I spoke English. With a brow of disgust for my skirts and sandals he said, 'You're in charge?' Modestly, I smirked that in a way I was, and then he burst out, 'Scandalous, disgraceful, outrageous, ought to be shot. . . .' " (*Seven Pillars*, 682)

What is noteworthy in all of these instances is not so much the narrow imaginations of the expatriate English as it is Lawrence's own almost sensual delight in both his appearance and their consternation. In Lean's film this is underscored by the fact that the scandalized major shortly encounters Lawrence once again at military headquarters, this time dressed in orthodox army garb, and begs the honor of shaking his hand. Asked drily by Lawrence whether they haven't met before, he fulsomely replies, "Oh, no, sir. I should remember *that*!"

To the Arab troops, however, Lawrence was a unique figure of a different kind, and also in part because of his costume. That the whiteness of his garments was part of their symbolic allure is evident from his account of his bodyguards, who "dressed like a bed of tulips, in every colour but white; for that was my constant wear, and they did not wish to seem to presume" (*Seven Pillars*, 475). "My clothes and appearance were peculiar in the desert," he reports with some pride. "It was notoriety to be the only cleanshaven one, and I doubled it by wearing always the suspect pure silk, of the whitest (at least outside), with a gold and crimson Meccan head-rope, and gold dagger. By so dressing I staked a claim which Feisal's public consideration of me confirmed."

What is the claim he here boasts of staking? Not only—I want to suggest—that of the English Arab chieftain, the Western prince of the desert, the white-skinned Arab soldier—but also that of Feisal's chosen, the clean-shaven Englishman whom, long ago, the Prince had dressed in wedding clothes.

Lawrence recalls in *The Seven Pillars of Wisdom* an intimate scene in Feisal's retreat at Aba el Lisan. The two men having discussed at leisured length "histories, tribes, migration, sentiments, the spring rains, pasture," Lawrence happens to mention that Allenby has given them the magnificent gift of two thousand camels, the means of victory. "Feisal gasped and caught my knee saying, 'How?' I told him all the story. He leaped up and kissed me." When Lawrence remarks that after the victory he can leave them, Feisal "protested, saying that I must remain with them always" (*Seven Pillars*, 541–42). The "magnificent gift" bestowed, paternally, by a superior officer; the grasp of the knee; the kiss—these iconographic indicators of fellowship are presented in a style at once artless and compelling. He wears, by design and designation, a costume based on wedding clothes intended for Feisal; he brings with him as Allenby's gift (a kind of "dowry") a vast number of camels, priceless contributions to the war effort; Feisal expresses the wish to have Lawrence remain with them (him) always. Lawrence seems oblivious to the iconography of marriage here, but its multiple inscription calls attention to itself repeatedly. Indeed, his own blindness to this recurrent thematic of his narrative adds to the sense of unwitting self-revelation that is a constant textual effect of his prose, and part of its considerable seductive power.

Lawrence's sexual ambivalences are clearly expressed throughout his memoirs, and have been much commented upon by biographers.[4] In his admiration for the "Eastern boy and boy affection which the segregation of women made inevitable," friendships that "often led to manly loves of a depth and force beyond our flesh-steeped conceit," and in which, "If sexuality entered, they passed into a give and take, unspiritual relation, like marriage," he idealizes the male companionships of the desert, describing one of his youthful servants as the "love-fellow" of the other, kneeling in appeal, "all the woman of him evident in the longing" (*Seven Pillars*, 244). And in his report of the confrontation at Der'a with the Turkish Bey, whose homosexual advances he spurned, he describes the experience of "a delicious warmth, probably sexual, . . . swelling through me" (*Seven Pillars*, 454) in the midst of the savage beating administered by the Bey's men.

His faltering confession of his pleasure at the hands of his torturers at Der'a marks a key turning point in *Lawrence of Arabia*, as it does in John Mack's psychologically compelling biography. Lawrence's discovery of sexual pleasure in the infliction of pain led to the elaborate arrangements for flagellation at the behest of an imaginary "uncle," who was punishing him for equally imaginary crimes: actually, for Lawrence's own guilt at his masochistic pleasure. The beatings he had sustained at the hands of his mother, whom he adored, the fact that he and his four brothers were illegitimate sons of a British peer—these may have played a part in opening his sensory responsiveness to the allure of pain and discipline. The ineluctable cycle of pleasurable punishment, guilt, punishment for that guilt, pleasure in the punishment, guilt again, and so on, dominated his final years.[5]

Like many exceptional and brilliant individuals, Lawrence's personal power came also from a sense of personal limitation; swerving, in effect, to avoid the "normal" social world of his Oxford upbringing, he displaced his enormous energies onto other, more global and more exotic realms where the family romance could be deployed to political as well as personal ends.[6]

For the adult Lawrence of *Seven Pillars* women occupy only a marginal and mysterious role. In a letter to a friend in the House of Commons he later wrote, "Women? I like some women. I don't like their sex: any more than I like the monstrous regiment of men. There is no difference that I feel between a woman and a man."[7] This offhand evocation of John Knox's Reformation-era tirade against women in authority (*The First Blast of the Trumpet against the Monstrous Regiment of Women*, 1558) will suggest something of the pressures Lawrence felt himself to be under in a world of sexuality and sociability. Without question, he was more comfortable with men than with women, and with "the plain man" rather than "the elaborated man," describing the sexual lives of such "plain men" (here, English soldiers in barracks), significantly, in terms of costume: "Sex, with them, is something you put on (and take off) with your walking-out dress: on Friday night, certainly: and if you are lucky on Saturday afternoon, and most of Sunday. Work begins on Monday again, and is really important."[8]

Throughout his life he seems to have been most comfortable in societies of men (his four brothers; his all-male school; his fellow archaeologists on a dig at Carchemis in Turkey; his army companions; his Arab associates). In this context, his own assumption of Arab dress, the white, flowing robes and gold headdress prescribed for him by Feisal, at once the sign of a warrior prince and a bride, paradoxically manly, even heroic, despite (or because of) his silk skirts—all this seems a mode of self-expression for Lawrence. He sees himself as at once self-demonstrative and self-denigrating, an apt guise for a complicated man who could write that he "liked the things underneath me and took my pleasures and adventures downward. There seemed a certainty in degradation, a final safety" (*Seven Pillars*, 581).

It is intriguing, in light of his later involvement with conventions of dress that cross boundaries of culture, gender, and class, to note that T.E. Lawrence's one attempt at a conventional male-female relationship itself began with a scene of cross-dressing. His one proposal of marriage—to a woman who would reject him in favor of his younger brother, and marry someone else when that brother was killed in the War—was made to an early childhood friend whom he initially mistook for a boy.

Janet Laurie had been the Lawrences' neighbor from 1894 to 1896, and later was sent to boarding school in Oxford to be near them. She and Lawrence saw a great deal of one another when he was an undergraduate, but the basis of their affection was begun in childhood. She was a tomboy, and he tended to tease her for "not being a boy" (Mack, 64). Laurie's own account of their first meeting, as recorded by John Mack, offers a fascinating point of entry into this scenario of courtship and misprision: "Her parents had wanted another son and so kept her hair short and dressed her like a boy. She was in church, and behind her were two or three Lawrence brothers with their nanny, Florence Messham. She heard one of the boys, who proved to be Ned, say to Miss Messham, 'What a naughty little boy to keep his hat on in church.' She turned around and put out her tongue and said, 'I'm not a boy, I'm a girl.' She overheard Miss Messham ('I took a great dislike to her') say, 'Well, she may not be a little boy, but she's a very rude little girl.' Thus the friendship began."[9]

So it seems that T.E. Lawrence's one serious attempt at a heterosexual relationship, the failure of which, some of his friends and biographers maintain, enforced his decision to live asexually among men, began in a moment of childhood cross-dressing and the misreading of children's dress codes. The one woman to whom Lawrence proposed was a woman he first met when she was dressed like a boy.

The *figure* of dress plays an important role, rhetorically as well as imaginatively, in Lawrence's writing. We have seen that he refers to sex, and sexual desire, as "something you put on (and take off) with your walking-out dress"—if you are so lucky as to be, unlike Lawrence himself, a "plain man." At another moment he speaks eagerly of a key meeting with superior officers, including Allenby, as an opportunity for "seeing the undress working of a general's mind" (*Seven Pillars*, 553). That he is *in* costume—that his robes are both naturalized and masquerade—is a constant theme of his letters to friends. "It's a kind of foreign stage, on which one plays day and night, in fancy dress," he wrote to an old Oxford schoolmate. "You want apparently some vivid colouring of an Arab's costume, or of a flying Turk, and we have it all, for that is part of the mise en scène. . . . Disguises and prices on one's head, and fancy exploits are all part of the pose."[10]

Lawrence's flair for self-theatricalization, his self-conscious awareness of his "silk-skirt[s]" and "fancy dress," are evident in the photographs of him taken in that period. Yet "I loathe the notion of being celluloided," he later wrote to Robert Graves. "My rare visits to cinemas always deepen in me a sense of their superficial falsity. . . . The camera seems wholly in place in journalism: but when it tries to re-create it boobs and sets my teeth on edge. So there won't be a film of me."[11] This spectacularly false prediction records his success at persuading Alexander Korda to abandon plans for a projected film of Lawrence's life.

It was Lowell Thomas who popularized the Lawrence legend in New York and London, Thomas who concocted the film-and-lecture shows that made "Lawrence of Arabia" a household name in the U.S. in 1919 even before he was celebrated in Britain. Lawrence was, characteristically, ambivalent about Thomas's glorification of him, and though he initially collaborated with the publicity effort, he came to resent it, calling Thomas "vulgar," a popularizer who indulged in "red-hot lying."[12]

He wrote to a man named Greenhill whom he had known in the desert campaign in Saudi Arabia, "For Lowell Thomas: I don't bear him any grudge. He has invented some silly phantom thing, a sort of matinee idol in fancy dress, that does silly things and is dubbed 'romantic.' Boy scouts and servants love it."[13] Boy scouts and servants; the class inflection, self-ironized, here underscores Lawrence's ambivalence toward his own "phantom" personae as officer and enlisted man. After the war he sent a letter to another acquaintance, disclaiming the heroics with which Lowell Thomas had credited him: "Only I was in fancy dress, & so I made a good 'star' for his film."[14] And to E. M. Forster, who had taken on the task of reviewing Thomas's book *With Lawrence in Arabia*, he wrote to correct the author's "rubbish," which he dismissed as "either invention or gossip": "I was never disguised as an Arab (though I once got off as a Circassian & nearly got on as a veiled woman!)" (*Selected Letters,* 283).

This tantalizing glimpse of a deliberately cross-dressed Lawrence, who "nearly got on as a veiled woman," remains itself a phantom, hovering at the margins of the legend. But the matinee idol, the "star," the European hero in Eastern "fancy dress," ambivalently sexual, masochistic, full of controlled violence: *this* phantom of the chic of Araby would be "celluloided," over and over again, in the years that immediately followed Lowell Thomas's famous footage of the Palestinian campaigns. The celebrity of Lawrence, the spectacular success of his story, that played to packed houses at Madison Square Garden in New York City in the spring of 1919, and the Royal Opera House in Covent Garden in the fall of the same year, itself contributed to the vogue for romantic films about "Arabia" that swept the U.S. in the twenties. In many ways Lawrence is the phantom presence behind the figure of the Western aristocrat in exotic "fancy dress," the sheik of Araby. And the incarnation of that fantasy was to be found in the spectacular success of an Italian-born actor, dressed in Arab robes, on the Hollywood screen.

RADICAL SHEIK

No single figure in the history of film has been more closely identified with passionate eroticism than Rudolph Valentino, whose appearance as Ahmed Ben Hassan in *The Sheik* (1921) set off a frenzy of response among (largely female) filmgoers. The story of the sheik's abduction of Lady Diana Mayo, whom he plucks from her horse and carries off to his tent, is full of the cartoon-like energy of sexual sadism. "Lie still, you little fool," the Sheik tells Lady Diana, and when she asks "Why have you brought me here?," he sneers, "Are you not woman enough to know?" The fantasy of abduction-turned-to-passionate-love in the desert made Valentino a star, and a love god.

Sheet-music vendors seized the moment to popularize *The Sheik of Araby*, Sheik fashions were worn by both women and men, men slicked their hair with Vaseline, and, in the sincerest form of flattery, imitation Sheik films quickly followed: *Arabian Love* starring John Gilbert, *Arab* with Ramon Navarro, and *Song of Love* with Edmund Carewe. "Shriek—For the Sheik Will Seek You Too!" invited the posters for Valentino's film, making sure audiences knew how to pronounce the new term—which promptly entered the dictionary with a second, slang meaning of "romantically alluring man" to second the original "Moslem religious official" and "leader of an Arab family, village, or tribe."[15]

The association of Valentino's role with unbridled sexual passion continues today in the merchandizing of an appropriate tie-in product: the Sheik condom, now available in a number of styles—traditional Non-Lubricated Sheik (with the picture of a brooding Mediterranean-handsome man in halftones on the box), Ribbed Sheik, Sheik Elite, and— the cross-dresser's special—new She's Sheik, still presumably to be worn by a male, but with larger-print warnings about the prevention of pregnancy and disease to recommend it to the prudent female customer.

One of the most curious, and yet predictable, features of *The Sheik*'s screenplay—based on a near-pornographic novel by an Englishwoman, Edith M. Hull, writing under the unisex initials E.M.—was that the Sheik himself turned out, in the course of the plot, not to be an Arab at all, but a Scot—in fact, the Earl of Glencarryl, a Scottish nobleman, who had been abandoned in the Sahara as a baby. This fortunate turn of events "legitimized" the relationship between Lady Diana and the Sheik, transforming an intended rape into a suitable love match; the family romance again, as so often, prevented interracial mixture, and preserved the honor of the "white" race. At the close of the film the lovers are en route "back to civilization on their honeymoon," according to *Exhibitors Trade Review*, which carried a synopsis of the plot.[16] A similar romance plot is found in Edgar Rice Burroughs's *Tarzan*, where the hero is discovered to be "really" Lord Greystoke— and, not incidentally, in the story of T.E. Lawrence, "Lawrence of Arabia," the illegitimate son of Sir Thomas Chapman. Thus Valentino (born Rodolpho Guglielmi) as Sheik Ahmed had all the advantages of desert attire, including a dazzling tan, a curving scimitar, and (incongruously but crucially) a cigarette holder, without the necessity of a correlative racial inferiority.

The sequel, *Son of the Sheik* (1926), based on Hull's book *Sons of the Sheik* but conflating the two "sons" in one—Valentino, who also played his own father in the film, thus rendering himself self-authored and doubly irreplaceable—adds elements of masochism to the already heady erotic brew. At one point Valentino is stripped to the waist and beaten (here we might recall the torture scene in *Lawrence of Arabia*, and Lawrence's own elaborately staged private beatings). The main plot involves, again, an abduction, but this time motivated by revenge rather than by love. His lovemaking, clearly as much desired as feared by his captive (Vilma Banky), is calculatedly cruel and explicitly misogynistic: as he lights his inevitable cigarette and strips off his robe and jeweled belt, he tells her, "All the beauties of the Arabian Nights being unveiled could not get a look from me."

In a famous still photo from *The Sheik*, Valentino's cigarette holder is counterposed by a revolver held in the hand of Agnes Ayres, as Lady Diana; the tacit switch of power tools underscores the riskiness of gender semiotics out of which the Sheik crafts his particular sexual appeal. Valentino's clean-shaven, boyish face, like his cigarette holder, became objects of defensive scorn for many self-identified "red-blooded-American-male" moviegoers, and sexual magnets for women—as well as for some men. As for Lady Diana, she is not just any old captive woman, but a militant feminist (again, see the gun) in pants. Once abducted by Ahmed, however, she quickly changes her tune, and her clothes, replacing her riding breeches with a skirt at his behest. Hull's novel describes her outfit and her sexual situation with lavish precision:

> Diana's eyes passed over him slowly till they arrested on his brown, clean-shaven face, surmounted by crisp, close-cut brown hair. It was the handsomest and the cruellest face that she had ever seen. Her gaze was drawn instinctively to his. He was looking at her with fierce burning eyes that swept her until she felt that the boyish clothes that covered her slender limbs were stripped from her, leaving her beautiful white body bare under his passionate stare. She shrank back, quivering, dragging the lapel of her riding jacket together over her breast with clutching hands, obeying an impulse that she hardly understood. "Who are you?" she gasped hoarsely.
> "I am the Sheik Ahmed Ben Hassan . . ."

Theorists of the gaze need look no further for its transfixing role in early film. *The Sheik* picked up on these plain hints, to foreground the elements of gender- and wardrobe-switching (Valentino in robes, Agnes Ayres in jodhpurs, both in eyebrow pencil and mascara), and added a spice of Middle Eastern pederasty—disclaimed, of course, by the closet-Scots hero. "You make a charming boy," the Sheik declares [and here the camp resonances of "boy" are to a modern audience unmistakable], "but it was not a boy I saw in Biskra."[17] The association of Araby with homoeroticism and boy love here has come full circle, as the "Lady" in pants displaces the "boy" as the object, at least the overt object, of the culturally cross-dressed, apparently "Oriental" Sheik's desire.[18]

TURKISH TROUSERS

> It is a strange fact but a true one, that up to this moment she had scarcely given her sex a thought. Perhaps the Turkish trousers which she had hitherto worn had done something to distract her thoughts.
> —Virginia Woolf, *Orlando*[19]

Orlando's transmutation from man to woman, which occurs in Virginia Woolf's narrative during the reign of Charles II, is enabled, sartorially speaking, by the costume of the country. As Ambassador of Great Britain at the Court of the Sultan in Constantinople, Orlando had dressed in Turkish style (though Woolf also endows him with that consummate originary sign of *English* cross-dress, the Order of the Garter). When the transformation takes place, overnight ("He stretched himself. He rose. . . . he was a woman" [*Orlando*, 97]), what remains *constant* for Orlando is not her *gender*, but her *clothes*.
The vogue for Turkish trousers, extremely ample in cut, and worn in Turkey by men

as well as women, became a fact of English women's fashion with the opening of trade and travel to the Middle East. Orlando's fictional Embassy to the Porte was, in the period 1716–1718, actually held by Edward Wortley Montagu, whose wife, Lady Mary, adopted the style with characteristic enthusiasm. As a woman, Lady Mary could enter into societies closed to men, and her visit to the Turkish baths is described in a number of remarkable letters, one of which more than a hundred years later influenced Ingres's painting *Le Bain Turc*.

At first Lady Mary attended the luxurious baths—five imposing domes of marble, filled with hot and cold fountains, sofas, cushions, and rich carpets—in her "travelling habit, which is a riding dress, and certainly appeared very extraordinary to them," especially, perhaps, because all the Turkish women were naked. The baths, which served as "the women's coffeehouse, where all the news of the town is told, scandal invented, etc." seem also to have been a locus of a kind of social democracy, since without clothing class indicators were, apparently, entirely lacking. On the sofas she saw "ladies, and on the second their slaves behind 'em, but without any distinction of rank by their dress, all being in the state of nature, that is, in plain English, stark naked."

Nonetheless Lady Mary was able to discern a kind of rank, since she reports that "the lady that seemed the most considerable amongst them" entreated her to undress and sit beside her, and her protests were unavailing until "I was at last forced to open my skirt and show them my stays, which satisfied 'em very well, for I saw that they believed I was so locked up in that machine that it was not in my own power to open it, which contrivance they attributed to my husband."[20] This naive concept she appears to have found amusing, although two sentences later she gives it a kind of credence, regretting that, although she wished to spend more time in the company of these Turkish ladies, she could not, since her husband was determined to pursue his journey the next morning, and she was forced to abridge her visit in order to go with him.

On the same day, April 1, 1717, she wrote to her sister, Lady Mar, a description of herself "in my Turkish habit," supplying full particulars, even though she intended to send a picture—i.e., a portrait—later.

> The first piece of my dress is a pair of drawers, very full, that reach to my shoes and conceal the legs more modestly than your petticoats. They are of a thin, rose-colored damask brocaded with silver flowers, my shoes of white kid leather embroidered with gold. Over this hangs my smock of a fine white silk gauze edged with embroidery. This smock has wide sleeves hanging half-way down the arm and is closed at the neck with a diamond button, but the shape and colour of the bosom very well to be distinguished through it. The *antery* [i.e., entari] is a waistcoat made close to the shape, of white and gold damask, with very long sleeves falling back and fringed with deep gold fringe.[21]

Half a dozen other details complete this toilette, which, though entirely feminine, is also virtually identical to the items worn by men, as Lady Mary's "translations" into an English sartorial lexicon—drawers, smock, waistcoat—make clear.

What Lady Mary is at special pains to point out to her sister, however, is the way in which the "perpetual masquerade" of the Turkish ladies makes sexual indiscretion not only possible, but undetectable. " 'Tis very easy to see that they have more liberty than we have." Since all Turkish women must wear two veils (or "muslins") and an item "not unlike a riding hood" whenever they go out into the streets, they are entirely unrecognizable. "You may guess how effectually this disguises them, that there is no distinguishing the great lady from her slave, and 'tis impossible for the most jealous husband to know his wife when he meets her" ("To Lady Mar," 111). Here is a characteristic paradox: the veiled Moslem women are capable of more flagrant transgressions than their less conforming English sisters. In the meantime, Lady Mary enjoys the freedom her "drawers" confer—a freedom as much psychological as actual, a sign of her participation in the "masquerade"—at a time, incidentally, when masquerade in England was all the rage, and the occasion for transgressions of gender boundaries as well as of station and rank. Masquerade was both "an intensely self-absorptive state of fantasy" and a cultural institution that allowed participation in "the anonymous collectivity of masks."[22] If it had this function in England, how much more intensive was the possibility of a "private vision of otherness" (Castle, 72) half a world away, in Constantinople? It is perhaps no accident that, in choosing an apt quotation to describe the morals of the Turkish women, Lady Mary elects to speak in the voice of Harlequin: "Tis just as 'tis with you" ("To Lady Mar," 111).

The billowing full-length "pair of drawers" has been in fashion with women intermittently ever since as "Turkish trousers" or "harem pants." Where Lady Mary seems to see her new "habit" as liberating as well as alluring, allowing both modest concealment and ease of movement (as contrasted with the "machine" of stays in which she was previously "locked up"), twentieth-century harem pants, as the name implies, suggest the aura of sexual fantasy in a male-centered culture. In effect, women of the 1950's donned "Turkish habits" to offer men the illusion of themselves as sultans, although the "dancing girls" of Araby—as we will shortly see—were very likely to have been boys.

But the leap from 1717 to 1950 passes over a period of particular interest in the history of "Turkish trousers" as a sign of women's independence, and of the reconfiguration of gender roles through the interposition of certain fantasy structures derived simultaneously from colonial dreams and colonial fears. On the British and American stage, in the years between Mrs. Siddons and Sarah Bernhardt, Aladdin was a favorite role for actresses, like Mrs. Charles Kemble and Mrs. Vining, in the tradition of the "Principal Boy" of the pantomime. And a wonderful photograph exists of Madame Celeste as the Wild Arab Boy in *The French Spy*, described in appreciative detail by an admiring modern critic: "As one's eye moves up topographically, it progresses from full Turkish pantaloons to slender waist to rounded bosom peeping archly from barest shoulder; the whole surmounted by a delicate military moustache!"[23] "Topographically" is an interesting choice of adverb here; Madame Celeste herself becomes a Middle Eastern landscape undulating before the gazer's eye, each contradictory gender clue a double sign. Like Aladdin, this "boy" could be read as male and female, "Arab" and European at once. That, indeed, was her charm.

Off the stage, however, the situation was quite different. In the 1850's "Turkish trousers" were introduced as liberating wear for American women. In 1851 Amelia Bloomer, owner and editor of the reform newspaper *The Lily*, introduced the Bloomer Costume, consisting of a short dress and Turkish trousers, as fashion wear for independently-minded women. Clothing reform was a long-standing issue among the social reformers of the period; the wasp waist and long flowing skirt then in style impeded breathing and scooped up mud and water from the streets, at least according to the reformers. By April 1851 Mrs. Bloomer had herself appeared in the costume that was subsequently to bear her name.

As an innovation, unfortunately, the Bloomer Costume ranks with the Susan B. Anthony silver dollar; only a few convinced individuals, and some utopian communities, adopted the style. The "Turkish" connotations attracted some unfavorable attention, despite the rage for artifacts *à la Turque* in style and home decoration. Some critics branded the costumes heathenish because of their association with Islam; a writer to the *New York Tribune* pointed out the lack of freedom of Middle Eastern women compared to Americans, and suggested that the spectacle of female reformers in Turkish trousers was properly a cause for cultural irony. Here we have the obverse of Lady Mary's observations about the freedom of "perpetual masquerade"—or rather, what *appears* to be the obverse; the *Tribune*'s correspondent in fact deploys American self-satisfaction with the (pre-feminist) status quo as a way of disempowering women in pants.

American dress reformer Mary Walker, who herself favored men's formal dress for its relative comfort and hygiene (compared to long skirts), wrote approvingly of Turkish trousers—in Turkey—as a boon to "women's physical being."

> In Turkey, the fact is recognized, that the women's limbs are flesh and blood, as well as the men's, and are therefore susceptible to the influences of the weather and need to be well protected; and hence the custom of the sexes dressing nearly alike. Those who would find fault with the men of that country, for *allowing* the women to dress like them, (instead of wearing our most fashionable clothes, or rather those of Paris), would immediately be credited with weak or bad motives.[24]

One particular nineteenth-century female reformer, however, perhaps best exemplifies the complex cultural transactions of Turkish costume with European sensibilities about gender and gender roles. I want therefore to turn next to a story about the French socialist and feminist Flora Tristan, which will point up not only the tensions around gender, costume, and nationality ("our most fashionable clothes, or rather those of Paris"), but also the way in which one set of racial or ethnic prejudices can be seen to underlie and be masked by another.

When Flora Tristan visited London in the 1830's she was appalled to find that the

House of Commons, "a body which claims to represent the *whole* nation . . . and which goes down upon its knees to receive the orders of a queen," refused to admit women to its chambers. Accordingly she sought out a male friend, a Tory, and asked him to lend her some men's clothes and take her with him to the sitting. "My proposal," she records, "had the same effect on him as had, in days gone by, sprinkling holy water on the devil! What! Lend men's clothes to a woman and insinuate her into the sanctuary of male power? What an abominable scandal, what depravity, what fearful blasphemy. My friend the Tory turned white with fear, red with indignation, snatched up his hat and stick, rose without a glance in my direction, and declared that he could have nothing more to do with me."[25]

Undeterred, Tristan altered her tactics. Since no Englishman was likely to assist her in her plan, she called on a succession of gentlemen attached to the French, Spanish, and German embassies. Again her proposal was rejected, not for the reasons given by her Tory acquaintance, but out of respect for the customs of the country.

Tristan persisted—she was in general a persistent woman—and ultimately she found a willing accomplice, in the person of "an eminent Turkish gentlemen, sent to London by his government, who," she writes, "not only approved my plan, but helped me carry it out by offering me a complete set of clothes, his admission card, his carriage, and his own amiable company as an escort" (Tristan, 59). On the appointed day, therefore, she repaired to his residence, where she changed into "an elaborate Turkish costume," which was much too big for her, and made her feel uncomfortable, "but he who desires the end must accept the means!" The odd couple, thus accoutered, set out for Parliament, and en route attracted immediate attention. No one seems to have been deceived about her gender. Murmurs rose around her: "The young Turk appears to be a woman," and several ladies, fixing their gaze on her, repeated this: "There's a woman in Turkish clothes!"

Her heart beating violently, Tristan records a feminine blush at this attention, but quickly recovers her calm demeanor, "for such is the influence of costume that, in donning the Turkish turban, I had acquired the serious gravity habitual to the Moslem." She and her host made for the back row, hoping to sit there in quiet anonymity, but rumors pursued her to the gallery. Here Tristan's indignation knew no bounds. For rather than respecting her incognito, they obsessively called attention to it, staring boldly through their lorgnettes, and speaking, for some reason, in French:

> "What is that woman doing in the House?"
> "What reason can she have for attending the session?"
> "She must be French: they have no respect for anything."
> "Such conduct is most improper."
> "The usher should make her leave."

As it turned out, Tristan and her friend had merely chosen the wrong House. When, after an hour, they proceeded across to the House of Lords, they met with a different—

one might say, a more Oriental—response: "There too they guessed my sex. . . . there were some smiles and whispers, but I heard no unseemly or discourteous remarks. I saw that I was in the presence of true gentlemen, tolerant of a lady's whims and even making it a point of honor to respect them" (Tristan, 57–62).

A number of points are worth noting in Tristan's spirited account. She chooses a transnational, trans-cultural disguise as a way of passing as a man, yet she is immediately "read" as a woman; she finds the wearing of Turkish clothing inspires a corresponding "Moslem" demeanor; and, despite her deliberate act of boundary-crossing or trespassing, she is indignant that the Englishmen in the Commons refuse to treat this "young Turk" with all the courtesies due to a Frenchwoman.

What is the place, in this narrative, of the "feminized" male "Oriental"? Would a Turkish man in traditional costume be treated with the same deference (and condescension) as a woman, in the context of Parliament? How did they treat her host? Might it not be argued that the members of the Commons, who see through her and want her ejected for transgressing the rules, are treating her with more gender equality than the Lords, who indulge a lady's whim? "Frenchness" seems here a medial term between English and Turkish; French manners, French political customs, and even the French language are at issue, though the French embassy was among those that refused to accommodate Tristan's request for "cover."

Flora Tristan's experiences with this double masquerade suggest that questions of gender and of nationalism (male/female, English/French) can be addressed, if not resolved, through a recourse to cultural "otherness" as represented by the intervening figure of the phantom "Oriental," the woman in Turkish trousers. The political binarism England-France is disrupted by this "Turkish" interloper, whose gender, not coincidentally, is radically put in question. Nor is it a coincidence that the two colonial powers who looked with such desire upon the Middle East should be again at odds when it comes to the sartorial politics of Middle Eastern gender.

DISPLACED PERSONS

In 1809, when Byron and his Cambridge friend John Cam Hobhouse set out on an Eastern journey that was to include Albania, Greece, and Turkey, they were warmly received by the famous Ali Pasha, a homosexual ruler who kept a court of handsome youths from whom he selected his officers, and whose grandsons, Byron wrote, "have painted complexions like rouged dowagers."[26] In Constantinople, among the Turks, the two men went to watch transvestite boy dancers in the coffeehouses.[27]

Of all the English writers who traveled to the Middle East, none found more literary pleasure in the tease of transvestism than George Gordon, Lord Byron. Byron's interest in the world of Islam was linked both to his bisexuality and to his fascination with the differing mores of the East. He was well versed in Turkish history, boasting in 1818 that he had read "Knolles, Cantamir—De Tott—Lady M. W. Montague—Hawkins' translation from Mignot's History of the Turks—the Arabian Nights—All travels of histories or books upon the East I could meet with . . . before I was *ten years old.*"[28]

Much Islamic poetry of the classical and medieval periods, whether written in Baghdad, Istanbul, Fez, or Seville, celebrates homoerotic passion, and Persian poetry was appearing in English translation in the eighteenth century for the first time. The scholars who brought these Eastern poems to Western eyes were often disparaging about their moral "depravities"; homosexuals in England were being prosecuted and even hanged at an alarming rate, and it was considered appropriate to veil the "unnaturalism" of these ancient affections while preserving the beauty of their expression. Thus in English translation the love objects of these poets were subjected to bowdlerization—were, in effect, transsexualized: as one editor noted with approval, "This disgusting object has, in obedience of decorum, been very properly translated by Sir William Jones . . . into a *damsel,* fair as a nymph of Paradise, by a licence of which we shall be found to have availed ourselves throughout these poems, and, we trust, for reasons too obvious to need any formal apology on our part."[29] Byron would shortly perform a similar act of poetic transsexualization in his elegiac verses, "To Thyrza," mourning the death of his beloved John Edlestone, whom he met when Edlestone was a Cambridge choirboy.[30]

But Byron was intrigued not only by literary and cultural representations of *homoeroticism* but also, quite specifically, by *transvestism*; in a letter to a woman friend describing his attachment to Edlestone in 1807, he had compared their friendship not only to the biblical Jonathan and David, and the Virgilian Nisus and Euryalus, but also to the celebrated contemporary cross-dressers, the "Ladies of Llangollen."[31]

When Byron and Hobhouse commenced their travels, they were excited to find themselves briefly in the same inn as William Beckford, the notorious exiled author of the Gothic novel *Vathek,* and tried in vain to meet him. Beckford's novel, which contained some tacitly homosexual passages, was originally to have been published together with a group of tales that made same-sex eroticism a more explicit theme, including one about an Arab prince who falls in love with a boy who later turns out to be a girl. Hearing about these unpublished "Episodes from Vathek," Byron asked a friend to obtain a copy in manuscript, but Beckford refused his request (Crompton, 122–23).

What literary connections could not secure, however, life would shortly provide. Byron's own amorous adventures were shortly to include a version of this transvestite story, in the guise of the female page familiar from Renaissance drama and prose romance, and recently employed by Sir Walter Scott in his 1808 poem *Marmion.* The celebrity of the handsome young poet attracted the attention of Lady Caroline Lamb, a romantic, free-spirited aristocrat; for two months she and Byron were lovers. As it happens, Lady

Caroline's maiden name was Caroline Ponsonby, and she was a second cousin once removed of Sarah Ponsonby, one of the famous Ladies of Llangollen. Cross-dressing, you might say, was in her family history.

Infatuated by her attentions, Byron rashly confided to Lady Caroline the story of his homosexual relationships in the East, and his affection for a young English boy, Robert Rushton, whom he had taken on as a page, but had sent home before the traveling party reached Turkey, ostensibly out of concern for Rushton's safety among the lecherous Turks. His passion for this young boy was so great that he persuaded Lady Caroline to rename her own page "Rushton."

It is not clear whether Lady Caroline already had knowledge of the Rushton affair when she sat for her own portrait in the costume of a page; either way, as uncanny presage or transvestite tease, the masquerade had its effect, especially when she also appeared in that disguise at Byron's door. She wrote to his valet a letter of instruction that sounds like an erotic scenario, with Lamb here dressed not as mutton but as fatted calf:

> I also want you to take the little Foreign Page I shall send you in to see Lord Byron. Do not tell him before-hand, but, when he comes with flowers, shew him in. I shall not come myself, unless just before he goes away; so do not think it is me.[32]

This plan was evidently put into effect at least once, as a visitor reports that in response to a letter from Byron to Lady Caroline, "the lady's *page* brought him a new letter."

> He was a fair-faced delicate boy of thirteen or fourteen years old, whom one might have taken for the lady herself. . . . I could not but suspect at the time that it was a disguise; if so he never disclosed it to me.[33]

Lady Caroline, woman and "page," was accessible to Byron as an erotic object who personated this fantasy, and represented at once herself—present in his chamber, sexually accessible—and the absent beloved Rushton.

One rumor also held that Byron kept a girl in boy's clothes at Brighton; Thomas Medwin claims in his *Conversations of Lord Byron* that the poet disguised a mistress as his brother Gordon, and a later story, discounted by a recent biographer, would suggest that his half-sister Augusta had accompanied him to Switzerland dressed as a page.[34] The existence of such rumors is in certain ways as interesting as their truth or falsehood, since they mark an area of speculation and intrigue. Byron and his pages—male and female—were to recur in the sexual mythology of the Byron story throughout his life.

Significantly, Byron also wrote a poem in which a male page is revealed to be a girl in disguise—*Lara*, the last of his four Oriental tales of 1813 and 1814. In it the mysterious hero Lara, who has just returned from the East, is threatened with the exposure of an undisclosed secret. Fighting on the popular side of a civil war, he dies in the arms of his page, who bears the Arabic name of Kaled; the true gender of the page is discovered when "he" dies of grief with his master in his arms.

The plot of *Lara*, like the masquerade of the fractious Lady Caroline, offers the same fantasy of transformation achieved by the prudish translators of Oriental homoerotic poetry. The boy page, with blushing cheek and hand "So femininely white it might bespeak/ Another sex, when matched with that smooth cheek" is attractive not so much in the resolution of his gender identity as in the refusal to be resolved. When Kaled is revealed to be a girl she is already dead; alive, he/she is precisely an enigma, neither the one nor the other. Byron's phrase "another sex" here signifies not, or not only, the female identity which is Kaled's ostensible secret, but the condition of cross-dressing itself that makes both/and possible—and desirable. To find the answer to this binary division is to find that the beloved is dead.

In a famous episode in *Don Juan* Byron continues the rhetoric of the alluring, sexually ambiguous male page in a fantasied "Eastern" setting—in fact the Turkey which, he reminds his readers, "charmed the charming Mary [Wortley] Montagu" (Canto 5.3). His hero, Juan is at sixteen "tall, handsome, slender, but well knit . . ./ Active, though not so sprightly as a page," so that "everybody but his mother deemed/ Him almost man" (1.54). The action of the poem moves swiftly from Spain to the Orient, where the captive Juan finds himself purchased by a black eunuch (described as "a black old neutral personage/ Of the third sex" [5.26]) who first tries to persuade Juan to be circumcised, as the Turks are, and then produces a woman's costume for him to wear.[35]

"I offer you a handsome suit of clothes,
    A woman's, true, but then there is a cause
Why you should wear them." "What, though my soul loathes
    The effeminate garb?" Thus after a short pause,
Sighed Juan, muttering also some slight oaths,
    "What the devil shall I do with all this gauze?" . . .

And then he swore, and, sighing, on he slipped
    A pair of trousers of flesh-coloured silk;
Next with a virgin zone he was equipped,
    Which girt a slight chemise as white as milk.
But tugging on his petticoat he tripped,. . . .

And now being femininely all arrayed,
    With some small aid from scissors, paint, and tweezers,
He looked in almost all respects a maid,
    And Baba smilingly exclaimed, "You see, sirs,
A perfect transformation here displayed." (5.73–80)

Since *Don Juan* is structured throughout on the alternation of masculine and feminine rhymes, it perfectly expresses Juan's predicament and the liberated, playful pleasure permitted by slipping into the feminine. Through Juan's naive indignation—expressed through words like "travesty," "effeminate," and "unsexed"—Byron himself travesties or parodies a whole Orientalist tradition of sartorial exchange. Juan's costume sounds enough like Lady Mary Wortley Montagu's by-now-famous "Turkish habit" ("a pair of drawers, very full . . . of a thin, rose-colour damask . . . [a] smock of a fine white silk gauze") to remind the reader of the *double* exchange involved, especially since the reader has been reminded of Lady Mary at the outset. Juan protests against wearing "effeminate garb" because he is being disguised as a woman, but Lady Mary, donning her new habit, is conscious that a Turkish woman wears trousers, smock, and waistcoat—items of clothing that in Europe would describe the wardrobe of a man. Thus Juan, "femininely all arrayed," makes his way to the imperial hall—cautioned by the eunuch Baba to stint his manly stride and affect a look of modesty, lest those whose eyes "may pierce [his] petticoats" (91–92) discover his disguise and toss him in the Bosphorus.

As things turn out, however, Juan has been purchased at the whim of the sultan's wife Gulbayez, and cross-dressed by Baba as a precaution against discovery rather than a transgressive erotic ploy. The powerful personage for whose sexual pleasure he is provided is a woman, not a man (although when the sultan himself arrives on this pan-erotic scene he glances over the assemblage, notes the disguised Juan, and praises the beauty of this latest "new-bought virgin").

Boldly, if imprudently, Juan proclaims that—like Hercules and other cross-dressed captives of Eastern queens—he cannot love "in this vile garb" (127), and is remanded to the seraglio, where "Juanna" is claimed as a bedfellow by several of the women. The scene that follows, the familiar male erotic fantasy of the disguised man in the harem, has the usual element of farce, for in the harem Juan possesses enormous sexual power by the very act of appearing to be powerless, and vigorous masculinity under the guise of impotence or femininity. The affectionate irony with which his hapless hero is treated suggests a double role for Byron: one, as the playfully voyeuristic poet exploring the Eastern regions of sexual ambiguity and women's desire; and the other, as the admirer of "pages," male and female, who serve at the behest of the aristocratic and bisexual Lord Byron.

The extraordinary transvestic materials of the poem clearly reflect upon Byron's own construction of "masculine" and "feminine" roles, as well as upon his fascination with the possibility of breaching or destabilizing them.[36] Equally clearly, gender dissymmetries, both cultural and personal, preclude Byron's championing of women's power in an uncomplicated and unambiguous way, as becomes clear in a later cross-dressing episode involving an aristocratic woman, the Duchess of Fitz-Fulke. Byron is both willing to be seduced by the temporary condition of female masquerade, and resistant—though even here his resistance is tempered by erotic attraction—to the spectacle of the politically and sexually empowered woman.

Yet, as Hazlitt suggests, the "great power" of the poem derives from Byron's ability to "turn round and *travestie* himself."[37] He himself is the transvestic figure inscribed on page after page. The poem's disparaging references to the "third sex" as castrati in Italian musical performances (4.86) and eunuch-servants in the seraglio (5.26) appear to belittle and contain these destabilizing presences by remanding them to the third worlds of Araby, or the servant class, or the stage, but such gestures of exclusion or encapsulation in fact call attention to what is apparently being dismissed. By locating transvestism, strategically, in an Eastern locale, Byron deploys the chic of Araby, its sexual and sartorial destabilizations, as a powerful fantasy as well as a social critique. The poem dramatizes transvestic disguise both as involuntary transformation and as wish fulfillment, while preserving—because of its "Oriental" setting—the escape hatch of the dream. Like the cross-dressed Juan—and the cross-dressed Duchess—his supporting cast of eunuchs, fops, and epicenes personify the very real power of transvestism not as a carnivalized stage elsewhere, an exotic other, but rather as a reminder of the repressed that always returns.

Like Byron, the Victorian explorer, travel writer, and Orientalist Richard Burton was fascinated by the literature and the erotica of the East. At personal risk of prosecution and imprisonment he translated and had privately printed a number of Eastern love manuals, including the *Kama Sutra* (1883). Of all his translations, however, he is probably best known for his sixteen-volume, unexpurgated version of the *Book of the Thousand Nights and a Night*, better known as the *Arabian Nights* (1885–86).

Burton's published translations of the *Nights* appended essays on homosexuality and pederasty, pornography, and the sexual education of women that anticipated in many of their insights some of the psychological theories of Sigmund Freud and Havelock Ellis. In his commentary on the *Arabian Nights* he distinguishes between "the funny form" of homosexual behavior in the *Nights* and its more vicious representations; by "the funny form," he means female cross-dressing.

Two significant tales of cross-dressed women are told in the *Arabian Nights*. In the first a queen, finding herself separated from her husband, dresses herself in male clothing to protect her virtue and, taken for a man, is made king of a country. In her male guise she commands that her husband be brought to her and tries to persuade him to go to bed with her. He at first resists, but finally agrees, and once in bed discovers that he was sleeping not with a man but with a woman, and, in fact, with his own wife.[38]

In the second and very similar tale, a slave girl becomes separated from her lover, assumes the disguise of a man, and, like the queen in the first story, becomes the ruler of a territory. Her lover, seeking her, comes into her city, and she sends for him, leading the people to comment that their king (the disguised slave girl) is in love with the young man. When he appears before her she commands that he rub her feet and calves, and he too resists the advances of this "king" at first, then succumbs, only to discover her identity as a woman and his beloved.[39]

These two tales, each featuring a powerful woman, a reluctant man, and the rewards of obedience to seduction, employ cross-dressing in a way that superficially resembles the plots of English Renaissance drama and romance: the woman is in distress because of the absence of her male lover, she acquires power through cross-dressing, but the result of that acquisition of power is to revalidate the man and the heterosexual experience. The option of homosexual union remains open, however, in the *Nights*, together with the implication that this was a common way to political advancement; the onlookers in the story of the disguised slave girl note that, since the "young man" has attracted the attention of the king, he will probably be made a general.[40]

Why does Burton find this kind of homosexual incident "funny," as contrasted with the narratives of pederastic seduction he deplores? Perhaps because female cross-dressing, and its attendant carnivalization, does not seem threatening to him—and because the power in the relationships depicted here is quickly restored to the man; Queen Burdur's husband swiftly discovers, once he is in bed with her, that she lacks a "tool like the tools of men." Burton is censorious of tales about the seduction of boys by older men, which he terms "perversion," and approves of those tales in which homosexuality is "wisely and learnedly discussed, to be severely blamed, by the Shaykhah or Reverend Woman."[41] But these tales of female transvestism, especially when they end with the revelation of the woman's "real" gender identity, may be "funny" rather than perverse to him in part because they are topsy-turvy, and represent the feminization of the man as only a temporary jest—one that parallels, in its structure of temporary female dominance, the frame-tale of Scheherazade and the King.

Like many other societies, including most in the West, the world of Islam maintains a double standard as regards cross-dressing. The Koran explicitly forbids extravagance in dress, stipulating certain garments and ornaments as appropriate for one sex and not the other. Men are not supposed to wear gold, silver, or silk, or any ring other than a signet ring.[42] Nonetheless, cross-dressing practices were well known in the East in Burton's time, and frequently transvestite rituals figured as part of the ceremonial processes of culture.[43] Burton reports that Afghan commercial travelers were accompanied in their caravans by so-called "travelling wives"—"boys and lads almost in women's attire, with kohl'd eyes and rouged cheeks, long tresses and hennaed fingers and toes," who rode luxuriously while "the husbands trudge patiently at their sides."[44] Notice Burton's phrase, "*almost* in women's attire"; again the peekaboo quality of both/and, male *and* female, seems for the European observer to be part of the fascination. In a society that cultivated transvestite "female" dancers and kept its "real" women veiled and shut off from the world, the construction of these two categories would allow fantasies of accessibility and inaccessibility to coexist without functional contradiction.

What is perhaps most interesting about Burton, however, is that his interest in disguise, cross-racial if not cross-gender, extended to his own practice; he himself, in an adventure that was to catch the popular imagination, journeyed to Mecca in Arab disguise, traveling to Cairo, Suez and Medina before entering the sacred city dressed as a Pathan, an Afghanistan Muslim. Burton had set off for Mecca in 1853 dressed as a "Persian prince"; when he landed in Alexandria, realizing that Persians were unpopular there, he altered his persona to that of a Sunni "Shaykh," declaring that "No character in the Moslem world is so proper for disguise as that of the Darwaysh [dervish]," since the dervish could be of any social station, of any age, of any region.[45] He acquired the special costume worn by male pilgrims, had the barber, as was customary, shave off the hair from his head, underarms, and pubic region, and entered the holy city. When he returned to his regiment, he retained his Arab dress, "not as a disguise but because he had virtually become an Arab" (Rice, 218).

Burton was not, as he himself pointed out, the first European to make this journey in disguise; one of his predecessors, the Swiss Johann Ludwig Burckhardt, had passed as an Arab, and then as a Syrian trader, on his own pilgrimage, reaching Mecca in 1815. But Burton's strategem and daring caught the imagination. His pilgrimage was reported in the London papers. He became a celebrity, as well as, in some quarters, an object of criticism, for he had himself "turned Turk," accepted the Muslim faith.

It is instructive to contrast Burton's journey to that of the equally intrepid English traveler Gertrude Bell, who traveled to to Persia, Syria, and Jerusalem in the 1890's and the early 1900's without disguise—and without the protection, as was customary, of a male European companion. She traveled as who and what she was—an English lady of a certain class, of formidable education and intelligence, who would later become an influential foreign policy adviser on Middle Eastern affairs. Bell wrote in her diary,

There are two ways of profitable travel in Arabia. One is the *Arabia Deserta* way,[46] to live with the people, and to live like them, for months and years . . . It's clear *I* can't take that way; the fact of my being a woman bars me from it.[47]

In her account of a 1905 journey through Lebanon, Syria, and Palestine, she reflected on the tolerance for diversity she encountered in those regions:

A man may go about in public veiled up to the eyes, or clad if he please only in a girdle; he will excite no remark. Why should he? Like everyone else he is merely obeying his own law. So too the European may pass up and down the wildest places, encountering little curiosity and of criticism even less. . . . he will be the wiser if he does not seek to ingratiate himself with Orientals by trying to ape their habits, unless he is so skilful that he can pass as one of themselves . . . For a woman this rule is of the first importance, since a woman can never disguise herself effectually.[48]

The double appearance of the word "pass" in this quotation is worth noting. In Bell's view, the European (male) may *pass* up and down freely either by "obeying his own law" or by "*pass[ing]*" as an Oriental, "one of themselves"—but only if he does it effectually, something a woman can never do. Nonetheless, Bell, a male-identified woman whose mentors were all men and who is frequently disparaging in her accounts of the intellectual qualities of her colleagues' wives, was on her own account treated on her travels like a "male" guest, entertained by men in the parts of their dwellings that were sexually segregated, like the guest house or the coffee hearth.[49] *Not* passing seems to have been Bell's way of passing. For her the body, and the costume, were separable from the mind, and from the construction of a social, intellectual, and political persona.

But let us return for a moment to Bell's gender rules for conduct in Arab lands. "A man may go about in public veiled up to the eyes, or clad if he please only in a girdle; he will excite no remark. Why should he?" while "A woman can never disguise herself effectually." The limits of this second assertion, and the complicated repercussions of the first, are exemplified in the stories of two extraordinary travelers, Isabelle Eberhardt and Michel Vieuchange. Eberhardt lived for years in the desert dressed as a man; Vieuchange journeyed to a forbidden city disguised as a woman.

THE TRANSVESTITE AS "BON GARÇON"

In a satiric episode in a play called *New Anatomies* by contemporary playwright Timberlake Wertenbaker, five women, four of them cross-dressed, appear in a cabaret bar. One is costumed as a man for "professional" reasons; she is a singer. Others explain their men's clothes as motivated by sexual orientation, or merely by willful choice.[50] All four, in a way, mirror the extraordinary life of the play's protagonist, Isabelle Eberhardt, a European woman who dressed like an Arab man, lived with the tribes of the North African desert, and manufactured for herself a new identity.

Isabelle Eberhardt was the illegitimate daughter of an aristocratic Russian woman and of the tutor engaged to care for her older children. Born in 1877, reared in exile in the outskirts of Geneva, Eberhardt was brought up like a boy, her hair cropped, her clothes boys' clothes, following Bakunin's instruction that "every child of either sex should be prepared as much for a life of the mind as for a life of work, so that all may grow up equally into complete men."[51] Educated bilingually in French and Russian, she learned Latin, Arabic, Italian, and a little English, and read Voltaire, Rousseau, Zola, and the Russian novelists. But her passion, following that of her biological father, Alexander Trophimowsky, was for Islam. By the age of sixteen she could read the Koran in Arabic, and inscribe classic Arabic calligraphy. She was enchanted by the Orientalism of Pierre Loti; the Near and Middle East and North Africa, which for the French was "the Orient," became her ideal fantasy place and then her home during a short, nomadic life that ended at 27 when her body, dressed like an "Arab cavalryman," was recovered from a flash flood in southwest Algeria.

Eberhardt's situation seems overdetermined both psychoanalytically and culturally. An illegitimate child, a girl, an exile relocated in a European country itself divided in language and cultural traditions, she early developed a fantasy parentage and a family romance: "As the daughter of a Muslim Russian father and Christian Russian mother," she wrote in a letter to a newspaper in 1903, a year before her death, "I was born a Muslim and have never changed my religion. My father having died shortly after my birth in Geneva, where he lived, my mother lived on in that city with my old great-uncle [Trophimowsky], who brought me up absolutely like a boy."[52] Her most recent biographer compares her, significantly, to T.E. Lawrence, another illegitimate child who was captivated by the East and the Arabs—and by their dress.

Eberhardt initially identified herself with her brother Augustin de Moerder, who was also, in all probability, Trophimowsky's child. Together they conceived the dream of going to North Africa. But Augustin, weak-willed and early addicted—as Eberhardt would later become—to drugs, continually disappointed his sister's expectations. Thus on the eve of moving her family to Algeria in 1895 she found Augustin missing and her mother ill. Instead of the journey to North Africa, Eberhardt was forced to settle, this time, for a trip to a photographer's studio.

The portrait photographer Louis David, a family friend, took two pictures which would become part of the Eberhardt legend: a full-length portrait of the young Isabelle in "Arab" costume, odds and ends from David's cupboard of Orientalist wares: a burnous, Turkish slippers clearly too large for her feet, an ornamented vest and dagger; and a close-up of herself in the costume of a sailor, wearing a hat with the name of the ship "Vengeance"— signifying, as she would remark to a friend and later inscribe in her diary, "the sacred aim of my life: revenge" for the injustices she felt had been wrought upon the de Moerder family.[53]

Cross-dressing for Isabelle Eberhardt thus became both a way of *obeying* the paternal and patriarchal law (Trophimowsky permitted her to go into Geneva only if she dressed as a boy) and a way of *subverting* it. "My life here is quite funny," she wrote to Augustin. "Just imagine—I go around dressed as a sailor, even in town, right under the noses of agents" (Kobak, 38). Dressed in this fashion, and drinking with friends, she made a bet with her companion, a married man five years older, that she would dare to kiss him in public. The "boy" in the sailor suit won the bet. Later, in North Africa, she took on the persona of a young Arab man, taking the name "Mahmoud Saadi." Under that name she spent her happiest years in the desert and in the town of El Oued, dressed in the traditional garb of the Tunisians: a burnous worn over a voluminous silk shirt, baggy trousers, white stockings, and yellow slippers. Her head was shaved completely, in the Muslim style, and she wore a tasseled fez. Casual acquaintances took her, unsurprisingly, for a young man.

Eberhardt appears to have taken a certain pleasure in gender indeterminacy. While she was still in Geneva and writing under a male pseudonym, "Nicholas Podolinsky," one of her correspondents—a Greek artillery officer—wrote to her with irritation, "I didn't know and still don't know what kind of a person I'm dealing with, what their real name is and to what sex or nationality he or she belongs. Meanwhile I haven't the time to write to unknown people behind diverse pseudonyms."[54] Another correspondent, the editor of a French journal who was to become a lasting friend, wrote in 1897: "Dear Mademoiselle and *confrère*, I easily forget in reading your letters whether you're a girl or a boy. If it weren't for your feminine handwriting, I'd believe the latter supposition more easily. In any case this proves you have an unusual virility. . . . Don't ever be completely masculine because a superior woman is superior to her masculine colleague . . . [don't get] too close to that other part of the human species that is egoism personified." [55]

Passing, while it was clearly a logistical asset for her in North Africa, was an option— in fact, an intermittent reality—for Eberhardt even in Geneva. A visitor to her family's home in 1897 reported that she observed "a young fellow of about sixteen . . . sawing wood in the courtyard. His delicate, elegant hands should have told us his sex, but we had no idea. It was only on the third visit that Monsieur Trophimowsky revealed the disguise to us. I warmed to the young lady, who was so gifted and so well-educated."[56] (It is interesting to speculate—given the dissymmetries of gender preconception—on whether the visitor would have warmed so readily to a young man she had mistaken for a young woman.)

A North African with whom Eberhardt had been corresponding under the name of Mahmoud—and who had seen and been struck by the photograph of her as a sailor— had a similar response when he met her for the first time at her family's new home in Algeria: "I shan't attempt to describe my astonishment on the quayside when, instead of shaking hands with a Mahmoud, I found myself in the presence of a young girl, very elegantly dressed" (Kobak, 54). The elegant female dress was Eberhardt's choice, deliberately putting in question her correspondent's assumptions, or, as she put it, his "prejudice[s]" (Kobak, 54). "*Bon garçonisme*," tomboyishness, is how she herself described to him the "mask" she wore toward the outside world, so full of "*pseudo-semblables*, so *dissemblables*" (Kobak, 55).

Later, in 1899, she again broke through her gender disguise, this time of necessity, since her passport described her as female; she therefore presented herself to the head of the Arab Bureau in Biskra, dressed as an Arab man, but announcing herself as a woman. Once more the doubleness of her gendered persona, the wearing and then the doffing of the mask, intrigued and attracted her associate; the colonel in charge invited her to lunch at his house, and then to dinner. Self-difference here is figured in the sequence *semblable/ pseudo-semblable/dissemblable*, in which *all* of the subject positions are occupied by Isabelle Eberhardt.

When in men's clothing, Arab or Western, she was often "read," like many cross-dressing women, as a "boy" rather than a man. Her "dainty hands"[57] and smooth complexion gave her away. Eberhardt seems sometimes to have believed that she was traveling incognito, or passing, when her Arab companions apparently knew of her "real" gender and were too polite, or too indifferent, to remark upon it: "Si Larbi never suspected that I was a woman, he called me his brother Mahmoud, and I shared his nomadic life and his work for two months," she wrote, with some complacency (Kobak, 97).

Eberhardt switched back and forth from male to female and from European to Arab costume throughout her life, largely in response to perceived political necessity, but also as a concession to her lovers' preferences. A Turkish diplomat to whom she was briefly engaged before her sojourn in North Africa wrote her requesting that she let her cropped hair grow out ("as I've let my beard grow") before their marriage.[58] Even the man she married, Slimène Ehnni, a young Arab officer from a regiment in El Oued, was at times ambivalent about her masquerade, fearing for her safety, and at one point she abandoned her male garb to dress in Arab women's clothes at his request.

When an assassination attempt upon her necessitated her appearance in court, the question of appropriate costume became an issue for debate between husband and wife. Slimène felt that European clothing would make a better impression, and she wrote back to him in some heat:

> You absolutely *must not buy European clothes, because you've no idea how much it costs and I formally forbid* you to contract a centime of debts. You know me and know very well that I'm prepared to obey you in everything, except when you're talking nonsense. One can tell you know nothing of what it *costs* to dress *not well*, but at least passably as a Frenchwoman: a wig (this costs, for a shaved head like mine, some 15 to 20 francs, because a simple plait won't do), a hat, underwear, corset, petticoats, skirts, stockings, shoes, gloves and so on. All I will concede is to stop *dressing as an Arab*, which is anyway the only thing which would prejudice the authorities against me. I shall therefore dress *as a European* [man], now that I'm properly equipped. I swear to you, *it's not for the pleasure of dressing up as a man*, but because it's *impossible* for me to do otherwise. At court-martial ... they always said to me, 'We quite understand that you wish to wear men's clothes, but why don't you dress as a European?' Anyway, that's all I have to say to you on the subject. It's impossible for me to do otherwise. ... I don't care if I dress as a *workman*, but to wear ill-fitting, cheap and ridiculous women's clothes, no, never ... (Kobak, 167)

In this letter, full of energetic underlinings and denials, class, gender, and nationality are deployed as categories that contain, or define, cultural anxieties. Eberhardt asserts her desire to present herself as a European—which is to say, a European man—as a strategic choice prescribed by economic and political factors. To dress as an Arab man is politically unwise, to dress as a Frenchwoman, economically impossible. The passionate rhetoric of the letter almost succeeds in repressing any more personal desire. But, like the delicate hands or *imberbe* face that give her away, the letter reveals what it seeks to conceal: "I swear to you, *it's not for the pleasure of dressing up as a man*."

Eberhardt was apparently willing to regard all of these categories as in play except one: willing, indeed apparently eager, to present herself as European or Arab, male or female, aristocrat or workman, depending upon the context, she was militant in her assertion of Muslim faith. As she wrote in an open letter to the *Dépêche Algerienne*:

> The investigating magistrates have repeatedly expressed their surprise at hearing me describe myself as a Muslim and an initiate of the Kadriya brotherhood at that; they also have not known what to make of my going about dressed as an Arab, sometimes as a man, and at other times as a woman, depending on the occasion, and on the requirements of my essentially nomadic life. . . .
>
> In order to avoid giving the impression . . . that in donning a costume and adopting some religious label I might be inspired by some ulterior motive, I wish to state unequivocally that I have not been baptised and have never been a Christian; although a Russian citizen I have been a Muslim for a very long time in fact.[59]

This emphatic declaration, which privileges religious faith so strongly over gender and nationality ("I have been a Muslim for a very long time"; "dressed as an Arab, sometimes as a man, and at other times as a woman, depending on the occasion, and on the requirements of my essentially nomadic life"), suggests that the mechanism of displacement may be at work, substituting for an element of "high psychical value"[60] (here, gender identity) one of comparatively low value (religion), so that what makes the writer most anxious is veiled, distorted, or censored, and replaced by something that provokes less anxiety. As we have noted, Eberhardt's situation was itself quintessentially that of multiple displacement; she is a "displaced person" in virtually every sense. In fact, her cross-dressing seems to mark and make legible the condition of category crisis itself. For Eberhardt is, in a sense, an example of the *personification of displacement*.

Lacan, following Roman Jakobson, associated displacement with metonymy, the chain of signification which "eternally stretch[ed] forth towards the *desire for something else*—of metonymy. Hence its 'perverse' fixation at the very suspension-point of the signifying chain where the memory-screen is immobilized and the fascinating image of the fetish is petrified."[61] Eberhardt's own desire for the towns and peoples of North Africa has inevitably been transmuted by her biographers, then and now, into a fetishizing activity of which cross-dressing was the sign. "Is what thinks in my place, then, another I?" Lacan asked, reading Freud's enigmatic "*Wo es war, soll Ich werden*." "Who, then, is the other to whom I am more attached than to myself, since, at the heart of my assent to my own identity it is still he who agitates me? His presence can be understood only at a second degree of otherness, which already places him in the position of mediating between me and the double of myself, as if it were with my counterpart" (Lacan, 171–72). For Eberhardt "Si Mahmoud Saadi," constructed of Arab cloth, was the self as *another* other, *semblable* and *dissemblable* at once, the one who mediates between: the transvestite. Thus a French Algerian writer records his first meeting with "two strangers in native costume":

One of the strangers was very dark-skinned and sickly-looking, but with regular and appealing features. He was called Si Slimane (sic) Ehnni. . . . His companion, elegant and slim, was a cavalier in a *haik* and a fine, immaculately white burnous. . . . "May I introduce Si Mahmoud Saadi," the dark visitor said, "that is his *nom de guerre*; in fact it is Mme. Ehnni, my wife."[62]

Slimène's rhetorical certainty—"in fact it is . . . my wife" is nicely contrasted with his acceptance of the other person who is also there, and who takes pride of place when being introduced: "Si Mahmoud Saadi" "his" *nom de guerre*. The diary Eberhardt began on the first of January 1900—the beginning of a new century—referred to herself regularly in the masculine gender [*je suis seul*], occasionally changing to the feminine. And a French brigadier-general wrote glowingly of her double-gendered persona:

We understood each other very well, poor Mahmoud and I, and I shall always cherish exquisite memories of our evening talks. She was what attracts me most in the world: a rebel [*réfractaire*]. To find someone who is really *himself*, who exists outside all prejudice, all enslavement, all cliché, and who passes through life as liberated as a bird in space, what a treat![63]

Through the shrewd manipulation of borders, identity papers, names and roles, Eberhardt, displaced and out of place in Geneva, became (at least for the popular press, and to a certain extent for herself) in effect a *spirit of place* in North Africa. The figure of clothing was for her a palpable sign; on January 1, 1900 she wrote in her diary that she wanted "to reclothe myself in that cherished personality, which in reality is the true one, and to go back to Africa again" (Kobak, 107).

Her critics tend to read her transvestism as the most vivid evidence that Eberhardt was "matter out of place," pollution, or dirt, in Mary Douglas's classic formulation,[64] but by animating the trope of displacement she reversed the paradigm. It is striking, for example, that the French journalist quoted above comments on the *cleanliness* of her garments.

When she participated in a desert *fantasia*, perhaps the only European woman to have done so, she described herself, tellingly, in a letter to her brother Augustin. For writing to this biological brother (who, though almost surely also the illegitimate child of Trophimowsky, had been given—unlike his sister—the "legitimate" family surname of de Moerder), Isabelle Eberhardt here triumphantly produces a family romance in which transvestite costume becomes the sign of recognition and decipherment. "You will see there," she wrote,

a cavalier mounted on a fiery little horse, wearing a gandoura and white burnous, with a high white veiled turban, a black rosary around his neck, and his right hand bound with a red cloth to hold the bridle better, and it'll be Mahmoud Saadi, adoptive son of the Great White Sheikh, son of Sidi Brahim.[65]

THE TRANSVESTITE *"EN FEMME BERBÈRE"*

In 1930 a young Frenchman, Michel Vieuchange, undertook an Arab journey in some ways the obverse of Eberhardt's, a journey by a *man* in the guise of an Arab *woman*. A passionate student of classical philology with a conservative French upbringing, Vieuchange was transformed by his military service in Morocco, and by his reading of Rimbaud, Nietzsche, and Walt Whitman. He threw himself initially into the writing of a novel and screenplays for the film industry, celebrating heroism and passion, and took as role models Leonardo da Vinci and Antonin Artaud. Vieuchange dreamed of a return to Morocco with an almost "demoniac" joy[66] even though—or perhaps because—the presence of fierce tribes in the Sahara virtually guaranteed him a fate of massacre or at the best, captivity. His goal was to reach the mysterious city of Smara. For this purpose he disguised himself as a Berber woman.

In September of 1930 Vieuchange joined the party of a native Mahboul of the region, and, together with three men and two women, set out for Smara. "Stripping himself of his European clothes," he "put on a white robe and wrapped a thick veil round his face, a veil almost opaque, and whose effect was to muffle his voice" (*Smara*, 1). His telltale white hands and feet were hidden by blue draperies, and his veil came just up to the level of his eyes, and across his nose. To Vieuchange all this cloth seemed excessive, but he capitulated to the instruction of his guides, and set off across the desert. His brother, with whom he had originally planned to travel, took home with him the rejected European garments. Two months later Vieuchange was dead, killed not by dissident Arabs but by a bout of dysentery contracted on the homeward journey.

Vieuchange's story is not one of overt transvestism of a psychological kind. In a way it is more fitting to compare him to Burton than to Eberhardt. His aim was clear; to adventure across the dangerous stretches of desert, the sole European in an Arab caravan, and reach a fabled Eastern city. He manifestly thought of himself as a man, increasingly protesting against the restrictions imposed by his enveloping female vestments, which changed even the sound of his voice. But his story itself seems curiously characteristic of the thirties, and of the European fascination with the sexual and social ambiguities of the East.

The quest for Smara, "the forbidden city," is in many ways cognate with the means of its access for a Western adventurer, the transvestite disguise, the marginal persona. Here is the testimony of Jean Vieuchange, describing the brothers' excitement when they sought to find the exact location of Smara on the map:

> The adventure began to take a definite shape when we saw, in that part of the map which is left white, one solitary spot, situated at the junction of a number of tracks, and said to be the lair of the Moors of the Atlantic Sahara, their center of brigandage and fanaticism: Smara.
>
> That spot, which some placed here, some there, became our objective. (*Smara*, 10)

But *where*, precisely, is Smara? "Some placed [it] here, some there." Like transvestism itself, "Smara" for the Vieuchange brothers reading the empty white map became not only a "solitary spot" but a space of possibility, a locus of desire. It seems all too fitting, then, that Michel Vieuchange, going one better the previous explorations of two of his fellow Frenchmen who had disguised themselves as native Muhammedans, should succeed in passing himself off as an Arab woman to tour the region. Transvestism is in a way the most "logical," or "appropriate," means of pursuing this quest, since Smara, the forbidden city, is its emblematic equivalent.

The adventure seemed at first something of a lark. Early in his travels, eager to have a record of the expedition and masquerade, Vieuchange expressed the desire to take some photographs. His diary notes show a sensitivity to the Arab unease about photography in general, and to the question of photographing women in particular; realizing that the Mahboul had departed and that the women of his party were unveiled, he wonders whether he would be committing a gaffe by doing so (*Smara*, 28). But he himself was photographed "*en femme berbère*" by the Mahboul, surrounded by grinning Arab companions, male and female. Another photograph shows him relaxing with friends, still in his women's clothes but his face unveiled. His anxiety about being trapped in the female role, however, became more acute as the journey continued.

Jean Vieuchange recalled the moment when Michel assumed his disguise *en route*:

> Michel got out of his European clothes, and El Mahboul helped him into the costume of a Berber woman. Michel stood, anxious as to the correctness of his veils, he allowed the elder of the two women [travelling with them] to adjust a knot here, a fold there. (*Smara*, 20–21)

Even in Jean's account, Michel's unease is palpable—unease not so much at the danger of the adventure (or "raid," as he decided to call it, stressing the element of border crossing) but at the fact of cross-dressing, the material impediment offered by the veil, which muffled his voice and restricted his movements. His very first journal entry complains about the discomfort of heelless slippers (worn by both Berber men and women). At first he is intrigued by his new identity, and the cross-dressing rituals that accompany it, shaving his legs at the first opportunity and staining his legs, arms and hands with permanganate of potash, since both he and his Arab companions are convinced that their whiteness (and especially the whiteness of his ankles) will give him away.

On this point, indeed, he seems more concerned than his guides. "An Arab, seeing my white ankles," he writes on September 15, "would say to El Mahboul, 'That isn't a woman you are taking along there, it is a man.' " In fact, he seems in a way to *want* to be recognized, or at least deciphered, decoded as a man rather than a woman; not only his ankles but his beard are cause for speculations about discovery. As the expedition proceeds he finds his veils, and the attendant inactivity of being a "woman," more and more vexing, and begins to protest against them in a kind of "feminist" rage:

I am compelled to travel completely veiled. How I want to have my face free, to walk in freedom. (*Smara*, 45)

It is impossible for me to say how difficult I find it to keep up this everlasting pretence. The heat, the fatigue, would be nothing; but this unending restraint! It drives me into an absolute frenzy of rage. . . . Everything annoys me: the women who giggle like idiots because I am irritated by these cloaks, beneath which I blow like a walrus. (*Smara*, 49)

The anomaly of Vieuchange's state is never more underscored than when he encounters a figure who might be considered his semiotic opposite, and with whom he becomes, for a little while, obsessed: the moustached woman, "our host's wife . . . with her hairy upper lip" (79). "Lhassen's wife and her moustache" (99) rather than her husband or his companions is somehow blamed as the "cause" of his constraint and incarceration. Everything is secondary to keeping from her the secret of his maleness—the secret of an identity which he is himself forced to put in question.

Yet there were compensations: for one, there was time to write. Over and over again in the diary a remark about the constraints of female costume is linked to an observation about his ability to write, which is enabled, rather than precluded, by his disguise. Another kind of compensation is the languid (homo)eroticism induced by his disguised state. He consistently describes the most ordinary activities in terms that seem, perhaps inadvertently, sexualized:

Lying drowsily beside Larbi, he touched me, and, showing me the half of a pomegranate, peeled off the yellow skin and gave me a handful of the seeds, which I took in the palm of my hand. . . . The juice spurted into my throat . . . (*Smara*, 28)

Or this, describing a drink in the midday sun:

El Mahboul unhooked the water-skin and, holding it above my head, gave me the first drink. Mouth glued to the opening, to the hairy skin, the water spurted down my throat in a stream, and flowed the length of my arms. I no longer noticed the earth or the foul taste of the water. . . . The women drank after me. (*Smara*, 46)

Encountering some unusual plants on a mountainside, he notes in particular

an oily plant shaped like a ball, emerald green: examined closely, a compact sheaf of [pillars] in the form of a phallus. El Mahboul hammered one of the balls with a stone, to show me the milky fluid which oozed out, and indicated his eyes, doubtless to say that it is blinding or harmful; I don't know. (*Smara*, 41)

This report reads almost like an unselfconscious masturbatory fantasy, in which forbidden ejaculation is punished by blindness, or like a manifestation of castration anxiety, provoked perhaps by his temporary transformation into a "woman." Yet another passage describes an attempt at picture-taking as in effect a scene of premature ejaculation with a consequent feeling of sadness and loss.[67]

In general Vieuchange's attitude vacillates between pleasure at the novelty of his position and the excitement of the quest, on the one hand, and frustration at his own feminized status, on the other. This frustration becomes even more acute when, because of increased danger and the onset of illness, he is transformed from "woman" to "fetus," and carried in a basket:

> I was put into a wicker hamper towards midday. Almost immediately I realized that it was not going to be amusing. . . . There, in the hamper, I was folded back on to myself like a foetus. That shell, that absolute powerlessness to make the slightest movement, hand or foot; strangling, almost agonizing when, finding it necessary to move my bruised foot, I found it impossible to do so. (*Smara*, 188)

The motif of the bruised or swollen foot is a constant theme in Vieuchange's narrative; he is constantly bandaging the toes of his lame left foot, chafed by the uncomfortable slippers. More than once this "Oedipal" thematic is acted out in a stage of forced infantilization, as in this account of what seems almost like a birth scenario:

> I let myself be put into the hamper, which suited me in the beginning almost better than the back of the animal. But very soon my bruises recurred; foot almost dead, while my hand felt as though it belonged to somebody else; thighs wedged; the animal, driving off the flies, rubbed his muzzle exactly where my feet were: all that made my mind disordered, put an end to thought, to the birth of ideas. Impatiently I waited for the halt. I demanded it. And at last I got it; but the Reguibat refused to let me come out of the hamper. . . . Shortly afterwards, the hamper fell from the side and I landed with my head among thorns. A mad rage; disgust; weariness perhaps; that crazy position, head lower than the feet; the stones that I felt. (*Smara*, 219)

Traveling, at least for the first stage of his journey, in a woman's clothes and veil, yet treated with more deference and consideration than any of the Arab women in the party (who walk when the men ride, who gather the wood and build the fires; at whose strength and energy he is continually marveling, even as he records his mingled desire and disgust for their unwashed bodies), Vieuchange is never really transformed into a woman, even symbolically. He rides; he drinks first; he is fed well and offered extra blankets. He pays. "Frenchman" here equals, not quite "woman," but rather some third kind—once more, the transvestite role is constituted as a third, as an alternative, not, or not necessarily, a mediation. And indeed, the rubric "Frenchman" is itself under erasure, for the fiction agreed upon, once he has doffed his female veils, is that he is not a Frenchman but an American trader.

Near the end of the journey his Arab hosts, registering his frustration, offer compliments—compliments couched, unsurprisingly, in terms of gender and race: "You are a man! Amazing (*mezian, mezian!*) You are strong! Strong as an Arab" (259). Less than three weeks later Vieuchange was dead.

What can we make of the contrast—and indeed of the similarity—between Vieuchange's story and that of Isabelle Eberhardt? Both are travelers, Westerners, Europeans—despite Eberhardt's Muslim faith and claim of Muslim ancestry. They appropriate and textualize the clothing they assume: textile for them is text, and tells a story of its own. Yet unlike Eberhardt, Vieuchange never constructs a personality, an other, from his transvestic experience. In fact he is not only relieved to assume men's clothing again at the first opportunity (*Smara*, 73) but also eager to record differences between him and the Arab women, as well as moments when his true gender identity is at risk of detection. In a way he wants, above all, to be recognized and acknowledged as a man.

Clearly, the political dissymmetry of gender roles inflects his response, and hers: Vieuchange experiences the repressions of a veiled female identity, Eberhardt the liberations of a male one, whether she is dressed in Western or in Arab clothes, despite—or perhaps, because of—the fact that when cross-dressed she is often recognized or deciphered as a woman. In her diaries, the cross-dressed woman is a powerful individualist, sexual libertine, dignified soldier on horseback, noble participant in the desert *fantasia*. In his diary, the cross-dressed man is a dependent foreigner, lame-footed social castrate, literal basket-case.

Like Eberhardt, the transvestic Vieuchange was suspected of being a spy. Under the veil, at least, only the eyes are visible. Thus in a letter to the *New York Times* the author of a book on present-day Afghanistan noted that "Afghans have long known the advantage of being unrecognizable. History has instances of men donning the traditional woman's garment when going against the authorities." Although veiling was made optional in Afghanistan in 1953, and until the Soviet invasion the number of women in traditional costume had diminished, it was once again, she reported, sometimes expedient to conceal the face. "Anonymity can be desirable, and the tentlike garment is the next thing to the legendary cloak of invisibility. There may even be men under some of them."[68]

But the irony of Vieuchange's story, at least as he tells it in his diary, is that while swathed in his protective veils he watched himself so closely, viewed himself as under watch. If displacement is the figure that perfectly describes Eberhardt's situation, in a different way it also describes Vieuchange. There is a pathos in his narrative that is not entirely produced by the brevity of his stay in Smara, or the death that overtook him at the end of the journey.

It is tempting to think of the transvestic journeys of Eberhardt and Vieuchange as symptoms of anxieties about gender and colonialism specific to a certain time and place, but present-day history gives such comfortable contextualizations the lie. In 1989, for example, actress Debra Winger arrived in Tangier for the filming of Paul Bowles's novel *The Sheltering Sky*, her hair cropped in the dramatic fashion of Bowles's late wife, Jane. The Bowleses became for her objects of intense fascination—and so did the Sahara Desert.

Among his other literary achievements, Bowles had been a leading figure in the restoration of Isabelle Eberhardt's reputation as a writer. He has remained deeply interested in gender-crossing, and—if published reports are correct—attracted to women who, like Eberhardt, Jane Bowles, and the transformed Winger, cross-dress and act out their multiple sexualities.

In Bowles's 1949 novel the American woman Katherine (Kit) Moresby (a thinly veiled portrait of Jane Bowles) goes off into the desert with a caravan headed by two Arab men; one of them becomes her lover, and ultimately dresses her in the clothes of a boy, taking her home with him as his "male" paramour. Tolerated in the household when the man's wives think she is a handsome Arab boy, she is attacked when they discover her real gender.[69] Cross-dressing and bisexuality function in this moment of the novel as figurative signs of the desert and the experience of North Africa; Kit's transformation is part of what it means to try—and fail—to annex another culture as a metaphor for one's own psychological dislocation: the fantasy of otherness as an achievable goal within the self.

But when Winger, as Kit Moresby, "disguised herself as a boy, and traveled, the only woman among men, deep into the Sahara with the Tuareg, a nomadic Hamitic tribe," her experience was one of uncanny recognition: "I realized I'd met the origin of my species with the Tuareg. Everything was familiar."[70]

The Tuareg of North Africa are a tribe of *veiled men*. The women of the tribe do not cover their faces, but the men do, shrouding themselves so completely that only their eyes show, and not removing the veil even to eat or sleep. However impelled by the plot of Bowles's novel, Debra Winger's self-transformation into a "Tuareg boy"—illustrated in *Vanity Fair* with a photograph of her in full Tuareg headdress and veil, only her eyes showing—may also be read as an appropriate, and appropriately complex, sign of the times. Described in the racy jargon of magazine prose as a "fast-living, chain-smoking, hard-drinking" woman who in her Hollywood career "played the game by men's rules and made no bones about it" (Collins, 248), Winger went to the desert cross-dressed and cross-shorn in the style of a celebrated bisexual woman, and then assumed the *veil* that distinguishes *maleness* in one of the desert's fiercest tribes. The conundrum of gender in Western appropriations of North Africa here re-poses itself in contemporary terms, the ennui and rootlessness of the Hollywood star displacing and replacing the quests of European romantic dreamers and postwar American intellectuals.

Debra Winger is an actress; her self-recognition as a Tuareg boy is, arguably, only one in a series of self-transformations that are part of the lingua franca of her trade. At one moment she is swathed in the dark veils of the Tuareg, and at the next she is being photographed in a silk sheath slit to the waist. As for Michel Vieuchange, as we have seen, he could hardly wait to rid himself of the trammeling clothing of Berber womanhood, and even Isabelle Eberhardt—whose reputation in this century was revived in part through the efforts of Paul Bowles—played deftly with the roles of "male" and "female," Arab and European, trying them on and taking them off like clothing.

When the concept of "the chic of Araby" comes, however, to encompass body as well as dress—when the transvestic impulse of the turn of the century is combined with, or overtaken by, the medical capacity to change the body through transsexual surgery—then the entire concept of "gender *roles*" is again, and fascinatingly, laid open to question.

THE EROTICS OF CULTURAL APPROPRIATION

In July 1972, James Morris, the noted British travel writer and foreign correspondent, booked himself a round-trip ticket to Casablanca, where he would visit the clinic of the famous Dr. B—and undergo the surgery that transformed him from a man into a woman.[71] Morris had been approved for surgery at home, in England, at the Charing Cross Hospital in London. In the narrative of this transformation, *Conundrum*, the woman who is now Jan Morris explains that the London surgeon would have required that James Morris divorce his wife before undergoing the operation, and that Morris, although willing to get a divorce eventually, resisted doing so as a condition of his surgery.

It seems clear, however, that for Morris, who had journeyed so extensively in Africa, North and South, Casablanca was a special, liminal place, the geographic counterpart of his/her psychological and physiological condition. S/he required a more exotic setting than Charing Cross for this most exotic of crossings. "I sometimes heard the limpid Arab music, and smelt the pungent Arab smells, that had for so long pervaded my life, and I could suppose [Casablanca] to be some city of fable, of phoenix and fantasy, in which transubstantiations were regularly effected, when the omens were right and the moon in its proper phase."[72]

For Renée Richards, another transsexual who traveled to Casablanca for the surgery, the city's exoticism evoked an opposite response; twice Richards, at that point still a man, went to the door of the Casablanca clinic, this "fantasy place" whose address he had long known by heart, and twice he left without entering (Richards, 246). When Dr. Raskin finally had the operation it was at home, in New York, on familiar ground. But for Jan Morris the lure of Casablanca was part of the process of transformation.

In the long period of probation before his surgery, when he took female hormones to change the contours and chemistry of his body, Morris imagined his indeterminate gender identity as a veil. "I first allowed my unreality to act as its own cloak around me," she writes, "or more appositely perhaps as the veil of a Muslim woman, which protects her from so many nuisances, and allows her to be at her best or her worst inside" (Morris, 113). For her, cross-gender is also imagined as cross-culture. What she describes as "our pilgrimage to Casablanca" (Morris, 172; where the plural denotes "mine and that of other transsexuals," but the implication of "James's and Jan's" remains latently powerful) is a literalization of a cultural fantasy that played itself out in cross-dressing as well as in homo- and bisexual relations between East and West, European and Arab.

"Paradoxically," writes Elizabeth Wilson in her book *Adorned in Dreams,* "in Islamic cultures women wear trousers and men robes."[73] The paradox, of course, is seen through Western eyes; it is likely that Western dress conventions seem equally paradoxical when viewed from some vantage points in Kabul or Algiers. Nonetheless, this simple reversal of expectation has enabled, in that part of the world often called the West (in practice, certain regions of Western Europe and North America), a wide range of transvestic practices and behaviors, from disguise to drag, from passing to protest.

That Jan Morris's pilgrimage should have as its ultimate destination not the heights of Eastern exoticism but a "flat in Bath" (Morris, 156) underscores the fundamentally ideological nature of the "conundrum" which she describes in biographical and biological terms. Morris is only exotic, magical, set apart, in the middle stages of the journey, as neither man nor woman, when the hormones have arrested and even reversed signs of age, have produced the illusion of a kind of Fountain of Youth or Shangri-La. Once tranformed, returned from Casablanca, Morris no longer inhabits that exhilarating no man's land. The biological clock, its works tinkered with but replaced, begins again to tick, and Morris finds herself, to her delight, transformed into a middle-aged suburban matron, who "wear[s] the body of a woman" (Morris, 159).

What seems so striking to me, though, is that James Morris sought to realize his dream in Casablanca. Transsexualism here presents itself as a literalization of the Western fantasy of the transvestic, pan-sexualized Middle East, a place of liminality and change.

APPOINTMENT IN MOROCCO

There is, in fact, more than a little appropriateness to the fact that Marlene Dietrich's signature costume of top hat and tails, the costume that signifies cross-dressing not only for her, in her own subsequent films and performances, but also for the legions of female impersonators who have since "done Dietrich" in drag, made its first appearance in a film called *Morocco.* Why cross-dressing in Morocco? Because the one was already, in European as in North American eyes, the figure for the other. Araby was the site of transvestism as escape and rupture.

Joseph von Sternberg's 1930 classic is the scene of multiple transvestic motifs—motifs that insistently put the sartorial rhetoric of gender in question. Dietrich, as the nightclub singer Amy Jolly, elegantly attired in her men's clothes, casually leans down to kiss a woman in the audience on the lips, and then reappears for her next stage turn dressed "as a woman," in a bathing suit and a feather boa. Her nightclub act is introduced by a bumbling male impresario in formal dress sporting a large hoop earring. Gary Cooper, as legionnaire hero Tom Brown, tucks a rose—Dietrich's gift to him—behind his ear. The master of ceremonies in his tuxedo begins to look like a drag version of Dietrich. So—although in a different tonal register—does Adolph Menjou when he comes to her dressing room in white tie and tails. The question of an "original" or "natural" cultural category of gender semiotics here is immediately put *out* of question. There is in the nightclub in Morocco nothing *but* gender parody.

The apparition of a woman in men's formal clothes (a spectacle that makes it clear that such "civilized" dress is *always* in quotation, no matter who wears it) is in this landmark film combined with a place, Morocco, and an object of clothing, the veil, that together constitute an interposition or disruption. The veil is to clothing what the curtain is to the theater. It simultaneously reveals and conceals, marking a space of transgression and expectation; it leads the spectator to "fantasize about 'the real thing' in anticipation of seeing it."[74]

The veil as a sign of the female or the feminine has a long history in Western culture, whether its context is religious chastity (the nun, the bride, the orthodox Muslim woman) or erotic play (the Dance of the Seven Veils). But presuppositions about the gendered function of the veil—that it is worn to mystify, to tantalize, to sacralize, to protect or put out of bounds—are susceptible to cultural misprision as well as to fetishization. Thus a German ethnologist who traveled for six months with the Tuareg of the North African desert felt called upon to report that there was "nothing effeminate about these Tuareg nobles . . . on the contrary, they are shrewd, ruthless men with a look of cold brutality in their eyes."[75] Although the Tuareg were known as fierce warriors, the fact that their men wore veils at all times while Tuareg women freely showed their faces was clearly a puzzle. The men's eyes, however, were still visible through a slit in the veil, and could be construed, at least by those who expected or hoped to find such a thing, as showing "cold brutality"—in other words, manliness. This Eurocentric obsession with the veil as female—with what is veiled as "woman"—is established early in *Morocco* as itself a mystification and a coded sign.

At the beginning of the film Arab women unveil themselves flirtatiously at Gary Cooper from the tops of city buildings. On shipboard en route from Europe Dietrich wears a fashionable *Western* veil of sheer black netting attached to a perky black hat, before making her appearance in male formal dress. Her sexual rival, the wife of the adjutant (superbly named "Madame Caesar" although—or because—she is emphatically *not* above suspicion), disguises herself in a Moroccan robe and veil in order to pursue Cooper. The distinction between the two women is both gendered and nationalized, though Madame Caesar's "Arab" costume is manifestly a kind of adventurer's fancy-dress, a colonial appropriation, not an acknowledgment of cross-national (or cross-racial) sisterhood. In the famous final scene, kicking off her sandals and tying her stylish neck-scarf around her head like a peasant kerchief, Dietrich joins the Arab women in the trek across the desert. Class markers are thus tied both to gender and to race; Dietrich "descends" from upper-class white tie and tails—the sign of the male, the aristocrat, or the high-style lesbian—to the status of a native camp follower. But what is most striking is the way in which von Sternberg's film puts the signification of gender in question, and does so in a particular locale.

Thus, in von Sternberg's *Morocco*, the "Foreign Legion," that colonial fantasy of amnesic brotherhood in which a recruit is permitted to put his past under erasure, is another version of this medial space. And so too is the boat that brings "Amy Jolly," the quintessential *jolie amie*, to Casablanca. That Amy Jolly's journey is twinned historically with Dietrich's (and von Sternberg's) passage from Germany to Beverly Hills underscores the transitional moment marked and encoded in the film. For Hollywood *was* Morocco, *was* Casablanca, as cross-dressing itself became, in the years that followed, nothing less than the radical of representation in film.

In cinematic representation the word "film" interposes itself, *like* a veil, as a space of multiple meaning: membrane or covering; photographic transparency; motion picture. The veil is a film, the film is a veil. What is disclosed *is* what is concealed—that is, the fact of concealment.

Here it is useful to recall not only Jacques Lacan's figure of the veil as a sign of latency,[76] but also the observations of Heinz Kohut, the pioneer theorist of narcissism, on theater and reality. Kohut notes that people "whose reality sense is insecure" resist abandoning themselves to artistic experiences because they cannot easily draw a line: "They must protect themselves, e.g., by telling themselves that what they are watching is 'only' theater, 'only' a play." So too with the analysand; only analysands "whose sense of their reality is comparatively intact will . . . allow themselves the requisite regression in the service of the analysis"—a regression that "takes place spontaneously, as it does in the theater."[77] This fear of blurring the line, of not being able to distinguish "reality" from "theater," this susceptibility to fantasy—to *cultural* as well as to intra-psychic fantasy— is, precisely, the stage (stage in both senses, both the process and the playing space) of the transvestite.

ANY WAY YOU SLICE IT, IT'S STILL SALOME

The picture is almost too eloquent. His wrists, fingers, and upper arms circled with jewels, his flowing locks adorned with an "Oriental" headdress, a jeweled belt at his ample waist, he kneels, with some little difficulty balancing his long skirt on his hips, and, all concentration, reaches out toward the head on the platter at his feet. The wig on the platter seems the mirror of the one that sits on his own head and cascades down his back, like a Burne-Jones in drag. It is Oscar Wilde in the costume of Salome.

The drag Salome is not a send-up but a radical reading that tells the truth. For the binary myth of Salome—the male gazer (Herod), the female object of the gaze (Salome);

the Western male subject as spectator (Flaubert, Huysmans, Moreau, Wilde himself) and the exotic, feminized Eastern Other—this myth, a founding fable of Orientalism, is a spectacular disavowal. What it refuses to confront, what it declines to look at and acknowledge, is the disruptive element that intervenes, the scandal of transvestism. It is no accident that the Salome story conflates the myths of Medusa and Narcissus, the decapitated head and the mirror image. This conflation was known to Donatello, who gave his Perseus the same face as his Medusa; it was known to Aubrey Beardsley, whose illustrations for Wilde's text clearly show Salome, in the act of kissing Iokanaan's dead lips, holding aloft the head with its snaky locks, transfixed by self-love on the bank of a reflecting pool. Self-love, and self-hatred.

The story of Salome and her mesmerizing Dance of the Seven Veils has become a standard trope of Orientalism, a piece of domesticated exotica that confirms Western prejudices about the "Orient" and about "women" because it is produced by those prejudices, is in fact an exercise in cultural tautology. In order to see what the story represses, let us first see what it purports to tell, and then take note of the ways it has been read and appropriated in European texts.

Here, in brief, is the familiar Salome story as it is reported by the Jewish historian Josephus and in the Gospels of Matthew and Mark. Herod watches Salome dance the Dance of the Seven Veils and is enraptured, inflamed. He says he will give her anything she wants, and she asks for the head of John the Baptist on a platter. Herod is dismayed by the request, but capitulates—yields up the head. Salome takes it and gives it to her mother.

Matthew's Gospel says she was prompted by her mother Herodias to ask for the Baptist's head in the first place. Mark tells it a little differently; her mother did not prompt her in advance, but was consulted on the spot. In both cases, though, the death of John is seen as the desire of the mother, not the daughter. The female subject is split, and the trajectory of the gaze doubled: Herodias gazes on Herod gazing on Salome. But John has already seen—and seen through—Herodias, denouncing her as an adulteress because she has married Herod after being married to his brother. The decapitation of the prophet is Herodias's revenge; she renders him powerless, and silences his tongue.

In neither Gospel, significantly, is Salome named; she is described only as the daughter of Herodias. Josephus mentions her name, but does not connect her with the death of John, nor does he record that she danced for Herod. Though both Gospels say she danced, neither mentions the famous Dance of the Seven Veils or, indeed, characterizes the dance at all: they say only that "the daughter of Herodias danced." Out of this thin stuff grew up the legend.

What is there here to stir cultural and sexual fantasy? Too much: parents and a willful child; incestuous desire; taboo; and a gap.

French writers and painters of the nineteenth century had a field day with Salome, and both feminists and deconstructive critics of the twentieth century have had a field day with them. A rich literature has grown up around the Salome story, filling in the blanks in the biblical account. Moreau's paintings, Huysmans's *A Rebours* and Flaubert's *Herodias* all focus largely on the dance itself.[78] Salome and her dance become a figure for that which can—and cannot—be represented, as well as for the putative cruelty and inscrutability of Woman.[79] "Salome's dance becomes the blind spot of writing to its own repression," suggests Françoise Meltzer, reading Salome's dance as an *aporia* which confounds logocentric "meaning" and puts the possibility of such meaning in question.[80] In its non-description, in its indescribability, lies its power, and its availability for cultural inscription and appropriation. "The ultimate veil," as Mallarmé declared, "always remains."[81]

In Egypt Flaubert watched the dance of the famous courtesan Kuchuk Hanem, and used her, it is claimed, as the model for his Salome, as well as for Tanit and Salammbô. Edward Said describes Kuchuk as a "disturbing symbol of fecundity, peculiarly Oriental in her luxuriant and seemingly unbounded sexuality,"[82] the embodied object of Flaubert's fantasies about the sensual, self-sufficient, emotionally careless Oriental woman. Yet Said overlooks or represses the fact that it is "not the female Kuchuk but a homosexual *male* who first catches the traveler's eye"[83]:

a male dancer—it was Hasan el-Belbeissi—in drag, his hair braided on each side, embroidered jacket, eyebrows painted black, very ugly, gold piastres hanging down his back; around his body, as a belt, a chain of large square gold amulets; he clicks castanets; splendid writhings of belly and hips; he makes his belly undulate like waves; grand final bow with his trousers ballooning.[84]

Hasan el-Belbeissi, like Kuchuk, could be induced to dance "the Bee" (Flaubert, 84), a celebrated performance in which the dancer sheds clothing as he or she dances, winding up, as Kuchuk does, "naked except for a *fichu* which she held in her hands and behind which she pretended to hide, and at the end she threw down the *fichu*" (Flaubert, 117). A curious feature of this dance is its aura of taboo: the musicians and other necessary members of the dancer's entourage are themselves veiled or blindfolded during the performance; Flaubert and his companions, alone, are permitted to watch. "That was the Bee. She danced it very briefly, and said she does not like to dance that dance."

As Joseph Boone points out, Said ignores the homosexual and homosocial aspects of Flaubert's account, and especially the salacious, erotically charged letters to his friend Louis Bouilhet, who features in a number of thinly veiled sexual reveries, and for whom the descriptions of the female courtesans and male bardashes seem explicitly intended. Boys, as well as girls, excited Flaubert's imagination in Egypt; he claims to have buggered a boy in a male brothel, on the custom-of-the-country principle, and intends to learn how to do it better—or so, at least, he writes to Bouilhet. Said is willing to note that Flaubert learned from his reading of W.E. Lane about both male and female dancers, but for Said, as for Flaubert, the Otherness that produces unbounded desire is a woman.

Boone's critique thus in effect proposes to substitute a dancing boy for the dancing girl, as an equally appropriate, and more destabilizing, reading of the Orientalist impulse in Western culture.

Renouncing the femininity of Salome is a task not only for gender theory, but for a new cultural criticism, since it challenges the construction of a feminized Orient subservient to the heterosexual masculinity of the Western observer. But as politically necessary as this substitution may be, it is not sufficient, in reading the riddle of Salome and her veils.

For Boone's salutary substitution, therefore, I want to suggest another—the substitution not of a regendered dancer but of a transvestite dance. I want to argue that on the level of the Imaginary, the dancer is neither male nor female, but rather, transvestic— that the essence of the dance itself, its taboo border-crossing, is not only sensuality, but gender undecidability, and not only gender undecidability, but the paradox of gender identification, the disruptive element that intervenes, transvestism as a space of possibility structuring and confounding culture. *That* is the taboo against which Occidental eyes are veiled. The cultural Imaginary of the Salome story is the veiled phallus and the masquerade. This is the latent dream thought behind the manifest content of Salome.

Subsequent retellings of Salome have come closer and closer to this unveiling; the veils drawn aside have been national as well as cultural, so that Oscar Wilde, an Irishman writing in French, can see through the necessary fictions of Flaubert and even Huysmans, as Ken Russell's American film, a triumph of postmodern trash cinema, sees through, as it re-stages, Wilde. In order to make this argument, it will be necessary to review, briefly, some of the details of the Salome tradition, and then to look at some evidence for peeking behind the veil.

Wilde begins, characteristically, by playing with the possibility of regendering the gaze. In his *Salome* the obsessive desire shared by Herod and the young Syrian Captain to look at Salome ("You look at her too much," each is told, over and over) is ultimately less compelling, and less compulsive, than Salome's own limitless desire to gaze upon Ioka-naan—and to have him return the gaze. ("Wherefore dost thou not look at me, Iokanaan? Thine eyes that were so terrible, so full of rage and scorn, are shut now. Wherefore are they shut? Open thine eyes!"[85]) The Medusa moment is doubled and literalized; not only is the gazing Herod (and before him the young Captain) destroyed, but so too is Salome. As she kisses the severed head, Herod gives the order for her to be killed. As we have noted, Aubrey Beardsley's famous illustration, aptly titled "The Climax," captures the regendering of the Medusa story and its conflation with the story of Narcissus.

Wilde seems, in fact, to have been at some pains to experiment with reversing the gender roles here. At an early stage of composition, he considered calling his play *The Decapitation of Salome*, and extending the plot to describe Salome's subsequent wanderings through deserts of sand and snow, and her spectacular accidental decapitation when she falls into a river of jagged ice.[86] In this fantasy, too, she becomes by reversal a female version of John the Baptist, ironically bathed in a river, dying a Christian and a symbolic castrate. Salome's extended praise of Iokanaan's body, hair, and mouth follow the incantatory rhetoric of the Song of Songs—"but," notes Richard Ellmann, "The Song of Songs describes a woman's beauty, not a man's" (Ellmann, 344). This is part of what makes Iokanaan's position intolerable to him; he is, in effect, feminized by the gaze of Salome.

Now, what if we were to take Wilde's gender hypothesis one step further, and ask what would happen if the object of the gaze were, not a woman or a man, but a transvestite? This is—I want to claim—in fact the substitution that Wilde's *Salome* enacts, a substitution radicalized and made visible in Ken Russell's 1988 film, *Salome's Last Dance*.[87] And this substitution is not only a rewriting of the Salome story but a rereading of it that makes all the sense in the world—makes sense, for example, of the cultural amnesia that omits to mention the dancer's name, or the name of her fabled dance. Let us see how that might happen.

Ellmann's biography of Wilde contains an amusing and disconcerting photograph of Wilde himself in the costume of Salome, a photograph I have already described above. The moment depicted is that which will lead to "The Climax": Wilde-Salome kneels, his/her bejeweled hands and arms outstretched, and gestures toward the head on the charger. The head itself is turned away, so that only its hair can be seen; it looks very like a wig. Thus: Wilde the author, Wilde the libertine, Wilde the homosexual, as Salome. The transvestite Wilde is yet another version of the "to seem" that replaces the "to have" in Lacan's trajectory of desire. Reaching toward the wig on the platter, he focuses attention on the materials of transvestite masquerade—on drag as and in theatrical representation.

In Russell's film, this substitution is brought to consciousness in the moment when the dancing Salome drops her final veil and appears naked, not as a woman *or* as a man but as two figures dancing side by side, one male and one female. This double image reduces to a single image of the boy, his whirling penis the center of the camera's (Herod's) astonished fascination—and then, the dance over, we see instead a naked girl, the Salome we thought we were watching all along. It is important to stress that this is *not* a hermaphrodite, despite the allure of Beardsley's illustrations. It is a stereo-optical intuition of transvestism (was it a boy? was it a girl?) apparently satisfied by the sight of the unveiled penis, then covered over again as the girl, her pubic area clearly visible, is wrapped in a robe and congratulated on her performance.

Let us now take note of Mallarmé's dictum, that the Dancer "delivers up to you through the ultimate veil that always remains, the nudity of your concepts and silently begins to write your vision in the manner of a Sign, which she is." And let us consider, in conjunction with it, Lacan's observation that "the phallus is a signifier, a signifier whose function, in the transubjective economy of the analysis, lifts the veil perhaps from the function it performed in the mysteries,"[88] and, even more centrally, the phrase of his that seems to have such pertinence to the transvestite masquerade: "[the phallus] can play its role only when veiled" (Lacan, 288). In other words, because human sexuality is constructed through repression, the signifier of desire cannot be represented directly, but only under a veil. Taken together, these somewhat abstract formulations about the dancer, the dance, and the veiled phallus, tell the story of the power of Salome—and the reason why the removal of the last veil is the sign of her death. For when the veil is lifted, what is revealed is the transvestite—the deconstruction of the binary, the riddle of culture.

What Oscar Wilde added to the long list of Symbolist Salomes was the realization that Salome was a figure for transvestism in its power to destabilize and define. What Russell added to Wilde was the literalization of the unveiled phallus—an interpretation of Wilde, not a rewriting of him, as Wilde read what was already inscribed in Salome, under the veil. And a key player in helping Wilde to reshape the role was Sarah Bernhardt.

Wilde, having written his play in French—an homage to the French preoccupation with the Salome story, to Flaubert as well as to Mallarmé, Moreau, and Huysmans—decided that the part of Salome should be played by Sarah Bernhardt. Wilde greatly admired Bernhardt. When she arrived in London in May 1879 he cast an armful of lilies beneath her feet as a carpet, and conceived a strong desire for her to act in one of his plays. Bernhardt had already become famous for her cross-dressed roles, of which she would play at least twenty-five in the course of her long career: Zacharie in Racine's *Athalie* and Zanetto, the strolling boy troubadour in Coppée's *Le Passant* in 1869 were among her early triumphs in breeches parts—later she would play Hamlet, in 1899, and Napoleon's doomed son, the Duc de Reichstadt, in a celebrated production of Rostand's *L'Aiglon* in 1900.

When, in 1892, Wilde replied to Bernhardt's request to write a play for her by saying, "I have already done so," he meant *Salome*, and she eagerly agreed to play the title role. The intended London production foundered on the licenser's ruling, but Wilde continued to hope that Bernhardt would stage his play.[89] Wilde, in other words, visualized his Salome as a woman who could play the part of a boy.

In Russell's film, Bernhardt plays a brief but crucial role as an absent presence; her relationship to *Salome* is tracked down and camped up. For at the end of the play-within-the-play Wilde, praising Lady Alice's performance as Herodias, remarks that no actress could have done better—except Sarah Bernhardt, who has something Lady Alice lacks. What's that?, Lady Alice asks, with hauteur. Why—a wooden leg, he replies.

In fact Bernhardt's leg was not amputated until 1915, twenty-three years after Wilde's initial suggestion that she should play the title part in his play, and the same length of time after Wilde's association with Alfred Taylor, the purported "historical" occasion of the film. Why, then, does *Salome's Last Dance* go out of its way to include an apparently anachronistic reference to Bernhardt's wooden leg?

Perhaps merely to give a sense of local color to this fantasy event; perhaps to underscore Wilde's misogyny; but perhaps, also, because the mention of Bernhardt's wooden leg here presents another detachable phallus, another sign of lack and its substitution in a phallic woman who happened to play, in the decades that she dominated the stage and the theatrical Imaginary, the parts of boys and men. That wooden legs played such a part in theatrical representation has been true at least since Marlowe's *Doctor Faustus*. But that the wooden leg should be a *woman's*—should be *Salome's*—reinforces the sense in which Salome herself is a transvestic construction. In other words, the wooden leg, though added after the fact as a sign of Bernhardt/Salome's amputation/castration, is part and parcel of the story here. And how does one dance with a wooden leg?

In the early, hopeful days when it looked as if Bernhardt could produce the play in London, before the intervention of the licenser of plays (the castrator of culture), the Marquess of Queensberry (the castrator as heavy father), and Mr. Justice Clark (the castrator of law), the designer Graham Robertson asked the actress whether she wanted a stand-in for the dance. Bernhardt replied equably, "I'm going to dance myself." "How will you do the dance of the seven veils?" he asked, and she answered, "smiling enigmatically," "Never you mind."[90]

So, once more, as always, the dance remains undescribable, undescribed—and, in the event, unperformed. Yet it may be that Bernhardt's refusal to involve herself in Wilde's misfortunes by purchasing the rights to *Salome* constituted an emblematic performance of the *Salome* part *par excellence*: indifferent, cruel, thoughtless. "Never you mind." This is the Dance of the Seven Veils as imagined by postmodernism, its ultimate performance, "the ultimate veil that always remains."

Let us now consider another post-modern drag Salome that addresses the issue of transvestism and the veil.

In *Pumping Iron II: The Women* (1985), a contest for female body builders, the entire competition is in effect one big Salome dance, as each woman performs a "free pose" routine, flexing her abs and delts for the judges to the tune of songs like "I'm Dangerous." But as aficionados (and aficionadas) of this film will know, a symptomatic narrative cross-cuts the docudrama of the competition; contestants and judges are racked by dissension about the meaning of the word "femininity": can it be used to characterize a woman with musculature so developed that she looks like a man? Although the word "lesbian" is never spoken, the subtext is perfectly clear. What threat do well-muscled women pose to the fantasy idea of "woman"? The controversy centers on Bev Francis, a former power lifter from Australia, whose appearance creates consternation in onlookers—and in the other contestants. Francis, the film's "heroine" and figure of ambivalent pathos, slims down to enter the contest and is immediately the cause of controversy, but some contestants—and one female judge—are virulent in their dislike of her body image. It will, says the judge, ruin the appeal of a growing sport: "Bev Francis doesn't look like a woman."[91] Bev herself, innocent of the heavy eye-makeup and teased hair of her American counterparts, worries anxiously after her "free pose": "Did my feminine quality come through? Are they going to say I'm too masculine?" In effect, they do; of the eight finalists, she comes in last.

But as the judges withdraw to consult about the rules (and the possible "new concept" of a woman's body), some entertainment is provided to keep the audience amused. An official spokesman for the contest describes this intervention, in unwittingly Lacanian terms, as "an exhibition to cover the gap." And the "exhibition" is, perhaps inevitably, a dance, performed by a figure swathed in veils.

The dancer's head and body are alike masked, so that it is at first impossible to determine its gender. But step by step the veils are discarded, disclosing at last the figure of Salome: a grinning *male* body builder, who pauses in his dance long enough to strip away a loincloth, revealing a skimpy G-string beneath. And the crowd roars. This dancer, who intervenes to "cover the gap" of judgment at a contest called—not entirely irrelevantly, in view of the Herodian context—"Caesar's World Cup for Women," literalizes the fantasy and fear that have been expressed throughout. Does she or doesn't she? Is she or isn't she? The game of phallic keepaway *is* the Salome dance. Here is an uncanny repetition of the scenario of Hasan el-Belbeissi, the male dancer who performed for Flaubert. The nameless male dancer of *Pumping Iron II*, so demonstrably and apparently unanxiously on display, doubles and translates the obsessive, unspoken question about Bev Francis and her sport that underlies so much of the film. "That *can't* be a woman." The cultural Imaginary of the Salome story is always the veiled phallus—and the threat (and promise) of its unveiling.

What is unveiled here—and I want to stress this—is not a man or a woman, not masculinity or femininity, but the specter and spectacle of transvestism: transvestism as that which constitutes culture.

SALOMÉ'S SALOME

> Freud was also interested in another type of woman, of a more intellectual and perhaps masculine cast. Such women several times played a part in his life, accessory to his men friends though of a finer caliber, but they had no erotic attraction for him. . . . Freud had a special admiration for Lou Andreas-Salomé's distinguished personality and ethical ideals, which he felt far transcended his own.[92]

It is almost irresistible to draw some connection between the psychoanalyst Lou Andreas-Salomé and her biblical namesake.

What are the limits of the power of signification? How does "Salome" as signifier encode a whole story below the line, below the surface: a story of dance, of the Orient, of enigma and narcissistic self-sufficiency, of castration and fetishism? Let us see.

In her childhood in Russia Louise von Salomé was given red-and-gold morocco slippers and was carried about by servants; "she would put on dancing shoes and go sliding over the parquet floors of their huge hall, liking the solitude as well as the movement."[93] Solitude and movement together continued to characterize her throughout her life, as did an enigmatic sexual appeal. Her marriage to the Iranologist Friedrich Carl Andreas was successful although apparently it was never consummated. Ernest Jones—perhaps protesting too much?—counted her among the women of "a more intellectual and perhaps more masculine cast," in Freud's life, and Freud himself, acknowledging that she had been a "Muse" to the weaker Rilke, contended that "those who were closer to her had the strongest impression . . . that all feminine frailties . . . were foreign to her."[94] "Frau Lou" as Salome? As the transvestite Salome?

Admired not only by Freud but also by Nietzsche, who proposed marriage to her and was refused, by Rilke (who was for many years her lover), and by the philosopher Paul Rée, Lou Salomé married an Orientalist and wrote—among many other things—essays on Islam. "Spectacular and seductive," with "a high forehead, generous mouth, strong features, and voluptuous figure," according to Peter Gay (who clearly both sees and tries to resist her appeal), she met Freud, who would later describe her as "a female of dangerous intelligence," at the Weimar Congress of psychoanalysts when she was already fifty years old. "Her appetite for men, especially brilliant men, was unabated," notes Gay, who characterizes her friendship with Freud as a mutual courtship ("Frau Lou had no monopoly on deploying the arts of seduction"[95]) that became also a relationship of intellectual respect.

When she became a practicing analyst Lou Andreas-Salomé's own work centered on narcissism, a subject on which she became a recognized authority, giving a much more positive valuation to self-love than did Freud, and anticipating some of the ideas of Kohut. In the course of her long correspondence with him she writes to Freud not only about narcissism but also about fetishism and castration anxiety, referring in particular to Rilke's confessions about "the penis as . . . 'the big one,' the extra-big, uncannily superior and uncontrollable one, haunting dreams and feverish nightmares"[96]; these led to the poet's "pleasure in masks and dressing up, as if he were protecting himself through disguises from something which nevertheless is himself and which on the other hand he would like to be rid of." Rilke's fear of the "too big" had in fact attached itself to Andreas-Salomé, whom he also associated with stone; the imagery of the "mother figure with a penis,"[97] which struck her in Freud's essay on "Fetishism," is clearly established in Rilke's confession to her: "I hated you as something *too big*."[98] The intersection of the myths of Medusa and Narcissus, which came together in the figure of the dancing Salome, come together again in Rilke's fantasy of Lou Andreas.

As for Freud (a Jew, a classicist, a fetishizer of antiquities), he referred to her in his letters as "Frau Andreas," and later as "Lou," never with the patronymic "Salomé" inherited from her Russian father—avoiding, we may say, or repressing, or disavowing the image of the dancer who held a king in thrall. Yet clearly Lou Salomé was for him, and apparently from the beginning, the object of specularity, as well as speculation, as a final piece of documentary evidence will suggest. Everyone who tells the story of Freud and "Frau Lou" takes note of his jealousy or pique when, briefly, she showed interest in the ideas of his former disciple Alfred Adler. Adler had split with Freud in part over the question of the fundamentally aggressive nature of human behavior—what Adler called the "masculine protest" over innate femininity in the (male) subject. Adler substituted aggression for sexuality as the foundational human activity, the male wish to conquer a female masquerading, in his view, as sexual desire. It is therefore particularly striking that Freud registered Andreas-Salomé's absence at one of his Saturday lectures, and associated that absence with her flirtation with Adler's ideas. Here is the letter he wrote to her, taking note of what was to be a temporary defection:

> I missed you in the lecture yesterday and I am glad to hear that your visit to the camp of masculine protest played no part in your absence. I have adopted the bad habit of always directing my lecture to a definite member of the audience, and yesterday I fixed my gaze as if spellbound at the place which had been kept for you.[99]

The ghostly absent presence of "Frau Lou," like the figure of Salome herself, is here invoked as the veiled phallus, the phallus under erasure, *not* masculine protest after all. For Freud, as in a different way for Rilke and for Nietzsche, Lou Andreas *was* Salome, compact of contradiction and category crisis: the seductive "masculine" woman, the female psychiatrist, the Oriental European, who, without herself cross-dressing, theorized the power of castration—and the power of transvestism.

MAN AND OMAN

I want to conclude this articulation of an abiding cultural fantasy and its effects by taking note of at least one Middle Eastern society in which cross-dressing has played a crucial defining role. As will be clear shortly, my interest in the Omani *xanith* is not so much in determining the precise social function this personage performs for his own culture as in the ways the *xanith* has recently come to signify something particular in, and for, a discourse of "third gender" roles in the United States and in Britain.

The association of the Middle East with transvestism and sexual deviance, and particularly with male homosexuality, reached what might be thought of as a theoretically inevitable stage with the discovery by an anthropologist, in 1977, of an Arabic culture that seemed to institutionalize the transsexual male as a third gender role. Writing in the British anthropological journal *Man,* Unni Wikan described the *xanith* of coastal Oman, effeminate males who wore pastel-colored *dishdashas*, walked with swaying gait and "reeked of perfume," who functioned as house servants and/or homosexual prostitutes, and who associated on most formal and informal occasions not with the men in this rigidly segregated Muslim society, but with the women. At a wedding Wikan observed *xanith* singing with the women, eating with them, even entering the bride's seclusion chamber and peeping behind her veil.

Wikan identified these *xanith* as "transsexuals," a term she defined as "a socially acknowledged role pattern whereby a person acts and is classified as if he/she were a person of the opposite sex for a number of crucial purposes." (This definition, which she attributed to Drs. Harry Benjamin and Robert Stoller, was later to be one of many points on which she was challenged.) The transsexuals of this Omani society—which she located in and around the small coastal town of Sohar, "reputed home of Sinbad the Sailor"— occupied, said Wikan, an intermediate role between men and women, a third position that was clearly demarcated by their dress.

> The transsexual . . . is not allowed to wear the mask [which covers forehead. cheeks, nose, and lips of Omani women from about the age of 13], or other female clothing. His clothes are intermediate between male and female; he wears the ankle-length tunic of the male, but with the tight waist of the female dress. Male clothing is white, females wear patterned cloth in bright colours, and transsexuals wear unpatterned coloured clothes. Men cut their hair short, women wear theirs long, the transsexuals medium long. Men comb their hair backward away from the face, women comb theirs diagonally forward from a central parting, transsexuals comb theirs forward from a sideparting, and they oil it heavily in the style of women. Both men and women cover their head, transsexuals go bareheaded. Perfume is used by both sexes, especially at festive occasions and during intercourse. The transsexual is generally heavily perfumed, and uses much make-up to draw attention to himself. This is also achieved by his affected swaying gait, emphasized by the close-fitting garments. His sweet falsetto voice and facial expressions and movements also closely mimic those of women.[100]

The transsexuals in Omani society, unlike women, according to Wikan, are deemed capable of representing themselves in a legal capacity; juridically, they are men, as they are grammatically, being referred to in the masculine gender. They are punished if they attempt to wear women's clothes. *Xanith*, biologically male, serve as passive homosexual prostitutes. If they wish to and can afford to, however, they may marry, and if they succeed in "perform[ing] intercourse in the male role" (Wikan, 308), and giving the traditional proof of defloration of the bride, they cease to be *xanith* and become men.

Thus Wikan suggests that it is the sexual act, and not the sexual organs, that defines gender in the society. Should he wish to, a *xanith* who has married may return to his former status, as some older *xanith*, once widowed, sometimes do; this change he signals by a public action (like singing at a wedding) that declares him to be no longer a man. The *xanith* can continue throughout his life to change from the role of "woman" to that of "man." Wikan explains the social necessity of this third gender role by the high standard of purity imposed upon Omani women; prostitutes are necessary, though held in low repute. *Xanith* are often "sexual deviants," who are attracted to their own sex; this the society accepts, though it does not approve. The Omani system thus protects women, while severely restricting their freedoms, and accommodates sexual variation as well as male sexual appetite by establishing a triad of gender roles, woman, man, and transsexual. About one in fifty males in Sohar become *xanith*.

The appearance of Wikan's article in the pages of *Man*—a journal whose complacent nineteenth-century title lent an unacknowledged irony to the succeeding exchanges—led to immediate and heated debate. The situation of the *xanith*, it was suggested by one scholar, was more likely the result of economic than of innate gender characteristics; a "man" is one who has the wherewithal to buy "himself" a bride—something, for example, that "dominant lesbian women" in a similar society of Muslims in Mombasa, Kenya, had perceived, choosing to have dependents rather than to be one. Poverty, not the demands of the male role, might be the cause of the *xanith*'s lifestyle.[101] Another correspondent accused Wikan of being "doggedly ethnocentric," and ignoring comparative materials from other cultures in order to make a claim for singularity in the case of the *xanith*. Citing articles on transsexuals in Aden, Australia, and Polynesia, as well as in the streets of Naples and Sydney, he urged anthropologists to come out of the closet and study the scene around them in the major cities of the West.[102]

Wikan retorted sharply, again in *Man*, flinging the charge of ethnocentrism back at her first critic; the argument that marriage creates an inequality in the status of women vis-à-vis men is "nothing less than straightforward and fashionable ethnocentricity," she declared. Indeed this epithet, which is clearly the worst possible insult to an anthropologist, surfaced yet again in Wikan's stinging reply to a *second* letter from the same critic ("less readiness to reshape . . . reality with ethnocentric—or Mombasa—concepts would protect her from pursing so many odd and fruitless tangents").[103] Citing the British explorer Richard Burton on the subject of pederasty among the Arabs and faulting Wikan for "assuming that in a sex act between men one partner is always a substitute woman," Gill Shepherd of the London School of Economics again contended that Wikan was overemphasizing gender and ignoring economic and class factors.

The controversy continued to occupy *Man* and its readers. A further pair of correspondents queried Wikan's use of the term "Oman"—which covers a wide variety of communities, all different from one another—suggested that (presumably like Margaret Mead) she "may possibly have been misled by her female informants," and challenged the notion of "intermediate gender" in particular and the role analysis mode of theorization in general.[104] And another writer challenged Wikan's use of the term "transsexual," pointing out that her definition (given above) differed sharply from Stoller's description of transsexuals as those who "contend from earliest childhood that they are really members of the opposite sex." "Anthropologists," the writer asserted, "would perhaps be better off just using ethnic labels in the analysis of cross-gender and sexual behaviour in other societies. Sufficient cross-cultural data are not yet available to make sound judgements as to how well Western *clinical* categories fit these behaviours in non-Western societies."[105]

This, in point of fact, seems to be not only a key problem in Wikan's argument but also a key factor raising the temperature (and the stakes) in the exchange that it provoked.

How possible is it to take a term like "transsexual," coined in 1949 to describe the condition of certain European and Anglo-American men, and translate it back into a culture which had been closed to the outside world (by Wikan's account) until 1971? What are the *ideological* and *political* implications of this cross-cultural labeling, and what if anything does it have to do with the constructed role of the Middle East itself as an "intermediate" zone, a place where pederasty, homosexuality, and transsexualism are all perceived (by Western observers) as viable options? If a Shangri-La for transsexualism as a "natural" development, a "third gender role" crucial to the social economy, were to be discovered *anywhere,* we should not perhaps be surprised to find that it is located in Oman, in the "reputed home of Sinbad the Sailor."

Nor should we be surprised that, whatever the methodological shortcomings of Wikan's research, or the unexamined implications discerned in it by feminists, Marxists, or comparative anthropologists, her argument for the *xanith* should be welcomed, uncritically, by another interested group; the editors, and presumably the readers, of *TV-TS Tapestry: The Journal for Persons Interested in Crossdressing and Transsexualism.* An article by "Nancy A.," entitled "Other Old Time Religions," cites Wikan's research extensively and straightforwardly, describing the dress and customs of the *xanith* in Omani society, and noting as well other transvestite or transsexual societies mentioned by Wikan or her various correspondents: the *berdache* of the Plains Indians, virtually the locus classicus of transsexualism in anthropology, and inevitably mentioned in survey studies of cross-dressing;[106] the *mahu* of Tahiti, who serves as a symbolic marker in his village, against which men can define their own role ("Since I am not the '*mahu*,' I must be a man," as Nancy A. puts it, though her source in the pages of *Man* is less liberally inclined; *his* imagined Tahitian villager says to himself, "this is what I am not and what I must not become"[107]).

At one point, after noting that *xanith* who wear women's clothes are imprisoned and flogged, the author comments in a somewhat wistful parenthesis "(I guess it's not so great after all)"—a reminder that "Nancy A." herself is a male-to-female cross-dresser. The final paragraph makes it clear that the *xanith* and the *mahu* are for *Tapestry*'s readers nothing less than role models, examples of societies in which the cross-dresser and transsexual have a crucial defining place. "I'm not sure," she concludes, "if these examples tempt you to fly to Tahiti or Oman . . . but at least you can see other societies' responses to a common phenomenon. Although we can't be as open as we would like, we can get out and help others understand and be more accepting. We have no clearly defined role, set rigidly in the society we live in, as do the others we have mentioned, so we have to make our own way."

Nancy A.'s article manifestly illustrates many of the dangers warned against by Unni Wikan's critics. Obviously a lay commentary and an unsophisticated one at that, completely unscholarly in style and method, it generalizes with unwarranted broadness and collapses distinctions that the warring anthropologists on the battlefields of *Man* are at great, and important, pains to draw. The ultimate epithet, "ethnocentric," could again be deployed against it, if so big a club is needed to swat so small a fly. Yet the very ethnocentricity of the piece is its political strength. Nancy A. espouses what might be described as an ethnocentric pluralism. The *xanith*, the *berdache*, and the *mahu* are her brothers—or her sisters. Her aims are frankly political and oppositional, her subject position as social marginal is her license to generalize and indeed to omit what does not suit her purposes. For example, she takes the title of Wikan's article, "Man Becomes Woman: Transsexualism in Oman as a Key to Gender Roles," and masterfully abbreviates it, in the manner of the *National Enquirer*, as "Man Becomes Woman," so that she can say, without overt irony, that Unni Wikan notes such-and-such "in her article, 'Man Becomes Woman' in the anthropological journal *Man*." This is a tour-de-force of titles and gender roles, and if *Man* does not become *Woman* as a result of such efforts, perhaps it ought to. Certainly the kind of -centrism indicated by *Man*'s nineteenth-century title is at least a little decentered in the course of these exertions, and feminists who cavil about welcoming male-to-female transsexuals in their midst might take note of the effectiveness of an interested critique from a position so culturally disadvantaged ("we can't be as open as we would like") that it mandates outreach as a condition for existence ("we can get out and help others understand and be more accepting"; "we have to make our own way").

The strictly veiled, strictly masked, strictly segregated women of the Sohari region of Oman, Wikan reasoned, were the precondition for the development of the *xanith* role. Men needed sex, women needed companionship, both needed servants; the *xanith* needed money, or sex, or acceptance, or all of these. The triadic structure she suggested, and that came under such sharp attack in part because it did posit a social logic, a story of positions and positionality, is a cultural reading of a social phenomenon, a reading clearly influenced, whether before or after the fact, by Wikan's discovery of a clinical literature of transsexualism. This move did not fully satisfy either anthropologists or clinicians. But it provided a necessary template for transsexuals and transvestites themselves—*some* transsexuals and transvestites, U.S. transsexuals and transvestites, not the *xanith*—to analyze and interpret the possibilities and dignities of their own social role.

This is another side to Orientalism; more than one kind of Western subject looks East, and sees himself/herself already inscribed there. What, finally, does the controversy around *Man* and Oman have to do with "the chic of Araby"? The *xanith* provided an uncanny "role model" for some observers specifically concerned with gender dysphoria and gender roles, and offered yet one more extraordinary example of the complex ways in which some Westerners have looked East for role models and for deliberate cultural masquerade—for living metaphors that define, articulate, or underscore the contradictions and fantasies with which they live.

13

THE TRANSVESTITE CONTINUUM
LIBERACE–VALENTINO–ELVIS

You don't understand. It's not that there's something extra that makes a superstar. It's that there's something missing.

George Michael[1]

Madonna announced to her screaming fans: "I want you all to know that there are only three real men on this stage—me and my two backup girls!"

Liz Smith, "Gossip"[2]

The television show "Saturday Night Live" once featured a mock game show called "¿Quién es mas macho?" in which contestants vied with each other to make gender distinctions. "¿Quién es mas macho?" "Fernando Lamas or Ricardo Montalban?" In Laurie Anderson's avant-garde film, *Home of the Brave*, this became a contest to distinguish between two objects: "¿Qué es mas macho?" Which *thing* is more macho? Pineapple or knife? Toaster or convertible? The choices here were deliberately self-parodic; it was culture itself that was being gendered. And the joke was further perpetrated by Anderson herself, deftly deploying a special microphone, or "audio mask," that lowered her voice to a "male" register. She appeared live onstage in a tuxedo-like black suit and white shirt, but within the film, for one startling moment, she cross-cross-dressed to play Eve in a gold-lamé skirt. *Qué es mas macho?*

Throughout this book I have tried both to theorize the question of transvestism and to demarcate certain structures that seem, sometimes surprisingly, to characterize or accompany it. As I have already noted, the more I have studied transvestism and its relation to representation the more I have begun to see it, oddly enough, as in many ways normative: as a condition that very frequently accompanies theatrical representation when theatrical self-awareness is greatest. Transvestite theater from Kabuki to the Renaissance English stage to the contemporary drag show is not—or not only—a recuperative structure for the social control of sexual behavior, but also a critique of the possibility of "representation" itself.

In order to make such large claims for transvestism as a social and theoretical force—in order to argue, as I have, that there can be no culture without the transvestite, because the transvestite marks the entry into the Symbolic—I need to test out the *boundaries* of transvestism, to see it or read it in places other than where it is most obvious. I need to argue, in other words, for an *unconscious* of transvestism, for transvestism as a language that can be read, and double-read, like a dream, a fantasy, or a slip of the tongue. In the domain of theater, which we have seen to be the self-reflexive locus of much transvestite activity, I want to hypothesize what might be called "unmarked" transvestism, to explore the possibility that some entertainers who do not overtly claim to be "female impersonators," for example, may in fact signal their cross-gender identities onstage, and that this quality of crossing—which is fundamentally related to other kinds of boundary-crossing in their performances—can be more powerful and seductive than explicit "female impersonation," which is often designed to confront, scandalize, titillate, or shock.

But first, let me discuss for a moment the "normative" case and the issues it raises. One clear space in which to explore the power of transvestism as theatricality is in contemporary popular culture, specifically the pop-rock-scene, where cross-dressing, "androgyny," and gender-bending have become almost de rigueur. David Bowie, Boy George, Kiss, Tiny Tim, Twisted Sister, Siouxie Sioux, the New York Dolls, from glam- and glitter-rock to heavy metal, from the seventies to the nineties, cross-dressing has meant deliberately and brashly—and politically—calling into question received notions of "masculine" and "feminine," straight and gay, girl and woman, boy and man. To give one random but suggestive example, Dee Snider, male lead singer of Twisted Sister, was voted one of the worst-dressed *women* of the year in 1984.[3]

When Boy George, in full makeup, wig, and flowing skirts, accepted a Grammy Award in 1984, he remarked to the television audience, "Thank you, America, you've got style and taste, and you know a good drag queen when you see one."[4] When he published a book of clothing patterns, complete with makeup instructions, it was immediately snapped up—by his *female* fans.[5] Let us agree to call Boy George (né George O'Dowd) a *marked transvestite*, a cross-dresser whose clothing seems deliberately and obviously at variance with his anatomical gender assignment.

Consider another telling instance of marked transvestism. At an event billed as "The First Annual Female Impersonator of the Year Contest" one of the broadcast commentators was short, plain, comic actress Ruth Buzzi, former star of "Laugh-In." As the curvaceous, stunningly coiffed and made-up contestants in their glittering gowns emerged, on-camera, from a door prominently marked "Men," and the camera panned back and forth between them and Buzzi, the audience was tacitly invited to speculate on the nature of "womanhood" or "femininity." This may well rank as a species of producer misogyny, but it also frames a question: if "woman" is culturally constructed, and if female impersonators are *conscious* constructors of artificial and artifactual femininity, how does a "female impersonator" differ from a "woman"? The question seems both ludicrous and offensive, but its theoretical and social implications are large and important. Female impersonators are often accused of misogyny (and regularly deny the charge), but in the female impersonator, the feminist debate about essentialism versus constructedness finds an unexpected, parodic, and unwelcome test.

Here is one drag queen's answer, describing the heyday of the London drag balls of the sixties: "there was a definite distinction then as there is now between the drag queens, who enjoyed masquerading as women, and the sex changes [that is, transsexuals], who regarded themselves, and were regarded, as real women."[6]

"Masquerading" versus "real" women. It makes sense that transsexuals, who have invested so much in anatomical alteration, should insist that the ground of reality is the feminized body: the body undergoing hormone treatment to develop breasts and hips, undergoing surgery to translate the penis into a vagina. But this binarism between "masquerading" and "real women" has been at the center of disputes and discussions among psychoanalytic critics, feminist film theorists, and, most recently, lesbian or self-described "queer theorists." Drawing on Joan Riviere's classic essay, "Womanliness as a Masquerade," and on Lacan's revision and extension of that essay in "The Signification of the Phallus," theorists have sought to define "woman" as a construct that depends, for reasons social and political as well as erotic, upon masks and masquerade.

Riviere had argued not only that "women who wish for masculinity may put on a mask of womanliness to avert anxiety and the retribution feared from men," but also that it was impossible to separate womanliness *from* masquerade:

> The reader may now ask how I define womanliness or where I draw the line between genuine womanliness and the "masquerade." My suggestion is not, however, that there is any such difference; whether radical or superficial, they are the same thing.[7]

The woman constructed by culture is, then, according to Riviere, already an impersonation. Womanliness *is* mimicry, *is* masquerade.

Here is Jacques Lacan, rewriting Riviere to describe "display in the human being," not just in the woman:

> the fact that femininity finds its refuge in this mask, by virtue of the fact of the [repression] inherent in the phallic mark of desire, has the curious consequence of making *virile* display in the human being itself seem feminine. ("The Signification of the Phallus," 291)

What does this mean? Is it that *all* display is feminine, because it is artifactual and displaced, a sign of anxiety and lack? Or that virile display *becomes* feminine because in being displayed it exhibits its own doubt? Or is it that the phallus is that which cannot be displayed? As we will see, the upshot of each of these three scenarios is the same.

As the Lacanian analyst Eugénie Lemoine-Luccioni explains, in a passage we have already noticed in connection with "fetish envy," "if the penis was the phallus, men would have no need of feathers or ties or medals. . . . Display [*parade*], just like the masquerade, thus betrays a flaw: no one has the phallus."[8]

In the same essay ("The Signification of the Phallus") Lacan had talked about the relations between the sexes as governed by three terms, not two: "to have" the phallus, which is what, in fantasy, *men* do; "to be" the phallus, the object of desire, which is what, in fantasy, *women* do; and the intervening term, "to seem." This intervention, of "seeming" (or "appearing"), substituted for "having," and protecting against the threat of loss, is, precisely, the place of the transvestite. So that, in psychoanalytic terms, the transvestite does represent a third space, a space of representation, even within a psychic economy in which *all* positions are fantasies. The theatrical transvestite literalizes the anxiety of phallic loss. The overdetermination of phallic jokes, verbal and visual, that often accompany transvestism onstage, is a manifestation of exactly this strategy of reassurance for anxiety through artifactual overcompensation.

Lacan's suggestion about "virile display" *seeming* feminine is a key one, because it is precisely this "curious consequence," paradoxical as it may seem, that characterizes the "transvestite effect" in what I am calling "unmarked transvestites." For while it is easy to speak of the power of transvestite display in figures like David Bowie, Boy George, and Annie Lennox, these overt cross-dressers, "marked transvestites," may in fact merely literalize something that is more powerful when masked or veiled—that is, when it remains unconscious.

I would now like to turn to three figures from popular culture in whom a certain consternation of gender is, to use a distinction from Roland Barthes, "received" but not "read."[9] ("The rhetorical or latent signified," says Barthes, discussing the ideology of fashion, is "the essential paradox of connoted signification: it is, one might say, a signification that is *received* but not *read*.") This is another opportunity to look *at* rather than *through* the transvestite, in this case by regarding the unconscious of transvestism as a speaking symptom, a language of clothing which is, tacitly, both dress and address. Unlike professional female impersonators, or comedians who affect travesty for particular theatrical ends (Milton Berle, Flip Wilson as Geraldine, Dana Carvey as the Church Lady), these performers do not think of themselves as transvestites. But—as we will see—the way they are received and discussed in the media, and, increasingly, the way they emphasize their own trademark idiosyncrasies of dress in response to audience interest all suggest that the question of cross-dressing, whether overt or latent, is central to their success, and even to the very question of stardom.

My first example may strike you as a bit too obvious to be considered completely unmarked, but he is, I think, at the origin of a certain theatrical worrying of exactly that borderline. I refer, of course, to the figure "known variously as Mr. Showmanship, the Candelabra Kid, Guru of Glitter, Mr. Smiles, The King of Diamonds, and Mr. Boxoffice," and described as "undoubtedly America's most beloved entertainer"[10]: Liberace.

Liberace, pianist, singer, tap dancer, and fashion plate, clearly regarded himself as a direct influence upon the pop stars of the eighties, citing Prince, Michael Jackson, Boy George, and Madonna as among those who had learned from him about "escapism and fantasy."[11] "There was a time," he reminisced, "when one woman might say to another, 'May I borrow your lipstick?' Now, it's not unusual for one male rocker to say to another, 'May I borrow your eyeliner?' And practically no man is above borrowing his best friend's skin bronzer" (Liberace, 222). "I was the first to create shock waves," he said. "For me to wear a simple tuxedo onstage would be like asking Marlene Dietrich to wear a housedress."[12]

The genial campiness of these remarks offers the retrospective view of a survivor. Yet Liberace's crossover career in fact tested boundaries with a singular combination of business acumen and purported self-revelation. Strikingly illustrating the notion I have developed above of the transvestite who emerges as sign of a "category crisis" located in a domain other than that of gender, he straddled the line between classical and popular music, all the while keeping his costume changes one jump (or one jumpsuit) ahead of the competition. A black diamond mink cape lined with Austrian rhinestones, weighing 135 pounds, so heavy that it gave one backstage worker a hernia. An ostrich-feather cape. A hundred-pound cape of pink-dyed turkey feathers for the Radio City Music Hall Easter Show, in which he planned to emerge from a giant Fabergé egg. "Quite frankly," grumped one critic, "all that pink and feathers make him look like a female impersonator auditioning for 'An Evening at La Cage.' "[13] A white fox fur cape with a long train which he wore for a command performance for the Queen. A matador's outfit that prefigures George Michael's—and Grace Jones's. A fancy-dress uniform with epaulets and gold braid that anticipates Michael Jackson in "We Are the World." Red, white, and blue hot pants that made him look like a drum majorette. His rings and jewelry were as extravagant as his furs and sequins. "To shake his hand," said the *New York Times*, "was to flirt with laceration."[14]

Liberace's appeal is often thought to have been largely or exclusively to older women, but at the peak of his popularity he was a culture hero to "girls and women of all ages— ready to squeal or swoon when they thought the occasion required it of them," and who responded with "hysterical adoration" to his appearance in 1956 at the Festival Hall— at least according to the customarily staid *Times* of London.[15] When the Liberace family— Lee, George, and their mother—arrived in London in 1956, he was welcomed by a crowd of over 3,000, mostly young girls and women, though the *Times* also notes the presence of "a few amused policemen [and] some ardent young men."[16] The British reviews are cautiously admiring, of his "resourceful" piano playing and "agreeable" singing and tap dancing as well as his "fancy dress": "with all his finery and his almost natural peaches and cream complexion," one noted, "he is a shy, quiet little man. . . . He did not swank or slobber, or flash diamond rings shaped like grand pianos at his admirers" (*Times*, October 2, 1956).

His performances were more like fashion shows than piano recitals. Parading up and down the stage in outfit after outfit ("Pardon me while I go slip into something more spectacular") he was in effect the first to mainstream "voguing"—the eighties dance craze, borrowed from male transvestite drag shows in Harlem in the sixties, that incorporates exaggerated fashion model poses. Liberace dressed for the stage, he said himself, "just one step short of drag" (Thomas, 215).

Displacing sexual questions onto sartorial ones with practiced ease, Liberace used the word "straight" to describe his "civilian" or offstage *clothes* (Liberace, 179). Although in his stage performances of the eighties he joked that he'd never wear in the street the clothes he wore on the stage, "or I'd get picked up, for sure," he preserved a theatrical space in which he could both assert and put in teasing question his heterosexuality and his biological or anatomical maleness. Thus the gag lines in his nightclub act about "streaking" with sex-symbol Burt Reynolds ("I've got the diamonds, he's got the jewels") and about the necessity of getting up from the piano from time to time ("it straightens the shorts").[17]

While he was not afraid of feminization, and in fact courted it, he steadfastly denied that he was gay, despite clear evidence to the contrary. He even went so far as to sue the London *Daily Mirror* columnist "Cassandra" (William Neil Connor, writing under a cross-gendered pseudonym) for using words like "fruit-flavored" and "it" to describe him. Cassandra had written—bizarrely, we may think—that Liberace was "the summit of sex—the pinnacle of masculine, feminine, and neuter. Everything that, he, she, and it can ever want." Masculine, feminine, and neuter. He, she, and it. Cassandra, oracularly, had consigned Liberace to the space of thirdness, the realm of the Lacanian Symbolic and of the transvestite. The space of desire.

The court case was itself a shrewd performance of transvestite theater stage-managed for optimal effect. Liberace's London barrister, dressed in his wig and robes, gestured toward the Beefeaters, the Knights of the Garter, and the guards at Buckingham palace as models of "glamour" "in these days of somewhat drab and dreary male clothing." "Look at me, My Lords and my learned friends, dressed in accordance with old traditions. We do not dress like this in ordinary trial testimony, nor does Liberace" (Thomas, 130–31) As if to make this point, Liberace had arrived in court wearing a conservative blue suit, white shirt, and necktie.

On the occasion of another law case, this one a palimony suit directed at him by a long-time male companion, a judge ruled in Liberace's favor when a woman process server said she had delivered a summons to him when he was dressed in a brown business suit. "That man wouldn't be caught dead in a brown business suit," said the judge (Thomas, 230). The plaintiff in the case, his former protegé, Scott Thorson, had told the scandal sheet *National Enquirer*, spitefully, that Liberace was almost totally bald and wore hairpieces on stage, and that he had had two major facelifts. "When he took me in his arms," Thorson testified with self-justifying "candor," "it revolted me at first." "I was unaccustomed to his full make-up." When asked if he himself was wearing makeup at the deposition, Thorson acknowledged that he was (Thomas, 228).

Makeup, wigs, face-lifts. This is the apparatus of "woman," that is to say, the artifactual creation of female impersonation and the drag queen on the one hand, and the youth culture on the other. "In fashion," says Roland Barthes, "it is age that is important, not sex." "Both sexes tend to become uniform under a single sign . . .: that of *youth*" (Barthes, 257, 258). By the end of his career Liberace's face looked as rigid and wooden as those of the mannequins at his Liberace Museum in Las Vegas ("the third most popular attraction in the entire state of Nevada"[18]), to which his old costumes, like Roy Rogers's stuffed horse, Trigger, were retired. As famous for his love of his mother as for supporting singlehandedly the entire Austrian rhinestone industry, he had somehow to remain a "boy," both in his private life as a gay man and in his public life as the crown prince of Mother's Day.

And this may be a reason for the one extraordinary and unexpected act of female impersonation that did become incorporated into Liberace's act: the aerial flying, back and forth across the stage, that developed into a regular feature of his performance. Already "ageless," a parodic version of the eternal "boy," with his face-lifts, hairpieces, and increasingly heavy makeup, he conceived of a desire to become (although he never says so): Peter Pan. Ostensibly this fantasy was triggered by the aerodynamic effect of his cape as he left the stage one night; soon he had enlisted Peter Foy, of the English Flying Foys, the man who had taught two generations of female Peter Pans, including Mary Martin, to "fly." Liberace here is, for a moment, a triumph of metonymic transvestism, a middle-aged man imitating a woman who plays a fantasy changeling boy.

It was not Peter Pan, however, who was Liberace's ideal, but rather a male star who had remained forever young by the unlooked-for expedient of dying early—his namesake, Rudolph Valentino. Liberace's mother, a great fan of the Latin lover, named her son Wladziu Valentino Liberace and, for good measure, also named his younger brother Rudolph. In many ways Liberace seems to have been haunted by the phantom of Valentino, "my namesake," as he described him to reporters (Thomas, 100). He had some of Valentino's elaborate costumes copied for stage performance. He bought Valentino's bed and put it in one of his guest rooms; he collected and exhibited at the Liberace Museum a pair of silver goblets said to have been intended as wedding gifts to Valentino and Pola Negri.

Furthermore, Valentino appears as a major figure in Liberace's personal social history of crossover style: "Years ago, both male and female movie legends influenced the fashion and cosmetic industries. All over the world, you could find copies of Dietrich's eyebrows, Joan Crawford's shoulder pads and shoes, Valentino's slave bracelet, as well as his slicked-back, glossy patent-leather hairstyle" (Liberace, 222). All of these, we might note, are cross-dressed or cross-gendered examples: a woman's shoulder pads, a man's bracelet, Dietrich's eyebrows.

He-man, heartthrob, movie idol, Valentino seems about as distant from Liberace—and from transvestism, marked or unmarked—as it would seem possible to get. Yet he is in fact an exemplary figure of unmarked transvestism, at once feminized and hypermale. His appearance in Arab robes, eyebrow pencil and mascara as the title character in *The Sheik* (1921), as we have noted, set off a frenzy of response among (largely female) filmgoers with its drama of sexual sadism amidst the tents of a "Middle Eastern" locale.

In fact the cross-dressing elements in Valentino's story are stronger and more omnipresent than the eye-makeup and the flowing robes. A notorious photograph of him as a faun, dressed in fake fur tights and playing a flute was exhibited in court. Valentino apparently tried to explain it as a "costume test" for a never-produced film called *The Faun through the Ages,* but it is more probable that he was posing in the Nijinsky role from *L'Après-midi d'un Faune* at the behest of his wife, the dancer Natacha Rambova. But then his wife—or rather, his wives—were part of his image problem, at least with men. For Rudolph Valentino, ballyhooed as the Great Lover, had married two women reputed to be lesbians, both members of the coterie surrounding the celebrated Alla Nazimova.[19] Rambova, his second wife, apparently had him prancing about in fur shorts; his first wife, Jean Acker, who according to one account "favoured a short, very masculine hairstyle, and wore a white blouse and tie under a rather severely cut suit,"[20] had locked him out of the marital bedroom and refused to consummate the marriage.

His unusual marital history, coupled with the masterful and pleasurable sadism of the original *Sheik* and the masochism and misogyny of its sequel have led some recent commentators to speculate about Valentino's own sexual orientation: "The obvious pleasure he sought from the company of young men, often as handsome as himself," writes one observer, "should not make us suppose he was homosexual." And, from the same source, "There is always something inherently feminine in the 'Great Lover,' for it is his own narcissistic reflection he seeks in the depths of his beloved's eyes" (Walker, 119). The campy appeal of Valentino to film audiences today exposes an inherent bisexuality in his self-presentation, again emphasized, if not in fact made possible, by the Arab dress he wore in his most famous film.

Valentino, as an immigrant from Italy who had worked as a gardener and a dance partner before making it in films, was first read as a foreign interloper replacing the image of the "All-American [i.e. Anglo] boy." This young Italian actor, despite the European specificity of his origins, became the prototype of the so-called "Latin lover"—the category to which, without saying so explicitly, the wits at "Saturday Night Live" had consigned the contestants for their "macho" contest, Fernando Lamas and Ricardo Montalban. (The Anglo television actor Jack Lord, star of "Hawaii Five-O," apparently "won" the contest.) In this catch-all categorization ethnic and racial distinctions become invidiously blurred, as Latino, Hispanic, Italian and presumably other dark-complected, dark-haired men are deliberately conflated as "Latin"—smooth, seductive, predatory, irresistible to women. And once again "hypermale" and "feminized" become, somehow, versions of the same description: these men are too seductive to be "really" men. As Miriam Hansen has noted, "the more desperately Valentino himself emphasized attributes of physical prowess and virility, the more perfectly he played the part of the male impersonator, brilliant counterpart to the female 'female' impersonators of the American screen such as Mae West or the vamps of his own films."[21] The mythical "Latin lover," like the "Third World," was an entity that could be simultaneously invented and manipulated. And chief among these fantasy figures, in the puritanically xenophobic imagination, was the dangerous Valentino. In other words, Rudolph Valentino was himself a significant figure of *crossover,* disruption, rupture. It was doubtless his foreignness, as well as his eye-makeup, his hair style, and his slave bracelet, that set up the confrontation between Middle East and American Midwest that led to the famous "Powder Puff" incident.

On July 18, 1926, the *Chicago Sunday Tribune* ran on its editorial page an article headlined "Pink Powder Puffs," which is worth reprinting here in its entirety:

A new public ballroom was opened on the north side a few days ago, a truly handsome place and apparently well run. The pleasant impression lasts until one steps into the men's washroom and finds there on the wall a contraption of glass tubes and levers and a slot for the insertion of a coin. The glass tubes contain a fluffy pink solid, and beneath them one reads an amazing legend which runs something like this: "Insert coin. Hold personal puff beneath the tube. Then pull the lever."

A powder vending machine! In a men's washroom! Homo Americanus! Why didn't someone quietly drown Rudolph Guglielmo, alias Valentino, years ago?

And was the pink powder machine pulled from the wall or ignored? It was not. It was used. We personally saw two "men"—as young lady contributors to the Voice of the People are wont to describe the breed—step up, insert coin, hold kerchief beneath the spout, pull the lever, then take the pretty pink stuff and pat it on their cheeks in front of the mirror.

Another member of this department, one of the most benevolent men on earth, burst raging into the office the other day because he had seen a young "man" combing his pomaded hair in the elevator. But we claim our pink powder story beats his all hollow.

It is time for a matriarchy if the male of the species allows such things to persist. Better a rule by masculine women than by effeminate men. Man began to slip, we are beginning to believe, when he discarded the straight razor for the safety pattern. We shall not be surprised when we hear that the safety razor has given way to the depilatory.

Who or what is to blame is what puzzles us. Is this degeneration into effeminacy a cognate reaction with pacificism to the virilities and realities of the war? Are pink powder and parlor pinks in any way related? How does one reconcile masculine cosmetics, sheiks, floppy pants, and slave bracelets with a disregard for law and an aptitude for crime more in keeping with the frontier of half a century ago than a twentieth century metropolis?

Do women like the type of "man" who pats pink powder on his face in a public washroom and arranges his coiffure in a public elevator? Do women at heart belong to the Wilsonian era of "I Didn't Raise My Boy to be a Soldier"? What has become of the old "caveman" line?

It is a strange social phenomenon and one that is running its course, not only here in America but in Europe as well. Chicago may have its powder puffs; London has its dancing men and Paris its gigolos. Down with Decatur; up with Elinor Glyn. Hollywood is the national school of masculinity. Rudy, the beautiful gardener's boy, is the prototype of the American male.

Hell's bells. Oh, sugar.[22]

Oh, sugar, indeed. Masculine cosmetics, depilatories, sheiks, floppy hats, and slave bracelets, effeminacy and a propensity for crime, pacifism, and communism—blame for all of these is placed squarely at the foot, or the braceleted wrist, of "Rudy, the beautiful gardener's boy." Here, without strain, the dark complected, hot-blooded Italian is conflated with the dark-complected, hot-blooded Sheik. No face-saving gesture reveals *this* Sheik as really a blue-blooded, white-skinned aristocrat. Instead his clean cut looks are attributed to an effeminate use of depilatories.

Valentino's taste for finery, including the infamous slave bracelets, laid him open to this kind of xenophobic attack from middle America in the midst of the summer doldrums. He took it personally, and very badly, issuing a challenge to his detractor, not to a duel, which the laws of the country forbade, but to a boxing or wrestling match, "to prove in typically American fashion, for I am an American citizen, which is the better man." The challenge concluded, "Hoping I will have an opportunity to demonstrate to you that the wrist under a slave bracelet may snap a real fist into your sagging jaw, and that I may teach you respect of a man even though he happens to prefer to keep his face clean, I remain, With utter contempt, Rudolph Valentino."[23]

Time magazine, reporting on the editorial and the challenge, described him as "a closely muscled man, whose sombre skin was clouded with talcum and whose thick wrists tinkled with a perpetual arpeggio of fine gold bangles, [who] read the effusion with rapidly mounting fury."[24] *Time* quoted him as saying that his profession required the makeup, while sentiment demanded the bracelets. But the editorial writer never revealed himself, and after a boxing match with a friendly New York sports reporter (which Valentino won, perhaps by this feat inspiring the mother of Cassius Clay to name her second son Rudolph Valentino Clay [Botham and Donnelly, 200]) he denounced the absent editorial writer as a coward: "The heroic silence of the writer who chose to attack me without provocation in the *Chicago Tribune* leaves no doubt as to the total absence of manliness *in his whole make-up*," Valentino wrote, with evident irony and, no doubt, unintended double entendre, his mind still dwelling on the powder puff incident.

Unavenged, the insult continued to rankle to the end of his life. When he was rushed into the hospital for the gastric ulcer and consequent peritonitis that would shortly lead to his death (though some claimed that he had been poisoned by a jealous rival), his first words on awakening from surgery were, reportedly, "Doctor, am I a pink puff?"[25] And in the final twist of fate, when his body lay in state at Campbell's Funeral Parlour in New York City, where an unprecedented 100,000 people filed by his catafalque, the mortician's art fulfilled his greatest fear: "Valentino lay in a half open casket, his hair slickered down into the familiar patent-leather imitation of life, his eyebrows freshly pencilled by a makeup man and his cheeks rouged in a manner that did indeed recall the gibe about the 'pink powder puff' " (Walker, 116).

Xenophobia, classicism, racism, homophobia. Notice that Valentino is not being explicitly described as gay, but as contributing to effeminacy and foppery, sapping the virility of the American Male. Again display and masquerade are perceived as feminine, and feminizing.

We have been looking at Rudolph Valentino as the unlikely role model for Liberace and as the equally unlikely object of what might be called "transvestification." Where Liberace was complicit with his cultural classification as a transvestite figure, instinctively understood its relationship to "star quality," and made it work for him, Valentino was both surprised and appalled, challenging the editorial writer to a boxing match to prove "which is the better man." But there is a third figure who stands in significant relation to these two, uncannily linked by circumstances that seem both bizarre and overdetermined, and that is the figure of Elvis Presley.

We have already noted that Liberace thought of himself as the precursor of glitter rock. But of all the show business "copies" to which Liberace laid claim, the one he most insisted upon was Elvis Presley. In his testimony in a British court in 1959 he maintained that he had to "dress better than the others who were copying me. One was a young man named Elvis Presley" (Thomas, 131). He made the same claim to the media on the occasion of his twenty-fifth anniversary in show business: "Because of Elvis Presley and his imitators, I really have to exaggerate to look different and to top them."[26] Elvis became a *cause* of feminine virile display.

There is a famous moment, a kind of sartorial primal scene, in which Elvis and Liberace themselves change clothes, become each other's changelings. In 1956 they met in Las Vegas, when Elvis appeared in the audience at Liberace's show. Liberace invited the young singer backstage, where, apparently at the suggestion of a press agent, Elvis put on Liberace's gold-sequinned tuxedo jacket, and Liberace donned Elvis's striped sport coat. They then swapped instruments, Liberace on guitar, Elvis on piano, and jammed together for twenty minutes on two of their signature tunes, "Hound Dog" and "I'll Be Seeing You." "Elvis and I may be characters," commented Liberace, "me with my gold jackets and him with his sideburns—but we can afford to be" (Thomas, 117).

This crossover moment between two crossover stars (Liberace traversing the boundary between pop and classical, Elvis between "white" and "black" music) has important implications beyond those of local publicity. The *New York Times* obituary for Liberace says, succinctly, about his gold lamé jacket, "Soon Elvis Presley was wearing a suit of gold lamé. Soon Elvis impersonators were wearing suits of gold lamé."[27] (So that Elvis impersonators are really Liberace impersonators.[28])

Predictably, the keepers of the Elvis legend are less forthcoming about any Liberace connection.[29] The film *This Is Elvis* shows a shot of the Riviera Hotel marquee proclaiming

"Liberace" in large letters, presumably to show what kind of entertainment Las Vegas was used to before the arrival of the King. An off-screen narrator impersonating the voice of Elvis says, "Liberace and his brother were one of the top acts of the time. I wasn't sure the place was ready for Elvis Presley." The point is contrast, disruption, not continuity.

Thirteen years later Elvis returned to Las Vegas, heavier, in pancake makeup, wearing a white jumpsuit with an elaborate jeweled belt and cape, crooning pop songs to a microphone: in effect, he had become Liberace. Even his fans were now middle-aged matrons and blue-haired grandmothers, who praised him as a good son who loved his mother; Mother's Day became a special holiday for Elvis's fans as it was for Liberace's.

A 1980 videotape of *Liberace in Las Vegas* (made, therefore, three years after Elvis's death), opens with a lush videotour of his home, including a tour of his closet. This is surely in part a camp joke, but the racks and racks of sequins, rhinestones, and furs—all of which we will shortly see him model onstage—will be oddly but closely echoed in the 1981 Elvis retrospective film, *This Is Elvis,* in which—also quite early in the film—attendants are shown readying his wardrobe for the show. Once again there are racks of clothes, jumpsuits with spangles and rhinestones, a whole rolling rack of jeweled belts. Watching the two films in succession it is difficult to tell whose closet is whose.

But something else, even more uncanny, ties Elvis and Liberace together. Both of them, remarkably, were twins, each born with a twin brother who immediately died. Both, that is to say, were—in the sense in which I have been using the term—changelings, changeling boys, substitutes for or doubles of something that never was.

Elvis Aron and Jesse Garon. *The Rolling Stone Illustrated History of Rock & Roll* notes that "His twin, Jesse Garon, died at birth, and he was always to be reminded of this absence ('They say when one twin dies, the other grows up with all the quality of the other, too . . . If I did, I'm lucky'), as if he were somehow incomplete, even down to his matching name,"[30] and almost all his biographers make some version of the same point.[31] Had Elvis's own child, Lisa Marie, been a boy, the parents intended to call him John Baron, continuing the rhyming line.

One biography of Liberace begins with a dramatization of the entertainer's momentous birth:

> "One of the babies was born under the veil," said the midwife in a voice shaded with sadness. "But the other one, my dear . . . " her voice suddenly joyful. "A *big* baby boy!"
>
> How pitiful the dead infant looked, its tiny body almost a skeleton, a film of placenta over its shriveled face like a cloth for burial . . .
>
> But the other baby—what a pulsing, squalling, robust piece of humanity. (Thomas, 1)

Uncannily enough, here is a *third* version of this changeling scenario, from the opening paragraphs of yet another biography.

Just before the turn of the present century, two bouncing babies were born who were to bring untold happiness into the lives of men and women all over the world.

One was the fledgling cinema. . . .

The other was Rudolph Valentino. . . .

As the babes grew up together, it was tragically ordained that so they would die.[32]

Jesse Garon Presley, Liberace's unnamed twin, the silent movie: three ghosts that haunt, and perhaps shape, the very notion of contemporary stardom.

Furthermore, Elvis, like Liberace, was obsessed with Rudolph Valentino, to whose celebrity (and spectacular funeral) his own were inevitably compared. The son of his promoter in the early Memphis days remembers that Elvis "aspired to be a second Rudolph Valentino" (Goldman, 129). Hence the sideburns, the "sullen, sultry leer" (the adjectives are those of Albert Goldman, a highly unsympathetic biographer), the photo sessions from this period stripped to the waist, the claim to friends that he had Italian blood.[33]

But it is the delicacy and vulnerability of the two men's visual images, as much as their sheer sexual power, that binds them. The pout, the curled lip (about which Elvis would joke onstage in his later Las Vegas years, "This lip used to curl easier"), the cool stare and contained sexuality, an auto-voyeurism incredibly provocative—all of these can be seen in Valentino's *Son of the Sheik,* an uncanny phantom of Elvis. Indeed Elvis made his own Sheik movie, *Harum Scarum* (1965), in which, dressed in "Arab" robes and headdress, pursuing the Princess Shalimar (played by Miss America Mary Ann Mobley), he is clearly intended to evoke memories of Valentino. Even the antics of the midget Billy Barty—seemingly gratuitous to the plot—echo, as if for emphasis, the hapless dwarf in *Son of the Sheik.* In an earlier—and better—film, *Jailhouse Rock* (1957), Elvis is stripped to the waist and beaten, in another clear citation from the popular Valentino film. In fact, the example of Valentino is one reason why he chose a movie career, and thus missed out on the early great days of what he himself had started—the theatricalization of rock and roll.

The comparison, explicit and implicit, is everywhere in the press. An article in *McCall's* (presumably a Bible for the matrons of fandom) described Elvis's bodyguards as "on a scale not seen in Hollywood since the days of Valentino and Fairbanks."[34] The *New York Times,* reporting on the hysterical scene at his funeral said, "Those old enough to remember said there had been nothing like it since Rudolf [sic] Valentino."[35] "Not since Valentino has a showbiz death so touched the national spirit," reported *People,*[36] and a Tennessee professor of psychiatry linked Elvis's superstardom with the American propensity for cult figures, suggesting, "Think of someone like Rudolph Valentino."[37] In 1989 a retro film was released about teen love in the fifties, which begins with the young hero purchasing Elvis's trademark car, a pink Cadillac; both the car and the film were called *Valentino Returns*—another evocation of the phantom, for Elvis, as we will see, is the other revenant, the other always-expected visitor, too-early lost.

Elvis, like Valentino, seemed to take the world by erotic surprise. Contrasted, again like Valentino, with a notion of the clean-cut all-American boy (represented in his case by Pat Boone), Elvis seemed for a time to stand as the personification of sex. But what does it mean to personify sex? And which sex?

The famous Ed Sullivan story—of how the camera filmed Elvis only from the waist up—has been told and retold, debunked as myth and explained as titillating publicity, a displacement upward that increased desire for a peek below. But what would that peek disclose?

"Is it a sausage? It is certainly smooth and damp-looking, but whoever heard of a 172-lb sausage 6 ft. tall?" This is the beginning of *Time* magazine's review of the film *Love Me Tender* in 1956. The referent, it soon becomes clear, is Elvis himself, not—as one might think—only a part of his anatomy. But Elvis as part-object, Elvis the Pelvis, became, not only a fan's fantasy and fetish but also, perhaps inevitably, his own. "The Pelvis"—an anatomical region which seems at first specific, but is in fact both remarkably vague and distinctly ungendered—became the site of speculation and spectatorship.

Thus, for example, an admiring male rock critic writing in 1970 praised Elvis as "The master of the sexual simile, treating his guitar as both phallus and girl. . . . rumor had it that into his skin-tight jeans was sewn a lead bar to suggest a weapon of heroic proportions."[38]

But a boyhood friend of Elvis's tells it somewhat differently, describing a stage ploy from the singer's early career, around 1955: "He would take the cardboard cylinder out of a roll of toilet paper and put a string in one end of it. Then, he'd tie that string around his waist. The other end, with the cardboard roller, would hang down outside his drawers, so as when he got onstage and reared back with that guitar in his hand, it would look to the girls up front like he had one helluva thing there inside his pants."[39]

Lead bar or toilet-paper cylinder, truth or rumor, this tale of Elvis stuffing his own pants with a prosthesis presents the Presley phallus as marionette, the uncanny as canny stage device, one that can manifest its phallic power automatically, so to speak, with the tug of a string or the backward push of the hips. Recall once more Lacan's paradox about virile display. The more protest, the more suspicion of lack. For this is what the phallus signifies: "its reality as signifier of lack." It is, as Stephen Heath points out, "the supreme signifier of an impossible identity."[40]

Psychoanalytically, transvestism is a mechanism that functions *by displacement* and *through fantasy* to enact a scenario of desire. In fetishistic cross-dressing, particular objects of clothing take on a metonymic role, displacing parts of the body, and especially the maternal phallus—that is, the impossible and imagined phallus which would represent originary wholeness.

What I am going to claim—what I have claimed throughout the book and will particularly want to argue here—is that transvestism *on the stage,* and particularly in the kind of entertainment culture that generates the phenomenon known as "stardom," is a symptom for the *culture,* rather than the individual performer. In the context of popular culture these transvestic symptoms appear, so to speak, to gratify a social or cultural scenario of desire. The onstage transvestite is the fetishized part-object for the social or cultural script of the fan.

One of the hallmarks of transvestic display, as we have seen repeatedly, is the detachable part. Wig, false breasts, the codpiece that can conceal male or female parts, or both, or neither. In the Elvis story the detachable part is not only explicitly and repeatedly described as an artificial phallus but also as a trick, a stage device, and a sham. Not for the first time the phallus itself becomes an impersonator—and, moreover, a female impersonator, for only a female would lack the phallus and need a substitute.

Elvis as female impersonator? Let us look further.

Elvis's appearance at the Grand Ole Opry, at the very beginning of his career, provoked a double scandal. His music was too black, and he was wearing eyeshadow. He was not asked back. For Chet Atkins, soon to become the organizer of Elvis's recording sessions in Nashville, the one lingering memory of Elvis at the Opry was his eye-makeup. "I couldn't get over that eye shadow he was wearing. It was like seein' a couple of guys kissin' in Key West."[41] (Notice here once again the conflation of cross-dressing, theatricality, and homosexuality.)

Elvis's hair created even more of a furor. It was like a black man's (Little Richard's; James Brown's); it was like a hood's; it was like a woman's. Race, class, and gender: Elvis's appearance violated or disrupted them all. His created "identity" as the boy who crossed over, who could take a song like "Hound Dog" from Big Mama Thornton or the onstage raving—and the pompadour, mascara, and pink and black clothing—from Little Richard, made of Elvis, in the popular imagination, a cultural mulatto, the oxymoronic "Hillbilly Cat," a living category crisis. Little Richard, defiantly gay, his conked pompadour teased up six inches above his head, his face and eyes brilliantly made-up, his clothes and capes glittering with sequins, appearing, as we have already noted "in one show dressed as the Queen of England and in the next as the pope,"[42] was vestimentary crossover incarnate,[43] not passing but trespassing. To put it another way, Elvis mimicking Little Richard is Elvis *as* female impersonator—or rather, as the *impersonator* of a female impersonator. And it is worth remembering that Richard attributes his adoption of bizarre costume in this period to *racial* crossover. "We were breaking through the racial barrier. . . . We decided that my image should be crazy and way-out so that the adults would think I was harmless" (White, 65–66). The year was 1956.

Elvis was the white "boy" who could sing "black," the music merchandiser's dream. And that crossover move was (perhaps inevitably) read as a crossover move in gender terms: a move from hypermale to hyperfemale, to, in fact, *hyperreal* female, female impersonator, transvestite.

It was in 1970, only two years after his much-heralded television "Comeback" performance, that Elvis made a striking vestimentary crossover in Las Vegas:

Not since Marlene Dietrich stunned the ringsiders with the sight of her celebrated legs encased from hip to ankle in a transparent gown had any performer so electrified Las Vegas with his mere physical appearance. Bill Belew [the costume designer], who had been very cautious up to this point about designing any costume that would make Elvis look effeminate, decided finally to kick out the jams. Now Elvis faced the house encased in a smashing white jumpsuit, slashed to the sternum and lovingly fitted around his broad shoulders, flat belly, narrow hips and tightly packed crotch. And then there were his pearls—loads of lustrous pearls, not sewn on the costume but worn unabashedly as body ornaments. (Goldman, 448)

"Not since Marlene Dietrich." This—in the voice of Elvis debunker Goldman—is Elvis precisely as female impersonator. Critic after critic notices that his sexuality is subject to reassignment, consciously or unconsciously, though the paradox—male sex symbol as female impersonator—remains perplexing and unexamined. "As for Elvis himself," writes one biographer, "he'll be gradually castrated into an everlasting pubescent boy. And as movie follows movie, each one worse than the last, he will actually start resembling a eunuch: a plump, jittery figure."[44]

Elvis moves in the course of his career along a curious continuum from androgyne to transvestite. This male sex symbol is insistently and paradoxically read by the culture as a boy, a eunuch, or a "woman"—as anything but a man.

His ex-wife Priscilla, the executive producer of the recent television series depicting Elvis's life, wanted in fact to repress, or expunge, the memory of his later years. "The problem," wrote one critic sympathetically, "is that Elvis left in such bad shape: over-weight, forgetting the words to his songs, wearing clownish rhinestone-covered jumpsuits. It's *that* Elvis—the one who keeps cropping up in books and TV-movies—that Priscilla wants to get out of people's minds." And, "if only Elvis had paid more attention to his image. Maybe he would have made it through the '70s, checked into the Betty Ford Center, turned on to aerobics. . . . "[45]

Overweight. Reviews and commentaries on Elvis in his last years speak frequently of him as having a "weight problem," as looking fat, not being able to keep the weight off. Of which gender do we usually speak in these terms? We may think of Elizabeth Taylor and her constant battle with extra pounds: Liz fat, Liz thin, Liz in and out of the Betty Ford Center. This is the spirit in which Elvis watchers watched Elvis watching his weight, as if the eternal boy within could be disclosed by the shedding of pounds, the disappearance of a telltale paunch. The comparable corpulence of wonder-boys Orson Welles and Marlon Brando, though remarked by the press, is not feminized in this way.

Yet the feminization and/or transgendering of Elvis begins much earlier than the Las Vegas jumpsuit days.[46] Whether through his mascara, his dyed hair, or his imitation of black music and style, Elvis was always already crossing over.

The 1990 debut of a weekly TV series on the life of Elvis Presley broke new ground for television programming, as John J. O'Connor noted in the *New York Times*. "It is," he points out, "the first weekly series built around the life of an actual entertainment personality"; "a decided rarity—a half-hour format devoted not to a sitcom but to straightforward biography." "Can," he wondered in print, "episodic biographies of Marilyn, Chaplin, Dean, et al., be far behind?"[47]

This list of celebrities to be compared to Elvis is instructive: Marilyn Monroe, Charlie Chaplin, James Dean. For all of them have been, like Elvis Presley, objects of imitation, repetition, replication—and re-gendering. (Think of Boy George's former boyfriend, the transvestite pop music figure Marilyn, with his long blond hair and hairy chest; of Lucille Ball's Chaplin [and Chaplin's own cross-dressing films[48]], of James Dean as lesbian butch idol, etc.) Andy Warhol, the master of pop replication, did multiple Elvises as well as Marilyns and James Deans, lots of them: a silkscreened print of Elvis's face reproduced 36 times (six across and six down); *Double* and *Triple Elvis; Red Elvis,* and a work called *Campbell's Elvis*—with Elvis's face superimposed over the label of a soup-can. Elvis was, in fact, the only pop figure Warhol carried over in his work from the fifties to the sixties. Critics have noted the affinities between the artist and the rock star: each "opted for a blank and apparently superficial parody of earlier styles which surprisingly expanded, rather than alienated, their audience." "[B]oth took repetition and superficiality to mask an obscure but vital aspect of their work: the desire for transcendence or annihilation without compromise, setting up a profound ambivalence on the part of both artist and audience as to whether the product was trash or tragedy."[49]

Newsweek read Warhol's interest in Elvis as the recognition of "an almost androgynous softness and passivity in his punk-hood persona,"[50] and the claim to androgyny, as we have seen, is not infrequently made as an explanation of Elvis's powerful appeal to women and men. But one of the things Andy Warhol may have seen in Elvis was the perfection of his status as a pop icon in his condition as always already multiple and replicated. The phenomenon of "Elvis impersonators," which began long *before* the singer's death, is one of the most startling effects of the Elvis cult.

What, then, is the relationship between transvestism and repetition? For one thing, both put in question the idea of an "original," a stable starting point, a ground. For transvestism, like the copy or simulacrum, disrupts "identity" and exposes it as figure. In one of the most famous of twentieth-century cultural analyses, Walter Benjamin noted the effect of mechanical reproduction on works of art like photography and film. "The technique of reproduction," he wrote (and think of *Elvis* here),

> detaches the reproduced object from the domain of tradition. By making many reproductions it substitutes a plurality of copies for a unique existence. And in permitting the reproduction to meet the beholder or listener in his own particular situation, it reactivates the object reproduced.[51]

In the mystical anagram adopted by his followers, "Elvis lives." (Or, to cite the slogan employed by Elvis's long-time manager Colonel Parker after his "boy" 's death, "Always

Elvis." That Colonel Parker deployed this slogan in the form of a rubber stamp says much about the reproduction of Elvis Presley. Had Colonel Parker known or cared anything about literary theory he might have had it read "Always already Elvis.")

Elvis made his public debut as a performer in 1954. By 1956—only two years later— the warm-up act for his show at the Louisiana Fair Grounds was performed by "exact replicas of Elvis Presley, doing his songs with his gestures and dressed in his clothes."[52] In Nashville one Wade Cummings, or "Elvis Wade," as he called himself, was described as the "first," or "original imitation Elvis," complete with paunch and flashy costume slit to the waist. According to him, "All Elvis impersonators are Elvis Wade impersonators." (So, in his view at least, there *was* an original, an original impersonator.) But there are hundreds of others. Notice here the relationship of the "impersonator" to Freud's "uncanny." The impersonator is something alive that seems almost like a machine. Is it possible that this is overdetermination through the dead brother, that all of these impersonators are some version of Jesse Garon Presley?

Most of these acts got their start *before* Elvis Presley's death; they were not only ghostly revisitations but also proliferations, multiplications. Some were even surgically reconstructed, like the man in Florida who had his nose, cheeks, and lip altered to look like the King. The surgeons "gave a slight millimeter push to the left-hand corner of [his] lip," to approximate the famous sneer.[53]

Indeed, the impersonation of Elvis always seemed to verge on the multiple, the replicated, as if one could never be enough. Two hundred Elvis impersonators were scheduled to perform at the birthday party for the Statue of Liberty. (Only seventy-five showed up.) What was this insatiable desire that could never be gratified?

After his death the Elvis impersonators assumed the magnitude of a major cult. "What, other than psychological transference," asked *People* magazine rhetorically one year later, "can explain the hysteria over the 100 or so ersatz Elvises around the country who are putting on eerie shows—complete with drum rolls from *2001*, sweaty scarfs tossed to screaming women, karate chops, bodyguards, sneers and bathos?"

Time magazine noted the success in Saigon of one Elvis Phuong, who, "complete with skintight pants and sneer, does Presley Vietnamese style."[54] Two Elvis impersonators in London, one Chinese, the other an Indian Sikh who wears a turban, prompted a two-page feature on the front page of the "Living Arts" section of the *New York Times* ("Honestly, not too many Chinese people do Elvis," Paul Chan confides to the *Times* reporter. "I think I must be the first Chinese Elvis in the world.").[55] And a routine news item in the entertainment pages of the *Los Angeles Times* noted a casting call for Elvis impersonators, "preferably overweight," for a "small but fun role" in *Robocop II.*[56]

At the First Annual EP (for Elvis Presley) Impersonators International Association Convention held in Chicago in June 1990, dozens of impersonators put in an appearance, including a female Elvis from Hertfordshire, England, a "Jordanian-American anesthesiologist Elvis" described by a Chicago newspaper as the "Hindu Elvis," and a seven-year-old Elvis from Brooklyn. The event was coordinated by a group that eventually hopes to develop a "Code of Ethics" for Elvis impersonators around the globe. "If the actual Elvis was at the convention," one reporter commented, "he might have been overlooked in the mob of look-alikes."[57]

One of the most popular sessions at the EPIIA, "How to Become an Elvis Impersonator," noted the three sartorial stages of Elvis's life as a performer: the fifties, or the Gold Lamé Period, the sixties, or the Black Leather period, and the seventies, or the Vegas Jumpsuit Phase, also known as the Aloha Years. Why do most impersonators choose the third phase, often believed to mark the decline of Elvis's career? This "question that has plagued Elvologists" was answered by the session leader in two ways: on the one hand, the seventies were the most visually exciting of Elvis's career; on the other, the "midlife demographics of the impersonator subculture" (largely over 40, largely working class) made the baritone, overweight Elvis an object of more ready—and more convincing—impersonation. As will be clear, I am suggesting a third reason for the appeal of the Vegas Jumpsuit Elvis, and also a link among the three vestimentary phases—a link for which "unmarked transvestism" might be thought of as a common term.

Here once again, in a passage of typically purple prose, is Elvis biographer Albert Goldman on the subject of this phenomenon of impersonation:

> What one saw after Elvis's death . . . was not just emulation but replication: the rite according to St. Xerox. Like those mythical soldiers sprung from dragon's teeth, there appeared overnight a new class of entertainers who were not so much mimics, impersonators or impressionists as Elvis clones. Some of these human effigies were so fantastically dedicated to their assumed identity that, like transsexuals, they submitted their bodies to plastic surgery so that their natural resemblance might be heightened to virtual indistinguishability. (Goldman, 584–85)

We are very close here to Freud's notion of the uncanny repetition-compulsion, the *heimlich* transformed into the *unheimlich,* castration anxiety, the multiplication of doubles, "something repressed which *recurs.*"[58] Meantime at Graceland, the Presley home (*Heim?*) and museum in Memphis, his costumes live, too, on mannequins (like Liberace's), for the delectation of the faithful. Elvis as ghost comes home to rejoin the ghostly twin brother whose grave has been moved to the Graceland memorial garden.

And these mechanisms of impersonation lead, with uncanny inevitability, to woman as Elvis impersonator. As Elvis's fame grew, and his looks became as famous as his sound, the hair and makeup began, fascinatingly, to cross *back* over gender lines. When his underage girlfriend Priscilla, later to become his wife, moved in with him in 1962, Elvis took charge of her appearance and turned her into a version of himself, insisting that she tease her hair up about twelve inches and dye it the same jet-black that his own hair was dyed. "In fact," writes biographer Goldman, "some people began to insist that Elvis and Priscilla were coming to look alike, that they were becoming twins" (355). Another set of uncanny twins: changelings.

As early as 1957 Little Richard toured Australia with a package of artists including Alis Lesley, billed as "the female Elvis Presley," complete with pompadour and low-slung guitar (White, 91). At the 1984 American Grammy Awards Show pop singer Annie Lennox of the Eurythmics, known for her close-cropped orange hair and gender-bending style, made a startling appearance "in full drag, as a convincing Elvis Presley."[59] In Jim Jarmusch's film *Mystery Train* (1989) a young Japanese Elvis fan assembles a scrapbook by pairing pictures of Elvis with the Buddha and two women: the Statue of Liberty and Madonna. "Elvis was even more influential than I thought," says her boyfriend. Canadian rockabilly star k.d. lang, who enjoys particular popularity with lesbian audiences, is famous for her short cropped hair and male attire. Often compared by critics to Elvis Presley, lang, whose lip in performance seems to curl, like Elvis's, of its own accord, did an Elvis impersonation on one of Pee Wee Herman's Christmas shows. And comedienne Roseanne Barr, who has achieved stardom by playing a fat, lower-middle-class housewife on television, appeared in a one-woman show where she made jokes about her weight, "handed out scarfs like Elvis," and "closed the show singing 'My Way' arm in arm with an Elvis impersonator."[60]

So that Elvis is impersonated and evoked on the one hand by female pop and rock stars (Alis Lesley, Annie Lennox, Madonna, k.d. lang) and on the other hand by an overweight comic actress. What I want to suggest is that these particular impersonations, impersonations of Elvis by women, were not only apt but in fact inevitable.

It is almost as if the word "impersonator," in contemporary popular culture, can be modified *either* by "female" *or* by "Elvis."

Why should this be? Why is "Elvis," like "woman," that which can be impersonated?

From the beginning Elvis is produced and exhibited as parts of a body—detachable (and imitable) parts that have an uncanny life and movement of their own, seemingly independent of their "owner": the curling lip, the pompadour, the hips, the pelvis.

Compare him, for example, with an All-American boy like Pat Boone, for whom the only detachable parts are his white bucks. The All-American boy doesn't have a body—or didn't until recently. Again it is useful to compare Elvis to Valentino, who replaced the All-American boy movie star with a model infinitely more dangerous and disturbing—because it had moving parts. Indeed, it could be said that a "real male" cannot be embodied at all, that embodiment *itself* is a form of feminization. If women, in the Western tradition, have been seen as the representatives of sex itself, then to personify sex on the stage must inevitably be to impersonate a woman.

Elvis is also—like a woman—not only a marked but a *marketed* body, exhibited and put on display, merchandised, not only by his manager Colonel Tom Parker, but also by Steve Binder, who invented the slick look of the 1968 TV "Comeback Special," leather suit and all, and by David Wolper, who produced the posthumous film *This Is Elvis* and also staged the Statue of Liberty extravaganza.

"The woman of fashion," writes Roland Barthes in a passage we have already had occasion to note, is a "collection of tiny, separate essences." "The paradox," he says, "is a generality of accumulation, not of synthesis: in Fashion, the *person* is thus simultaneously impossible and yet entirely known" (Barthes, 254–55.) Here Barthes says "person," but, earlier, "woman." It is "woman" whom fashion creates as this illusion of parts. And "woman" is what can be known, exhibited, disseminated, replicated—while at the same time remaining "impossible."

Elvis, too, is simultaneously impossible and entirely known. Much as he is exhibited, he is also withheld from view: in the army, in Hollywood, holed up at Graceland. At the end of every performance, while his fans screamed for more, an announcer would solemnly intone, "Ladies and gentlemen, Elvis has left the building." Like the changeling boy, Elvis is always absent or elsewhere. Indeed as always already absent, Elvis himself was the best, and the most poignant, of Elvis impersonators, staging a much-heralded "comeback" in 1968 at the age of 30, and, in another comeback, revisiting his classic crossover rock songs of the fifties from the curious vantage point of Hawaii or Las Vegas in the middle seventies. Like a revenant, he just never stops coming back. (Here we might recall the story of the phantom hitchhiker in the film *Mystery Train*—who turns out, of course, to be the ghost of Elvis heading for Graceland.)

We have briefly noted the fact that Elvis in effect sat out the rock revolution that he himself had started. Instead of taking to the concert stage like the Beatles, he went to Hollywood to become a "movie star," following the game plan of Colonel Parker, but also, presumably, his own dream of being a Valentino. Like Flaubert writing for the French theater, he was a genre behind. He missed his own moment—the moment that he had engendered—and spent the rest of his career as he had spent the beginning, being always too early or too late to be the Elvis that he was.

Is it possible that this is the essence of stardom, of superstardom? To be simultaneously belated and replicated; not to be there, and to cover up that absence with representations?

In a recent essay on camp, Andrew Ross has suggested that "in popular rock culture today, the most 'masculine' images are signified by miles of coiffured hair, layers of gaudy make-up, and a complete range of fetishistic body accessories, while it is the clean-cut, close-cropped, fifties-style Europop crooners who are seen as lacking masculine legitimacy" (Ross, 164). As a cultural observation this is shrewd, yet it reinscribes the binary *within* the reassuring domain of the masculine. Ross underestimates the power of the transvestite as that spectral other who exists only in representation—not a representation of male or of female, but of, precisely, itself: its own phantom or ghost.

The argument from "masquerade" tries to establish "woman" as artifactual, gestural, a theatrical creature who can be taken apart and put back together. But what has become clearer and clearer is that "man"—the male person—is at least as artifactual as "woman." Mechanical reproduction is the displacement into its opposite of the fear of artifactuality and dismemberment.

"Which is most macho"? The answer can come only from the impersonator. For by enacting on the stage—or the video screen—the disarticulation of parts, the repetition of images that is the breakdown of the image itself, it is only the impersonator who can theorize gender. Let me quote once again from Roland Barthes.

> As for the human body, Hegel had already suggested that it was in a relation of signification with clothing: as pure sentience, the body cannot signify; clothing guarantees the passage from sentience to meaning; it is, we might say, the signified par excellence. But which body is the Fashion garment to signify? (Barthes, 258)

What are the choices? An article in the gay and lesbian journal *Out/Look* called attention to the power of "The Drag Queen in The Age of Mechanical Reproduction," because the drag queen foregrounds illusion and falsehood as material reality: "being a drag queen means the constant assertion of the *body*."[61] But again, *which* body? The fashion garment of the drag queen signifies the absent or phantom body. Paradoxically, the body here is no body, and nobody, the clothes without the Emperor.

It is epistemologically intolerable to many people—including many literary and cultural critics—that the ground should be a figure. That gender exists only in representation. But this is the subversive secret of transvestism, that the body is not the ground, but the figure. Elvis Presley watching *his* figure, as his weight balloons up and down, Elvis deploying his lips and his hips to repeat by an act of will and artifice the "natural" gestures that once made them seem to take on an uncanny, transgressive life of their own, Elvis Presley, male sex symbol as female impersonator, becomes the fascinating dramatization of the transvestite effect that underlies representation itself.

CONCLUSION *A TERGO:*
RED RIDING HOOD AND THE WOLF IN BED

Long ago
there was a strange deception:
a wolf dressed in frills,
a kind of transvestite.
But I get ahead of my story.
In the beginning
there was just Red Riding Hood.
                    —Anne Sexton, "Red Riding Hood" (1971)

Why is it that in discussing transvestism in literature and culture we seem to have run into Red Riding Hood and the wolf at every turn? In Richard Wright's "Man of All Work," for example, we saw that the story of "Little Red Riding Hood" was explicitly invoked by the innocent Lily Fairchild as she plies the cross-dressed "maid" Carl Owens with the tale's traditional catechism: "your arms are so big"; "and there's so much hair on them"; "your voice is heavy, like a man's"; "your face is rough," and so on. "Mama, does Lucy know about Little Red Riding Hood," Lily asks her mother, and Carl (dressed as "Lucy") answers, truthfully, "Miss Lily, I know all about her." Djuna Barnes, describing the moment when Nora Flood finds Doctor O'Connor in his nightgown, wig, and rouge, evokes the tale of Red Riding Hood as a subtext-on-the-surface for this scene of discovery: "Red Riding Hood and the wolf in bed."

Indeed, like some Lacanian signifier gone mad—or lycanthropic—the wolf inscribes itself all over the text of transvestism, from Virginia *Woolf*'s *Orlando* to Albee's *Who's Afraid of Virginia Woolf?* In a short story about a medical sex-change procedure the German writer Christa *Wolf* explores the complexity of post-modern gender identity through the fiction of an experimental subject given a sex-changing drug—a drug that turns the unnamed female narrator into a transsexual man called "Anders" (literally, "other"). And one of the aliases of the Chevalier d'Eon—that paradigm of gender undecidability—was, as we have seen, "William *Wolff*."

Recent analyses of "Red Riding Hood" by folklorists have produced a similar overdetermination of the name. Thus for example *Wolf*ram Eberhard writes about Chinese analogues to the tale made famous in the West by Perrault and the Brothers Grimm; *Wolf*gang Mieder offers an extraordinarily entertaining account of modern versions of the story, including cartoons (an account described without guile by one bibliographer as " 'Little Red Riding Hood' in modern dress"), and Hans-*Wolf* Jager, whose name encompasses both wolf and hunter, has published a significant essay on Red Riding Hood and the French Revolution.[1]

Is the Red Riding Hood story, as modern interpreters have wanted to see it, a feminist fairy tale about a resourceful little girl's initiation into sexuality and adulthood? Jack Zipes suggests that Little Red Riding Hood reflects "men's fears of women's sexuality—and of their own as well."[2] The wolf and the gamekeeper, wild but natural appetite and the restraining authority of the law, are split versions of the same figure of "maleness," male desire and male governance. Or is the wolf a werewolf in the older sense, a human being who crosses a boundary between civilization and wildness—the male counterpart of the female witch? Is it the figure of the male as female, the wicked wolf as benign (grand)-mother, that terrifies and pleases, seduces and warns? Or is it perhaps something else?

Why is the wolf cross-dressed? In many illustrations of the tale, he is not; he accosts Red Riding Hood on the road in his own shape—that of an animal, or a man in hunter's or courtier's garb; even in bed dressed as "grandmother" he wears only a frilly cap, no real disguise.

The protagonist of the story I am about to tell was himself as haunted by the wolf as signifier as are the scholars of "Red Riding Hood"—or the pages of this text. The sobriquet given him by his doctor was a wolf-name, derived from the patient's own obsessive and disabling dream. Years later, when he had made an entire career based upon his fame as an analytic subject, he began to have trouble with his teeth (he had too fierce a bite) and consulted a dentist, whose name was *Dr. Wolf*. Dr. Wolf predicted that he would lose all his teeth because of the violence of his bite, at which point he went in search of another, less ominous dentist. A little less than a year later, after having consulted several medical specialists, including two dermatologists and several dentists, he was referred to a dentist who was described as "a man of great judgment and experience," "a dean among dentists."[3] And this dentist of dentists was named—*Dr. Wolf*. The second Dr. Wolf confirmed the diagnosis of the first—the patient had a "hard bite" and might lose all his teeth. Depressed for this and for other reasons shortly to be noted, the patient sought a new analyst—this one, perhaps not surprisingly, a woman.

There is, I want to suggest, considerable appropriateness in finding the wolf and Red Riding Hood embedded in this particular story: for it is the story, itself, of the primal scene, Freud's "From the History of an Infantile Neurosis" (1918)—better known as the "Wolf-Man Case." I will have a few things to say about Freud's own transcription of the case, and his relationship to his patient, an impoverished Russian nobleman. But my chief interest is in the point at which the latent dream thoughts of the case, the materials of transvestism, somewhat occluded in Freud's original discovery and retelling of the fairy tales behind the wolf-dream, become manifest: when the patient begins to dream of his new, female analyst as a cross-dressed man.

I want therefore to turn to the aftermath of Freud's famous "Wolf-Man Case," a rewriting of the Red Riding Hood story as a story of transvestism in which not only the *wolf* but also the *woman as cross-dresser* is repeatedly, even obsessively, evoked, in order to pose the question Djuna Barnes asks, but, provocatively, does not answer: what is it that fascinates about Red Riding Hood and the wolf in bed? Of what, precisely, is this a primal scene?

THE WOLF WHO CRIED BOY

For five months, from October 1926 to February 1927, Freud's former patient, known as the Wolf-Man, consulted another psychoanalyst, Dr. Ruth Mack Brunswick, to whom he had been referred by Freud himself. The immediate cause of this consultation was the return of the Wolf-Man's neurosis, this time manifesting itself in a "hypochondriacal *idée fixe*" : a fixation, not to put too fine a point upon it, on his nose, which he declared to have been disfigured by a dermatologist's bungling, an ill-advised electrolysis, which had left him with a scar, or a hole in his nose. Obsessed by this disfiguration (which was completely invisible to the naked eye) he carried about with him a pocket mirror which he constantly pulled out in order to inspect it.

> He neglected his daily life and work because he was engrossed, to the exclusion of all else, in the state of his nose. On the street he looked at himself in every shop-window; he carried a pocket mirror which he took out to look at every few minutes. First he would powder his nose; a moment later he would inspect it and remove the powder. He would then examine the pores, to see if they were enlarging, to catch the hole, as it were, in its moment of growth and development. Then he would again powder his nose, put away the mirror, and a moment later begin the process anew. His life was centered on the little mirror in his pocket, and his fate depended on what it revealed or was about to reveal. (Brunswick, 265)

Dr. Brunswick viewed the new treatment as, in essence, a continuation of the old: "The source of the new illness was an unresolved remnant of the transference, which after fourteen years, under the stress of peculiar circumstances, became the basis for a new form of an old illness" (Brunswick, 266). The "peculiar circumstances" in question included the Russian Revolution and the First World War. The Wolf-Man, born to a wealthy Russian family, had undergone a radical change in economic status, and was now a stateless person with a sick wife, working at a minor bureaucratic post in Vienna and living on an annual dole collected by Freud from the analytic community for "this former patient, who had served the theoretical ends of analysis so well" (Brunswick, 266). The original analysis undertaken with Freud had disclosed a strong desire on the patient's part for love from his father, whom he also regarded (in an important variant of the Oedipal story) as the castrator.

The Wolf-Man's own psychic history was one of a struggle between a passive homosexual desire for his father and an active identification with him in his sexual encounters with housemaids and other women of lower-class status—and also an identification with his elder sister, the father's favorite and the more "masculine" of the two children, whose early death by suicide may have precipitated her incorporation into his intrapsychic life. Readers of Freud's "From the History of an Infantile Neurosis," with its suggestively fragmented title, would have no knowledge of either the Wolf-Man's subsequent marriage to the slightly exotic Therese (a dark-eyed, dark-haired nurse with Spanish [or Jewish?] antecedents whom he met during a brief stay in a Munich sanatorium) or of the nose fetishism that was to bring him back to Freud's—and Dr. Brunswick's—consulting room.

Yet Freud, as Brunswick instantly saw, was the father to the Wolf-Man: the representative of the biological-familial father (the Wolf-Man sought, for example, Freud's permission to marry Therese at the conclusion of his analysis, and exulted in his praise of this "breakthrough to the woman"[4]) and, at the same time, the father of psychoanalysis, the revolutionary methodology which was to make the "son" famous, and thus make the Wolf-Man the heir to a new patriarchal estate.[5] The annual payment collected for him by Freud for six years replaced the lost Russian inheritance, an inheritance that had doubled, to the Wolf-Man's pleasure, upon the death of his sister-rival, and had then been lost during the Revolution. It was, indeed, only by taunting the Wolf-Man about his claim to be Freud's favorite son that Dr. Brunswick was able to precipitate the second analysis. And here, not surprisingly, is where cross-dressing enters the story.

But first let us recall the symptom, the telltale nose and the pocket mirror that disclosed—to the Wolf-Man alone—its tale of mutilation. Where did he get the mirror? As it happens, he borrowed it from his wife. "The patient," writes Brunswick, "borrowed first his wife's mirror, in order to examine his nose, and then, as it were, her feminine habit of frequently looking at herself in it" (Brunswick, 281). There is something ambivalent in the attitude toward women expressed in this statement ("her *feminine* habit"), as, more directly, in the female analyst's assertion that Therese, "*womanlike*," advised the Wolf-Man not to tell Freud about his recovery of some of the family jewels from Russia, lest the annual payments cease. But it is difficult to be sure where Brunswick leaves off and free indirect paraphrase takes over: the characterization of Therese's "feminine habit" and "womanlike" duplicity may be the analyst's translation of her patient's gender attitudes rather than her own. As she writes, "The concealment of the jewels, the casual acceptance of the yearly money, the petty dishonesties, were all a mystery to him. And yet their secret lay in his remark about his wife: 'Women are always like that—distrustful and suspicious and afraid of losing something.'" The Wolf-Man, in short, had—in this respect—become a "woman," become his wife.

The pocket-mirror and its powder compact, the ineffectual dabbing at the invisibly mutilated nose—these were another kind of "breakthrough to the woman": not the repression of homosexuality in the choice of a wife, but the identification with the woman's role. The fantasy of castration embodied in the nose-fixation (for it was the Wolf-Man who also furnished Freud the unforgettable bilingual puzzle in the essay on "Fetishism" about the "shine" or "glance" on the nose) here finds its specific enabling object in the woman's, the wife's, narcissistic accessory.

The analysis with Brunswick, like the analysis with Freud twenty years previously, became stalled by the patient's own leisurely pleasure in the process. The Wolf-Man was perfectly content to talk. His satisfaction with the daily conversation itself impeded progress. Freud, faced with this situation, had imposed a time limit on the analysis.[6] Brunswick, in a similar situation, attacked the father-son fantasy, the Wolf-Man's smug acceptance of himself as Freud's favorite and his heir, the recipient of the annual money, the man who discovered Freud and made him famous. The result of this attack was a series of cross-dressing dreams, in which Brunswick appears as a ludicrous imitation man.

> My technique [writes Brunswick] therefore consisted in a concentrated attempt to undermine the patient's idea of himself as the favorite son, since it was obvious that by means of it he was protecting himself from feelings of a very different nature. I drove home to him his actual position with Freud, the total absence (as I knew from Freud to be the case) of any social or personal relationship between them. I remarked that his was not the only published case—this being a source of enormous pride to the patient. He countered with the statement that no other patient had been analysed for so long a period: this too I was able to contradict. From a state of war we now reached a state of seige.
>
> As a result of my attack, his dreams at last began to change. The first of this period reveals a woman wearing trousers and high boots, standing in a sleigh which she drives in a masterful manner, and declaiming in excellent Russian. The patient remarked that the trousers were a little humorous, and not, like a man's, entirely practical. . . .
>
> Two factors were evident here: first, the contempt for me, and secondly, the wish to be back in analysis with Freud. (Brunswick, 284–85)

The Wolf-Man resisted these deductions, asserting that he was getting all the benefits of Freud's insights without coming directly under his influence, since, he said, he was quite sure that Brunswick discussed all the details of the case with Freud in order to get his advice. When she denied this, he stormed out of her office, furious at Freud's neglect, and promptly dreamt another dream in which his father, in the dream a professor, has a long, hooked nose like a Jew, and is emblematically castrated. So much for Freud. But what about the trousered woman with the high boots and the masterful driving style? Brunswick, as she points out, knew no Russian. The dominatrix in the dream does seem to be a commentary on the woman-as-analyst, in her humorous trousers, not entirely practical since she has no penis and therefore no need of a fly. But the dream seems also a fantasy of the Wolf-Man as woman, in the driver's seat, restored to power and to a time before the Revolution—to, in fact, the Russia of his childhood.

Here is another cross-dressing dream from the same period, again as recorded by Ruth Mack Brunswick:

> The patient is in the office of a doctor with a full, round face (like Professor X.). He is afraid that he has not enough money in his purse to pay the doctor. However, the latter says that the bill is very small, that he will be satisfied with 100,000 Kronen. As the patient leaves, the doctor tries to persuade him to take some old music, which, however, the patient refuses, saying he has no use for it. But at the door the doctor presses on him some coloured postcards, which he has not the courage to refuse. Suddenly the patient's (woman) analyst appears, dressed like a page in a blue velvet knickerbocker suit and three-cornered hat. Despite her attire, which is boyish rather than masculine, she looks entirely feminine. The patient embraces her and takes her on his knee. (Brunswick, 294)

And here is Brunswick's interpretation of the role she plays:

> It will be remembered that the patient was seduced at an early age by his elder and always precocious and aggressive sister. This seduction activated his latent passivity, directing it toward the woman. Thus my boyish costume has several meanings: first, the historic one of the sister's aggression; secondly, my role, as analyst, of a father-substitute; and thirdly, an attempt on the part of the patient to deny the castration of the woman, and attribute a phallus to her. In the dream I resemble those pages on the stage whose parts are usually and obviously taken by women. Thus I am neither man nor woman but a creature of neuter gender. However, the attribution of the phallus to the woman turned into a conquest for the patient who immediately discovers her femininity and proceeds to make love to her. Thus an additional purpose of her masculinity is disclosed: the patient has granted her the phallus in order to take it away from her, in other words, to castrate her in his father-identification as he has in the past wished to be castrated by that father.

This was the first dream the Wolf-Man presented to Brunswick in which he displayed his own heterosexuality and a positive erotic transference toward his female analyst. As she notes, "an element of identification with the woman is undoubtedly present, but the patient's leading role is a masculine one. Apparently only now has his father-identification become strong enough to enable him to develop a normal, heterosexual transference to me" (Brunswick, 295). Brunswick, like Freud, sees heterosexuality and normality as equivalent. She resists his "identification with the woman," as she resists the idea of a sexual economy without women altogether. But so, increasingly, does the patient, whose marriage is regarded by him, as by all of his analysts, as itself a manifest sign of functional health.[7]

Whatever we may think of the sexual politics of classical analysis, however, it appears that the fantasy of the cross-dressed woman is enabling for the Wolf-Man in both dreams. Dominatrix or page boy, the woman in male attire but clearly readable as woman ("a little humorous . . . not, like a man's, entirely practical"; "boyish rather than masculine"), occupied a liminal space between the Wolf-Man himself (passive, latently homosexual, economically castrated, and obsessed with his little mirror) and the beloved father-analyst-castrator. Significantly, the apparent disfiguration of his nose was suggested to him in part by the presence (and periodic disappearance) of a wart on his mother's nose and a pimple on his wife's. These women, culturally and economically dependent, bearing on their faces as elsewhere on their bodies the signs of their own castration, are the converse of the cross-dressed analyst in the Wolf-Man's dreams of 1926–27.

Brunswick begins her explication of the page-boy dream by reminding the reader of the Wolf-Man's seduction by his older sister—a seduction deduced by Freud in the course of the original analysis. ". . . the patient was seduced at an early age by his elder and always precocious and aggressive sister. . . . Thus my boyish costume has several meanings: first, the historic one of the sister's aggression." When we turn to the Wolf-Man's own chronicle of his childhood, "The Memoirs of the Wolf-Man," which he wrote at the invitation of Muriel Gardiner and signed with the name by which psychoanalysis had made him famous, we find yet another scenario of cross-dressing, this one directly involving his sister Anna—and situated, appropriately enough, in the inverted or topsy-turvy context of carnival:

> At carnival time Anna and I were invited to a children's fancy dress party, where Anna planned to appear in a boy's costume. I do not remember how old Anna was at the time; at any rate she was old enough for Mademoiselle [the Swiss governess] to feel concerned about Anna's good reputation as a young girl. Perhaps she also hoped to take this opportunity to regain her lost influence over Anna. Our discussion of Anna's costume took place one day at lunch. My father thought there was no reason at all why Anna should not wear boy's clothes to the party. Mademoiselle, on the other hand, contended that it was not seemly for "*une jeune fille comme il faut*" to appear publicly in trousers. So a vehement argument developed between my father and Mademoiselle, who went so far as to declare in a resolute voice that, even though my father had given his permission, she, as Anna's governess, nevertheless forbade her to go to the party in boy's costume. Now Mademoiselle had overstepped the limits, and accordingly received a severe rebuke from my father. (Gardiner, 17).

This passage is worth quoting at length because it contains a number of crucial details that will repeat in the history of the Wolf-Man. The time is *carnival*, the liminal, festive period in which inversion is not only permitted but valorized. As Terry Castle, among others, has pointed out, carnival and masquerade were often directly associated in the European public mind with transvestism and, in consequence, with homosexuality. "The implication . . . that sodomy follows from transvestism—became a standard notion in the eighteenth century"; "to don the garments of the opposite sex was to enter a world of sexual deviance."[8]

Characteristically, it is the bold and precocious sister, and not the Wolf-Man himself, who expresses the wish to cross-dress at the party. Several times in his case history Freud comments on gender role reversal between brother and sister; in the Wolf-Man's childhood "they used to say of him that he ought to have been the girl and his elder sister the boy" (Freud, "Infantile Neurosis," 15), "as a child she was boyish and unmanageable"

(21), the boy's playing with toy soldiers was seen as a gender-appropriate displacement of his desire to play with dolls, and so on. The father is also described as preferring his daughter to his son; "his father had an unmistakable preference for his sister," writes Freud (17). Indeed, the analysts Abraham and Torok posit the idea of an incestuous relationship between father and daughter that haunts the Wolf-Man throughout his life.[9]

Anna's wish to cross-dress is remembered by the Wolf-Man specifically as a testing ground of female authority: the governess may have hoped to "take this opportunity to regain her lost influence over Anna." The father, on the other hand, welcomes the cross-dressing plan: "there was no reason at all why Anna should not wear boy's clothes to the party." The episode ends with a row in which the father exerts his authority over "Mademoiselle," rebuking her and (briefly) causing her to contemplate leaving his employ ("after the insults inflicted on her by our father she could no longer remain in our house"). In the end, however, the governess is reconciled to the reversal of her social judgment, and begins—to the mother's surprise—to speak in highly complimentary (and oddly gendered) terms about the father once again: *"Monsieur est si délicat"* (Gardiner, 17).

In this memory the Wolf-Man can associate himself with his sister's boldness with impunity. The sister herself is not punished for her desire to cross-dress; quite to the contrary, her plan is upheld by the father, and the real "boy" of the family is supported by the patriarch in a striking show of "male" solidarity. What costume the young Wolf-Man was to wear is never disclosed.

If in his retrospective imagination he translates this into a personal desire for masquerade, transvestism, and homosexual passivity or sodomy ("father has given permission to cross-dress and carnivalize"), it is because he identifies with, or has incorporated into himself, the persona of the now-dead Anna, whose suicide made him the father's favorite. He is only a spectator in the memory; Anna's wish, Anna's fantasy, can be tested out in terms of family and gender power relations without direct threat to himself. And, in fact, Anna *is* punished, after all; she dies. Does this mean that cross-dressing is culpable? Or only that girls and women should not pretend to have the power of boys and men?

There is a sense in which the story of the costume party lends credence to a lesson about the erasure of all female roles ("father has given Anna permission to be a boy, too; 'Mademoiselle' has no power, and girls in general have power only insofar as they can become boys"). In other words, a cultural gender dissymmetry reinforces the family's internal power relations. The Wolf-Man contemplates from an apparently safe distance the idea of the governess's self-exile ("she could no longer remain in our house"). But is he not, in this recuperated memory, putting himself in the place of the disempowered, gender-coded, class-marked governess ("Mademoiselle"), as well as of the boundary-crossing sister who wants to appear publicly in trousers?

The Wolf-Man's "Memoirs" were written in 1970, at the behest of Muriel Gardiner. As a written document, then, they postdate Freud's case history (which the Wolf-Man clearly knew by heart) by over fifty years, and Ruth Mack Brunswick's "Supplement" by more than forty. The two cross-dressing dreams reported by Brunswick are thus textually prior, although biographically subsequent, to the memory of Anna's transgressive adolescent transvestism. If the Wolf-Man knew Freud's case history, he also knew Brunswick's, and it may be that the "Memoirs" reflect and respond to the "Supplement." In any case, the costume worn by the female analyst in the second dream ("dressed like a page in a blue velvet knickerbocker suit and three-cornered hat . . . boyish rather than masculine") suggests the context of masquerade and carnival and the omnipresent theatrical figure of the female page.[10]

Without a description of Anna's "boy's costume" we can only speculate about its nature, but it seems plausible to associate this boyish page suit with the Wolf-Man's recollection of his sister. The elaborateness of the materials and details of the blue velvet knickerbocker suit and tricorn hat suggest both wealth and aristocratic leisure; surely it is more likely that Anna intended to wear a costume of this kind than the outfit of a peasant boy or even ordinary clothes like her younger brother's, since there would be little exoticism in cross-gendered mufti, and a children's "fancy dress party" for the children of pre-Revolutionary Russian noblemen implies a certain expenditure of money and imagination.

Where else would this highly particularized costume description have come from? Possibly from the theater, of which the Wolf-Man was an aficionado. But the interconnectedness of the two narratives remains striking. Recall Brunswick's reading of the page-boy dream:

> [M]y boyish costume has several meanings: first, the historic one of the sister's aggression; secondly, my role, as analyst, of a father-substitute; and thirdly, an attempt on the part of the patient to deny the castration of the woman, and attribute a phallus to her. In the dream I resemble those pages on the stage whose parts are usually and obviously taken by women. Thus I am neither man nor woman but a creature of neuter gender. . . . an additional purpose of her masculinity is disclosed: the patient has granted her the phallus in order to take it away from her, in other words, to castrate her in his father-identification as he has in the past wished to be castrated by that father.

This, I suggest, is a cogent analysis of the costume party scene as well as of the dream. That the sister is dead renders her doubly a castrate, without power—and even more emphatically neither man nor woman, "a creature of neuter gender."

We may also call to mind the fact that in the first Brunswick cross-dressing dream of 1926–27 the woman is wearing trousers and high boots and is declaiming Russian verse while driving a sleigh in a masterful manner. And this too may connect with the costume party, in which the governess declared it inappropriate for a nice girl to appear publicly in trousers. Brunswick interprets the Russian declamation as mockery, since she herself understands no Russian at all, not even the occasional phrases the Wolf-Man interjects into his German sentences. But the sister, of course, spoke Russian flawlessly; it was her native language, and she "produced imaginative writings of which her father had a high opinion" (Freud, "Infantile Neurosis," 21). The sleigh, too, suggests a Russian landscape, and the time of childhood, before the Revolution (and before Anna's death).

In other words, the interpolation of the memory of the fancy dress party with its scenario of Anna's cross-dressing and the Wolf-Man's displaced desire for gender reversal (would the transvestite child be punished? would a fantasy of transvestism earn the father's love?) offers an augmented insight into the two cross-dressing dreams from Ruth Mack Brunswick's supplementary case history. The "historic" aggression of the sister noted by Brunswick is itself supplemented by a concrete and specific memory of the sister as cross-dresser, a memory that once again casts the pre-adolescent Wolf-Man in the role of spectator to mysterious interactions between his father and a(nother) woman: the sister, the governess (who finally described the father as "délicat"), the "astonished" mother (Gardiner, 17).

The master-trope of Freud's Wolf-Man case was, of course, the demonstration of the primal scene, whether as actuality or as primal fantasy, and the location, therefore, *pace* the rebellious psychoanalytic sons Jung and Adler, of the real stuff of the psyche in *infantile* neurosis. As Brunswick herself points out, this second analysis was a leftover part of the first; this second, cross-dressed transference was a working out of materials left undigested from the first analysis, the analysis with Freud, the primal analytic scene which, in his case history, established Freud's own promulgation of psychoanalysis as itself the initiatory and constitutive moment.

"I was the first—a point to which none of my opponents have referred—to recognize both the part played by phantasies in symptom-formation and also the 'retrospective phantasying' of late impressions into childhood and their sexualization after the event" (Freud, "Infantile Neurosis," 103n). "*I was the first.*" The assertion of primacy is clear, as is the irritation on the part of the father of psychoanalysis toward the sons: "I did not require the contributions of Adler and Jung to induce me to consider the matter with a critical eye." If he has resisted the suggestion that later life, rather than infantile experiences, established these symptoms and memories or fantasy-traces, "it has been as a result of arguments such as are forced upon the investigator by the case described in these pages or by any other infantile neurosis" (296n).

So something has been forced upon the investigator; he has been compelled to look upon a puzzling and counterintuitive scenario, just as the Wolf-Man beheld (or fantasized) the coital scene between his parents.

Freud's investigation traced the wolf phobia to two fairy tales, "Little Red Riding Hood" and "The Wolf and the Seven Little Goats," which were read to the young child by his governess from a book with memorable illustrations. At first it seemed as if "Red Riding Hood" must have been the principal fairy tale source, until Freud raised the question of the "six or seven wolves" in the dream.

> I raised a doubt whether the picture that had frightened him could be connected with the story of "Little Red Riding-Hood." This fairy tale only offers an opportunity for two illustrations—Little Red Riding-Hood's meeting with the wolf in the wood, and the scene in which the wolf lies in bed in the grandmother's nightcap. There must therefore be some other fairy tale behind his recollection of the picture [of the erect, striding wolf]. He soon discovered that it could only be the story of "The Wolf and the Seven Little Goats." Here the number seven occurs, and also the number six. . . . (Freud, "Infantile Neurosis," 31)

The patient obligingly supplies this additional story, in which a wolf disguises himself as the kids' mother in order to enter their house and eat them. Freud goes on to point out correspondences between the two fairy tales, in both of which the wolf becomes a threatening father figure, devours the child or children, and ultimately has his belly slit open and stones substituted for the ingested children, who are rescued unharmed. But these two tales also have something else in common, something more fully articulated in "Little Red Riding Hood" (the patient's first choice as source material) but present in both, and that element, as any reader of "Little Red Riding Hood" will recall, is cross-dressing.

The wolf, having met Red Riding Hood on the path and learned from her the way to her grandmother's house, lets himself into the house and devours the grandmother. "Then he put on her clothes, dressed himself in her cap, laid himself in bed and drew the curtains."[11] In "The Wolf and the Seven Little Goats" the goats' mother has warned them against the wolf's rough voice and black feet, so he disguises his voice with chalk and his feet with flour, and passes himself off as their mother. " 'First show us your paws that we may know if you are our dear little mother,' " they cry. "Then he put his paws in through the window, and when the kids saw that they were white, they believed that all he said was true, and opened the door" (Grimm, 40). This is the detail of the story that recommends it to Freud, who is seeking for the reason that the dream wolves are white. But what he does not point out is that in both stories the wolf is a (grand)mother as well as a father-substitute, and that in both he is masquerading as a woman.

Bruno Bettelheim, commenting on "Red Riding Hood," describes it in terms very close to Freud's account of the primal scene: "Most children," he says, "view the sexual act as an act of violence which one partner commits on the other." "I believe," he adds, "it is the child's unconscious equation of sexual excitement, violence, and anxiety which Djuna Barnes alludes to when she writes: 'Children know something they can't tell; they like Red Riding-Hood and the wolf in bed!' "[12] But the context of Barnes's exclamation, or rather of her character Nora's, is—as we have already noted—one of the most disquieting cross-dressing scenes in all twentieth-century literature, the moment when Nora Flood comes at three in the morning to visit Doctor Matthew O'Connor:

> In the narrow iron bed, with its heavy and dirty linen sheets, lay the doctor in a women's flannel nightgown.

The doctor's head, with its over-large black eyes, its full gun-metal cheeks and chin, was framed in the golden semi-circle of a wig with long pendent curls that touched his shoulders, and falling back against the pillow, turned up the shadowy interior of their cylinders. He was heavily rouged and his lashes painted. It flashed into Nora's head: "God, children know something they can't tell; they like Red Riding Hood and the wolf in bed!"[13]

Bettelheim's text betrays nothing of the strangeness of this scene, and his footnote directs the reader to T.S. Eliot's introduction (which cites the sentence in question) rather than to the novel. But his allusion to *Nightwood* seems to me to be uncannily apt, despite itself, and to point to something revealing about the Wolf-Man case. The primal scene toward which it gestures is not, or not only, that of parental coitus, the Shandyean moment of self-conception witnessed, impossibly and indelibly in its repetition, by the terrified and fascinated child. What the child knows and can't tell is another and even less explicable truth, the fact of blurred gender as figured in the eroticism of cross-dressing. When the little goats open the door to the wolf, it is the black paw made white that holds their attention; when Red Riding Hood interrogates the wolf in the bed it is the anomalies of "grandmother's" appearance that attract her. And when Nora intrudes upon Doctor O'Connor, making her way past the perfume bottles, rouges, powder puffs, laces, and ladies' underclothing to his bedside, she is "dismayed" at first, because what she witnesses is not a revelation but a recognition: "He had evacuated custom and gone back into his dress" (*Nightwood*, 80).

The phrase "evacuated custom" has always struck me as a peculiar one, even for the baroque elegance of Barnes's phrasing. It is further disconcerting, to a non-folklorist, at least, to discover that evacuation, or defecation, was part of the traditional Red Riding Hood story, at least before it was sanitized for court use by Charles Perrault in 1697. Realizing at the end of her litany ("how hairy you are," "what big ears you have," etc.) that her "grandmother" was in fact a predatory impostor whose "big mouth" was "the better to eat you with," the resourceful Red Riding Hood claimed a sudden call of nature as an excuse to go outside. This motif has been traced not only in early European versions of this very popular story but also in Chinese examples of the tale.[14] As Alan Dundes points out, "this explicit anal component of 'Little Red Riding Hood' has received virtually no attention from commentators, probably because it was one of the 'ruder' elements presumably intentionally omitted by Perrault" (Dundes, 224). Dundes deduces a pattern of oral, anal, and finally genital motifs in the tale, and concludes that it is "full of infantile fantasy" (225).

Whether or not Barnes's word "evacuated" is a kind of textual effect, a latent recollection of one of the "ruder versions" of Red Riding Hood, it is clear that at least one auditor of Red Riding Hood would, without question, have been interested in this detail, and that is the Wolf-Man, whose obsessive interest in—and difficulty with—evacuation led Freud to write a whole section of his case history under the title "Anal

Erotism and Castration." Defecation for the Wolf-Man was the one way to remove the "veil" which, he told Freud, interposed itself between himself and the world.

> The veil was torn, strange to say, in one situation only; and that was at the moment when, as a result of an enema, he passed a motion through the anus. He then felt well again, and for a very short time he saw the world clearly. (Freud, "Infantile Neurosis," 99)

The Wolf-Man remembered that he had been told that he had been born with a caul (German *Glückshaube*, literally "lucky hood"). "The caul was the veil which hid him from the world and the world from him." "But what," asks Freud, rhetorically, "can have been the meaning of the fact that this veil, which was now symbolic but had once been real, was torn at the moment at which he evacuated his bowels after an enema. . . . The context enables us to reply. If the birth-veil was torn, then he saw the world and was re-born. The stool was the child, as which he was born a second time, to a happier life" (Freud, 100). And since, as Freud goes on to point out, the sensation of rebirth could only take place if the enema were administered to him by a male attendant, the Wolf-Man's fantasy of rebirth was a version of the homosexual wishful fantasy, the wish, in this case, to have intercourse with his father, and present him with a child. Anal erotism became a strategy for escape, or delay, as well as for pleasure. But it also became a figure for childbirth, the action parodied by the hunter's slitting of the wolf's belly to release Red Riding Hood and her grandmother.

In Freud's reconstruction of the primal scene, of which the wolf-dream is a transposition, he ultimately adduces a detail which he himself repressed from the narrative for more than forty pages: the fact that the dreamer, the Wolf-Man, "interrupted his parents' intercourse by passing a stool, which gave him an excuse for screaming" (Freud, "Infantile Neurosis," 80). Freud sees this as a sign of infantile sexual excitement; he himself proposes an additional detail—that the father was annoyed at being interrupted—but has reluctantly to drop it, since "the material of the analysis did not react to it" (80). The empathetic identification of analyst with father here, apparently, suggests its own limits. (Freud also claims that defecation is more "feminine" than urination in this circumstance, presumably because it involves the anus and not the penis. The resistance of the analyst throughout this case to regarding male homosexuality as in any way healthy or functional is one of the least "modern," and most obtrusive and obstinate, of the text's own symptoms.)

What does this analytic adventure tell us about the primal scene of cross-dressing? First of all, it suggests that the experience itself, of confrontation with the wolf in bed, is pervasively and complicatedly erotic, not least so at the moment of disclosure—as any child knows—when the wolf reveals "his" real identity, and moves to gobble up the transfixed and giggling child. The Wolf-Man, despite his sobriquet, was himself the Red Riding Hood figure, the child with the "lucky hood"; after the analysis with Freud, his female analyst—a substitute for the feared and loved father figure—became the cross-dressed wolf, bringing to consciousness the fantasy that lay behind the two wolf-tales originally discussed by analyst and patient—a fantasy that Freud, as much as his patient, apparently declined to explore.

THE PRIMAL SCENE OF CROSS-DRESSING

Defending the notion of the "primal scene" against his critics, Freud insists on the importance of the infant observer: his rivals' "low estimate of the importance of early infantile impressions and . . . unwillingness to ascribe such enduring effects to them" (49) blocks, in his view, any full understanding of either "primal scenes" or—what others would prefer to regard them as—"primal phantasies."

In a note added to his account of the Wolf-Man case Freud himself backs down from his original assertion that the Wolf-Man, when an infant, must actually have observed his parents' lovemaking, the "primal scene." Instead he holds up the possibility that the boy had seen copulation between animals (sheep-dogs standing in for wolves), and then transferred this new understanding onto the puzzle of parents in bed together (Freud, "Infantile Neurosis," 57–60). But in his "Introductory Lectures on Psycho-Analysis" he articulates what is, for him, the ultimate form of the primal scene: "The extreme achievement on these lines," he writes, "is a phantasy of observing parental intercourse while one is still an unborn baby in the womb."[15]

This concept of the "primal scene" has been worrisome, as well as fascinating, to subsequent observers, in part because it seems, as Freud himself repeatedly acknowledged, to exist on the borderline between the *scene* (or the "seen") and the *fantasy*. "What Freud seems to be getting at," suggest the psychoanalysts Laplanche and Pontalis, "is the idea that this scene belongs to the (ontogenetic or phylogenetic) past of the individual and that it constitutes a happening which may be of the order of myth but which is *already given* prior to any meaning which is attributed to it after the fact."[16] Lacan has his own version to propose. Freud, he says, offers the primal scene as a gaze upon that which cannot be uttered, that which renders the subject absent, empty, "beyond intersubjectivity," in that space-which-is-not-a-space that Freud elsewhere describes, so evocatively, as "the navel of the dream":

> To Freud, the vision of the dream seems like the reversal of the fascination of the gaze. It is in the gaze of these wolves, so anxiety-provoking in the account of it given by the dreamer, that Freud sees the equivalent of the fascinated gaze of the infant confronted with the scene which profoundly marked him in the imaginary and redirected his entire instinctual life. We find there something like a unique and decisive revelation of the subject, in which an indefinite something that is unsayable is concentrated, in which the subject is lost for a moment, blown up.[17]

"Something like a unique and decisive revelation of the subject, in which an indefinite something that is unsayable is concentrated." Why should the Wolf-Man case in its extended form, and the Red Riding Hood story that supplies one of its textual cruxes, be so fixated on the conundrum of cross-dressing? For no less a reason, I want to contend, than that *cross-dressing is itself a primal scene.*

We have noted that what ties together cross-dressing and the Red Riding Hood story and Freud's account of the Wolf-Man is that all of them have something to do with the primal scene in general. Red Riding Hood, in fact, is the primal scene of narrativized cross-dressing, the story that is told over and over again in a multiplicity of versions, when the child, the innocent gazer (Lily Fairchild, Nora Flood), comes upon the spectacle of cross-gender representation: that which—like parental coitus—seems inexplicable, unimaginable, fascinating, taboo. When we find the Red Riding Hood story in Freud, we find it in the case history that is about the primal scene. So that even for Freud "Red Riding Hood" is a primal scene—a primal scene, so to speak, within the narrative of the *Urszene*, the ur-primal scene.

"I was three or perhaps four years old when I realized that I had been born into the wrong body, and should really be a girl," writes Jan Morris at the beginning of *Conundrum*. "I was sitting beneath my mother's piano." Nora Ephron rather tartly suggests, in her review of Morris's book, that a boy sitting beneath the piano would be looking up his mother's skirt, and that a visit to a Freudian analyst to recover this scenario might have saved Morris the trouble and expense of transsexual surgery.[18] But such scenes, such scenarios of looking, are part of the very structure of the recognition scene we have noted in figures from Radclyffe Hall's lesbian cross-dresser Stephen Gordon opening the pages of Krafft-Ebing to Peter O'Toole's Lawrence of Arabia, curtseying to his robed shadow in the desert sun. The very existence of transvestite theaters, from Shakespeare's cross-dressed "heroines" to the contemporary drag show, testifies to the primacy of cross-dressing as spectacle, as that which purports both to conceal and to reveal. Conceal what? Reveal what? When the wig is doffed, ceremonially, at the end of a transvestic stage performance, what is the "answer" that is disclosed? Only another question: is *this* the real one? In what sense real? What is the "truth" of gender and sexuality that we try, in vain, to see, to see through, when what we are gazing at is a hall of mirrors?

I began this book by noting how frequently the phenomenon of cross-dressing, or transvestism, is looked *through* rather than *at* in critical and cultural analyses—how often, indeed how insistently, cultural observers have tried to make it mean something, anything, other than itself. If cross-dressing is, in fact, a primal scene, that which is not only constitutive of culture but also, by the same repressive mechanism, a deferral and a displacement, in Lacan's terms "a unique and decisive revelation of the subject, in which an indefinite something that is unsayable is concentrated, in which the subject is lost for a moment, blown up"—if, that is to say, cross-dressing is not only found *in* representations of the primal scene, but also itself *represents* a primal scene, then the secondary revision of commentators upon this phenomenon can be regarded as part of the mechanism. Cross-dressing is about gender confusion. Cross-dressing is about the phallus as constitutively veiled. Cross-dressing is about the power of women. Cross-dressing is about the emergence of gay identity. Cross-dressing is about the anxiety of economic or cultural dislocation, the anticipation or recognition of "otherness" as loss. All true, all partial truths, all powerful metaphors. But the compelling force of transvestism in literature and culture comes not, or not only, from these effects, but also from its instatement of metaphor itself, not as that for which a literal meaning must be found, but precisely as that without which there would be no such thing as meaning in the first place.

NOTES

NOTES TO INTRODUCTION, CLOTHES MAKE THE MAN

1. Sigmund Freud, "Femininity," in *New Introductory Lectures on Psycho-Analysis* (1933). *The Standard Edition of the Complete Psychological Works of Sigmund Freud*, general editor James Strachey (London: The Hogarth Press and The Institute for Psycho-Analysis, 1964), 22:113.

2. Jan Morris, *Conundrum: An Extraordinary Narrative of Transsexualism*,(New York: Henry Holt and Co., 1974; 1986), 110.

3. Sandra Salmans, "Objects and Gender: When an It Evolves into a He or a She," *New York Times*, November 16, 1989, Bl. See Jo B. Paoletti and Carol L. Kregloh, "The Children's Department," in *Men and Women: Dressing the Part*, ed. Claudia Brush Kidwell and Valerie Steel (Washington: Smithsonian Institution Press, 1989), 22–41. Paoletti, whose research is cited in the *Times* article, had no explanation for the shift in public perception.

4. Feminist Charlotte Perkins Gilman was one of the few to protest against "the premature and unnatural differentiation in sex in the dress of little children," arguing that "a little child should never be forced to think of this distinction." Charlotte Perkins Gilman, "Children's Clothing," *Harper's Bazaar*, January 1910, 24.

5. Kenneth S. Lynn, *Hemingway* (New York: Simon and Schuster, 1987), opposite 289. Lynn's captions for other childhood photographs of Hemingway point out that his mother raised him and his older sister Marcelline as "twins," dressing them both in the clothing of the same gender, sometimes male, sometimes female. That Hemingway's youngest son Gregory should himself have become a cross-dresser (*Exposure* 3,2 [July 1990]: 109) is probably a coincidence—but nonetheless adds another twist to the fascinating and complex Hemingway story.

6. *Fortune,* August 27, 1990, 14.

7. Vern L. Bullough, *Sexual Variance in Society and History* (Chicago: University of Chicago Press, 1976), 610. Bullough speculates interestingly about "whether homosexuals had earlier adopted red as a color in Chicago or whether they wore red because Havelock Ellis told them it was the thing to do." Bullough, 611.

8. Havelock Ellis, *Studies in the Psychology of Sex* (New York: Random House, 1936), l:299–300.

9. Sally Jacobs, "You Do What You Need to Do," *Boston Globe*, August 2, 1988, 2.

10. Jacobs, "You Do What You Need to Do," 2.

11. For example, Marguerite Waller, "Academic Tootsie: The Denial of Difference and the Difference It Makes," *Diacritics* 17, 1 (Spring 1987): 2–20.

12. Elaine Showalter, "Critical Cross-Dressing: Male Feminists and the Woman of the Year," *Raritan* 3,2 (Fall 1983):138.

13. Teresa de Lauretis, *Alice Doesn't: Feminism, Semiotics, Cinema* (Bloomington: Indiana University Press, 1984), 57. See also Rebecca Bell-Metereau, *Hollywood Androgyny* (New York: Columbia University Press, 1985).

14. Vito Russo, *The Celluloid Closet: Homosexuality in the Movies*, rev. ed. (New York: Harper & Row, 1987), 323.

15. Pauline Kael, review of *Tootsie*, *New Yorker*, December 27, 1982, 71.

16. See Stephen Orgel's essay on Renaissance theatrical conventions, "Nobody's Perfect: or Why Did the English Stage Take Boys for Women?" *South Atlantic Quarterly* 88, 1 (Winter 1989):7–30.

17. Robert J. Stoller, Chapter 18, "Transvestites' Women," in *Sex and Gender* (London: The Hogarth Press and the Institute for

Psycho-Analysis, 1968), 1:206–217; Ann Woodhouse, "Forgotten Women: Transvestism and Marriage," *Women's Studies International Forum* 8, 6,(1985): 583–592. Virginia Charles Prince, *The Transvestite and His Wife* (Los Angeles: Argyle Books, 1973); J.T. Talamini, *Boys Will Be Girls* (Washington, D.C.: University Press of America, 1982); Richard F. Docter, *Transvestites and Transsexuals: Toward a Theory of Cross-Gender Behavior* (New York: Plenum Press, 1988), 167–193; "He/She, We & They, Partners of Transvestites," booklet prepared by a group of wives at Fantasia Fair, Provincetown, MA., *Tapestry* 50 (1987): 62–65; Heather Peerson, "The TV's Wife," *Tapestry* 51 (1988): 77–78; Thomas S. Weinberg and Vern L. Bullough, "Women Married to Transvestites: Problems and Adjustments." *Tapestry* (1988): 37–42.

18. Played, as Elaine Showalter nicely points out in "Critical Cross-Dressing," by Dabney Coleman, who was cast in a similar role in the 1980 film, *Nine to Five*. Showalter observes about this intertextuality that "Insofar as *Tootsie* is a commentary on the woman's movement, teaching women how to stand up for their rights, it borrows what little politics it has from *Nine to Five*" (137). As will be clear, my idea of the politics of the film differs from Showalter's.

19. Sigmund Freud, "Fetishism" (1927), *SE* 21: 152–57, and "Femininity" (1933), *SE* 22: 24,126, 130. See also Stoller, *Sex and Gender*, 1:177ff.

20. Susan Gubar, "Blessings in Disguise: Cross-Dressing as Re-Dressing for Female Modernists." *Massachusetts Review* (Autumn 1981): 447–513. Sandra M. Gilbert, "Costumes of the Mind: Transvestism as Metaphor in Modern Literature," *Critical Inquiry* 7,2 (Winter 1980): 394. Both essays are reprinted, in a combined and revised form, in *Sexchanges*, Vol. 2 of Gilbert and Gubar's *No Man's Land* (New Haven: Yale University Press, 1988), 324–76.

21. Stephen Greenblatt, *Shakespearean Negotiations: The Circulation of Social Energy in Renaissance England* (Berkeley: University of California Press, 1988), 92–93.

22. Walter Cohen, "Political Criticism of Shakespeare" in *Shakespeare Reproduced: The Text in History and Ideology*, ed. Jean E. Howard and Marion F. O'Connor (New York: Methuen, 1987), 38.

23. Théophile Gautier, *Mademoiselle de Maupin*, trans. Joanna Richardson (Harmondsworth: Penguin Books, 1981), 329–30.

24. Carroll Smith-Rosenberg, *Disorderly Conduct: Visions of Gender in Victorian America* (New York: Oxford University Press, 1985); Stephen Greenblatt, "Fiction and Friction," in *Shakespearean Negotiations*; Stephen Orgel, "Nobody's Perfect"; Maxine Hong Kingston, *The Woman Warrior* (New York: Knopf, 1976).

25. Fredric Jameson, "Imaginary and Symbolic in Lacan: Marxism, Psychoanalytic Criticism, and the Problem of the Subject," *Yale French Studies* 55/56, *Literature and Psychoanalysis, The Question of Reading: Otherwise*, ed. Shoshana Felman (New Haven: Yale French Studies, 1977), 384.

26. Jacques Lacan, "The Agency of the Letter in the Unconscious," in *Ecrits: A Selection*, trans. Alan Sheridan (New York: W.W. Norton, 1977), 151.

27. Patricia J. Williams, *The Alchemy of Race and Rights* (Cambridge: Harvard University Press, 1991), 122–125.

28. See below, Chapter 4.

29. Jan Morris, *Conundrum*, 110–11.

30. Such genetic markers have been helpful, for example, in trying to identify carriers of Huntington's Disease, which does not manifest itself overtly in the body until the later years of life.

NOTES TO CHAPTER I, DRESS CODES, OR THE THEATRICALITY OF DIFFERENCE

1. *Soushen ji (Seeking the Spirits)* (Beijing: Zhonghua, 1979) 7:79 193. I am grateful to Judith Zeitlin for this reference from her study of Pu Songling's *Records of the Strange*, forthcoming as a book from Stanford University Press.

2. "Fashion Statement: Students Wear Ties," *New York Times*, October 27, 1990: 28.

3. Joseph Berger, "Legal or Not, Principal Plans a Dress Code," *New York Times* October 19, 1990: B1–B3.

4. Sumptuary laws were proposed, promulgated, and administered at the national (and occasionally the city) level in England and France, but they also figured prominently in the semi-independent states and cities in Germany (Nuremberg, Strassburg, Hamburg, Lübeck and many other cities in central Germany) and in the cities of Zurich, Basel, and Bern in Switzerland. Dating from as early as the Roman Law, and drawing force in Europe from the strength of religious, guild, and other paternalistic organizations in the middle ages, these laws, which sought to regulate clothing and social behavior (including the consumption of certain kinds of food and drink) continued to be passed and fitfully enforced in Switzerland through to the eighteenth century, although in

England sumptuary legislation *per se* came to an end with the accession of James I to the throne. See, for example, Frances Elizabeth Baldwin, *Sumptuary Legislation and Personal Regulation in England* (Baltimore: The Johns Hopkins University Press, 1926); Wilfred Hooper, "The Tudor Sumptuary Laws," *English Historical Review* 30 (1915): 433–49; and John Martin Vincent, *Costume and Conduct in the Laws of Basel, Bern, and Zurich, 1370–1800* (Baltimore: The Johns Hopkins University Press, 1935).

5. Susan Chira, "In Japan, the Land of the Rod, an Appeal to Spare the Child," *New York Times*, July 27, 1988: 1,7.

6. Baldwin, *Sumptuary Legislation*, 137. As so often, a narrative thread pulled becomes the fabric of a whole new story. The history of knitted stockings as an item in the industrialization of fashion goes back to Queen Elizabeth, who refused a patent to the Rev. William Lee, the inventor of the first knitting machine, because his stockings were coarser than the fine silk wear imported from Spain. Lee improved his machine to the point where it produced a finer stocking, but was again denied a patent because the Queen now feared that the machine would lead to economic hard times for hand knitters. Lee died in poverty, in France, in 1610; his knitting machine, introduced into England by his brother, remained the standard model used by the industry for hundreds of years, and its needle design is still used today in the manufacture of full-fashioned stockings.

7. Carol Barkalow, with Andrea Raab, *In the Men's House* (New York: Poseidon Press, 1990), 53–54; 38; 74; 58.

8. William Perkins, *Cases of Conscience* (1608). Sig. 2G2v. See Jonas Barish's invaluable study, *The Antitheatrical Prejudice* (Berkeley: University of California Press, 1981), for a more extended discussion of the resistance to theater and actors in Renaissance England.

9. There are records of such proclamations in 1562, 1563, 1572, 1576–77, 1579–80, 1587–88, and 1597. For a good overview of sumptuary laws in Renaissance England, see Cumberland Clark, *Shakespeare and Costume* (London: Folcroft Library, 1977), as well as the more specific accounts noted below.

10. William Jerdan, ed., "The Rutland Papers," in Camden Society Publications, no. 22: 247.

11. *Sermons or Homilies Appointed to Be Read in Churches in the Time of Queen Elizabeth* (Oxford: Clarendon Press, 1814), 262.

12. See, for example, what is probably the most compelling modern account of this appearance, in Louis Adrian Montrose, "Shaping Fantasies: Figurations of Gender and Power in Elizabethan Culture," *Representations* 44:2 (Spring 1983), 61–94. But all extant descriptions of Elizabeth cross-dressed on that occasion date from long after Tilbury, and are almost surely creations of a nostalgic cult of Elizabeth rather than accurate accounts of a historical event.

13. Quoted in Paul Johnson, *Elizabeth I: A Study in Power and Intellect* (London: Weidenfeld and Nicolson, 1974), 320.

14. John Louis Vives, "Of raiments," in *Instruction of a Christian Woman* (1529), trans. Richard Hyrde (1557), Book II, Chapter viii.

15. Philip Stubbes, *Anatomy of Abuses*, ed. Frederick J. Furnivall (London: New Shakespeare Society, 1877), 73 (Sig.F5v).

16. John Rainolds, *Overthrow of Stage Playes* (New York: Johnson Reprint Corp., 1972), 34–35, 10–11. J.W. Binns, "Women or Transvestites on the Elizabethan Stage?: An Oxford Controversy," *Sixteenth Century Journal* 5,2 (October 1974): 95–120.

17. Sigmund Freud, "Fetishism" (1927), trans. Joan Riviere. *SE* 21:154.

18. Middleton, *Works*, ed. A. H. Bullen (Boston: Houghton Mifflin, 1885–86), 8 vols. 3: 130–44; Alan Bray, *Homosexuality in Renaissance England* (Boston: Gay Men's Press, 1988), 87.

19. For these examples, and for much of the historical argument summarized here, I am indebted to Jean Howard's thorough and helpful essay, "Crossdressing, The Theatre, and Gender Struggle in Early Modern England," *Shakespeare Quarterly* 3,4 (Winter 1988): 418–40. Howard cites as her source for these court records the research of Professor R. Mark Benbow on the records of the Repertories of the Aldermen's Court in the London City Record Office and from the Bridewell Court Minute Books between approximately 1565 and 1605.

20. Samuel R. Gardiner, *Documents Relating to the Proceedings Against William Prynne in 1634 and 1637*, in Camden Society Publications, new series, #18: 4.

21. *Calendar of State Papers and Manuscripts Relating to English Affairs, Venetian Series* (London, 1864—),15: 111–112.

22. R.H.F. Scott, ed., *The Transvestite Memoirs of the Abbé de Choisy* (London: Peter Owen, 1973), 131.

23. *Calendar of State Papers, Domestic, James I*. Public Records Office (rpt. Kraus Reprint, 1970), ed. Allen B. Hinds. 10:116.

24. *Hic Mulier: Or, the Man-Woman: Being a Medicine to Cure the Coltish Disease of the Staggers in the Masculine-Feminines of Our Times* and *Haec Vir: Or the Womanish-Man: Being an Answer to a late Booke intituled Hic-Mulier.*(University of Exeter: The Rota, 1973). Sig A4v.

25. Jonathan Dollimore raises this same point in an excellent brief treatment of Renaissance cross-dressing, "Shakespeare, Cultural Materialism, Feminism and Marxist Humanism," *New Literary History* 21,3 (Spring 1990): 483.

26. Stephen Greenblatt, *Renaissance Self-Fashioning: From More to Shakespeare* (Chicago: University of Chicago Press, 1980), 1–9.

27. Especially at risk was the "masculine" self; men in women's clothes could all too easily "turn into" women if they were not careful. Laura Levine, "Men in Women's Clothing: Anti-theatricality and Effeminization from 1579–1642," *Criticism* 28 (1986):126, 128, 136. Recent work on the homoerotics of English Renaissance drama and on the emergence of the concept of homosexual

identity in the period has challenged this idea of translation into women, while drawing renewed attention to the construction of sexuality and the fact that "gender difference is also class difference" (Jonathan Goldberg, "Making Sense," *New Literary History* 21:3 (Spring, 1990): 461. Goldberg's paper "Playing the Sodomite" also speaks tellingly to this point.) See also Dollimore, "Shakespeare, Cultural Materialism, Feminism and Marxist Humanism."

28. Charlton Ogburn, *The Mysterious William Shakespeare* (New York: Dodd Mead, 1984), 177.

29. *Boston Globe*, July 15, 1989: 17.

30. *Time*, July 24, 1989: 52.

31. Michael Billington, "Lasciviously Pleasing," in Garry O'Connor, *Olivier: In Celebration* (New York: Dodd Mead, 1987): 71.

32. Hugo Vickers, *Times* (London). Blurb from the dustjacket of Anthony Holden, *Laurence Olivier*.

33. Anthony Holden, *Laurence Olivier* (New York: Atheneum, 1988), 234–35.

34. Thomas Platter, narrative of his travels in 1595–1600, written in 1604–5. Cited in B. Binz, *Anglia* 22,456, translated and reprinted in E.K. Chambers, *The Elizabethan Stage* (Oxford: Clarendon Press, 1923), 2:365. See also Clark, *Shakespeare and Costume*, 170 and Theodore Komisarjevsky, *The Costume of the Theatre* (London: Geoffrey Bles, 1931), 73–93.

35. Stephen Gosson, *The School of Abuse* (1579); rpt. in Arthur F. Kinney, *Markets of Bawdrie: The Dramatic Criticism of Stephen Gosson* (Salzburg: Salzburg Studies in English Literature, 1974), 96.

36. *Calendar of State Papers, Domestic Series* (London, 1856–72), 1:269.

37. Natalie Zemon Davis, "Women on Top," in *Society and Culture in Early Modern France* (Stanford: Stanford University Press, 1985), 136, 150.

38. *The Statutes of the Realm*, 11 vol.,1810 (rpt. London, 1963, 12 vol.) 2: 399; *Rotuli Parliamentaorum ut et Petitiones et Placita in Parliamento* (Great Britain: Record Commission). Cited in Baldwin, *Sumptuary Legislation*, 103, 218, 228.

39. *Exposure* 3, 2 (July 1990): 51.

40. Although the British materialist critic Jonathan Dollimore, in a recent article, imagines a production of *Antony and Cleopatra* in which the Egyptian Queen is played either by "Peter Stallybrass of the University of Pennsylvania or . . . Gary Taylor, editor of the Oxford Shakespeare," with "Antony . . . played by a woman—ideally Marjorie Garber of Harvard." Dollimore, "Shakespeare, Cultural Materialism, Feminism and Marxist Humanism," 490.

41. Arthur Holmberg, " 'Lear' Girds for a Remarkable Episode," *New York Times*, May 20, 1990: H7.

42. Mervyn Rothstein, "An Artful Falstaff Who Transcends Sex," *New York Times*, June 7, 1990: C17, C20.

43. Richard Gilman, "Princely Role of Hamlet—Every Actor's Dream," *San Francisco Chronicle*, May 27, 1990: 32.

44. Edward P. Vining, *The Mystery of Hamlet* (Philadelphia: J.B. Lippincott and Co., 1881), 48.

45. Vining, 59. Vining's book was dedicated to Horace Furness, the eminent scholar who edited the Shakespeare Variorum and who coincidentally, as we will see, starred as a Harvard undergraduate in 1854 as the first great cross-dressed Hasty Pudding "diva."

46. Following Vining's theory that Hamlet was a woman. See Lawrence Danson's forthcoming article on the Nielsen film, "Gazing at Hamlet, or the Danish Cabaret," *Shakespeare Survey* 24.

47. Rothstein, C20. A letter to the *New York Times* pointed out that Carroll's Falstaff was in fact *not* the first; the British actress Juliana (or Julia) Glover (1779–1850) played Falstaff at the Haymarket Theater, where she was apparently not a success, although she had allowed herself to become "monstrously fat" for the role. Ludia Webb (d.1793), a comic actress, is said to have played the "other" Falstaff, the Falstaff of the history plays, in a Haymarket production in 1786. Caldwell Titcomb, letter to the editor, *New York Times*, June 29, 1990: A10.

48. Patricia Parker, *Literary Fat Ladies* (London and New York: Methuen, 1987), 21–22; Valerie Traub, "Prince Hal's Falstaff: Positioning Psychoanalysis and the Female Reproductive Body," *Shakespeare Quarterly*, 40, 4 (Winter 1989): 456–74; Nancy Cotton, "Castrating (W)itches: Impotence and Magic in *The Merry Wives of Windsor*," *Shakespeare Quarterly* 38,3 (Autumn 1987): 320–26. Coppélia Kahn, *Man's Estate* (Berkeley: University of California Press, 1981), 72–73; Laurie A. Finke, "Falstaff, The Wife of Bath, and the Sweet Smoke of Rhetoric," in *Chaucerian Shakespeare*, E. Talbot Donaldson and Judith J. Kollman, eds. (Detroit: Michigan Consortium, 1983), 7–24; Anne Parten, "Falstaff's Horns: Masculine Inadequacy and Feminine Mirth in *The Merry Wives of Windsor*," *Studies in Philology* 82, 2 (Spring 1985): 184–99; W.H. Auden, *The Dyer's Hand and Other Essays* (New York: Random House, 1962), 195–96.

49. John Downes, *Roscius Anglicanus, or an Historical Review of the Stage* (London: H. Playford, 1708), 26. A footnote to this account added that "After the Restoration (we are told by old Mr. Cibber) it was a frequent practice of the ladies of quality, to carry Mr. Kynaston the actor, in his female dress, after the play [which began then at three o'clock] in their coaches, to Hyde-Park."

NOTES TO CHAPTER 2, CROSS-DRESS FOR SUCCESS

1. Mike Barnicle, *Boston Globe*, July 24, 1988: 21.

2. *San Francisco Chronicle*, May 24, 1990: E4.

3. John T. Molloy, *The Woman's Dress for Success Book* (New York: Warner Books, 1977), 28.

4. Ruth La Ferla, "His, Now Hers," *New York Times Magazine*, April 25, 1988: 94.

5. Woody Hochswender, "Patterns," *New York Times*, June 28, 1988.

6. Mary Randolph, quoted in Tom Goldstein, "In Vanguard of Do-It-Yourself Law Movement," *New York Times*, March 11, 1988.

7. John T. Molloy, *Dress for Success* (New York: Warner Books, 1975), 119.

8. *Information for the Female-to-Male Crossdresser and Transsexual*, 2nd ed.(San Francisco: L. Sullivan, 1985), 22.

9. The passage is from Robert J. Stoller, *Sex and Gender: On the Development of Masculinity and Femininity* (London: The Hogarth Press and the Institute of Psycho-Analysis, 1968), 1: 195.

10. *Information for the Female-to-Male Crossdresser and Transsexual*, 7.

11. Kay Gould, "Mystique of Make-Up," *Tapestry* 50 (1987): 74.

12. Anonymous, "Woman to Woman," *Tapestry* 51 (1988):67–69. Reprinted from the SHAFT Newsletter and the Beaumont Bulletin.

13. See, for example, Stoller's chapter on "The Mother's Contribution to Boyhood Transsexualism," 108 and 125, and his comments on close mothers and absent fathers as hospitable conditions for the development of cross-dressing children throughout the book.

14. *Information for the Female-to-Male Crossdresser and Transsexual*, 41.

15. *Under Construction*—as the name implies, a group largely for transsexuals; it also publishes *The Los Angeles Transsexual Yellow Pages*.

16. *Boston Globe*, December 20, 1987: A25.

17. *San Francisco Chronicle*, July 23, 1990: F1.

18. Letter of Robert Livingstone to Mr. Lowndes. *Calendar of Treasury Papers, 1702–1707*. ed. Joseph Redington (London, 1874), 3: 512.

19. Lewis Morris, February 7, 1707/8, in E.B. O'Callaghan, *Documents Relative to the Colonial History of the State of New York; Procured by John Romeyn Brodhead*, 11 vols.(Albany, 1855) 5:38.

20. Elias Neau, Letter, February 27, 1708/9, in George Morgan Hills, *History of the Church in Burlington, New Jersey*, 2nd ed. (Trenton, New Jersey, 1885), 89.

21. Lord Sylvester Douglas Glenbervie. *The Diaries of Sylvester Douglas (Lord Glenbervie)*, ed. Francis Bickley, 2 vols. (London: Constable; Boston: Houghton Mifflin, 1928) 1:77.

22. Patricia U. Bonomi, "A Portrait Questioned," letter to the *Times Literary Supplement*, May 4–10, 1990: 473.

23. Jonathan Katz, *Gay American History: Lesbians and Gay Men in the U.S.A.* (New York: Thomas Crowell, 1976), 570.

24. David Nyhan, "Bush Will Be Held Accountable for the Cheap Shots Against Dukakis," *Boston Globe*. August 22, 1988: 19.

25. *New Orleans Times-Picayune*, December 28, 1988: A8.

26. Charles McCool Snyder, *Dr. Mary Walker* (reprinted New York: Arno Press, 1974). Vern L. Bullough, *Sexual Variance in Society and History* (Chicago: University of Chicago Press, 1976), 597–99.

27. Max Beerbohm, *Letters to Reggie Turner*, ed. Rupert Hart-Davis (London: Hart-Davis, 1964), 103.

28. George L. Mosse points out that "Hirschfeld never publicly admitted he was a homosexual, though he lived with a friend." Mosse, *Nationalism and Sexuality: Middle-Class Morality and Sexual Norms in Modern Europe* (Madison: University of Wisconsin Press, 1985), 141.

29. This phenomenon, and particularly the existence of cross-dressed female soldiers, sailors, and cavalrymen in the armed forces of Europe and the U.S. has been the subject of a number of recent biographies, reprints, critical essays, and works of fiction, from *The Cavalry Maiden*, the journal of a cross-dressed woman in the Polish army during the Napoleonic Wars (Nadezdha Durova, trans. Mary Fleming Zirin [Bloomington: Indiana University Press, 1988]) to *The Female Soldier: Or, The Surprising Life and Adventures of Hannah Snell*, a recently reprinted eighteenth-century pamphlet about a woman who joined the army in 1745, dressed as a man ([1750] intro. Dianne Dugaw [Los Angeles: Clark Library, Augustan Reprint Society, 1989]) to *High Hearts*, Rita Mae Brown's popular novel about a cross-dressed woman officer in the Confederate Army during the U.S. Civil War (New York: Bantam, 1986). The renewed popularity of this genre testifies once again to the fascination of the later twentieth century with the possibilities of masquerade and self-transformation offered by transvestic disguise. These recent retellings almost all focus on some external rationale for cross-dressing—Hannah Snell and Brown's Geneva Chatfield, for example, are both said to enlist to join

their husbands, though both become soldiers in their own right, surpassing and leaving behind the men they sought to imitate. For other case histories of female soldiers and sailors, see Bullough, *Sexual Variance*, 599–600.

30. Magnus Hirschfeld, *Die Transvestiten: Eine Untersuchung über den erotischen Verkleidungstrieb* (Berlin: Alfred Pulvermacher, 1910). Leslie Martin Lothstein, *Female-to-Male Transsexualism: Historical, Clinical, and Theoretical Issues* (Boston: Routledge and Kegan Paul, 1983), 22.

31. Joint Army and Navy Committee on Welfare and Recreation, *A Report on Army Special Service Activities and Facilities* (Washington, D.C.: United States Government Printing Office, 1942).

32. Allan Bérubé, *Coming Out Under Fire: The History of Gay Men and Women In World War Two.* (New York: Free Press, 1990), 69–70.

33. Rosamund Gilder, "You Bet Your Life," *Theatre Arts* (September 1944): 521–27. Bérubé, *Coming Out*, 94.

34. Quentin Crisp, *The Naked Civil Servant* (New York: New American Library, 1983), 153.

35. Kris Kirk and Ed Heath, *Men in Frocks* (London: Gay Men's Press, 1984), 31.

36. Homer Dickens, *What a Drag: Men as Women and Women as Men in the Movies* (New York: Quill, 1984), 78.

37. *South Pacific.* Music by Richard Rodgers, Lyrics by Oscar Hammerstein II, Book by Oscar Hammerstein II and Joshua Logan (Williamson Music, 1949).

38. See Vito Russo, *The Celluloid Closet: Homosexuality in the Movies.* rev. ed. (New York: Harper & Row, 1987), 54, 162.

39. Grant's appearance in a woman's robe in Howard Hawks's *Bringing Up Baby* has been cited by both film critics and biographers as a significant moment within that film. As David Huxley, a shy paleozoologist pursued by Katherine Hepburn (in the role of a dizzy, accident-prone heiress), he finds himself emerging from the shower in her Connecticut home suddenly bereft of his clothes; in a tactical maneuver to keep him from leaving the premises she has sent them off to the cleaner. When Hepburn's wealthy aunt comes to the door, Grant snatches up the nearest garment, a white robe trimmed with fur or marabou, and explains to her in exasperation, when she demands to know why he is wearing those clothes, that he just "went gay all of a sudden."

"Gay," in 1938, meant approximately what it means today; Gershon Legman's "The Language of Homosexuality," which listed "words and phrases current in American slang, argot, and colloquial speech since the first World War, and particularly during the period between 1930 and 1940," defines *gay* as "an adjective used almost exclusively by homosexuals to denote homosexuality, sexual attractiveness, promiscuity . . . or lack of restraint, in a person, place, or party" (Jonathan Ned Katz, *Gay/Lesbian Almanac: A New Documentary* [New York: Harper & Row, 1983] 571, 577). What did Grant—or Howard Hawks—think the audience would hear in the word? And *which* audience?

A recent biography of Grant describes the woman's garment he is wearing in *Bringing Up Baby* as "a fluffy nightgown" (Charles Higham and Roy Moseley, *Cary Grant* (New York: Avon Books, 105); Stanley Cavell, in his reading of the film, calls it a "negligee" (Cavell, *Pursuits of Happiness: The Hollywood Comedy of Remarriage,* Cambridge: Harvard University Press, 1981: 115). But a "negligee" (or a nightgown) is usually made of a delicate, soft fabric, often translucent and revealing. What Grant wears is instead something more like a "peignoir," an elegant dressing-gown, feminized but opaque and shaped, hanging rather than clinging, not at all revealing except for its plunging neckline. Yet, like H.D.'s Freudian "slip," this feminine garment names its own disorder, for something is indeed *negligée* here, something is being neglected.

Biographers have presented evidence that Grant himself was gay or bisexual, citing his relationships with Randolph Scott and others. His bisexuality was apparently well known in Hollywood circles, where it occasioned considerable concern, at least among studio executives. Grant's exasperated declaration within the film ("I went gay all of a sudden") might thus be read as a wink to the gay audience ("We know what we're talking about, however silly this picture—and my relationships with the women in it—might seem to be"), as a condition-contrary-to-fact, a denial ("I'm saying this because it's so patently ridiculous, as even you should be able to see") or as a double bluff of the purloined letter variety ("Grant declares this openly; therefore it can't be true, no matter what you've heard").

Cavell's reading stresses a heterosexual male anxiety of artifice, through the constant iteration of the word "bone" (penis; erection): the film opens with Dr. Huxley debating where a particular bone should go on the reconstructed skeleton of a brontosaurus, much of the action involves the recovery of a missing dinosaur bone without which Huxley feels his work will be forever incomplete, and Hepburn, casting about for an alias for him, seizes in desperation on the name "Bone." But looked at more closely these references are all double-edged. As Cavell acutely notes, the "bone" is closely linked in the film to the "behind." When Huxley ruminates, in the opening sequence, "I think this one belongs in the tail," his fiancée, the serious, mannishly dressed, and suggestively named "Miss Swallow" (who thinks that honeymoons and children are irrelevant to marriage), tells him "You tried that yesterday." In a comic scene in a posh restaurant Hepburn splits the tails of Grant's coat, and he in turn accidentally tears off the back of the skirt of her evening gown, so that he has to stand very closely behind her (to conceal the missing dress panel) as they maneuver their way out. Cavell calls this "more or less blatant and continuous double entendre,"—but what is *entendu*? And, again, what is *negligée*?

In another Hawks film, *I Was a Male War Bride* (1949), Grant was the "bride"—and had to cross-dress as a WAC.

40. Andrew Fineberg, "When the Boss Wears a Hula Skirt," *New York Times*, Business Section, Part 2, March 25, 1990: 33.

41. *Harvard Graduates' Magazine*, April, 1893, quoted in Anthony Calnek, *The Hasty Pudding Theatre: A History of Harvard's Hairy-Chested Heroines*, with a foreword by Alistair Cooke (New York/Milan: A.D.C. in association with A.M.O.F., 1986), 13.

42. "Certain Orders by the Schollars & officers of the Colledge to bee observed, written 28 March 1650." In *The College Book N*.1*. 49–54. Reprinted in *Publications of the Colonial Society of Massachusetts, Collections: Harvard College Records, Part I* (Boston: Colonial Society, 1925), 15:37–38.

43. *The Lawes of the colledge published publiquely before the Students of Harvard Colledge May 4, 1655* ("the Chauncey Code") MSS UA I.15.803VT; UA I.15.805 VT. Reprinted in *Publications of the Colonial Society of Massachusetts, Collections: Harvard College Records, Part III* (Boston: Colonial Society, 1935) 31:330.

44. Clifford K. Shipton, *Biographical Sketches of Those Who Attended Harvard College in the Classes 1713–1721*, in *Sibley's Harvard Graduates* (Boston: Massachusetts Historical Society, 1942), 6:91–2. "In the Colledge-Hall, June 17* 1712," in *The College Book, N* 4*. 43. Reprinted in *Publications of the Colonial Society of Massachusetts, Collections: Harvard College Record, Part I* (Boston: Colonial Society, 1925), 15: 402; John Leverett, *Diary of John Leverett as President of Harvard College*. Harvard Archives UA I.15.866.VT.

45. *The College Book N* 1*. 182–206. "This body of laws for Harvard College was made by the President & Fellows thereof, and consented to by the Overseers of Said College, Anno Domini 1734." Reprinted in *Publications of the Colonial Society of Massachusetts, Harvard College Records, Part I*, 15: 141.

46. Ralph Werther/Jennie June ("Earl Lind"), *The Female-Impersonators* (New York: The Medico-Legal Journal, 1922), 100.

47. "Bare Leg Ban Hits Harvard: The Actors Must Wear Stockings in Boston," *Boston Post*, March 15, 1917.

48. *Boston Post*, op. cit., and "Casey Doesn't Fall For This Harvard 'bunk,' " *Boston Traveller*, March 15, 1917.

49. "Yale Limits Skirt Wearing," *New York Times*, December 11, 1915: 22, col. 3.

50. "College Athletes Act Best in Skirts," *New York Times*, December 12, 1915: Section II, 16, col. 1.

51. "Year Limit for Actors at Harvard," *Boston Post*, May 8, 1916.

52. For a discussion of the term "effeminate" and how it has changed over time, see Chapter 6, "Breaking the Code: Transvestism and Gay Identity."

53. Presumably very few, if any, members of the NYU class of 1915 would have been dockhands; this was still an era in which attending college was a privilege of the well-to-do. So "dock hand" is probably as artificial as "woman" here, and is a marker of fictive "class" aligned with the fictive "gender" of the performers.

54. Joan Vennochi, "Men Only—For Now," *Boston Globe*, October 13, 1988: 85, 87.

55. Philip Weiss, "Into the Woods: Bohemian Grove Confidential," *Spy* (November 1989): 60.

NOTES TO CHAPTER 3, THE TRANSVESTITE'S PROGRESS

1. *New York Times*, February 2, 1989: A18. Associated Press report, citing an interview with Tipton's son, Jon Clark, in the *Spokane Spokesman-Review*.

2. Jonathan Katz, ed. *Gay American History: Lesbians and Gay Men in the U.S.A.* (New York: Thomas Crowell, 1976), 222.

3. John D'Emilio and Estelle B. Freedman, *Intimate Matters: A History of Sexuality in America*. (New York: Harper & Row, 1988), 125.

4. *Information for the Female-to-Male Crossdresser and Transsexual*. 2nd ed. (San Francisco: L. Sullivan, 1985), 10.

5. Ann M. Butler, *Daughters of Joy, Sisters of Misery: Prostitutes in the American West, 1865–1890* (Urbana: University of Illinois Press, 1985), 144. Emilio and Freedman, *Intimate Matters*, 124.

6. Juliet Wheelwright, *Amazons and Military Maids: Women Who Dressed as Men in the Pursuit of Life, Liberty and Happiness* (London: Pandora, 1989), 1–6. "Colonel Barker in the Dock at the Old Bailey," *Daily Herald*, April 25, 1929.

7. Sigmund Freud, "Fetishism" (1927), *SE* 21, 156.

8. For a fuller discussion of how gay lifestyles intersect with cross-dressing, see Chapter 6, "Breaking the Code: Transvestism and Gay Identity."

9. New York, Ballantine Books, 1981: 108.

10. Oscar Wilde, *The Picture of Dorian Gray*. (London: Penguin Books, 1985; orig. pub. 1891), 103.

11. Théophile Gautier, *Mademoiselle de Maupin*, trans. Joanna Richardson (Harmondsworth: Penguin Books, 1981), 246–47.

CHAPTER 3

12. Jacques Lacan, "The Signification of the Phallus," in *Ecrits: A Selection*, trans. Alan Sheridan (New York: W.W. Norton, 1977), 287.

13. Stephen Greenblatt, "Fiction and Friction," *Shakespearean Negotiations* (Berkeley: University of California Press, 1988), 90–91. For an excellent treatment of the relation of the boy actor to fears and assumptions about women in the Renaissance, and in these plays, see Stephen Orgel, "Call Me Ganymede: Shakespeare's Apprentices and the Representation of Women" (forthcoming in *Why Did the English Stage Take Boys for Women?* Routledge, 1992).

14. Otto Weininger, *Sex and Character* (London: William Heinemann, 1906), 67. See also below, "Breaking the Code."

15. Angela Carter, *The Passion of New Eve.* (London: Victor Gollancz, 1977; rpt. Virago Press, 1987), 132.

16. Alan Bray, *Homosexuality in Renaissance England* (London: Gay Men's Press, 1982; 2nd ed. Boston: Gay Men's Press, 1988), 65.

17. Shaun Considine, *Barbra Streisand: The Woman, the Myth, the Music* (London: Century, 1985), 345.

18. Freud's note comes in the context of a discussion of the Wolf-Man's fears of castration and his association of it with "the ritual circumcision of Christ and of the Jews in general."

    Among the most tormenting, though at the same time the most grotesque, symptoms of [the Wolf-Man's] later illness was his relation to every tailor from whom he ordered a suit of clothes: his deference and timidity in the presence of this high functionary, his attempts to get into his good books by giving him extravagant tips, and his despair over the results of the work however it might in fact have turned out. [The German word for "tailor" is "*Schneider*," from the verb "*schneiden*," ("to cut"), a compound of which, "*beschneiden*," means "to circumcise." It will be remembered, too, that it was a tailor who pulled off the wolf's tail.] Sigmund Freud, *From the History of an Infantile Neurosis* (1918), *SE* 17: 86, 87n.

19. James Brady, "In Step with: Amy Irving." *Parade Magazine*, October 30, 1988.

20. Rebecca Bell-Metereau, *Hollywood Androgyny* (New York: Columbia University Press, 1985), 231. See also Jack Kroll, "Barbra, the Yeshiva Boy," *Newsweek*, November 28, 1983, 109; David Denby, "Educating Barbra," *New York*, November 28, 1983, 111; Pauline Kael, "The Perfectionist," *New Yorker*, November 28, 1983: 176.

21. Johnny Carson, *Tonight Show* February 16, 1984. Considine, *Barbra Streisand*, 356–58.

22. Sigmund Freud, "Revision of the Theory of Dreams," in *New Introductory Lectures on Psycho-analysis* (1933), *SE* 22:24.

23. Sigmund Freud, "Medusa's Head" (1922), *SE* 18: 273.

24. *New York Times*, January 29, 1984.

25. Isaac Bashevis Singer, "Yentl the Yeshiva Boy," trans. Marion Magid and Elizabeth Pollet, in *Short Friday and Other Stories* (New York: Fawcett Crest, 1978), 160.

26. George Puttenham, *The Arte of English Poesie,* intro. Baxter Hathaway (Kent, Ohio: Kent State University Press, 1970 [facsimile reproduction of 1906 reprint]), 183–84.

27. J.M. Barrie, *Peter Pan* (Harmondsworth: Puffin Books, 1986 [orig. publ. London: Hodder & Stoughton, 1911]), 116.

28. The term is one that Girard used throughout his writings on Shakespeare. See, for example, René Girard, "The Politics of Desire in *Troilus and Cressida*." *Shakespeare and the Question of Theory*, ed. Patricia Parker and Geoffrey Hartman (New York: Methuen, 1985), 188–209.

29. Cesare Vecellio, *Habiti antichi e moderni di tutto il mondo*, Venice, 1590, cited in Lynne Lawner, *Lives of the Courtesans* (New York: Rizzoli, 1987), 20.

30. Lawner, *Lives of the Courtesans*, 21.

31. Pietro Aretino, *The Letters of Pietro Aretino*, trans. Thomas Caldecott Chubb (Hamden, Connecticut: Archon Books, 1967) 6:249.

32. Edgar Wind, *Pagan Mysteries in the Renaissance* (Harmondsworth: Penguin Books, 1967), 53. Erwin Panofsky, *Studies in Iconology* (New York: Oxford University Press, 1939), 95–128.

33. Virgil, *Aeneid*, trans. Robert Fitzgerald (New York: Random House, 1983), 1:660–719.

34. A great deal has been written in recent years on the phenomenon of the boy actor and the implications for gender roles on and off the stage in the English Renaissance. See, for example, Laura Levine, "Men in Women's Clothing: Anti-theatricality and Effeminization from 1579 to 1642," *Criticism*, 28 (1986), 121–43; Lisa Jardine, " 'As boys and women are for the most part cattle of this colour': Female Roles and Elizabethan Eroticism," *Still Harping on Daughters: Women and Drama in the Age of Shakespeare* (Totowa, N.J.: Barnes and Noble Books, 1983), 9–36; Kathleen McLuskie, "The Act, the Role, and the Actor: Boy Actresses on the Elizabethan Stage," *New Theatre Quarterly*, 3 (1987), 120–30; Phyllis Rackin, "Androgyny, Mimesis, and the Marriage of the Boy Heroine on the English Renaissance Stage," *PMLA*, 102 (1987), 29–41; Catherine Belsey, "Disrupting Sexual Difference: Meaning and Gender in the Comedies," *Alternative Shakespeares*, ed. John Drakakis (London: Methuen, 1985), 166–90; Jean E. Howard, "Crossdressing, The Theatre, and Gender Struggle in Early Modern England," *Shakespeare Quarterly* 39:4 (1988), 418–

440, and Stephen Orgel, "Nobody's Perfect: Or Why did the English Stage Take Boys for Women?" *South Atlantic Quarterly* 88:1 (1989), 7–30.

35. Edward Albee, *Who's Afraid of Virginia Woolf?* (New York: Atheneum, 1962; rpt. Signet/ New American Library, 1983), 47.

36. George describes Martha as "braying" in the opening moments of Albee's play. (George: "Do you want me to go around all night *braying* at everybody, the way you do?" Martha (*Braying*): "I DON'T BRAY!" George (*Softly*): "All right . . . you don't bray.") Albee, 7.

37. Ronald Smothers, "Embryos in a Divorce Case: Joint Property or Offspring?" *New York Times*, April 22, 1989: Section 1, 1. In a recent updating of this case, the divorced "parents" of the embryos, Mary Sue Davis Stowe and Junior Lewis Davis, were awarded joint custody (*New York Times* September 14, 1990: B5).

NOTES TO CHAPTER 4, SPARE PARTS

1. Robert J. Stoller, *Sex and Gender: On the Development of Masculinity and Femininity* (London: The Hogarth Press and the Institute of Psycho-Analysis, 1968), 1:186.

2. Robert J. Stoller, *Observing the Erotic Imagination* (New York: Oxford University Press, 1985), 30.

3. Here are some selections from a vast (and growing) medical literature: Harry Benjamin, *The Transsexual Phenomenon* (New York: Julian Press, 1966); Havelock Ellis, *Studies in the Psychology of Sex* (New York: Modern Library, 1942); Otto Fenichel, "The Psychology of Transvestism," *International Journal of Psycho-Analysis*, 11 (1930): 111–27; Emil Arthur Gutheil, "Analysis of a Case of Transvestism," in Wilhelm Stekel, ed., *Sexual Aberrations* (New York: Liveright, 1930); John Money, *Gay, Straight, and In-Between: The Sexology of Erotic Orientation* (New York: Oxford University Press, 1988); Virginia Prince and Peter M. Bentler, "Survey of 504 Cases of Transvestism," *Psychological Reports* 31 (1972) 903–17; L.H. Rubenstein, "The Role of Identification in Homosexuality and Transvestism in Men and Women," in Ismond Rosen, ed., *The Pathology and Treatment of Sexual Deviation* (London and New York: Oxford University Press, 1964).

4. Sigmund Freud, "Fetishism" (1927), trans. Joan Riviere *SE* 21: 149–57.

5. See, for example, Richard F. Docter, *Transvestites and Transsexuals: Toward a Theory of Cross-Gender Behavior.* (New York and London: Plenum Press, 1988), esp. Chapter 8; Prince and Bentler, "Survey of 504 Cases"; Deborah Feinbloom, *Transvestites and Transsexuals* (New York: Dell, 1976); J.T. Talamini, *Boys Will Be Girls* (Washington D.C.: University Press of America, 1982). Some critics maintain that respondents to such surveys are likely to conceal or minimize their homosexual experiences or identities, but most spokespersons for transvestite groups endorse these statistics as valid. For a fuller discussion of transvestism and gay identity, see Chapter 6 below.

6. Alfred Adler, "The Masculine Protest as the Nuclear Problem of Neurosis," paper read to the Vienna Society in 1911. Published, with another relevant paper, "Some Problems of Psychoanalysis," in *Heilen und Bilden* (with C. Furtmuller, Munich, 1914), 94–114.

7. Renée Richards, with Jack Ames, *Second Serve* (New York: Stein and Day, 1983), 56–57.

8. Jan Morris, *Conundrum: An Extraordinary Narrative of Transsexualism* (New York: Henry Holt and Co., 1974; 1986), 152–53.

9. Henry Reed, "Lessons of the War" (1946) in *A Map of Verona* (London: Jonathan Cape Ltd., 1956).

10. Stoller, *Observing the Erotic Imagination*, 135.

11. See, for example, Naomi Schor, "Female Fetishism: The Case of George Sand," in Susan Rubin Suleiman, ed., *The Female Body in Western Culture* (Cambridge: Harvard University Press, 1986), 363–72. Schor cites medical as well as literary arguments in her bibliography.

12. Robert J. Stoller, *Splitting* (New York: Quadrangle, 1973).

13. One such "pre-op" transsexual, in this case a male-to-female transsexual, Merissa Sherrill Lynn (born Wade Southwick), is the founder of the International Foundation for Gender Education, an organization for transvestites and transsexuals based in Waltham, Massachusetts. Lynn was recently interviewed by the *Boston Globe*, and the interview transcript as printed in the newspaper manifested pronominal anxiety in an extreme degree:

> "The bottom line is that it is a turn-on," said a smiling Lynn, smoothing *her* blue and white floral print dress with well-manicured nails.

> "This is all me," Lynn said, squeezing *his* breast through *his* dress. "I don't have a double D-cup, but this keeps

me stable and happy. It gives me peace." (Sally Jacobs, "You Do What You Need to Do," *Boston Globe*, August 2, 1988 [emphasis added])

14. Leslie Martin Lothstein, *Female-to-Male Transsexualism: Historical, Clinical and Theoretical Issues* (Boston: Routledge and Kegan Paul, 1983), 6–7, 14.

15. The case is well argued by Catherine Belsey, in a deliberately polemical articulation of "the construction of the subject":

> Man, the centre and hero of liberal humanism, was produced in contradistinction to the objects of his knowledge and in terms of the relations of power in the economy and the state. Woman was procured in contradistinction to man, and in terms of the relations of power in the family. (Belsey, *The Subject of Tragedy: Identity & Difference in Renaissance Drama* [London: Methuen, 1985], 9)

16. Sigmund Freud, "Femininity" (1933), *SE* 22: 114.

17. J. Gelb, M. Malament, and S. LoVerme, "Total Reconstruction of the Penis," *Plastic and Reconstructive Surgery* 24 (1959): 62–73.

18. John Money, *Gay, Straight, and In-Between: The Sexology of Erotic Orientation* (New York: Oxford University Press, 1988), 58.

19. According to Money, the term "transexual" was coined by D.O. Caudwell in an article, published in 1949, "Psychopathia Transexualis," *Sexology* 16. Dr. Harry Benjamin popularized the term in his 1966 textbook (the first on the topic), *The Transsexual Syndrome* (New York: Julian Press). Benjamin's spelling, with two "s"s, is thus the one most generally in use (Money, 88). I have spelled "transsexual" in the conventional way except when quoting Money directly.

20. Nora Ephron, "Conundrum," *Crazy Salad: Some Things About Women* (New York: Bantam, 1976), 203.

21. Peter Alfano, with Michael Janofsky, "A Guru Who Spreads the Gospel of Steroids," *New York Times*, November 19, 1988: 49.

22. For another approach to this question based on medical evidence viewed in a social and gendered frame, see Suzanne J. Kessler, "The Medical Construction of Gender: Case Management of Intersexed Infants" *Signs* 16 (Autumn 1990): 3–26. Kessler's fascinating article, which appeared after a version of "Spare Parts" had been published in *differences* (l,3: Fall, 1989), shares many of the concerns and doubts voiced here about the "objectivity" of medical judgments on gender identity.

23. For a discussion of women who lived their lives as men, see Chapter 3.

24. See, for example, Nancy J. Vickers' reading of Petrarch, "Diana Described: Scattered Woman and Scattered Rhyme," in *Writing and Sexual Difference*, ed. Elizabeth Abel (Chicago: University of Chicago Press, 1982), 95–110 and Barbara Johnson's discussion of the Romantic predilection for dead women as erotic (poetic) objects, "The Lady in the Lake," in *A New History of French Literature*, ed. Denis Hollier (Cambridge: Harvard University Press, 1989), 627–632.

25. Mary Wollstonecraft Shelley, *Frankenstein, or, the Modern Prometheus* (1818 text), ed. James Riger (Indianapolis: Bobbs-Merrill, 1974), 48–49.

26. Bill Henkin, *The Rocky Horror Picture Show Book* (New York: Hawthorn/Dutton, 1978), 127.

27. Carrie Rickey, "Let Yourself Go," *Film Comment* 18 (March–April 1982): 44.

28. Harry Benjamin, *The Transsexual Phenomenon* (New York: Julian Press, 1966).

29. Christine Jorgensen, *Christine Jorgensen: A Personal Autobiography*, (New York: Bantam, 1967), 131.

30. Jacket copy for videotape of *Glen or Glenda*, by Admit One Video Presentations.

31. Christa Wolf, "Self-Experiment: Appendix to a Report," trans. Jeanette Clausen, *New German Critique* 13 (Winter 1987): 109–131. See Anne Hermann's discussion of this story, "The Transsexual as *Anders* in Christa Wolf's 'Self-Experiment," *Genders* 3 (1988):43–56.

32. "Vidal Looks for Myra," *Variety*, April 3, 1968: 6.

33. Rebecca Bell-Metereau, *Hollywood Androgyny* (New York: Columbia University Press, 1985), 162.

34. John Lithgow, "My Life as a Woman," *Mademoiselle*, September 1982: 46–47.

35. Thomas Harris, *The Silence of the Lambs* (New York: St. Martin's Press, 1988), 149.

NOTES TO CHAPTER 5, FETISH ENVY

1. Robert J. Stoller, *Observing the Erotic Imagination* (New Haven: Yale University Press, 1985), 155.

2. Gladys Perint Palmer, "Fashion famine plagues London," *San Francisco Examiner*, October 22, 1989: E3.

3. David A. Raphling, M.D., "Fetishism in a Woman," *Journal of the American Psychoanalytic Association* 37:2 (1989): 465–91.

4. Naomi Schor, "Female Fetishism: The Case of George Sand," in Susan Rubin Suleiman, ed., *The Female Body in Western Culture*. (Cambridge: Harvard University Press, 1986), 371.

5. Eugénie Lemoine-Luccioni, *La Robe* (Paris: Seuil, 1983), 34.

6. For a cinematic realization of this fantasy attributed to women, see the film *Personal Best* (1982), in which Mariel Hemingway "progresses" from a lesbian affair to a heterosexual one, and playfully insists on holding her lover's penis as he urinates—much to his initial discomfiture. *Personal Best*, directed by Robert Towne, was, as Vito Russo points out, "too straight for gay audiences and much too gay for conservative straights." Russo, *The Celulloid Closet: Homosexuality in the Movies* (New York: Harper & Row, rev. ed. 1987), 271.

7. Sigmund Freud, "On Transformations of Instinct as Exemplified in Anal Erotism" (1917), trans. E. Glover, *SE* 17: 129.

8. Sigmund Freud, "Fetishism" (1927) *SE* 21: 157.

9. Jacques Lacan, "Guiding Remarks for a Congress on Feminine Sexuality," in *Feminine Sexuality: Jacques Lacan and the école freudienne*, ed. Juliet Mitchell and Jacqueline Rose, trans. Jacqueline Rose (New York: W.W. Norton, 1982), 96.

10. Stoller, *Observing the Erotic Imagination*, 135–36.

11. Octave Mannoni, " 'Je sais bien . . . mais quand même,' la croyance," *Les Temps Modernes* 19: 212 (1964): 1262–86.

12. Sarah Kofman, *The Enigma of Woman*, trans. Catherine Porter (Ithaca: Cornell University Press, 1985), 87.

13. Jacques Derrida, *Glas* (Paris: Éditions Galilée. 1974), 232ff.

14. Jacques Lacan, "The Signification of the Phallus," in *Ecrits: A Selection*, trans. Alan Sheridan (New York: W.W. Norton, 1977), 289.

15. G. Blakemore Evans, et al, *The Riverside Shakespeare* (Boston: Houghton Mifflin, 1974), 349.

16. A.R. Humphries, *Much Ado About Nothing*, The Arden Shakespeare (London: Methuen, 1981), 161.

17. Jim Beckerman, "A Cheer for Standing Lear on Its Ear," *The News Tribune* (Woodbridge, New Jersey) January 10, 1988: C-11.

18. See, for example, Peter Erickson, "The Order of the Garter, the Cult of Elizabeth, and Class-Gender Tension in *The Merry Wives of Windsor*," in *Shakespeare Reproduced*, ed. Jean E. Howard and Marian F. O'Connor (New York: Methuen, 1987), 116–40.

19. *Eric Partridge's Dictionary of Slang and Unconventional English*, ed. Paul Beale, 8th ed. (London: Routledge and Kegan Paul, 1984).

20. Indeed, we might even consider "cod" as in "codfish." It is no accident, I think, that one of the most overt and outrageous Dame figures of the twentieth-century stage, Captain Hook of Barrie's *Peter Pan*, is taunted by Peter in a famous scene in which Peter calls him a "codfish." Hook is of course the living embodiment of castration and consequent phallic display, his right hand having been severed by Peter in an earlier encounter. See Chapter 7, "Fear of Flying, or, Why Is Peter Pan a Woman?"

21. *Opinions of the Press of Emma Waller . . .* [c.1876]. Harvard University Library (Newspapers cited are: the Chicago *Herald*, New Orleans *Picayune*, St. Louis *Herald*, Boston *Transcript*, Cincinnati *Commercial*, Cincinnati *Index*, Buffalo *Post*, Buffalo *Express*, Memphis *Bulletin*, Memphis *Avalanche*. Cited in Frank W. Wadsworth, "Hamlet and Iago: Nineteenth Century Breeches Parts," *Shakespeare Quarterly* 17 (1966): 137.

22. I am grateful to Nancy Vickers for initially calling both the video and the awards show to my attention.

NOTES TO CHAPTER 6, BREAKING THE CODE: TRANSVESTISM AND GAY IDENTITY

1. Hugh Whitemore, *Breaking the Code* (New York: Samuel French, 1987), 102.

2. Beth Winship, *Ask Beth*. San Francisco Chronicle, April 29, 1990: 4.

3. *Donahue* transcript #01194 (Cincinnati: Multimedia Entertainment, 1984), 2.

4. *Donahue* transcript #02034 (Cincinnati: Multimedia Entertainment, 1984), 11, 4, 10.

5. *Donahue* transcript #02187 (Cincinnati: Multimedia Entertainment, 1987), 1, 2.

6. "Crossdressers & The Women In Their Lives," *Geraldo*, transcript 363 (New York: Investigative News Group, 1989), February 6, 1989: 2.

7. Doris Kearns Goodwin, "Gay Soldiers: They Watched Their Step," *New York Times Book Review*, April 8, 1990: 9.

8. Alan Bray, *Homosexuality in Renaissance England* (London: Gay Men's Press, 1982), Thomas Middleton, *The Works of Thomas Middleton*, ed. A.H. Bullen (London, 1886) 3: 130–34.

9. Charlotte Wolff, *Magnus Hirschfeld: A Portrait of a Pioneer in Sexology* (London: Quartet Books, 1986), 107–8. Vern L. Bullough, *Sexual Variance in Society and History* (Chicago: University of Chicago Press, 1976), 644–45. Peter Ackroyd, *Dressing Up* (New York: Simon and Schuster, 1979), 30–31; 64.

10. Richard F. Docter, *Transvestites and Transsexuals: Toward a Theory of Cross-Gender Behavior* (New York: Plenum Press, 1988), 9.

11. On "female impersonators" in New York City in the early decades of the twentieth century, see the autobiographical memoir *The Female Impersonators* by Ralph Werther/Jennie June ("Earl Lind") first published in 1922 (New York: Arno Press, 1975), 104.

12. John Money, *Gay, Straight, and In-Between: The Sexology of Erotic Orientation* (New York: Oxford University Press, 1988), 102.

13. Joann Roberts, "Critical Expressions II: Open vs. Closed Gender Groups," *Gender Expressions* 1,2 (April, 1989): 7–9.

14. Oscar Wilde, *The Picture of Dorian Gray* (1891) (London: Penguin Books, 1988), 187.

15. Vito Russo, *The Celluloid Closet: Homosexuality in the Movies* (New York: Harper & Row, 1987), 440.

16. Virginia Woolf, *Orlando: A Biography* (Harmondsworth: Penguin Books, 1970), 98.

17. Sandra M. Gilbert and Susan Gubar, *No Man's Land 2: Sexchanges* (New Haven: Yale University Press, 1989).

18. Carroll Smith-Rosenberg, *Disorderly Conduct: Visions of Gender in Victorian America* (New York: Oxford University Press, 1985), 272.

19. Richard von Krafft-Ebing, *Psychopathia Sexualis with Especial Reference to the Antipathic Sexual Instinct* (Stuttgart, 1886), trans. F.J. Rebman (Brooklyn: Physicians and Surgeons Book Co., 1908), 355.

20. Radclyffe Hall, *The Well of Loneliness* (New York: Avon Books, 1981), 204. Such scenes of gay self-discovery through reading are not uncommon. We might compare the one in *The Well* to that related by the pseudonymous "Diana Frederics" in *Diana: A Strange Autobiography* (New York: Dial Press, 1939):

    Browsing in my father's library one night, I came upon a book on sex. I had seen it many times. I had read parts of it, but now I saw a section I had never noticed before. One detailed chapter was on homosexuality. I read and reread, eager, fearful, and finally sick in the pit of my stomach. (Frederics, 20)

21. Edward J. Kempf, *Psychopathology* (St. Louis: Mosby, 1920), esp. chapter 10, "The Psychology of the Acute Homosexual Panic," 477–515. Jonathan Ned Katz, *Gay/Lesbian Almanac* (New York: Harper & Row, 1983), 374n.; 391–92. Eve Kosofsky Sedgwick, *Between Men: English Literature and Male Homosocial Desire* (New York: Columbia University Press, 1985).

22. Quentin Crisp, *The Naked Civil Servant* (New York: New American Library, 1983), 43.

23. John Waters, "The Man Who Stayed in Bed," review of *Serious Pleasures: The Life of Stephen Tennant*, by Philip Hoare (New York: Hamish Hamilton/ Viking, 1991), *New York Times Book Review*, February 3, 1991: 11.

24. Teresa Riordan, "Lights, Camera . . . Makeover," *San Francisco Chronicle*, Sunday Punch, 3 (Spy Publishing Partners, 1990).

25. The OED cites Shakespeare's *Richard III* as the locus classicus—"we know your tenderness of heart,/And gentle, kind, effeminate remorse" [*R.III.* 3.7.209–10], a citation that is profoundly ironic, since the context is Buckingham's glozing public entreaty to an ostensibly reluctant Richard that he should accept the English crown—in quest of which he has already murdered or defamed all his relations. "Effeminacy"—even in this apparently benign sense—thus again contains a hidden sting: untrustworthiness, two-facedness, duplicity. The "effeminate" Richard—as in Olivier's production—is "bitchy," even, at times, "hysterical." For another account of the permutations of the word "effeminate," see Bray, *Homosexuality in Renaissance England*, 130–31. Bray, whose book is concerned with male homosexuality, does not take note of the stigmatization of women.

26. Havelock Ellis, *Sexual Inversion* (Philadelphia: F.A. Davis Co., 1901), 283.

27. *The Ladder*, no.1 (May, 1957): 28.

28. Joan Nestle, *A Restricted Country* (Ithaca: Firebrand Books, 1987), 101.

29. "Prostitutes wore the *toga* like men." . . . "[I]n Castres (in 1375) the statutory sign was a man's hat and a scarlet belt." William Sanger, *History of Prostitution: Its Extent, Causes and Effect Throughout the World* (New York, 1876), 75, 80. Cited in Nestle, *Restricted Country*, 162. See also the wearing of trousers by Venetian courtesans in the Renaissance, in Chapter 3, "The Transvestite's Progress."

30. Although these terms may have begun as ironic parodies or critiques of heterosexual practice, they soon obtained, as Alan Bray points out, a contextual currency of their own. See Bray, *Homosexuality in Renaissance England*, 86.

31. Sally Jessy Raphael, "I'm Prettier Than My Wife," Transcript 642, February 20, 1991: 1.

32. Sigmund Freud, letter to Wilhelm Fliess, September 21, 1897. *The Complete Letters of Sigmund Freud to Wilhelm Fliess, 1887–1904*, trans. and ed. Jeffrey Moussaieff Masson (Cambridge: Harvard University Press, 1985), 266.

33. Helena Michie, personal communication.

34. Nantucket *Inquirer and Mirror*, June 14, 1990: 7C.

35. Judith Butler, *Gender Trouble* (New York: Routledge, 1990), 31.

NOTES

36. Kris Kirk and Ed Heath, *Men in Frocks* (London: Gay Men's Press, 1984), 106.

37. "Miss Manners" (Judith Martin), *San Francisco Chronicle*, May 9, 1990: B6.

38. See, for example, "The Future of Gay America," *Newsweek*, March 12, 1990: 24–25.

39. This is a project recently and admirably undertaken by a number of critics, among them Teresa de Lauretis, "Sexual Indifference and Lesbian Representation," *Theatre Journal* 40 (1988): 155–177; Sue-Ellen Case, "Toward a Butch-Femme Aesthetic," in *Making a Spectacle: Feminist Essays on Contemporary Women's Theatre*, ed. Lynda Hart (Ann Arbor: University of Michigan Press, 1989), 283; Henry Abelove, "Some Speculations on the History of Sexual Intercourse during the Long Eighteenth Century in England," *Genders* 6 (November 1989): 125–130; Jonathan Goldberg, "Not Playing the Sodomite," lecture delivered at the conference on Gender at the Crossroads, Stanford University, March 1990.

40. John A. Hules, letter to the editor, *Out/Look* 3, 1 (Summer 1990): 79–80. *Newsweek*'s article on "The Future of Gay America" (cited above) quotes Frank Kameny, "a veteran gay activist," as saying, "I've never heard a rational explanation for the prejudice against [gay marriages]—after all, marriage licenses aren't rationed, so we wouldn't be taking them from someone else" (25). *Newsweek* also reports on an article in the *New Republic* by Andrew Sullivan that argued that marriage was good not only for gays but also for society at large because it would promote social and economic stability.

41. *General Evening Post*, July 24, 1790. In Elizabeth Mavor, ed., *A Year with the Ladies of Llangollen* (Harmondsworth: Penguin Books, 1986), 135. Burke, writing to Eleanor Butler, commiserated with her on this "base publication" and urged her to consider that "you suffer only by the baseness of the age you live in" (July 30, 1790; Mavor, 136).

42. John Lockhart, letter to his wife, August 24, 1825. In Mavor, *A Year*, 162.

43. Charles Mathews, letter to Mrs. Mathews, September 4, 1820. Mavor, *A Year*, 178–79.

44. Charles Mathews, letter to Mrs. Mathews, October 24, 1820. Mavor, *A Year*, 200–201.

45. Prince Puckler Muskaus, letter to "Julia," July 1828. Mavor, *A Year*, 142–43.

46. Colette, *The Pure and the Impure*. trans. Herma Briffault, intro. Janet Flanner (New York: Farrar, Straus & Giroux, 1967), 127. (French edition, *Ces plaisirs*, pub. 1941)

47. Shari Benstock, *Women of the Left Bank* (Austin: University of Texas Press, 1986), 177.

48. Anonymous, "S/M Aesthetic," *Out/Look* 1,4 (Winter 1989): 43.

49. "The idea that butch and femme are in some sense 'replicas' or 'copies' of heterosexual exchange," writes Judith Butler with compelling clarity, "underestimates the erotic significance of these identities as internally dissonant and complex in their resignification of the hegemonic categories by which they are enabled. Lesbian femmes may recall the heterosexual scene, as it were, but also displace it at the same time. *In both butch and femme identities, the very notion of an original or natural identity is put into question*; indeed, it is precisely that question as it is embodied in these identities that becomes one source of their erotic significance" (Butler, *Gender Trouble*, 123, emphasis added).

50. "Butch-Femme Relationships: Sexual Courage in the 1950s," in Nestle, *Restricted Country*, 106–7.

51. Case, "Toward a Butch-Femme Aesthetic," 283.

52. Nestle, *Restricted Country*, 107.

53. Lee Lynch, *The Amazon Trail* (Tallahassee, Florida: Naiad Press, 1988), 12.

54. Hall, *The Well of Loneliness*, 165.

55. Richard Saul Wurman, *SF Access* (New York: Access Press, 1987), 132.

56. Arlene Stein, "All Dressed Up, But No Place to Go? Style Wars and the New Lesbianism," *Out/Look* 1,4 (Winter 1989): 38.

57. Oscar Montero, "Lipstick Vogue: The Politics of Drag," *Radical America* 22,1 (January–February 1988): 41.

58. Mick LaSalle, "Garland—More or Less," *San Francisco Chronicle*, October 12, 1989: E3.

59. Scott Alarik, "Jim Bailey's triumphant turn as Judy Garland," *Boston Globe*, June 8, 1989: 84.

60. *De donde son los cantantes* (1967; *From Cuba with a Song*) in which a transvestite entertainer named Lotus Flower is murdered by a Spanish general, and two white transvestites carry a statue of Christ (symbolic of Fidel Castro) from Santiago to Havana. *Cobra* (1972; *Cobra*) features a transvestite entertainer who has undergone a sex-change operation and her double, La Cadillac, who has had the same operation in reverse; *Colibri* (1982; *Hummingbird*), set in a brothel run by an aging transvestite whose establishment caters to the sexual fantasies of rich oilmen.

61. Severo Sarduy, "Writing/Transvestism," *Review* 9 (Fall 1973): 33. Italics in the original.

62. The phrase "the reverse of the medal" also calls to mind Derrida's phrase "the tain of the mirror." "Philosophy," writes Derrida, is "incapable of inscribing (comprehending) what is outside it otherwise than through the appropriating assimilation of a negative image of it, and dissemination is written on the back—the *tain*—of that mirror." For Derrida the limits of reflection are tied

up with undecidability, with the "floating indetermination that allows for substitution and play," that claims as its "propriety or property" "impropriety or inappropriateness," evading mediation between binaries by "mimic[king] it, indefinitely preventing it, through . . . ironic doubling." Jacques Derrida, *Dissemination*, trans. Barbara Johnson (Chicago: University of Chicago Press, 1981), 32–33; 93.

63. Esther Newton, *Mother Camp: Female Impersonators in America* (Englewood Cliffs: Prentice-Hall, 1972), 101–3. Judith Butler underscores the fact that this tension among anatomical sex, gender identity, and gender performance denaturalizes "gender"— and heterosexuality: "In imitating gender, drag implicitly reveals the imitative structure of gender itself—and its contingency" (Butler, *Gender Trouble*, 137).

64. Lisa Duggan, *Out/Look* 1,1 (Spring, 1988): 64.

65. Victoria Glendinning, *Vita* (New York: Quill, 1983), 95.

66. Janet Flanner, Introduction to Colette, *The Pure and the Impure*, n.p.

67. For d'Eon's story see below, Chapter 10, "Phantoms of the Opera."

68. James E. Lebensohn, "Eyeglasses," *Encyclopaedia Britannica* 9:14. (Chicago: Encyclopaedia Britannica, 1965), 9:14.

69. We might recall here Freud's reading of the figure of the optician Coppola, who offers "fine eyes" (spectacles) for sale, and sells instead a pocket (one-eyed) spy-glass to the student Nathaniel in E.T.A. Hoffmann's *Sand-Man*. Sigmund Freud, "The 'Uncanny' " (1919) *SE* 17:228–32. That blinding is a dream symbol for castration is, of course, a consistent argument of Freud's work, and especially of his understanding of the Oedipus story. Sigmund Freud, *The Interpretation of Dreams* (1900), *SE* 5:398 and 398n.

70. Sigmund Freud, "The Psychogenesis of a Case of Homosexuality in a Woman" (1920), *SE* 18:163.

71. Jacques Lacan, *The Four Fundamental Concepts of Psycho-Analysis*, trans. Alan Sheridan (New York: W.W. Norton, 1981), 104, 107.

72. Terry Castle, personal communication to the author, April 27, 1990.

73. Havelock Ellis, "Sexual Inversion in Women," *Alienist and Neurologist* (St. Louis) 16,2 (1895): 152–54.

74. Sigmund Freud, "Three Essays on the Theory of Sexuality" (1905), *SE* 7:182.

75. Colette, *The Pure and the Impure*, 65.

76. Michael Specter, *Washington Post*, reprinted as "New Cigaret for 'Virile Females,' " *San Francisco Chronicle*, February 17, 1990: A2.

77. William Safire, "Virile Women Target Tobacco Men," *New York Times Magazine*, March 11, 1990: 18.

78. Quoted by Sujata Banerjee in the *Baltimore Evening Sun*. Reprinted as "The Lusty Look of Female Smokers," *San Francisco Chronicle*, February 24, 1990: C10.

79. J.D. Reed, "They're Puttin' on the Vogue," *Time*, May 22, 1989.

80. Terence Rafferty, "Realness," *New Yorker*, March 25, 1991: 72.

81. Daniel Goleman, "Studies Discover Clues to the Roots of Homophobia," *New York Times*, July 10, 1990: B1.

82. Marshall Kirk and Hunter Madsen, *After the Ball: How America Will Conquer Its Fear and Hatred of Gays in the 90s* (New York: Doubleday, 1989). Kirk and Madsen describe a "rift in the gay community" between men they call "R-types," who think of themselves as "straight gays," and "Q-types," "homosexuals on display," who "jauntily assume any one of several recognizable public personas: the long-haired androgyne or permed 'fem,' the titanic leather master, the dude-ranch cowboy, the clipped clone, the Bruce Weber hyperboy, and others. (Manliness, you see, is troublesome to Q's and must be deflated by burlesque)" (258). They see no resolution in the "cold war" between Q's and R's, but urge activists to "strike a better balance between the values and imagery of Q's and R's in public. This will help teach straights that a great many nonstereotypic gays do, in fact, exist. At the same time it will build support for the movement among R's" (260). Kirk and Madsen themselves describe the "stereotypic" gay at considerable length in their book, ostensibly in the context of accounting for straight assumptions and misreadings of gay people (see esp. 18–26, "All Gays Are Easy to Spot: There Are Telltale Signs!"). Although the book talks about "gay life," as the authors admit, their observations "relate largely to gay *men*—admittedly a defect of the whole of this book" (277).

83. Esther Newton, "The Myth of the Mannish Lesbian," in *The Lesbian Issue*, ed. Estelle B. Freedman, Barbara C. Gelpi, Susan L. Johnson, and Kathleen M. Weston (Chicago: University of Chicago Press, 1985), 25. Orig. pub. in *Signs: Journal of Women in Culture and Society* 9,4 (Summer 1984):555–75.

84. David Joselit, "Robert Mapplethorpe's Poses," in *Robert Mapplethorpe: The Perfect Moment*, ed. Janet Kardon (Philadelphia: Institute of Contemporary Art, University of Pennsylvania, 1988), 19.

85. Janet Kardon, ed., "Robert Mapplethorpe Interview," in Kardon, *Mapplethorpe*, 28.

86. Gloria Moure, *Marcel Duchamp* (New York: Rizzoli, 1988), 16.

87. This is the way the show was mounted in the Berkeley Art Museum, where I saw it in 1989.

NOTES TO CHAPTER 7, WHY IS PETER PAN A WOMAN?

1. Letter to Dulce Wroughton April 7, 1908, Mrs. A. Lunn Collection. In Tim Jeal, *The Boy-Man: The Life of Lord Baden-Powell* (New York: William Morrow, 1990), 86.

2. Roger Lancelyn Green, *Fifty Years of Peter Pan* (London: Peter Davies, 1954), 123. The establishment of Peter as a star part for women began surprisingly early in its stage history, and is a testimony to both the play's and the part's peculiar appeal. Gladys Cooper, who played Peter in 1923 and 1924, wrote in her autobiography, "People say that every actress wants to play Peter Pan, and . . . I was tremendously keen to do so in my turn." *Gladys Cooper* (1931) 187–92; quoted in Green, *Fifty Years*, 125.

3. Michael Billington, *Guardian*, December 17, 1982. Jacqueline Rose, *The Case of Peter Pan, or The Impossibility of Children's Fiction* (New York: Macmillan, 1984), 113.

4. Irving Wardle, *Times*, December 18, 1982. Rose, *The Case of Peter Pan*: 113.

5. Andrew Birkin, *J.M. Barrie and the Lost Boys: The Love Story That Gave Birth to Peter Pan* (New York: Clarkson N. Potter, 1979), 180.

6. *Omnibus* interview with Richard Baker, BBC Television, January 16, 1983. Rose, *The Case of Peter Pan*, 113.

7. Birkin, *J.M. Barrie*, 105.

8. Denis Mackail, *Barrie, The Story of J.M.B.* (London: Peter Davies, 1941), 368.

9. J.M. Barrie, *Peter Pan* (Harmondsworth: Puffin Books, 1986), 71. Reprint of *Peter and Wendy* (London: Hodder & Stoughton, 1911).

10. Pauline Chase, *Peter Pan's Postbag* (London: Heinemann 1909). Green, *Fifty Years*, 124.

11. *Peter and Wendy*, 199; reprinted as *Peter Pan*, 19–20. *Peter Pan; or, the Boy Who Would Not Grow Up*, in *The Uniform Edition of the Plays of J.M. Barrie* (New York: Charles Scribners' Sons, 1928). To avoid confusion with the play, the novel version will henceforth be abbreviated as *PW* in the text, the play as *PP*.

12. The equivalence of Never Land and dream seems clearly established in Barrie's text by the fact that the Darling children *recognize*, rather than merely discover, the features of the Never-landscape ("I say, John, there's your flamingo." "Look, Michael, there's your cave." "Wendy, I do believe that's your little whelp." (*PW*, 60)

13. J.M. Barrie, *Margaret Ogilvy* (1896), in *The Works of J.M. Barrie* (Peter Pan edition; New York: Charles Scribners' Sons, 1930), 8:12.

14. Tim Jeal, *The Boy-Man*, 35, 54, 66, 74–78, 86–87.

15. J. M. Barrie, *Tommy and Grizel. The Works of J.M. Barrie* (Peter Pan edition; New York: Charles Scribners' Sons, 1930), 6:491, 266.

16. J.M. Barrie, *Tommy and Grizel* (New York: Charles Scribners' Sons, 1900), 51.

17. J.M. Barrie, *The Little White Bird* (1902). *The Works of J.M. Barrie* (Peter Pan edition; New York: Charles Scribners' Sons, 1930). 7:60–61.

18. Rose, *The Case of Peter Pan*, 38.

19. Birkin, *J.M. Barrie*, 239.

20. Birkin, *J.M.Barrie*, 242.

21. Peter Llewelyn Davies, *Some Davies Letters and Papers, 1874–1915*, unpublished. Quoted in Birkin, *J.M.Barrie*, 235.

22. Thus Naomi Lewis, in her introduction to the Puffin Classics *Peter Pan*, notes that the book may be preferable in some ways to the stage production, since "in the theatre, Peter, and Wendy too, may look confusingly like certain well-known actresses." *Peter Pan* (Harmondsworth: Puffin Books, Penguin Books, rpt.1986), 10.

23. See Rose, *The Case of Peter Pan*, 100–102.

24. Peter Ackroyd, *Dressing Up* (New York: Simon and Schuster, 1976), 102.

25. One exception, as we will see in Chapter 11, is the minstrel show.

26. Rose suggests that "what is at stake in *Peter Pan* is the adult's desire for the child" (Rose, *The Case of Peter Pan*, 3) and touches briefly on transvestism and the pantomime tradition only to look through it, at what she discerns as beneath the surface, the link between sexuality and the child. Thus she writes that "What *Peter Pan* gives us better than pantomime, more of than pantomime (perhaps this is the essential difference) is the right to look at the child. On stage, Peter Pan is, of course, both child and woman. The transvestism was not new, and it goes beyond the traditional role of the principal boy. The preponderance of young women in the cast (the 'mass transvestism' of the procession on stage)," Rose notes, "is a skilful recombination of all [the] components of late Victorian theatre" as a way of repackaging a voyeuristic interest in the child as a form of innocence (Rose, 98–99). The term "mass transvestism" is quoted from Michael Booth's *Victorian Spectacular Theatre (1850–1910)* London: Routledge and Kegan Paul, 1981), 79.

27. Rose, *The Case of Peter Pan*, 4, 6, 25.

CHAPTER 7

28. Green, *Fifty Years*, 146–47.

29. B.R. Burg, *Sodomy and the Pirate Tradition: English Sea Rovers in the Seventeenth-Century Caribbean* (New York: New York University Press, 1984). Originally published as *Sodomy and the Perception of Evil*.

30. Frank Sherry, *Raiders and Rebels: The Golden Age of Piracy* (New York: William Morrow, 1986), 214.

31. Captain John Evans, in Daniel Defoe, *A General History of the Robberies and Murders of the Most Notorious Pyrates*, ed. Manuel Schonhorn (orig. pub. 1724; 2nd ed. 1728; Columbia, South Carolina: University of South Carolina Press, 1972), 69–70.

32. Jean-Baptiste Labat, *Memoirs of Père Labat*, 239–240.

33. Jacques Lezra, "Pirating Reading: The Appearance of History in *Measure for Measure*." *ELH* 56, 2 (Summer 1989): 288 fn. 22.

34. A.L. Lloyd, *Folk Song in England*, 2nd ed. (New York: International Publishers, 1967), 15.

35. For explorations of the figure of the "warrior woman," see, for example, Dianne Dugaw, *Warrior Women and Popular Balladry 1650–1850* (Cambridge: Cambridge University Press, 1989), Julie Wheelwright, *Amazons and Military Maids* (London: Pandora, 1989), Simon Shepherd, *Amazons and Warrior Women: Varieties of Feminism in Seventeeth-Century Drama* (New York: St. Martin's Press, 1981), and Abby Kleinbaum, *The War Against the Amazons* (New York: New Press, 1983).

36. Terry Castle, *Masquerade and Civilization: The Carnivalesque in Eighteenth Century English Culture and Fiction* (Stanford: Stanford University Press, 1986), 64.

37. Dan Kiley, *The Peter Pan Syndrome: Men Who Have Never Grown Up* (New York: Avon Books, 1983), 31.

38. Chase, *Peter Pan's Postbag*; cited in Birkin, 215.

39. Simon Frith, "Oh Boy!" in *Music for Pleasure* (New York: Routledge, 1988), 169–70. Originally published in the *Village Voice*, 1985.

40. Mary Drewery and Olave Baden-Powell, *Window on My Heart: The Autobiography of Olave, Lady Baden-Powell, GBE, as told to Mary Drewery* (London, Hodder and Stoughton, 1973), 78–79. Rose Kerr and Alix Liddell, *The Story of the Girl Guides* (London, Girl Guides Association, 1932; 1976), 163. Jeal, 436–37.

41. Steve Perry, "Ain't No Mountain High Enough: The Politics of Crossover," in *Facing the Music*, ed. Simon Frith (New York: Pantheon, 1988), 51–87.

42. J. Randy Taraborrelli, *Call Her Miss Ross* (Secaucus, New Jersey: Carol Publishing, 1989), 475.

43. Michael Jackson, *Moonwalker* (New York: Doubleday, 1988), 274, 275.

44. *Life*, special issue, "The 80s," 12, 12 (Fall 1989), 77.

45. Steve Dougherty, Todd Gold, David Marlow, Robin Micheli, Andrew Abrahams, and Sabrina MacFarland, "Madonna & Michael," *People* 35, 14 (April 15, 1991): 68.

NOTES TO CHAPTER 8, CHERCHEZ LA FEMME

1. Sue Grafton, *"D" is for Deadbeat* (New York: Bantam Books, 1988), 229.

2. P.D. James, *Devices and Desires* (New York: Alfred A. Knopf, 1990) [orig. publ. London: Guilding, 1989].

3. Charlotte McLeod, *The Corpse in Oozak's Pond* (New York: Mysterious Press, 1987), 187.

4. Ellery Queen, *The Last Woman in His Life* (New York: New American Library, 1970).

5. Arthur Conan Doyle, *A Study in Scarlet* (1887) in *Sherlock Holmes: The Complete Novels and Stories* (New York: Bantam, 1986), 1: 38–39.

6. Ruth Rendell, *A Sleeping Life* (Bantam Books: Garden City, N.Y., 1986; orig. publ. Doubleday, 1978).

7. Dorothy L. Sayers, "The Entertaining Episode of the Article in Question," *Lord Peter Views the Body* (New York: Avon Books, 1969; orig. publ. 1928), 25–35.

8. See Mary S. Gossy, *The Untold Story: Women and Theory in Golden Age Texts* (Ann Arbor: University of Michigan Press, 1989). The hymen, a piece of flesh, a piece of cloth, a text, as Derrida points out, is the space of "in-between-ness," the ultimate undecidable: "neither desire nor pleasure, but in between the two. Neither future nor present, but between the two. . . . With all the undecidability of its meaning, the hymen only takes place when it doesn't take place, when nothing *really* happens." Jacques Derrida, *Dissemination*. trans. Barbara Johnson (Chicago: University of Chicago Press, 1981), 212–13.

9. "A Scandal in Bohemia," Arthur Conan Doyle, *Sherlock Holmes: The Complete Novels and Stories* (New York: Bantam Books, 1986), 1: 209.

10. Edgar Allan Poe, "The Purloined Letter," in John P. Muller and William J. Richardson, *The Purloined Poe: Lacan, Derrida, and Psychoanalytic Reading* (Baltimore: The Johns Hopkins University Press, 1988), 8.

11. Josephine Tey (pseud. for Elizabeth MacKintosh), *To Love and Be Wise* (New York: Pocket Books, 1977; orig. pub. 1951), 26.

12. "Women, especially if they grow up with good looks, develop a certain self-contentment which compensates them for the social restrictions upon them in their choice of object. Strictly speaking, it is only themselves that such women love with an intensity comparable to that of the man's love for them. . . . The importance of this type of woman for the erotic life of mankind is to be rated very high. Such women have the greatest fascination for men, not only for aesthetic reasons, since as a rule they are the most beautiful, but also because of certain interesting psychological factors. For it seems very evident that one person's narcissism has a great attraction for those who have renounced part of their own narcissism and are in search of object-love. The charm of a child lies to a great extent in his narcissism, his self-sufficiency and his inaccessibility, just as does the charm of certain animals which seem not to concern themselves about us, such as cats and the large beasts of prey. Indeed, even great criminals and humorists, as they are represented in literature, compel our interest by the narcissistic self-importance with which they manage to keep away from their ego anything that would diminish it." Sigmund Freud, "On Narcissism: An Introduction" (1914), *SE* 14:88–89.

13. Dora Siggins's name may be yet another oblique Tey clue. Dora Sigerson Shorter was the author of a poem called "A Vagrant Heart," which begins "O to be a woman to be left to pique and pine," and includes the sentiment "there is joy where dangers be—Alas to be a woman and the nomad's heart in me." Julie Wheelwright uses "A Vagrant Heart" as the epigraph to her book on female-to-male cross-dressers, *Amazons and Military Maids* (London: Pandora, 1989).

14. Bruno Bettelheim takes issue with the idea that the similarity of French *vair* (variegated fur) and *verre* (glass) led to Perrault's changing a fur slipper to one made of glass (*The Uses of Enchantment: The Meaning and Importance of Fairy Tales* [New York: Alfred A. Knopf, 1965], 251). The predominance of castration figures in many versions of the "Cinderella" story (the sisters' mutilation of their feet to fit the slipper, their eventual punishment by having their eyes pecked out) suggests considerable anxiety about gender roles as well as about the sexuality noted by Bettelheim, and adds to the pertinence of Grant's and Dora's exchange of pleasantries about the dancing shoes. *Cinderella* is also, of course, one of the most famous of Panto plays, with adult men in drag playing the roles of the Ugly Sisters.

15. June Rose, *The Perfect Gentleman* (London: Hutchinson, 1977), 12.

16. Captain William Henry Dillon, in Rose, *Gentleman*, 33.

17. Count de Las Casas, in Rose, *Gentleman*, 34. Emphasis in the original.

18. Rose, *Gentleman*, 141.

19. Rose, *Gentleman*, 152. Other biographies of Barry are Isobel Rae, *The Strange Story of Dr. James Barry* (London: Longmans, Green, 1958), Jessica Grove and Olga Racster, *Dr. James Barry—Her Secret Story* (London: G. Howe, 1932).

20. D.R.B. McKinnon, in Rose, *Gentleman*, 13.

21. Colonel Rogers. Cited in Rose, *Gentleman*, 124.

22. George A. Bright, "A Female Member of the Army Medical Staff." Letter to the Editor, *The Lancet* (October, 12, 1895), 959.

23. A.M.S., Letter to the Editor, *The Lancet*, October 19, 1895, 1021.

24. E. Rogers, Letters to the Editor, *The Lancet*, October 19, 1895, 1021; October 26, 1895, 1086–7; November 16, 1895, 1269; May 2, 1896, 1264.

25. Janet Carphin, Letter to the Editor, *The Lancet*, October 19, 1895, 1021.

26. George Chamberlayne, Letter to the Editor, *The Lancet*, November 16, 1895, quoted in Rogers, 1269.

27. Anonymous, "A Female Medical Combatant," *The Medical Times and Gazette*, August 26, 1865, 225.

28. Edward Bradford, "The Reputed Female Army Surgeon," Letter to the Editor, *The Medical Times and Gazette*, September 9, 1865, 293.

29. Sigmund Freud, *Psycho-Analytic Notes on an Autobiographical Account of a Case of Paranoia* (1911), *SE* 12:3–82. Daniel Paul Schreber, *Memoirs of My Nervous Illness*, trans. and ed. Ida Macalpine and Richard A. Hunter (Cambridge: Harvard University Press, 1988). Passages from Schreber hereafter quoted in the text are given in the translation of the *Standard Edition* of Freud's works, by Alix and James Strachey. The editors include the following note to the reissue of the *Standard Edition* in 1958:

"An English translation of the *Denkwürdigkeiten* by Dr. Ida Macalpine and Dr. Richard A. Hunter was published in 1955 (London: William Dawson). For various reasons, some of which will be obvious to anyone comparing their version with ours, it has not been possible to make use of it for the many quotations from Schreber's book which occur in the case history. There are clearly special difficulties in translating the productions of schizophrenics, in which words, as Freud himself points out in his paper on "The Unconscious" (*SE* 14: 197ff.), play such a dominating part. Here the translator is faced by the same problems that meet him so often in dreams, slips of the tongue, and jokes. In all these cases the method adopted in the *Standard Edition* is the pedestrian one of where necessary giving the original German words in footnotes and endeavoring by means of explanatory comments to allow an English reader some opportunity of forming an opinion of his own on the material." (*SE* 12:7–8)

Since I am in this chapter principally interested in Freud as detective, rather than in Schreber, I will cite from the *Standard Edition* whenever passages from Schreber's *Memoirs* are translated there. When quoting from *SE* I will cite in the text the page numbers for Freud and for Schreber (i.e., the German edition, *Denkwürdigkeiten eines Nervenkranken*, Leipzig, Oswald Mutze, 1903) cited by Freud. Macalpine and Hunter also key their translation to this German edition, so the versions can be readily compared. When I cite from a passage not directly discussed by Freud, I use the version of Macalpine and Hunter, and will so indicate in the text.

30. "The process of unmanning consisted in the (external) male genitals (scrotum and penis) being retracted into the body and the internal sexual organs being at the same time transformed into the corresponding sexual organs" (Schreber, 53).

Macalpine and Hunter, the translators of Schreber's *Memoirs*, include the following note:

> Unmanning: *Entmannung*. The authorized translation of Freud (1911) uses the term "emasculation." We have chosen "unmanning" because the primary meaning is "to remove from the category of men," which is what Schreber intended. Only its fourth definition in the Oxford English Dictionary is given as castration. Emasculation, on the other hand, has castration as its primary meaning, i.e., rendering sterile. From the pages immediately following, as well as from Schreber's further text, it is quite obvious that he meant transformation by an evolutionary process into a reproductive woman which was to render him fertile. Schreber himself stresses this by usually putting "change into a woman" in brackets after the word "unmanning." (361)

It is also "quite obvious" that Freud took Schreber to mean, consciously, or unconsciously, castration, since it is upon that supposition that his whole Oedipal reading of the *Memoirs* depends.

31. Macalpine and Hunter (181) translate this term "picturing": "the picturing of female buttocks on my body."

32. Joan Riviere, "Womanliness as a Masquerade," in *Formations of Fantasy,* ed. Victor Burgin, James Donald and Cora Kaplan (New York: Methuen, 1986), 39–40.

33. Robert J. Stoller, *Observing the Erotic Imagination* (New Haven: Yale University Press, 1985), 155.

NOTES TO CHAPTER 9, RELIGIOUS HABITS

1. Sydney Smith, *Lady Holland's Memoir* (London, 1855), 1: 9.

2. *Christian Century*; quoted in the *Church Times*, February 15, 1980. Cited in Janet Mayo, *A History of Ecclesiastical Dress* (London: B.T. Batsford, 1984), 9.

3. Boy George, in Kris Kirk and Ed Heath, *Men in Frocks* (London: Gay Men's Press, 1984), 112.

4. Mablen Jones, *Getting It On: The Clothing of Rock 'n' Roll* (New York: Abbeville Press, 1987), 144.

5. In "Like a Prayer," as Susan McClary points out, Madonna is drawing upon "two very different semiotic codes associated with two very different forms of Christianity: Catholicism and the black Gospel church." Susan McClary, "Living to Tell: Madonna's Resurrection of the Fleshly" *Genders* 7 (March 1990), 14.

6. Mayo, *History of Ecclesiastical Dress*, 80.

7. F.W. Fairholt, *Costume in England*, enlarged and revised by H.A. Dillon (London: G. Bell and Sons, 1885), 1: 319.

8. Letter from Horace Walpole to Lord Hertford, 12 February 1765; *Letters*, 6: 188. Mayo, *History of Ecclesiastical Dress*, 82.

9. Kirk and Heath, *Men in Frocks*, 19.

10. Vern L. Bullough, *Sexual Variance in Society and History* (Chicago: University of Chicago Press, 1976), 367. Jerome, *Commentarius in Epistolam ad Ephesios*, 3:5 (658), in J.P. Migne, *Patrologiae Latinae* (Paris: Garnier Bros, 1884) 26: 567.

11. In Spain she was known as Librada, in northern France Livrade, in southern France Debarras, all from *Liberata*; in Germany she was Onhkummer, in Flanders Ontcommer, in England Uncumber, from German *kummer*, trouble. Bullough, *Sexual Variance*, 368.

12. *Butler's Lives of the Saints*, ed. Herbert Thurston and Donald Attwater (New York: P.J. Kennedy & Sons, 1956), 3:151–52; 4:36–37.

13. John Anson, "The Female Transvestite in Early Monasticism: The Origin and Development of a Motif," *Viator: Medieval and Renaissance Studies* 5 (1974), 30.

14. W.P. Barrett, trans. *The Trial of Jeanne d'Arc* (London: G. Routledge, 1931), 152–54.

15. Marina Warner, *Joan of Arc: The Image of Female Heroism* (New York: Vintage Books, 1982), 146.

NOTES

16. Catherine Clément, *Miroirs du sujet* (Paris: C. Bourgeois, 1978), 83–84. Warner, *Joan of Arc*, 158.

17. So said her squire, Jean d'Aulon: "I've heard it said by many women, who saw the Maid undressed many times and knew her secrets, that she never suffered from the secret illness of women and that no one could ever notice or learn anything of it from her clothes or in any other way." Jean Baptiste Joseph Ayroles, *La Vraie Vie de Jeanne d'Arc* (Paris: Gaume, 1890–1902), 4:215. Warner, *Joan of Arc*, 19. The same claim was later made in the *Almanach de Gotha* (Gotha, Germany: Justus Perthes, 1822) , 63 and by Jules Michelet (*Histoire de France* [Paris, 1844], 5:53).

18. See, for example, Régine Pernoud, *Joan of Arc*, trans. Edward Hyams (New York: Stein & Day, 1966), 220.

19. Andrea Dworkin, *Intercourse* (New York: The Free Press, 1987), 100.

20. Holly Hill, ed., *Playing Joan: Actresses on the Challenge of Shaw's Saint Joan* (New York: Theater Communications Group, 1987), 135.

21. Barbara Ferraro and Patricia Hussey with Jane O'Reilly, *No Turning Back: Two Nuns' Battle with the Vatican over Women's Right to Choose* (New York: Poseidon Press, 1990), 139.

22. Henry Adams, *Mont Saint Michel and Chartres* (London, 1913). Cited in Warner, *Joan of Arc*, 188.

23. Natalie Zemon Davis, "Women on Top" in *Society and Culture in Early Modern France* (Stanford: Stanford University Press, 1985), 137.

24. As Eve Sedgwick points out, "Matilda's whole appeal to Ambrosio is couched in the eloquence of the monastic habit and the parts of the body that peek through it." Eve Kosofsky Sedgwick, "The Character in the Veil: Imagery of the Surface in the Gothic Novel." *PMLA* 96 (1981), 257.

25. Matthew Lewis, *The Monk* (New York: Oxford University Press, 1973), 58 (vol.1, ch.2).

26. Sedgwick, "The Character in the Veil," 258.

27. George Gordon Lord Byron, *Don Juan*, ed. T.J. Steffan, E. Steffan, and W.W. Pratt (London: Penguin, 1987), 16:527.

28. Terry Castle, *Masquerade and Civilization: The Carnivalesque in Eighteenth-Century Culture and Fiction* (Stanford: Stanford University Press, 1986) 40, 63.

29. Vito Russo, *The Celluloid Closet: Homosexuality in the Movies* (New York: Harper & Row, 1987), 184.

30. Vincent Canby, "A Tale of Two Hoods in 'Nuns on the Run,' " *New York Times*, March 16, 1990: B5.

31. My thanks to John Coventry for this eyewitness account.

32. Tony Bizjak, "The Sobering of Sister Boom Boom," *San Francisco Chronicle*, October 24, 1989: B3–4.

33. Kirk and Heath, *Men in Frocks*, 100.

34. Charlotte Brontë, *Villette*, intro. Margaret Drabble (Dent: London, 1983), 364.

35. Sandra M. Gilbert and Susan Gubar, *The Madwoman in the Attic* (New Haven: Yale University Press, 1979), 426.

36. Eve Kosofsky Sedgwick, *The Coherence of Gothic Conventions* (New York: Arno Press, 1980), 140.

37. Mary Jacobus, *Reading Woman: Essays in Feminist Criticism* (New York: Columbia University Press, 1986), 52.

38. Sigmund Freud, "Sketches for the 'Preliminary Communication' of 1893" (1892), *SE* 1:153.

39. "A Case of Successful Treatment by Hypnotism" (1892–93), *SE* 1:126.

40. This blessing, from the Mishna *Menachot* 43B, is one of three ancient prayers. The other two thank God for not making the speaker a heathen or a bondman. An Orthodox Jewish woman prays thanking God "who hast made me according to thy will." For further information on these prayers, see Rafael Posner, *Jewish Liturgy* (Jerusalem: Keter Publishing House Jerusalem, 1975) and Elie Munk, *The World of Prayer* (New York: P. Feldheim, 1954–63). I am grateful to Adam Z. Newton for these references.

41. Homer Dickens, *What a Drag: Men as Women and Women as Men in the Movies* (New York: Quill, 1984), 65.

42. Diane Owen Hughes, "Distinguishing Signs: Ear-Rings, Jews and Franciscan Rhetoric in the Italian Renaissance City," *Past and Present* 112 (August 1986): 17–18.

43. Otto Weininger, *Sex and Character* (London: William Heinemann, 1906), 314.

44. Sander L. Gilman, *Difference and Pathology* (Ithaca, NY: Cornell University Press, 1985), 33–35. Charlotte Perkins Gilman, "Review of Dr. Weininger's *Sex and Character*" *Critic* 12 (1906): 414.

45. Sigmund Freud, Preface to the Hebrew Translation of *Totem and Taboo* (1930), *SE* 13:xv.

46. Sander L. Gilman, *Sexuality: An Illustrated History* (New York: John Wiley and Sons, 1989), 265, citing Alexander Pilc, *Beitrag zur vergleichenden Rassen-Psychiatrie* (Leipzig: Franz Deuticke, 1906), 18.

47. George L. Mosse, *Nationalism and Sexuality: Middle-Class Morality and Sexual Norms in Modern Europe* (Madison: University of Wisconsin Press, 1985), 135; 142.

48. "Höre, Israel," *Die Zukunft*, March 6, 1897, 454–62. S. Gilman, 267.

49. Terry Castle, *Masquerade and Civilization*, 35–36.

50. Marcel Proust, *Remembrance of Things Past*, trans. C.K. Scott Moncrieff and Terence Kilmartin (Harmondsworth: Penguin, 1986), 2:639. Djuna Barnes, *Nightwood* (New York: New Directions, 1937). Radclyffe Hall, *The Well of Loneliness* (New York: Avon Books, 1981).

51. Adolf Hitler, *Mein Kampf*, trans. Ralph Manheim (Boston: Houghton Mifflin, 1971), 56.

52. Max Nordau, *Zionistische Schriften* (Cologne: Jüdischer Verlag, 1909), pp.379–81. Mosse, *Nationalism and Sexuality*, 42. Gilman, *Sexuality*, 267.

53. A.J. Langguth, *Saki: A Life of Hector Hugh Munroe* (New York: Simon and Schuster, 1981), 258, 83. Mosse, *Nationalism and Sexuality*, 121.

54. Benedict Friedländer, cited by Karl Franz von Leexow, *Armee und die Homosexualität* (Leipzig, 1908), 5, 61–3. Mosse, 41.

55. David Friedrich Strauss, *Der alte und der neue Glaube: Ein Bekenntnis* (Leipzig: G. Hirzel, 1982), 71; Gilman, *Sexuality*, 267.

56. Marjorie Garber, "Freud's Choice: 'The Theme of the Three Caskets,' " in *Shakespeare's Ghost Writers* (London: Routledge, 1987), 75–86.

57. *The Complete Letters of Sigmund Freud to Wilhelm Fliess, 1887–1904,* trans. and ed. Jeffrey Moussaieff Masson (Cambridge: University Press, 1985), 45–51, 113–18.

58. Stanley Cavell, *The Claim of Reason* (New York: Oxford University Press, 1979), 480.

59. *The Merchant of Venice*, ed. Horace Howard Furness. A New Variorum Edition of Shakespeare (1888) (New York: American Scholar, 1965), 383.

60. Cited from the *Literary Digest*, October 26, 1929, in Toby Lelyveld, *Shylock on the Stage* (Cleveland: Western Reserve University, 1960), 126.

61. Sandra Gilbert and Susan Gubar, *No Man's Land*. Vol. 2: *Sexchanges* (New Haven: Yale University Press, 1989), 333–4.

62. James Joyce, *Ulysses* (New York: Random House, 1961), 493.

63. S. Lindner, "Das Saugen an den Fingern, Lippen etc. bei den Kindern (Ludeln.)," *Jahrbuch fur Kinderheilkunde und physische Erziehung* 14 (1879). Sigmund Freud, *Three Essays on Sexuality* (1905), SE 7:179–85; Gilman, *Sexuality*, 265.

64. Jean-Paul Sartre, "The Childhood of a Leader," in *The Wall (Intimacy) and Other Stories*, trans. Lloyd Alexander (New York: New Directions, 1948), 86.

65. Alice Yeager Kaplan, *Reproductions of Banality* (Minneapolis: University of Minnesota Press, 1986), 18.

66. Ilan Avisar, *Screening the Holocaust* (Bloomington: Indiana University Press, 1988), 170.

67. Jeremy Gerard, "Milton Berle Browses at Home and The TV Audience Gets a Treat," *New York Times*, December 11, 1990, C15. Asked why he had had so many extra-marital affairs, Berle told an interviewer, "Maybe I had to prove my manhood to the outside world that always saw me with my mother and wearing dresses in my act. Is she his 'beard'? Is he gay? Maybe that's why I played around so much." Dotson Rader, "The Hard Life, the Strong Loves of a Very Funny Man," *Parade* magazine, *The Boston Globe*, March 19, 1989: 6.

NOTES TO CHAPTER 10, PHANTOMS

1. Sally Jacobs, " 'You Do What You Need to Do' ". *The Boston Globe*, August 2, 1988: 2.

2. Chapman Pincher, *Traitors* (New York: Penguin Books, 1987), 104–5.

3. *The* (London) *Times*, May 6, 1986; *Daily Mail*, May 6 and 7, 1986. Pincher, *Traitors*, 105.

4. Joyce Wadler, "For the First Time, The Real-Life Models for Broadway's *M. Butterfly* Tell of Their Very Strange Romance," *People* 30:6 (August 8, 1988): 91.

5. David Henry Hwang, *M. Butterfly* (New York: New American Library, 1989). I am grateful to David Henry Hwang and to John Lithgow, who graciously allowed me to see the playscript before *M. Butterfly* appeared in published form.

6. A. Mapa, the actor who succeeded Wong in the role, used the same device of onomastic occlusion, which had become by that time—if it was not originally—part of the mystification of gender and sexuality disclosed (and dis-clothed) on the stage.

7. Antonin Artaud, "On the Balinese Theater," in *The Theater and Its Double*, trans. Mary Caroline Richards (New York: Grove Press, 1958), 61.

8. Many observers during the opera's European visit commented on similarities between the Chinese and the Elizabethan theaters,

including the paucity of scenery, the absence of stage lighting to indicate night, and the commotion of eating, drinking, and talking that took place in the audience during the performance.

9. Leonard Cabell Pronko, *Theater East and West* (Berkeley: University of California Press, 1967), 151.

10. Pronko, *Theater East and West*, 44.

11. In both China and Japan *female-to-male* transvestite theaters have also enjoyed a considerable popularity. In contemporary Japan, for example, the Takarazuka Young Girls Opera Company presents all-female productions in which the male roles are played by women, while recent films like Shusuke Kaneko's *Summer Vacation: 1999* (1990), starring four young actresses as schoolboys in a drama of uncanny homoerotic substitutions, problematize gender roles and sexual fantasies.

All-female troupes were popular during the Ming and Qing dynasties in China (Colin P. Mackerras, *The Rise of Peking Opera, 1770–1870* [London: Oxford University Press, 1972], 45–47). It is striking that many of the Chinese plays and tales that focus on female cross-dressing turn on a moment of reversal or disclosure, in which the woman pretending to be a man is revealed in her imposture, often through an inadvertent glimpse of her tiny bound feet. This sign of "nature" was in fact a sign of culture, since the cultural aesthetic of foot-binding produced an ideal of beauty that was the effect of mutilation and deformity. The small size of the appendage is a mark of femininity, artificially and painfully wrought. Theatrically produced as a device of discovery, the female foot that trips up the masquerading "general" or "statesman" becomes a displacement *downward* that marks the site of anatomical gender. Thus, for example, in the play *Ideal Love-Matches* by dramatist Li Yu a woman disguised as a man discloses her gender identity when she takes off her shoes. "With those black boots off, his feet are little 'three-inch lotuses.' It means he must be a girl!" (Patrick Hanan, *The Invention of Li Yu* [Cambridge: Harvard University Press, 1988], 175).

Similarly, in a tale called "Miss Yan" or "Yanshi" by the seventeenth-century author Pu Songling, an intellectually gifted woman who has disguised herself as a man in order to substitute for her less studious husband at the candidates' examinations reveals her gender to an incredulous aunt by pulling off her boots and displaying her bound feet; the men's boots have been stuffed with cotton wool. Another tale by the same author, subsequently expanded by him into a long vernacular play, describes a young woman's quest for revenge on her father's murderers. Disguising herself as a young male entertainer, the heroine, Shang Sanguan, takes the fancy of the murderer, a village bully; they retire together for the night, and in the morning servants discover that the bully has been beheaded, and the young "boy" has hanged himself. When they attempt to move the "boy's" body the servants discover to their surprise that "his socks and shoes felt empty, as if there were no feet inside. They took them off and found a pair of white silk slippers as tiny as hooks, for this was in fact a girl."

As Judith Zeitlin notes, "bound feet, those man-made fetishes which had become the locus of the erotic imagination in late Imperial China, are transformed into a *natural* and *immutable* proof of true femininity" and "It is almost irresistible to explore the allure of bound feet in Freudian terms as representations of the female genitals—as mutilated appendages with *something missing*" (Zeitlin, *"The Painted Wall": Pu Songling's Records of the Strange* [forthcoming, Stanford University Press, ms. 167]).

12. Earle Ernst, *The Kabuki Theatre* (Honolulu: University Press of Hawaii, 1956; 1974), 10–11.

13. Peter Ackroyd, *Dressing Up* (New York: Simon and Schuster, 1979), 94.

14. Yoshizawa Ayame (1673–1729), *Ayame-gusa*. Quoted in Ernst, 195.

15. Thomas Coryate, *Coryate's Crudities* [1611] (New York: Macmillan, 1905). W. Robertson Davies, *Shakespeare's Boy Actors* (London: J.M. Dent, 1939), 34.

16. John Downes, *Roscius Anglicanus, or an Historical Review of the Stage* (London: H. Playford, 1708), 26.

17. Kenneth Tynan, *Tynan on Theater* (Harmondsworth: Penguin Books, 1964), 108.

18. Ian Buruma, *Behind the Mask* (New York: New American Library, 1984), 117–118.

19. Jean-Paul Sartre, Introduction to *The Maids and Deathwatch, Two Plays by Jean Genet*, trans. Bernard Frechtman (New York: Grove Press, 1961), 10.

20. Jeremy Gerard, "David Hwang: Riding on the Hyphen," *New York Times Magazine*, March 13, 1988: 87.

21. Wadler, *People*, 96.

22. Roland Barthes, *The Fashion System*, trans. Matthew Ward and Richard Howard (New York: Hill and Wang, 1983), 254–55.

23. Denis Diderot, *The Paradox of Acting*, trans. William Archer (New York: Hill and Wang, 1957), 19.

24. Honoré de Balzac, *Sarrasine*, in Roland Barthes, *S/Z*, trans. Richard Miller (New York: Hill and Wang, 1974), 236.

25. Barbara Johnson, "The Critical Difference: BartheS/BalZac." in *The Critical Difference* (Baltimore: Johns Hopkins University Press, 1980), 10.

26. Charles Burney, *An Eighteenth-Century Musical Tour in France and Italy*, ed. Percy A. Scholes (London: Oxford University Press, 1959), 247.

27. Enid Rhodes Peschel and Richard E. Peschel, "Medicine and Music: The Castrati in Opera," *The Opera Quarterly* 4,4 (Winter 1986/87): 22.

28. Jacques Casanova, *The Memoirs of Jacques Casanova de Seingalt*, trans. Arthur Machen (New York: Dover Publications, 1961), 3:1737.

29. Angus Heriot, *The Castrati in Opera* (New York: Da Capo Press, 1975), 188.

30. Roger Baker, *Drag: A History of Female Impersonation on Stage* (London: Triton Books, 1968), 113–114. Vern L. Bullough, *Sexual Variance in Society and History* (Chicago: University of Chicago Press, 1976), 491–92.

31. Sir Thomas Overbury, *The Overburian Characters* [1614], ed. W.J. Taylor (Oxford: Basil Blackwell, 1936), 77.

32. Wilfred Blunt, *Slow on the Feather* (London: Russell, 1986), cited in Pincher, *Traitors*, 163.

33. In *Traitors*, a book notable for its thoroughgoing and largely unconscious homophobia (the author refers throughout to homosexuality as a "compulsion," an "abnormality," and a "stigma"), Chapman Pincher nonetheless observes that, although many traitors have been homosexual (Roger Casement, John Vassall, Guy Burgess, etc.), the link between sexuality and treason was socially constructed—they were already "gay deceivers"—rather than innate. Sexual object choice—gay or straight—is one thing, and cross-dressing and transvestism are often quite another. Yet this is another crossover pattern worth noting.

34. Among them, Loretta Janeta Velasquez, author of *The Woman in Battle*, ed. C.J. Worthington (Hartford, Connecticut: T. Belknap, 1876) and Sarah Emma Edmonds (pseud. of Sarah Emma Edmundson), who titled her memoir *Nurse and Spy in the Union Army: Comprising the Adventures and Experiences of a Woman in Hospitals, Camps, and Battle-fields* (Hartford, Connecticut: W.S. Williams & Co., 1864, rpt.1865; also issued as *Unsexed: or, The Female Spy in the Union Army* [Boston: DeWolfe, Fiske, 1864]). Bullough, *Sexual Variance* (599–600), is slightly skeptical about Velasquez's claims, but is convinced of the accuracy of Edmonds's.

35. Jean Le Royal d'Alembert. *Oeuvres Philosophiques, Eloge de Choisy* (Paris: 1805), 8.

36. *The Transvestite Memoirs of the Abbé de Choisy and the Story of the Marquise-Marquis de Banneville*, trans. R.H.F. Scott (London: Peter Owen, 1973).

37. Besides his ecclesiastical biographies, his history of Louis XIV, his journal of the Siam expedition, there exists another curious text that has been attributed to the Abbé de Choisy, though some claim that it was at least in part written by the celebrated author of fairy tales, Charles Perrault. "The Story of the Marquise-Marquis de Banneville" is the tale of the young Marquise de Banneville, born a boy, but brought up as a girl by "her" mother because her father had died in the war, and the mother feared a boy child would suffer the same fate. Little Marianne, "*la belle Marianne*" as she became known, was famous for her wit and beauty, and attracted the attention of many suitors, as well as the protection of the Comtesse d'Alitref (an anagram for Choisy's friend, Madame de La Fayette). Dressed in the height of the day's fashion, with ear pendants, dangling tresses, and face patches (except in church, where she—like Choisy—went modestly coiffed and patch-less), the little Marquise was, at nearly fourteen years old, the toast of Paris, and sublimely unaware of her "real" gender.

    One day at the Comédie—the invariable scene of such revelatory exchanges of the gaze, as the church was to Dante and Petrarch—she saw in the next box a handsome young man, with dazzling diamond rings in his ears and three or four patches on his face. When she calls the attention of the Comtesse to this handsome newcomer, the Comtesse complains that "he makes himself pretty, and that does not suit a man. Why does he not dress as a girl?" (116). This undefined gender status is part of what attracts the Marquise, as she later remarks to him : "You can wear patches and bracelets with no opposition from us. You will not be the first, for these days the young men adorn themselves like girls" (118). The phrase "no opposition" is double here, and key: not only no resistance, but no complement. "These days" young men and girls are alike. How alike, the rest of the story will show.

    When, inevitably, the Marquise and her friend fall in love, her mother, scenting danger, tells "her" (somewhat belatedly, we may think) the truth: "I gave birth to a boy, and had him brought up as a daughter."

    "Oh, madame," cried the little Marquise, "could it be possible that I am. . . ."

    "Yes, my child," her mother said, kissing her, "You are a boy."

    In profound distress, the little Marquise wonders whether her admirer knows this awful secret, since he asks only friendship from her, and resists when she speaks of their marrying. But soon her pleasure in his company makes her forget, or disbelieve, what her mother has told her, and all goes on as before, until a grave illness forces the mother's hand. In extremis, she tells her brother "the truth of her daughter's birth," and promises him that his children will inherit her estates, since the little Marquise can obviously never marry.

    After her mother's death and the required period of mourning, the Marquise becomes an object of scandal, constantly seen at the Opéra, the Comédie and the balls with her friend, and she resolves to quiet the gossips by going through with her original plan to marry him. This he consents to do only if they will live together as brother and sister, marrying only in the public eye. On the wedding night, needless to say, both young people confess: *each* has been cross-dressing all his or her life. Overjoyed, and now with "no doubts that she was a boy" as her "husband" encourages her to touch his "lovely bosom," the "little Marquise," now described in the text with the pronoun "*il*," expresses a desire to remain cross-dressed for the rest of her life: "How could I wear a man's hat?"

    "Let us remain as we are," he agrees. "Rejoice, beautiful Marquise, in all the charms of your sex, and I shall enjoy all the freedom of mine." The story ends on a sober note of patriarchal economics, promising that the birth of a boy will take away from the wicked Uncle (who shed no tears for his dead sister) any hope of inheritance. But consider the language of this final exchange: "all the charms of *your* sex, and . . . all the freedom of *mine*." "Charms" are traditionally feminine, and "freedom" masculine. Despite the author's pronominal gender switch, then, the Marquise and Marquis are perfectly content to define themselves as members of the sex in which they have been dressing all their lives. And this is indeed what makes the story both an allegory and a fairy tale. What they wish comes true.

38. Among the many books and articles on this enigmatic figure, see J. Buchan Telfer, *The Strange Career of the Chevalier d'Eon de Beaumont* (London: Longmans, Green, 1885); Ernest Alfred Vizatelly, *The True Story of the Chevalier d'Eon* (London: Tyson and Edwards, 1895); Marjorie Coryn, *The Chevalier d'Eon 1728–1810* (New York: Frederick A. Stokes, 1932); Edna Nixon, *Royal Spy: The Strange Case of the Chevalier d'Eon* (New York: Reynal and Co., 1965); Cynthia Cox, *The Enigma of the Age: The Strange Story of the Chevalier d'Eon* (London: Longmans, Green, 1966); Michel de Decker, *Madam le Chevalier d'Eon* (Paris: Perrin, 1987), and Gary Kates, "d'Eon Returns to France: Gender and Power in 1777," in *Body Guards: The Cultural Contexts of Gender Ambiguity*, ed. Julia Epstein and Kristina Straub (New York: Routledge, 1991).

39. Edna Nixon, in *Royal Spy*, reports the cross-dressing in Russia as a fact, citing portrait evidence. Bullough (*Sexual Variance*, 488) disputes this, arguing that there is no evidence to support such a claim. Versions of the Russia story appear in all biographical accounts. Telfer, *Strange Career*, 14, notes that "if there is no direct proof in substantiation of the oft-told tale that d'Eon appeared at the Court of Elizabeth in female attire, there is at least valuable evidence in support of it." What comes out clearly here, as I have already suggested, is the desire to believe this story, or at least to have evidence that makes belief credible.

40. Telfer, *Strange Career*, 208.

41. The Count de Broglio to Louis XVI, May 30, 1774. M.E. Boutaric, *Correspondance secrète inédite de Louis XV. sur la politique étrangère* (Paris, 1886), 2: 392.

42. November 16, 1774.

43. Ackroyd, for example, supports the idea that Beaumarchais was actually persuaded that d'Eon was a woman (*Dressing Up*, 78); Vern Bullough (*Sexual Variance*, 489) believes that Beaumarchais knowingly went along with the fiction.

44. *Morning Post and Daily Advertiser, &c.*, November 10–11: 1775.

45. *Morning Post and Daily Advertiser, &c.*, November 13–14: 1775.

46. To the Count de Broglio, December 5, 1775. Frédéric Gaillardet, *Mémoires sur la Chevalier d'Eon, etc.* (Paris, 1866), 249.

47. *Gentleman's Magazine*, vol. 44; quoted in Telfer, *Strange Career*, 286–287.

48. *Scots Magazine*, vol. 39; quoted in Telfer, *Strange Career*, 287.

49. August 15, 1777.

50. Order signed in the King's name by Gravier de Vergennes, at Versailles, August 19, 1777. See Telfer, *Strange Career*, 289.

51. Telfer, *Strange Career*, 293.

52. Cox, *The Enigma of the Age*, 166.

53. Letter to d'Argental, March 17, 1777; quoted in Telfer, *Strange Career*, 300.

54. Letter to the Count de Maurepas, February 8, 1779; quoted in Telfer, *Strange Career*, 305–6.

55. Letter to the Count de Maurepas, February 8, 1779.

56. Christie MSS, quoted in Telfer, *Strange Career*, 309.

57. Ackroyd, *Dressing Up*, 78.

58. Letter to the Count de Broglio, February 10, 1775. *Le Secret du Roi, correspondance secrète de Louis XV avec ses agents diplomatiques, 1752–1774,* 3rd ed. (Paris, 1879), 2:563.

59. Nixon, *Royal Spy*.

60. Letter from George Silk to Robert Slade, May 27, 1810. Quoted in Telfer, *Strange Career*, 332.

61. Robert J. Stoller, foreword to Richard Green, *Sexual Identity Conflict in Children and Adults* (New York: Basic Books, 1974), 8. See also C. Bulliet, *Venus Castina: Famous Female Impersonators, Celestial and Human* (New York: Civici, Friede, 1928); E. De Savitch, *Homosexuality, Transvestism, and Change of Sex* (London: William Heinemann Medical Books, 1958); O. Gilbert, *Men in Women's Guise* (London: John Lane, 1926).

NOTES TO CHAPTER 11, BLACK AND WHITE TV

1. Frances E. W. Harper, *Iola Leroy, or Shadows Uplifted*. With a new introduction by Hazel V. Carby (Boston: Beacon Press, 1987), ix.

CHAPTER II

2. Zora Neale Hurston, *Their Eyes Were Watching God* (Urbana: University of Illinois Press, 1978), 10.

3. Alice Walker, *The Color Purple* (New York: Harcourt Brace Jovanovich, 1982), 230.

4. Laura Shapiro, "Who Dares to Be Bare?" *Newsweek,* November 19, 1990: 84.

5. Jerry Crimmins and Robert Davis, "Student's Painting Creates Stir," *Chicago Tribune,* May 12, 1988: B1.

6. Robert Davis and Ann Marie Lipinski, "Politics Takes Its Place in World of Art," *Chicago Tribune,* May 13, 1988: A1.

7. "The Righteous Act of Being Wrong," Editorial, *Chicago Tribune,* May 13, 1988: A20.

8. All of the images reproduced in this book show persons in theatrical or cinematic performance, or voluntarily posed for the artist or the camera. Although the artist who painted "Mirth and Girth," David K. Nelson, and the photographer who took a picture of the painting, Jim Prinz, were both willing to have it shown here, to do so would have violated the principle that has guided the selection of images throughout.

9. Bob Greene, "Editors Choose Just to Say 'No,'" *Chicago Tribune,* May 18, 1988: E1.

10. Robert Davis and Maria Hunt, "Clergy Vow Action over Art Policy," *Chicago Tribune.* May 14, 1988: A5.

11. "Some Things We Should Never Forget," Editorial, *Chicago Tribune,* May 17, 1988: A20.

12. Davis and Lipinski, "Politics Takes Its Place in the World of Art."

13. Davis and Hunt, "Clergy Vow Action Over Art Policy," 5; Clarence Page, "The People's Republic of Chicago," *Chicago Tribune,* June 26, 1988: D3.

14. Sue Taylor, "School for Scandal," *Art News,* 87, 9 (November 1988): 37.

15. May 13, 1988: A20.

16. Quoted in William H. Honan, "Artists React to Grant Withdrawal," *New York Times,* November 10, 1989: B13.

17. Myra Jehlen, "The Ties That Bind: Race and Sex in *Pudd'nhead Wilson,*" in Mark Twain's *Pudd'nhead Wilson: Race, Conflict, and Culture,* ed. Susan Gillman and Forrest G. Robinson (Durham, North Carolina: Duke University Press, 1990), 112.

18. David Gates, "The Faking of the President," *Newsweek,* November 27, 1989: 84–85.

19. Donald Bogle, *Blacks in American Films and Television: An Illustrated Encyclopedia* (New York: Simon and Schuster, 1988), 468.

20. Henry Louis Gates, Jr., *The Signifying Monkey: A Theory of Afro-American Literary Criticism* (New York: Oxford: 1988), 135–136. James Albert Ukawsaw Gronniosaw, *A Narrative of the Most Remarkable Particulars in the Life of James Albert Ukawsaw Gronniosaw, An African Prince, As Related by Himself* (S. Hazard, 1770).

21. And even of the prison chain that binds together two bitter comrades, Sidney Poitier and Tony Curtis, in the film *The Defiant Ones* (1958)—a film that Pauline Kael, curiously, once described as "*The Thirty-Nine Steps* in drag." Pauline Kael, *Kiss Kiss Bang Bang* (Boston: Little, Brown, 1968), 206.

22. Sterling Brown, "Negro Character as Seen by White Authors," *The Journal of Negro Education* 2 (1933): 179–203. See also Henry Louis Gates, Jr., "TV's Black World Turns—But Stays Unreal," *New York Times,* November 12, 1989: B40.

23. Donald Bogle, *Toms, Coons, Mulattoes, Mammies, & Bucks: An Interpretive History of Blacks in American Films* (New York: Continuum, 1973; updated 1989).

24. David Bradley, "Foreword" to *Eight Men: Stories by Richard Wright* (New York: Thunder's Mouth Press, 1987), xxii.

25. Woody Hochswender, "Vogueing Against AIDS: A Quest for 'Overness,'" *New York Times,* May 12, 1989.

26. Terence Trent D'Arby, Interview in *Q,* October 1987. Quoted in Steve Perry, "Ain't No Mountain High Enough: The Politics of Crossover," in *Facing the Music,* ed. Simon Frith (New York: Pantheon, 1989), 82. As Perry points out, D'Arby's anger at these artists' perceived accommodation leads him to neglect to mention his own kind of career crossover, from the U.S. to Britain, "where the racial equation is different, at least for American blacks" (Perry, 83). In Perry's opinion "What's disturbing about the whole notion of compromising, of making accommodations, is not compromise itself, but the implication—dating all the way from 19th-century black minstrelsy to Michael Jackson's multiple nose jobs—that the compromises are motivated by racial self-hatred" (Perry, 83).

27. Dave Hill, *Prince: A Pop Life* (New York: Harmony Books, 1989), 2.

28. Ralph Ellison, "Change the Joke and Slip the Yoke," *Shadow and Act* (New York: Random House, 1964), 63–64.

29. Homer Dickens, *What a Drag: Men as Women and Women as Men in the Movies* (New York: Quill, 1984), ii.

30. Olive Logan. "The Ancestry of Brudder Bones," *Harpers'* 58 (1878–79): 698–99.

31. Robert C. Toll, *Blacking Up: The Minstrel Show in Nineteenth-Century America* (New York: Oxford University Press, 1974), 142. T. Allston Brown, *History of the American Stage* (New York: Dick & Fitzgerald, 1870), 216–17; George C. D. Odell, *Annals of the New York Stage* (New York: 1927–49) 8:220; 351–52; 392.

32. New York *Clipper,* Jan. 13, 1873; May 16, 1874. Quoted in Toll, *Blacking Up,* 142.

NOTES

33. New York *Clipper,* December 13, 1881; June 2, 1883; October 21, 1882. Quoted in Toll, 144.

34. "Phoebe Anna White," *Songs of Kunkel's Nightingale Opera Troupe* (Baltimore, 1854), 18–19; Toll, *Blacking Up,* 162–63.

35. Alan Bérubé, *Coming Out Under Fire: The History of Gay Men and Women in World War Two* (New York: Free Press, 1990), 79–80.

36. Dickens, *What a Drag,* 170.

37. Jonathan Ned Katz, *Gay/Lesbian Almanac* (New York: Harper & Row, 1983), 442–444. Other blues singers of the period also sang songs that acknowledged lesbianism in black culture, like Lucille Bogan's "B.D. [Bulldagger] Woman's Blues" and Bessie Smith's "Foolish Man Blues" with its reference to "mannish acting women." See Eric Garber's article on Gladys Bentley, noted below.

38. Eric Garber, "Gladys Bentley: The Bulldagger Who Sang the Blues," *Out/Look* 1,1 (Spring 1988), 58. John D'Emilio and Estelle B. Freedman, *Intimate Matters: A History of Sexuality in America.* (New York: Harper & Row, 1988), 227. Late in her life, perhaps under pressure from the homophobia of the McCarthy years and the need to support herself and her mother, Bentley recanted her lesbianism—and her trousers—in an article for *Ebony* called "I Am a Woman Again" (Garber, "Gladys Bentley," 60).

39. Phyllis Rose, *Jazz Cleopatra: Josephine Baker in Her Time* (New York: Doubleday, 1989), 24, from an interview with Mura Dehn, December, 1984. See also Marcel Sauvage, *Les Mémoires de Joséphine Baker* (Paris: Editions Kra, 1927), 89.

40. Pierre de Regnier, "Is it a man? Is it a woman?": "La Revue nègre," in *Candide,* November 12, 1925, Arsenal Pressbook (RO 15-702), 123. Rose 19. I am indebted to Rose's book for all subsequent references to Josephine Baker.

41. Lynn Haney, *Naked at the Feast: A Biography of Josephine Baker* (New York: Dodd, Mead, 1981), 156–58; Josephine Baker and Jo Bouillon, *Josephine,* trans. Mariana Fitzpatrick (New York: Harper & Row, 1977), 80–81.

42. While this is in part doubtless due to "the temper of the times" (for example, the determinedly "decadent" Berlin of the twenties) it is also, I think, something more. Consider this disparate, but cumulatively suggestive, collection of instances.

    —At a party in Berlin in February 1926, dressed only in a pink apron and surrounded by men in evening clothes, Baker performed a lively solo, and danced into the arms of a woman in a tuxedo. This was the young Fraülein Landshoff, the mistress of her host, the playwright Karl Gustav Vollmoeller. Immediately another guest, the art collector and diarist Count Harry Kessler, conceived of a "pantomime or ballet" featuring Landshoff as Solomon and Baker as the Shulamite; Solomon was to wear a dinner jacket, the Shulamite—predictably—little or nothing, but in "ancient style," and the work would be performed to music "half jazz and half Oriental" (Otto Friedrich, Introduction to *In the Twenties: The Diaries of Harry Kessler,* trans. Charles Kessler [New York: Holt, Rinehart and Winston, 1976]. Rose, *Jazz Cleopatra,* 85). Kessler, in other words, at once read Baker as transgressive, and read her transgression as related to, or explicable by, a story about cross-dressing.

    —The Folies-Bergère of the same year, 1926, featured a skit about Louis XIV and his mistresses in which the Sun King was played by a woman. (The "King's" costume of wig and high heels made this spectacle itself a kind of double-cross-dressing.) In the remainder of the show precision dancers appeared as "dinner-jacketed men, as flagellants, as Pacific prawns, as transported slaves, [and] as rabbits" (Rose, *Jazz Cleopatra,* 99). Baker herself, this time dressed in a grass skirt with feathers around her neck, starred in a famous scene in which she danced the Charleston frenetically on the surface of a mirror. Moreover, even this Cubist spectacle had its transvestic edge: the Charleston episode was framed by a sketch in which a comic "professor" falls ludicrously in love with the dancing Baker. She deftly evades his clutches by substituting a black *male* dancer for herself, and the myopic professor fails to notice the difference. (Rose, *Jazz Cleopatra,* 282n.)

    —At Christmas in that same year Baker appeared as Santa Claus in a free matinee performance for the children of Paris' traffic cops at the Folies-Bergère. (No photograph exists which could be compared to the Santa of Mr. T., but the repetition is a curious one, nonetheless.)

    —Janet Flanner, commenting on Baker's return to Paris as a more sophisticated entertainer in 1930, regrets the fact that she "has, alas, almost become a little lady," "almost civilized"; "on that lovely animal visage lies now a sad look, not of captivity, but of dawning intelligence." "One is surprised," Flanner wrote, "that she doesn't want to play Othello" (Janet Flanner, *Paris Was Yesterday: 1925–1939,* ed. Irving Drutman [New York: Viking 1972], 72–73).

    —Like so many other female entertainers of her time, Josephine Baker performed upon occasion in the costume Marlene Dietrich had made famous: a man's formal dress of white tie, top hat, and tails. In Phyllis Rose's recent biography, a photograph of a smiling Baker in this regalia, holding a cigarette at a jaunty angle, is captioned, perhaps tongue-in-cheek, "No more bananas."

43. Lynne Carter, quoted by Marian Christy, *Boston Globe,* March 12, 1971. Also Judy Klemesrud, "Lynne Carter, Female Impersonator Who Will Perform at Carnegie Hall," *New York Times,* January 16, 1971. Rose, *Jazz Cleopatra,* 252.

44. "By the time I finished the book," Rose writes, "I was taken aback to realize that after five years I had come to see her in a number of ways as not all that different from myself. It made me wonder if I had not imposed on her some of my own sensibility, and perhaps I have." And, again, "If I didn't have my say about Josephine Baker, people might not credit the degree to which, in our fantasies at least, we cross, the degree to which she wanted to be remembered for her ideas or the degree to which in my dreams I am onstage in fox and feathers with an audience madly applauding. To consider us so different that we could have nothing to say about each other flattens us both and minimizes our common cultural heritage, not to say our humanity." Rose, *Jazz Cleopatra,* x–xi.

45. "The Theatre," *Time,* February 10, 1936.

46. New York *Clipper,* November 23, 1872. Quoted in Toll, *Blacking Up,* 142.

47. Barbara J. Fields, "Ideology and Race in American History," in *Region, Race, and Reconstruction,* ed. J. Morgan Kousser and James M. McPherson (New York: Oxford University Press, 1982), 143–177.

48. Madison Grant, *The Passing of the Great Race, or The Racial Basis of European History* (New York: Scribner's, 1918; orig. publ. 1916), 18.

49. William and Ellen Craft, *Running a Thousand Miles for Freedom, or The Escape of William and Ellen Craft from Slavery. Great Slave Narratives,* ed. Arna Bontemps (Boston: Beacon Press, 1969), 271.

50. Jean Fagan Yellin, *The Intricate Knot: Black Figures in American Literature, 1776–1863* (New York: New York University Press, 1972), 168.

51. Harriet Beecher Stowe, *Uncle Tom's Cabin* (New York: Signet, 1966), 410.

52. John William Ward, Afterword to the Signet edition, 491.

53. Leslie Fiedler, *The Inadvertent Epic* (Toronto: Canadian Broadcasting Corporation, 1979), 33.

54. Jean Genet, *The Blacks: A Clown Show,* trans. Bernard Fretchman (New York: Grove Press, 1960), 124.

55. Mark Twain, *Following the Equator: A Journey Around the World* (New York: Harper and Brothers, 1929), 7. Susan Gillman's description of this servant as "situated in a world *between:* between black and white, masculine and feminine" (Gillman, *Dark Twins: Imposture and Identity in Mark Twain's America* [Chicago: University of Chicago Press, 1989], 100) aptly locates the alluring transgressiveness for Twain of both racial- and gender-crossing.

56. Twain's short story "1,002nd Arabian Night" (1883) involves the fantasy of babies switched at birth, each growing up with the interests of his/her *biological* rather than *cultural* gender ("people came to observe that Selim Mahomet-Abdullah, the ostensible *boy,* always interested herself in feminine matters, and that Fatima, the ostensible *girl,* always interested himself in masculine things"). When the two marry and have twins, the same populace exclaims over the fact that "the father, and not the mother" is "the mother of the babes!" (*Mark Twain's Satires and Burlesques,* ed. Franklin P. Rogers, [Berkeley: University of California Press, 1967], 132; Gillman, *Dark Twins,* 200, n.18). In "Hellfire Hotchkiss" (1897), set in the same Dawson's Landing (a fictive version of Hannibal, Missouri) as *Pudd'nhead Wilson,* biology is no longer destiny; Rachel "Hellfire" Hotchkiss and Oscar "Thug" Carpenter are, respectively, "the only genuwyne male man in this town and . . . the only genuwyne female girl, if you leave out sex and just consider the business facts" (Rogers, 187). But Hellfire, confronted with the realization that society will not accept them in their present social styles, determines to abandon her "boyish" ways. In "Wapping Alice" (1898, 1907), which Gillman considers the best of the transvestite tales, there is a *male* transvestite, whose identity is suddenly disclosed by Twain on the second page: "Some of the ridiculous features of the incident," says his narrator, "will be better understood if I expose Wapping Alice's secret here and now in the beginning—for she had a secret. It was this: she was not a woman at all, but a *man*" ("Wapping Alice," ed. Hamlin Hill [Berkeley: Keepsake series, 1981], 42). As for "Alice's" motivation, "Why he unsexed himself was his own affair." In 1907, revising this story in his Autobiographical Dictation for 10 April, he altered what he described as a "fictitious" but "non-essential detail; "For my own pleasure I wish to remove that fictive detail now, and replace it with the fact. . . . Wapping Alice was a *woman,* not a man" ("Wapping Alice," 71). Gender indeterminacy here extends even to authorial design. As Gillman remarks, in a fascinating treatment of the whole question of the "transvestite tales," "sexual difference turns out to be at its origin unstable and unprovable" (Gillman, *Dark Twins,* 111).

57. In one of these, "Feud Story and the Girl Who Was Ostensibly a Man" (ca. 1902; ed. Robert Sattelmeyer, *Missouri Review* 10 [1987]: 97–112; Gillman, *Dark Twins,* 201 n.25) [unpublished in Twain's lifetime] the cross-dresser, forced by a bitter old man to assume her transvestic disguise, is claimed as the "father" of her child by a pregnant young woman who engineers their marriage. The couple, Twain's manuscript indicates, "do not live together"; in the final sentence we learn that "At last the child was born—a boy." This is yet another example of the phenomenon of the changeling boy, whose apparently definitive maleness replaces the transvestite "father'"s gender-under-erasure, as was the case with Singer's "Yentl."

58. Mark Twain, *The Tragedy of Pudd'nhead Wilson* (New York: Signet, 1964), 29.

59. W.E.B. Du Bois, *The Souls of Black Folk* (1903) (New York: Avon, 1989), 3.

60. "Metaphor, Metonymy and Voice," in *A World of Difference* (Baltimore: The Johns Hopkins University Press, 1987), 166.

61. It is suggestive to compare the veil image in *Pudd'nhead Wilson* with Freud's reading of the veil in the "Wolf-Man" case. See below, "Conclusion." "The tearing of the veil was analogous to the opening of his eyes and to the opening of the window [in the Wolf Man's dream]. The primal scene has become transformed into a necessary condition for his recovery." (Sigmund Freud, "From the History of an Infantile Neurosis" [1918] *SE* 17:75: 99–101). Tom Driscoll's desire to obliterate the traces of his black mother, to be solely the son of his fantasy "father," Judge Driscoll, leads him to become the "veiled young woman" from whom he can be "born a second time into a happier life"—in this case by killing the adoptive-father and implicating a pair of innocent male twins in the crime.

NOTES

62. Richard Wright, "Man of All Work," in *Eight Men* (New York: Thunder's Mouth Press, 1987), 118–19.

63. For an excellent essay on *Imitation of Life*, see Lauren Berlant, "National Brands/National Body: *Imitation of Life*," in *Comparative American Identities: Race, Sex, and Nationality in The Modern Text*, ed. Hortense J. Spillers (New York: Routledge, 1991), 110–40.

64. Michael Jackson, *Moonwalker* (New York: Doubleday, 1988), 38–39.

65. *Moonwalker*, 229; Taraborrelli, 407. In his autobiography Michael Jackson also includes a photograph of himself and Sophia Loren in which the two stars look startlingly similar (*Moonwalker*, 125).

66. *Vanity Fair* 52, 12 (December 1989), 170.

67. Leonard Maltin and Richard W. Bann, *Our Gang: The Life and Times of the Little Rascals* (New York: Crown Publishers 1977), 42. Recall that Julian Eltinge himself performed in transvestite blackface in the early years of his career.

68. The comparison to Sapphire is made more piquant by the fact that Sapphire, of course, had originally been played on radio by a white man, when the program originated nationwide in 1929; it was not until the thirties that "Amos 'n' Andy' "s creators, Freeman Gosden and Charles Correll, brought in black actors to play the radio roles. (The series was moved to television in 1951 with an all-black cast, including Tim Moore—who had played a female impersonator in *Boy! What a Girl*—as Kingfish.)

69. *Time* 99, 5 (January 31, 1972), cover story, "When You're Hot, You're Hot," 56–60. *Ebony* 2, 2 (December 1970), cover article, Louie Robinson, "The Evolution of Geraldine," 176–82.

70. C. H. Hughes, "Postscript to Paper on 'Erotopathia,'" in *The Alienist and Neurologist* 14 (October 1893), 731–732. Cited in Vern L. Bullough, *Sexual Variance in Society and History* (Chicago: University of Chicago Press, 1976), 613–14.

71. C. H. Hughes, "Homo Sexual Complexion Perverts in St. Louis," *The Alienist and Neurologist* 28 (1907), pp. 487–488. Bullough, *Sexual Variance*, 164.

72. David Frechette, "What's Wrong with This Picture," *Black Film Review*, 5,3 (Summer 1989), 23.

73. Richard modeled his hairstyle and his makeup after blues entertainer Billy Wright and a flamboyant gay pianist who called himself Esquerita. Richard wore Pancake # 31 throughout his career, together with eye-makeup, mascara, and gaudy, glittering robes. Charles White, *The Life and Times of Little Richard* (New York: Pocket Books, 1984), 26,30.

74. Hill, *Prince: A Pop Life*, 129.

75. The term, which I think perfectly describes the complex transactions involved, is Nancy Vickers's. See her work on George Michael, "The Art of the Double Cross," delivered as a lecture at the conference on "Gender at the Crossroads," Stanford University, March 1990.

NOTES TO CHAPTER 12, THE CHIC OF ARABY

1. T.E. Lawrence, *Secret Dispatches from Arabia*, ed. Arnold Lawrence (London: Golden Cokrell Press, 1939), 37–38 (from *Arab Bulletin* 1,32 [November 26, 1916], 482).

2. T.E. Lawrence. *Seven Pillars of Wisdom* (London: Jonathan Cape, 1935; rpt. Harmondsworth: Penguin Books, 1986), 129.

3. In a strong essay published after I had completed this chapter, Kaja Silverman also notes the telling detail of the wedding clothes, which she regards as an aspect of Lawrence's "double mimesis," his insertion of himself into the structural positions occupied by certain Arabs (like Feisal) who became ego ideals for him, and with whom he aligned his own "fantasmatic." "To wear [Feisal's wedding garments] is to be in a position to love that image of the Other's virility which has become the 'self' " (Silverman, 26). Where my reading of the white wedding costume differs from hers is in my sense that Lawrence (and by "Lawrence" I mean here, on the one hand, the author of *Seven Pillars*, and on the other, the protagonist of David Lean's film) could simultaneously regard himself as Feisal's "other" and as his *bride*. Silverman, whose chief interest is in the transformation of Lawrence's "reflexive masochism" into "feminine masochism" after the rape and beating incident at Der'a, does not see the early Lawrence of the Arabian campaign as "feminized." Yet, as I have been arguing, there is no necessary inconsistency between a hyper-virilized and a feminized position *from the point of view of the reader or viewer* regarding a cross-dressed subject. Silverman, "White Skin, Brown Masks: The Double Mimesis, or With Lawrence in Arabia," *differences* 1, 3 (Fall 1989), 3–54.

4. Richard Aldington, *Lawrence of Arabia: A Biographical Enquiry* (London: Collins, 1955), and, especially, the fine biography by John E. Mack, *A Prince of Our Disorder: The Life of T.E. Lawrence* (Boston: Little, Brown, 1976).

5. Searching his personal history for earlier beatings that might have given pleasure, Mack finds that it was Lawrence's mother, not his father, who beat him, since his father was apparently too tender-hearted to do so. But with this mother, who was in many ways as strong-willed as Lawrence himself, he enjoyed an extremely affectionate relationship, and seems to have had a relatively happy boyhood, despite the stain of illegitimacy that marked him and his four brothers. Indeed—and this is the point—he seems

in some ways never to have progressed beyond boyhood into an adolescence of courtship and awakening sexuality, hetero- or homosexual. His adventures in the East, his archaeological researches, his remarkable success with the Arab revolt, were in a way a translation of his boyhood fascination with the medieval world, the crusades, and Richard I, the Lionhearted.

6. One of the major displacements in his life was, apparently, that of the sexual object. C.F.C. Beeson, a close friend in his years of adolescence, reports that Lawrence showed no interest in girls; Arnold Lawrence, T.E.'s youngest brother, claimed that he died a virgin (Mack, *A Prince*, 25; 67).

7. To Earnest Thurtle. *The Letters of T.E. Lawrence*, ed. David Garnett (London: Cape, 1938), p.649. This droll reference to John Knox's *First Blast of the Trumpet against the Monstrous Regiment of Women* (1558), punning on the military sense of "regiment" as well as Knox's primary sense of "rule," is characteristic of Lawrence's deployment of his extraordinarily wide reading.

8. To James Hanley, 1931. *Letters of T.E. Lawrence*, 728.

9. Mack, *A Prince*, 20. Interview with Janet Laurie Hallsmith, March 25, 1965.

10. Letter to Vyvyan Richards, July 15, 1918. Malcolm Brown, *T.E. Lawrence, The Selected Letters* (New York: Norton, 1989), 149, 151.

11. Letter to Robert Graves, February 4, 1935, *Selected Letters*, 520.

12. Letter to E.M. Forster, June 17, 1925. *Selected Letters*, 283.

13. Letter to Greenhill, March 20, 1920. Humanities Research Center, University of Texas, Austin. Mack, *A Prince*, 277.

14. Letter to Miss Fareedah El Akle, January 3, 1921. *Selected Letters*, 183.

15. *American Heritage Dictionary* (Boston: Houghton Mifflin, 1973), 1193. The current fashion among TV newscasters to pronounce this word "shake" rather than "sheek" is not a correction of an earlier vulgar error on the part of American filmgoers, but—at least according to the dictionary—an alternative, and equally (but not more) correct pronunciation. That Dan Rather and others would rather say "shake" than "sheek," however, seems to me to suggest that they want to distance themselves, and today's Middle Eastern dignitaries, from the Hollywood image made so popular by Valentino.

16. *Exhibitors Trade Review*. November 19, 1921, 1763. *There is a new star in heaven . . . Valentino: Biographie, Filmographie, Essays*, ed. Eva Orbanz (Berlin: Verlag Volker Spiess, 1979).

17. Alexander Walker, *Rudolph Valentino* (London: Elm Tree Books/Hamish Hamilton, 1976), 43–51, 110–23. On Valentino's life and films, see also Jack Scagnetti, *The Intimate Life of Rudolph Valentino* (New York: Jonathan David, 1975), 30–36, 106–18, 138–40; Noel Botham and Peter Donnelly, *Valentino: the Love God* (London: Everest Books, 1976), 70–75, 102–8, 194–206; Orbanz, *There is a new star in heaven*.

18. For a valuable discusson of Valentino from the point of view of cinematic spectatorship, see Miriam Hansen, "Pleasure, Ambivalence, Identification: Valentino and Female Spectatorship," *Cinema Journal* 25, 4 (Summer 1986): 6–32. Hansen's article, which came to my attention after I had written the analyses of Valentino that appear both in this chapter and in Chapter 13, argues from a similar vantage point about his gender re-coding and the way it is inflected by class and race.

19. Virginia Woolf, *Orlando: A Biography* (1908) (London: Penguin, 1970), 108.

20. To Lady ——, Adrianople, April 1, 1717. *Embassy to Constantinople: The Travels of Lady Mary Wortley Montagu*. ed. Christopher Pick (London: Century Hutchinson, 1988), 97–98.

21. To Lady Mar, Adrianople, 1 April, 1717. *Embassy to Constantinople*, 108–9.

22. Terry Castle, *Masquerade and Civilization: The Carnivalesque in Eighteenth Century Culture and Fiction*. (Stanford: Stanford University Press, 1986), 72–73.

23. Frank W. Wadsworth, "Hamlet and Iago: Nineteenth-Century Breeches Parts," *Shakespeare Quarterly* 17 (1966): 129–39.

24. Mary Edwards Walker, *Hit* (New York, 1871), 62–63.

25. *The London Journal of Flora Tristan, 1842, or The Aristocracy and the Working Class of England*, trans. Jean Hawkes (London: Virago, 1982), 58.

26. Prevesa, November 12, 1809. *Byron's Letters and Journals*, ed. Leslie A. Marchand (Cambridge: Belknap Press of Harvard University Press, 1973–82), 1:228.

27. Hobhouse found the demonstration "beastly"; Byron's response, Crompton notes, is not recorded. Louis Crompton, *Byron and Greek Love* (Berkeley: University of California Press, 1985), 143–44. Leslie A. Marchand, *Byron: A Biography* (New York: Alfred A. Knopf, 1957), 1:243.

28. Isaac Disraeli, *The Literary Character of Men of Genius*, 3rd. ed. (London: John Murray, 1822), 101–2.

29. John Hindley, *Persian Lyrics, or Scattered Poems from the Diwan-i-Hafiz* (London: E. Harding, J. Debrett, and West & Hughes, 1800), 33n.

30. The identity of "Thyrza," given Byron's celebrity and reputation for amorous amplitude, was a subject of highly interested dispute;

Lady Falkland, whom Byron had assisted financially but did not know, wrote him passionately asserting that she must be "Thyrza," and Byron's contemporary biographer, Thomas Moore, was at pains to describe Thyrza as not a real person at all, but a myth.

31. July 5, 1807. Marchand, *Byron's Letters and Journals*, 1:124.

32. Byron, *The Letters and Journals*, ed. R.E. Prothero (London: John Murray, 1989), 2:116n.

33. R.C. Dallas, *Correspondence of Lord Byron with a Friend* (Paris: Galignani, 1825), 3,41–42. This and the previous quotation are cited by Crompton, to whose fascinating book on Byron's bisexuality and its political as well as personal consequences I am much indebted.

34. *Medwin's Conversations of Lord Byron* (1824), ed. E. J. Lowell, Jr. (Princeton: Princeton University Press, 1966), 67. Crompton 110, 209, 243.

35. George Gordon, Lord Byron, *Don Juan*, ed. T.G. Steffan, E. Steffan and W.W. Pratt (London: Penguin Books, 1987). Byron wrote to Henry Drury, "I see not much difference between ourselves and the Turks, save that we have foreskins and they have none— that they have long dresses and we short, and that we talk much and they little." May 3, 1810. Marchand, *Byron's Letters and Journals*, 1:238.

36. In an essay on cross-dressing and the politics of gender in *Don Juan* Susan Wolfson notes that Byron's relation to his own mother gives biographical plausibility to Juan's role as phallic woman, and observes that the real power of transvestite transformation lies in the other major transvestic figure in the poem, the woman cross-dressed as a man, the Duchess of Fitz-Fulke. " 'Their She Condition': Cross-Dressing and the Politics of Gender in *Don Juan*," *ELH* 54,3 (Fall 1987): 611.

37. William Hazlitt, "Lord Byron," *The Spirit of the Age* (1825), reprinted in *The Complete Works of William Hazlitt*, ed. P.P. Howe, 21 vols (London: J.M. Dent, 1930–34), 11:75.

38. "The Tale of Kamarr al Zamamn," 216th Night. *The Book of the Thousand and One Nights and a Night*, trans. and annotated by Richard F. Burton (rpt. New York: Heritage Press, 1934), 2:1150–52.

39. "The Tale of Ali Shar and Zumurrud," 326th Night. Burton, *Nights*, 3:1475.

40. Vern L. Bullough, in *Sexual Variance in Society and History* (Chicago: University of Chicago Press, 1976), sees this as a probable echo of the mameluke period, "when the slave (*mameluke* means 'owned') who became the favorite of a ruling Sultan could expect to advance rapidly" (226).

41. Burton, "Terminal Essay," *Nights*.

42. Koran, trans. Mohammed Marmaduke Pichthall (New York: New American Library, 1953), 7 (The Heights): 25. Ali ibn Bakr, Burhan al-Din, al-Marghinani, *The Hedaya or Guide: A Commentary on the Mussulman Laws*, trans. Charles Hamilton, preface and index by Stanish Grove Grady, ed. (rpt. Lahore, West Pakistan: Premier Book House, 1957), 4: 597 (Book 54, sec.2).

43. The nineteenth-century Egyptologist William Edward Lane reported that boys about to undergo the rite of circumcision were dressed in girls' clothing. Among the Muslims of Egypt Lane describes female impersonators called *khawals*, "dancers" (and others, called *gink*, "a term that is Turkish, and has a vulgar signification which aptly expresses their character"), who wore their hair long and braided, plucked out the hair of their beards, applied kohl and henna to their eyes and hands in imitation of women, and danced to the accompaniment of castanets. Their costumes, "as if to prevent their being thought to be really females," were "partly male and partly female: it chiefly consists of a tight vest, a girdle, and a kind of petticoat." When walking in the streets, these men frequently veiled their faces, "not from shame, but merely to affect the manners of women." W.E. Lane, *Manners and Customs of the Modern Egyptians* (1860; rpt. London: Everyman's Library, 1963), 551, 388–89. Vern Bullough noted in 1976 that boys were still sometimes dressed as girls in Egypt to avoid the evil eye, since boys were thought more vulnerable to the "eye" than girls. *Sexual Variance*, 233.

44. Burton, "Terminal Essay," *Nights*.

45. Edward Rice, *Captain Sir Richard Francis Burton* (New York: Scribners', 1990), 181, 184.

46. Charles Montagu Doughty's *Arabia Deserta* chronicled Doughty's arduous trip through the Arabian peninsula in 1876–78. Doughty, an ardent Evangelical Christian, criticized Burton, and Burton's *Personal Narrative of a Pilgrimage to El-Medinah and Meccah*, for accepting Islam, and with it the comforts of Arab hospitality. Doughty's account records his suffering from the hardships of the desert, the heat, and the cruelty of the Bedawin.

47. E. Burgoyne, ed, *Gertrude Bell—From her personal papers* (London: E. Benn, 1958–61), 2:296–97.

48. Gertrude Bell, *The Desert and the Sown* (London: William Heinemann, 1907; rpt. Boston: Beacon Press, 1987), Preface (unpaged).

49. Sarah Graham-Brown, "Introduction" to Bell, *The Desert and the Sown*, ix.

50. Mel Gussow, "A Sexual Cover-Up in 'New Anatomies,' " *New York Times*, February 22, 1990.

51. Cited in Annette Kobak, *Isabelle: The Life of Isabelle Eberhardt* (New York: Alfred A. Knopf, 1989), 16.

52. Letter to *La Petite Gironde*, 1903. Kobak, *Isabelle*, 29.

53. Diary, January 18, 1900; quoted in Kobak, *Isabelle*, 33.

54. Christos Christidi, 1896; quoted in Kobak, *Isabelle*, 39.

55. J. Bonneval, January 1897; quoted in Kobak, *Isabelle*, 43.

56. Mme. Casson, quoted in Kobak, *Isabelle*, 49.

57. Recall the advice of *Information for the Female-to-Male Crossdresser and Transsexual*, 2nd. ed. (San Francisco: L. Sullivan, 1985), 24.

58. Ahmed Rachid, letter to Eberhardt, July 5, 1898, quoted in Kobak, *Isabelle*, 71.

59. *The Passionate Nomad: The Diary of Isabelle Eberhardt*, trans. Nina de Voogd (Boston: Beacon Press, 1987), 53.

60. Sigmund Freud, *The Interpretation of Dreams* (1900), *SE* 4: 307.

61. Jacques Lacan, "The Agency of the Letter in the Unconscious, or Reason Since Freud," *Ecrits*, trans. Alan Sheridan (New York: W.W. Norton, 1977), 167.

62. Robert Randau, *Notes et souvenirs* (Algiers: Charlot, 1945), quoted in Kobak, *Isabelle*, 195.

63. General Herbert Lyautey, letter to Victor Barrucand. Quoted in Kobak, *Isabelle*, 212.

64. Mary Douglas, *Purity and Danger* (London: Routledge and Kegan Paul, 1966), 40.

65. Letter to Augustin de Moerder, November, 1900, quoted in Kobak, *Isabelle*, 139–40.

66. Michel Vieuchange, *Smara: Chez Les Dissidents du Sud Marocain et du Rio de Oro*, ed. and introduction by Jean Vieuchange (Paris: Librairie Plon, 1932), xxi. Translated by Fletcher Allen, *Smara: The Forbidden City* (New York: E.P. Dutton, 1932; rpt. New York: Ecco Press, 1987).

67. I was very anxious to take a photograph of El Akhsas, probably never photographed before. I made a first effort; but, once up, and having the three men around me, they suddenly became afraid [that his identity might be detected] and forced me to sit again. So I sat down again and waited for half an hour. Then I fixed two pins so that my blue veil would not move, and I could operate beneath it without being seen ... for the second time, Larbi and El Mahmoul pressed so much against me, jostling me, that the shutter worked before I was ready. It was the last on the spool, so there was no remedy ... bad night ... I took a considerable risk trying to get that photograph, and I misfired. I should have been so glad to get it. (*Smara*, 44)

68. Rhea Talley Stewart, "Afghanistan Lifted the Veil Decades Ago," *New York Times*, May 22, 1989, A16.

69. Paul Bowles, *The Sheltering Sky* (New York: Vintage Books, 1949; 1990). In the scene of transvestic transformation, Kit pulls on the "full soft trousers" and the "loose vests and the flowing robe" her lover provides for her "with growing delight," noting that "she looked astonishingly like an Arab boy" (290–91).

70. Nancy Collins, "Winger on the Wild Side," *Vanity Fair*, October 1990, 194.

71. Dr. Georges Burou. Morris's omission or suppression of "Dr.B—'s" surname, whether motivated by discretion or stylistic verve, makes the whole episode into a novelistic adventure with something of an eighteenth-century flavor.

72. Jan Morris, *Conundrum: An Extraordinary Narrative of Transsexualism* (New York: Henry Holt and Company, 1974; 1986), 136. Renée Richards, with Jack Ames, *Second Serve* (New York: Stein and Day, 1983).

73. Elizabeth Wilson, *Adorned in Dreams: Fashion and Modernity* (Berkeley: University of California Press, 1985), 162.

74. Ludmilla Jordanova, *Sexual Visions: Images of Gender in Science and Medicine between the Eighteenth and Twentieth Centuries* (Madison: University of Wisconsin Press, 1989), 90.

75. Peter Fuchs, *The Land of Veiled Men*, trans. Bice Fawcett (New York: Citadel Press, 1956), 49.

76. Jacques Lacan, "The Signification of the Phallus," in *Ecrits: A Selection*, trans. Alan Sheridan (New York: W.W. Norton, 1977), 287–88.

77. Heinz Kohut, *The Analysis of the Self* (Madison, Connecticut: International Universities Press, 1971; 1987), 210–11.

78. For example, René Girard, "Scandal and the Dance: Salome in the Gospel of Mark," *New Literary History* 15, 2 (Winter 1984): 311–24, and in the same issue, Françoise Meltzer, "A Response to René Girard's Reading of Salome"; Linda Seidel, "Salome and the Canons," *Women's Studies* 2 (1984): 29–66; Françoise Meltzer, *Salome and the Dance of Writing: Portaits of Mimesis in Literature* (Chicago: University of Chicago Press, 1987), 13–46.

79. Huysmans's Des Esseintes finds in Salome "the symbolic incarnation of undying Lust, the Goddess of Immortal Hysteria, ... the monstrous Beast, indifferent, irresponsible, insensible." Joris-Karl Huysmans, *A Rebours*. Translated as *Against Nature* by Robert Baldick (Baltimore: Penguin, 1959), 66.

80. Françoise Meltzer, *Salome and the Dance of Writing*, 46.

81. In a passage that has been allusively linked to Salome, describing the power of Dance upon the spectator, Mallarmé makes the connection between femininity and textuality explicit, while retaining the emphasis upon the poet as gazing subject and the

dancer as "illiterate" (*illettrée*), "unconscious" (*inconsciente*) object of the gaze, who becomes the catalyst for the male poet's creativity:

> par un commerce dont paraît son sourire verser le secret, sans tarder elle te livre à travers le voile dernier qui toujours reste, la nudité de tes concepts et silencieusement écrira ta vision à la façon d'un Signe, qu'elle est.

> [through a commerce whose secret her smile appears to pour out, without delay she delivers up to you through the ultimate veil that always remains, the nudity of your concepts and silently begins to write your vision in the manner of a Sign, which she is.]

Stephane Mallarmé, *Oeuvres complètes* (Paris: Pleiade, 1946), 307. Translated by Barbara Johnson, in her essay, "Les Fleurs du Mal Armé: Some Reflections on Intertextuality," *A World of Difference* (Baltimore: The Johns Hopkins University Press, 1987), 127.

82. Edward Said, *Orientalism* (New York: Vintage Books, 1978), 187.

83. Joseph A. Boone, "Mappings of Male Desire in Durrell's *Alexandria Quartet*," *South Atlantic Quarterly* 88, 1 (Winter 1989): 81.

84. Gustave Flaubert, *Flaubert in Egypt: A Sensibility on Tour*, ed. and trans. Francis Steegmuller (London: Bodley Head, 1972), 39.

85. Oscar Wilde, *Salome, A Tragedy in One Act*, trans. Alfred Douglas (New York: Dover Publications, 1967), 64.

86. Richard Ellmann, *Oscar Wilde* (New York: Alfred A. Knopf, 1988), 344.

87. Russell's film is clearly indebted to the earlier Alla Nazimova silent film version of Wilde's play, a clear case of camp *avant la lettre*.

88. Lacan, "The Signification of the Phallus," 287.

89. Cornelia Otis Skinner, *Madame Sarah* (New York: Paragon House, 1966) 63, 123–24, 260–70. Ellmann, *Oscar Wilde*, 371. After his arrest in 1895 Wilde sent a friend to ask her to assist him by paying four hundred pounds for the rights to *Salome*, but although she expressed sympathy, she delayed and did nothing. Ellmann, *Oscar Wilde*, 458; Skinner, *Madame Sarah*, 123–24.

90. [Walford] Graham Robertson, *Time Was: The Reminiscences of W. Graham Robertson* (London, 1931; New York: Quartet Books, 1981, 125–27. Ellmann, *Oscar Wilde*, 372.

91. The "typical response" to Bev Francis's body, according to *Newsweek*, was "that *can't* be a woman." Charles Leerhsen and Pamela Abramson, "The New Flex Appeal," *Newsweek*, May 6, 1985, 82. See also Laurie Schulze, "On the Muscle," in *Fabrications: Costume and the Female Body* (New York: Routledge, 1990), 59–78.

92. Ernest Jones, *The Life and Work of Sigmund Freud*, edited and abridged in one volume by Lionel Trilling and Steven Marcus (New York: Basic Books, 1961), 377.

93. Angela Livingstone, *Salomé, Her Life and Work* (Mt. Kisco, New York: Moyer Bell, 1984), 18.

94. Sigmund Freud, "Lou Andreas-Salomé" (1937), trans. James Strachey. *SE* 23:297.

95. Peter Gay, *Freud: A Life for Our Time* (New York: W.W. Norton, 1988; Doubleday Anchor, 1989), 193.

96. Letter to Freud, October 19, 1917, in Ernst Pfeiffer, ed., *Sigmund Freud and Lou Andreas-Salomé, Letters*, trans. William and Elaine Robson-Scott (New York: W.W. Norton, 1966), 66–67.

97. Letter to Freud, November 6, 1927. In Pfeiffer, *Letters*, 168.

98. Letter from Rilke to Lou Andreas-Salomé, 1898, quoted in Angela Livingstone, *Salome, Her Life and Work*, 126.

99. Letter from Freud to Andreas-Salomé, November 10, 1912. Pfeiffer, *Letters*, 11.

100. Unni Wikan, "Man Becomes Woman: Transsexualism in Oman as a Key to Gender Roles," *Man* NS 12 (1977): 307. Reprinted in a somewhat expanded form as "The *Xanith*: A Third Gender Role?" in Unni Wikan, *Behind the Veil in Arabia: Women in Oman* (Baltimore and London: The Johns Hopkins University Press, 1982), 168–86.

101. Gill Shepherd, "Transsexualism in Oman?" (letter), *Man* NS 13 (1978): 133–4.

102. Robert Brain, *Man* NS 13 (1978): 322–23.

103. Shepherd, "The Omani *xanith*," *Man* NS (1978), 663–71; Wikan, response, 667–71.

104. G. Feurstein and S. al-Marzooq, *Man* NS 13(1978), 665–67.

105. J.M. Carrier, "The Omani *xanith* controversy," *Man* NS 15 (1980): 541–42.

106. For example, Peter Ackroyd, *Dressing Up* (New York: Simon and Schuster, 1979), 37. Ackroyd classifies the *berdache* with Tahitian, Brazilian, Aztec and Inca tribal transvestites as members of an "honorary third sex" in a section of his book called "Transvestism Accepted." Nancy A., "Other Old Time Religions," *The TV-TS Tapestry Journal* 40: 70–72.

107. The example of the *mahu*, from Robert I. Levy, "The Community Function of Tahitian Male Transvestism: A Hypothesis," *Anthropological Quarterly* 44 (1971), 12–21, is cited in Brain's letter to *Man*.

NOTES TO CHAPTER 13, THE TRANSVESTITE CONTINUUM

1. *George Michael: Music, Money, Love, Faith* (MTV Networks, 1988). I am grateful to Nancy Vickers for this reference.

2. *San Francisco Chronicle,* May 9, 1990: E1.

3. Mablen Jones, *Getting It On: The Clothing of Rock 'n' Roll* (New York: Abbeville Press, 1987), 129.

4. Andrew Ross, "Uses of Camp," in *No Respect: Intellectuals and Popular Culture* (New York: Routledge, 1989), 165.

5. Mablen Jones, *Getting It On,* 144.

6. Kris Kirk and Ed Heath, *Men in Frocks* (London: Gay Men's Press, 1984), 58.

7. Joan Riviere, "Womanliness as a Masquerade," in *Formations of Fantasy,* ed. Victor Burgin, James Donald and Cora Kaplan (London: Methuen, 1986), 38. Jacques Lacan, "The Signification of the Phallus," in *Ecrits: A Selection,* trans. Alan Sheridan (New York: W.W. Norton, 1977).

8. Eugénie Lemoine-Luccioni, *La Robe* (Paris: Seuil, 1983), 124.

9. Roland Barthes, *The Fashion System,* trans. Matthew Ward and Richard Howard (New York: Hill and Wang, 1983), 231–32.

10. Dustjacket copy for *The Wonderful Private World of Liberace,* by Liberace (New York: Harper & Row, 1986).

11. Liberace, *The Wonderful Private World of Liberace,* 171.

12. Bob Thomas, *Liberace* (New York: St. Martin's Press, 1987), 243.

13. Dick Maurice, *Las Vegas Sun,* March 1986. Thomas, *Liberace,* 254.

14. William E. Geist, "About New York: Liberace Is Here, With His Glitter Undimmed," *New York Times,* April 3, 1985: B5.

15. *Times* of London. October 2, 1956: 3.

16. *Times* of London, September 26, 1956: 6.

17. Videocassette, *Liberace: Behind the Music.*

18. Dick Alexander, "A Las Vegas where there's no bettor fun," *San Francisco Examiner,* July 22, 1990: T4.

19. Alexander Walker, *Rudolph Valentino* (London: Elm Tree Books/Hamish Hamilton, 1976), 32–33, 99. The desire of critics to accept allegations that Acker and Rambova were lesbians may suggest something of their own ambivalence toward Valentino's love-god image; thus one biographer comments, for example, on Valentino's statement that "a man may admire a woman without desiring her." "It has been reported that Natacha construed this as a veiled reference to her Lesbianism, and, on reading it, slapped Valentino's face. But such a report is necessarily hard to confirm" (Walker, 99).

20. Noel Botham and Peter Donnelly, *Valentino: the Love God* (London: Everest Books, 1976), 70.

21. Miriam Hansen, "Pleasure, Ambivalence, Identification: Valentino and Female Spectatorship," *Cinema Journal* 25,4 (Summer 1986): 25. Hansen also has excellent things to say about the Latin Lover, the discourse of exoticism, and the "repressed desire of miscegenation" in the U.S.

22. *Chicago Sunday Tribune,* July 18, 1926: A10.

23. *Chicago Herald-Examiner,* quoted in Botham and Donnelly, *Valentino,* 196–97.

24. Botham and Donnelly, *Valentino,* 200.

25. Jack Scagnetti, *The Intimate Life of Rudolph Valentino* (Middle Village, New York: Jonathan David Publishers, 1975), 115.

26. *Time,* the *New York Times,* and the *Los Angeles Times* all carried articles on him. Thomas, *Liberace,* 173.

27. James Barron, "Liberace, Flamboyant Pianist, Is Dead," *New York Times,* February 5, 1987: B6.

28. There have, in fact, been numerous Liberace imitators, as Dick Alexander notes in the *San Francisco Examiner,* July 22, 1990: T4.

29. Although at least one, Jac L. Tharpe, points it out in passing. Tharpe, "Will the Real Elvis Presley . . . ", in Tharpe, *Elvis: Images and Fancies* (Jackson: University Press of Mississippi, 1979), 4.

30. Peter Guralnick, *The Rolling Stone Illustrated History of Rock & Roll,* ed. Jim Miller (New York: Random House/Rolling Stone Press, 1980), 21.

31. Nik Cohn's novel, *King Death* (1975), speculates on what would have happened had Jesse lived. Albert Goldman comments that "This spirit brother is one of the most important characters in the life of Elvis Presley." Albert Goldman, *Elvis* (New York: McGraw-Hill, 1981), 65.

32. Norman A. Mackenzie, *The Magic of Rudolph Valentino* (London: The Research Publishing Co., 1974), 11.

33. "This surprising identification with the film idol of the silent era, a man who was dead before Elvis was born," writes Albert Goldman, "is the first unmistakable sign that Elvis had discovered the essence of his appeal and was starting to cultivate a

corresponding image. It is also a sign of prescience, for nothing better defines Elvis' future role than the formula: teen Valentino. If you add to the basic image of the sultry Latin lover the further garnishings of an erotic style of music and dance, the tango for the twenties, rock 'n' role for the fifties, the parallel is perfect. Soon Elvis would even have crow-black hair" (Goldman, *Elvis*, 129).

34. Vernon Scott, "Elvis Ten Million Dollars Later," *McCalls*, February 1963: 124.

35. Molly Ivins, "Presley Fans Mourn in Memphis . . . ". *New York Times*, August 18, 1977: C18.

36. "The King Is Dead, But Long Lives the King in a Showbiz Bonanza." *People* 8,15 (October 10, 1977), 29.

37. Werner T. Mays, in John Edgerton, "Elvis Lives!" *The Progressive* 43, 3 (March 1979): 23.

38. George Melly, *Revolt into Style* (Harmondsworth: Penguin, 1970), 36–37.

39. David Houston. Goldman, *Elvis*, 157.

40. Stephen Heath, "Joan Riviere and the Masquerade," in *Formations of Fantasy*, 53.

41. Goldman, *Elvis*, 122. Patsy Guy Hammontree, *Elvis Presley, A Bio-Bibliography* (Westport, Connecticut; Greenwood Press, 1985), 13.

42. Charles White, *The Life and Times of Little Richard* (New York: Pocket Books, 1984), 66, 69.

43. Charles White, *The Life and Times of Little Richard* (New York: Pocket Books, 1984), 69.

44. William Allen Harbinson, *The Illustrated Elvis* (New York: Grosset & Dunlap, 1977), 93.

45. J. David Stern, "The King Is Back," *TV Guide* 38,7 (February 17, 1990), 6–7.

46. Albert Goldman, whose view of Elvis often borders on the vitriolic, puts the turning point at his army experience, which was traditionally supposed to make a man of him: "The Elvis who had appeared on the Dorsey, Berle, and Sullivan shows, who had starred in *Loving You* and *Jailhouse Rock*, was butch. He had a chunky, clunky aura. . . . After the army, Elvis appears very delicate and vulnerable. . . . With his preposterous Little Richard conk, his limp wrist, girlish grin, and wobbly knees, which now turn out instead of in, he looks outrageously gay" (Goldman, *Elvis*, 329–30). Goldman targets, especially, what he describes as "his queer showing on *Frank Sinatra's Welcome Home Party for Elvis Presley*." "When he confronts the much smaller but more masculine Sinatra, Elvis's body language flashes, 'I surrender, dear.'"

Goldman's hostility toward (and fascination with) his subject is clear, as is his desire to pop-psychoanalyze and re-gender him. Thus he describes the 21-year-old Elvis's "Girlish boudoir," full of Teddy bears (picture caption, Goldman 289ff.), observes that "throwing things like a hysterical woman was one of Elvis's more dangerous habits" (Goldman, 337) and claims that he was so sensitive about his uncircumcised state that "instead of pissing in a urinal . . . he would always go inside, like a woman" (Goldman, 339). When it comes to accounting for the singer's popularity, Goldman has recourse again to gender and to a kind of instant cultural criticism. "Much of Elvis's power over young girls came not just from the fact that he embodied their erotic fantasies but that he likewise projected frankly feminine traits with which they could identify. This AC/DC quality became in time characteristic of rock stars in general, commencing with Mick Jagger and the Beatles (who had such ravishingly girlish falsettos) and going on to include Jim Morrison, David Bowie, Elton John and many figures of the punk pantheon" (Goldman, 345).

47. John J. O'Connor, " 'Elvis' The Series: Poor Boy Makes Good," *New York Times*, February 6, 1990: B1.

48. *The Masquerader*, 1914; *The Woman* 1915. Of *The Masquerader*, *Bioscope* wrote, "Mr. Chaplin gives a really remarkable female impersonation. The makeup is no less successful than the characterization, and is further proof of Mr. Chaplin's versatility." *The Films of Charlie Chaplin*, ed. Gerald D. McDonald, Michael Conway, and Mark Ricci (Secaucus, New Jersey: The Citadel Press, 1971), 62.

49. John Carlin, *The Iconography of Elvis*, as quoted in Victor Bockris, *The Life and Death of Andy Warhol* (New York: Bantam Books, 1989), 124–25.

50. *Newsweek*, August 29, 1977. Cited in Tharpe, *Elvis: Images*, 4.

51. Walter Benjamin, "The Work of Art in the Age of Mechanical Reproduction," *Illuminations*, trans. Harry Zohn (New York: Schocken Books, 1969), 221.

52. Goldman, *Elvis*, 229.

53. "Elvis Presley Imitations in Spirit and Flesh," *Rolling Stone* 261 (March 23, 1978).

54. *Time*, April 9, 1990: 38.

55. Sheila Rule, "The Men Who Would Be Elvis," *New York Times*, June 26, 1990: B1.

56. "Beauty Pageant's 'Roger & Me' Lesson," "Outtakes" column, reprinted from the *Los Angeles Times*. *San Francisco Chronicle*, February 12, 1990: F3.

57. Alice Kahn, "A Whole Lotta Elvis Going On," *San Francisco Chronicle*, June 11, 1900: B3.

58. Sigmund Freud, "The Uncanny" (1919) *SE* 17:241.

59. Simon Frith, "Confessions of a Rock Critic," in *Music for Pleasure: Essays in the Sociology of Pop* (New York: Routledge, 1988), 193.

60. *San Francisco Chronicle,* February 22, 1990.

61. Mark Leger, "The Drag Queen in The Age of Mechanical Reproduction," *Out/Look* 6 (Fall 1989): 29.

NOTES TO CONCLUSION, RED RIDING HOOD AND THE WOLF IN BED

1. Wolfram Eberhard, "The Story of Grandaunt Tiger," in Alan Dundes, *Little Red Riding Hood: A Casebook* (Madison: University of Wisconsin Press, 1989), 21–63; Wolfgang Mieder, "Survival Forms of 'Little Red Riding Hood' in Modern Society," *International Folklore Review* 2 (1982), 23–40; commentary, Dundes, *A Casebook*, 243; Hans-Wolf Jager, "Is Little Red Riding Hood Wearing a Liberty Cap? On Presumable Connotations in Tieck and Grimm," Dundes, *A Casebook*, 89–120.

2. Jack Zipes, *The Trials and Tribulations of Little Red Riding Hood: Versions of the Tale in Sociocultural Context* (South Hadley, Massachusetts: Bergin & Garvey, 1983), 57.

3. "A Supplement to Freud's 'History of an Infantile Neurosis' (1928)," by Ruth Mack Brunswick, in *The Wolf-Man by The Wolf-Man*, ed. Muriel Gardiner (New York: Basic Books, 1971), 268, 277.

4. "But for Freud the 'breakthrough to the woman' could under certain circumstances be considered the neurotic's greatest achievement, a sign of his will to live, an active attempt to recover." The Wolf-Man, "My Recollections of Sigmund Freud," in Gardiner, *The Wolf-Man*, 138. Here the "breakthrough" signals the successful repression of homosexuality as a self-regulating therapeutic act.

5. The Wolf-Man, an excellent analytic pupil, also saw this point clearly (at least in retrospect), as he wrote to Muriel Gardiner in a letter dated October 23, 1970: "Regarding my treatment with Freud specifically, in every psychoanalysis—and Professor Freud himself often emphasized this—the transference of the father-complex to the analyst plays a very great role. In this respect, the situation was most favorable for me when I came to Professor Freud. For, in the first place, I was still young, and the younger one is, the easier it is for him to form a positive transference to the analyst. In the second place, my father had died only a short time before, and Professor Freud's outstanding personality was able to fill this void. So I had found in the person of Professor Freud a new father with whom I had an excellent relationship." Gardiner, *The Wolf-Man*, 89.

6. Sigmund Freud, "From the History of an Infantile Neurosis" (1918), *SE* 17:11. See also "Analysis Terminable and Interminable" (1937), *SE* 23:217.

7. "The Wolf-Man had come to Freud 'entirely incapacitated and completely dependent upon other people.' . . . He had had no satisfactory relationship with a woman. . . . After his analysis with Freud, the Wolf-Man. . . . was able to marry, and he supported and cared for his wife during the twenty-three years of their marriage." Muriel Gardiner, "The Wolf-Man in Later Life," in *The Wolf-Man*, 365.

8. Terry Castle, *Masquerade and Civilization: The Carnivalesque in Eighteenth-Century English Culture and Fiction* (Stanford: Stanford University Press, 1986), 46, 47.

9. Nicolas Abraham and Maria Torok, *The Wolf Man's Magic Word: A Cryptonomy*, trans. Nicholas Rand (Minneapolis: University of Minnesota Press, 1986).

10. See Castle, *Masquerade and Civilization*, 47ff.: "Several contemporary accounts describe scenes of homosexual flirtation, though usually between men only, and always in extremely coy terms. Typically a sartorial error is invoked to explain such incidents, but only after piquant images have been presented to the reader. As on the Shakespearean stage, men fall in love with 'boys' at the masquerade who turn out to be women. . . . In an episode from James Boaden's account of the life of Elizabeth Inchbald, the scandal is reversed. Inchbald (who had played Bellario on the London stage) attended a masquerade in male dress in 1781 and was subsequently 'charged with having captivated the affections of sundry witless admirers of her own sex.' Boaden records that the experience put Inchbald in mind of 'the beautiful equivoque in the character of Viola.' "

11. *The Complete Grimm's Fairy Tales* (New York: Pantheon Books, 1944), 140.

12. Bettelheim, *The Uses of Enchantment: The Meaning and Importance of Fairy Tales* (New York: Alfred A. Knopf, 1976), 175–76.

13. Djuna Barnes, *Nightwood* (New York: New Directions, 1937), 79.

14. Zipes, *The Trials and Tribulations of Little Red Riding Hood*, 5–6; Paul Delarue, "The Story of Grandmother," in Dundes, *A Casebook*, 16; Eberhard, "The Story of Grandaunt Tiger," in Dundes, *A Casebook*, 24, 44; 57; P. Saintyves, "Little Red Riding Hood or the Little May Queen," in Dundes, *A Casebook*, 82; Géza Roheim, "Fairy Tale and Dream," in Dundes, *A Casebook*, 163, 164; Dundes, "Interpreting 'Little Red Riding Hood' Psychoanalytically," in Dundes, *A Casebook*, 198; 201,224.

NOTES

15. Sigmund Freud, "Introductory Lectures on Psycho-Analysis (1916–1917)" (Part II), *SE* 16:369–70.

16. J. Laplanche and J-B. Pontalis, *The Language of Psycho-Analysis*, trans. Donald Nicholson-Smith (New York: W.W. Norton, 1973), 336.

17. Jacques Lacan, "Beyond the Imaginary, The Symbolic or From the Little to the Big Other," *The Seminars of Jacques Lacan, Book II, The Ego in Freud's Theory and in the Technique of Psychoanalysis 1954–55,* trans. Sylvana Tomaselli (New York: W.W. Norton, 1988), 176.

18. Jan Morris, *Conundrum: An Extraordinary Narrative of Transsexualism* (New York: Henry Holt and Co., 1974; 1986), 3. Nora Ephron, "Conundrum," *Crazy Salad: Some Things About Women* (New York: Bantam, 1976), 203.

INDEX

INDEX

INDEX

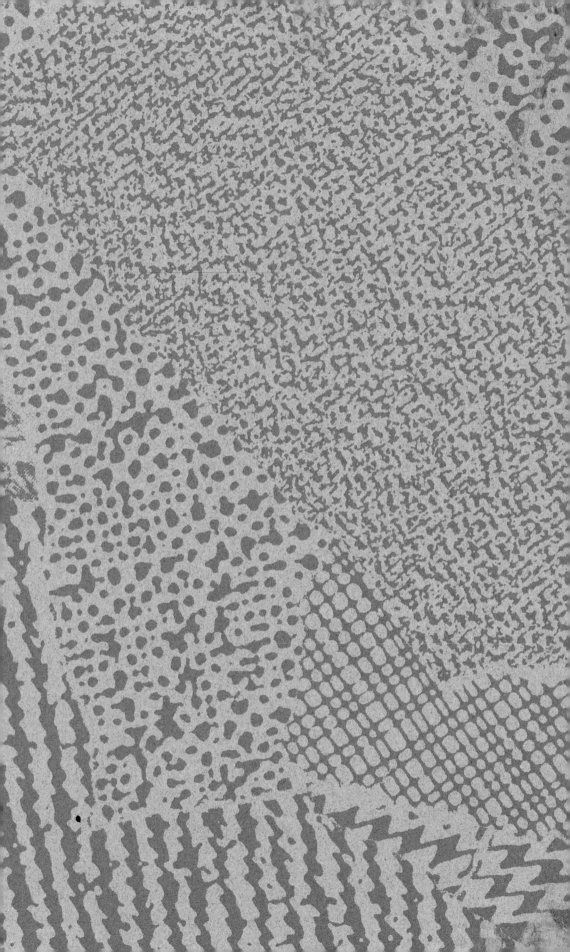